Afro-Brazilians

Rochester Studies in African History and the Diaspora

Toyin Falola, Senior Editor
The Frances Higginbotham Nalle Centennial Professor in History
University of Texas at Austin

(ISSN: 1092–5228)

A complete list of titles in the Rochester Studies in African History and the Diaspora, in order of publication, may be found at the end of this book.

Afro-Brazilians

Cultural Production in a Racial Democracy

Niyi Afolabi

UNIVERSITY OF ROCHESTER PRESS

Copyright © 2009 Niyi Afolabi

All rights reserved. Except as permitted under current legislation, no part of this work may be photocopied, stored in a retrieval system, published, performed in public, adapted, broadcast, transmitted, recorded, or reproduced in any form or by any means, without the prior permission of the copyright owner.

First published 2009

University of Rochester Press
668 Mt. Hope Avenue, Rochester, NY 14620, USA
www.urpress.com
and Boydell & Brewer Limited
PO Box 9, Woodbridge, Suffolk IP12 3DF, UK
www.boydellandbrewer.com

ISBN-13: 978-1-58046-262-4

ISSN: 1092-5228

Library of Congress Cataloging-in-Publication Data

Afolabi, Niyi.
   Afro-Brazilians : cultural production in a racial democracy / Niyi Afolabi.
     p. cm. — (Rochester studies in African history and the diaspora ; 39)
   Includes bibliographical references and index.
   ISBN-13: 978-1-58046-262-4 (hardcover : alk. paper)
   ISBN-10: 1-58046-262-6 (hardcover : alk. paper) 1. Democracy–Brazil.
2. Africans–Brazil. 3. Racism–Brazil. 4. Africans–Brazil–Ethnic identity.
5. Brazil–Civilization–African influences. I. Title.
   HM477.B6A36 2009
   305.896'081–dc22
                                                                2008047629

A catalogue record for this title is available from the British Library.

This publication is printed on acid-free paper.
Printed in the United States of America.

To
The Glory of God

א ✝ ת
איהא רשא איהא

[The Alpha and Omega
The I Am That I Am]

Contents

Notes on Yoruba Orthography	viii
Preface	ix
Acknowledgments	xi
Introduction: Negotiating Cultural Production in a Racial Democracy	1
1 Two Faces of Racial Democracy	22
2 Quilombhoje as a Cultural Collective	51
3 Beyond the Curtains: Unveiling Afro-Brazilian Women Writers	80
4 (Un)Broken Linkages	108
5 The Tropicalist Legacy of Gilberto Gil	127
6 Afro-Brazilian Carnival	151
7 Film and Fragmentation	169
8 Ancestrality and the Dynamics of Afro-Modernity	193
9 The Forerunners of Afro-Modernity	207
10 (Un)Transgressed Tradition	239
11 Ancestrality, Memory, and Citizenship	267
12 *Quilombo* without Frontiers	302
13 Ancestral Motherhood of Leci Brandão	357
Conclusion: The Future of Afro-Brazilian Cultural Production	376
Notes	381
Bibliography	397
Index	417

Notes on Yoruba Orthography

The transnational nature of this book makes having notes on Yoruba orthography as used in both Yoruba and Brazilian contexts necessary. Selecting one standard form for the entire book was a difficult choice to make. Other than the direct quotations in which cultural producers use one form as opposed to the other, I have adopted the continental Yoruba as the uniform usage. Yoruba is a tonal language and as a result, the three tones, namely, high, mid, and low, may vary the meaning of a given word. While the high tone is represented with an acute accent (á, é, ẹ́, í, ó, ọ́, and ú), the low tone is represented with a grave accent (à, è, ẹ̀, ì, ò, ọ̀, and ù), and the mid tone is not marked at all. Due to colonialism, some words were, however, "corrupted" by the English because producing certain Yoruba sounds was difficult for the missionaries, such as the "ṣ," which was rendered as 'sh.' For example, Antônio Olinto, the Brazilian writer discussed in chapter 4, uses this colonial rendition as in "**sh**ango"; perhaps due to his writing in the context of a newly independent Africa that was still struggling with the vestiges of colonialism. In Portuguese, the same sound is written with an "**x**" so that Ṣàngó, in Yoruba of Western Nigeria, will be written as **X**angô in Brazil. Other orthographic variations between the continental Yoruba and the Brazilian include Èṣù (Exu), Ọ̀ṣun (Oxum), Ògún (Ogum), Òriṣànlá (Oxalá), Ọya (Oiá, Iansan, Yansã), Yemọja (Yemanjá, Nanã, Iemanjá), *àṣẹ* (axé), *ẹbọ* (ebó), and *òrìṣà* (orixá, orisha).

Preface

This book synthesizes my research, over the years, in the "Land of Carnival" and the "Racial Paradise," as Brazil is often commercially and exotically marketed to the rest of the world. My curiosity about Brazil started in 1982 while I was an exchange student in São Paulo. While I valued the opportunity of studying with Brazilians and being able to use the language of Luís de Camões, Machado de Assis, and José Craveirinha with such ease and facility, I was appalled by the absence of Afro-Brazilians on the Universidade de São Paulo (USP) campus, where I was with six other students from Nigeria. That was my first lesson in racial exclusion. Young and naive though we were at the time, it did not take us long to understand that we were privileged to be studying at that foremost Latin American university. Whenever we met Afro-Brazilians working in menial positions on or off campus, we were often asked questions such as "Are you diplomats?" "How did you get into USP?" "Are you on scholarship?" It was inconceivable to them that Afro-Brazilians could afford a university education or would have the intellectual preparation to sit with other Brazilians in an academic setting. To our amazement at the time, even almost one hundred years after abolition, the psychology of slavery was still very much alive in the minds of many. We could see other faces of color in the classroom, especially the Japanese, but blackness was an anomaly. This was quite saddening in a country that preached and continues to preach "racial democracy." I was reminded of Abdias do Nascimento's *Racial Democracy: Myth or Reality?* in which he exposes this hypocrisy, and this idea has stuck with me for many years. It took seventeen years to be able to meet Baba Abdias in person after my many visits to Brazil. His immeasurable contribution to the advancement of Afro-Brazilian dignity and Pan-African consciousness—scientifically, politically, culturally, and spiritually—surely deserves a Nobel Prize.

Although the situation of Afro-Brazilians has changed somewhat since 1982, my visits to Brazil in the 1990s and more recently do not indicate significant progress even decades after the centenary celebration of the abolition of slavery in 1988. And therein lies the motivation for this book: a retrospective and prognostic view of the challenges faced by Afro-Brazilians in the last two centuries. The deluding concept of racial democracy is still sacredly sanctioned in all spheres of Brazilian life. Afro-Brazilians are still poorly educated, have little in terms of political influence, and in contrast to whites, are the most powerless. Abdias do Nascimento, Gilberto Gil, Benedita da Silva, and some of the leaders of the *blocos afro(s)* are a few examples of Afro-Brazilians who have managed to attain some political power through struggle. Although Afro-Brazilians continue to be visible in sports, entertainment, music, and other areas of creative expression, in the political arena, the ultimate location of power, a considerable vacuum remains to be filled. This book is both a celebration and an invitation to all on the African continent and in the diaspora to look beyond their location and appreciate that we are all united by a vital force.

I thank Christopher Dunn and Idelber Avelar, my Brazilian(ist) colleagues at Tulane University and the African and African Diaspora Studies Program. Equally deserving of my gratitude is the Tulane University Council on Research and the Stone Center for Latin American Studies, whose research grants supported my work at different stages—especially the research trips to Brazil from 1998 through 2001. I must also thank the anonymous readers for their cogent critiques that helped me recast some of my positions.

Niyi Afolabi
University of Texas at Austin

Acknowledgments

The publication of this book benefited from a number of generosities in the very last stages of production. I would like to express my gratitude to the Department of Spanish and Portuguese and the Warfield Center for African and African American Studies at the University of Texas at Austin for their financial support. I also acknowledge a University Co-operative Society Subvention Grant and a Special Research Grant awarded by the University of Texas at Austin. I would equally like to thank the Office of Research and the Dean of the College of Liberal Arts of the University of Massachusetts at Amherst for their support. I must not forget those graduate students at Tulane University who took my course on Afro-Brazilians and with whom I first shared some of the ideas of this book. At the University of Rochester Press, I am grateful for the professionalism of the editorial team, especially its meticulous attention to details. It was a pleasure working with Suzanne Guiod, Katie Hurley, and Tracey Engel. Finally, this book represents a timely testament and a modest tribute to the struggles of Afro-Brazilians. Viva Zumbi! Viva Quilombo dos Palmares!!

Introduction

Negotiating Cultural Production in a Racial Democracy

> I sing to *Palmares*[1]
> without complex or jealousy
> of Virgil, Homer or Camões
> for my song
> is a cry of a people
> in plain struggle for freedom.
>
> —Solano Trindade

Brazil, the most racially diverse Latin American country, is also the most contradictory. It is a country that has been able to maintain fantasy as reality through the myth of racial democracy for many centuries. Enshrined in that mythology is the masking of an exclusionism that strategically displaces and marginalizes Afro-Brazilians from political power. A democracy that subjugates a section of the population by virtue of the color of their skin cannot be said to be in the interest of that segment of the population but the perpetrator of segregation and dehumanization. In *Racism in a Racial Democracy*, France Winddance Twine highlights the word *shock* as in the shock of racism, to problematize a dual feeling of action and nonaction on the part of Afro-Brazilians in the face of racism. She suggests that in order to contain the shock of racism, Afro-Brazilians have become silenced, coerced, and self-secluded. As a result, the more volatile act of challenging racism openly and directly is traded for "harmonious relations" thereby leaving white supremacy untouched. At work in this truism is what I call "vital force": that ancestral strength and energy with which Afro-Brazilians cope and regenerate themselves through creative and cultural strategies that have their political implications even when they are not forcefully or apparently articulated.

In this vital force, which among Afro-Brazilians is generally referred to as *axé*, resides that muse of cultural resistance and production without which their spiritual survival is not only impossible but practically illusory. This book provides an analysis of the strategies of survival in the various spheres of cultural production—verbal and visual, social and political—while focusing on significant historical, literary, and popular manifestations in the nineteenth and twentieth centuries. Aside from using canonical and emerging writers as well as exponents of popular culture as my primary sources of analysis, I also integrate personal interviews wherever relevant. I begin by suggesting that these cultural strategies serve as a "veil" à la Robert Stepto—the metaphor of deliberate masking through which the invisible subject subverts invisibility in order to negotiate visibility and become self-empowered.[2] I then go on to problematize and reject "racial democracy" through a contrastive and dialogic approach. This dialogic approach contrasts the discourses of racism with carnivalesque strategies of subversion in order to highlight the missing link in redressing the processes of subjugation and marginalization in the Brazilian context.

The multiple interconnected ideas in this book—namely, vital force, Afro-Brazilian identity, racial democracy, ancestrality, Afro-modernity, and cultural production—stem from that same source of vitality that enriches Afro-Brazilians as they redefine themselves, engage mythologies and stereotypes that have been used to define and distort their realities, and finally, turn such "new" discourses into tools of cultural production, resistance, and survival. I use "vital force" here as a grounding trope of analysis in order to uncover those strategies deployed by Afro-Brazilians to retain their dignity and sanity in the face of racial discrimination and inequalities. Some of these strategies include writing, performance, and celebrating Afro-Brazilian heroes through symbolic actions such as organizing visits to the tomb of Luís Gama, a celebrated nineteenth-century Afro-Brazilian poet in São Paulo. While I agree with Edimilson de Almeida Pereira that it is almost impossible to write about Afro-Brazilian culture in absolute, integral, and symmetrical terms, most of the cultural producers included in this study are Afro-Brazilians who have become recognized writers and performers to the point of being representative of the affluent segment of the Afro-Brazilian population. At the same time, Afro-Brazilian culture, as appropriated by these cultural producers, would be nonexistent without the primacy of the Afro-Brazilian masses, who themselves constitute the contributive essence of the culture. This is an intricate and inextricable relationship between the culture, the site or location of culture, and the producers themselves.

Inspired by the Yoruba concept of àṣẹ—which simply means "amen" "so be it" or "may it come to pass"—it is the sealing of a prayer or supplication made to the gods. In the Brazilian context, the orthography has been changed to *axé*, and the meaning also slightly modified. Rather than a word uttered forcefully to fulfill a "litany," Candomblé worshippers use the term to mean spiritual energy that descends upon their congregation like a blessing. For example, to lay the foundation of a *terreiro* (temple), the worshippers must plant an *axé*, an offering in recognition of the spiritual power and legitimacy of the shrine. Vital force thus captures the totality of power, strength, authenticity, energy, and legitimacy—a combination that culminates in forceful articulation embedded in cultural production.

Within the incisive mythology of racial democracy, those known as Afro-Brazilians are not that easy to define. For my purposes, these are individuals and their descendants who have been forcefully removed from the African continent and transported to Brazil, to a new and alienating environment where they have had to abandon their own languages and assimilate the culture of the Portuguese, in particular. Without the religious and cultural elements that these African descendants brought with them from Africa, it would be even more difficult to call anyone *Afro*-Brazilian. Yet despite African descendants' primary claim on Afro-Brazilian identity, Brazilian racial complexity makes any absolute categorization problematic due to race mixture as well as the affinities shared by other Brazilians with Afro-Brazilian culture. While the process of "whitening" has done much to minimize the racial injustices suffered by blacks in general, especially by suggesting that Brazil is a "raceless" society, that fantasy does more disservice to racial relations. White writers and performers such as Jorge Amado and Caetano Veloso do have a claim to "Afro-Brazilianness," but none of them claims that association with pride. Caetano Veloso and Jorge Amado would conveniently see themselves as *baianos* (Bahians), that is, natives of Bahia, without necessarily identifying or aligning themselves with blackness. This confirms the hypocrisy that pervades all Brazilian racial relations. The nonalignment posture of Veloso and Amado may not necessarily stem from a sense of "ambiguity" between their promotion of an Afro-Brazilian image nationally and internationally on the one hand, and their whiteness as opposed to blackness on the other, but from a sense of political expediency facilitated by that very ambiguity.

By racial democracy, I refer to the official adoption of the myth of harmonious coexistence and lifestyles between the masters and their slaves as developed by Gilberto Freyre in his now canonized *Casa grande e senzala* (The Masters and the Slaves). Since the publication of this book in 1933, critics on both sides of the debate have been busy trying to justify or attack this well-packaged ideological and racist treatise.[3] Instead of confronting the reality of racism, the mostly white-dominated Brazilian government spends energy trying to defend racial democracy that is nonexistent. Maria Alice de Aguiar Medeiros captures this paradox in a rereading of *Casa grande e senzala* that she appropriately titles *O elogio da dominação*, that is, "In Praise of Domination." Indeed, racial democracy sounds more like racial domination for it forces the conformist and nonperceptive Brazilian to believe that everyone is "Brazilian" and "color-blind." For Medeiros: "It is traditionally believed that the non-white population of the country enjoys a privileged social situation, thus insulated against any discriminatory attitudes. Obviously, there is a major discrepancy between this official rhetoric and the 'racist' praxis which has, over time, segregated and maintained blacks and mulattoes in the lowest position of social hierarchy" (*O elogio* 71).[4] The question, then, is how Afro-Brazilians cope with this myth, especially in their cultural production.

Cultural production becomes an ideological tool even in its most entertaining mode. By this concept, I mean the sum total of cultural manifestations from performative, and artistic to intellectual production. The performer in this context is a warrior on stage and on the streets. The fine artist visualizes a world that may not be immediately feasible in reality, but he or she conjures it up through the stroke of the brush and imagination, paying homage to the gods, and asking them to bring about change in a world that is resistant to change. Likewise, intellectual producers, writers and professors alike, are warriors who use the pen instead of spears and guns to combat the enemies of progress. The commonality here is the energy and ideology that inform that production. Each poem, each song, each painting, each novel, each play, each performance by an Afro-Brazilian cultural producer is a dialogue with Brazilian racial democracy. It is a strategic mode of exposing the inequalities through a variety of veils that entertain, ridicule, invoke, provoke, protest, and demand for change at the same time.

Clóvis Moura, in *Sociologia do negro brasileiro,* suggests that racial democracy negates ethnic identity and thus propagates the elimination of the so-called inferior races through "whitening." By that same logic, or lack of it, creative works by Afro-Brazilians are thus relegated to lacking in "culture" and reduced to exotic objects of study. Moura calls for the study of Afro-Brazilians from their own perspectives, through how they define themselves and not through others' definitions. In this sense, I subscribe to Raymond Williams's notion of culture in *The Long Revolution,* where he states:

> Culture is a description of a particular way of life, which expresses certain meanings and values not only in art and learning but also in institutions and ordinary behavior. The analysis of culture, from such a definition, is the clarification of the meanings and values implicit and explicit in a particular way of life, a particular culture. Such analysis will include the organisation of production, the structure of family, the structure of institutions which express or govern social relationships, the characteristic forms through which members of the society communicate. (57–58)

This notion of "particular culture" and "particular way of life" explains our position to let Afro-Brazilian voices speak for themselves and not be projected by the eye of the other.

Taking the premise of Raymond Williams, Afro-Brazilian cultural production has indeed been a "long revolution" that is yet to come full circle in order to achieve that most desirable goal of social equality and change, especially in ideological orientations and racist stereotypes. Historically, Afro-Brazilians may be said to have started producing their culture right from their Atlantic passage to Brazil when the seeds of slavery were first planted and where acts of protest and rebellion were met with corporal and mental flagellation. Since slaves were considered "property" and "objects," they were denied the opportunity to learn to write and memory became the most viable tool of "documentation." It is this collective memory that is usually passed down orally through storytelling from generation to generation that Castro Alves, the "singer-poet of slaves," as he is called, reenacts in his epic poem *O navio negreiro* (The Black Slaveship), later parodied by Solano Trindade in *Cantares ao meu povo*.[5] Instead of the romantic rendition of the ship by Alves, Trindade paints it as a vehicle of pain and death thereby demystifying the role Castro Alves's poetry played for the Afro-Brazilian cause.

While I have some historical motivation in the conception of this book, I did not set out to be chronological. Instead, I have selected topics, issues, and significant figures in Afro-Brazilian cultural production who best illustrate the complexities of racial democracy and its bearing on Afro-Brazilians and the relevance of this myth in the broader and more marginalizing political sphere. In my choice of issues to cover, ranging from the literary to popular culture and visual arts, I seek to be more inclusive and panoramic than specialized or restrictive. In so doing, I hope to bring together many voices from various cultural compartments to dialogue with racial democracy. The choice of Machado de Assis and Lima Barreto to provide a nineteenth-century context and illustrate opposing views on racial democracy stems from the fact that both writers are mulattoes from Rio de Janeiro who lived in the same era but did not have the same reception and "popularity." One was easily co-opted within the official mythology, while the other was not. A similar comparative study could be done on Jorge Amado and Abdias do Nascimento, Jorge de Lima and Solano Trindade, Mário de Andrade and Cruz e Souza. Beyond this innovative reading of canonical writers, Quilombhoje as well as women writers fill the lacuna between the complacency of the modernist movement and the emerging trends in Afro-Brazilian discourse. Antônio Olinto is then situated as a transition between literature and popular culture, between Africa and Brazil, as his works take the reader on a journey from Brazil to West Africa.

On the popular cultural terrain, Gilberto Gil is a significant voice whose musical phenomenon oscillates between culture and politics. The biographical approach allows for a closer analysis of the emergence of a major Afro-Brazilian icon whose contribution will continue to resonate in Brazilian music for decades to come. In problematizing Afro-Brazilian carnival, I take the position that the manifestation has been reduced to a mere annual celebration to promote tourism, hence the actual producers of that "marketable culture" remain marginalized and objectified as mere local color as soon as Carnival is over. It is that cycle of alienation and disenfranchisement that I call into question. The cinematic perspective is quite significant in the structure of the book. In addition to covering films that have been adapted from emblematic works such as Mário de Andrade, *Macunaíma;* Jorge Amado, *Jubiabá;* Dias Gomes, *O pagador de promessas;* Vinicius de Moraes, *Orfeu da conceição;* João Felício dos Santos, *Xica da Silva,* and Gianfrancesco Guarnieri, *Eles não usam Black Tie,* it also provides an overview of Afro-Brazilian cinematic history since the fifties to date.

Chapter 1, "Two Faces of Racial Democracy," comparatively engages in a discussion of two canonical Brazilian writers of the turn of the twentieth century: Machado de Assis and Lima Barreto. Machado is heralded as the greatest Brazilian writer of all times in spite of his marginal and demeaning treatment of black characters; Barreto is marginalized and forgotten given his ferocious attack on the myth of Brazilian racial democracy. In rereading Machado de Assis, I suggest that the philosophical dimension of the writer has often overshadowed the fact that he is Afro-Brazilian. Can a writer be philosophical yet racially conscious at the same time? Other than being the greatest Brazilian writer of all time, what has he contributed to advance the cause of Afro-Brazilians? This is where Lima Barreto compellingly contrasts with Machado. Against Clóvis Moura's premises of "co-optation" and "dignification" in *Sociologia do negro brasileiro,* I compare and contrast the legacies of both writers in Afro-Brazilian letters.

Chapter 2, "Quilombhoje as a Cultural Collective," examines, celebratorily, Quilombhoje's existence as a black literary movement following the great tradition of emblematic writers in the regeneration of Afro-Brazilian personality and dignity. In addition to providing a survey of the emergence, travails, and achievements of the group in terms of a cultural movement that can be said to be an offshoot of the Unified Black Movement of the 1970s, this chapter focuses primarily on two anniversary editions: *Cadernos negros: Os melhores poemas* (1998) and *Cadernos negros: Os melhores contos* (1998). Funded by São Paulo's Ministry of Culture, these special editions are testimony to the relevance of Afro-Brazilian cultural production although the group had been in existence and self-publishing for more than two decades before such a national recognition, an ironic coming of age after so many years of radical struggle against invisibility.

Chapter 3, "Beyond the Curtains," locates prominent yet emerging players in Afro-Brazilian women's writing through Miriam Alves and Durham's *Enfim nós/Finally Us* and a selection of poetic and narrative works by "representative" Quilombhoje female members and authors over the years of the group's existence such as Alves, Esmeralda Ribeiro, and Sônia Fátima da Conceição. In addition to focusing on these three established writers, I provide an overview of the concerns, styles, and values of a cross-section of Afro-Brazilian women voices. In a combination of the will to overcome their multiply marginalized status, these writers expose what it means to be

Afro-Brazilian, women, writers, mothers, and lovers at the same time. The need to justify their identity and relevance forces Alzira Rufino to assert in a definitive and declarative tone:

> I am a black woman period
> return my identity to me
> tear up my birth certificate
> I am a black woman without ellipses
> without commas, and without anything missing
> I no longer want in-betweens
> I am a black woman "cannon ball"
> I am a black night weariness
> I am a black woman period. (*Finally Us* 35)

Such a recuperative and empowering assertion makes reading Afro-Brazilian women's writing a mixed task of process of working out their pain, as if the writing process domesticates and releases the anguish.

Chapter 4, "(Un)Broken Linkages," examines the ancestral linkages between freed African slaves from Brazil who returned to Nigeria after abolition of slavery and their adaptation and reintegration into a society their ancestors left over three centuries before. Close readings of *Brasileiros na África* and the Afro-Brazilian trilogy *A casa da água*, *O rei de Ketu*, and *Trono de vidro* in light of "postcolonial" theory reveals (un)broken linkages between the returnees and the new/old community they forge in West Africa, especially in Lagos (Nigeria), Cotonou (Benin), and Lomé (Togo). The case is made for the consideration of Olinto as a Yoruba diaspora writer in a way Jorge Amado, a celebrated Brazilian writer, does not qualify. Unlike Amado, who superficially uses African elements such as customs and religious traditions as local color, Olinto descends into the West African communities, living the experiences through interviews and documentation, and finally transposes that experience into credible works of cultural memory.

Chapter 5, "The Tropicalist Legacy of Gilberto Gil," examines the irony in Gilberto Gil's artistic acclaim and "marginalization" (in contrast to Caetano Veloso) in the Tropicalist and Afro-Brazilian discourse as well as discusses his larger political contribution to Brazilian cultural and aesthetic production through an analysis of *Gilberto Gil: Todas as letras*. Gil's contribution to Afro-Brazilian culture is unparalleled by all musical standards. A syncopated voice of reconciliation between the many strands of competing racial "hegemonies" within Brazil, he represents that fluid personality that the Brazilian government would like as a nonthreatening Afro-Brazilian achiever who "knows his place." Yet, this is only in appearances, hence my biographical approach. Gil's emergence in the era of countercultural waves reveals this visionary as a rebel with a cause. His lyrics combine love for humankind with love for politics and recuperation of Afro-Brazilian heritage in all its forms. As the current minister of culture in the Luiz Inácio Lula da Silva administration, Gil's political and cultural achievements need to be weighed against his overall contribution to the Afro-Brazilian cause—where he remains wanting and unpopular among the majority of Afro-Brazilians.

Chapter 6, "Afro-Brazilian Carnival," investigates the operational, structural, and cultural hindrances to popular participation through a case study of carnivalesque manifestations in Bahia, especially the Ilê-Aiyê organization in Salvador, Brazil. This study problematizes the "exotic" and "commercial" images of Brazil's most popular cultural manifestation. Behind those "happy" faces and, underneath those colorful, elegant, and exorbitant costumes are silenced voices who see Carnival as a yearly routine to escape poverty and social stagnation. The critique of the *blocos afro(s)* as organizations that claim to be "popular" and yet must survive through the contributions of their mostly "poor" members examines the paradoxes of popular participation. Aside from the tourist attraction, Carnival is the time for these organizations to recover from the year's low financial income. Ilê-Aiye's current move and investment in educational projects, especially among the youth, is one step in the right direction toward investing in the community and overcoming the seasonal carnivalesque theatrics.

Chapter 7, "Film and Fragmentation," offers a critical discussion of select Brazilian films produced between 1950 and 2000 for the purpose of highlighting the processes of dehumanization of Afro-Brazilian actors as "domestics" and "buffoons" as well as an examination of a few cases of subtle yet questionable resistance and subversion. Aside from providing the different categories of Afro-Brazilians projected on the screen by white film directors, and the transfer of the "whitening" logic to the cinematic industry, the chapter also focuses on a number of significant films that confirm the notion of fragmentation in the representation of Afro-Brazilians. These select films include *Orfeu negro, O pagador de promessas, Macunaíma, Xica da Silva, Eles não usam Black Tie, Quilombo,* and *Jubiabá*. Until we see a rise in accomplished Afro-Brazilian film producers, such as Joel Zito Araújo, the Afro-Brazilian will likely continue to be projected by others for exploitative motives.

To appreciate the full import of Afro-Brazilian cultural production, one must also understand the history of Africans' contribution to Brazil as a whole since the advent of slavery in 1535 through its abolition in 1888 and the struggles toward true emancipation and empowerment to date. The primary compelling legacy is that of the slave condition. Regionally located, the slaves had to adjust to the environmental reality and the economic exploitation to which they were subjected in each region. In the early years of slavery, Africans were concentrated in the agrarian areas of Pernambuco, Bahia, Minas Gerais, Maranhão, and later in Rio de Janeiro. Due to the coffee economy in São Paulo, the African presence increased in this southern region in the nineteenth century. Slaves' productivity was basically conditioned by the economy and what they were made to produce, not what they would have liked to produce, in terms of their cultural values for example. The movement of slaves was equally restricted. One aspect of the master-slave condition was that the master could have sexual relations with any of his female slaves, which resulted in the creation of the mixed-race mulatto. Mulattoes later exemplified the Brazilian theory of miscegenation and upward mobility, as captured in the sugarcane plantation and gold and diamond mines in which they struggled to carve a niche for themselves.

In the slave condition where Africans found themselves, they had to learn to be of good service in all areas to satisfy their masters. Instead of the African drums they were used to, they were compelled to play the flute, work as carpenters, masons, shoemakers, as well as carry out plantation-related duties such as sugarcane growing, tobacco planting, and gold and diamond mining. These assigned roles and functions continued into the late nineteenth century even after abolition since Afro-Brazilians could only fit into certain job categories such as cooks, servants, and messengers. Even in the twentieth century, most of the achievements of black movements that brought about racial consciousness were stifled by the paradox of racial democracy and by internal conflicts within the movements. The denial of racism, especially by mulattoes has not helped the situation. An example cited by Michael Hanchard is quite typical. A São Paulo taxi driver in 1988 claimed there is no race problem in Brazil because his wife is a blonde (*Orpheus and Power* 67). Such an ignorant view of a serious problem tends to undercut the efforts of Afro-Brazilians to organize and effect change. Hanchard goes on to suggest that "it is the relative lack of power of Afro-Brazilians that determines the forms that their resistance assumes" (67). Despite some achievements of the black movements as have spilled over into the carnivalesque groups in Salvador, Bahia, in the twenty-first century, though greeted with optimism and hope, the dream continues to be deferred.

In the field of cultural production, Afro-Brazilians occupy a significant place in the Brazilian artistic crucible that includes musical styles and creative works that have gradually become defining elements of the complex Brazilian "national character." From artistic and cultural manifestations such as Carnival, capoeira, samba, dramatic and visual arts including film and television (where, admittedly, their images are mostly distorted and fragmented), through literary works by such writers as Luís Gama, Cruz e Souza, Machado de Assis, and Lima Barreto, Afro-Brazilians are a force to be reckoned with. My position about the "co-optation" of Machado de Assis does not undermine his accomplishments as the premier Brazilian writer. In this regard, it is worth noting that although colonial Brazil produced many educated mulattoes who would later champion the Afro-Brazilian cause in terms of their artistic contributions, the significance of this foundation must not be minimized. One of the paradoxes of some of these cultural figures lies in their marginalization in spite of their national contribution and significance. Through popularity or revival, often posthumous, these producers of culture become irrelevant, especially if what they are saying contradicts the official position about racial harmony. Such are the sad cases of Cruz e Souza and Lima Barreto, while Machado de Assis represents the exception to the rule.

In music specifically, Afro-Brazilians were often considered naturally gifted since they had opportunity to sing on numerous occasions, while working in the field, in religious ceremonies, and during festivals. This inherent musicality will later develop into the formation of the *escolas de samba* (samba schools) for the purpose of the annual Brazilian passion: Carnival (Port. *Carnaval*). Though a priest, Father José Maurício is considered one of the greatest musicians Brazil has ever produced. His *Requiem* testifies to Afro-Brazilian genius. Other musicians of the colonial era include José Joaquim Emerico Lobo Mesquita, Marcos Coelho Netto, and Francisco Gomes da Rocha. This group formed the so-called Minas school. Modern composers whose erudite compositions used Afro-Brazilian elements include Villa-Lobos, Alexandre Levy, Francisco Mignone, Alberto Nepomuceno, Itiberê da Cunha, Francisco Braga, Basílio Itiberê, Luciano Gallet, Jaime Ovale, José Siqueira, Pixinguinha, Donga, João da Baiana, and Ernesto Nazaré. Unlike those musicians who thematized African elements in popular Brazilian music, such composers as Zé Kéti, Cartola, Martinho da Vila, Milton Nascimento, Gilberto Gil, and the mulatto Dorival Caymmi are considered great composers and passionate interpreters of Afro-Brazilian culture.

In addition to these individual artists and performers, the samba schools in Rio de Janeiro as well as *blocos afro(s)* in Bahia (especially Ilê-Aiyê and Olodum) served and continue to serve as a training ground for the successful musicians we know today. Among these musical stars who have had international exposure and success we can name Gerônimo, Daniela Mercury, Alcione, Edson Gomes, and Carlinhos Brown. Visits by internationally acclaimed performers such as Paul Simon[6] and Michael Jackson,[7] who performed with Olodum for example, are an evidence of efforts toward globalization. Other developments point to the restlessness of Bahian youth and the search for an outlet through protesting lifestyles in the *favelas*, or ghettos, and through urban violence. This outlet is found in the message of frustration and defiance in their records. These Brazilian hip-hop artists or groups include Racionais MCs, Sistema Negro, GOG, Face da Morte, and Ndee Naldinho, among others. These are compelling voices of the Brazilian new wave as music takes on a more combative function in the resolution of racial discrimination and social injustice. These urgent and youthful producers can only hope that the targeted audience is listening to their desperate voices crying out for intervention and transformation.

In the field of literature, including the dramatic production of *Teatro Experimental do Negro* (Black Experimental Theater), led by Abdias do Nascimento, Afro-Brazilians' contributions cannot be ignored. For the sake of convenience, Afro-Brazilian literary production may be divided into two significant "moments": objectification and subjectivity. Objectification comprises the arrival of Africans in Brazil and the aftermath of slavery, the memory of slavery as projected by both blacks and whites, the modernist movement and the exclusion of black writers, and the subsequent thematization of Afro-Brazilians. Subjectivity concerns the search for the Afro-Brazilian voice and the black movements of the 1970s as well as the gradual process of legitimization of the Afro-Brazilian voice in the 1980s and 1990s, through postabolition centenary protests and increasing internationalization and visibility. Both moments reflect contrastive attitudes with respect to the Afro-Brazilian. The first moment has to do with literature about the Afro-Brazilian, while the second engages literary production from the viewpoints of Afro-Brazilians themselves.

Although the descendants of today's Afro-Brazilians first set foot in Brazil in the sixteenth century as slaves, they became quickly enmeshed in the cultural fabric of Brazil's heritage as early as the seventeenth century due to the condition of slavery that put both masters and slaves into a community-like commercial arrangement except that the labor was forced. For my purposes, I take this entry point of the African into Brazilian literature from the founding father of Brazilian literature, Gregório de Matos, in whose satirical poems are early references to blacks as "objects" in the Bahian colony thus qualifying their place in the social hierarchy:

> Who are her sweet objects? . . . Blacks.
> Are there others more appreciable? . . . The Métis.
> Who among these are appreciated? . . . Mulattoes.[8]

Following Gregório de Matos is Domingos Caldas Barbosa,[9] whose rhythmic poetry makes Edimilson de Almeida Pereira consider him the marker of Afro-Brazilian literature ("Survey," *Callaloo* 18.4 [1995]: 875). Due to his Indian-African heritage, Gonçalves Dias deserves a passing mention as far as Brazilian nationalism goes, although his penchant was for Indianism more than Africanism. Luiz Gonzaga Pinto da Gama, a mulatto of African-Portuguese parentage, moved away from the typical monotony of the praise of the white woman and replaced it with the sensibility of the black woman. He was an abolitionist who has been compared to Abdias do Nascimento,[10] an honor for both freedom fighters.

Controversial as he is in life and in death, Machado de Assis is the foremost Brazilian writer and founding president of the Brazilian Academy of Letters.[11] A genius by all artistic standards, he wrote in all literary genres leaving such canonical works as *Dom Casmurro, Epitaph of a Small Winner, Quincas borba* (Philosopher or Dog), and *Iaiá Garcia,* among others. The debate surrounding his blackness and commitment stems from his neutral position toward the abolition of slavery although as a renowned journalist at the time he had a chance to influence public opinion and voice his support in the same way Castro Alves did in his poetic works and passionate declamation, which gained him the accolade "singer of the slaves."[12] Beyond Machado, another significant writer of the nineteenth century is Lima Barreto, who, in contrast to Machado's silence, portrayed the injustices of slavery and racial discrimination in such works as *Recordações do escrivão Isaías Caminha, Clara dos Anjos,* and numerous incisive short stories. Other writers include Tobias Barreto de Menezes, a poet, sociologist, and philosopher, who could be considered a proponent of the myth of racial democracy *avant la lettre;* Antônio Gonçalves Crespo; José Patrocínio; and João da Cruz e Souza, a fine symbolist poet whose works still need more critical attention for their Afroconsciousness. These writers, among others, laid the foundation for the transitional phase of Afro-Brazilian literature, the *Semana de arte moderna* (Week of Modern Art), considered the marker of Brazilian modernism in 1922.

Brazilian modernism marks the beginning of the emergence of the AfroBrazilian voice even if at the outset it was a thematic voice rather than that of the subject. The conscious rediscovery and reevaluation of what is authentically Brazilian led to the revitalization of traditionalism, primitivism, regionalism, and the contribution of the Afro-Brazilian civilization, among others, to the Brazilian crucible. As Benedita Damasceno observes, "The climate of intellectual freedom sponsored by modernism led to the appearance of other intellectual and Black militant movements calling for the recognition and appreciation of black cultures and color" (*Poesia negra* 61). In this sense, modernism opened the gates for already well germinated and incubating ideas that were waiting to explode. And explode they did with the emergence of such Afro-Brazilian newspapers as *O clarim da alvorada* (1924), founded by Jaime de Aguiar, which demanded the immediate and nationwide integration of Afro-Brazilians; *A voz da raça* (1939), the official bulletin of Afro-Brazilian intellectuals who frequently met in São Paulo under their formal organization Frente Negra Brasileira. In addition, an Afro-Brazilian Congress was organized in 1940 by Nascimento, Edson Carneiro, and Guerreiro Ramos. Abdias do Nascimento crowned this moment by founding the highly regarded Afro-Brazilian theater *Teatro Experimental do Negro* (*TEN*) in 1944. Despite these achievements, one must ask why Afro-Brazilians were not participants at the significant Week of Modern Art.

The reasons are manifold. First, Mário de Andrade (1893–1945), who led the modernist movement, was a mulatto, a condition that is reflected in his often-cited statement "I am three hundred," as if to suggest that he has so many cultures and races in him that he would rather not defend or claim any one. In essence, he fits into that convenient frame of racial democracy that confirms his most "nationalistic" project in *Macunaíma*. Subtitled, "A Hero without Any Character," the work, also classified by the author as a "rhapsody," synthesizes the different traditions, customs, values, and folklore of Brazil into the multiple character of the protagonist name *Macunaíma*. Second, Afro-Brazilian writers such as Lino Guedes, Jorge de Lima, and Solano Trindade who were already writing poetry at the time were not considered "mature" and were marginalized yet. It was many years and decades after the modernist explosion before Afro-Brazilian writers finally emerged to recuperate their long-silenced voices. These voices include those of Jorge de Lima, who is renowned for his African rhythmic poems such as "Essa negra Fulô" (This Negress Fulô) and his epic poem "Invenção de Orfeu" (Invention of Orpheus); Jorge Amado, a white Bahian writer who contributed significantly to the spread of Afro-Brazilian culture through his novels, especially *Tenda dos milagres, Mar morto,* and *Jubiabá,* but who ironically, does not consider himself Afro-Brazilian; Solano Trindade, a contemporary of Abdias do Nascimento, a people's poet who used his poetry to sing and fight for freedom.

Abdias do Nascimento deserves a special mention due to his overall contribution to the general advancement of the dignity of Afro-Brazilians. He is widely considered an icon of the theater and an activist. He used his leadership of *TEN* to bring about social transformation through consciousness and rootedness in African mythology and culture. His play *Sortilégio* (Sortilege) betrays the contradictions and anguish of the alienated Afro-Brazilian who must be brought back to his roots through religious rites of passage and symbolic sacrifice. Beyond theater, Nascimento is also a visual artist, a professor, and ultimately, an elected senator between 1983 and 1997. His achievements are truly unique among Afro-Brazilians currently living.

The *movimento negro* (Black Movement), which can be said to have started in the 1950s, continued and became even more dynamic in the 1960s and most significantly in the 1970s during the era of the Black Power movement in the United States. One of the results of these ideological and militant agitations is the formation of a new cadre of writers who, for the sake of facility, could be called postmodernist black writers. Most of these writers would reject and resist this alienating label and would prefer to be called "ancestralist writers," for drawing inspiration from their African past.[13] This is the generation that was born during the fifties and sixties, in the heat of Afro-Brazilian struggles for equality and true emancipation. *Cadernos negros,* a literary series that started in 1978, is a brainchild of such a movement, organized and published through cooperative collaboration and donations by Quilombhoje, as the group came to be known since 1980.

In studying Quilombhoje as a cultural group and an integral part of contemporary Afro-Brazilian literature as a whole, I have arrived at a theoretical six-part categorization of the emerging tendencies, concerns, and patterns in their works. The first, which I have denominated the forerunners of Afro-modernity, includes the honorary members of the group. This is the "old guard" who are more like mentoring voices for the younger generation. The concerns here range from struggles for the affirmation of Afro-Brazilian identity to the preservation of collective memory. This category includes Oswald de Camargo, Abdias do Nascimento, and Eduardo de Oliveira. The second category, multiplicity and form, whose concern deals with aesthetic experimentation and multiplicity in the struggle with form, includes writers such as Cuti (Luíz Silva), Arnaldo Xavier, Ronald Tutuca, Carlos de Assumpção, and Landê Onawale. Often going beyond the racial problematic and ideological limitations of their predecessors, these writers entrench their discourse in issues of origin, religion and social problems.

The third, tradition and memory, combines their penchant for tradition and ancestral consciousness on the one hand with collective memory and the transgression of that same tradition on the other. These writers include Miriam Alves, Abelardo Rodrigues, Abílio Ferreira, Geni Guimarães, and Esmeralda Ribeiro. The fourth, regional consciousness, includes those writers who are not otherwise known beyond their regions of operation, such as Aline França, Jônatas Conceição da Silva, José Carlos Limeira, Adão Ventura, Oliveira Silveira, and Edimilson de Almeida Pereira. As is to be expected, their immediate concerns lie in the social problems of their regions as well as the beauty of their respective landscapes. The fifth, universality and transformation, brings together those writers who succeed in blending the racial with the universal in their concerns to dignify the human spirit beyond the confines of race. The form here is sophisticated and varied, terse and dramatic, succinct, subtle, and yet, accusatory. The final category, populism and ideology, refers to those writers who situate their ideology within the ancestral paradigm and the challenges of operating in such a traditional context within the daily constraints of rampant racism. These writers include Oubi Inaê Kibuko, Sônia Fátima, Conceição Evaristo, and Jamu Minka.

While this group collaborates to publish their works, most of them have branched off into publication of their individual works. The group itself has a policy of publishing an individual writer by ballot and quality of their work. Although this new generation of writers has this avenue for their outlet, some writers have gained recognition while others have not. A foremost Bahian storyteller, Deoscoredes M. dos Santos, better known as Mestre Didi, deserves a special mention. His stories, such as *Contos Crioulos da Bahia*, reflect the continuity of African oral traditions in Brazil; the recent publication in honor of his eightieth birthday, *Ancestralidade Africana no Brasil* (1999), is very commendable.

In terms of contemporary historiography, the most recent Afro-Brazilian work that has been heralded as a major achievement in Afro-Brazilian cultural production is Paulo Lins's *Cidade de Deus* (1997). Lins uses the trope of "God's own city" to capture the violence, fear, terror, misery, racism, and survival of slum life, particularly concerning drug trafficking. Although this slum actually exists, the name itself is the most compelling metaphoric paradox of living in the city of God and yet living like the devil incarnate. This is the best account of slum life since *Pixote*, a film that looks at the children of the street, and Carolina Maria de Jesus's rendition of poverty and survival in *Child of the Dark*. Another movie that is worth seeing is the new rendition of the classical *Black Orpheus* film, now simply titled *Orfeu* (Orpheus), directed by Carlos Diegues. Like *Cidade de Deus*, *Orpheus* is quite realistic, combining the carnival setting and a love story with the realities of slum life in Brazil. This reflects new aesthetic trend in Brazilian direction: the need to capture reality as it truly is without distortion. From music and carnival through literature, theater, and film, Afro-Brazilians have contributed significantly to the making of Brazil and deserve to be heard and to be subjects of research—hence my closing of this survey with a review of the state of the field.

A cursory bibliographic review is hopeful for it shows a surging interest in Afro-Brazilian studies at least in North America. Among the more compelling works include Roger Bastide's *Estudos Afro-Brasileiros*, Pierre Verger's *Flux e reflux de la traité de nègres entre le Golfe de Bénin et Bahia de todos os santos* and *Orixás*, David Brookshaw's *Race and Color in Brazilian Literature*, Carl Degler's *Neither Black nor White*, Thomas Skidmore's *Black into White*, Giorgio Marotti's *Black Characters in the Brazilian Novel*, Benedita Gouveia Damasceno's *Poesia negra no modernismo brasileiro*, Abdias do Nascimento and Elisa Larkin Nascimento's *Africans in Brazil*, George Reid Andrews's *Blacks and Whites in São Paulo*, David Hellwig's edited volume *African American Reflections on the Brazilian Racial Paradise*, Michael Hanchard's *Orpheus and Power: Racial Politics in Contemporary Brazil*, Robert Stam's *Tropical Multiculturalism*, France Winddance Twine's *Racism in a Racial Democracy*, Kim Butler's *Freedoms Given, Freedoms Won*, and Larry Crook and Randal Johnson's edited volume *Black Brazil*.[14]

On the political front, Brazil remains enigmatic even in the era of a seemingly new dispensation that was once thought inconceivable: affirmative action. Brazil has formally come to terms with racism and is attempting to redress the hypocrisy of the past through a rejection of the myth of racial democracy. For the last fifty years or so, the discussion of race has been structured and sponsored by the state to the extent that any position that differed from the denial of racism was considered an affront to state policy and security. With the exception of Afro-Brazilian activists and social science scholars who have consistently articulated the persistence of racial inequalities, Brazilians are generally hostile to the notion that racism is a fact of life in Brazil. Their arguments are often simplistic and unpersuasive: how can there be racism in a multiracial, multicolored, and multicultured national society? The combination of presidencies of Fernando Henrique

Cardoso and Lula seems to have ushered in a new way of thinking about race; acceptance of the notion of racial democracy as a myth is the first point of departure. Why would affirmative action policies be necessary if there is not a consensus about racial inequalities and racism? Mala Htun's optimistic stance on the changing state policy on race in Brazil provides provocative insights on Brazil's trajectory from official racial democracy to sponsor and advocate of affirmative action: "The culture celebrates mixity, and racial categories are fluid and ambiguous. Yet Brazil is profoundly stratified by color, and for decades, the state did nothing to alter the situation. In fact, it suppressed efforts to challenge the racial democracy myth and sought to whiten the population by encouraging European immigration. In the early 2000s, policy changed radically. The government admitted Brazil is racist and endorsed an extreme form of affirmative action—quotas—to address racial inequality" (61).

Brazil's admission of racism by default raises a number of issues on how to perceive Brazilian racial politics in the new millennium. The fact that state policies are being implemented to counter the extensive damage caused by racism over the years speaks to the heart of changing state consciousness and conviction. Htun attributes the following factors to the sudden change in policy: first, policy discourse mobilized by Afro-Brazilian activism; second, Brazil's political gain in marketing its liberal credentials to the rest of the world; third, the World Conference on Racism held in Durban, South Africa, in 2001, during which Brazilian policy makers pledged to institute changes on racial inequalities; and fourth, a dialectic process between social mobilization and presidential initiative framed within the international context.

Although it is too soon to assess the effects of these policy changes on inequalities in Brazil, such concrete measures as the presidential creation of an affirmative action program; introduction of quotas for blacks, women, and the physically challenged; an initiative to increase blacks' presence in the diplomatic sector; and gradual expansion of university admissions to reserve 40 percent of slots for Afro-Brazilians are beyond cosmetic, but must also not be seen as a guarantee of future improvement. If it has taken decades for Brazil to change its position of legal racial discrimination, it will probably take some time to see the results of these new transformative initiatives.

Márcio Barbosa completes his survey of the Quilombhoje group on an optimistic yet challenging note by saying, "O grande desafio é não parar" (The ultimate challenge is not to lose momentum).[15] Indeed, Afro-Brazilians have come a long way in creatively overcoming the immense odds against them. It is through their persistent sacrifices over the years that the notion of affirmative action has become a reality. Hopefully, racial democracy can be reconstituted and remedied in the years to come. In this era of globalization and cultural studies, and given the resonances between Brazil and the United States, it is worthwhile conducting comparative studies between the Afro-American and Afro-Brazilian experience in order to elicit commonalities and differences. Drawing such connections helps compare, for example, how Afro-Brazilians perceive Afro-Americans and vice versa, as well as the achievements of each group in the struggle for full citizenship and true democracy.

The notion of Afro-modernity in Brazil is indeed a political statement, for it encapsulates how Afro-Brazilians negotiate their African heritage and culture within shifting global processes of modernization and its attendant gains, losses, and contradictions, especially in the political domain. Beyond examining the "racist caricature" and folklorization of Afro-Brazilian culture that begun in the nineteenth century and still continues today, this section of the book sets out to fulfill three main objectives. First, it theorizes on the notions of ancestrality and modernity in Afro-Brazilian culture. Second, it exposes about forty cultural producers who are yet to receive due critical attention for their contributions to Brazilian culture as a whole. Third, it attempts to demarginalize Afro-Brazilian culture by exposing it to an English-speaking audience (obviously, most books on Afro-Brazilian affairs are written in Portuguese). The study itself crystallizes my own research in Brazil over the last twenty-five years. During these years, I had the opportunity to rekindle interactions with significant and emerging cultural producers whom I have known since the early eighties. Twenty years after these initial contacts, something continues to baffle me about the Afro-Brazilian experience and condition: the continued state of disempowerment and lack of political participation. The Lula presidency inaugurated in January 2003 seems to have ushered in a "new era" with what I call three "black faces of power" in his new administration. Until recently, Gilberto Gil was minister of culture; Benedita da Silva occupied the Ministry of Social Action, while Marina Silva continues to serve as the minister of the environment. While Lula's appointments are commendable, three of about forty ministerial positions makes for a paltry level of representation for a country that continues to sell the claim of "racial democracy" to the rest of the world. Afro-Brazilians, after all, constitute at least half of the population. This is why, contrary to the official illusion that Brazilians are living in a raceless society, race cannot but be part of any discussion of modernity in Brazil.

Chapter 8, "Ancestrality and the Dynamics of Afro-Modernity," asserts the validity of the ancestral paradigm within the modernist and postmodernist manifestations of Afro-Brazilian culture. It engages a number of cultural theorists, such as Paul Gilroy, Abdias do Nascimento, Terry Eagleton, Michael Hanchard, Júlio Braga, and Birago Diop, while arguing that the African diaspora must not be seen as the "appendage" of European or Western modernity but a shifting atemporal process of adaptation, innovation, and renewal of African values that people of African descent took with them during the transatlantic passage to their new locations. Despite the depiction of Africa by colonialists and enslavers as a "primitive" continent that the West actually tried to save from itself, and the appropriation of such myths in the contemporary discourse on race relations and racial discrimination, the juxtaposition of modernity with tradition in this section reveals the value of ancestral strength as a necessary instrument of disalienation from a systematic alienation of Africans in Africa as well as in the diaspora.

Chapter 9, "The Forerunners of Afro-Brazilian Modernity," exposes four writers, namely Solano Trindade, Abdias do Nascimento, Eduardo de Oliveira, and Oswaldo de Camargo—all of whom belong to the vanguard era of Afro-Brazilian culture. Born between the early twentieth century and the thirties, they represent the voices that were already mature in the seventies to articulate their protest against racial oppression in Brazil and in consonance with the civil rights and Black Power movements in the United States. In their different styles, they communicate their frustrations that may be summed up as the burden of blackness. Comparable to Langston Hughes in his poetic imagination, and with special concern for the poor and the downtrodden in society, Solano Trindade sings and cries for freedom. Abdias do Nascimento uses African mythology and religion to challenge Afro-Brazilians to appreciate and take pride in their African origin. He is also an avid critic of racial democracy in Brazil. His outspokenness forced him into exile in the early years of Brazil's military dictatorship, and his theory of *Quilombismo* is acknowledged in Afro-Brazilian studies. Eduardo de Oliveira adopts the formal style of Parnassianism in his poetry, but he is no less an activist who propagates black beauty, pride, and personality. Like Oliveira's, Oswaldo de Camargo's works have an engagement with form, but he is not as politically committed as Oliveira. Camargo's attitude to the Afro-Brazilian condition can be characterized as a refusal to accept the position of a victim. Instead, he searches for perfection in style and life as a way of proving his humanity and moving beyond the stigma of blackness. These four pioneer cultural producers laid the foundation for the proclamation of Afro-Brazilian modernity and postmodernity that flourished in spite of nonrecognition of their efforts in the eighties.

Chapter 10, "(Un)Transgressed Tradition," discusses the possibility and pitfalls of transgressing blackness and Afro-Brazilian tradition through aesthetic experimentation with multiple forms. This chapter argues that the cultural producers such as Cuti, Arnaldo Xavier, and Ronald Tutuca do not succeed in moving beyond their identity despite their efforts to write in sophisticated media. Although they write about freedom from bondage, their attempts to move beyond the racial problematic are negated by their constant referential discourse on African origin, religion, and social problems, which results in the conscious use of the very instrument of their subjugation for their liberation. The struggle faced by this younger generation of writers goes beyond the ideological limitations of their predecessors. On the one hand, they are compelled to modify the rules of engagement since the militant phase of the movement has waned. On the other hand, they have also realized the importance of communicating with a wider audience, especially university-based critics who will undoubtedly subject their works to Western standards. If consciousness of an esoteric audience is responsible for the abstruse writing by Xavier and Tutuca especially, they have also inadvertently succeeded in alienating themselves from their primary audience—Afro-Brazilians. As a result, it is questionable whether this group of intellectual cultural producers is communicating with the people or in actuality simply communicating with a bourgeois Brazilian population who may or may not sympathize with the overall cause of the masses of Afro-Brazilians.

Chapter 11, "Ancestrality, Memory, and Citizenship," discusses the works of Esmeralda Ribeiro, Miriam Alves, Abílio Ferreira, and Geni Guimarães to ascertain how they negotiate their ancestral consciousness and memory with the contradictions of a citizenship they are still struggling to attain. By citizenship, I suggest that Afro-Brazilians are yet to strip themselves of the mantle of slavery, which inhibits true political participation. Each of these cultural producers adopts a different approach in their "cry for freedom." For Ribeiro, a simple piece of telephone apparatus inherited from her father is used to dramatize the importance of heritage and sense of ownership through articulation and assertion. The transformation of this material "inheritance" into a "community action" through its insertion into the samba school serves to illustrate the community ties Afro-Brazilians share and yet confirm that political power is only limited to popularized performative spirituality and culturalism. Ancestrality for Alves lies in the spiritual performance and homage to the African goddesses believed to control the four elements of nature: earth, water, air, and fire as a pretext to tell the story of the transatlantic passage comparable to *I Is a Long-Memoried Woman*. As the most prolific of Afro-Brazilian women writers, Guimarães considers the process of production as that of childbirth. *Terceiro filho* (Third Child) confirms this position as she exposes autobiographical elements concerning unreciprocated love in her passionate relationships and her struggles to overcome that feeling of emptiness. What is curious in Guimarães's writing is a certain distance from open engagement with racism. Perhaps she is too involved with being loved that discrimination has become nonexistent or minimized in her own mind. Remarkably, Ferreira succeeds in condensing the individual concern with the collective in "A casa de Fayola" (Fayola's House)—an archetypal text that sums up the challenges of modernity and tradition as Afro-Brazilians grapple with their ancestrality and the exigencies of modernity in the Brazilian racial "paradise."

Chapter 12, "*Quilombo* without Frontiers," analyzes the cultural production of regional writers from Bahia and Minas Gerais with particular emphasis on their unity and diversity. Covering an extensive array of cultural producers, it uses the trope of the "*quilombo*" as a point of commonality in their manifestation of protest and decolonized consciousness. These two regions are significant in Brazilian intellectual and political history since they represent two historical eras with different racial tensions both of which have their origins in slavery and colonialism. Bahia has often been referred to as the "Black Rome," a befitting accolade for a cultural and religious space that replicates African presence, and the relics that Africans brought as slaves to Brazil, through torturous memory and resilient performances. With its different "*engenhos*" (sugar plantations) and reminiscent of the "*pelourinho*" (the place of flagellation), Minas Gerais also is noted for cattle raising, which did not make slave labor and culture any less traumatic. In the poetic world of Antônio Vieira, the memory of Africa is recollected during many journeys across Africa and North America, a form of "reverse diaspora" that confirms the poet as an invocator of Africa, a contemporary Castro Alves who not only laments the horrors of the transatlantic passage but pays homage to the strength and beauty of Africa through nostalgia. Jônatas Conceição da Silva engages the "margins" as a formidable trope to capture the displacement and dispossession of Afro-Brazilians in their daily lives. José Carlos Limeira is an activist poet in the sense that he seems to consciously seek out situations that embarrass and ridicule white oppressors by contrasting them to Afro-Brazilian heroic historical figures such as Zumbi dos Palmares and Luíza Mahin. I consider Aline França one of the Afro-Brazilian women voices caught in the structural invisibility engineered by Brazilian society itself. A well-rooted Bahian woman, she sings about the prophetic salvation of her people from the hands of white oppressors and environmental abuse. In their varied stylistic approaches, the Afro-Mineiro cultural producers such as Adão Ventura, Edimilson de Almeida Pereira, Marcos Dias, Ricardo Aleixo, Waldemar Pereira, and Anélito de Oliveira equally indict the burden of blackness and the need to move beyond the stigma. This extensive chapter demonstrates the richness and diversity of Afro-Brazilian cultural production in the modernist frame.

Chapter 13, "Ancestral Motherhood of Leci Brandão," analyzes the Yoruba ancestral and Afro-Brazilian connections that motivate Leci Brandão's cultural production. Unlike Daniela Mercury, the Bahian solo performer who has popularized the songs of many Afro-Bahian Carnival groups, Brandão is still shrouded in regional oblivion, but she can no longer be neglected. Continuing the legacy of such eminent singers as Alcione and Beth Carvalho, whose samba lyrics continue to be heard in the mouths of Brazilians, especially in the *pagode* circles, Brandão has produced a significant lyrical output with political sensibility that deserves to be brought to light. Given the limited research done on her to date and the scanty bibliographic resources, this chapter situates her work within the entire spectrum of Brazilian popular music in order to assess her full importance, focusing in particular on her 2005 performance, with other major *pagode* talents, in *Raça brasileira/Casa do pagode (20 anos)*.

A pluralistic society such as Brazil ought to be multifaceted in its critical perspective. The current tendency of elitism and politicization of critical outlets for the dissemination of Afro-Brazilian culture does a disservice to the producers of that culture. As the Afro-Brazilian interviewee notes in the movie *King for a Day*, the producers of Afro-Brazilian culture are no longer in charge of their own culture but are treated as petty informants to the professional exploiters and beneficiaries of that culture through the latter's economic power and control—a condition that is only tangentially redressed during Carnival celebrations. This book is my own modest contribution to what I see as a lifelong struggle to see Afro-Brazilian culture recognized as part of Brazilian culture, as a fully integrated element that is not just a subject of study. Likewise, Afro-Brazilian cultural producers highlighted in this book are only a sampler of so many more that deserve close critical attention. The Afro-Brazilian cultural producers highlighted herein demonstrate, through both their Afro-modernity and ancestral connections, how the people's common African history, including the traumatic experience and survival of slavery, has led to imaginative strategies for coping with the ramifications of marginality. Ultimately, new aesthetic models expressing frustrations and renewed resolve serve to indicate how Afro-Brazilians continue to make sense of their present conditions.

1

Two Faces of Racial Democracy

> To make believe color is not noticed in social situations is to end up permitting discrimination by default. To recognize that discrimination is an ever-present tendency in any society in which there is a physically identifiable group is to take the first step in guarding against prejudice.
>
> —Carl Degler, *Neither Black nor White*

> Analyzing today's [1968] reality we could almost say that the Golden Law was signed yesterday. The situation of the free Negro has changed a little in the 80 years since abolition: low social, educational, economic, political, and sanitary status, and the list of frustrations transformed into a strong potentiality of just resentments by the race.
>
> —Abdias do Nascimento, *O negro revoltado*

Many are the masks of inequality in Brazil and limited are the strategies of resistance: Carnival, samba, capoeira, and the representation of the mulatta in Brazilian literature and culture are a few of the cultural manifestations competing for a place in the exportation of myth and the exploitation of the Afro-Brazilian experience. Even the most casual observer of Brazil is easily co-opted into believing that, somehow, it is possible to live in a world free of prejudices and inequalities given a racial mixture that facilitates harmony and racial blindness. Roberto Schwarz captures this blindness in *Misplaced Ideas* when he cites sarcastically: "Better [to] have good Negroes from the African coast, for our happiness and theirs, notwithstanding the Briton, with his morbid philanthropy, which makes him forget his own home and allows a poor white brother to die from anger, a slave without a master to pity him; the hypocritical and stupid Briton, who oversees the destiny of our happy slave and thus exposes himself to the ridicule of true philanthropy" (19). Hence cultural contact between Africa and Brazil through the intermediary of the Portuguese colonizer was a "harmonious" and "happy" and "beneficial" one to both parties.

Here slavery is manipulated and projected as a noble and philanthropic project in favor of the slave. The three hundred years of slavery in Brazil and the subjugation and rape of the Afro-Brazilian mind and soul prove otherwise.

Ironically, some Brazilians have been so brainwashed that this perspective remains engrained within the myth of racial democracy that pervades Brazilian identity, life, and culture as manifest, above all, in the legitimization of racism. To the student conscious of Brazilian racial relations, nothing can be further from the truth. For how can there possibly be discrimination in a racial democracy? And how can Afro-Brazilians be marginalized and alienated in a so-called racial paradise to which they supposedly belong? These are pertinent and larger rhetorical questions that orient our discussion in the specific field of Afro-Brazilian literature with particular focus on Lima Barreto and Machado de Assis. As this study will show, "racial paradise" translates into a matter of perception, a normalized absurdity that finds justification in the institutionalized myth of *mestiçagem* or *miscigenação* (race mixture). The comparative discussion of Machado and Barreto raises a number of questions. While I take the position that Machado's criticism of social injustices is less forthright relative to Afro-Brazilians than the open attack by Barreto, Machado is considered by many as a refined parodist, a subtle and ironic writer—hence the propensity for critics to misread his intentions. Edimilson Almeida de Pereira suggests, for example, that "art frees the artist," but the individual's freedom is far less significant than the collective, especially in the preabolition era when energies were directed toward freedom for the slaves. I take issue with Pereira's complacent position in the sense that Machado de Assis cannot be considered incisive and straightforward in his criticism of Brazilian society if all he did was avoid confrontation of volatile political issues through deft use of ambiguity.

Within the limits of this comparative exposition, the frank articulation of a black/mulatto consciousness in the case of Barreto and the deliberate assumption of a "false" identity through denial of blackness and a "strategic" alliance with the white establishment as in Machado's writing, provide a viable prism for the analysis of the Brazilian dilemma. And a dilemma it is, for while Machado de Assis is constantly heralded as the greatest Brazilian writer of all times, Lima Barreto is marginalized and relegated to the place of a melancholic singer of blues in life and death. The irony of this differential critical reception and success is perhaps most compelling in our engagement with the life, works, and times of these singular Brazilian writers. By exploring racial consciousness and implications for inequalities in late-nineteenth-century and early-twentieth-century Brazil, the select works of these two canonical writers contrastively confirm and question the myth of racial democracy—for example, Barreto's *Recordações do escrivão Isaías Caminha* and *Clara dos Anjos* and Machado's *Iaiá Garcia*. While these works are meant as pathways into the literary and cultural theories of each writer, they also share a commonality: coming to terms with the perception of the Brazilian racial reality through the landscapes of Rio de Janeiro and the representation of the Afro-Brazilian during slavery and abolition. Contextually, both writers paint the drama of Rio de Janeiro at the turn of the nineteenth century but differ in their sociothematic concerns. While Lima Barreto identifies with the pain and struggles of the urban periphery, Machado de Assis identifies with the urban bourgeoisie. The contrast is not only an interesting one, it has implications for the respective writers' construction of their own identities as conditioned by societal façade and self-conscious allegiances. The confessional mode relative to the burden of being black or mulatto in Barreto contrasts with Machado's attempt at escaping his African origin and identity thus making himself a recluse within that false "mulatto escape hatch." The attitudes of Machado and Barreto toward their origin and Afro-Brazilian identity are viable case studies in "escape" as an aesthetic form of dealing with reality. For Machado, escape translates into a denial of the racial dilemma, a form of deliberate amnesia that appeals to the carioca, and by extension the Brazilian upper class, through skillful ambiguity. For Barreto, however, escape is through the power of the pen, a constructive and well-channeled anger, partly accusatory and partly therapeutic, with the ultimate goal of recuperating and negotiating Afro-Brazilian identity and humanity. *Recordações* and *Clara dos Anjos,* situated between the earlier and later phases of Barreto's career, provide ample evidence of the ideological stance of the writer against racial discrimination, while *Iaiá Garcia* belongs to the intermediary phase of Machado's literary development, the transition between the romantic and realist eras. Regardless of *when* they wrote, *how* and *what* they wrote about are even more relevant if we are to understand their opposite ideologies, which in turn nourished their differing creative impulses. The unity of these three works lies in the manipulative problematic of love, be it self-love or the lack of it, as in Machado's works or self-love by protest as in Barreto's.

In his seminal work *Sociologia do negro brasileiro,* which vividly captures the essence of these works, Clóvis Moura affirms that the literary representation of the Afro-Brazilian is a direct reflection of the social structure. Urgently calling for a revisionist approach to the study of Afro-Brazilian literature, he cites Machado de Assis as a typical example of a whitened writer who is bent on whitening his characters as well:

> Temos o exemplo de Machado de Assis que escreve durante a escravidão como se vivesse uma realidade urbana européia, querendo branquear os seus personagens, heróis e heroínas. Toda a primeira geração romântica, por isto mesmo, é uma geração cooptada pelo aparelho ideológico ou burocrático do sistema escravista. Por isto mesmo não podiam criar uma literatura que refletisse o nosso *ser* cultural. (27)

[We have the example of Machado de Assis, who writes during slavery as if he were living an urban European reality, intent on whitening his characters, heroes, and heroines. Hence the entire first romantic generation is a co-opted generation within the ideological and bureaucratic apparatus of the slave system. That was why they could not portray *our* cultural reality in their literary works.]

Unlike Machado, Barreto was not able to be co-opted partly due to his consciousness of his racial identity and the burden that accompanied blackness in Brazil of the colonial era. Moura goes on to praise Barreto as the writer who dignifies the Afro-Brazilian as a fictional character who is not only human but who articulates his own individuality. It is against the background of these contrastive metaphors of "co-optation" and "dignification" that we situate our readings of Machado de Assis and Lima Barreto.

Machado de Assis: A Co-opted Writer

The "co-optation" of Machado de Assis is voluntary and self-conscious. In order to anchor himself on the Aryan pedestal, he must not only claim his "mulatto-ness," but must also deny his blackness. Born a mulatto in 1839 to poor parents, a white mother from the Azores Islands and a black father, his ambition to transcend the limitations associated with blackness and poverty forced him to distance himself both publicly and privately from issues related to slavery. While he rose steadily on the social ladder, he sacrificed his most valuable weapon (his voice) by not openly speaking out against slavery. While Maria Luisa Nunes in her article "The Artist's Identity" attempts to rationalize Machado's indifference, claiming that Machado's detractors are motivated by "envy and intrigue further elaborated upon by a large dose of racism" (189), I insist that social mobility is no excuse for Machado's cynical silence and ambiguity in the face of slavery and the abolitionist movement. One need not be socially mobile in order to pay allegiance to one's race.

In his obsession with rising socially, Machado focuses his energy on the creation of characters who have appeal only to the bourgeoisie while ridiculing his few black characters by assigning them marginal roles as happy slaves, domestic servants and suckling black mothers among others. Machado's evident need to please his favored white upper-class audience continues to earn him stiff criticism among some Afro-Brazilian intelligentsia. I consider this attitude of Machado, even when subconscious, as a quintessential case of social and moral irresponsibility. By the time of his death in 1908, Machado had accomplished perhaps what a black Brazilian could only dream of at the turn of the twentieth century: acceptance by the cultural elite into the aristocratic society, along with the founding presidency of the Academia Brasileira de Letras, literary fame, recognition, and popular acclaim. But at what price? The most virulent criticism of Machado's lack of contribution and commitment to the Afro-Brazilian cause is to be found in Mário de Andrade's conclusion in *Aspectos da literatura brasileira*. Sarcastically describing Machado as "um homem que me desagrada e que eu não desejaria para o meu convívio" (103; an unpleasant fellow I would not like to have around me), Andrade dissects the motives and limitations of Machado's creative imagination emphasizing the permanent scar on his otherwise fine accomplishments as a foremost Brazilian writer:

> Machado de Assis é um fim, não é um começo e sequer um alento novo recolhido em caminho. Ele coroa um tempo inteiro, mas a sua influência tem sido sempre negativa. . . . Machado de Assis não profetizou nada, não combateu nada, não ultrapassou nenhum limite infecundo. Viveu moral e espiritualmente escanchado na burguesice do seu funcionarismo garantido e muito honesto, afastando de si os perigos visíveis. . . . E se o Mestre não pôde ser um protótipo do homem brasileiro, a obra dele nos dá a confiança do nosso mestiçamento, e vaia os absolutistas raciais com o mesmo rijo apito com que Himanitas vaio o sedentarismo das filosofias de contemplação. (107–8)

> [Machado de Assis is an end, not a beginning, not even a fresh breath of air taken on the way. He crowns an entire period, but his influence has always been negative. . . . Machado de Assis prophesied nothing. He did not combat on behalf of any cause, nor did he transcend the limits of his own *myopic fecundity*. Morally and spiritually, he sat on the fence and safety nest of bourgeois values, security and respectability of his status as a civil servant, protecting himself from all visible danger. . . . But creative works are more valuable than their creators. And if the Master could never be a true prototype of Brazilian man, his work encourages us to be proud of our mixed descent, and ridicule racial absolutes in the same blatant way that Humanities mocked the sedentary philosophies of contemplation.] (Emphasis added)

In the process of protecting himself from his own skin, which is laden with countless stereotypes, Machado "sold out" to the Europeanized cultural values that enslaved and still enslave Afro-Brazilians. How can one be proud of a "mixed descent" when one significant part of that descent is neither recognized nor accepted? Racial absolutism may be a backward reasoning, yet the survival of one race is as important as the other and that is where the notion of racial democracy is a hypocritical illusion.

For a writer of national and international fame, the legacy of Machado de Assis in Brazil remains that of a "great" writer for all times. Yet, to Afro-Brazilians, those I consider his "neglected people," he is nothing but a cowardly traitor whose self-centeredness, alienation, and reliance on the so-called "mulatto escape hatch" combine to disqualify him as a deserving contributor to the cause of black liberation, especially during the era of the abolition struggle. Of his numerous chronicles, short stories, and novels, only a handful feature black characters even when they are of secondary importance. In most of these works, Machado either privileges the master-slave relationship even when the slave has been set free, as in the plight of Raimundo in *Iaiá Garcia,* or describes the slave condition indifferently without any comment on its oppressive and degrading effects on the human condition, thereby reinforcing the status quo, as found in short stories like "Pai contra Mãe," "O Caso da Vara," "Mariana," and countless chronicles in which Machado depicts the Afro-Brazilian as a powerless and voiceless prey in the hands of the oppressive master and system.

Even in *Iaiá Garcia,* published in 1878, ten years before the official abolition of slavery, where there is a full development of a black character, what is the social status of this character? As to be expected, another loyal, faithful, and "happy" ex-slave! There is no attempt to highlight any significant changes in the plight of the former slave whose relationship remains slavish toward the former master. Although Machado may have been unaware of the implications at the time, it behooves the critic to uncover the mentality behind such an indifferent attitude and construction, especially when the writer was a mulatto. As the last novel of his romantic phase, *Iaiá Garcia* combines the romantic theme of love with larger sociopolitical issues of slavery, abolition, bondage, freedom, and human degradation.

Machado's co-optation is betrayed in his skillful treatment of color, class, and culture as it relates to the problematic of marriage and social impediments in *Iaiá Garcia.* The theme of triangular love is superimposed on the dilemma of pride as well as the place of the Afro-Brazilian as a "loyal" ex-slave. Although Raymond Sayers, in *The Negro in Brazilian Literature,* gives more credit than necessary to Machado's portrayal of Raimundo, the ex-slave, we suggest that any critical reception that considers *Iaiá Garcia* as "Machado's tribute to the Negro" (207) is as faulty as Machado's "prejudiced" representation. The excuses enumerated by Sayers (203), from Machado hating his own race to the writer's acceptance of human misery are myopic and apologetic. That the Afro-Brazilian was not a suitable subject for Machado's satire given his "fixed" position as slave in Brazilian society is equally debatable. A character need not be a "free agent" (204) to be used as a subject of satire. In fact, Raimundo's portrayal as an "ex"-slave is satirical in itself. Although "free," he is still playing the role of a loyal slave. What can be more ironic? Since my interest here goes beyond Machado's philosophy of *humanitas,* the notion of competition, individualism, and survival of the fittest and strongest ("Ao vencedor as batatas"—Victory to the winner!), I will focus on the development or nondevelopment of Raimundo as an Afro-Brazilian character and its implication for Machado's co-optation in this novel.

Iaiá Garcia explores the complex drama of Jorge and Estela, whose relationship fails due to a combination of factors: lack of will on the part of one of them, Jorge. Beyond the dilemma of passionate but "weak" Jorge, social conventions play another role as reflected in the class discrimination represented by Valéria, a rich widow and Jorge's excessively controlling mother. In order to ensure Jorge does not marry Estela, Valéria seeks the services of Luís Garcia, a widowed public servant, to convince Jorge to serve his country (Brazil) in the Paraguaian War under the guise of patriotism.[1] Jorge leaves for the battlefield where he fights valiantly to "escape" his frustration and "rejection" by Estela. Concerned with Jorge's imminent return, Valéria quickly arranges a marriage of convenience between Estela and Luís Garcia, father of a thirteen-year-old named Iaiá Garcia (Lina). In spite of their age difference, Luís and Estela get married and live happily with Iaiá, while Valéria soon dies.

At the end of the Paraguaian War, which lasted five to six years, Jorge returns to Rio triumphantly and well decorated. As a family friend, he falls in love with Iaiá. Sick and dying, Luís asks Jorge to take good care of his wife and daughter. Meanwhile, Iaiá had always doubted Estela's love for Jorge, and she becomes his fiancée in order to ensure peace in her father's marriage. Once engaged to Jorge, Iaiá realizes the old passion between Jorge and Estela, her stepmother. A cold war of suspicions soon ensues between Iaiá and Estela. Luís dies oblivious to it all. Iaiá calls off the engagement and offers herself instead to fifty-year-old Procópio Dias, who has always admired and desired her, so as to allow Estela to marry Jorge. Iaiá's feelings fluctuate between resentment and understanding. Estela confesses to Iaiá that she does not love Jorge, thus facilitating a rekindling of love and engagement between Iaiá and Jorge. However, there is a snag: in order to avoid an impending tragedy, Raimundo, the ex-slave, fails to deliver Iaiá's love letter to Procópio and as a result, Iaiá and Jorge marry for love while Estela leaves Rio to become a teacher in São Paulo.

Iaiá Garcia's complex plot structure clearly privileges upper-class characters like Valéria, the powerful, calculating, and rich matchmaker who forbids Jorge's romance with Estela due to the latter's lower-class status; Luís Garcia, Iaiá's father, who inherits not only monetary properties from his father but also a human "property" such as the ex-slave, Raimundo; Iaiá Garcia, Luís's daughter, whose pragmatism and affluence are critical in the manipulation of the multiple love triangles (Luís–Estela–Jorge; Luís–Estela–Iaiá; Jorge–Iaiá–Procópio; and Iaiá–Jorge–Estela). We are left with Raimundo having no significant function, nor does he fit into a triangle where he might play any dynamic role. Rather content to be the happy "ex-slave" in the hands of Machado, grateful to be a "good" and "faithful" servant, he is a willing tool of manipulation and exploitation. The differential representation of the characters among whom Raimundo is the least developed and complicated makes obvious Machado's co-optation. While Raimundo's role may be said to be critical as the facilitator of the happy union between Jorge and Iaiá at the end of the story, it is nevertheless a subservient one. Raimundo, the letter-carrier, decides not to deliver the message to Procópio Dias in order to save his former master's daughter from any heartache. Indeed, Raimundo seems to have been a "slave" to three generations of masters: Luís Garcia's father, Luís Garcia himself, and now, the latter's daughter, Iaiá. Raimundo does not have a life of his own; he is always at the service of others—a domesticated figure from the beginning to the end of the novel. The question, then, for Machado is: Is this all Raimundo is good for? The answer lies in the marginal character development of Raimundo in *Iaiá Garcia*. It is safe to consider Raimundo as a flat figure and not necessarily a character in the novel. And this is where critics who praise or defend Machado for his modest contribution are subjective and overbearing.[2] The representation of Raimundo is merely a representation of local color to reinforce and legitimize the "passive," "cordial," and "subservient" stereotypes of Afro-Brazilians in racist discourse.

For Machado, Raimundo is just a useful structural frame for the "sandwiched" love triangles and episodic plot structure. He first appears at the beginning of *Iaiá Garcia* as a symbolic figure whose ultimate role at the end of the story is not surprising: he ends up in the same role as when he was first introduced despite the express freedom granted him by Luís Garcia. The reader's first encounter with Raimundo is appalling, pathetic, and humiliating. It is a portrayal that may be acceptable to the upper-class audience of Machado, yet is insulting to the intelligence and humanity of the freed slaves after 1888:

> Raimundo parecia feito expressamente para servir Luís Garcia. Era um preto de cinqüenta anos, estatura mediana, forte, apesar de seus largos dias, um tipo de africano, submisso e dedicado. Era escravo e livre. Quando Luís Garcia o herdou de seu pai,—não avultou mais o espólio,—deu-lhe logo carta de liberdade. Raimundo, nove anos mais velho que o senhor, carrega-o ao colo e amava-o como se fora seu filho. Vendo-se livre, pareceu-lhe que era um modo de o expelir de casa, e sentiu um impulso atrevido e generoso. Fez um gesto para rasgar a carta de alforria, mas arrependeu-se a tempo. Luís Garcia viu só a generosidade, não o atrevimento; palpou o afeto do escravo, sentiu-lhe o coração todo. Entre um e outro houve um pacto que para sempre os uniu.
>
> —És livre, disse Luís Garcia; viverás comigo até quando quiseres. (14–15)

> [Raimundo seemed expressly made to serve Luís Garcia. He was a black man in his fifties, of medium stature, strong in spite of his years, a type of African that was submissive and dedicated. He was a slave though free. When Luís Garcia inherited him from his father, he did not count him as part of the spoils but immediately gave him a certificate of freedom. Raimundo, nine years older than his master, had carried the latter in his arms and awakened him in the morning as though he were his own son. Finding himself free, he felt that

his freedom was a way of being expelled from the home; and he experienced a daring though generous impulse: he made a gesture as though to tear up the enfranchisement letter. But he repented in time. Luís Garcia noticed only the generosity, not the boldness. He was touched by the slave's affection and understood his sincerity completely. Between the two a closer tie was woven which united them forever.

"You are free," said Luís Garcia; "you may live with me as long as you like."]

The notion of being "expressly made to serve Luís Garcia" is a loaded life sentence from which there will be no clemency for Raimundo throughout the novel. What is more interesting is how Machado, a master of ambiguity and irony, blames Raimundo's continued enslavement on his own choice to remain within the Garcia household in order not to lose the benefits of family security even though his place remains that of a perpetual servant. This description of Raimundo as "submissive," "dedicated," and "generous" betrays Machado's attitude toward the slave condition in late-nineteenth-century Brazil. How can an old man in his fifties, nine years older than Luís Garcia himself, be "happy" to be his slave? What kind of permanent "tie" of subjectivity and subservience can be so cordial, unresisting, and "understanding"? Of course, we may blame Raimundo for being so passive and subservient, yet within the context of slavery, that was all he could be. But Machado is being crafty and engaging in double-speak, hence his depiction of Raimundo as "a slave though free" as if to be simultaneously in favor of and against abolition.

By complicating Raimundo's plight, Machado may in fact be playing on his art of ambiguity while at the same time foreseeing the era of abolition and its ambiguous implication for the freed slave. Since *Iaiá Garcia* was published ten years before the abolition of slavery, Machado seems too cautious to articulate any opinion that will set him at odds with the dominant white elite. Even if caution, tact, and diplomacy were his intentions, they are ideologically misplaced and compromised. Here is an opportunity to show what freedom could do for the slave. Here is an opportunity for Raimundo to rebel and show a certain amount of self-dignity. Instead, Machado's argument seems to be that the slave will continue to be a slave even when set free. In fact, by turning the argument around, Raimundo is made to look like the architect of his own plight, his eternal slave condition. He has been set free by "his master"—the same child he once "carried . . . in his arms . . . as though he were his own son"—yet, due to the master-slave/father-son type of "bond" between them, Raimundo is reluctant to leave. Ironically, Raimundo has in fact become the child and Luís Garcia, once a child, is now his new master, the same way he will go on to be of service to Iaiá, later on in the story. In addition, the mere idea of having to leave the relative "comfort" of enslavement is not conceivable to the slave. Freedom, then, is still slavery by choice according to Machado, and the denial of freedom may be said to be a generous act and a favor to the slave. And this is where Machado's thesis completely falls apart. I remain unconvinced that Machado had any abolitionist spirit and was speaking against slavery between the lines. At best, Machado's legacy will always be that of a master of ambiguity and ideological nonalignment.

Even Raimundo's "impulso rebelde" (rebellious impulse) that Raymundo Faoro contends is born out of disappointment is questionable since it was a moment of decision and self-discovery for Raimundo.[3] Weighing the odds and options available to him, Raimundo settles for what I consider oppressive comfort. What is rebellious about simply taking the easy way out? What is rebellious about being happy to be a slave? The psychological analysis Machado paints of Raimundo fits well with the racist thesis that the slave needs the master to be human just the same way the master needs the passivity of the slave to feel wholesome and in control. On a closer analysis, Raimundo's rebellion lies somewhere else as Machado puts it in his description of Raimundo: "he felt that his freedom was a way of being expelled from the home." His "rebellion," in fact, stems from his reaction to the prospect of his expulsion from the house—an unconscious betrayal of the inner fear of having nowhere to go, the ultimate fear of displacement from the oppressive security he has known now for two generations. Raimundo therefore felt consoled when Luís Garcia reassured him that he could stay on as long as he wished: "És livre, disse Luís Garcia; viverás comigo até quando quiseres" (14–15; "'You are free,' said Luís Garcia; 'you may live with me for as long as you like.'") And this is what should be "disappointing" for Raimundo—the prospect of dying a slave and not experiencing true freedom.

The next phase in Machado's character nondevelopment is to consolidate the master-slave relationship post-"freedom," such as when Raimundo offers to continue playing music for the master:

> Raimundo foi dali em diante um como espírito externo de seu senhor; pensava por este e refletia-lhe o pensamento interior, em todas as suas ações, não menos silenciosas que pontuais. Luís Garcia não dava ordem nenhuma; tinha tudo à hora e no lugar competente. Raimundo, posto fosse o único servidor da casa, sobrava-lhe tempo, à tarde, para conversar com o antigo senhor, no jardinete, enquanto a noite vinha caindo. Ali falavam de seu pequeno mundo, das raras ocorrências domésticas, do tempo que devia fazer no dia seguinte, de uma ou outra circunstância exterior. Quando a noite caía de todo e a cidade abria os seus olhos de gás, recolhia-se eles a casa, a passo lento, à ilharga um do outro.
>
> —Raimundo hoje vai tocar, não é? dizia às vezes o preto. (14–15)

[From then on, Raimundo was like an external soul of his master. He thought for him, and reflected for him his very thoughts. In all of his actions, he was no less silent than punctual. Luís Garcia never gave any orders; he had everything he needed at the right time and in the proper place. Although he was the only servant in the house, there was time left over in the afternoon for him to walk with his former master in the little garden as night descended. There they spoke of their small world, of unusual everyday occurrences, of what the weather would be like the following day, of this and that outward circumstance. When night had completely fallen, and the city was opening its "gas" eyes, they would return to the house, walking slowly side by side.

"Raimundo is going to play for you today, isn't he?" the Negro sometimes said.

This is a well-understood pact in which Luís Garcia need not give orders for the slave to know what to do; he was a competent slave, well trained for the benefits of the master and the "privileges" he stands to gain, however pathological the relationship may be. What seems to change concerns mode-of-address terms such as "antigo senhor" (old master) and "ex-escravo" (ex-slave). Marotti captures this new but questionable relationship when he confirms that it is nothing but a façade that reinforces the status quo: "There is a form of recognition of the freedom of slaves so long as everything else stays the same; masters and slaves remain in their places and everybody is happy. Is this perhaps another way of eliminating the problem, by avoiding it?" (116). And that is the crux of the problem: through denial, racial and social inequalities are supposedly washed away and neutralized since "quaisquer que fossem as diferenças civis e naturais entre os dois, as relações domésticas os tinha, feito amigos" (Machado, 15; whatever their civil and natural differences, domestic rapport has made them close friends). Nothing can be further from the reality: what kind of relationship can there be between an ex-slave and an ex-master under the same roof, especially when one is powerful and rich and the other powerless and poor?

In avoiding the problem of slavery, Machado does not eliminate it; rather, he succeeds in displaying his indifference and confirming his status as a co-opted writer within the prejudiced Brazilian society of his time. The fact that Raimundo gets to walk "side by side" with Luís Garcia in the afternoon or that he assumed the "external soul" of his former master by providing him his needs with dedication and precision does not elevate the status of a so-called happy ex-slave. In all of these cosmetic benefits or privileges, the relationship is unbalanced from the viewpoint of freedom of thought, action, and movement. Instead, Raimundo thinks *for* Luís Garcia and not for himself. Raimundo walks *with* the ex-master not when he himself wants to walk but when the ex-master needs him. In addition, Raimundo needs to get permission to play music *for* the pleasure of the master, not for his own pleasure. The catalogue of mindlessness, dispossession, and dependence is limitless as Raimundo becomes the quintessential metaphor for the passive, pacified, and objectified figure.

On the other side of Raimundo's "static" frame lie his qualities as a "thinker," and reluctant decision maker. Machado seems to be compensating for the flat, almost insignificant nature of Raimundo's portrayal throughout the novel. Yet, in this new/old role of a "servant," Raimundo's thought is premised upon the sense of being a "faithful slave" who protects the master and his loved ones against bad occurrences as in the drama of Iaiá's letter to Procópio Dias, her admirer. Once Iaiá comes to terms with the passionate intrigue continuing between Estela (her stepmother) and Jorge, her fiancé, she sets up her own intrigue by proposing to Procópio through the letter that Raimundo never delivered.

Taking Raimundo's "goodwill" act as a crafty gesture on the part of Machado to show that the slave could reason and may even be said to have a mind of his own, I find so many limitations in this role of a letter-carrier and facilitator of happy unions among the upper-class characters. Like a secondary character typical of Machadian representation of the Afro-Brazilian, Raimundo will have few occasions and instances in which he can at least "hesitate," "reflect," or "decide" as to what action to take. Like the Shakespearean "walking shadow," or the more subversive protagonist in Ellison's *Invisible Man*, Raimundo remains a fictional flash who comes on and off life's stage for a few moments of glory, and then disappears, only to reappear when needed again at the end of the story. In this Machadian drama of temporary visibility and perpetual invisibility, however, I suggest that Raimundo's actions and nonactions are geared toward satisfying someone else other than himself:

Raimundo, chamado para levar essa carta, recebeu-a depois de alguma hesitação. Olhou para o papel e para a sinhá-moça. Depois sacudiu a cabeça com um ar de dúvida. Iaiá simulou não ver nada, mas o gesto do preto impressionou-a. Ia afastar-se, Raimundo reteve-a dizendo:

—Iaiá me desculpe . . . esta carta . . . Raimundo não gosta de falar àquele homem.

—Não lhe fales; basta deixar a carta em casa dele.

Raimundo não insistiu; acampanhou com os olhos a filha de seu antigo senhor, abanando a cabeça com o mesmo ar de alguns momentos antes. Depois olhou para a carta como se quisesse adivinhar o que ia dentro. . . . O coração do preto dizia que aquela carta era alguma coisa mais do que um recado sem conseqüência. Quis levá-la a Estela; mas rejeitou o expediente, por lhe parecer infidelidade. Dez minutos depois saiu em direção à casa de Procópio Dias. (132)

[Raimundo, who had been summoned to deliver the letter, accepted it after some hesitation. He looked at the paper and at the young girl. Then he shook his head with an air of doubt. Iaiá pretended not to notice, but the black man's gesture made an impression on her. She was about to leave; Raimundo held on to it saying:

"Iaiá will forgive me . . . this letter . . . Raimundo doesn't like to speak to that man."

"Don't speak; all you need to do is leave the letter at his house."

Raimundo didn't insist. He accompanied the daughter of his former master with his eyes, shaking his head with the same air as before. Then he looked at the letter as if he wanted to guess the content. . . . The black servant's heart told him that letter was something more than an inconsequential message. He wanted to take it to Estela; but he rejected the idea because it seemed a disloyal act. Ten minutes later, he left in the direction of Procópio Dias's house.]

Here is a case of negotiation and not absolute articulation of freedom of will. Although Raimundo's initial act of hesitation had an impact on Iaiá, the latter ended up having the upper hand as she dismissed his argument saying: "Don't speak; all you need to do is leave the letter at his house." He would not like to argue with the daughter of his ex-master, except for an ineffective passing hesitation. Likewise, Raimundo would hesitate to show the letter to Estela so as not to betray Iaiá's trust; a constant case of wanting to have integrity, to please, and to make others (masters) happy at his own expense.

In the final chapter, where once again Iaiá must verify whether Raimundo delivered her letter to Procópio, the loyalty of Raimundo is put to the test. To her disenchantment, she finds out that Raimundo has been "disobedient" but with good intentions. To reach this resolution, he has been to Procópio's house three times, and on all three occasions, he hesitated due to the extended background of fidelity and devotion he has for the Garcia family:

Iaiá foi ter com Raimundo.

—Entregaste?

—Não entreguei, disse o preto.

Iaiá ficou alguns instantes imóvel. Raimundo tirou a carta do bolso, e esteve com ela nas mãos, sem atrever-se a levantar os olhos; levantou-os enfim e disse resolutamente:

—Raimundo achou bonito que Iaiá escrevesse àquele homem, que não é seu pai nem seu noivo, e voltou para falar a nhanhã Estela.

—Dê cá, disse a moça secamente; não é preciso.

Raimundo entregou-lhe a carta, e sacudiu a cabeça encanecida, como se quisera repelir os anos que sobre ela pesavam, e retrodecer ao tempo em que Iaiá era uma simples criança, travessa e nada mais. (138)

[Iaiá went to meet Raimundo.

"Did you deliver it?"

"No, I didn't, said the black man."

Iaiá remained motionless for a few moments. Raimundo took the letter from his pocket and held it in his hands without daring to raise his eyes; finally he did raise them and said firmly:

"I didn't think it was right for you to write to that man, who is neither your father nor your fiancé, so I came back to speak to Mistress Estela."

"Give it to me," said the girl abruptly. "You don't need to."

Raimundo gave her the letter and shook his grizzled head, as if he wanted to deny the years that weighed upon it and retrogress to the time when Iaiá was merely a child—mischievous and nothing more.]

Raimundo justifies his decision not to deliver Iaiá's letter based on two interrelated reasons: moral grounds and family loyalty. He would rather have Iaiá be with Jorge—a relationship he sees as more genuine, well intentioned, and promising. Raimundo's ethical standards are quite high, yet he is unable to see how his continued presence in an oppressive environment jeopardizes his own chances of ever being free. This is why Raimundo's character as constructed by Machado is so illusory, unexalting, and demeaning for the collective Afro-Brazilian psyche.

Although these two episodes of "hesitation" may be seen as resistance by some readers, they do not go beyond the attitude of a slave being a slave in order to please his master. Despite all his efforts, Raimundo is insulted and disrespected by Iaiá. While Iaiá's reaction made him reflect about when she used to be a little girl, his inner anguish stems more from his helplessness and powerlessness even while dealing with a third-generation master represented by Iaiá. In spite of his good heart and goodwill, Raimundo remains a slave at the mercy of his owners.

As a name derived from an unusual character, "Raimundo" is deserving of interpretative analysis. Taken as a symbolic microstructure, Raimundo, or "raio do mundo" ("the ray/light of the world"), may be interpreted as the hopeful/hopeless sign of things to come postabolition, a ray of light in the dark prison of slavery or the notion that the only choice left for the slave is to be a "good freed slave." This character contrasts with other Machadian protagonists, especially of the author's "realist" phase. In contrast to Raimundo with his instinctive devotion, care, concern, honesty, and blind loyalty to a fault of self-detriment, Machado favors his later protagonists like the crafty Dom Casmurros of the society in *Dom Casmurro,* the demented Rubiãos as in *Quincas borba,* and the self-centered Braz Cubas in *Memórias póstumas de Brás Cubas.* In helping others shine and succeed in life, Raimundo fails to shed light on himself, thus remaining a shadow of others.

Conceptually and thematically, *Iaiá Garcia* is the singular text of optimism in the entire Machadian creative imagination, given its happy culmination in the marriage between Jorge and Iaiá. Principally associated with pessimism and human misery, Machado's works have a penchant for the macabre, the somber, and the gloomy, where interests overlap and only the strong survive and where only those who know what they want and how to get it win. It should not be a matter of surprise that Machado is more often on the side of the winner, and never the loser. The characters of his prolific works attest to this central philosophy. Who are the winners and losers in *Iaiá Garcia?* Or is the text so "optimistic" that there are no losers? First among losers is "societal convention," epitomized by Valéria and Estela due to their pride. While Valéria's pride is hypocritical, that of Estela is genuine yet unrealistic. Then we have Luís Garcia, who allows himself to be coerced into marrying someone he does not love him (Estela) only to have the latter betray him with Jorge. Jorge and Iaiá are winners because they know what they want and how to get it.

By Machado's standards, Raimundo loses for lack of self-awareness and self-love. Although this should be a virtue, it does not fit Machado's mode of winning. In his selfless love for others, he forgets himself and persists as a tool in the fulfillment of others. While pride may be seen as a tragic flaw in Valéria and Estela, the opposite is what we find in Raimundo. The total lack of a sense of who he is, where he hails from, and where he is going further complicates and shapes his vision of the world. We have only his moral and physical characteristics but nothing of his origin other than the fact that he is black. The different terms used to qualify him range from "escravo" (slave), "ex-escravo" (ex-slave), and "meu preto" (my black man) to simply "o preto" (black man)—all carry subtleties and nuances that are still informed by subservience and patronizing. Having gained his freedom, perhaps what he could ask from Luís Garcia is not food and shelter within the same household that kept him in bondage for two generations. Rather, a conscious Afro-Brazilian as is found in such heroes as Ganga Zumba and Zumbi dos Palmares would do anything (including rebel violently) to be free, to do for themselves and be responsible for themselves. Just as "alguma coisa escapa do naufrágio das ilusões" (142; something escapes the shipwreck of illusions) in Machado's conclusion of *Iaiá Garcia*, there can be no further delusions about Machado's ideological co-optation as depicted in his callous portrayal of Raimundo. Against the background of Raimundo's insignificant character and ghostly existence for which Machado stands accused, Barreto provides us with a compelling contrast.

Lima Barreto: An Advocate for Afro-Brazilian Dignity

In contrast to Machado de Assis's lukewarm attitude toward the dilemma of blackness, Lima Barreto carries the burden to a compelling degree that also accounts for his rebellion and forthright criticism of inequalities and injustices in his works. His approach is quite unlike the apologetic and co-optive representation of the Afro-Brazilian in Machado's works. In his novels, Barreto stands out as the voice of courage who defies the society and its hypocrisies and urges a conscious project of dignifying the Afro-Brazilian subject. For Barreto, although a mulatto, his black consciousness was a matter of pride not shame, a virtue not a vice; and ultimately, a cause for which he was prepared to ridicule his prejudiced society even at a cost of his career and recognition. Barreto considers racism and social injustice as diseases that must be diagnosed and remedied before they become too delayed to the extent that cure becomes impossible. He is in this sense the very opposite of Machado de Assis, and he does not even hide his position on Machado maintaining that the latter was never his model in terms of inspiration or influence:

> Não lhe negando os méritos de grande escritor, sempre achei no Machado muita secura de alma, muita falta de simpatia, falta de entusiasmos generosos, uma porção de sestros pueris. Jamais o imitei e jamais me inspirou. Que me falem de Maupassant, de Dickens, de Swift, Balzac, Dandet—vá lá, mas de Machado, nunca! Até em Turguenev, em Tolstoi, poderiam ir buscar os meus modelos; mas em Machado, não! (Cited in **Figueiredo**, *O romance*, 12–13)

[While not denigrating his merits as a great writer, I always found Machado to be cold-hearted, unsympathetic and expressly ungenerous, a kind of emotionally disturbed figure. I never imitated him and he never inspired me. Tell me about Maupassant, Dickens, Swift, Balzac, Dandet—and whathaveyou, but Machado, never! You can even look as far as in Turgenev and in Tolstoy for my models; but Machado, oh no!]

In listing writers who inspire him, Barreto suggests that literature must have a social function and must not distance itself from the people it is supposed to represent. Machado, in this sense, is an "alienated" writer whose love for philosophical abstractions, ambiguity, and use of distant and mostly aristocratic language and characters end up situating his works more within the Westernized tradition than the Brazilian sociocultural reality that Barreto strives to capture through a colloquial use of language.

Unlike Machado's fondness for upper-class urban carioca personages, Barreto's heart lies with the "povão" (masses), while his settings reflect the realities of the "anonymous people, the minor employees, the faceless copyists, the workers, the seamstresses, the failures, the disinherited" (Marotti, *Black Characters*, 173), all of whom remind him of his own modest background. Born in 1881, seven years before the abolition of slavery in Brazil, to middle-class mulatto parents who tried to provide him with the best education and cultural exposure they could offer, he will later become rebellious due to personal setbacks (such as his mother's death when he was seven years old) and professional failures related to what Francisco Barbosa calls "inexplicável esquecimento"[4] (inexplicable obscuration) that led this ambitious mind to alcoholism and an early death in 1922 at age forty-one. In spite of the brevity of his life, Barreto for Afro-Brazilian, is larger than life. He remains the voice of the oppressed and the voiceless, the rebel with a cause, the nonconformist whose contribution to Brazilian letters can no longer be obscured, negated, or diminished—as is manifest in the renewal of interest in this articulate writer.

As one dissects the heart of Brazil's societal sickness, two emblematic works by Lima Barreto that ridicule racial democracy come to mind. *Recordações do escrivão Isaias Caminha* and *Clara dos Anjos* confront the myth of the Brazilian "racial paradise" in a way that Machado de Assis would rather not. Both works deal intimately with racial prejudice from a quasi firsthand perspective. Because of his bohemian and marginal lifestyle, Barreto translates with extreme sensitivity, his observations of societal corruption and inequalities into crude, caricatural, and vivid tableaux. This was the postabolition, premodernist era of conservative and backward Rio de Janeiro when "freedom" from slavery did not quite translate into equality of opportunities. It was the era when Barreto earned the accolade of "the novelist of the First Republic" for his ferocious criticism of its bourgeois mentality. As Abdias do Nascimento puts it, it was as if "the Golden Law was signed yesterday" (*O negro revoltado* 21). In every text, and on every page, Barreto articulates his anger and disenchantment, his frustration and yet optimism of at least making a difference through his confrontational legacy against a racist society. While Machado at the turn of the century almost did not place the Afro-Brazilian on the map of human dignity, Barreto pushed the limits by doing just that at the beginning of the twentieth century through a literary defense against oppression.

In *Recordações*, published in 1909, Barreto pays a tribute to the struggles of the common people, through the confessions of Isaías Caminha, a journalist, who represents a prototype of the oppressed mulatto who must first discover himself in order to revolt against the mediocrity and hypocrisy of a society that oppresses him. In essence, this semiautobiographical work is a ritualist journey not only into adulthood but also into the writing process wherein the writer dialogues with himself and the implied reader about his inner doubts, insecurities, and travails in the hope that by writing about his experiences, he or she can touch the world, transform society, and rehumanize what is left of society's dehumanization of his very soul and spirit.

As Barreto clearly demonstrates in *Recordações*, a tormented life is only meaningful if the anger can be creatively controlled and transformed into a weapon of change, whether the approach is decent or vulgar. In confessing what motivated his creative impulses while writing *Recordações*, Barreto states:

> O meu fim foi fazer que um rapaz nas condições de Isaías, com todas as disposições, pode falhar, não em virtude de suas qualidades intrínsecas, mas batido, esmagado, prensado pelo preconceito, com o seu cortejo, que é, creio, fora dele [. . .]. Se lá pus certas figuras e o jornal, foi para escandalizar e provocar a atenção para a minha brochura. Não sei se o processo é decente, mas foi aquele que me surgiu para lutar contra a indiferença e má vontade dos nossos mandarins literários. (Barbosa, *Lima Barreto e a reforma da sociedade*, 41)

> [My goal was to make a young man in Isaía's situation, with everything at his disposal, fail, not due to his intrinsic qualities, but solemnly beaten, smashed, squeezed due to prejudice, which I think is beyond his control. . . . If I portray certain characters and the press in my work, the idea was to scandalize and call attention to my chapbook. I don't know if the approach was appropriate, but that was my instinctive reaction and the way I knew to fight against the indifference and ill-will of our literary mandarins.]

Barreto's caricatural assault on his society is caustic and unforgiving yet apologetic in tone as if to reach out to the larger society and call for awareness that can lead to change in racial attitudes.

The "Breve notícia" (Brief Notice) that prefaces the text is no less confessional, as the reader confuses Isaías Caminha with Lima Barreto since the notice is signed by each. This crafty "confusion" between the protagonist and the implied author only adds to the autobiographical texture of *Recordações*. In this preface/notice, Barreto provides a background to his decision to write. He picked up a national magazine one day in which Afro-Brazilians have been depicted as degenerates, a description that made him reflect on his own past that somewhat confirmed the writer's opinion, since at the time, he was only an ordinary clerk in a remote neighborhood, contrary to the dreams of greatness he had in his childhood. And it is the anguish and verity of these memories that gave birth to the novel. As he puts it, *Recordações* was partly a response to the author of that derogatory piece in the magazine "dei razão ao autor do escrito" (18; I felt like an evidence of the author's write-up). Yet, Barreto subconsciously apologizes to his readers, in a disclaimer of sorts, urging the reader to be open-minded since he has been pushed to respond in self-defense:

Não é meu propósito também fazer uma obra de ódio; de revolta; mas uma defesa a acusasões deduzidas superficialmente de aparências cuja essência explicadora, as mais das vezes, está na sociedade e não no indivíduo desprovido de tudo, de família, de afetos, de simpatias, de fortuna, isolado contra inimigos que o rodeiam, armados da velocidade da bala e da insídia do veneno. (19)

[It is neither my intention to produce a work of hate or revolt, but my defense against superficially deduced accusations that essential basis is in the society and not in the individual deprived of everything—family, affection, sympathy, material possession—isolated among enemies armed with bulletlike velocity and insidious venom.]

The accusations and defenses aside, through the prism of Isaías Caminha, Barreto exposes disturbing skeletons in the cupboard of a society that claims to be racially democratic. As we follow him in his search for understanding of the myths and the realities, we discover along with the protagonist the hostilities and ambiguities of the society, as well as his own instability and fragmentation.

Isaías's life journey is a mix of dreams and deceptions, expectations and frustrations that are somewhat representative of what the average dark mulatto underwent in the Rio de Janeiro of the turn of the century. While Robert Herron's argument that "Isaías's failure in the novel is caused by factors much more complex than his color or his poverty" (26) is a valid one, his arguments of "lack of determination and will power . . . laziness and inertia" on the part of Isaías fall within stereotypical characterization of blacks. I suggest that discrimination against his color, his social class, and the entire "whitened" society and culture combine to produce significant powerlessness that can potentially deprive a soul of its energy, determination, and willpower. In defense of Raimundo, let me argue that lethargy and laziness are symptomatic of a larger societal dysfunction. In fact, when lethargy is considered as a strategic means of conserving one's energy, it becomes not only subversive, but provides a regenerative ground for a counteroffensive.

An intelligent but poor boy, an idealist by right and nature, Isaías dreams of leaving the suburbs of Espírito Santo for Rio de Janeiro in order to become a "doutor" ("doctor" or educated figure) and improve his lot in life. His parents are generally supportive, but his mother is somewhat reluctant. He craftily convinces his uncle, Valentino, to recommend him, through a colonel/family friend, to an influential congressman in Rio de Janeiro, Dr. Castro. For a boy of twelve, the prospect of beginning a new life in Rio brings such ecstasy that he begins to dream of the future: "Ouvia uma tentadora sibila falar-me, a toda a hora e a todo o instante, na minha glória futura" (21; At every turn and moment, I kept hearing a seductive witch tell me about my future glory). Convinced of his prospective success in Rio de Janeiro, he reflects:

> A minha situação no Rio estava garantida. Obteria um emprego. Um dia pelos outros iria às aulas, e todo o fim do ano, durante seis, faria os exames, ao fim dos quais seria doutor!
>
> Ah! Seria doutor! Resgataria o pecado original do meu nascimento humilde, amaciairia o suplício premente, cruciante e onímodo de minha cor. (26)
>
> [My place in Rio was guaranteed. I would have a job. I would take classes with others and at the end of every year, for six years, I would sit for exams, at the end of which I will become a doctor!
>
> Ah! I would be a doctor! I would redeem the original sin of my humble birth; I would soothe the urgent, crucial, and singular pain of my color.]

Isaiás's reflection about the future sets the tone for the series of dramas that will ensue toward the gradual unmasking of a fatal destiny.

Although he recognizes the positive influence of his father in terms of the latter's encouragement that he get an "elitist" education, the first few lines of the text set a more urgent tone by virtue of the protagonist's resolve to leave the environment he was born into for greener pastures: "A tristeza, a compreensão e a desigualdade de nível mental do meu meio familiar, agiram sobre mim de um modo curioso: deram-me anseios de inteligência" (21; The sadness, the understanding, and mental inequality of my family ambience curiously affected me: they gave me a thirst for knowledge). Why does

Barreto set up his protagonist for a journey about which he seems already to have a premonition? Isaías represents a paradox of paradoxes, an embodiment of struggling forces, those of an aspiring poor man in Brazil, ambitious and bent on improving himself, and yet doomed by the very force of social power he seeks. Once he begins to associate among the ranks of power, he becomes a threat to the very institution he challenges and the society in which he is trying to be upwardly mobile. He must be checked, put back in his figurative "place," as Isaías finds out in Rio de Janeiro—all too soon, too quickly, too painfully.

For Barreto, the ironic effect of the story his protagonist is narrating, its twists of fate that accompany his drama, is as important as the story itself for it is in the paradox that the story captures the aesthetic and transformative imagination of the reader. A few episodes provide case studies of the illusions and disillusions of Isaías Caminha. First, Isaías arrives in Rio in search of Dr. Castro, the congressman to whom he had been commended. He meets a parade of characters who quickly school him about Brazilian sociopolitical realities, preparing him for his ultimate encounter with the congressman: the arrogant bread seller Laje da Silva, who insults him; a senator on the public bus who engages in obscene antics; congressmen sleeping on duty. These sights, coupled with an exposé of a whole world of opportunism, corruption, and indifference, begin to lead to Isaías's gradual disillusionment, culminating in his meeting with the congressman:

> Entreguei-lhe a carta. Leu-a num instante, tendo na testa uma ruga de aborrecimento; depois perguntou-me:
>
> —É o senhor?
>
> —Sim senhor
>
> —Você (mudou logo de tratamento) sabe perfeitamente como as coisas vão: o país está em crise, em apuros financeiros, estão extinguindo repartições, cortando despesas; é difícil arranjar qualquer coisa; entretanto . . .
>
> —Mas doutor eu não queria grande coisa. . . . Cem mil-réis por mês me bastava. . . . Todos por aí arranjam eu. . . .
>
> —Sim . . . Sim . . . Mas têm grandes recomendações, poderosos padrinhos— eu, o que valho? nada! Ainda agora o Ministro do Interior não nomeou o meu candidato para juiz do júri. (54)

> [I gave him the letter. He read it quickly, his wrinkling forehead betraying disgust; then he asked me:

"Are you the one, sir?"

"Yes, sir."

"You (he soon changed the form of address) are quite familiar with how things go: the country is in crisis, in financial problems, they are eliminating branches, cutting costs, I cannot help you out; meanwhile . . ."

"But sir, I wasn't looking for anything spectacular. . . . A hundred thousand reis a month would be enough for me. . . . Everyone out there gets something but me . . ."

"Yes . . . yes . . . But you have great recommendations, powerful godfathers—And me, what am I worth? nothing! Recently, the Interior Minister did not nominate me for judgeship."]

Obviously shocked by the congressman's utter indifference, he feels alone and abandoned in a major city. Humiliated and forced to check out of the hotel due to lack of money, wrongfully accused, imprisoned, and later released, he becomes melancholic and totally dejected that introspection and meditation become his therapeutic outlets.

In one such meditative moment, he reflects on his dissatisfaction—blaming it partly on the pain of having to remember the unpleasant events in his life. In putting it down on paper, the protagonist shares an intimate monologue with the reader about the sheer mysteries of life:

Por que não estou satisfeito? Não sei. E quem o poderá saber! Há em nós tanta coisa misteriosa, tantos sentimentos cujas origens nos escapam, que me esforço em vão por explicar este meu atual estado de alma. . . . Penso—não sei o quê—que é este meu livro que me está fazendo mal. . . . E quem sabe se excitar recordações de sofrimentos, avivar as imagens de que nasceram não é fazer com que, obscura e confusamente, me venham as sensações dolorosas semimortas? Talvez mesmo seja angústia de escritor, porque vivo cheio de dúvidas, e hesito de dia para dia em continuar a escrevê-lo. Não é o seu valor literário que me preocupa; é a sua utilidade para o fim que almejo. (65)

[Why am I not satisfied? I don't know. And who can know! There are so many mysteries in us, so many feelings the source of which we cannot explain as I try in vain to explain my current state of mind. . . . I think—you know what—that it is this my book that is hurting me so much. . . . And who knows, perhaps the excitation of memories of suffering, reliving the episodes that inspired them may actually be partly and confusingly responsible for these painful and semimortified sensations? Perhaps it is the writer's anguish, because I live filled with fears and I hesitate from one day to the next in continuing to write the book. What matters to me is not its literary merit but its ultimate utility.]

Here is perhaps a fundamental moment of crisis and revelation in the fictional and autobiographical trajectory of Barreto/Isaías. This episode combines the frustrations of daily living of an aspiring young Afro-Brazilian with those of an aspiring writer. The question of memory is vital as well. By asserting the pain of remembering, Isaías actually "authenticates" his reflections by suggesting that he is compelled to go back in time to relive those memories as he recollects them on paper. At the same time, this is equally a testament on Barreto/Isaías's aesthetic philosophy, in particular with regard to the function of literature. For Barreto, literature must have a social function; he minimizes his artistic accomplishment when he states that he is preoccupied not with the "valor literário" (literary value) of his works but with their ideological impact on the society as an instrument of change. The anguish of writing, as Barreto notes, compounds the anguish of the lived experience, and the constant doubts of whether to continue to write may not necessarily mean lack of creative ability but of the physical energy to continue reliving the pain through the writing process.

In spite of his social and professional melancholy as a writer, Isaías often consoles himself with doses of humor, especially in situations that are beyond his control, and the novel is filled with quite a number of these. He takes advantage, for example, of his arrest and interrogation to expose the reader to the corruption and abuse of power by the police as he describes not only Captain Viveiros ("o seu olhar cúpido e a sua papada farta") (63; his greedy looks and fat chin) but also the police officer interrogating him: "O delegado pareceu me um medíocre bacharel, uma vulgaridade com desejos de chegar a altas posisões" (63; The officer looked like a mediocre holder of a bachelor's degree, a vulgar person with keen eyes on upward mobility). However, the most acute humor lies in Isaías's bold response motivated by anger and the need to fight back for his self-dignity when the officer persists in humiliating and insulting him with a barrage of questions:

> Por aí, houve em mim o que um autor russo chamou a convulsão da personalidade. Todo eu me agitei, todo eu me indignei. Senti num segundo todas as injustiças que vinha sofrendo; revoltei-me contra todos os sofrimentos que vinha suportando. Injustiças, sofrimentos, humilhações, misérias, juntaram-se dentro de mim, subiram à tona da minha consciência pelos meus olhos e então expectorei as sílabas:
>
> —Imbecil!
>
> —Que diz! perguntou ele com autoridade.

—Que você é um imbecil, ouviu? (64)

[At this point, I felt inside of me what a Russian writer called a convulsion of personality. I became all agitated and all offended. I instantly felt all the injustice I have been suffering; I revolted against all the suffering I had had to bear. Injustice, suffering, humiliation, misery, all came together inside me to the level of my consciousness, passing through my eyes and I articulated the words:

"Imbecile!"

"Excuse me!" he retorted with authority.

"I said you are an imbecile, you heard me!?"]

Isaías's "convulsion of personality" is justified and well channeled in the face of injustice and inequality. Of course, he was quickly thrown in jail, but this encounter is one of the many episodes in the novel when Isaías just could not take it anymore, having to vent his anger and struggle for his own self-preservation and self-dignity. Disturbed yet resolved to confront his tormentors, Isaías speaks for the new Afro-Brazilian personality, which questions stereotypical treatment of a "marginalized" sector of the citizenry struggling for respect and recognition of their contribution.

After a series of tribulations, Isaías finally makes a dramatic entry into the world of hegemonic "power" in the Brazilian hierarchy of letters: he is employed by *O globo* as a servant, thanks to a friend, Gregoróvitch. However, this new position forces him to become subservient in a desperate compulsion to survive and maintain his mental and physical well-being. There is, after all, something humbling about suffering, but not when it is racially motivated. Isaías, while appreciative of the opportunity to mingle with power players, is quick to point out his limitations and imposed passivity. He aspires to become, but is not yet satisfied; he may be close to power, but is not powerful himself. He seems to be content with just being part of the production of power represented by *O globo,* a situation he captures so sarcastically when he ridicules the entire hypocritical operation of the press:

> Em menos de ano e tanto, tinha já construído uma pequena consciência jornalística para meu uso. Julguei-me superior ao resto da humanidade que não pisa familiarmente no interior das redações e cheio de inteligência e de talento, só porque levava tinta aos tinteiros dos repórteres e dos redatores e participava assim de um jornal, onde todos têm gênio.... Aquela casa, como todas do seu feitio, em que se fabricam novidades para o público, era uma colmeia de gênios. Colmeia é bem o termo porque era pequena e acanhada. (101)

[Within less than a year or so, I had developed a small journalistic consciousness for my use. I saw myself as better than the rest of humanity who are not familiar with the internal workings of the press supposedly full of talent and intelligence, simply because I supply reporters and editors with ink and thus participate in a Press where everyone is a genius. . . . That house, with all its workmanship, in which news is produced for public consumption is a beehive of geniuses. Beehive is the right term because it is small and narrow.]

For Isaías, *O globo* becomes a laboratory of societal analysis, where the writing experience collides with an intimate search for self-understanding. *O globo* then becomes a subtext within the entire semiautobiographical novel. Isaías's criticism of the press betrays Barreto's own disenchantment with its mediocrity and abuse of power. The "beehive" metaphor is double-edged. On the one hand, it captures the restlessness and productive energy of bees, and on the other, it reflects the narrow-mindedness of the colony of bees (journalists, feature writers, reporters, editors).

Isaías's association with the press will affect his life significantly. Gradually, he becomes constrained and conditioned by the owner's (Loberant) iron hand of discipline to ensure the newspaper is on the stand the following day. Although he tries to mingle with his co-workers, he is perceived as hardly human, much less as an equal partner, by these colleagues, who only participate tangentially in his existential drama: Gregoróvitch's stylistic carelessness and opportunism; the grammarian Lobo's narrow-mindedness; routine subservience of secretary Leporace; Losque and Lara's programmatic humor; Aires d'Ávila's editorial rascality and Floc's intellectual constraint even as the literary critic of the newspaper, all combine to introduce him to a world of invented news and praise-singing of false "heroes" and the powerful. It is a world where the mere act of discovery of the suicide of Floc earns him a new position of reporter.

Isaías is excited about his new position, about his social mobility and feeling of power. In a total sense of fulfillment and ecstasy, he states:

Nos meus primeiros meses de reportagem foi quando amei mais ativamente a vida. Não porque me visse adulado pelos almirantes e capitães-de-mar-e-guerra, mas porque senti bem a variedade onímoda da existência, a fraqueza dos grandes, a instabilidade das coisas e o seu fácil deslizar para os extremos mais opostos. Dois meses antes era simples contínuo, limpava mesas, ia a recados de todos; agora poderosas autoridades queriam as minhas relações e a minha boa vontade. (157)

[I had never passionately liked life more than during my first months as a reporter. Not because of the feeling of flattery I felt from admirals and captains, but because I felt the ominous variety of existence, the weakness of the top brass, the instability of things, and the easy slide toward opposite extremes.

Two months earlier, I was only a servant cleaning tables and taking messages for everyone. Now, people in powerful positions of authority depend on my relations and goodwill.]

However, this turns out to be a short-lived sense of power as the reality of being Afro-Brazilian soon sets in, as expressed in his final reflections in the novel. Now bestowed with "power" that was once elusive, he must also pay a price of integrating himself into a society in which he does not have absolute faith.

In the final analysis, once realized, Isaías's power translates into multiple symbolic acts of moral fragmentation and instability, of which his defeat of Leporace and his encounter with an Italian prostitute are prominent episodes. The episode with the Italian prostitute (Leda) is particularly striking to the extent that Isaías realizes a consciousness of his social position and function. While pursuing the opportunity for sexual conquest and fantasies, he recalls his father as well as the life of his mother, a loaded combination that suddenly causes a feeling of disillusionment and cyclic dissatisfaction with his own life:

Lembrava-me da vida da minha mãe, da sua miséria, da sua pobreza, naquela casa tosca; e parecia-me também condenado a acabar assim e todos nós condenados a nunca a ultrapassar.

A Italiana conversava com o remeiro sobre a pesca. Ela conhecia a vida e fazia perguntas nítidas. . . .

Lembrava-me de que deixara toda a minha vida ao acaso e que não pusera ao estudo e ao trabalho com a força de que era capaz. Sentia-me repelente, repelente de fraqueza, de falta de decisão e mais amolecido agora com o álcool e com prazeres. . . . Sentia-me parasita, adulando o diretor para obter dinheiro.

Âs minhas aspirações, àquele forte de sonhar da minha meninice eu não tinha dado as satisfações devidas. (166)

[She reminded me of my mother's life, her misery, her poverty, in that clumsy house; and it seemed as if I were equally doomed to end up the same way without all of us ever overcoming this burden.

The Italian woman was having a conversation with the paddler about fishing. She was familiar with the profession and asked precise questions. . . .

She reminded me that I had always left my life to chances and had not exerted much energy toward studies or work. I felt repugnant, repugnant to a fault, for my indecision and now even more weakened by alcohol and pleasures. . . . I felt like a parasite, singing the praises of the boss for monetary gains.

My aspirations, those strong youthful dreams, I had not pursued satisfactorily.]

In this episode of coming to terms with a failed life, Isaías's reflections may be seen as a larger concern for the plight of Afro-Brazilians in general in their challenging struggle for equality and justice. While his memories of his mother's misery and poverty during his childhood and his prophecy that "todos nós" (all of us) may not overcome sound defeatist, they must also be seen within the context of his arduous trajectory of social mobility, painful adventures, and discoveries. Isaías, like the implied author, Barreto, recognizes Leda as the former lover of the congressman who was to help him break into the carioca power circles and feels partly responsible, as a member of the paternalistic club that oppresses lower-class women, for her plight. Hence, he resists the temptation of sexual indulgence and consequently fails to fully integrate himself with the upper class. I might add that Barreto's example of Isaías's unsatisfied libido stresses the impossibility of the Brazilian mulatto's or *mestiço*'s (mestizo) achieving total integration except in the case of conscious co-optation (as with Machado). Reminiscent of his desire for power, Isaías's sexual desire cannot be truly fulfilled since satisfaction lies somewhere else: in the fluid ambiguity that facilitates social change. Once secure, Isaías is unable to enjoy what he has always sought after as the determinant of his poverty: oppression and alienation within the Brazilian socioracial reality, which forms the essence he sets out to assault. The final note of blaming the inequalities of Brazilian society of the time, and even today, is an indictment that will also echo in *Clara dos Anjos,* a novel with a similar problematic but with a female protagonist.

Although posthumously published in 1948, *Clara dos Anjos* may have been written between 1904 and 1908 (even before the publication of *Recordações* in 1909), at least sometime before 1922. The fundamental commonality between both works, as depicted in the dramas of Isaías and Clara, lies in the psychological trauma caused by social rejection or inequality due to one's race. As Guaraciaba Micheletti points out in the preface to *Clara dos Anjos,* "Em Lima Barreto, o mesmo determinismo social que torna os homens impotentes confere às mulheres fragilidade e ausência de vontade própria6" (6; In Lima Barreto, the same social determinism responsible for men's impotence confers fragility and absence of self-will on women). While Isaías's "impotence" is premised on a social power structure that limits the degree of his ascendancy as well as the possibilities of self-fulfillment, Clara is conditioned by the same impotence complicated by the status of womanhood in Brazil at the turn of the twentieth century. Isaías's and Clara's conditions are, to a significant extent, microcosms of the yoke weighing on all Afro-Brazilians, male and female, as they penetrate a society laced with countless illnesses against which they are neither inoculated nor adequately prepared to combat. Comparatively, the social determinism of Barreto's character, Isaías, differs from Machado de Assis's character, Raimundo, in the sense that Isaías is well aware of the social forces against him even though he believes he could somehow overcome those forces through intelligence, hard work, and struggle. For his part, Raimundo seems to be positioned as a weak and hapless figure who allows others to determine his fate. Both are victims of slavery and its psychological frustrations and consequences. One's activism as opposed to the other's passivity is the essential distinguishing element in their social determinism.

Clara's drama may be considered a feminine version of Isaías's in the sense that she is confronted by the same battered dreams and hopes of ascendancy due to the color of her skin and social class. She is unable to marry Cassi Jones de Azevedo, a womanizer of a higher social class, because Cassi's family, and by extension the society, makes it difficult. Yet, within the frame of "racial democracy," she must undergo that illusion of inclusion by being seduced and finally abandoned, facing the reality of rejection by the very character who once promised her heaven, earth, and happiness under the sun. Similar to Isaías's confession, and coming to terms at the end of his journey of self-discovery, the narrator of *Clara dos Anjos* captures the fact that Clara's status is diminished by her erroneous perception of a racist society:

> Agora é que tinha a noção exata da sua situação na sociedade. Fora preciso ser ofendida irremediavelmente nos seus melindres de solteira... para se convencer de que ela não era uma moça como as outras; era muito menos no conceito de todos....
>
> A educação que recebera, de mimos e vigilâncias, era errônea. Ela devia ter aprendido da boca dos seus pais que a sua honestidade de moça e de mulher tinha por inimigos.... Ora, uma mulatinha, filha de cateiro! O que era preciso, tanto a ela como às suas iguais, era educar o caráter, revestir-se de vontade... para se defender de Cassis e semelhantes, e bater-se contra todos os que se opusessem, por este ou aquele modo, contra a elevação dela, social e moralmente. Nada a fazia inferior às outras, senão o conceito geral e a covardia com que elas o admitiam. (133)

> [Only now did she perceive her actual place in society. It was necessary to be fatally offended in her bashfulness as a single lady... in order to be convinced that she was not a young woman like others; she was much more minimized in everyone's view....
>
> The education she had received in sweetness and vigilance was faulty. She ought to have learned from her parents' mouths that a young woman's and a

lady's honesty foments enmity. . . . Worse still, a mulatta, daughter of a letter-carrier! What was necessary for her and her equals was to build the character, renew the will . . . in order to defend themselves against the Cassis and their ilk and confront headlong, all oppositions blocking her progress, socially and morally. Nothing made her inferior to others except the general bias and the cowardice with which she and others like her accept this bias.]

And perhaps this is where Clara differs from Isaías. While the latter sought to belong to the white world of power and cease to be powerless, Clara seems to have discovered the obstacles in her social mobility and is now more determined than ever to combat these societal ills in spite of her own cowardice.

As in Barreto's juxtaposition of the corrupt world of the press with that of Isaías's struggle to become accepted in that same world, Clara's impossible marriage with Cassi Jones de Azevedo reflects another juxtaposition of an innocent, poor mulatta with a rotten, corrupt, and amoral upper class. These social tensions, while located within the individual or the family, confirm Barreto's implied and larger thesis at the end of *Clara dos Anjos* that "nós não somos nada nessa vida" (133; we don't amount to anything in this life). Although desperate and defeatist in tone, it is equally an indictment of the society and, above all, a cry for intervention without which symbolic protest cannot become an explosive action in the direction of change through awareness.

Contrasting Racial Consciousness: Machado versus Barreto

The three symbolic black/mulatto(a) characters of Machado de Assis and Lima Barreto as explored in *Iaiá Garcia, Recordações do escrivão Isaías Caminha,* and *Clara dos Anjos* provide ample evidence of a contrastive racial consciousness and commitment between the two writers. In the case of Machado, the aesthetic combines with ideological co-optation since the writer favors upper-class characters while marginalizing and stereotyping black characters—a case of betrayal constructed under the guise of fallacious racial democracy for which Machado proves a revered exponent as seen in the demeaning representation of Raimundo in *Iaiá Garcia*.

For Barreto, the consciousness of blackness constitutes an ideological paradigm founded on the premise that being mulatto in a racist society does not in any way improve the privileges of mixed-raced persons. Through a careful sociopsychological characterization of Isaías Caminha and Clara in *Recordações* and *Clara dos Anjos*, respectively, Barreto painstakingly destroys the myth of Brazilian racial democracy by subjecting these emulative characters to rigorous self-discoveries that force them to revolt and question the contradictions of the so-called racial paradise.

2

Quilombhoje as a Cultural Collective

> The hero or heroine of an immersion narrative must be willing to forsake highly individualized mobility in the narrative's least oppressive social structure for a posture of relative stasis in the most oppressive environment, a loss that is only occasionally assuaged by the newfound balms of group identity.
>
> —Robert Stepto, *From Behind the Veil*

> A enunciação em primeira pessoa revela a determinação do poeta de desvencilhar-se do anonimato e da "invisibilidade" a que relegou sua condição de descendente de escravos ou de ex-escravos e, mesmo após a Abolição, sua situação estranhamento em uma sociedade que não o convocou a participar em igualdade de condições.
>
> [The first-person articulation reveals the poet's determination to defend himself from the anonymity and "invisibility" to which his condition of descendant of slaves or ex-slaves has relegated him—in a society that even after Abolition, strangely, did not invite him to participate in equal opportunities.]
>
> —Zilá Bernd, *Literatura negra*

When in 1975 Thales de Azevedo, in *Democracia racial*, predicted a possibility of an "Afro-Brazilian Literature," little did he know that twenty-five years after that prediction there would actually be a set of works on that very subject with a prominent status by that name. In Azevedo's formulation, Afro-Brazilian literature is by nature, an arm of protest, "sendo embora de protesto contra a situação social de contato com a sociedade *branca*, não tem o negro condições de escapar à própria contra-imagem que dele faz o branco" (105; given its nature of protest against social conditions fomented by its contact with the white society, the Afro-Brazilian cannot escape a counter-image against that projected by whites). In view of this combative context of emergence, for the Afro-Brazilian writer writing is compelled to be political while the written word represents only a "veil" with a larger signifying and transformative function. And it is within this perspective that the emergence of the Quilombhoje group in São Paulo in 1978, three years after Azevedo's assertion, must be contextualized.

Drawing on Stepto's thesis of "call and response," Afro-Brazilian literature can equally be constructed against the Afro-American literary tradition. Similar to the manner in which prefiguring texts such as nineteenth-century slave narratives constitutes a "call" that will later necessitate a "response" in the modern era through "ascent and immersion" or even what Stepto calls the "prologue to the epilogue of a prologue" (xi), Quilombhoje offers *Cadernos negros* as an appropriate response not only to the call of slavery but also to the preabolition and postabolition literary movements. And it is in this sense that we consider the group as representing the continuity of black consciousness within the cultural and political movement established by entities like Frente Negra Brasileira and Movimento Negro Unificado.

As an offshoot of a set of movements—literary, cultural, and political— Quilombhoje can be situated as a response, within a response, especially in the postmodernist sense. The *Semana de Arte Moderna* (Week of Modern Art) of 1922, which inaugurated Brazilian *modernismo*, must also be seen as a laboratory of contradictions that Quilombhoje tried to resolve through collective engagement and dialectical dialogue with the past. Stepto signals a note of caution as to the myriad possibilities and implications of a response when he posits that "a response is fundamentally an artistic act of closure performed upon a formal unit that already possesses substantial coherence. There can be no one response, no one and final closure; there can only be appropriate and inappropriate responses, and what is appropriate is defined by the prefiguring call that has come before" (xi). Quilombhoje's response begins where the preabolition and postabolition writers left off, carefully dialoguing with their currents while at the same time renewing and redefining their own commitments and significance. The choice of a group identity stems from the idea of a literary movement intent on maintaining a continuity of tradition while at the same time helping emerging writers to improve.

Following the great tradition of emblematic writers such as Castro Alves, Luís Gama, Cruz e Souza, Lima Barreto, Lino Guedes, Jorge de Lima, and Solano Trindade among others, Quilombhoje as a group has been producing *Cadernos negros* since 1978, alternating poetry and short stories consistently. These young and bohemian writers primarily from São Paulo, together with other regional writers from all over Brazil, have one common goal: the commitment to establish a literary tradition as in continuity with the great Afro-Brazilian literary tradition while addressing current social issues that face the Afro-Brazilian community. The works produced since 1978 have ranged in thematic and stylistic concerns from an ideological resistance to racism to the recuperation of black cultural heritage that was denigrated due to slavery, to revalorization of cultural values with homage paid to African religions through Candomblé rites, issues of family values and hetero/homo-sexual relationships and a dialogue between tradition and modernity.

This study focuses primarily on two twenty-first-anniversary editions by Quilombhoje: *Cadernos negros: Os melhores poemas* (1998) and *Cadernos negros: Os melhores contos* (1998). Navigating a hidden world of the contemporary Afro-Brazilian experience in Brazil, Quilombhoje is that primary source of inspiration that has produced quality collective and individual works that challenge not only the myths of the enslaved and ex-slave but also that of racial democracy and its related stereotypes. Within the context of the etymology of the group's name, Quilombhoje derives from *quilombo*, a typical settlement of runaway slaves who not only resisted slavery but chose to be free at whatever cost. But the addition of "hoje" (today) to *quilombo* makes it contemporary and more relevant to the challenges of being Afro-Brazilian in the second half of the twentieth century and after. It is in this sense that the movement and its literary production qualify as a postmodernist enterprise that is verifiable in its sociothematic concerns, stylistic experimentation, and finesse.

The two anniversary editions, in addition to providing us with a literary trajectory of the Quilombhoje group after twenty-one years of existence, also provide us with a sampling of its best works of poetry and prose where the respective writers engage with the preservation of Afro-Brazilian cultural heritage in the face of multiple threats of racism, urban violence, modernity, ignorance, and urgent social issues. The dynamics of the stories and poems lie in the ability of the writers to capture individual dramas in their collective social implications. Race, class, and gender intermingle with issues of survival of the family and the challenge of protecting children from social decay and the threat of violent extinction at the hands of hooligans. Quilombhoje is indeed a social organization beyond its primary function of a black literary and cultural movement. The attempt here is to provide a window into the stubborn hopes, the inspiring travails, and the compelling contradictions of this contemporary Afro-Brazilian movement for equality and justice.

In his comparative study of the *Movimento negro* of Rio de Janeiro and São Paulo, *Orpheus and Power* (1994), Michael Hanchard argues painstakingly and convincingly about the challenges and social impact of black movements. He states that in their struggle against dominant racial hegemony, these movements are co-opted into that same oppressive structure through culturalism and economic dependence. Hanchard sees this as an unfortunate paradox that compels these organizations to engage in "meta-politics, that is, a politics once removed from direct action and engagement with forces of white dominance" (159). These limitations, which often compel black movements to subject themselves, consciously or otherwise, to cultural folklorization despite explicit articulation of dissent, tend to cripple "alternative, sometimes directly confrontational, political practices" (159), which Hanchard calls their "Gramscian problematic" (159). In resolving this problematic productively, dialogue with the historicized past becomes a primary strategy of not just survival but negotiation toward a more political and transformative participation: "The continuous present, rather than a folkloric past, must be historicized if black and white critical intellectuals are to reveal ongoing, racialized disjunctures in Brazilian society. If the movimento is to avoid Orpheus' fate, there needs to be greater critical activity *within* the movimento, not only for exploding both self-laudatory and demeaning accounts of an Afro-Brazilian past, but most importantly, to historicize and thereby de-folklorize an Afro-Brazilian present" (167). The implications of Hanchard's call for historicism and dialogue must be drawn out. It is the first step toward creating a mutually strategic agenda for change and validation. Although the allusion to Orpheus's fate may suggest not "looking back" and thus not historicizing, we believe the sense of negotiation here implies not dwelling on the past but using it as an instrument of reappropriation toward rendering Afro-Brazilian reality a serious issue of study and consideration as opposed to the current simplification and folklorization typical of Carnival, capoeira, samba, and other cultural manifestations that have been commercialized and co-opted.

Historical Background

Of the different pieces of history written individually or collectively on the Quilombhoje group in the form of introduction or preface (Cuti in vol. 8, Carolyn Richardson Durham, Esmeralda Ribeiro, Márcio Barbosa, and Sônia Fátima in vol. 20), among others intended for special anniversary editions (Benedito Cintra and Cuti in *Os melhores poemas* and Aldo Rebelo and Cuti in *Os melhores contos*), Márcio Barbosa's piece in *Thoth* on *Cadernos negros* is the most comprehensive and authoritative to date.[1] Divided into three periods (1970s, 1980s, and 1990s), the essay situates the years of learning, growing, producing, distributing, and appealing to the immediate and larger community for recognition. Barbosa combines the emergence of Quilombhoje with the challenges of maintaining a collective project as well as situates the group within overall place of Black literature in Brazilian letters. For Barbosa, Afro-Brazilian literature is a rich defining emblem that denotes rapport with Africa as well as a symbolic spiritual continuity in the diaspora:

> A literatura negra evidencia um modo de estar no mundo e atualiza uma herança cujas raízes estão no continente que deu origem ao homem moderno: a África. África onírica, África ancestral, África que gerou em nosso inconsciente

coletivo uma forma singular (embora dinâmica e aberta) de nos relacionarmos com a natureza e com as outras pessoas. (211)

[Afro-Brazilian literature exudes a mode of being in the world and updates a heritage rooted in the continent that begets the modern man: Africa. Oneiric Africa, ancestral Africa that cultivates in us a unique collective consciousness (albeit dynamic and open) in our relationship with nature and other people.]

Barbosa's universalistic tone does not minimize his black consciousness and his sense of collective belonging to Africa, for it is this essential communion with Africa that defines the Afro-Brazilian as a people with a past, a history and an ancestry. And it is this search for belonging, identity, and place in the world that motivated the founding of Quilombhoje.

The year 1978 was decisive for Quilombhoje; it was a period of national unrest and protest against the military dictatorship as well as demand for civil rights for Afro-Brazilians. Among active organizations at the time were the MNUCDR (Movimento Negro Unificado Contra a Discriminação Racial—Unified Black Movement against Racial Discrimination), FECONEZU (Festival Comunitário Negro Zumbi—Black Zumbi Community Festival), and Grupo Palmares from Porto Alegre, which had demanded November 20 as Black National Day, as opposed to May 13, the official date of commemoration of abolition. It was against this background, and to the credit of Cuti and Hugo Ferreira, that the first *Cadernos negros* was launched with eight poets in 1978. As Barbosa noted, this was not the first attempt at anthologizing young Afro-Brazilian poets; similar efforts had been made in previous years, such as Hamilton Cardoso's *Negrice* (1977) and *Coletânea de poesia negra* (organized by a black group in Santos, a São Paulo neighborhood). Although the context of emergence was a political one, that of agitation for better conditions for blacks in a racist society, Barbosa is quick to point out the dilemma Quilombhoje faced. It was almost inconceivable for black movements to agree with a black group writing about their experiences since literature was considered a "passatempo burguês" (a pastime of the elites). Within this context, the group had already faced resistance since its inception.

Paying homage to the generation of writers before *Cadernos negros*, Barbosa acknowledges the influence of the following writers, as the group met to read and discuss their works: Cruz e Souza, Luís Gama, Lima Barreto, Machado de Assis, Aimé Césaire, Richard Wright, and Lino Guedes among others. The consistent production of *Cadernos negros* in the early years of formation and the following decade was made possible through self-financing on the part of the members of Quilombhoje. It was not until 1994 that a progressive publisher, Anita Garibaldi, offered to coedit with the Quilombhoje. Also in 1998, twenty-one years after publication of first volume, the

Ministry of Culture decided to participate in the promotion of its activities by sponsoring four works launched at once. While it took this long, one can say that Quilombhoje and *Cadernos negros* have finally arrived—but at what price?

Barbosa notes the importance of the group as a continuation of the black social movement, since the "dinâmica do movimento" (dynamic of the movement) depends on collaboration and sacrifice on the part of the participants, such as through all-night debates and discussions of collective and individual works:

> Varávamos a madrugada discutindo poesia, mergulhando em cada um dos textos trazidos pelos presentes, procurando refletir sobre a nossa condição de criadores negros numa sociedade racista. A tarefa da produção de livros e o ativismo literário impulsionaram-nos para outras atividades. (213)

> [We stayed up all night discussing poetry, immersing ourselves in each of the texts brought by the members present, trying to reflect on our condition as black writers in a racist society. The task of production and literary activism motivated us into various other activities.]

These meetings were a period of intellectual and organizational ferment where ideas germinated and the process of production became part and parcel of the group's involvement and function. With time, collective works also led to the inauguration of "Livro do autor" (The Author's Book Series), which allowed members to publish their individual works.

For any organization to function and survive, organize events, and carry through with activities, the issue of discipline must become a question to be pondered. Many were resolved to debunk the myth that Afro-Brazilians are habitual late-comers and can neither be punctual nor organize themselves without the help of someone else. The group then decided to limit the number of absences after which a member would be compelled to leave the group. This decision led to a partial disintegration of the group as two important members, Miriam Alves and Jamu Minka, had to leave. The challenges were manifold: from financial and logistical obstacles to a lack of critical reception or reception from a misguided anthropological perspective. In addition, the personal financial sacrifices of some without immediate rewards caused internal conflicts, resulting in more members leaving the group:

> A expectativa de ver o texto causar impacto, ser lido por muitos, não se concretizava no curto prazo. De compensações financeiras, é bom nem falar. Os desgates passaram a minar a resistência dos quilombhojeiros. Muita dedicação e pouco retorno são ingredientes fatais. O grupo não tinha dívidas, mas

também nunca tive dinheiro suficiente para contratar profissionais. Todo trabalho era voluntário. (215)

[The hopes of seeing our works have an impact and be read by many were not being fulfilled in the short term. As for financial gains, better to not even think about it. The cost was affecting the resistance of Quilombhoje members. A lot of dedication and minimal reward was a fatal combination. The group did have debts yet never had enough money to hire professionals. All the work was done by volunteers.]

The loss of members was not to end as Cuti and Oubi withdrew from the group in 1994 and 1995, respectively. These withdrawals coupled with the prior departure of Miriam Alves and Jamu Minka were devastating but did not cause the group to break up. It was about this time that the group obtained an outlet through the coeditorship of Anita Garibaldi, who had better recognition in terms of publishing and marketing.

Barbosa sums up his historical survey with a balancing act, enumerating the travails and achievements and ending on a tone of optimism and yet of challenge in terms of the future of Quilombhoje and *Cadernos negros*. By 1999, Quilombhoje had over 30 thousand copies in circulation. Among these works are twenty-one collective volumes, ten individual works, and two books of essays. For a self-sustaining group, this is a huge achievement. Although Barbosa ends with a line of "pessi-optimism," "O grande desafio é não parar" (The ultimate challenge is not to lose momentum), he notes that the achievements of Quilombhoje are minimal if compared to the larger Brazilian publishing market that has marginalized the group for so long. It is some consolation that despite the withdrawal of certain members, the same continue as contributors although no longer integrally involved. Barbosa notes that after 1995 the group was organized by three members: Esmeralda Ribeiro, Sônia Fátima, and Barbosa himself.

The following analysis is a celebration of the group over twenty years through the works of Abílio Ferreira, Conceição Evaristo, Cuti, Éle Semog, Esmeralda Ribeiro, Eustáquio José Rodrigues, Jônatas Conceição da Silva, José Carlos Limeira, Lia Vieira, Márcio Barbosa, Miriam Alves, Oswaldo de Camargo, Oubi Inaê Kibuko, Ramatis Jacino, Ricardo Dias, Sônia Fátima da Conceição, Jamu Minka, Carlos de Assumpção, Jorge Sequeira, Landê Onawale, Teresinha Tadeu, and Waldemar Euzébio Pereira. These writers also represent the emerging and regional diversity of the group's collaborators from São Paulo, Rio de Janeiro, Minas Gerais, Bahia, Pernambuco, and Rio Grande do Sul. Much is to be expected from this group, especially in serving as an avenue for "unknown" or marginalized regional writers who have something to say and need greater visibility in order to say it effectively.

Os Cadernos negros: Os melhores poemas (Black Notebooks: Selected Poems)

Zilá Bernd, in her discussion of the characteristic elements of "minor literature" in *Introdução à literatura negra* (45–93), identifies the following: a presence of a strong coefficient of deterritorialization, that is, an effort at recuperating lost Afro-Brazilian cultural "territories" and giving them new meaning; the predominance of the political, such as the denunciation of racism; and the emergence of a collective and revolutionary voice, such as what Bernard Mouralis refers to as "contraliteratura" or the "completely engaging discourse of the Self that the Other can neither obscure nor subvert,"[2] hence its nature of protest against the dominant culture.

In the area of postabolition poetry, Bernd goes on to elaborate such additional characteristics as the emergence of the individual voice or the "eu enunciador" (77) in which the Afro-Brazilian writer becomes self-conscious toward a rewriting of history from his/her point of view; the construction of the Afro-Brazilian epic by placing emphasis on heroes such as Zumbi dos Palmares; the reversal of values, such as juxtaposition of Afro-Brazilian values against the white dominant values; and the creation and manipulation of symbolic structures against stereotypical images associated with blackness, night, evil, sin, tam-tam, sacrifice, and so on. As a postmodernist literary production, the poetry of *Cadernos negros* is located somewhere between the individual and the collective, between the epic and the antiepic, between history and antihistory since it must mobilize by being relevant while at the same time culturally rooted so that it can survive various currents, both institutionalized and economical. It is against this background that the variety of poems contained in *Os melhores poemas* must be appreciated since they cover the period between 1978 and 1998 of Brazil's cultural and political history.

The context, volatilely and vigorously enacted by Benedito Cintra's preface, uses the Macdonald metaphor to capture the currents and limitations within which *Cadernos negros* has had to operate over the years. According to his "Negritude e Arte":

> Nossos inimigos querem impor o individualismo como prática social, política e cultural. Querem destruir as formas coletivas de pensar e agir. Ancorados pela grande mídia, esta sempre em uníssono, querem excluir a crítica, a controvérsia, o debate. Objetivam impor uma visão única e reacionária sobre a realidade e os acontecimentos. Mais recentemente, vêm incentivando a mediocridade cultural, um esoterismo banal, a despolitização, a anti-brasilidade, o besteirol. No fundo, querem *macdonaldizar* a nossa cultura. Afinal, "tudo se resolve pelo mercado" que eles mesmos manipulam. (17)

[Our enemies want to impose individualism as a social, political, and cultural practice. They want to destroy our collective way of thinking and acting. Supported by the almighty media, all in unison, they want to exclude criticism, controversy, debate. They intend to impose an exclusive and reactionary vision on reality and events. More recently, they are giving incentives to cultural mediocrity, a banal esotericism, depoliticization, anti-Brazilianness, and absurdities. In essence, they want to "McDonaldize" our culture. After all, "everything is resolved through the market" that they themselves manipulate.]

Here is a powerful synthesis of the challenges Quilombhoje faces as a cultural group struggling to make a difference. Apart from the difficulty writers have in working regular jobs in addition to their creative vocation, the combination of racial discrimination on the home/work front can be devastating and discouraging; however, the group must be praised for squarely facing these odds and yet producing works of a very high quality.

On a more specific note of appreciation, Cintra sees *Os melhores poemas* as "um pouco do universo simbólico e do cotidiano do negro; dos seus sonhos, de sua indignação, seu protesto" (17; a sample symbolic universe and the quotidian reality of the Afro-Brazilian—his dreams, his indignation, his protest). *Os melhores poemas* is thematically multivocal and stylistically enriched in its varied poetic experimentation. Painting a stifled world where the oppressed person must articulate his/her voice from the very abyss of social structure, challenging the anomalies and affirming self-dignity and love even in the midst of protest. From issues of identity, protest, love/pleasure/sex, and solidarity, to homage and evocations of heroes, the volume captures the tapestry that Afro-Brazilians represents in their fragmentation and struggle for cohesion of affirmation. As Edimilson de Almeida Pereira observes, "African-Brazilian literature is part of the fractured tradition of Brazilian Literature." This "fractured" element is manifest not only in the Afro-Brazilian personality but also as translated into literature:

> African-Brazilian Literature written in this system is Brazilian Literature, as well, albeit a literature that expresses a world view specific to African-Brazilians. The dynamics of tensions and contradictions present in this literature help us to understand the attitudes of the authors who either downplayed, denied, or made their ethnic origin central to their identity; clarifies the necessity to denounce social oppression and gives evidence to a new sensibility that aesthetically apprehends the universe of African-Brazilian culture. (*Callaloo* 18.4 [1995]: 876)

This "new sensibility" translates the inner will to create works that reflect the realities of the Afro-Brazilian as a distinct experience from the dominant culture. In this sense, it is partly creative in vocation and yet revisionist in its intentions, as we verify in a few examples.

A quantitative breakdown of the fifty-one poems in this volume reveals an interesting pattern in thematic concerns. About 40 percent deals with protest, followed by the issue of identity with 30 percent, issues of love/pleasure/sex, evocations of Pan-African heroes or ancestrality, and questions of solidarity are 15, 10, and 5 percent, respectively. This "revelation" accentuates the question of protest as a more pressing problematic since this is the area of racial discrimination that affects everything else. Through protest, the Afro-Brazilian voice comes alive as it relates the daily experiences of inequalities and injustice toward the goal of cultural affirmation and demand for change.

The Afro-Brazilian voice, captured figuratively in Abelardo Rodrigues's "Garganta" (Throat) must be properly cleansed from the uncertainty, insecurities, and passivity of the past in order to produce, in the urgency of the moment, a carnivalesque voice, apt at regeneration and subversion:

> Uma garganta não é corpo/flácido
> É sangue escorrendo em leilão de cais.
> Tua garganta, irmão
> é uma quarta-feira de cinzas. (*Cadernos negros/Black Notebooks* 246)
> [A throat is not a weak body, / it is blood flowing in public outcry. / Your throat, brother, / is an Ash Wednesday.]

Once cleansed, such a voice can only produce, according to Oubi Inaê Kibuko's theory of committed poetry, a "poema armado" (armed poetry):

> Que o poema venha armado
> e metralhe a sangue-frio
> palavras flamejantes de revoltas
> palavras prenhes de serras e punhais. . . .
> E construa solidamente
> uma fortaleza de fé
> naqueles que engordam
> o exército dos desesperados. . . .
> E nem mais se sustente
> com carne, suor e sangue
> dum povo emparedado e sugado
> nos engenhos da exploração! (114–15)

> [Let the poem come armed / and attack in cold blood / words burning with protest / words pregnant with saws and daggers . . . / And construct solidly / a fortress of faith / in those who multiply / the army of desperate people . . . / And no longer live / by meat, sweat, and blood / of a walled-in and extorted people / in the plantations of exploitation!]

The construction of a "fortress of faith" is the nourishing element for a tired and restless body, calling out for intervention and yet determined to be always prepared for any eventuality.

A fortress is always constructed as a shield against attack, in a constant state of readiness in a society that attacks its own citizenry and leaves them for dead in mind and soul. Hence Lepê Correia's faith in the struggle, defiance, and affirmation of his negritude, his blackness, and his humanity, as in "Teimosa presença" (Stubborn Presence):

> Eu continuo acreditando na luta
> Não abro mão do meu falar onde quero
> Não me calo ao insulto de ninguém
> Eu sou um ser, uma pessoa como todos
> Não sou um bicho, um caso raro
> ou coisa estranha
> Sou a resposta, a controvérsia, a dedução
> A porta aberta onde entram discussões
> Sou a serpente venenosa: bote pronto
> Eu sou a luta, sou a fala, o bate-pronto
> Eu sou o chute na canela do safado
> Eu sou um negro pelas ruas do país. (92)

> [I continue to believe in the struggle / I speak wherever I please / I don't keep quiet at anyone's insult / I am a human being, a person like any other / I am not an animal, a rare specie / or something strange / I am the response, the controversy, the deduction / An open door that allows arguments / I am the poisonous snake: quick bite / I am the struggle, the speech, the ready beat / I am the soccer boot in the shin of the trickster / I am black on the streets of this country.]

This cry of protest coupled with self-definition and self-affirmation has a declarative tone as if the poetic voice is enumerating what he is not, as well as what he is, in order to have an unmistaken and balanced perspective of his identity and what he stands for ideologically.

Correia's poem of protest and identity finds numerous echoes in Éle Semog's "Dançando negro" (Dancing Black), Cuti's "Quebranto" (Exhaustion) and "Para ouvir e entender 'estrela,'" (In Order to Hear and Understand the "Star"), Oliveira Silveira's "Outra negra fulô" (Another "Neggress"-Flower), all of which poems redefine blackness from their own perspective. They challenge current stereotypes, such as the myth within a myth of a white Santa Claus, the contrast between the dancing black and the thinking white, the anger that accompanies police brutality, the sense of exhaustion and frustration and the solace found in indiscriminate drunkenness as captured by Cuti in "Quebranto." But it is in Celinha's "Negritude" that we find a synthesis of the burden of blackness flowing like "a warrior chant" in response to mental and physical anguish and oppression:

> De mim
> parte *um canto guerreiro*
> um vôo rasante, talvez rumo norte
> caminho trilhado da cana-de açúcar
> ao trigo crescido, pingando de sangue
> do corte do açoite. Suor escorrido
> da briga do dia
> que os ventos do sul e o tempo distante
> não podem ocultar. (34; emphasis added)

[From me / emerges *a warrior chant* / a smooth flight, perhaps northward / path mapped from sugarcane to / growing wheat, trickling blood / from cuts sustained from lashes. Sweat flowing / from the day's battle / that the southern winds and distant time / cannot hide.]

As "a warrior chant," the poem takes on an ideological significance. Not only is orality implied, and by extension a veneration of the ancestral past, but its ultimate power lies in its politics and commitment: visible, defiant, indicting, and self-defensive, it forewarns the oppressor/enemy of its readiness to attack and self-defend simultaneously. The element of surprise then becomes, for both parties, a matter of aptitude and will as to who makes the first move.

For the warrior to have a lasting impact on the community, the members of that same community must be mobilized or at least made aware of the imperative and significance of the war being waged. Miriam Alves's "MNU," Oswaldo de Camargo's "Em maio," and Jamu Minka's "Cristovão-Quilombos" take a more collective and historical approach to revisionism by engaging significant issues affecting the entire Afro-Brazilian community, such as misery, commemoration of slavery, and the myth of colonial "discoveries." For Alves, knowledge of one's condition is the basis of power not only for negotiation but also for denunciation, such as in "MNU," which stands for the Unified Black Movement:

> Eu sei:
> Surgiu um grito na multidão
> um estado seco de revolta
> Surgiu outro
> outro
> e
> outros
> aos poucos, amotinamos exigências

querendo o resgate
sobre nossa forçada
miséria secular. (105)

[I know: / a cry emerged from the multitude / a dry state of revolt / Another emerged / another / and others / gradually, we make demands in mutiny / we demand ransom / for our forced / secular misery.]

Alves's compassion for the collective pain of history is complemented by Camargo's juxtaposition of the claims and contradictions of May 13 as the official date of the abolition of slavery in Brazil. Camargo ridicules the hypocrisy of the dominant culture in wanting to remember a past favorable to them as "masters" and also of the ignorance of the former slaves, the elderly in particular, who feel they achieved something, however insignificant to the youth who refuse to celebrate:

A liberdade que sei é uma menina sem jeito,
vem montada no ombro dos moleques
e se esconde
no peito, em fogo, dos que jamais irão
à praça.
Na praça estão os fracos, os velhos, os decadentes
e seu grito: "Ó bendita Liberdade!"
E ela sorri e se orgulha, de verdade,
do muito que tem feito! (112)

[The liberty I know is a clumsy little girl, / on the shoulder of rascals / hiding out / in the burning chest of those who will never go / to the square. / In the square, you have the weak, the old, the decadents / and their shout: "Oh blessed Liberty!" / And she smiles, and truly proud / of all that has been accomplished.]

The seeming irony here is more of a paradox. On the one hand, the elderly are celebrating freedom while the young ones still see the chains of slavery dangling on their necks and feet as they are still "subdued" by the same mentality that effectuated slavery in the first place. On the other hand, the former masters are eager to display history from the perspective of benevolence. The implied intergenerational conflict among Afro-Brazilians serves not as a divisive measure on the part of the dominant culture but as an intellectual opportunity for Afro-Brazilians to redefine strategies toward a continuous reprogramming of the youth toward pragmatic black consciousness. Alves speaks about the division between the commitment of the youth as opposed to that of the adults. By contrasting the "freedom" the poetic voice feels in the arms of rascals who, like her, avoid the independence celebrations of the adults and the oppressed who show up at the square, Alves ridicules the celebration as a hypocritical festivity that does affect the lives of ordinary people but only to reinforce their powerlessness and ignorance.

Jamu Minka's "Cristovão-Quilombos" applies that "pragmatic consciousness" when it subjects the European "explorer/discoverer" of the Americas to a rereading and reversal of his name within an ideological context. Instead of Cristovão Colombo, Minka renames, re-creates, and reinvents, partly suggesting a self-discovery and partly indicting and rejecting the myth of European discovery:

> Piratas no paraíso
> Europa rouba tudo
> Ouro e prata, milho, batata
> cana e canga em corpos de América e África
> Pós impacto do primeiro engano
> —a visita era conquista e seus horrores—
> deuses invadidos trovejam tambores
> e cospem flechas de rebeldia
> Depois de Colombo e sua maldita herança. (77)

[Pirates in paradise / Europe steals everything / Gold, silver, corn, potatoes / sugarcane, and slave cargoes from America and Africa / Aftermath of the first deception /—the visit was conquest and its horrors—/ invaded gods drum their tam-tams / and eject arrows of rebellion / Against Columbus and his accursed patrimony.]

By trading "Quilombos" for "Colombo," the poetic voice takes an ideological stance against an agelong claim, suggesting that only Afro-Brazilians can discover themselves just like the *quilombos* or settlements organized by rebellious/runaway slaves in nineteenth-century Brazil.

Celinha's voice takes on this catalogue of protest with a Pan-African vision when in "Um sol guerreiro" (A Warrior Sun), dedicated to "todas as crianças negras assassinadas em Atlanta e muitas outras crianças assassinadas todos os dias no ventre da humanidade" (all black children assassinated in Atlanta and many other children killed every day in the womb of humanity), she evokes optimism and hope for the suffering community of blacks all over the world. As a consolation, she turns to the children, constructed as the future of tomorrow, and attempts to provide them hope symbolized by the rising and warrior sun in the midst of hopelessness and persistent darkness:

> Cante, menino
> cante uma canção que emudeça os prantos,
> que repique os ataques
> e ensurdeça os gritos

Porque amanhã não haverá mais
nenhum resto de esperança
não haverá mais um outro amanhecer,
pois certamente muito antes
de surgir um novo dia
um sol, guerreiro, há de raiar
à meia-noite, para despertar o teu sono,
Como uma nova alvorada. (37)

[Sing, young one / sing a song that silences the wailings, / that rekindles the attacks / and deafens the cries / Because tomorrow / there will no longer be / any hope left / there will no longer be a sunrise / for certainly before / the rise of another day / a warrior sun must shine / at midnight, to wake you from slumber / like a new dawn.]

The imperative tone of this poem gives it the power of certainty and hope that usually accompanies optimism.

Another consistent problematic in the poetry volume is the question of identity. As Bernd points out, "A identidade da poesia negra é dada principalmente pela intenção que contém de recriar e de reconstruir um mundo que seja diferente do mundo dos brancos" (*Literatura negra* 87; The identity of black poetry is principally marked by the intention of re-creating and reconstructing a world different from that of whites). The issue of identity, especially in a pluralistic society, is a constant debate that echoes in the case of Brazil, a collateral issue of national culture. As a matter of convenience for the dominant establishment, Afro-Brazilian culture is only relevant during commercialized cultural expressions and manifestations such as Carnival, samba, and capoeira. Without sounding essentialist, Brazilian culture and identity in general are defined and manipulated by the dominant culture, which claims a racial democracy where there is none, which faults the marginalized for being "lazy" and "sensual" and hence unable to climb rapidly in the social hierarchy. As Renato Ortiz points out in *Cultura brasileira e identidade brasileira*, "Toda identidade se define em ralação a algo que lhe é exterior, ela é uma diferença" (8; Every identity is defined in relation to something that is foreign to it, that amounts to its difference). From this perspective, Afro-Brazilian identity is primarily defined in relation to the dominant culture, hence the constant juxtaposition and polarity between white and black metaphors in most of Afro-Brazilian poetry, such as in "Linhagem," "Negritude," "Mineiridade," "Outras notícias," "Olhar negro," "Raça e classe," "Ser e não ser," and "Efeitos colaterais."

Carlos de Assumpção, in "Linhagem" (Lineage), sets the tone for the discussion of identity in *Os melhores poemas* since he combines the present with the ancestral past, as well as a consciousness of protest even to the point of universality:

> Eu sou descendente de Zumbi
> Zumbi é meu pai e meu guia
> Me envia mensagens do orum
> Meus dentes brilham na noite escura
> Afiados como o agadá de Ogum. (31)

> [I am a descendant of Zumbi / Zumbi is my father and guide / He sends me messages from heaven / my teeth shine in dark night / sharp-edged like Ògún's sword.]

While Zumbi, the Afro-Brazilian hero, is given primary focus, Africa is however foregrounded through allusions to "orum" (heaven) in Yoruba and the reference to Ògún the Yoruba god of iron and the road, as equally syncretized and adopted in Brazilian religious rites such as Candomblé.

This sense of fragmentation and being different from the African and yet a descendant is best captured by Esmeralda Ribeiro in "Olhar negro." While Assumpção draws inspiration from an Afro-Brazilian who is relevant to the immediate experience of liberation in Brazil, Ribeiro finds in this new personality a possibility for regeneration as she enumerates the varied fragments of her being as reflected and recomposed by the sun, in front of the mirror, in the consolation that comes from drinking *cachaça* (sugarcane liquor) or under the psychological stress caused by day-to-day afflictions, in the struggle to be a woman, and in the hope of putting the pieces together:

> Mas
> não desisto
> vou
> atravessando o meu oceano
> vou
> navegando
> vou
> buscando meu
> olhar negro
> perdido no azul do tempo. (66)

> [But I don't give up / I continue crossing my ocean / I continue navigating / I continue searching my / black gaze.]

Ribeiro speaks for most Afro-Brazilians in terms of their current dilemma of trying to put the fragmented self together after the curse and pain of slavery, which Jamu Minka captures vividly in "Raça e Classe":

Nossa pele teve maldição de raça
e exploração de classe
duas faces da mesma diáspora e desgraça. (75)

[Our skin was cursed by virtue of race / and exploration due to class / two faces of the same diaspora and misfortune.]

Minka cogently enumerates the adverse consequences of racial and class discrimination. He further exposes the detrimental impact of slavery on Afro-Brazilians. Minka points out the difficulty of being doubly discriminated against due to one's race and class, which, according to the poetic voice, should be considered more as complimentary features than shameful attributes.

Minka's exposition of the problem of race and class is an indirect invitation to a larger discussion of racial democracy as captured in his "Efeitos colaterais" and in Oliveira Silveira's "Ser e não ser." Minka subjects the myth of the "racial paradise" to rigorous scrutiny when he faults the propaganda for the hypocrisy and imposed dictatorship under which Afro-Brazilians are compelled to deny their racial reality or else face the consequences of oppressive and technical invisibility:

Negros de alma negra se inscrevem
naquilo que escrevem
mas o Brasil nega
negro que não se nega. (76)

[Blacks with black souls inscribe themselves / in what they write / but Brazil denies / Any black who does not self-deny.]

As if to agree with Minka, Silveira equally ridicules Brazilian hypocrisy in her contradictory claim of racial equality:

O racismo que existe,
o racismo que não existe.
O sim que é não,
o não que é sim.
É assim o Brasil
ou não? (108)

[Racism exists / Racism doesn't exist. / Yes that means no / No that means yes. / Such is the reality of Brazil / or not?]

This disease, disguised as a mask of democracy, lies at the heart of Brazil's contradictions as a nation. By insisting that the individual black is to blame for being marginalized or poor, the dominant classes argue that the society provides avenues for social ascension. The opportunities may be there, but the fact is they are hardly meant for blacks, and a wide range of excuses abound for not allowing blacks to participate, the most obvious premised on the charge of laziness. This further complicates the psyche of the Afro-Brazilian as some, like the case of mulattoes, would rather associate with the white establishment for the meager gains that accompany denial of blackness.

Taking the evocation to a more Pan-African level, Márcio Barbosa, in "Mandela," offers the most engaging and political portrayal of Nelson Mandela as a symbol of resistance. The highly revered hero of the African continent was imprisoned for twenty-six years by the former South African apartheid regime due in effect to his insistence on equal rights for blacks and whites. Barbosa's poem combines passion with a powerful dose of optimism as he asserts that no prison will be able to hold a people intent on liberty:

> Nenhum cárcere pode prender, entre paredes de pedra e musgo, a música das passeatas, a voz rebelde dos jovens, o beijo de amor das mulheres no rosto negro dos homens, a aurora do novo mundo nos bairros de lata e pólvora. . . .
>
> Nenhum estupidez escraviza o negro ao branco e permanece impune. . . .
>
> Não, nenhum cárcere detém o crepúsculo ou impede a marcha sangrenta das horas. (100–101)
>
> [No prison can hold, between stone walls and moss, the music of passers-by, the rebellious voice of the youth, the women's loving kiss on black men, the aura of the New World in neighborhoods constructed with iron and gun powder. . . . / No stupidity will enslave blacks while whites go unpunished. . . . / No, no prison will stop sunrise or the bloody march of the times.]

In addition to serving as an inspiration to Afro-Brazilians, Mandela is mythicized; he becomes a legend whose ideals the black community aspires to achieve for the Afro-Brazilian community. Here is a voice of resistance, of protest, of courage, and of optimism that contributes to the regeneration of Afro-Brazilians in their current struggle for civil rights in a racist society.

Cadernos negros: Os melhores contos (Black Notebooks: Selected Short Stories)

Quilombhoje's choice of the short story as the genre to alternate with poetry has multiple rationales: the experimental nature of the group when it first started in 1978, the limited means of self-sponsored production, and the brevity of the genre, given that most of the contributors had other vocations in addition to writing. These limitations raise a more serious problem of critical reception and the reading public. As if the battle of creating the time to write is not enough, these committed writers must also become their own critics. While there may be a few pages here and there by such critics as Zilá Bernd, Oswaldo Camargo, and David Brookshaw, on select writers or a panoramic overview of the group, *Cadernos negros* contains a limited amount of *Cadernos negros* general literary criticism. The two volumes of criticism produced by the group, *Reflexões: Sobre a literatura afro-brasileira* (1985) and *Criação crioula: Nu elefante branco* (1987), are perhaps the most comprehensive but both need updating since the critical commentary focuses more on the plight of being an Afro-Brazilian writer in a racist society than on actual textual analysis. The 1995 special edition of *Callaloo* was a laudable step in that direction, but it was still too panoramic to represent the significance of *Cadernos negros* in contemporary Afro-Brazilian literature.

Os melhores contos offers the best selection of stories written by Quilombhoje's membership to date. Of the seventeen stories taken from the different volumes over the years, we find Abílio Ferreira's "A casa de Fayola," Conceição Evaristo's "Ana Davenga," Cuti's "O batizado," Éle Semog's "A seiva da vida," José Carlos Limeira's "Tanclau," Márcio Barbosa's "Quando o malandro vacila," Miriam Alves's "Alice está morta," and Oubi Inaê Kibuko's "Reencontro" particularly engaging and worthy of analysis. As Aldo Rebelo's preface, "A arte da resistência" (13–16), indicates, the stories have a wide range of appeal and concerns: from female oppression to the marginality of young and old, male and female, and overall racial discrimination that has devastated the Afro-Brazilian community.

In oppositional response to the stereotypical images of the Afro-Brazilian found in works by white writers or unconscious black/mulatto writers—the buffoon, the rogue, the slave, the vagabond—the stories in *Cadernos negros: Os melhores contos* portray characters that reflect immediate sociopolitical realities of the Afro-Brazilian person and community, hence the creation of heroes and heroines with their strengths and weaknesses. Miriam Alves captures this attitude of response when she asserts rhetorically:

> Fica a questão se a literatura feita por nós rompe estas imagens ou as personificam?—Rompe quando nos propomos a falar do nosso lugar, de nossa interioridade. A nossa fala desvela, delata, relata, invade quem ouvi-la ou lê-la. Ela é a própria personificação do negro sendo, re-sendo, mudando, re-mudando, sentindo, re-sentindo. A exterioridade assume simbolismos próprios, extravasando o texto, assumindo sentidos da nossa singularidade e pluralidade neste Brasil-social-injusto.

(*Cadernos negros* 8 [1986]: 13)

[The question remains, does our literature change these images or personify them? It changes them when we are bent on speaking about our place, our inner being. Our writing watches, denounces, exposes, invades whoever hears or reads it. It is the self-personification of the Afro-Brazilian, being—being reborn, changing, and rechanging, feeling and refeeling. The exteriority assumes our own symbols teasing meaning out of the text, assuming significations of our plurality in this socially unjust Brazil.]

The focus on the inner self, on the need to self-define as opposed to being the object of external or imposed definition of the Afro-Brazilian, is what Bernd refers to as the "eu enuciador" ("I" the speaker) without which others continue to speak for Afro-Brazilians. Unlike in poetry, where the poetic "I" is commonplace, there is a mix of the subject in the short stories since the characters need to be more developed and there is a deliberate distancing even when the narrative voice may be that of the implied author.

Abílio Ferreira's "A casa de Fayola" (Fayola's House) constitutes a paradigmatic text of the central conflict facing the Afro-Brazilian community today. Issues such as the conflict between tradition and modernity, religion and progress, alienation and resistance, and the old versus the new merge into a central pretext of a failed amorous relationship between Fayola and Alexandre, and of the attempt by Afro-Brazilians to grapple with changing realities and times. In naming the protagonist and the antagonist, there is a subtle implication of giving the "traditionalist" character an Afrocentric, Yoruba-sounding name while Alexandre sounds more Portuguese, more Eurocentric, more "alienated." Fayola lives in a villa with a strong African influence and with Afro-Brazilian religious rites such as Candomblé, while Alexandre is only returning after a long time away with new ideas about progress and modernity. The opening of the text foregrounds the immediate setting of the action as Alexandre returns: "Enfurnou-se na vila antiga que ficava muito abaixo do nível da rua, como um vale anacrônico no meio da cidade" (21; He stepped into the old villa, which was located way below the level of the street like an anachronistic valley in the middle of the city). The "anachronistic" reference carries with it a sense of something obsolete and decadent that needs to be abandoned if not renovated. But Alexandre's perception of reality differs from Fayola's and therein lies their conflict as well as the irony for both: while one wants change, the other resists any change that means abandoning her well-rooted cultural values and identity. A series of heated dialogues, debates, and arguments reveals their irreconcilable differences stemming from cultural influences from which they seemed conditioned and doomed:

Fayola está firme.

—Aí a gente luta pela vila. . . .

Mal ela termina de falar, a voz forte de Alexandre se impunha.

—Lutar de que jeito? Vocês são pequenos, não têm força.

—Nossa força é a união e o amor pelas nossa coisas.

—Ah é? Pois quando o poder cair em cima de vocês, eu serei o primeiro a querer saber como é que você vai evitar que os seus queridos menininhos negros se tornam marginais e onde é que vai funcionar o seu ridículo terreiro de candomblé. Você vai ter de acabar com a feira de artesanato e com o bloco de afoxé. Não haverá mais lugar pra vocês. Pensa um pouco, Fay. O fim dessa comunidade é questão de tempo! (25)

[Fayola remains adamant.

"Over there, we fight for the villa. . . ."

She had hardly finished, when Alexandre retorted,

"Fight in what way? You are few, you don't have a power base."

"Our power lies in our unity and love for what belongs to us."

"Really? Once the hand of the higher power comes down on you, I will be the first to inquire how you will avoid your beloved Afro-Brazilian children not becoming marginals and where will your ridiculous Candomblé temple be? You will end up joining the artifact's open market and the *afoxé* carnivalesque group. There will no longer be any space for you. Just think about it, Fay. The end of this community is only a matter of time!"]

Alexandre's pessimism is understandable. Having acquired an erudite education abroad, earning a decent salary, and being relatively comfortable, he is now poised to do away with his cultural values while encouraging Fayola to come with him to the city. Although well meaning, he is the prototype of the alienated Afro-Brazilian who is also living in the colonial past due to his mentality. There is no reason why the traditional and the modern cannot merge in a viable anthropophagic fluidity.

In contrast to Alexandre, Fayola possesses a perspective that must be understood within a cultural and ideological context. Her insistence on staying in the villa signifies her attachment to the ideals of cultural nourishment without which she will probably die. From the beginning of the relationship, she was forthright: "Eu disse desde o começo que daqui eu não sairia" (24;

I made it clear from the outset that I would not leave here). She goes on to say that her happiness and spiritual well-being are tied to the villa in a tellurian relationship that is inseparable: "Sou feliz aqui. Você sabe, sempre soube que eu jamais deixaria a vila. Não saio daqui por nada. Terão de nos tirar daqui a força" (25; I am happy here. You know, and always knew that I would never leave this villa. Nothing will make me leave. They will have to force us out of here). In spite of her optimism and defiance, Fayola does not seem to see beyond her cultural values, not even for the sake of love, and Alexandre's insistence only falls on deaf ears. Alexandre sounds like a "rational" person, trying to understand Fayola's rigidity of mentality:

> Você pretende passar o resto dos seus dias aqui. A troco de quê? Fay, isso é uma tolice. Isso aqui não vale esse sacrifício. Toda a sua vida por uma fantasia? Um sonho? . . . Pobreza! Mas que merda! Essa gente vai morrer no esquecimento, porque logo alguém muito poderoso manda demolir esta bosta toda para construir um prédio de apartamentos, o que, convenhamos, é útil e dá dinheiro. Ou então, o governo transforma essa velharia num enorme museu. (24–25)

[You plan to spend the rest of your days here. In exchange for what? Fay, this is stupidity. What you have here is not worth this sacrifice. Your entire lifetime for a fantasy? A dream? . . . Poverty! What a shit! These people will die in oblivion because soon some top brass will order this place demolished and construct an apartment complex, which, we must admit, is useful and lucrative. Or rather, the government can turn this old settlement into a museum.]

As the text clearly suggests, the origin of this rivalry and conflict between Fayola and Alexandre lies in their different upbringing and family expectations. While Alexandre's family sees the past as an impediment to progress, Fayola's roots are well entrenched in the community, and it is this contrast in what they both stand for that will make their union impossible as Alexandre reflects:

> Procurava lembrar-se de tudo o que lhe ocorrera: o crescimento dos dois, juntos, naquela mesma vila; a adolescência, as rodas de capoeira, os sonhos de seus pais (a família de Fayola lutara por um futuro de caráter complementamente diferente daquele que seu velho pai sonhara para ele, Alexandre, único filho). Agora parecia-lhe fácil compreender o clima de rivalidade que havia persistido, até a morte, entre as duas família. (26–27)

[He was trying to remember everything that happened to him: the growth of both of them together, in that same villa; their adolescence, the capoeira circles, their parents' dreams (Fayola's family fought for a future of a character totally different from that of his old father's dream for him, Alexandre, the only son). Now, it seemed easy to understand the permanence of rivalry between the two families even till death.]

Against this background, it is as if their relationship was doomed from the start. Their lack of mutual understanding of their plight further complicates the plot. While it would be easy enough for them simply to separate, their continued passion keeps drawing them together in a relationship that moves fast to a tragic closure. Even when Alexandre tries to convince Fayola about "o nosso povo" (our people) and the implication of their living in a "futile" and "backward" past, Fayola quickly defends the past, which for her continues to represent the present: "Mas não é apenas o passado que vejo. A vila é a vida da gente, mesmo que tentemos negar. Ela é o tempo presente que vamos construindo e que nos constrói a cada minuto" (27; But it is not only the past I see. The villa is our life even if we try to deny it. It is the present we continue to construct and which, in turn, constructs us every minute.) Fayola does have a point, for if the dwellers of the villa, which can also be a symbolic representation of the favela, do not have or know any other life, to simply abandon their connection to existence is to sign their own death warrant. In their inability to have a productive dialogue, Alexandre and Fayola must come to terms with their fundamental differences and let go.

The plot, however, gets complicated as Alexandre resorts to violence, setting Fayola's house on fire while she was asleep inside, leaving her for dead:

A vila acordou sobressaltada aos gritos de "Fogo! Fogo!"

Em pouco mais de meia hora, tudo dentro do pequeno cômodo era cinza, mas antes que o fogo se alastrasse para as outras casa, a tempestade já o havia exterminado, tamanha a força com que voltara a cair. (29)

[The villa woke up in a panic to the shouts of "Fire! Fire!"

In less than half an hour, everything in the small household was nothing but ash, but before the fire could spread to other houses, the force of the damage had already extinguished it.]

There are fundamental questions to be asked given the tragic end of the story: Why did Alexandre have to destroy the house as well as kill Fayola in the process? What is the symbolism of Fayola's death within the larger context of Afro-Brazilian culture and community? In addition to the implied portrayal of Alexandre's violence, which we see from the beginning in terms of his jealousy and ambition when he first returns to the villa to look for Fayola: "Se houver um homem aí dentro, mato os dois" (21; Should there be any man in there, I will kill both of them). Although Alexandre did not meet any man with Fayola, the premonition of Fayola's death remains constant throughout the story, although not necessary. Ferreira may be challenging Afro-Brazilians to some of the realities they take for granted, such as the issue of class struggle. In going beyond the racial dilemma, Ferreira's thesis in "A casa de Fayola" reconstructs the notion of racial discrimination and calls attention to the prospect of ideological and class discrimination and the accompanying intolerance, all of which are as destructive as racism.

From a gendered point of view, the dynamics of male-female relationship in the Afro-Brazilian community are further subjected to a critique if Fayola's death is perceived as inevitable, and ultimately a reflection of violence and chauvinism perpetrated by the male figure. In addition to emotional conflicts, there is indeed a pronounced power struggle between Alexandre and Fayola. The violent elimination of Fayola betrays a deep-seated frustration on the part of Alexandre—a psychological condition that blinded him from carefully exploring the various options available to him before resorting to the questionable and tragic "solution." Dialogue was not an option since Fayola is portrayed as intransigent and belligerent for reasons understandable within the logic of self-preservation and cultural preservation. Yet, death and violence are completely avoidable if only Alexandre could walk away from the impending tragedy in search of an alternative significant other who fits his "cosmopolitan" and "civilized" profile and posture. "A casa de Fayola" is undoubtedly a valid treatise on the imperative of intraracial tolerance, which is as critical as interracial harmony.

Similar to the drama of Fayola in "A casa de Fayola," Ana Davenga's predicament in Conceição Evaristo's "Ana Davenga" confirms the terrible decadence that has befallen the Afro-Brazilian community, especially at the hands of their men. These stories are moving away from a centrality of preoccupation with racism that once dominated poetic expression to more compelling realities of the family and male-female relationships. Both stories take place in the domestic space and in a setting comparable to the favela where crime and insecurity are the norms coupled with a strong sense of group solidarity and identity. Unlike "A casa de Fayola," in which the story is told from two perspectives, those of both Fayola and Alexandre, "Ana Davenga" seems to be told primarily from Ana's perspective although narrated by an omniscient narrator who also echoes the voice of the implied author. Unlike Fayola who is portrayed as strong, roots-conscious, and defiant, Ana Davenga lives in the shadow of her husband, Ana Davenga, even to the extent of adopting his name: Ana then becomes Ana Davenga. Davenga's vagabondesque and roguish lifestyle remains something of a mystery to Ana even though she benefits materially to such an extent that she may be seen as a silent participant in his mischievous and clandestine operations. Although Fayola dies along with the symbolic death of her "house" or strong beliefs, Ana is such an undeveloped and incredible character that her death at the end of the story has nowhere near the same effect as Fayola's. She dies after being struck by stray bullets from the police as Davenga resists arrest, and the unborn child in Ana's womb dies along with her:

> Davenga vestiu a calça lentamente. Ele sabia estar vencido. E agora, o que valia a vida? O que valia a morte? Ir para a prisão, nunca? A arma estava ali, debaixo da camisa que ele ia pegar agora. . . . Davenga pegou a camisa, e desse gesto se ouviram muitos tiros. . . . Na favela, os companheiros de Davenga choravam a morte do chefe e de Ana, que morrera ali na cama, metralhada, protegendo com as mãos um sonho de vida que ela trazia na barriga. (41)

> [Davenga put his trousers on slowly. He knew he was defeated. And now, what is the point of living? What's the value of death? Go to prison? Never! The gun was there, under the shirt he was about to remove from the bed. . . . Davenga picked up the shirt and many gunshots were heard. . . . In the shack, Davenga's companions lamented the loss of their chief and of Ana, who lay dead on the bed with many gunshot wounds, her hands protecting the dream of life she was carrying in her womb.]

A shadow in life and death, Ana Davenga represents an objectified Afro-Brazilian woman who must not only be submissive and passive, but must also be nice to the entourage of her bandit-husband. Like her husband, she lives on the edge of society, concerned about the future of her children but not really doing anything about it. But could she do anything in her situation? As Anne duCille points out in *The Coupling Convention,* "Coupling in the modern black feminist text is more often fictionalized as marital horror than as hearthside harmony" (145). While Fayola and Ana differ in their social and ideological disposition toward their men, their physical and psychological disposition is not questionable. Both women, despite their "disagreements" with their lovers, will always open their doors and hearts to them and try to satisfy their emotional needs albeit temporarily. This lack of real harmony is accounted for by socioeconomic conditions which women are often subjected, which duCille calls "the explicit impossibilities of the actual social and material conditions of most Americans, especially most black Americans" (143). In questioning the participation of Afro-Brazilian women in their own destruction, Evaristo's story makes an appeal to both men and women to rethink their roles and how their weaknesses contribute toward the failure of the Afro-Brazilian family and, by extension, the community at large. The Fayolas, Alexandres, Ana Davengas, and Davengas of the Afro-Brazilian community must have a change of attitude if not for themselves then at least for the survival and future of their survival and posterity.

Evaristo's appeal for redress is further echoed in Miriam Alves's "Alice está morta," a title that must not be read simplistically but ideologically. Alice may be dead physically in the sense of being tired, beaten down, and ultimately giving up the ghost, yet it could be a cry of protest signifying a new personality, a new Alice who will never be the same again. Her "death" can be read symbolically as an opportunity for regeneration. Like Fayola and Ana Davenga, the Afro-Brazilian women pay with their lives for the unrealistic expectations of their lovers, husbands, or boyfriends. The case of Alice is fascinating: she is considered the "par perfeito" (130; the perfect other) since she never demands anything. Her docility and readiness to satisfy her boyfriend sexually is what keeps the relationship alive. Both Alice and her boyfriend have strange expectations of each other. Being unmarried, they have a "living arrangement" that is ambiguous and based primarily on the fulfillment of sexual pleasures and desires. This convenient arrangement can not last because it is flawed from the beginning: it is not based on love.

The occasional arguments and complaints by both parties lead to an impasse as one faults the other for the failure of their fantastic relationship, which lacks a solid foundation in the first place. Suddenly, the narrator-boyfriend realizes he loves and hates Alice at the same time as he complains and reflects on the routine nature of their lives:

> Convivência sem grandes encantos. Eu e ela na casa de cômodos, escorando-nos. Meus filhos soltos neste mundo sem notícias. Trabalho. Noite. Dia. Sexo. Um pouco de choro de vez em quando. Odiei Alice. Culpei-a. Realidade insuportável. . . . De repente entendi: eu amava Alice. . . . Monótono e cotidiano. (132)

> [Coexistence without any great enchantment. She and I live in a comfortable house, leaning on each other. My children are here and there, without my hearing much from them. Work. Night. Day. Sex. A little sobbing once in a while. I hated Alice. I blamed her. Unbearable reality. . . . Suddenly I understood: I loved Alice. . . . Daily and monotonously.]

The fragmentation and nonchalance of the description by Alice's lover's of their love/hate relationship betrays a frustrated lover looking for a way out and yet consoling himself that it is not that bad, that it is a situation of mixed feelings, loving and hating at the same time. But it is a "consolation" without basis. The "happiness" continues until Alice herself starts complaining about everything. What she could not resist with her body she resists with her mouth. Her voice becomes her self-defense, an insulting weapon that her lover can not take anymore. He reflects again:

> Começou a esmurrar-me. Exigia suas alegrias de volta. Arranhou-me o rosto na altura da barba recém-escanhoada. Doeu. Doeu mas não ter o que ela

pedia. Não havia nem para mim. O poço estava seco. Tinha apenas para continuar acordando, dormindo, trabalhando, tomando cerveja nos dias de pagamento. . . . O ódio brotou. (133)

[She started to punch me. She was asking to regain her happiness. She cut my face while [I was] having a close-shave. It hurt. It hurt but I did not have what she wanted. I did not have it even for myself. The well was dry. All that was left was to continue waking, sleeping, working, and drinking beer on payment days. . . . Hate flourished.]

And it is this hate that will finally lead to the climax as the lover silences his loved/hated "ribanceira" (133; ravine) by throwing her through the window like a sacrificial lamb to Èṣù, god of the crossroads. Only then does she keep quiet. In silencing his lover through death, Alice's lover displays a lack of consciousness for the needs of the Afro-Brazilian community. His likes are a disgrace to the cause of Quilombhoje even as he is a prototype of the social misfit whom the group tries to educate and free from his/her psychological entrapment and ignorance.

Among the other stories, Cuti's "O Batizado" explores the devastation of alcoholism and prostitution in the Afro-Brazilian community; Éle Semog's "A seiva da vida" ridicules the myth of sex as a "nigger's game" of rejuvenation as portrayed by the racist media thereby objectifying and stereotyping the Afro-Brazilian male; José Carlos Leira's "Tanclau" both entertains and critiques, the art of lying as a strategy of survival for the Afro-Brazilian. Márcio Barbosa's "Quando O malandro vacila" further probes the disillusionment of the Afro-Brazilian in the face of so many dashed hopes despite persistent struggle. Esmeralda Ribeiro's "Guarde segredo" is a rereading of Barreto's *Clara dos Anjos* with a contemporary twist and expresses vengeance over the manipulative Cassi Joneses of the society who abandon their women after getting them pregnant. As its title suggests, Eustáquio José Rodrigues's "Pão da inocência" is a grotesque indictment of hunger, another disease afflicting certain individuals, especially abandoned children on the streets of Brazil's cities.

The concerns of many of the stories are multiple in that they cover a wide range of not just Afro-Brazilian reality but the larger Brazilian experience as well. Lia Vieira's "Operação candelária," for example, ridicules bureaucratic stupidity and hypocrisy, which is a nationwide phenomenon inherited from the Portuguese. Oubi Inaê Kibuko's "Reencontro" superimposes a simple train journey with a spiritual awakening through a reencounter with the narrator's historical past and cultural values. Oswaldo de Camargo takes a critical and violent jab at the contradictions of civilization, as his title "Civilização" reveals. Sônia Fátima's "Obsessão" explores the foibles of human obsession with vanities, while Ramatis Jacino's "Os espiões" fantasizes on how a narrator deals with imaginary spies whom he thought he got rid of with his newly acquired revolver. Perhaps as a philosophical closure, Ricardo Dias's "Vida provisória" contemplates the futility and temporality of our lives through a trivial episode of life and death. As a unified construct, these stories bring together a catalogue of stereotypes and counter-stereotypes, mystifications and demystifications, myths and realities, in an effort to provide the reader a balanced perspective of contemporary Afro-Brazilian reality.

For a people who have been historically uprooted, displaced, marginalized, misinformed, exploited, and taken for granted, the relevance and contribution of Quilombhoje and *Cadernos negros* in Brazilian letters and culture cannot be overemphasized. In terms of contextual quality of material and stylistic strategies, Quilombhoje has perhaps recuperated in three decades what took centuries to destroy. It is a matter of pride that a long-overdue season of recognition and critical reception has begun in critical circles. Behind and beyond the veil of words, pain, agony, aspirations, and dreams contained in the pages of *Cadernos negros*, a political Afro-Brazilian intellectual emerges. The juxtaposition of Afro-Brazilian values with those of the dominant culture has a political implication: change. Likewise, the social ills within the Afro-Brazilian community, such as violence, crime, and alcoholism, also cry for a remedy. And therein lies the politics of Quilombhoje as a transformative Afro-Brazilian cultural movement.

Concluding his seminal work, *Orpheus and Power*, Hanchard uses the gaze of Orpheus as a signifying metaphor, appealing to black movements to choose dialogue as opposed to confrontation or looking back: "Orpheus believed he could simply exchange the limitations of dialogue for the selective expansiveness of meaning and memory, and in doing so retain the Eurydice of his past. But Death, knowing fully that dialogue, however fragmented, was worth far more than memory, refused to be shortchanged. Hopefully the movimento negro will not succumb to the same frustrations, and will choose dialogue over the backward glance" (167). Hanchard, in this sense, echoes what Márcio Barbosa calls the challenge of continuity of the movement, looking forward but not being burdened by past or present challenges: "O grande desafio é não parar" (The ultimate challenge is not to lose momentum). In not looking back like Orpheus does, Quilombhoje is faced with various challenges: maintaining the group identity in spite of challenging economic limitations, exercising caution within the prospects of co-optation now that the group has become more visible and recognized nationally and internationally, and finally, the issue of critical reception and continued existence as a movement. Dialogue must not translate into passivity and renewed servitude. Rather, it should be a meeting ground for negotiation.

The way forward lies not only in getting more accreditation, visibility, and promotional opportunities but in safe-guarding the history and achievements of the group. "Fragmentation" is a concept that featured in both creative and critical discourses of Quilombhoje, and it is imperative to guard against such a tendency, especially with respect to greater popularity and internationalization. The example of the Afro-Brazilian cultural group Olodum is a case in point. The commercialization of the group may be a good thing as far as keeping the organization running, but it brings with it the dangers of co-optation and abandonment of primary ideological principles, which must be resisted at all cost. Quilombhoje is bound to go places, discover the world, and dialogue with similar entities in the African diaspora.

Esmeralda Ribeiro vividly captures this optimism in her *Malungos e milongas* (Brothers and Sisters). Ribeiro has definitely favored dialogue over confrontation and seems to take Hanchard's line of thinking in *Orpheus and Power*. To look back is to rehash the wounds and make solidarity impossible. At the same time, looking back allows for the identification of enemies of progress such as Mr. Eduardo, the white boss in Ribeiro's work. In this parabolic story, there may be a lesson for Quilombhoje as a group movement where brothers and sisters need each other. To what extent must the group identity take precedence over individual interests? The public space is one of competing interests, and where demands for change are made collectively, the likelihood of being taken seriously is greater. The anniversary editions are ample proof of greater things to come out of Quilombhoje.

3

Beyond the Curtains

Unveiling Afro-Brazilian Women Writers

> I want to speak about us, because time has always left us behind the curtains, camouflaging us generally as domestics.
> —Esmeralda Ribeiro

> I cannot deny the contradictions within me.
> —Miriam Alves

The complexity and inherent contradictions of the place of the Afro-Brazilian woman in the larger context of Brazil's so-called racial paradise can be summed up by what Marilena Chaui, in *Conformismo e resistência*, describes as the drama of the family setting through which pleasure is provided but which is also a "nucleus of tension and conflicts" (145). In this mixture of social conformism and resistance, the Afro-Brazilian woman is multiply burdened. Oftentimes fulfilling the roles of mother, lover, provider, spokesperson, encourager, and nourisher, she becomes fragmented in an effort to assert her individuality amid social conventions and racial stereotypes. To break with these stereotypical roles, the Afro-Brazilian woman must not only break the conventional rules; she must also compound her roles even further by becoming militant and subversive as opposed to being subordinate. And this is where, in most cases, the recurrent concern lies in self-mystification in order to recuperate the dignity of that fragmented construction.

Dating from the era of slavery, the Afro-Brazilian woman has been portrayed as a slave, a domestic servant, a black mammy, or at best, a "mulatta," a sexual and sexualized object whose function is to satisfy the perverse desires of the master without any hesitation. In contrast to these images, contemporary Afro-Brazilian women writers articulate, through the written word, their once silenced and marginalized voices, demanding respect and dignity as well as the freedom to be who they are without being apologetic or patronized.

As Yêda Pessoa de Castro points out in "Também mulher, imagem de Deus" (Woman as Well, Image of God), Afro-Brazilian women's writing attempts to "rescue the image of the Afro-Brazilian woman from the folkloric arena and plot in which she has been subjected as an absent protagonist" (cited in Quintas, *Mulher negra*, 88). The notion of the "absent protagonist" captures Miriam Alves's allusion to Esmeralda Ribeiro's assertion that "I want to speak about us, because time has always left us behind the curtains, camouflaging us generally as domestics" (23). And this zealous will to go beyond socially imposed curtains lies at the heart of *Enfim nós/Finally Us* and specific texts by Alves (*Momentos de busca* and *Estrelas no dedo*), Ribeiro (*Malungos e milongas*), and Fátima (*Marcas, sonhos e raízes*) that form the analytical basis of this study. Although the poetry written by female members of Quilombhoje predominates and has varied social and individual concerns, the prose works by male and female members alike have been unduly neglected in critical terms.

Finally Us: A Primer of Afro-Brazilian Women Writing

Quilombhoje's collective dilemma of getting recognized by commercial publishers and university presses features as a familiar constant in the case of women writers who are even more marginalized than their male counterparts. Although the categories of "male" and "female" are reductionist when it comes to writers, being black and female in Brazil can be a double bind of invisibility. And it is against this background that the publication of *Finally Us* sets an encouraging precedent in the dissemination of quality writing by Afro-Brazilian women. In their diversity and richness, the stories in this collection reveal salient preoccupations that challenge and engage these writers who have chosen the word as a weapon against silence and subjugation in a society that still claims to be racially democratic. The celebrative tone of relief captured in *Finally Us* is evidence of many years of work, hoping, anguishing, and yet not giving up, as Miriam Alves's prologue clearly puts it:

> *Finally Us* . . . exposes naked intimacies and sharp sentiments with agile, languid, and sensual curves, without false modesty. It rebels with its poetic action, reclaiming the ownership of the body, going on to being the subject of desire and pleasure, de-objectifying itself. Black women's writing with this attitude rejects the common notion of the Black woman's passivity, of the so-called "mulatta" who is always portrayed as the object of pleasure, in constant prostitution and without any other perspectives. (25)

I will navigate and highlight the inherent rebelliousness in the "poetic action" that most of these poems represent. For structural purposes, the variety of concerns is categorized as follows: being a woman as identity, the warrior woman, the Pan-Africanist woman, the strong woman, the grateful woman, the marginalized woman, the defeated woman, the victimized woman, and the hopeful woman.

Afro-Brazilian womanhood is captured in poems articulating issues of desire and universality, such as "Resgate," "Verídico," and "Eu-mulher." Alzira Rufino's "Resgate" (Ransom) debunks and protests the myth of racial democracy in Brazil when she affirms her blackness in a declarative tone:

> I am a black woman period
> return my identity to me
> tear up my certificate
> I am a black woman without ellipses . . .
> I am a black woman period. (35)

In a similar poem, "Verídico" (Truthful), Rufino juxtaposes the myth with reality while indicting the discriminatory subjugation implied in the color of the skin:

> I am a decent Creole woman
> My color frightens
> "this race offends" I heard it said . . .
> I see shackles in the alley . . .
> in the hopeless skins
> in the torrents of no's. (41)

Beyond Rufino's black consciousness, Conceição Evaristo takes her womanhood to a universal plane in "Eu-mulher" (I-Woman), as the poetic voice becomes the universal woman endowed with visionary and procreational powers and attributes:

> I-Woman in red rivers
> inaugurate life . . .
> I foresee
> I anticipate
> I live beforehand . . .
> I-Woman
> shelter of the seed
> continual motion
> of the world. (71)

The essence of these poems lies in the affirmation of the Afro-Brazilian woman's black identity and humanity.

Celinha's "Cantiga," "Um Sol Guerreiro," and "Resistência" capture the warrior's song of protest as she engages the condition of the ex-slave and its attendant depersonalization and oppression remembered through the symbolic act of hair-braiding:

> To braid your hair black woman is
> To remember passionate songs of the sunny days
> and the cold
> nights of seasons . . .
> like ropes, like shackles and whips . . .
> It is to trace the lines
> of the map of a nation. (55)

Memory then triggers not only protest but anger contained by the hope of tomorrow and in solidarity with other oppressed brothers and sisters all over the world: "We shall not dazedly protest / eruption of anger on the continents" (57). Celinha's Pan-Africanist consciousness blossoms in "Um sol guerreiro" (A Fighting Sun), a passionate elegiac homage she pays to "all black children murdered in Atlanta and to many children murdered every day in the womb of humanity" (64), refusing to weep "because the crying is muted / on my lips" (64) but hopeful of tomorrow's regeneration: "I sang because now the rain / will spring forth the earth" (64).

Rufino takes on Pan-African sentiments where Celinha left off when, in "Apartheid," she questions the "logic" of segregation as was practiced in South Africa and everywhere else a white minority oppresses a black majority:

> People make dividing lines
> geographical difference
> they alter language
> they worship the rationality
> of the machine. (39)

The Afro-Brazilian woman, however, discovers her strength through resistance against injustice as she affirms her possibilities and capabilities through her female identity, as in Evaristo's "Eu-mulher." For Celinha, being a woman is a virtue to celebrate, something to be grateful about as she captures in "Caué":

> Caué
> I dedicate myself to you
> I offer myself to you
> I thank you
> for this life
> so full of dreams
> and of life, of life, of life. . . . (67)

In dreaming, the Afro-Brazilian woman does not lose the sense of her struggle against a marginalized status, as Rufino cryptically points out in "Sinais" (Signs):

> I read faces
> melancholy
> latifundium resists
> life aborts
> I, a product from this clay
> and everything multiplies itself. (33)

Although hopeful of victory and recuperation of her fragmented body and identity, the Afro-Brazilian woman sees herself as "defeated" and "victimized" in the present, as reflected in Eliana Potiguara's "Neste século de dor" (This Century of Pain) and Adrea Branco's "Tolices" (Foolishness). In "In This Century of Pain," Potiguara captures the pain and protest of the poetic voice in her negation of conception and procreation. She is triply marginalized as black, Native American, and female, hence her fury:

> In this century of pain we will no longer have pussies
> Because to be a mother in this century of death
> Is to be in a fever in order to subsist. (79)

Branco, in "Tolices," questions the passivity of the Afro-Brazilian woman who, despite the lover's deceit and empty promises, continues to wait "stupidly" yet rebelliously:

> You promise, and I wait
> You undo everything that I did
> You make love to me . . . and I don't reject you
> since fool that I am, I still love you.(47)

This tone of helplessness in love is equally found in Esmeralda Ribeiro's "Rotina," a violent repulsion against machismo. Yet, what makes life worth living is the stride and sense of humor with which these challenges are taken and transformed into hopeful vestiges in the midst of tremendous oppression.

Alves and Durham's *Enfim nós/Finally Us* remains the most comprehensive panorama of Afro-Brazilian womanhood since the publication of Carolina Maria de Jesus's *Quarto de despejo* (1960; Beyond All Pity, 2005) in the United States. Additionally, Benedita da Silva's trajectory of victory as the first Afro-Brazilian to be elected to the Brazilian Congress sends a positive signal of greater things to come. However, the present repressed and oppressed Afro-Brazilian voices continue to demand dignity and equity as well as the imperative of recognition and intervention by the same society that claims to be racially democratic. Published three years after *Finally Us*, the anniversary editions of *Cadernos negros: Os melhores poemas* provide an additional significant window into the world of Afro-Brazilian women writers.

In contrast to the racial democracy propaganda expressed and critiqued by both Jamu Minka and Oliveira Silveira in their works,[1] Conceição Evaristo stands out as a poet of both black and regional consciousness. For her, being "Mineira" is all she could wish for, and each time she has to return to Rio de Janeiro, it is as if she is being uprooted. The melancholy and homesickness captured in "Mineiridade" pay homage not only to regional identity but also to an implied rejection of the myth of national identity:

> Quando chego de Minas
> trago sempre na boca um gosto de terra.
> Chego aqui com o coração fechado
> um trem esquisito no peito.
> ....
> É duro, é triste
> ficar aqui
> com tanta mineiridade no peito. (40)

[When I arrive from Minas / I always bring memories of the land in my mouth. / I arrive here with a closed heart / a strange train in my heart . . . / It is hard, it is sad / to remain here / with so much Minas identity in my heart.]

In addition to her consciousness of being a native of Minas Gerais, Evaristo equally engages the issue of gender and specifically of being an Afro-Brazilian woman as she declares in "Eu-mulher." In this vein, Ribeiro's "Vários desejos de um rio," Sônia Fátima's "No regresso," Lia Vieira's "Nós voláteis," and Cuti's "É tempo de mulher" and "Mar glu-glu" focus on the issue of Afro-Brazilian womanhood. As Benedito Cintra observes in her preface to *Os melhores poemas*, Afro-Brazilian women not only contribute their writing about specifically female experiences; they equally participate significantly in the organization of the volume. In this sense, they cease being marginal or secondary characters, but instead are equal partners with men:

> Estão aqui e ali, na essência de muitos versos, não como coisa, objeto, mas como guerreiras ou como referência militante na história e no tempo. Também como negras que questionam, agem, reivindicam, expondo a beleza e a sensualidade que lhes são intrínsecas. (17)

[They are here and there in the essence of the poems not as objects, but as warriors or militant reference be it historical or temporal. As black women also, they question, act, and make demands, demonstrating the beauty and sensuality that are intrinsic to their nature.]

As equal partners, Afro-Brazilian women decide how they want to articulate their feelings and enact varied acts of desire. In some cases, articulation of desire is also an act of protest. For Evaristo, desire in "Eu-mulher" takes the form of affirmation of the place of the woman in the world: she is likened to milk that flows in her breasts, to the blood that flows through her thighs, and to her vague words that imply instead of being explicit. It is as if she substitutes for her voice her corporeal acts of desire and nonetheless communicates through her actions. In addition, she is a visionary:

Antevejo
Antecipo
Antes-vivo
Antes—agora—o que há de vir" (41)

[I foresee
I anticipate
I live before time
Before—now—and yet to come.]

She represents something of the divine in her quality as the embodiment of the past, the beginning, the present and the future; a refuge-machine that keeps the world alive:

Eu fêmea-matriz.
Eu força-motriz.
Eu-mulher
abrigo da semente
moto-contínuo
do mundo. (41)

[I, the core of womankind / I the motion force / I, woman / refuge of the seed / continuity machine / of the world.]

Unlike Evaristo with her universal vision of womanhood, Ribeiro in "Vários desejos de um rio" (Various Desires of a River) contemplates the evolution of the woman from childhood to adulthood, enumerating her varied desires over the years. Through these homages to her past, the poetic voice relives and recaptures the joys of innocence as the ideal moment of fluidity similar to the river to which she likens herself, without any complexities or constraints of adulthood:

> Eu queria entender
> esta cantiga de criança:
> "A menina pretinha será rainha, olê, seus cavaleiros!
> Mas está presa no castelo, olê, olê, olá!
> E por que ela não foge?, olê, seus cavaleiros!
> Mas com quem está a chave?, olê, olê, olá! (243)

> [I would like to understand / this childhood song: / "The black young girl will be a queen, hurrah! gentlemen! / But she is stuck in the castle, hurrah! gentlemen! / And why won't she escape? hurrah! gentlemen! / But who has the key? hurrah, gentlemen!"]

While Ribeiro takes the liberty to express her womanhood through a regression into her innocent past, Cuti indulges himself in an erotic muse, paying homage to the physical manifestation of desire when the woman plays the hard-to-get game only to finally give in to her own subconscious mystery and desired fulfillment from which an initial kiss, however timid, finally leads to the opening of the "céu ao meio" (the sky in the middle) where love is consumed.

Cuti subverts the notion of the oppressed woman, giving her control over her own body yet making her a participant in a mutual act of obsession with desire. After all,

> É tempo de mulher
> é tempo de colher
> orgasmos de mulheridade. (53)

> [It is time of the woman, / it is time of harvesting / orgasms of womanhood.]

Similarly, Lia Vieira, in "Nós voláteis" (Volatile Us), freely contemplates the act of lovemaking albeit through an intellectual fantasy in which the poetic voice imagines dwellers of the upper floor of her apartment complex making love, giving her mixed sensations in her own solitary state. The poem captures an unsatisfied libido struggling for fulfillment through fantasies:

> Atentou para o ruído e
> percebeu que a libido no apartamento de cima começara.
> Estavam literalmente fodendo na sua cabeça.
> Aqueles rangidos e gemidos ritmados
> lhe despertavam desejos adormecidos até então. (96)

[She was attentive to the ripples and / realized that the libido in the upper apartment was unleashed. / They were practically fucking in her head. / Those rhythmical gnashing and trembling acts / were provoking desires once dormant in her.]

In line with the escapist fantasies adopted by Lia Vieira, Sônia Fátima reflects on what it will be like when her lover returns in "No regresso" (Upon Return). This contemplation has both philosophical and physical functions in the dramatization of desire and pleasure. In transporting the mind through a sea of imaginary desires, the physical merges with the psychological as the poetic imagination takes off. Far from mere hallucinations, these are conscious ambiguous desires that may be sexual, resistant, and intellectual:

No dia em que retornares
....
Usarei o xampu que dará
mobilidade aos meus cabelos
farei teatro em tua presença.
Te convencerei de que minha disposição
é a mesma, te envolverei de tal forma. . . .
Te carregarei para o inferno
em que minha vida transformaste. (119)

[The day you return / I will use shampoo that will / enhance my hair / I will do theater in your presence. / I will convince you that / nothing has changed, will get you so involved. . . . / I will transport you to hell / into which my life has been transformed.]

Read more closely, "No regresso" is in fact a poem of protest against abandonment. For the "hell" her life has become is the same hell the poetic voice seems to be preparing for the returning lover. By convincing the ex-lover of her continued loyalty, she sets the stage for disappointment and revenge. Here is a classic example of a poem of ambivalence where fantasy could actually mean a song of defiance and rebellion and not simply an amorous longing.

As these examples indicate, the Afro-Brazilian woman is ultimately the decision maker of her manifestation or denial of pleasure/desire. Similarly, the Afro-Brazilian woman can protest machismo in a patriarchal society as in Ribeiro's "Rotina," where in an indicting tone the poetic voice denounces the varied and overwhelming role of the man in her life. From father to husband to boss, men are constantly dominating her life:

Há sempre um homem
me dizendo
o que fazer. (60)

[There is always a man / telling me / what to do.]

And yet, as Conceição Evaristo points out in "Malungo, Brother, Irmão," a call for solidarity, Afro-Brazilian women need their men and vice versa:

No fundo de calumbé
nossas mãos sempre e sempre
espalmam nossas outras mãos
moldando fortalezas esperanças,
heranças nossas divididas com você:
Malungo, brother, irmão. (45)

[In the interior of the diamond vessel / our hands forever and ever / rub against each other's hands / shaping fervent hopes / our heritage divided with you: / Malungo, brother, irmão.]

As if echoing this call for solidarity, Carlos de Assumpção's "Batuque" calls for intraracial as well as interracial solidarity through the formation of a multiracial "quilombo":

Batuque batuque bate
Tambor que bate
O toque de reunir
Todos os irmãos
De todas as cores
Sem distinção. (28–29)

[Batuque Batuque beat / Drum beat / the clarion call / to all brothers / of all colors / without distinction.]

While this idea may be naive and controversial, it is indeed strategic in the sense of having a dialogue with other races. Such a solidarity, if at all feasible, will go a long way toward expanding the parameters of Afro-Brazilian relations with the rest of the world.

Dialogue with the world through inversion is an effective means of reversing the image of the Afro-Brazilian. Such dialogue is thus not conditioned by the world but is initiated by the evocation of Afro-Brazilian heroes/heroines, ancestors, and by extension, heroes of the world, such as in Abelardo

Rodrigues's "Zumbi," Márcio Barbosa's "Mandela," and Miriam Alves's "Mahin Amanhã." While Bernd asserts that the construction of the Afro-Bahian epic sets out to correct and "fill the gaps" (80) left in the traditional historiography in which black contributions are either minimized or completely distorted, Rodrigues takes it a step further when through what he calls "silêncio no grito" (silence of the shout) he appeals to Afro-Brazilian warriors to honor Zumbi:

> em mão feito lança
> na voz feito nós . . .
> Sim,
> 20 de novembro
> é uma canção
> guerreira. (25)

[with sword-carrying hands / with our collective voice . . . / Yes, / November 20 / is a warrior song.]

Unified in voice and action, the poetic voice mobilizes Afro-Brazilians into a commemoratory song in honor of the death of Zumbi on November 20, thus juxtaposing this date with that imposed by the dominant culture (May 13).

Miriam Alves complements the heroic portrayal of Zumbi in "Mahin Amanhã," where she pays homage to Luiza Mahin, an Afro-Brazilian heroine and significant symbol of resistance, especially to Afro-Brazilian women. But her significance goes beyond gender and captivates the entire Afro-Brazilian community:

> A cidade toda se prepara
> Malês
> bantus
> geges
> nagôs
> vestes coloridas resguardam esperanças
> aguardam a luta
> Arma-se a grande derrubada branca
> a luta é tramada na língua dos Orixás. (104)

[The whole city is getting ready / Malês / bantus / geges / nagôs / multicolored outfits rekindle hopes / they await the battle / the great white overthrow is ready / the battle is plotted in the language of the òrìṣà.]

In this reverence for Afro-Brazilian religion, Alves's objective is twofold. In addition to depicting the heroism and significance of Mahin, of the Ewe ethnic group, who contributed to the planning of the Malê (Muslim slaves) Rebellion of 1835, she also uses her portrayal to revisit the unspoken battle between blacks and whites in a racist and hypocritical society. By privileging blacks with the language of the gods (the òrìṣàs), it is implicit that whites lost the battle, especially when Alves actually refers to the rebellion as the "white overthrow."

Miriam Alves: Redignifying Afro-Brazilian Womanhood

Among the foremost contemporary Afro-Brazilian women writers, Miriam Alves stands out among her peers as a fearless voice seeking equality and justice on behalf of countless voiceless women in the Afro-Brazilian community. Her commendable effort to publish these "silenced" voices in *Finally Us* amply signals a visionary with a mission. Alves, who spent a career as a social worker, has transcended the limits of poetic imagination and finds solace in synchronizing the poetic, the mythical, the political, and the sociocritical in a nexus of lived and desirable experiences. As her individually published titles, *Momentos de busca* (Moments of Inquiry, 1983) and *Estrelas no dedo* (Stars on the Fingerpoint, 1985) reflect, Alves seems obsessed with discovery and illumination through a conscious spiritual search for the unknown. Her poetic corpus may be said to be defined by rewriting history and defragmenting the self. While *Momentos* can be summed up in three major movements—fragmentation and ambiguity, defragmentation and unmasking, and a process of reconstruction through hope—*Estrelas* further develops this optimism with assurance and confidence.

Articulate and assertive in the various interview sessions I conducted with her, Alves makes no apology for challenging the establishment to gain a hearing for black voices that had been silenced and misrepresented.[2] For her, the contemporary Afro-Brazilian reality must not only be portrayed; it must be rehistoricized and rewritten. While Alves denies being an official member of the group since she left it in 1995, she continues to participate in the collective production of the *Cadernos negros* series at least as a contributor. Asked about its importance, she asserts: "As long as we define our place our own way, we are saying things that many people do not want to hear, or are afraid to hear. And it is through such acts that we remove the mask of invisibility that has been imposed on us by those who want to deny our existence or who want to see us their own way, in a way that simply portrays us as subservient . . . , like rogues, . . . suspicious characters, . . . fools" (*Cadernos negros* 8 [1986]: 13). In her characteristic declarative style, Alves articulates the relevance of the group effort to combat racism and restore the dignity of Afro-Brazilians at the same time.

Miriam Alves's works constitute a perplexing and renewing search, a preexisting state of crisis foregrounding what is known as a point of entry into the unknown. Even to the poetic voice, the search is mysterious as she ponders in "Estranho indagar" (Strange Questioning):

> What am I looking for?
> I don't know
> What am I hiding?
> I don't know . . .
> The flames are engulfing me
> making my body boil. (*Momentos* 11)

While deliberately ambiguous, the poetic voice is conscious of a warring duality of wanting to confront the present and yet being cautious about the implied pain in the inevitable resort to the past, as captured in "História":

> I have a history
> the peddlers of human cargo and ideas
> don't want to hear.
> A history of those sold over there
> three centuries ago
> at the square of histori-city.
> History of struggle and resistance. (Camargo, *A razão da chama*, 95)

Yet, armed with this knowledge, Alves's poetic vision is that of chaos and fragmentation, where emotions travel freely through internal and external journeys in search of an elusive resolution and coherent arrival. As Abelardo Rodrigues points out in his preface to *Momentos*, it is a mixed journey in which "various levels of poetical questioning merge with the experiential in a process of addition and subtraction" (7).

In most of her poetry and narratives, Alves locates Afro-Brazilian womanhood in the need to reinvent the stereotypical image associated with slavery and scientific racism. The Afro-Brazilian woman's fragmentation is best captured in "Pedaços de mulher" (Pieces of a Woman), where a woman recalls her objectification and anguish as she tries to reconstruct herself into a subject who can revolt and fight against imposed amnesia:

> Woman—shards
> of flesh drying
> in the back yard
> a prisoner in the house of amnesia
> Woman—revolt
> I move against the clothes pins
> that hold me on this clothesline. (*Callaloo* 18.4 [1995]: 801)

The second movement of *Momentos* unmasks social realities responsible for the Afro-Brazilian woman's fragmentation. "Vidranças quebradas" (Broken Mirrors), "Cristo atormentado" (Tormented Christ), "Lamento" (Lament), "Depreendendo" (Depressing), "Cena do cotidiano" (Daily Scene), and "Indo" (Going) attest to the issues of oppression, depression, and hunger as the poetic voice struggles to survive and remain whole in a world that is tearing her all apart. In "Vidranças quebradas," the protected, frightened, and timid inner self is shaken to its foundations as the broken mirrors reflect

> The vulnerable interior
> visible to all eyes, seemed whole
> timid and shamed
> in front of the astute
> malicious spectator. (52)

With the inner self vulnerable, secrets are revealed as in the personified image of the anguished Christ in "Cristo atormentado," hunger and emptiness in "Indo," sadness and numbness in "Lamento," a sense of defeat and depression in "Depreendendo" and the overwhelming daily torture and cry for help as in "Cena do cotidiano":

> I am crying
> asking for help . . .
> Hunger is killing me
> I know it is not death
> nor is it hunger
> It is everything I cannot understand. (25)

The process of searching by itself implies a lack of understanding and vulnerability, an ignorance that can only be rectified through conscious rites of passage.

The third perceptible movement of *Momentos* is a reformulation of the fragmented selves and experiences into a meaningful anchor of hope as found in "Magma," "Luta do ideal" (Struggle for the Ideal), "Imaginando o mundo" (Imagining the World), and the title poem, "Momentos de busca" (Moments of Inquiry). For the love of the world, the poetic voice imagines a flourishing moment in the life of a "magma," inorganic matter that could be a metaphor for regenerative impulses of the act of lovemaking or of replenishing the world:

> I scourge the world
> flames want it destroyed

> to see it reconstructed
> every morning
> depriving it of seeds of hope
> of will
> of love
> of desire
> without knowing (will I see it flourish?). (*Momentos* 33)

To which, she adds her wish for the world to be a better place, to live and prosper without seeing the fruits of her labor constantly die in the mouth of the oppressor:

> The world, see it in movement
> I want to see it
> going . . . going . . .
> in the direction of (I don't know)
> anything better
> any other better place. (34)

While part of self-discovery requires a significant dose of optimism for any fulfillment, Alves does not believe in a blind hope. Instead, she comes to terms with the imperative of struggle in order to achieve her lofty aspirations of a better world. As she declares in "A luta do ideal," the construction of a new and better world requires a new, more militant warrior:

> Armed for war . . .
> My crazy throat rekindled . . .
> I shouted to myself:
> "I am going to war!!!
> I am going to struggle!!!
> I defend an ideal . . .
> True and for real."
> coming out
> with a sword in hand
> legacy of the past
> in the struggle of effect. (45)

As a warrior, the tone is set for ultimate liberation and limitless possibilities that the poetic voice has sought for since her opening lines in "Estranho indagar."

The search is no longer "strange"; it is real: the poetic voice can now contemplate the world as in "Imaginando o mundo":

> And this is the world
> of creative liberty

> the space of the being (of being)
> limitlessly.... (55)

As if coming full circle, the poetic voice rejoices as she finds fulfills her aspirations, the journey seems complete and she discovers herself in a tone of celebration, completeness, and wholeness:

> Ah!! my world
> is not where
> my feet lead
> the world is three-dimensional
> there is a time of the mind
> the space of the soul
> of creative and imaginative
> liberty
> of the simple,
> good and free human being. (56)

The optimistic closure of *Momentos* sets the tone for *Estrelas no dedo* and for a possible characterization of the poetic art of Miriam Alves. In addition to creative liberty, central to Alves's heart is the liberty of the Afro-Brazilian woman and, by extension, the Afro-Brazilian community.

Estrelas no dedo picks up from *Momentos* in a dualistic trajectory toward self-fulfillment. Here, poetry is also desire; it is struggle; it is hope; it is, above all, futuristic in its premonition of life after death as captured in "Quando" (When):

> When nothing else is left
> my memories remain
> of clenched fists
> contemplating what I could have been. (50)

Mystical and prophetic, the poetic voice feels fulfilled in her "gritos de fogo" (shouts of fire), and this volume of poetry is distinctly more mature, lyrical, experimental, cogent, and economical than *Momentos*. Perhaps a commonality between the two volumes lies in the passion for reconstruction, a penchant for specificity in universality, and a sense of fulfillment in the creative liberty to contemplate literature in its multiple possibilities.

Structurally, *Estrelas* is laced with visual images of the sea, the sky, the bird, the clouds, and the wind, as if the poetic persona sees herself as a creative bird—unlimited in her flights, restless yet gliding energetically toward her set goals and priorities. And it is against this background that we situate the aesthetic and ideological tropes of *Estrelas*. For Miriam Alves, the voice is the foundation of expression without which ideas, however significant, lose their social impact. Like an "Arte poetica," Alves begins the collection with a testament as in "Voz" (Voice) that can be read as the Afro-Brazilian voice:

> I am the voice of the wind
> I break the silence of the planet
> soothing the loneliness of homes. (15)

From this empowerment of the voice, the sky is no longer the limit as the poet-persona captures, through memory and contemplation, countless possibilities of poetic action: music, desire, chant, identity, aspirations, burden, solitude, rebellion.

Through her voice, Alves finds an outlet for her inner secrets as reflected in nature in "Guardiãs" (Ancestors), uses the wind as an echo of her hidden feelings in "Nuvens" (Clouds), awakens dormant desires in "Vontade" (Wish), while renewing her voice in "Saber da chama" (Knowledge of the Charm). But these desires to be in communion with nature must not in any way be confused with art for art's sake. Indeed, the voice is an instrument of rebellion and protest as evident in "Revolta de desejos" (Revolt of Desires):

> Our desires
> suffocate the arms
> which hold us
> in the conventional warmth
> called Love. (46)

And similarly in "Revolta dos atos" (Revolt of Acts), in which doubts, uncertainties, and illusions get in the way of possible union and consummation of love:

> I was solitude
> I am the illusion of an encounter
> I am the undefined assumption
> in the subtle lines of affirmation.
> ....
> I am weariness
> I carry with me the repugnance
> of always stopping
> on the way
> to encounters. (47)

But it is in "Carregadores" (Carriers) that we find the ultimate burden of being Afro-Brazilian, where the pain of the past is transformed into a weapon of resistance and of hope by those who are burdened beyond limits:

> We carry on our shoulders
> vivid burden
> the struggle, the pain of the past
> We carry on our shoulders
> vivid sting
> the shame that is not our own
> We carry on our shoulders
> vivid burden
> the iron mark of the oppressor
> We carry in our hand
> vivid spear
> the hopes of things to come. (30)

The transformation of the shoulders carrying the burden into the hand carrying a weapon of resistance craftily inverts the values of oppression and replaces them with resistant values, as in the concluding, title poem, "Estrelas no dedo":

> One day the future will come
> bringing stars in the hand
> honey on the lips
> hopes on our feet. (49)

Here, the sweet voice and the shining hand become partners in the redignification of Afro-Brazilian identity and gender. Like *Momentos de busca*, *Estrelas no dedo* ends equally on a note of optimism, making Miriam Alves a conscious poet of the regenerative possibilities of hope.

Esmeralda Ribeiro: Politicizing the Afro-Brazilian (Female) Voice

Unlike Miriam Alves's lyricism and mysticism, Esmeralda Ribeiro's criticism of the Afro-Brazilian condition is caustic and political. In addition to her search for solidarity between the sexes, Ribeiro sees the female voice as a political weapon that should not become subservient but must dialogue at the same level with that of men in general and male authority figures in particular. A personable, dynamic, yet assertive critic, she combines with her role as present editorial member of Quilombhoje/*Cadernos negros* with being a mother and wife of Márcio Barbosa, a fellow Quilombhoje editor. Ribeiro does not mince words in her attack of white supremacy or racial democracy, which for her is nothing but racial hypocrisy. A modern and seasoned griot by all definitions and standards, Ribeiro is the creative and critical conscience of the subaltern in the Afro-Brazilian community. Her criticism goes beyond the issues of gender, race, and class to include the plight of children and the Afro-Brazilian family. Her most fascinating poetic piece ever is found in "Rotina" (Routine), where she protests the fact that as a woman she has to answer to men in some form or another:

> There's always a man
> telling me
> what to do. (*Finally Us* 91)

Laconical and provocative, in three lines, Ribeiro condenses her fury and anguish while asking for redress. To rush to dub her "feminist" is to miss the essence of Ribeiro. For in a similar economical use of poetic language, she captures the reality of slavery in today's Brazil in "Fato" (Fact):

> They abolished slavery as an institution
> But
> Not as a condition (*Finally Us* 87)

And it is against this background that Ribeiro must be understood: a critical voice against all forms of domination and injustice.

As a critic, Ribeiro is direct to the point of being polemical and sarcastic. On her view of the relevance of Quilombhoje and *Cadernos negros,* she writes:

> Racists lace my identity with blue and pink ribbons and promote me in a small box of matches with the most current packaging. They offer their hypocritical hands trying to push me, betrayingly, toward the gulf of the unknown, but they fail to realize that I protect myself with chords of poems, in the language of the story and through the memory of the griots. Writers who don't conceive of Afro-Brazilian literature as a weapon of intellectual distancing from my community will succeed in removing literature from the moribund dust of the shelf, by taking it to the streets, crossing traffic lights with it, crossing stations, overcoming the limitations of knowledge. (*Cadernos negros* 8 [1986]: 10)

Here is the voice not just of the Afro-Brazilian woman writer but also of the militant, the intellectual in spite of herself, the critic whose combative scope goes beyond the immediate Afro-Brazilian community to a Pan-Africanist consciousness typical of a nationalist heroine.

From an intertextual perspective, we have in Ribeiro's *Malungos e milongas* a postcolonial rendering of Chinua Achebe's *Things Fall Apart* (*O mundo se despedeça*) in the sense that "things fall apart" not exclusively because of the white man but because of the uncritical adoption, by Afro-Brazilians, of the seeds of discord that are inherent in individualism and corrupt competition. These are vices not restricted to interracial relations but also intraracial conflict situations. Instead of working together, we are working apart; instead of getting stronger, we are being weakened by the legacy of the postcolonial condition institution we want to combat: racism, intolerance, jealousy, and other ills. Ribeiro's "conto" (short story), as she calls it, is the sixth in the series "Livro do Autor" that has produced individual works such as Oubi Inaê Kibuko's *Poemas para o meu amor,* Miriam Alves's *Estrelas no dedo,* Jamu Minka's *Teclas de ébano,* Cuti's *Quizila,* and Márcio Barbosa's *Paixões crioulas.* These efforts are commendable in going beyond collective limitations to embrace an expansive individual creative muse.

Malungos e milongas captures the multiple skeleton in the Afro-Brazilian communal closet, especially as it relates to the central issue of discord and betrayal in the struggle for survival, social mobility, and competitive edge. The disruption of harmony is deadly, as Ribeiro points out; it is a disease that eats into the family fabric, turning brothers and sisters into bestial victims of greed at the hands of the Mr. Eduardos of Brazilian society who incite members of the same family against each other while sadistically enjoying the painful disintegration of a once cohesive family unit. Taken as a metaphor of "brotherhood and sisterhood," which appropriately translates Ribeiro's title, the "short story" calls attention to one of the unspoken ills that has eaten up the many years of struggle and the dangers of allowing it to continue. It is painful enough to have been enslaved—more painful and devastating still to permit intolerance and "divide-and-conquer" tactics to rob the black movement of what has taken many years to achieve. Perhaps the challenge lies in not losing sight of the collective good that comes with the sacrifices of cooperation.

Although the plot seems a little oversimplified, the style overtly simple, and the overall construction somewhat lacking in complication, the message here is more important than the form. The omniscient narrator presents us with a work setting that overlaps with a family setting in a drama of competition, backbiting, jealousy, and distrust. *Malungos e milongas*'s characters, the four brothers and sisters Carlos Gabriel, Marta, Mauro, and Ruth, are between the ages of twenty-four and thirty years. In a ten-episode portrayal, we follow the ties that bind these contemporaries together as well as the intrigues that will make them fall apart. Each episode offers an illuminating window into the conflicts within Afro-Brazilian society as well as the conflict and contradiction of individual aspirations with those of the community.

In the opening episode, "Quadro" (Frame), the four primary characters are introduced. They possess all the good qualities of a mutually-dependent family: supportive, cordial, and cooperative. In addition, their features consist of values inherited from their parents, ranging from regenerative attributes to womanizing tendencies. Yet, what binds them is cooperation: "Cooperation bound them in one fellowship of feelings. Mauro could feel. He was no good. Too much of a womanizer. He had 'affairs' here and there. Consequently, he has a good number of children spread over the map of his life. In order to avoid his responsibilities with the courts, he distributed presents here and there. Ruth was the one helping him with payments" (9). While this portrayal stresses the cooperation of the family members, it also reveals their darker sides, especially the womanizing and irresponsibility of Mauro. Ribeiro is thus not just painting a "romantic" picture of Afro-Brazilians; instead, she is calling attention to the ugliness and painful realities that threaten the continuity and survival of the family setting as the narrator forewarned, however ambiguously: "But destiny, secretly, was threatening to wipe out that unity" (10). Of course, destiny plays itself out for better or for worse at the end of the story.

Conflict arises among brothers and sisters when, as co-workers in the same firm in the episode "O começo inesperado" (The Unexpected Beginning), the President of the firm orders the foreman to appoint one of them, Ruth, as the Executive Manager:

> For the brothers and sisters, they have been working peacefully in that firm. They were closely knit as if they were children of the same *orixá* [god]. That energetic power was also instrumental in keeping them working together. It has been seven years of tranquility until that day when the foreman came to their section and put his game on the table:
>
> "People! I have good news for you. The President has charged me to choose, among you, the new Executive Manager." (14)

Ordinarily, this revelation should have been good news indeed. Yet, as brothers and sisters suddenly faced with the prospect of promotion, competitive greed and selfishness set in. Ironically, Ruth, who was named by the President for the position, did not have a chance in the eyes of the foreman since she had frequently dismissed his unwanted advances. Her disregard for Mr. Eduardo, the foreman, comes in different tones as she insultingly describes him on at least two occasions as a worm: "You are a worm" (13); "that worm-looking face" (23). The foreman was set in his revenge as he assured himself: "I will be the one to choose," he thought: "You will see Mr. President. You will see" (14). In carrying out a personal vendetta against Ruth, Mr. Eduardo compromises his judgment and integrity as he sets out to disrupt the unity among brothers and sisters at all cost. And therein lies the suspense and the agitation, for every character must now contemplate and wish to be the chosen one. True to his dubious character, Mr. Eduardo knows how to play upon these vulnerabilities.

In spite of the various scenes of brutal rivalry and instigated competition among the siblings, Carlos Gabriel and Ruth, the oldest brother and the youngest sister, would have their moments of reflection as they dialogue in "O diálogo" (The Dialogue) on the devastation of the bond that used to hold them together and the sense that it was not worth the price they are paying as a family in disarray:

"Brother, this cacophony spreading around in the firm about some promotion only confirms my suspicions that such a promotion is only a ploy to destroy our unity." She sighed and continued to develop her thoughts: "I never imagined we could be in such a disarray. Just imagine, our father and mother went to live in the interior due to our conflict"—and nostalgia forced a honeylike tear drop from his eye. (42)

Their exchange of feelings and ideas finally make them come to the realization that Mr. Eduardo must be seen as the enemy that he is and not some saint who wishes them well:

"People like Mr. Eduardo pollute our lives. It seems like the ghost of the small boss is in the center of events. . . . On the other hand, I cannot trust his kiss as if he were being supportive. Who is our enemy? Who???!!!" And then she concluded: The moment we turn our backs, they betray us at the next available opportunity. (41–42)

Through the narrative voice as well as the voice of Ruth, Ribeiro hits the nail on the head when she identifies the likes of Mr. Eduardo as enemies of progress in the Afro-Brazilian community. In addition, the beneficiary here is neither the brothers and sisters nor Mr. Eduardo, for in the final analysis Ruth was not chosen, and the chosen one, Mauro, was not excited. Perhaps the paradox is meant to be the moral of the story: that unity and strength are better attributes for the community than individualism and selfishness.

The closing of the story, in which Ruth invites Carlos Gabriel to another project (Projeto Xingu) is very significant. Instead of lamenting the losses and crying over the evil that has already been perpetrated, Ruth envisions the way forward in building other alliances such as an equally compelling project that she was able to involve herself in. Taking the story to a positive conclusion may be seen on Ribeiro's part as a signal that despite the conflicts and negativity brought about by all involved, there is hope if only the brothers and sisters can come together again in a consciousness of solidarity. In *Malungos e milongas,* the gallery of characters suggests group effort was more productive and healthy until the seed of discord and competition was sown amidst the quartet. At the same time, individualism was only compensated as a form of "co-optation" as in the character of Mauro, who is selected for the position due to his patronizing attitude. In the process, he loses the respect and collaboration of his group members and, by implication, loses his "authority." Of what use is an Executive Manager without his employees? Of what use is a foreman without his workers? Mr. Eduardo may not have thought all this through when he allowed his own self-interest to cloud his judgment.

Ribeiro's plea against disintegration is a genuine effort toward rescuing perhaps the most sacred value system of Africanity: communality. As the text alludes, the seven years of tranquility are better looked upon as the years of sowing, cultivating, and germinating. The years ahead are full of promising harvests, and they should not be hampered by self-interest. Ruth's decision to leave with Carlos Gabriel is not a sign of abandonment of the group; rather, it hints at the importance of making a conscious effort to change the course of one's destiny in a positive way.

Sônia Fátima: Conflicts and Pitfalls of the Black Movement

Fátima's *Marcas, sonhos e raízes* takes on preoccupations similar to Ribeiro's in *Malungos e milongas* but with more depth and African ancestral consciousness. Reflecting on Afro-Brazilian literature and the import of *Cadernos negros*, Fátima, in "Being Black, Human, and a People: 'A Situation of Urgency,'" lays out what she perceives as the contradictions of contemporary Afro-Brazilian literature: the need to promote blackness in relation to whiteness as if the Afro-Brazilian is still insecure about his/her color, looking for every opportunity to prove to the white establishment the opposite of the images made of him, and exposing the injustices and ending up taking the role of a victim. Fátima finds this situation pathetic and reactionary, calling otherwise for a more dynamic assessment of blackness, not through the lenses of whites as if writing for them, but writing for blacks and about their ancestral connections: "In this manner, the transformative character of literature loses its affirmative function since Afro-Brazilian literature is expected to be reactionary. It seems to me that the Afro-Brazilian finds himself/herself locked within a prison whose keys are held by whites. He thus does everything to be noticed by whites, and for his plight as victim to be noticed without looking for other means of self-liberation" (*Reflexões* 89). This cogent appraisal of the psyche of the Afro-Brazilian writer may not be true of all writers but is nevertheless quite compelling of analysis and concern. Its truism reflects in the amount of dialectical writing, especially in the wake of abolition and later. Fátima's call has not gone unheeded since 1985, three years before the centenary of "official" abolition, as manifest in the amount of writing now focused more on the Afro-Brazilian community and interpersonal conflicts than on the issue of color. And it is within this context that Fátima situates her own aesthetics.

Fátima's thematic concerns range from the issue of love to that of African spirituality and ancestrality. But the most engaging concern lies in the issue of the black movement and the contradictions of the struggle. And this is what is unique about contemporary Afro-Brazilian literature. Female writers are distinguishable not necessarily in their individual concerns, which are typically first race-bound before being gender focused. The overlap results from the immediacy of black consciousness that forces Afro-Brazilian women to be their own spokespersons for equality alongside their male counterparts. Zilá Bernd captures this essential characteristic in her comparison of Afro-Brazilian women writers to their counterparts in the United States:[3] "Contrary to North-American female writers who do not get involved with the black movement which, in a certain way, cast them from political action as if political action was the prerogative of male sex, Brazilian female writers participate actively mainly in literary groups" (28). While Bernd's position may be highly exaggerated, to the extent that African American women may not be functioning within group dynamics; yet as individuals, they boast of equal if not greater achievements in the political and participative arena. Contemporary Afro-Brazilian feminine discourse is doubly yoked and could also be ambiguous, as we find not only in Fátimá's *Marcas, sonhos e raízes* but also in many of her poems, such as "Desejo" (I Want), which captures her poetical testament:

> I want
> to slide into the river waters
> to embrace the shadows of waterfalls
> to greet the orishas in the forests
> to adorn myself with stars
> to sparkle in the night
> to smile. (*Finally Us* 219)

The process of sliding, embracing, adorning, and sparkling yields positive attributes for someone who is declarative and precise in her intentions. The feminine gesture of adorning herself combines with the need to be happy and dignified while at the same time not losing her connections with her ancestral protectors—the *òrìṣàs!* All these attributes have a commonality that tends to universalize Fátima's concerns even in their specificity: harmony with nature and life.

Harmony and disequilibrium, trust and betrayal in love and in the struggle are only a few of the overlapping conflicts that *Marcas, sonhos e raízes* engages with incisive dedication as if exposing the horrors and indicting the perpetrators at the same time. Craftily constructed around a love story that is in itself a reflection of the struggle, Fátima exposes a hidden yet devastating sore of the Afro-Brazilian community that calls for remedy and therapy. Similar stories by fellow Quilombhoje members such as Abílio Ferreira's "A casa de Fayola" and Conceição Evaristo's "Ana Davenga" reflect a pattern of self-analysis that departs from the we-them, racistanti-racist discourses, to a more focused attention on the ills of the community and the holding responsible of members for their actions and inaction. Weaving the plot around the Movement of Black Militants (MMN, a pseudonym for MNU perhaps) and one of its active members, Jofre, is also curious.[4] Could this be a criticism of the leadership of black movements? Charity, they say, begins at home. If these leaders cannot get their relationships and family situations together, how can they expect to recruit and retain members in a cause that may be defeated even before it starts by the irresponsible example of the leadership? Under the guise of a love affair and relationship, Fátima puts the Unified Black Movement on trial while at the same time calling attention to the urgency of intervention.

When a woman writer writes from the viewpoint of a male protagonist, it also raises questions. Why is the protagonist, Jofre, portrayed as a male? Could the active participant in the movement not be a woman? Is Fátima suggesting that men are solely to blame for the disintegration of the movement? How does an intimate relationship carry over into the commitment of the protagonist to the movement? These are questions that Fátima asks albeit in a subtle fashion. And that is why the story must not be read simply as a love affair or failed relationship. Indeed, we consider the relationship a metaphor for the movement's relationship with its members. How so? Take Jofre and Beokis and Suzana, for example. Here we have a triangular relationship that developed swiftly almost before any of them could think about what he/she was getting into? Is this situation any different from real-life relationships and their twists?

Jofre's drama is an interesting one. His commitment to the movement is unquestionable, yet the temptation of new passions and affairs at first sight is equally overwhelming. Between this need to be disciplined and the weakness of the flesh lies the conflict of human nature, as Jofre himself reflects when he loses his love, Beokis, due to his affair with Suzana: "'Who has never fallen in love with another woman?' He thought. 'She should understand the difference between men and women.' Jofre understood the situation as a game of life. The apartment was always empty during the daytime. Beokis only returned at night. On that afternoon, the òrìṣàs (Yoruba deities) did not intervene. Jofre did not forgive himself for not being perceptive. He suffered a lot with that lack of judgment" (21). Jofre's sense of self-disappointment is understandable. He has been described as a man of his word, a dedicated activist and leader whose life is an embodiment of the movement in its entirety: "Twenty-seven years old, relatively strong, medium build, Caucasian-type mouth, ebony nose. The hefty Rastafarian was a fan of Bob Marley. Living, for Jofre, was a struggle against discrimination headlong and fearlessly. He felt like a true soldier in the midst of a battlefield" (11). And yet, he is not without his flaws despite these positive promovement attributes and commitment.

The reader is left puzzled at the end of the story: what is Fátima trying to do in this novella? Is this a case of urgency that must be portrayed as such or is this a deliberate exaggeration? Following the drama of Jofre and his fellow "militants" is one thing; Fátima's pessimistic vision is another.

Jofre is completely crushed in this representation, a case of dashed hopes and aspirations that are true to the Afro-Brazilian social reality yet surrealistic from the viewpoint of the outsider looking into the inner workings of the black movement. Are things this disorganized and chaotic? What motivation is left to continue the struggle if members constantly argue over petty disagreements and only help each other out after humiliating the needy member? The closure is that of disillusionment, and this is where *Marcas, sonhos e raízes* creates a gulf instead of bridging it. From a feminist perspective, Fátima may be said to be offering a counterbalancing and demeaning picture of the oppressive and insensitive male, but here the love-family question seems like a subtext within a macro-text of the black movement. Which is what makes this a compelling reading, especially for different black entities and organizations. It seems Fátima's concern is a larger question of the community and the lack of cohesion that can easily lead to the disintegration of the movement.

The various discussions among the group members (Jofre, Dacolé [Joel], Carlos, Valter, Lina, Armando, and Maria Clara) especially in "Na sede" (At the Headquarters) and "A reunião" (The Meeting) reveal many contradictions and challenges faced by the black movement in Brazil. On the one hand, these are struggling members, often without regular employment, possessing a basic education but financially needy; and on the other hand, they are poised to combat a society that keeps them subjugated without any material or human resources. Yet, the choice of a leader turns into a circus of personal antagonisms and attacks that ends up causing more conflict without resolving the issues at hand. The issues of discipline and punctuality, for example, are important for the survival of any organization, but conflating these matters with personal attacks, as in the case of Jofre's financial and personal family problems, is misplaced since it distracts the organization from its collective mission to combat the so-called enemy successfully.

Although Jofre's attack on tardiness is a laudable one, by blowing it out of proportion he incites criticism from others about his own "irresponsibility." According to him: "Our problem is that we all make irresponsibility the order of the day. That is why every meeting starts an hour and a half late" (26). Instead of giving this problem serious thought and due discussion, another member, Dacolé, is quick to digress from that point to the issue of cleaning up the Headquarters as if to insinuate that they should live by example and not by speeches alone: "What about starting with cleaning the Headquarters?" (26). The personal attacks continue unabated to the point where Jofre, a dedicated member, becomes defensive and provocative: "Of course, comrade, my situation is such because I set high goals. I gave my life to the movement. That may be fine with me. But if each one of us only thinks of himself or herself, the movement cannot progress" (29). As an individual, Jofre can only do so much; besides, his personal problems stemming from his separation from Boekis have not helped the situation. It actually diminished his leadership qualities and effectiveness. And this is where the problem lies. If every potential leader is dismissed due to his/her personal problems, the alternative may be total disintegration, and that is exactly the situation of the movement here.

Of course, Jofre's act of infidelity is reproachable, and he has paid for it by being thrown out by Boekis. But does it help to ostracize him to the extent of losing sight of his overall potential contribution to the success of the organization? Is this the time to criticize and condemn Jofre, broke and homeless, for his misfortunes? Or is this the time to rally around and provide him comfort even while rebuking him? After a futile discussion, it is resolved that Jofre will stay temporarily (for the night only!) with Armando, another dedicated member. And it is only after this resolution that the actual meeting starts. Again, the discussion is not on what to do in the community but about the criticism of the likes of Pelé, who did not use his position to improve the situation of Afro-Brazilians. And in this sense, the point is well taken, but of what use is dwelling on what Pelé did, did not do, or could have done? It is puzzling that so much energy is spent on the issue of leadership that individual responsibility is ignored and minimized. In the final analysis, it is as if Jofre has become a personal target of humiliation at the hands of his fellow militants. Instead of being encouraged, he becomes disillusioned: "Jofre has gotten very weak. He felt the presence of betrayal at every corner. The day has been tense. In the corners, from everyone's mouth and in his own thoughts. He anguished at the fate of the papers and posters he had left in the hostel and what Dona Maria could have done with them" (49). But Fátima comes to the rescue of her protagonist: Jofre consoles himself with the òrìṣàs, where he finds spiritual refuge.

Fátima's ultimate unveiling of the hard reality of the Afro-Brazilian community lies in her representation of the "O casarão" (The Big House) where Jofre is supposed to be squatting with Armando while trying to redeem his deteriorating plight. We are faced with a disturbing reality of ghetto life where humans become bestial and revert to a survival of the fittest mentality. As the narrator recounts: "The impression that the same person was the property of a slave owner was an issue of daily reality. There was an air of dubiousness in everyone; a sign of exploitation is manifest in every tenant. Twelve families altogether. They brushed each other off in an ambience of dissatisfaction that results from living in an environment that is not meant for humans. . . . Armando's salary made it impossible for him to leave that setting. He was hurting living with that painful reality" (53). And this is the reality the movement must face and combat. Yet, for some, this reality is what defines the Afro-Brazilian community. The permanent conflict comes from wanting change, on the one hand, and wanting to keep things as they are, on the other. It is a dilemma captured by the symbolic drama of the living-dead.

From the examples of Miriam Alves, Esmeralda Ribeiro, and Sônia Fátima, perhaps the compelling challenge for Afro-Brazilian women writers lies mostly in the recognition of the inseparability of their femininity from their black consciousness. In this sense, some "curtains" still need to be pulled back to allow for more compelling discussions of such issues as motherhood, heroism, participation, equal opportunity, and empowerment, as well as transnational issues beyond race and gender. In the final analysis, it is only through acceptance and due recognition that these writers can be seen as equal partners in the cultural production of Brazilianness and not just bearers of burdens and shakers of shackles that continue to bind and brutalize Afro-Brazilians.

4

(Un)Broken Linkages

By all accounts, Antônio Olinto, whose works have been translated into at least seven languages, deserves to be considered a Yoruba diaspora writer given his contributions to establishing connections between Yorubaland and its foremost and richest extension in the Americas: Bahia, Brazil. My personal experience in Salvador, Bahia, led to a reawakening of my own Yoruban diaspora consciousness.

Because I was born and raised in the bubbling heart of Lagos, Nigeria, Olinto's narratives, especially *A casa da água,* bring back memories of familiar settings. I can hear echoes of hustling street traders, the nocturnal pleasantries of celebrants barricading whole blocks for extravagant open-air parties, the playground in Campos Square (*Praça campos*) that serves as a point of encounter for students, truants, and adults who have come together to play soccer. Most significant is the Brazilian Quarter sandwiched between Kakawa, Broad, and Bamgbose Streets, as well as the relics of Brazilian architecture on Bamgbose, Simpson, and Oshodi Streets where the Iron Gate and a few other structures seem to transpose the northeast of Brazil, especially Bahia, into a Nigerian reality. Olinto's narratives depict an unbroken connection in this sense—a linkage that is easily made, a kinship that can neither be denied nor minimized. In addition, the names of my Lagosian friends and childhood classmates quickly come to mind: Vera Cruz, Da Costa, Pinheiro, Olympio, D'Almeida, Sho Silva, Gomez, Ferreira, Da Rocha, and Da Silva—all Brazilian names and families who returned to Nigeria and Benin after the abolition of slavery in Brazil in 1888.

Politics of Return and Resettlement

While the rationale to return home after abolition can be linked to the strong religious ties some of the slave groups who arrived in Brazil in the latter phase of slavery, especially the Yoruba, had with Africa, it is questionable whether that was the only determining factor. Other factors relate to the sense of Afro-Brazilians' total estrangement and displacement even after abolition due to lack of dignity and economic sufficiency to start a life on their own. A critic has suggested that the latter was in fact the most compelling reason for the return to Africa:

> For most, homecoming was a unique experience in many respects. It meant an end to the life on the plantations and the endless affronts to their dignity. There was also the opportunity to regain some form of respect among people of their own color. Thus, the fear of repeating the harrowing crossing did not deter many, among whom were those born in captivity, and the others called "passengers," "Africans transported twice, the first time in ships which took them 'to receive an education in Brazil' and the second when they returned to the fatherland that had sold them." (Amosu, "The Jaded Heritage," 43)

Amosu's notion of a "jaded heritage" aptly captures the paradoxical lifestyle of the returnees who on the one hand desperately wanted to return home to Africa, and on the other hand felt a certain nostalgia for Brazil as they struggled to keep Northeastern Brazilian traditions alive such as *Bumba-Meu-Boi, Careta,* and the Yoruba-Portuguese words corrupted upon their return, such as *frejon* for *feijão* (beans), *imoyo* for *molho* (soup), and *farofa* for cassava flour dipped in tempered soup. Although the first generation of returnees had significant influence in Lagos due to their artisan and architectural skills, through marriage and education over the years, later generations of returnees were transformed into civil servants and have gradually lost their original affluence. What is left, then, are Brazilian-style buildings, festivals, and the Brazilian Descendants' Union, which serves as a forum for preservation of their fast-fading heritage.

Aside from these gradually disappearing and unkempt traditions and connections, two cultural events serve as reminders of this compelling legacy: FESTAC (Festival of Arts and Culture), held in Nigeria in 1977, and the Third International Congress of Òrìṣà Tradition and Culture, held at the University of Ife, Nigeria, in 1986. In addition to bringing together brothers and sisters from all over the globe, members of the same lineage long separated and dispersed by geographical and historical accidents, these events also provided a moment of reflection on the richness of African cultures and their survival in the New World. For the first time, African artists, writers, performers, and cultural producers in general could exchange views on their commonality and diversity, be they from Cuba, Trinidad, Brazil, Senegal, or even Nigeria, where they were being hosted. Popular musicians like Gilberto Gil, Fela Anikulapo-Kuti, and Abdias do Nascimento quickly became household names on Nigerian television while daily FESTAC activities gave Nigerians much to ponder in terms of lost legacies and kinship. In the same vein, the richness of the diaspora also became apparent to our visitors as they confirmed the connections between practices that we as Africans have taken for granted and that they are compelled to keep intact. In this sense, Africa and the diaspora are mutually enriching.

From this background, Antônio Olinto represents that missing voice in Nigerian-Bahian and Yoruba diasporic discourse. A native of Ubá, Minas Gerais, Olinto was born on May 10, 1919. Trained in a Catholic seminary before taking to journalism as a career, he also served as Brazilian cultural attaché to Nigeria and Britain. As a journalist, literary critic, and creative writer, Olinto combines that rare gift of observation with an ability to convey critical commentary that qualifies him as a public intellectual. Aside from anthropologist Pierre Fatumbi Verger, who documented slave trade routes from coastal West Africa to Brazilian ports, especially Salvador, Bahia, and Deoscoredes, and the commendable efforts of Maximiliano dos Santos (Mestre Didi) in literature, no attempt has been made to recuperate this fascinating memory and establish connections as Olinto has done.[1,2] His corpus includes *Brasileiros na África* (Brazilians in Africa) and the Afro-Brazilian trilogy of *The Water House*, *The King of Ketu*, and *Glass Throne* the primary texts analyzed in this chapter. In producing these significant works, Olinto has been influenced by his sojourn in Nigeria in the 1960s and 1970s as a cultural attaché to the Brazilian Embassy in Lagos. A close friend of Jorge Amado, the celebrated Brazilian novelist, Olinto has done for both Africa and Brazil what Jorge Amado did principally for Bahia and the rest of the world.[3]

Considered within all of Afro-Brazilian letters, Olinto may not be as popular as Amado but he is to the Yoruba diaspora what Amado is to Brazil. While Amado may not assume his affinity to Afro-Brazilian culture in terms of defining himself as such, his choice to simply be called "Brazilian" betrays an identification with the racial myth of whitening and its implied differentiation between mulattos and the rest of the black population whom he contradictorily portrays in his "Afro-Brazilian" works. By contrast, Olinto, although white, is very passionate about these connections through his incursions into Yoruba mythology, customs, and traditions. In addition to the Afro-Brazilian trilogy and *Brasileiros na África* under examination, Olinto has written poetry and other narratives among which are *Nagasaki* (1956), *O dia da ira* (1959; *Day of Wrath*), *Teorias* (1967; *Theories and Other Poems*), *O cinema de ubá* (1972; Ubá's *Cinema House*), *Copacabana* (1975), *Tempo de palhaço* (1989; *Time of the Buffoon*), and more recently, *Sangue na floresta* (1992; *Blood in the Forest*). Here is a literary odyssey that cannot be ignored, for Olinto's concerns range compellingly from Afro-Brazilian roots in Africa to humanity in general, hence his natural disposition as a Brazilian cultural attaché in Nigeria.

Brasileiros na África (Brazilians in Africa)

Published in 1964, *Brasileiros na África* is a collection of essays on the author's experiences in Africa, primarily during the euphoric epoch of independence. In addition to following the political events in Africa in general,

Olinto dedicates a substantial part of the book to the activities of Brazilian descendants in Nigeria, especially their cultural, literary, political, and economic influence on the Lagosian sociopolitical structure as a whole. Those who really need this book are dispersed in Nigeria, Benin, and Togo, as well as among the current wave of the "New Diaspora" (that is, those Africans who voluntarily left Africa to "settle" in the West in search of a better quality of life). The section on "Brazilians in Africa" offers firsthand accounts of Nigerian Brazilians in Lagos.

Opening with numerous black-and-white photographs of Brazilian descendants, the two sections focusing on Nigerian Brazilians detail the lifestyles, challenges, and achievements of this unique group of the Lagosian elite. The photographs document family portraits, monuments, and architecture, including the celebrated Water House on Kakawa Street, and the *sobrado* (two-story building reminiscent of a wealthy plantation owner's house) on Tokunboh Street, which was built by Lázaro Borges da Silva; as well as the Afro-Brazilian festivals and arts that are now part of the Lagosian cultural heritage, such as *Bumba-Meu-Boi* and *Gueledé*. Of the family portraits covering the entirety of West Africa, from Nigeria through Togo, a few are worth mentioning, including one of Antônio Olinto and his wife, Zora Seljan. The families include those of Romana da Conceição, Maria Ojelabi, Joseph Sebastian Nicholas, Isabel Souza, Júlia da Costa, Dona Sophia Marilewa da Silva, Lázaro Borges da Silva, Albino Taiwo Gansallo, Germana Afanu, Dona Angêlica Thomas, Dona Luiza Ebun Turton, Padre Thomas Moulero, Clément da Cruz, Xaxá de Souza I, and Epiphanio Olympio. This is a rich "family album" for in addition it includes the membership of the *União Descendentes Brasileiros* (Brazilian Descendants' Union). The photographic collection captures more in images than words can ever record.

The Brazilian Quarter, or "Popo Aguda" as Yorubas in Lagos call it, lies between Tinubu Square and Campos Square. Running parallel to the Quarter are three main streets: Bamgbose, Igbosere, and Tokunbo. Other lateral streets are Harley, Carrena, Campos, Okesuna, Kakawa, and Odunlami. One wonders how the mix of Brazilian descendants and the emerging Lagosian elite came to be in the heart of Lagos Island, a city that was colonized by the British, not the Portuguese. Prior to the abolition of slavery, especially in the first half of the nineteenth century, African slaves were already returning with their families to Nigeria. Between 1840 and 1859, these former slaves started building Brazilian-style houses, some of which still stand, forming the architectural relics of the Brazilian Quarter. By extension, the Holy Church Cathedral, which is often referred to as "Ijo aguda" (The Church of Brazilian Descendants), remains one of the landmarks of Brazilian architecture that survives in Lagos.

In one of the interviews he conducted with the older generation of the descendants, Olinto captures these intimate confessions from Romana da Conceição, who lived at 196 Bamgbose Street, and who had arrived in Lagos in 1900 at the age of twelve. She actually lived just a few yards from where I was born on Bamgbose Street: "'Where were you born, my auntie?' 'I am from Pernambuco. In Recife. I still recall many things from there, but Bahia is more vivid in my memory because I went to live in Salvador at the age of nine'" (165). According to Romana, the trip from Salvador to Lagos lasted six months on the ship called *Aliança* (Alliance) and there were about sixty returnees altogether. About a dozen people died in the course of the seemingly endless journey. Although Romana was happy to have returned to Nigeria, she often had nostalgic thoughts of going back to Brazil to visit in order see Bahia, and practice her beloved Brazilian Portuguese. For this Afro-Brazilian woman, there is an ongoing sense of being displaced: "I am here, but it is as if I am in Bahia. Out there, I see the hills of Pelourinho, I see street vendors and hawkers, I see relatives passing by" (167). These reminiscences of living in Lagos and missing Salvador, and of living in Salvador and wanting to return to a free home in Nigeria, capture the dilemma of the floating migrant in the specific case of slavery, abolition, and return. Romana's case may be different from the exile, but not so different in terms of the nostalgia and "double consciousness" she feels about being both Nigerian and Brazilian.

The second part of Olinto's fascinating account focuses on the life and times of Maria Ojelabi, another Brazilian returnee who had arrived in Lagos in the company of Romana da Conceição and others on the *Aliança*. Maria was born in Nazaré das Farinhas in Bahia, and her story is somewhat tragic and sad. She attended a convent located around Badagry between 1900 and 1903 but later married Mr. Ojelabi, from whom she got her new last name. Although she never had any children of her own, she took good care of other relatives' children, such as Migué and Elza Maria. She became sick from a nail that punctured one of her shoes and entered her foot; although advised to go to the hospital, she refused for fear of injections. The bruised area quickly became infected with tetanus and within two weeks, on November 9, 1963, she died. Romana da Conceição, who considered her like a sister, became her immediate family since Maria did not have any close family members. Many Brazilian friends, including representatives of the Brazilian Embassy in Lagos, attended the funeral ceremonies and festivities. During the celebrations, many "lost" Brazilian songs were revived by attendees in homage to Maria Ojelabi, who was renowned for her popular songs. One of her favorite songs was called "Enganadora" (Swindler):

> Oh swindler,
> Don't come to deceive me,
> Oh swindler,
> Don't come to deceive me,

Don't take away from me the payment
That someone else has come to make
Oh swindler,
Get out of here. (*Brasileiros na África*, 209)

As Olinto points out, even Romana often claimed that Africans did not know how to have fun until Afro-Brazilians returned to Lagos. She cited Brazilian feasts like São João, firecrackers, *bumba-meu-boi*, picnics, and street dancing as just a sampling of the Brazilian lifeways brought back to enrich life in Lagos.

Brazilians who returned to West Africa have a lot to celebrate and reminisce about. In the first instance, through the survival of African religions in Brazil and specifically the preservation of the Yoruba language in Candomblé religious practices, which blend Catholicism with Yoruba traditional religion, it was possible for Afro-Brazilians to integrate into Lagos life and build churches, schools, and houses according to their needs. In the second instance, through births, marriages, and deaths, the cohesive and distinct community forged at the turn of the nineteenth century began to fade, including the use of Portuguese language. Instead, Yoruba and English became the operative languages for the newly forged Nigerian-Brazilian identity. While this dual heritage is worth celebrating, it is also of concern that many of these buildings, festivities, memories, and the skilled labor that made the returnees economically viable are gradually giving way to new challenges of modernity and nationality. Examination of *The Water House*, *The King of Ketu*, and *Glass Throne* illuminates these challenges while grounding the paradox of the return journey to Africa in contextual and theoretical perspectives.

Postcolonial theory offers us the possibility for alternate reading practices beyond the limits of the dominant paradigm. But it also poses some problems. One such problem is the term *postcolonial* itself; to a significant degree, it fails to convey the continuum of the colonial experience. I propose that the term "postcolonial" is misleading, and that "neocolonialism" is more useful because the former is premised on an unfounded assumption of a definite rupture from the colonial condition. Neocolonialism implies a colonial continuum despite apparent attempts by former colonized regions of the world at political self-determination and self-expression. The problematics of a postcolonial reading (that is, reading as though there were some remarkable break between two historical-political modes) can be explored by examining Olinto's 1969 trilogy.

A casa da água (The Water House)

In *The Water House*, Olinto, profoundly influenced by his sojourn in Nigeria in the sixties, reconstructs Afro-Brazilian history through the depiction of an

Afro-Brazilian family who returned to Nigeria after emancipation in 1888. The story begins in 1898 in Brazil, where Grandmother Catarina, taken there as a slave in her girlhood from Abeokuta, Nigeria, and later emancipated, decides to return to her homeland with her two daughters. On arrival in Lagos, Mariana, Catarina's thirteen-year-old eldest daughter, emerges as the heroine of the family (and will become the heroine of the novel). Her efforts to obtain an education, to preserve the family, and to launch its business ventures make her one of the most extraordinary figures in a long line of black literary matriarchs. Recalling her rural Brazilian past, she hits upon the idea of digging a well in the backyard of their new island home in Lagos, at a time when the shortage of water makes it a precious and valuable commodity. The well succeeds and becomes the basis for a family dynasty that extends from Lagos to Dahomey and Togo. Olinto takes the title of the book, *The Water House,* from this crucial event.

The novel skillfully depicts the life of returned Brazilian communities in Africa, especially the lasting influence of those people who have come to represent a distinguished and respected elite in Nigeria. Generation after generation is traced on its steady march upward toward social prominence, a mobility based on acquisition of overseas educational qualifications. Births and marriages, deaths and separations, all the struggles of life are seen through the perspective of Mariana and her impressive offspring. Their reintegration into Yoruba society and values, and their retention of continued family and commercial links with Brazil and with the descendants of the returned Brazilians is depicted with care and nuance. Olinto adds the spice of cosmopolitanism as one son acquires a Parisian education and Togolese bride, one daughter returns from England a qualified physician and marries a leading Nigerian barrister, and an adopted grandson makes his way to Brazil to take up a position teaching Yoruba. The story ends with the overthrow by the military of Mariana's Paris-educated son. He becomes the first president of the fictional independent Republic of Zorei, which a reader familiar with West African political instability and constant military intervention can easily decipher as Nigeria.

In this context, there are two settings of colonialism and post/neocolonialism. The first location is colonial Brazil, where Catarina was enslaved under Portuguese domination; the second is fictional Zorei (Nigeria) upon the family's return to another colonial experience, under the British. Rather than return to a "precolonial" reality under which Catarina had originally left Nigeria or a "postcolonial" reality following emancipation, she finds her family returning to another colonial situation. For the family, this could be interpreted as a transfer to a neocolonial condition. The assumed "postcolonial" situation comes only with the independence of the Republic of Zorei. But we should note that this postcoloniality is attended by a tone of pessimism. The end of the narrative expresses the very issues of the appropriateness of the term "neocolonialism" as opposed to postcolonialism. As

Mariana's Paris-educated son and president-elect, Sebastian, informs his village in his farewell speech:

> Independence has given us all an aura of euphoria. And it's quite right that it should. But it's also dangerous. We tend to think now that all our problems have been solved automatically. We are independent, and it's as if some heavenly power will see to everything, increase production, balance our budget, make the people happy. But we know that this is not going to happen. On the contrary, independence is going to increase our problems. . . . We have a culture, we have a civilization in no way inferior to those of any European power, but often we are lacking in even the most rudimentary technical skills. And that is why we must strive toward a state of self-awareness; we must realize that the date of our independence was only the beginning of our fight for true independence. (349–50)

Sebastian Silva's appeal that his people look beyond independence is visionary, but the rhetoric is all too familiar. Having been educated in Europe, Sebastian is more than delighted to return to his roots in order make a difference. He has the perspective of a well-informed and educated citizen who can evaluate the challenges of independence as well as offer practical solutions to the problems of underdevelopment. This well-meaning appeal for a "spirit of sacrifice, hard work, and integrity" (350), however, is cut short by the military coup d'état that overthrows Sebastian's regime and his subsequent assassination. Although reactions to his speech vary from those who consider him pessimistic to those who agreed with him, Sebastian's character is typical of the post-independence African leader who sets out to transform a former colony into a truly independent nation, and yet is faced with the vestiges of neocolonialism, as corruption and greed force political actors to work against themselves by betraying their leader through sabotage and assassination. Given the coincidental parallel between his dream and death, Sebastian's vision of a truly independent Zorei remains a desirable but elusive ideal.

The trajectory of Catarina and Mariana's family is more an exercise in genealogical documentation than an attempt to place events in historical perspective. Although Olinto provides the reader with a chronology at the beginning of the text, his project is a fictional reconstruction of history, not a conscious effort to authenticate the novel. The effect of this is to focus attention on the characters, particularly Mariana, the principal character, whose strength and dynamism is reflected in the construction of the "Water House," which we might read as a symbol of the leadership lacking in neocolonial Africa. Mariana's stature as a heroine is well deserved; she has gone to great lengths to overcome the odds of adjustment to a new setting by finding a commercial niche and quickly investing in the building of the "Water House," which continues to be a family and communal legacy.

Olinto's text departs from the traditional temporality and historicity by which most African novels are structured and read, and because of which many have been tagged postcolonial. Simon Gikandi refers to such a temporal critical reading as a "secure framework" typical of the Lukacsian concept of the novel.[4] Olinto's text has a double setting, Africa and Brazil, and a double temporal frame, postabolition Brazil and (British) colonial Nigeria. Each location and timeframe functions to comment on the other. Mariana becomes the locus in which both periods and both locations exist simultaneously. The complexity of this setting as explored by Olinto may be challenging to the reader unfamiliar with the Afro-Brazilian literary tradition. Such unfamiliarity can lead to the type of myopic review that described *A casa da água* as "a magnificent attempt that failed."[5] Such paternalistic, condescending, and regressive criticism occurs because a reader neglects Olinto's conscious displacement of time as central to the novel's meaning. He replaces a focus on time with a narrative focus on the female hero, Mariana, from whose point of view the story is told. Olinto thus combines the African and Brazilian locations of the novel in Mariana, who, indeed, is an embodiment of the two cultural ambiences (as she is the ancestor of four generations of Afro-Brazilian descendants on two continents).

The limits of the term "postcolonial" have been explored by numerous critics. The central argument challenging its validity remains that of the limits of commonality of experience within the diversity of colonized Third World countries. Ella Shohat's "Notes on the 'Post-Colonial'" provides an in-depth interrogation of the concept of "postcoloniality" by examining its ambivalence and convenience in relation to other "post-" terms, such as postmodernism or postindependence as opposed to "neocolonialism" and "Third World." Shohat points out that the terms "postcolonial" and "postindependence" suggest a discontinuity of colonialism while "neocolonial" affirms a continuity, and "Third World" a commonality of concerns. As Shohat contends:

> The term "postcolonial" carries with it the implication that colonialism is now a matter of the past, undermining colonialism's economic, political, and culturally deformative traces in the present. The "postcolonial" inadvertently glosses over the fact that global hegemony, even in the post–Cold War era, persists in forms other than overt colonial rule. As a signifier of a new historical epoch, the term "postcolonial," when compared with neo-colonialism, comes equipped with little evocation of contemporary power relations. (*Social Text* 31–32, 105)

"Postcolonial," in contrast to a more politically explicit term such as "neocolonialism," thus tends to obscure the permanence of the colonial legacy and its structural relics that continue to haunt and hinder any attempt at true rupture and self-determination.

In Olinto's work, we can see how the relics of colonialism persist through the mirroring effects of alienation and economic servitude. One example is the sense of alienation that the conversation between Epifania and Teresa, who keeps referring to non-Brazilians as Africans as if she were not one of them, reveals:

"Why do you call them Africans?"

"Because they are Africans."

"Then what are we?"

"We are Brazilians. You have just arrived and you don't know what things are like here. We are civilized people, different from these others. It was us who taught the people here joinery; we taught them how to build big houses, and churches; we brought cassava, cashews, cocoa, dried meat, coconuts. They stare at you with big round eyes and don't know how to enjoy themselves. The only thing they know is to cause trouble at our parties." (78–79)

This example reveals the effects of displacement and internalized complexes that attend any form of subjugation. In this case, Teresa as an Afro-Brazilian who has returned to the African continent feels she is superior to Africans on the continent, thereby allowing herself to be duped psychologically: a perfect case of a the neocolonial mentality.

In her article, "The Angel of Progress: Pitfalls of the Term 'Post-Colonial,'" Anne McClintock equally struggles with postcoloniality as used to reflect departure or "progress" from the colonial experience. Instead, she calls for a return to the Fanonian ideal in which the colonized person uses the past (history and memory) to open up the future. Her call for engagement in the "politics of affiliation" that reflects power relations between the center and the periphery, between the dominator and the dominated, is striking. Olinto illustrates these power relations in the dichotomy between the former colonialists and their subjects; likewise between slave owners and their slaves. In the contemporary setting represented by the "Water House" and its economic importance, Mariana represents the "periphery," as she tries to change the power structure through economic empowerment and enterprise. Her attempt to balance her status as a descendant of slaves and her new status as a businesswoman able to sponsor her children abroad for their education changes the dynamics of power. One of her children, Sebastian Silva, ultimately returns to Zorei to be elected president of the new republic. Mariana does become the catalyst who, through her resolve and dynamism, upsets the balance of power relations, thus becoming a participant in the center, hence an affiliate rather than a representative of the periphery.

118 *(Un)Broken Linkages*

As opposed to the sheer convenience of Western critical paradigms, the term "neocolonial" offers a sense of history and specificity of experience. By contrast, postcolonial theory attempts to be all-encompassing or hegemonic. Ella Shohat argues that this tendency results in problematic "hybridities" that are limiting in perspective and detrimental to a negotiation of positionalities:

> As in the term "postcolonial," the question of location and perspective has to be addressed, i.e. the differences between hybridities, or more specifically, hybridities of Europeans and their off-shoots around the world, and that of (ex)colonized peoples. And furthermore, the difference among and between Third World diasporas, for example, between African American hybrids speaking English in the First World and those of Afro-Cubans and Afro-Brazilians speaking Spanish and Portuguese in the Third World. (110)

Olinto, like other Afro-Brazilian writers, communicates the specifics of this hybridity by adopting an African lexicon in the Portuguese language of Brazil, a feature that not only distinguishes Brazilian Portuguese from the continental but also attests to a conscious effort on his part to preserve his African heritage in his works through the infusion of African elements.

In *A casa da água*, Olinto's use of Yoruba exemplifies resistance to the colonial language. One such effect is the obligation that every one of the recently arrived Afro-Brazilians learn English in order to continue transacting business with the government. Seu Machado, a patriarch and elderly member of the family protests and declares his preference for Yoruba: "English is a foreign language. Portuguese is a foreign language. What we ought to speak is Yoruba" (145). Examples of the spiritual bond Mariana's family has with Yoruba abound in the text. A sign reading "Water," advertising the product of the "Water House," is written in Yoruba, for example. Mariana also makes occasional reference to the language as if trying not to forget simple greetings such as "e karo" (good morning), "o dabo" (good-bye), and "mo fe je" (I want to eat) (21). Finally, the book contains constant references to Yoruba gods, called *òrìṣàs* and to Ifà (Yoruba system of divination)—both of which seem to have left Africa, traveled across the Atlantic, and come back to Africa with the returnees. In such instances, Olinto's text suddenly turns poetic, as in the singing of *oríkì:* "O mistress of the land, O powerful mistress of the coconut palms, may Oshun bring you many riches and much happiness" (201). Another expression of cultural resistance is the singing about Ifà:

Ifà wanted something to eat
Ifà wanted to eat the tortoise
Sadly the tortoise stuck out its head
And begged: Spare me! Spare me!
Let me survive your gracious desire. (202)

This conscious use of Yoruba language and culture gives Olinto's text its African frame of reference.

In their own formulation of the postcolonial concept, Bill Ashcroft, et al., suggest that there is a "continuity of preoccupations" in the culture of all countries affected by imperialism from colonialism to the present. This "presentness of the past" colonial experience contradicts the use of the prefix *post* in "postcoloniality":

> What each of these literatures has in common beyond their special distinctive regional characteristics is that they emerged in their present form out of the experience of colonization and asserted themselves by foregrounding the tension with the imperial power, and by emphasizing their differences from the assumptions of the imperial center. It is this that makes them distinctively postcolonial" (*The Empire Writes Back* 2).

The "foregrounding [of] the tension" notwithstanding, the acknowledgment of colonial experience and its continuity is more fundamental to any discussion of "postcoloniality." And Olinto exemplifies this continuum in his portrayal of Mariana as a character who represents slavery, colonialism, and the aftermath; therefore, we can locate a fiction such as Olinto's within the continental African imagination as well as within the diasporic cultural outpouring. Abiola Irele's assertion that "Black writing in the New World has a certain claim to be considered as an avatar of the African imagination" (*Research in African Literatures* 21 [1989]: 65) can be thought of as embodied by Olinto's text. Indeed, his assertion complements a call by the Nigerian government in the early days of independence that Brazil should be given express membership in the Organization of African Unity.[6] *A casa da água* forms part of a long-neglected heritage of the African imagination by giving fictional form to a paradigm that can also be considered the neocolonial situation.

The challenge posed by Olinto's imagination lies in the problematization of location characterized by a "double consciousness," à la W. E. B. Du Bois, in both spatial and psychological terms. The Afro-Brazilian family leaves Brazil, a postabolition space, to return to a colonial reality, which upon attaining independence becomes a "post"-colonial one. My contention here is that this same double consciousness is true of the African on the continent. Indeed, it is appropriate to state that my reading of Olinto's text becomes a paradigm for how contemporary Africans struggle with the supposed end of colonialism. There is, on the one hand, a conscious effort to step beyond the colonial heritage and mentality, and on the other hand, the unconscious inability to step out of it despite independence. The continuum of the African experience as manifest in the literature of the New World presents a parallel with the continuum of colonialism as expressed by neocolonialism. The African diasporic heritage is not negatable in the New World nor the colonial erasable by the prefix "post." The effort to discard the colonial self for a postcolonial identity continues to be hindered by the contradiction of defining the self in relation to borrowed theories as well as by the assumption of living in a postcolonial condition.

O rei de Ketu (The King of Ketu)

Written by a "son of the soil" who, though born and raised in Minas Gerais, is versed in Yoruba language, culture, traditions, and customs, *The King of Ketu* is a celebration of those lived memories of Nigeria and West Africa as recounted by an Afro-Brazilian. Perceptive in its descriptions of minute details of religious beliefs, social interactions, and lifestyles, *The King of Ketu* naturally connects with *The Water House* as a sequel in Olinto's trilogy. Along with *Glass Throne,* the narratives complete a metaphorization of Nigeria, and Benin, and the fictionalization of Afro-Brazilian experience in West Africa in general. The narrative captures the commercial adventures and memories of Abionan as he sells his merchandise in different villages on a daily basis. More compelling, however, is the problematic of social death and political instability that echoes the concerns of Ben Okri's *Famished Road.*

The five-part construction blends commerce with in-depth knowledge of Yoruba culture. The omniscient narrator brings the reader into intimate contact with Yoruba cosmogony, betraying the possibilities of the work as a semiautobiographical novel. While the author is not a merchant in real life, his position as a cultural attaché in Lagos gives him firsthand exposure to the mysteries and idiosyncrasies of West African life.

Using the metonym of Ketu as a dual trope for market and kingdom, the king of Ketu, called Alaketu, is then symbolized in the character of Abionan, the market woman–protagonist who is destined to be the king's mother. The narrative opens with an *oríkì* (Yoruba praise-poetry) of the king's mother in an homage appropriate to her significant role and to the memory of her deceased son:

> I sing of the market woman as she sits on her wooden stool, setting out yams on a board with a basket of potatoes on the ground and green leaves in a corner while the scent of peppers from the next stall was mingling with the sun; I sing of her at the moment when she gathers her painted mat up, and once she had one with a colorful peacock but had learned that it would bring her ill-luck. . . . I sing of her on that dawning day as the *adiré*-seller is hanging out her bluish-indigo cloths. . . . I sing of her at the encounter as she recalls her son and the days when she bore him on her back, without him her body is lighter, the son who was to be Alaketu or the king of Ketu, yet how could he have died so tiny when he was not even ill? . . . I sing of her with that recollection in which she feels herself to be once more the mother of the king of Ketu; I sing of her at the start of her tale in Ketu. (1)

The paradoxical opening (praise and mourning) notwithstanding, the somber note does not overshadow the beauty of the description and the dignity of the market woman in spite of her agony of loss and the pain of remembering. A journalist, literary critic, and writer, Olinto appreciates and plays with the value of memory and the spirit of enterprise that the typical African market woman represents in the African society.

Olinto's Yoruba epigraph at the beginning of the book—"Iya ni wura, baba ni jigi," which translates as "Mother is gold, father is mirror"—captures the importance of the female subject in this novel, as in *The Water House*. Through this popular saying, mothers are generally held in the highest esteem by their offspring in Yoruba culture. It is a salutary way of appreciating the sacrifices of one's mother in terms of her months of pregnancy, her labor, her many years of nursing and compelling love. While the setting in this case is the marketplace, situated more in old Dahomey (now Benin) than in Lagos (the old capital city of Nigeria), and while Mariana, the heroine of *The Water House*, is a character of the past, it is in her granddaughter, young Mariana, that we find a symbolic reincarnation.

Structurally, each of the five parts re-creates the market scene as Abionan goes to sell her wares in four different markets, only to return to the first one in the fifth part as if to suggest a completion of the cycle. From the "Ketu Market," "Opo Meta Market," "Idigny Market," "Iro Kogny Market," through "Ketu Market Once Again," these market adventures and journeys are also symbolically linked with the Yoruba "market days" that Olinto craftily explores. In the first, third, and fifth parts, Olinto opens each section with a "song" reminiscent of the *oríki*, in which the author pays homage to the market woman. Each of these songs captures the actions and state of mind of the market woman in a psychological portrayal. Using this plot structure to map the development of Abionan as she moves from a simple "market woman" in the first part, to a "childless woman" in the second, and finally a "weary woman" in the fifth, Olinto displays a profound consciousness not only of the poet but of a sympathetic and sensitive observer as we accompany Abionan on her daily adventures to the market.

Although there is no mention of specific days of the week in the five parts, Olinto creates a new mythology by weaving the celebration of specific gods with certain days of the week, thus creating new meanings. In Yoruba culture, the days of the week have their symbolic meanings and Yorubas tend to be cautious not to conduct business or travel on certain days because of the beliefs associated with them.[7] The worship of the gods interests Olinto more than the traditional days of the week. He gives subtitles to the five parts as follows: *Ojo awo* is associated with "day of secrecy, day of Ifá and Eshu"; *Ojo Ogun* is linked to the day of Ògún, the god of iron; *Ojo jacuta* relates to the day of Ṣàngó, god of thunder; *Ojo Obatala* is dedicated to . . . **bàtál á**, god of heaven; while the fifth part begins the cycle again as *Ojo awo*. Olinto has been influenced here by the Candomblé religion in Brazil with its specific days set aside for the worship of different Yoruba gods that have been transposed into Brazil through slavery.

At work in *The King of Ketu* is the dual consciousness of Yoruba and Afro-Brazilian mythologies, especially those concerning the cycle of life, death, and rebirth—generation, degeneration, and regeneration. The fifth part, which completes the narrative structure of the novel, demands a closer examination in this respect. In this section, the yearnings, adventures, and dreams of Abionan come to a problematic denouement in a pivotal moment of secrecy and divination. The opening captures the weariness and anxieties of Abionan as she wakes up from a deep sleep: "I sing of her amid that final stillness that takes charge of her whole body; I sing of her in the void that invaded her, in that dreamless sleep and in that white utter sleep into which she dropped" (227). She has been to four different markets and has now come full circle by returning to Ketu Market. In her profound sleep, she had a dream about her son being pursued by a hunter on a hilltop; she had seen a red-stained sheet, an *osumare* (rainbow), and a line of people filing past her child. After her consultation with the *babalawo* (diviner) for the dream's interpretation, *Ifá* (the oracle of divination) revealed that her son will suffer before assuming such an important position as becoming a king. By using a pretext of dream and its interpretation, Olinto reconstructs the Yoruba belief in divination and gives Abionan an opportunity to rechart the course of her life and destiny by deciding to rekindle a dormant loving relationship with Ademolá, who belongs to a line of kings, with the result that her new son will become the king of Ketu.

Amidst the fulfillment of Abionan's destiny and that of her yet-to-be-born son who will be king, is the demise of Abionan's mother, Aduké. This blend of celebration and mourning is what defines duality in Yoruba culture. When someone has lived a good life, Yorubas usually celebrate even as they mourn the dead. Yet, for Abionan, the conflict arises from her uncertainty that her mother lived a good life. Only Abionan understood her mother's silent moments, her days of sickness and anguish, as well as possible moments of happiness about having such a wonderful daughter. The intricate connection between the dead, the living, and the unborn is best captured by Abionan's self-reflection about her deceased son and mother:

> Abionan had thought of her child's death, for it was as if her child had died a second time; she had lost him in the market and she had lost mother by the sea; the little boy had been buried at the foot of a baobab that wasn't on her land, though it was the spot where she had been born, but mother would be buried on her own land and would not be far from the child; both would be sleeping close to the road that ran from Ketu to Opo Meta, and thus deep down in the depths of herself the deaths of Aduké and Adeniran conjoined—

it has been one single death; the little boy had died and now the little girl into which mother had been transformed had died too. (271)

The deaths of mother and child are, for the grieving Abionan, symbolic of transformation from the physical to the spiritual realm. While her mother has been considered the reincarnated spirit of her departed son in the sense of a living metaphor of continuity, this unified death of both members of the family represents both consolation and disappointment that now leave Abionan desolate and lonely, with no other choice than to pursue the rebirth of the deceased Adeniran.

The King of Ketu closes with the internment of Abionan's mother and hope for the future through the birth of a new Adeniran; thus, the new king of Ketu has some significant implications in the overall construction of the novel. Life translates into a series of journeys during which various acts such as the adventures of Abionan condense into a metaphor of a market. As the saying goes, "Ile aiye ni oja, orun ni ile" (The world is a marketplace), and, as such, life becomes a marketplace in its own right since marketers leave home to conduct business in a neutral milieu only to return "home," which metaphorically means the afterlife. The different market days equally symbolize chapters of life in the drama of Abionan, whose name also signifies "the one born on the road." By implication, market, journey, road, and adventure mesh in the myriad possibilities life represents. Through these chapters, journeys, or adventures, the king of Ketu, who ironically is the only one who does not physically exist, is only discussed in the past and future tenses, never in the present. He represents the essence of Yoruba mythology, the world of the unborn, the dead, and the living, from the viewpoint of communal existence that derives its nourishment from the belief in life's continuity despite its apparent cessation.

Trono de vidro (Glass Throne)

While *The Water House* and *The King of Ketu* capture the life and times of Afro-Brazilian returnees in their land of origin, the last of the trilogy, *Glass Throne*, transcends the initial euphoria of return and reencounter, turns it into a nostalgic account of both Brazil and the symbolic Republic of Zorei (Nigeria), and also depicts the returnees' struggle to attain political power in the new setting. Complete by itself, the narrative is more political than previous two novels, which focus on cultural matters. The disillusionment of the principal characters in *Trono de vidro* situates the work as well as the previous narratives within the postcolonial and postslavery context. Divided into three parts—"The Long Waiting," "The Campaign," and "The Multitude"—*Trono de vidro* follows the expectations of the people of Zorei who are willing to support Mariana's candidacy to the presidency given the legacy of her father, Sebastian Silva. Young Mariana's involvement in the politics of the fictional Republic of Zorei as a third-generation returnee has implications for the integration of the returnees in their beloved African setting. While feeling welcome in their long lost "home," the returnees must also deal with displacement from Brazil for which they occasionally feel nostalgic. In the short term, they must continue their struggle for political power already set in motion from the first narrative, *The Water House*.

The notion of a spiritual rebirth of Sebastian Silva, the great former president of Zorei, in the person of his daughter Mariana, runs through the narrative. Although Mariana is somewhat reluctant, the persuasion of family members such as Abionan and Tomás da Silva give her a sense of solidarity and mobilize her toward the formation of the political movement to be called Sebastianism:

> "We have groups of people in all cities and villages who are waiting for your approval to start a movement."
>
> "Is it going to be a revolution?"
>
> "No. At least, not necessarily. The dictatorship will react, but the union of popular will with the support of the international community will change the situation without any eruption of violence or armed struggle." (21)

Here is where politics unusually blends with tradition and religion, for the belief in ancestral connections and continuity makes it imperative for Mariana to pursue such political dreams even if she must be persuaded by the community to do so.

Trono de vidro not only documents a period in African history; it also bears witness to one of the continent's significant waves of political change, namely the battle for an egalitarian society in South Africa. Apartheid, the policy of forced legal separation of blacks and whites, was one of the issues Mariana promises to combat if elected president of the Republic of Zorei. In addition, she adopts a Yoruba name not only for political reasons or because it was fashionable at the time, but for ideological and spiritual reasons. In an interview with a reporter, Mariana elaborates her political mission and agenda:

> "Why did you change your name to Ilufemi?"
>
> "I added a Yoruba name because, until recently, I only used my two Brazilian names, Mariana Silva, and I felt it was important to affirm my Africanity."

"Don't you think this change is pedestrian and pretentious given what the name means—'the country wants me to be president'? . . ."

"It's not exactly that, but it sums up the idea. If I feel the people want me and are behind me, I will be better motivated to fight."

"What contribution do you think that a young woman like you can contribute to a country with myriad problems such as Zorei?"

"The same contribution that a man, old [or] young . . . could make. I agree that my age may be a barrier, but I was raised in a political and university environment. . . . I took a course in Political Science and have analyzed what my dad did for this country. . . ."

"What do you feel about the struggle against apartheid in South Africa?"

"We must all be involved in the struggle. There needs to be an organization, a bigger one than the one we have now among African countries, to force the racist regime in South Africa to bring about universal elections and a majority rule." (128)

Sounding more like a seasoned than an amateur politician, Mariana displays knowledge of strategic imperatives in order to gain local popular support and to emphasize the need for Zorei to become involved in international politics.

During the election campaign, Mariana derives energy from the legacy of her father, Sebastian, going to his tomb to ask for his blessing. She wants to be a "revival of his life," an "imitation of her father," and wishes her father could bless her so as to honor his palace and throne (185). Perhaps this is where the title is taken—the fact that Mariana is sitting on a crystal throne that used to belong to her father, hence the illuminating glow emanating from her father's spirit. Even in this search for ancestral support and strength, Mariana is tapping a cultural source of energy, the vital force that protects the living and the unborn while recognizing the spiritual presence of the dead. Olinto's weaving of these Yoruba beliefs into a narrative that is essentially political in construction is reminiscent of his own rootedness in Afro-Brazilian cultural memory.

As a typical postcolonial African country, Zorei must deal with her propensity for corruption, and guard against excesses. In many speeches and discourses, Mariana has denounced all acts of corruption and reiterated her faith in the people, who for her represent the government. Her priorities to improve the quality of life in democratic Zorei include improving food, housing, health, and education. These priorities, however, are tied to external aid, especially from the World Bank in the form of X-ray machines and medical supplies. Although Olinto chose to end the trilogy on an optimistic note, he simultaneously reminds the reader of Africa's ongoing hardships and struggles.

On one hand, Olinto's trilogy establishes connections between West Africa and Brazil, particularly between Yorubaland and Bahia; on the other hand, it calls attention to the challenges of postcolonial states such as Nigeria, Benin, or Togo, struggling to recuperate vital heritages on the brink of oblivion. While the connections are worth preserving and are commendable, the fragmented linkages due to the passing of generations of returnees must be repaired through a cooperative partnership that will give Brazilian descendants in West Africa the opportunity to reestablish contact with families left behind in Brazil, while offering those families the pleasure of visiting Africa voluntarily. Such an opportunity can surely be facilitated by the Brazilian and West African governments in the name of maintaining cultural ties and preserving national heritage.

5

The Tropicalist Legacy of Gilberto Gil

> I will move on with faith since faith does not usually fail. The happiness of man is a warrior-like happiness.
>
> —Gil, *O poético e o político*

Music, like poetry, has often been considered the language of the soul and an outlet for feelings. But music can also be visionary in its search for untraveled "outlets" such as the Brazilian Tropicalist wave of the mid-1960s spearheaded by Gilberto Gil and Caetano Veloso. At the dawn of the twenty-first century, Gil is credited with approximately five hundred musical pieces, an amount that underscores the productive energy of "Baba Alapala," as he is often called. If there is anything simultaneously distinguishing and complementary about Gil and Caetano, it is the individual and collective rebelliousness inherent in their involvement with the short-lived but influential pop-cultural movement otherwise known as *Tropicalismo* or *Tropicália*. In spite of their shared innovative styles and philosophies, especially against the military dictatorship that ultimately drove them into exile in the late sixties, they do differ in their sociopolitical commitment and engagement. While Gil is more politically conscious, vocal, and critical, Caetano is more reserved, subtle, and delicate. And therein lies a fundamental contrast that partly explains Caetano's popularity and Gil's lack of recognition in the Tropicalist discourse, given Brazilians' complacency in the arena of political and social change. In addition to an analysis of Gil's lyrical output in the course of his musical career, especially as compiled by Carlos Rennó in *Gilberto Gil: Todas as Letras*, this chapter seeks to answer two fundamental questions: why has Gil been an "appendix" to the Tropicalist phenomenon, while Caetano seems to enjoy a "forerunner" status; and why has Gil's intellectual contribution been omitted in the larger context of his Brazilian cultural production?

The Tropicalist Pioneer, or the Gil Phenomenon

In terms of enigma, exuberance, and presence, Gil is a close parallel to Fela Anikulapo-Kuti, the internationally acclaimed Nigerian musician-cum-rebel, and constant thorn in the flesh of every military government that has ruled Nigeria until Fela's untimely death in 1998. Echoing Gilberto Freyre's "lusotropicalist" myth of Portuguese adaptability in the tropics, and a subversion of that same unfounded claim of racial equality and harmnoy, *Tropicalismo* was indeed an innovative and revolutionary movement that sought to "anthropophagize" or "cannibalize" traditional Brazilian musical styles through the incorporation of international styles such as British rock 'n' roll and North American rhythm and blues.[1] Founded by Gilberto Gil and Caetano Veloso in 1968 with enthusiasts such as Gal Costa, Chico Buarque, Torquato Neto, Augusto de Campos, José Carlos Capinam, Tom Zé, and Rogério Duprat, *Tropicalismo* transformed bossa nova as we knew it, giving it a hybrid texture and tenor through musical collages, montages, and experimentation reminiscent of *concretismo*. As Gerard Béhague points out, "Tropicália composers deliberately avoided the dancing character of classic urban popular music" (1980: 451) as a form of protest against musical limitations and lack of sociopolitical commitment. In this sense, Gil can be said to be the most visible exponent of this political transformation. As Veloso conceded, the political function of art cannot be limited, but is something intangible: "I do think music makes some things move and create differences.... But it's very difficult to be conscious of what kind of differences it can make" (Schnabel, *Rhythm Planet*, 146), and this is where both artists differ, yet complement each other, since for Gil consciousness is at the very heart of any artistic production.

Born Gilberto Passos Gil Moreira in Salvador on June 26, 1942, of José Gil Moreira and Claudina Passos Gil Moreira, he grew up in Ituaçu, in the interior of Bahia, and later returned to Salvador for his primary and secondary education. At a very early age, Gil was fascinated by Luiz Gonzaga, the popular Northeastern singer who universalized the music of the *sertão* (backlands) and from whom he took private music lessons. Gil later learned the accordion and the guitar while perfecting his skills through years of experimentation, practice, and performance. Perhaps his most significant influences derive from his involvement with the Tropicalist movement, his imprisonment in the hands of the Brazilian military dictatorship in 1969, and his subsequent three-year, self-imposed exile in London along with Veloso.

Before the advent of *Tropicalismo* in the sixties and seventies, Brazilian popular music was immersed in the bossa nova trends of the fifties with such prominent exponents as João Gilberto, Antônio Carlos Jobim, and Vinícius de Moraes, among others, interpreting urban realities, albeit from the viewpoint of the upper middle class. This class issue, in relation to representation, generated heated criticism on the part of those interpreters of culture who saw bossa nova as elitist and alienated due to its approximation to jazz, hence a "foreign" influence on Brazilian music, which at the time was primarily made up of different varieties of samba. The *tropicalistas* wanted to modernize and innovate Brazilian popular music through the introduction of electric guitars and experimental rhythms. Taking their cue from the tenets of *modernismo* of the 1920s, Tropicalists, in music, translated this philosophical and aesthetic movement into "an aggressive attack on traditional middle-class values and on the sacrosanct dialectic reason of Western culture so much rooted in Brazilian traditions" (Béhague 1980, 448). In so doing, the contradictions of Brazilian modernism seem reconciled forty years after with *Tropicalismo* since the exponents were rebelling against redundancy and traditionalism and not necessarily against Western values. As Béhague notes: "The ideological attitude of Tropicália musicians did not entail a rigorous and everlasting dogma. As a truly socio-political action, 'tropicalismo' did not, in retrospect, intend to perpetuate anything; rather it was meant to awaken the consciousness of the middle class to the Brazilian tragedy of poverty, exploitation, and oppression, and to point out the true nature of the modern Brazilian reality" (449). And this is where Gil, like Veloso, gets his musical and poetical license in terms of limitless innovation and experimentation.

Given this limitless liberty of musical expression, Gil became not only very eclectic in his manipulation of international styles; he equally became highly critical of the dominant class in contrast with the masses whose modest life he identifies with in "Refavela," a sense of returning to his Afro-Brazilian roots. In addition to joining the *afoxé* Filhos de Gandhi, an Afro-Bahian carnival group, he synchronized rhythms from rock, reggae, and African juju in order to produce a new Brazilian beat that captures the negritude movement that was emerging in Brazil in the early seventies. Although Gil continues to parade annually with Filhos de Gandhi, he occasionally makes performance appearances with Ilê-Aiyê, an exclusively black carnival group led by Vovô. Gil's black consciousness and spirituality, coupled with his collaborative project with the Wailers in Jamaica, led to the production of one of his most significant album to date, *Raça humana* (Human Race). In spite of his imprisonment and exile, Gil has not ceased to be controversial in his criticism of social injustices. As Pamela Bloom notes: "Gil is still provoking the establishment—turning inward for insight and outward for influence. . . . Gil's *Raça humana* scans the world, sniffing out the perfect beat. Aided by muses like King Sunny Ade, Jimi Hendrix, and Bob Marley. . . . Gil's rhythmic expression alone is a tour de force" (71). It is this unique blend of the magical, the passionate, the lyrical, and the philosophical with the political that makes Gil a phenomenon, a sort of enigma in spite of himself, a free spirit captured in an enchanting, reggae-infused, and electrifying cut, "Esotérico" (Esoteric), which has remained for us a trademark of "Gilmania," a mystical staccato that does not lose its message of the divine in human nature:

> No point even abandoning me
> Because mystery is just part of life
> . . . .
> In fact, not even that esoteric
> If I am an incomprehensible fella
> My God is even more so
> Mystery is just part of life. (*Todas as letras* 181)

In an interview conducted by Robert Meyers, "Brazilian Popular Music in Bahia 'The Politics of the Future': An Interview with Gilberto Gil," Gil elaborates on his emergence, his significant influences, his rapport with other artists such as Veloso and Gal Costa:

> And then I was ready for something new, so to speak. And then I heard João Gilberto. And that was a bomb. Extraordinary. I was extremely impressed by that. I thought there was a mixture of ingredients that was intoxicating, seductive, an irresistible form. . . . I turned into an interpreter, composing and singing, looking for a personal message, cultivating my own sound, because João Gilberto stimulated me unconsciously to find what I had of the musical in me. . . . Soon afterwards I met Caetano, Gal, Bethânia. We were asked to do work with Alcione, Tom Zé, Fernando Lobo, Djalma Correia—with other people who were becoming interested in bossa nova. Caetano was also. Our interests converged in a common area of the new. And the rest is history. (Meyers, "Brazilian Popular Music in Bahia" 302, 304)

And the rest is indeed history, because in no time, the interactions with the new and old musicians forged a totally different product coupled with international musical influence such as The Beatles, leading the new group to professionalize, moving from north to south in search of musical legitimacy and expansion: And with The Beatles we had the desire to do something beyond bossa nova, which in Brazil came to be called *tropicalismo*. It was really an impulse to create a music that was a little freer of the thematic chains of the romantic sentiment, everything that was Dorival Caymmi, João Gilberto, the samba of Rio de Janeiro, something that would be more the cry of the machine, the messianic quality of modern life. And it was through the rock of The Beatles that we tried to create a version of The Beatles in Brazil. (Meyers, 302, 304)

The boldness of *tropicalistas* to construct a Brazilian version of an alien expression was not without personal and political sacrifices; that boldness landed both Gil and Caetano in jail. From the perspective of the political and cultural establishment that was yet to be comfortable with *modernismo*, these young exponents were going against the norm, against the grain, and against the general mood of Brazilianness in their own radical quest for postmodernity:

Everyone thought our position was very much that of rebels and iconoclasts. We were vocalizing, let's say, a violent new instinct, the tempestuous instinct of post-modernism from Brazil. It was no longer modernism. Whereas bossa nova wrapped up modernism into something comfortable, *tropicalismo* was already the discomfort of post-modernism, a fragmented explosion of post-modernism, that only now has come to be understood as post-modernism, even though it was already a fact during that time. So, I heard a lot of rejection in the artistic community, from the consumer, from the institutional powers in the society, from dominant stratas [*sic*], from powerful sectors of the government. (Myers, 304)

From his Tropicalist phase in 1968 to his post-Tropicalist years marked with ideological, spiritual, entrepreneurial, cultural, political, and lyrical growth, Gil evolved into an international musical legend. Not only did he experiment with Brazilian, British, American, African, and Caribbean rhythms, he also redirected his energy to Eastern philosophy in his 1997 album, *Quanta* (Quantum), in which science blends with art. To situate Gil within *tropicalismo* exclusively is to limit the multifaceted and multivocal nature of the Gil phenomenon. Yet, after thirty years, *Tropicália* continues to influence and encourage innovation and experimentation in Brazilian popular music. Parodying Gonçalves Dias's nostalgic-romantic poem "Minha terra tem palmeiras" (My Land Has Palm Trees), Gilberto Gil, with Torquato Neto, provides in "Marginália II" (1967), a cogent testament of *Tropicália* beyond "Geléia geral" (General Jam), which is often considered the Tropicalist Manifesto:

i, Brazilian, i confess
my guilt, my exile
dry daily bread
tropical melancholy
solitary blackness
here is the end of the world
my land has palm trees
where the wind blows strongly
with hunger and fear
above all, with death
Oh le-le-le-la-la
. . . .
here is the end of the world
here is the end of the world
here is the end of the world. (Favaretto, *Tropicália*, 143–44)

Taken as a lamentation construct, "Marginália II" takes an incisive jab at the anomaly of Brazilian social reality where, instead of the romantic bounty and exaggeration of Gonçalves Dias, the lyrical voice condemns the permanence of hunger and the fear of the unknown, of tomorrow, and of death. Instead of the palm trees producing food for the masses, they are producing hunger. The repetition of "here is the end of the world" accentuates the urgency of Brazil's haunting dilemma and, ironically, indicts the government of the day (a military dictatorship) under which Brazilians are condemned to marginality, hopelessness, and frustration. The burden for Gil is to sing of hope and promise in the midst of despair. And perhaps that is the puzzle that defines the Gil phenomenon.

The Tropicalist Griot: An Endless Lyrical and Spiritual Trajectory

Gil's musical career can be divided into seven phases, following Rennó's *Gilberto Gil: Todas as letras:* 1962–66 (formative years, public praise-singing); 1967–69 (pre-Tropicalism, Tropicalism, and post-Tropicalism); 1970–74 (exile in London, back in Brazil, back in Bahia); 1975–78 (from *Refazenda* to *Doces bárbaros*); 1979–83 (from *Realce* to *Um banda um*); 1984–89 (from *Raça humana* to *O eterno deus mudança*); and the 1990s (from *Parabolicamará* and *Tropicália 2* to *Quanta*). In this trajectory, we will attempt to highlight significant moments and lyrics in each phase while focusing on the context of emergence to better appreciate the total import of "Gilmania" and the life of this poet, performer, songwriter, and politician.

The formative years for Gil served as a training ground for self-discovery and self-definition. While most of his lyrics were laden with issues of lost love and unrequited passion, Gil's politics were also becoming manifest in those few songs concerned with his state of origin, Bahia; Northeastern migrants; and African deities such as Yemọja and Ọṣun. We consider these years of interior journey a prelude to the Tropicalist rebellion, the offshoot of troubled beginnings, and an era of reflection in search for the meaning of life. While personally engrossed in the quest for the future and love, Gil was also deeply concerned with questions of identity, justice, and equity in his native Bahia, from which everything else seems to flow, and to which his ties are unquestionable not only to the land and its people but also to their well-being and peace. This period is significant in Gil's career because, in 1966, after producing his initial musical jingles and meeting and performing with like-minded artists such as Caetano, Gal, Bethânia, Tom Zé, Capinam, Torquato Neto, he decided to make music his professional life, resigning his administrative position with Gessy Lever Company in São Paulo and leaving with his family for Rio de Janeiro.

In four songs written in 1962 and recorded during his formative years, "Vida sem vida" (Lifeless Life), "Sonho triste" (Sad Dream), "Você" (You), and "Bem devagar" (Very Slowly), Gil reflects on the ephemeral nature of life, dreams, and love, often sounding melancholic and disillusioned, yet hopeful in his passion, faith, and memories of love. In essence, these tracks represent the explosion of a budding bohemian sensibility here, a romantic heart struggling with the harshness and brutality of social reality. In "Vida sem vida," happiness is elusive; peace, tenderness, and love are all illusions; and the poet-singer is left with nostalgic memories of the past and painful lamentations about the present:

> My summer days are no longer warm
> My moon-inspired night no longer poetic
> And the garden flowers no longer colorful
> For me, the word "happiness" ceases to exist. (42)

Through love, however, the poetic voice regains itself, consoles itself, as in "Sonho triste," especially in "Você":

> In you I found the truth
> Of a love without vanity
> Of a love without passion
> I found in you in this world
> Something beautiful and profound
> For my heart. (43)

It is a consolation that comes slowly but surely as in "Bem devagar," in which love is likened to a revolving door, taking in a newly-found romance and letting go of an old one, and once again, having a feeling of happiness regained:

> Without running
> Slowly
> Happiness returned to me
> Without perception
> Without suspicion
> My heart allowed you to emerge. (44)

In four other songs written between 1964 and 1965, "Eu vim da Bahia" (I Came from Bahia), "Iemanjá" (Yemọja [Yoruba sea goddess]), "Retirante" (Migrant), and "Roda" (Circle), there is a shift from the search for love and affection to a search for identity, spirituality, social equality, and justice.[2] This is the transitory phase for Gil's political and cultural consciousness that may be called *Pré-Tropicalismo* (pre-Tropicalism). While struggling to professionalize, Gil traveled to the south of the country in search of greener pastures, where he paid tribute to his Bahian identity in "Eu vim da Bahia," in which he promises always to return to his home state, perhaps in a nostalgic moment of delirium:

> I come from Bahia
> I come from Bahia to sing
> I come from Bahia to sing
> So many beautiful things that
> Bahia has, which is my place
> My earth, my sky, my sea. (58)

It is only in his praise of "Iemanjá" that Gil's love for Bahia is betrayed. For Gil, Yemọja becomes the symbolic life of *baianos* (Bahians), for they depend on this sea goddess for the fish they eat and sell. And above all, Yemọja is beautiful, a queen who radiates the beauty of Bahia!

In "Roda," a composition by João Augusto but performed by Gilberto Gil, the gap between the rich and the poor in Brazil is accentuated, but the piece invites both classes to a philosophical lesson on (in)equality in life and death:

> If the rich dies and the poor
> Buries the rich and I
> Want to see who will separate
> The remains of the rich from mine
> If equality exists down there
> It must exist up here too
> Whoever wants to be more than he is
> Must one day suffer. (52)

While the moral here about human exploitation is direct and laconic, in "Retirante" Gil hides under the metaphor of the migrant to expose the anguish and tenacity of the backland dweller, the *sertanejo*, who is compelled to migrate due to drought. Yet, Gil partly sees in this reality of the migrant the defining characteristic of his own Northeasternness:

> I have to return
> I have to return
> I have to see if time
> Has made the forest green
> For which the hinterland has always hoped. (53)

In giving expression to Gil's penchant for personal landscapes and memories, this formative phase reflects autobiographical moments that may be lost to ideology as we move into the next phase where contradictions transform into grotesque parody.

Gil's Tropicalist years are perhaps the most engaging and revolutionary as they combine shocking musical novelties and manifestations with moments of incarceration and ultimate entrance onto the international stage of protest and renewal. "Soy louco por ti, América" (I Am Crazy for You, America), "Domingo no parque" (Sunday in the Park), "Luzia Luluza," "Cérebro eletrônico" (Electronic Brain), "Vitrines" (Windows), "Volkswagen Blues," "Aquele abraço" (That Embrace), and "Futurível" (Into the Future) all composed and performed between 1967 and 1969, testify to a sober and somber period in the life of Gilberto Gil. While "Domingo no parque" (Sunday in the Gardens) uses the capoeira musical background and rhythm to capture Brazilian regionalism, flavor, and folklore in the rendering of an otherwise moral tale of jealousy, passion, revenge, and death, "Soy louco por ti, América" (I am Crazy About You, America) evokes more of a conscious continentalism where Brazil represents a microcosm of Latin America. The mixture of Portuguese with Spanish is also strikingly novel, suggesting the breaking down of linguistic as well as cultural barriers.

The other six songs express some of the darkest moments of Gil's life, as he faced imprisonment and departure from his beloved country because of a conviction on political charges of subversion. The lyrics of "Cérebro eletrônico" were deliberately written as classic prison notes. The song captures Gil's depression and mental encounter with death in search of an explanation for his physical enclosure and limitation. It is a moment of deep reflection about the function of the brain and the mind when subject to enforced immobility. The brain then becomes an "electronic" gadget struggling for control between the imprisoned self and the state. Yet, the ultimate will to live determines the survival or death of the incarcerated soul:

> I can decide if I live or die
> Because
> Because I am alive, I live like a dog
> And I know
> That no electronic brain will rescue me
> From my inevitable valley of death
> . . . .
> I know that death is our primitive impulse. (103)

And no one captures these reflective moments better than Gil as he reminisces and philosophizes simultaneously:

> The fact that I was basically violated and stripped of my existential condition—my body—and seeing myself denied of my freedom of action and movement, of my basic control over my space and time, wish and free will, perhaps, must have transported me in my reflections of alternative possibilities and unconsciously made me think of the mental and physical limits of man, his mechanical creativity, the uncontrollable energies that increase his mobility and capacity to function and create. (103)

That unique opportunity to be "free," even for a few moments, finally came when he was visited by relatives. The visit became something of a dream fulfilled, a desired escape expressed in "Volkswagen Blues":

> Let me present to you
> My Volks-Volkswagen blues
> Ready to carry me away
> A long way to reach the moon. (107)

It was indeed a shame that a patriotic mind like Gil's was exiled. Perhaps the most painful thing for Gil is saying good-bye to Brazil and to his loved ones; these mixed feelings are expressed in "Aquele abraço":

> My path in the world I cultivate
> Bahia has already given me royalty and compassion
> I am the one who knows about myself—that embrace!
> For you who forgot me—that embrace!
> Hello, Rio de Janeiro—that embrace!
> All Brazilian people—that embrace! (110)

Here is a convergence of pain and consolation as the poet faces the inevitability of exile. It is a decision that has not come easily, hence the need to bid farewell to everyone: Bahia, Rio, friends, family, and country, as if seeking their approval and blessing.

In spite of these gloomy moments, "Vitrines," "Luzia Luluza," and "Futurível" provide a window of opportunity for passionate memories, love, and contemplation of the future. In "Vitrines," the poetic voice/eye televises a woman he had fallen in love with and for whom he had bought a pair of glasses through which he now sees her blue eyes.[3] In "Luzia Luluza," the poetic voice contemplates the possibility of marriage to Luluza, and for himself, the certainty of fame in the future. In line with this future is the image of the computer that "Futurível" sees as the ironic and mutating source of happiness: "Happiness is made of metal" (105). These lyrical enclosures and poetic implosions reveal the fragility of the human being as well as its stoic survival instinct when pushed to the edge. In this postadolescent trajectory that gives birth to *tropicalismo*, there seems to be a direct connection between Gil's creative rebellious impulses in search of novel forms and rhythms, and the rebellion that is contained in the search for identity and self-affirmation. To divorce one from the other is to minimize this symbiotic rapport.

As Gil's eclectic and innovative nature continues to pour forth through his music, the gaps between the personal, the poetic, and the political shrinks considerably. Although the lyrics composed between the period of exile and return to Brazil (1970–74) were written at different intervals, the preoccupations with existentialism, orientalism, Bahian identity and traditions, futurism, and love remain constant. During this phase, seven songs highlight Gil's creative and political prowess: "Cálice" (Chalice), "Oriente" (Orient), "Expresso 2222" (Express 2222), "Nega" (Black Woman), "Filhos de Gandhi," "Tradição" (Tradition), and "Back in Bahia." Of these, we find "Cálice" to be a classic due to its direct yet ingenious criticism of censorship under the military dictatorship. The structuring motif here can be summed up under the rubric of brutality-silence-ordeal. Composed and performed in conjunction with Chico Buarque, the piece taps the biblical imagery of Gethsemane and the moment of agony when Jesus was cried out to his Father to take away this painful cup, or "cálice" (chalice), an ambiguous construction that implies wine or blood, burden or censorship that imposes a disquieting silence on the citizenry:

> How does one drink this bitter drink
> Gulp down the pain, swallow the task
> Even muting the mouth, the heart remains
> Silence is not heard in the city
> Why be a son of a saint
> Better be a bastard
> Another less mortified reality
> So much deception, so much brute force
> Father, take away this chalice
> Father, take away this chalice
> Father, take away this chalice
> Of bloody red wine. (138)

Here is the poetic and musical gem by which any dictatorship is disempowered. And the story goes that when Gil and Chico Buarque were about to perform this caustically critical song, the microphone was turned off, and as Gil puts it, "we carried out a civil disobedience and insisted on singing the song" (139).

The symbols manipulated here are numerous: chalice, father, silence—all find their dialectical relationship in an ambiguous construction that requires a deeper analysis. Chalice is symbolic of the Last Supper's wine, which in this case connotes blood—something that cannot be easily gulped down as the lyrics sarcastically suggest. Likewise, the son prefers to be a bastard, hence rebellious, instead of a docile, saint-like son who will simply do as the father says. The "father" here refers to the state and the image of the dictatorship, while "silence" actually becomes subverted since "the heart remains," and "silence is not heard in the city"—as if to suggest that censorship has failed in its mission, as the citizenry continues to "make noise" and vocalize their anguish and oppression through the power of music, as the ambivalence of

"Cálice" attests. Gil and Chico Buarque are commendable for forging this artistic and political alliance, in raising and mobilizing the consciousness of Brazilians against a brutal military dictatorship.

While "Cálice" presents a national political emergency through the muse of music, other songs present emotional and international as well as national concerns. "Nega" translates blissful moments in exile (in London) with a black woman; "Oriente" captures Gil's abiding fascination with the East and a passing wish to do his postgraduate studies there; "Tradição" translates the poet's memory of an obsession with the "Garota do Barbalho" (a Bahian lady from Barbalho), an older girl who was a "sexual object" to Gil and to whom Gil was a "cultural object." "Filhos de Gandhi" betrays Gil's renewed interest in his African roots, hence his association with this *afoxé* carnival group since his return from exile. But it is in "Back in Bahia" and "Expresso 2222" that I appreciate Gil's ability to reminisce on a regional level while being visionary at the same time. Gil laments his separation from Bahia after three years of exile, expressing joy and pleasure to be back in his native state, his native land:

> There in London, I often felt far from here
> . . . .
> Today I feel
> As if it was necessary to return
> So much lively
> Life divided, here and there. (130)

As in "Back in Bahia," where "Bahia" functions as an idealistic metaphor, Gil idolizes a childhood train (222) in "Expresso 2222," transforming it into an aesthetic vehicle not of his past but of the future by adding another numeral, hence the year 2222, a futuristic symbol of movement, spirituality, and renewal:

> Never does one reach the concrete Christ
> Be it through material or anything real
> After 2001 and 2002 outside
> Christ is like the one seen ascending into the heavens
> Ascending into the heavens
> In bright celestial garment ascending into the heavens. (129)

The year or number 2000 translates into an allegory of the end of time or life, likened perhaps to the poet's life in Brazil before exile. Since he spent three years in exile, the "2001 and 2002 outside" may be read as the years beyond the "end of the world" that Brazil under military domination represented. This notion also echoes the allusion in "Marginália II," in which Gil compares the political and social situation in Brazil to the end of the world.

Another dimension in this metaphoric ascension into heaven is the bohemian and troubled season of the 1960s when drugs, especially hemp, were the norm of rebellious identity. Gil's fascination with the image of Christ seems to come from a prophetic and spiritual consciousness, which he then expresses in his lyrics even when depicting banal or romantic scenarios.

Since his return from London, Gil seems to have reached a professional prime as testified to by the prolific production of the mid-seventies and beyond of which the following cuts are significant samples: "Niguém segura este país" (No One Can Bear This Country), "Refazenda" (refarming), "Retiros espirituais" (Spiritual Withdrawals), "Esotérico" (Esoteric), "Chuck Berry Fields Forever," "Alapala," "Refavela" (Re-Slum), "Balafon," "Refestança" (Re-Party), "Não chore mais" (No Woman, No Cry), and "The United States of My Life." As a "son of the soil," Gil radicalizes his roots in his native Bahia, paying homage not only to the Oriṣa but to their origins in Africa as well as to their diasporic manifestations. In "Alapala," "Balafon," and "Chuck Berry Fields Forever," Gil identifies with African rhythms as well as the subversion of slavery.[4] Although Gil pays homage to African musical instruments as sources of spiritual and ancestral power, he uses this song to re-historicize and remythicize African gods by tying Afro-Brazilian consciousness into an otherwise praise-singing of Ṣàngó, the Yoruba god of thunder:

"My grandpa, your grandpapa's
Daddy was born in Africa
A king, a tribal king Yoruba"
"So you, my boy, you've got to be
Yourself a little new Ṣango
Oh, Aganju, baba Alapala
. . . .
And that is why you should be proud, my boy. (185)

This movement to re-Africanize, or to create an Afro-consciousness, as it was called, emerged in the mid-1970s along with the Movimento Negro Unificado (Unified Black Movement), which clamored for black rights all throughout Brazil. Perhaps this explains the three interconnected cuts—"Refazenda," "Refestança," and "Refavela"—all searching for alternative communities to relieve the discomfort and displacement of a new but equally enriching world, where the body and mind are transported and purified through dance and musical bacchanal.

Apart from the recognition of African beats and historicity, spirituality also serves as the missing link in this seemingly severed but unbroken connection between Africa and Brazil. In "Retiros espirituais," "Esotérico," and "The United States of My Life," Gil throws himself into mystical meditations and spirituality, exploring dreams, uncovering mysteries, and searching for the divine even in the mundane. Here is a moment of discovery in "Retiros espirituais":

> In my spiritual withdrawals
> I discover certain abnormal things
> Like some vacillating and lonely moments
> Just with you and me
> Soon, about to come
> A new moment
> The wind blowing like a dream
> On the destruction of everything
> Which crazy people like to dream about. (172)

Craftily, the abnormality of the first stanza changes to normalcy in the second and then banality in the third, forming what Gil calls his favorite paradigm: thesis-antithesis-synthesis. As if this contemplation is not deep enough, Gil becomes a prophet in "Esotérico," my favorite song, which captivatingly welcomed me to Brazil in 1982 and remained number one on the national radio chart for some time:

> No point even abandoning me
> Because mystery is just part of life
> ....
> People will love you even more
> Even more difficult for you than for me
> Be it one, two, ten, ten million
> All the same. (181)

It is not so much the lyrics but the electrifying beats, synchronous, syncopative throbbing, and enchanting rhythms of this cut that send the listener on an "esoteric" journey and engender appreciation for Gil's pulsating eccentricity and philosophy. He could be dubbed the Brazilian Bob Marley.

Gil's search for the divine and the spiritual is reflected in his fascination with Jamaican reggae, especially his composition of "Não chore mais," an adaptation of Bob Marley's "No Woman, No Cry." This tune was not only pioneering in terms of reggae influence on Brazilian music; it soon became such a success nationwide that it transformed Afro-Brazilian popular music as a whole, especially in Bahia, among the carnival groups—hence the denomination "samba-reggae." This was the time of "poder negro" (Black Power) of the seventies—an era when black pride and African personality became revived in Bahia and Brazil as a whole, in particular among members of the Unified Black Movement. Thus, any connection with the African diaspora was always welcome in the name of solidarity in the struggle.

Yet, in his usual ambivalent style, Gil used the music, especially the "No, cry no more" adaptation as a metaphor for the period following sociopolitical repression in Brazil as if that period was one of mourning and lamentation, which in fact it was:

> Friends locked up
> Friends disappearing just like that
> Never to be seen again
> Such memories
> Images of evil per se
> Better to let it go
> No, cry no more
> No, cry no more. (204)

In "The United States of My Life," Gil captures the feeling of sharing the burden of others, of an entire nation languishing under a dictatorship in the land of carnival and contradictions, of fragmentation as well as hope for the future:

> Tomorrow
> I'll be free from any pain or sorrow
> I'll still be high to the highest I can grow
> I'll still be here, there, now, and then. (206)

This is exactly what Gil wants: to be free and limitless, to be "here, there," yet timeless and sufficiently optimistic about the future to be "now, and then," and, in the process, to grow to the fullest by overcoming and transforming pain into a means of growth.

The fifth phase (1979–83) in Gil's career is marked by a period of meditation and transnationalization, reaffirmation of his love for Jamaican reggae through co-performance with Jimmy Cliff, and a continued manifestation of Afro-consciousness through the incorporation of Afro-Brazilian religious elements in his music. In "Realce" (Splendor), "Palco" (Stage), "Serafim" (Seraphim), "Andar com fé" (Walk in Faith), and "Raça humana" (Human Race), Gil displays a penchant for the universal through introspective moments of dream and faith. In "Realce" Gil provides hope for the struggles of the human condition, resorting to the myth of eternal return and rebirth from ashes:

> Don't despair
> When life hurts, hurts,
> And no magic interferes
> If life hurts

> Like the sensation of brightness
> Suddenly, we will shine. (222)

As Gil explains, the piece was prompted by a moment of reflection when he considered abandoning his musical career, or what he saw as a "stage." Gil was obviously not without his fears and experience of crisis as he considered the relationship between composition and performance—one solitary and selfless, the other public and self-promoting: "Musical composition is a phenomenal accomplishment, a transcendental pride for life.... It is very vain to be on stage and produce instantaneous pleasure for all—an animistic assertion of musical life through the energies of live human bodies. On stage, aside from the fun, the feeling is that of sharing, of one man giving to another" (239).

This sense of being a source of fulfillment for others, of life being a series of gradual sacrifices in the construction of infinite possibilities, as in "Serafim," is first hinted at in "Andar com fé" and later synthesized in "Raça Humana" where faith remains the life force behind the regeneration of human frailty and nature:

> Human race is
> A week
> Of God's work
> Human race is the burning wound
> A beauty, a rottenness
> Eternal fire and death
> Death and resurrection. (261)

In this community of world citizenship, Gil equally pleads for human solidarity with homosexuals in "Veado" (Gay). He suggests, "If you are an artist, you must learn to be gay. I am an example: I am a learner" (268). This assertion clarifies and obfuscates at the same time. While not denying his fascination with homosexuality, he is at the same time suggesting that he has the artistic liberty to be both homosexual and heterosexual simultaneously. Gil's confession confirms Pamela Bloom's statement that Gil is "a noted bisexual" ("Raça humana/Human Race" 71).

Beyond his identification with marginality and homosexuality, Gil constantly returns to his Afro-Bahian roots, whether physically or inspirationally. Born, raised, and proud to be Bahian, Gil's ultimate solidarity is first with Bahia, the "Mecca" of African culture in Brazil, and then with the world. The praise of Bahia in its human elegance and physical beauty are captured in "Bahia de todas as contas" where

> Our culture is root
> Tenderness is our leaf

Sweetness is our fruit
This is how our God wanted it. (274)

as well as in "Toda menina baiana" (Every Bahian Girl), which is dedicated to his daughter, Nara, with whom he performed the song:

Every Bahian girl has a God-given deity
Every Bahian girl has a God-given charm
Every Bahian girl has a God-given style
Every Bahian girl has a God-given limitation as well. (226)

This lyric reveals Gil's total sensibility and impartiality. By enumerating both merits and demerits of the typical "Bahian girl," Gil is affirming her actual "humanity"—her perfection in imperfection.

Gil's Afro-consciousness transcends Bahia as he celebrates Afro-Brazilian heroes such as Ganga Zumba and Zumbi as well as historical memories such as the *quilombo*, the settlement of resistant and runaway slaves, and the *afoxé*. In "Axé, Babá" (Supreme Power) Gil intercedes with Òrişànlá (Oxalá), the supreme god, asking for blessing, love, and power in a ritualistic song of praise:

My father Oxalá
Give us happiness
Bread of our vitality
Of your power
Of your love
Of your power
Of your love. (243)

By the same token, Gil defines the essence of the *afoxé*, such as the Filhos de Gandhi, the most traditional Afro-Brazilian carnival group that still sings Yoruba ancestral songs in its carnival parade:

Afoxé moves on
Always moved
Will continue to move
With black devotion
And the blessing of Oxalá. (246)

In addition to being spiritual, Afro-Brazilians are thought to have a warrior's nature inherited from their ancestors, hence Gil's homage to Zumbi: "Black happiness is a warrior-like happiness" (276). But it is in "Quilombo," a song composed for the movie of the same title, that Gil demonstrated his ability to be lyrical and ideological at the same as he puts the Quilombo (settlement of the runaways during slavery) on a musical map, thereby calling attention to the fate of Afro-Brazilians during slavery as well as to their resistance during the same period:

> Quilombo
> Which they created with all the gods watching
> Quilombo
> Which they irrigated with wailing waters
> Quilombo
> For which they had to fall armed and fighting
> Quilombo
> Which we all still desire so much today. (274)

For Afro-Brazilians, the *quilombo* is that image of their resistance at its best, their sacred territory, their "black Eldorado."

Gil's sixth phase, which we may call the midlife years (1984–89) or the moment of political legitimacy and defiance, captures the regrouping and remapping of ideals that have always concerned this musician-composer: social equity, political participation, black rights, and antiracist rhetoric through musical power and prowess as well as spirituality. In this combination, there is a subtle development of ambivalence or revisionism, especially in "A mão da limpeza" (The Cleaning) where Gil challenegs the image of the Afro-Brazilian as a "dirty" being in the sense of his/her being "the hand that tarnishes things" instead of a (positive) builder, constructor, creator. Gil confronts this stereotype forthrightly:

> The white man invented the story that if
> the black man doesn't tarnish on his way in
> He will tarnish on his way out, hmmn!
> Just imagine that!
> He will tarnish on his way out, hmmn!
> Just imagine that!
> What a damned lie, hmmn! (278)

Instead of limiting his efforts to poetic and musical correction of the different myths of Afro-Brazilians' diabolical instinct, Gil took his battle to the political arena by campaigning for mayor of Bahia in 1988. Unfortunately for Gil, he did not receive the nomination of his own party, the PMDB (Brazilian Democratic Movement Party). In an anguished indictment of this discrimination, Gil composed "Pode, Waldir?" in which he attacks the fabric of Brazilian racism:

> The argument is that it is a delicate moment
> And for any such sin

There may not be forgiveness
Change is very risky, better change to aldermanship
But the candidate
That he cannot change
The candidate must be a moderate person
Without any past ripples
A puppet of the status quo. (326)

Apparently irritated, Gil turns sarcastic in the interrogative title wondering: if the candidate could not be a mayor, what is the likelihood or guarantee that he would make a proper alderman? Is Gil's sentiment a matter of paranoia or a concrete and legitimate diagnosis of social decay? In "Vamos fugir" (Let's Escape), although composed in a different context and thus not directly related, Gil seems to be tired of fighting the same battles and consoles himself with fantasies of escape, perhaps to Jamaica or to Japan, with his loved one, away from this place that constantly bars his progress:

Let's escape
From this place, Baby
I'm tired of waiting
For you to take me. (287)

But through new songs, new landscapes, new pleasures, and new challenges, the spiritual mind will always find a way.

New landscapes, for Gil, lie in paying homage to globally renowned artists of like mind, such as Stevie Wonder, Bob Dylan, and Bob Marley, and other musical giants. In "Só chamei porque te amo," a Gilian interpretation of Wonder's "I Just Called to Say I Love You," Gil revisits his nostalgic passion for Brazilian festivities unlike the North American celebrations captured by Wonder in the original cut:

Neither carnival
Nor even São João festival
. . . .
When nostalgia comes, there is no explication
. . . .
I just called because I love you
I just called because you are a great passion
I just called because I love you
From the very bottom of my heart. (296)

Given Gil's unprecedented sensibility and prolific eclecticism, he is able not only to redefine and adapt songs by other artists who inspire him but equally able to project himself beyond Brazil, as in his fascination with the Oriental world and philosophy captured in "Do Japão" (From Japan):

> From Japan
> I want a geisha that can change my attitude
> Show me desires that I never knew
> We'll take a plane to a forbidden altitude
> Without a pilot knowing what to do
> We'll go and live together in another world. (324)

The obsession with "another world," with something different and new, personified by a geisha in this case, has been a preoccupation of Gil's for quite some time, and his desire and ability to travel and acquire new values often translate into a better appreciation of himself, hence the constant retrospection evident in "Quarto Mundo" (Fourth World). In this song the poet-musician resolves to gain a better understanding of his "tropical music" in the "room of the world" (320) where all cultures and memories meet in a spaceless and timeless communion. Ultimately, Gil concludes in Mario Puzoan lingo that life is so beautiful in "É bom estar vivo" (It's Good to Be Alive):

> The same man I've been I will stay
> I'll better stay no matter how long
> Until it finally comes, the day
> I hear inside the sound of the gong
> Then now I'll certainly give away
> My possessions
> All my possessions
> All my songs
> . . . .
> Good enough baby, just to sing a song. (309)

These sober and reflective moments serve as a prelude to Gil's final phase, with its air of the supernatural, of magical realism, of contemplation of the beyond.

The seventh phase (the 1990s) of Gil's musical trajectory is what I call his futuristic, spiritual, and introspective years. In addition to a continued alliance with the black world, not only as a source of inspiration but also through expressions of solidarity with countries in crisis such as Haiti and South Africa, Gil turned his focus on the African diaspora and its echoes in Brazil. For example, Gil uses "Haiti" (coproduced with Caetano) as a trope for problematizing the oppression of blacks, mulattoes, and poor whites in Brazil, suggesting that Brazil's situation is comparable to the Haitian dilemma:

> No one is a citizen
> Whether you go to see festivities in Pelô
> Whether you don't go
> Think about Haiti
> Pray for Haiti
> Haiti is here
> Haiti is not here. (350)

This song is significant because it marked the reunion of Gil and Caetano for *Tropicália* 2 (1993) in celebration of twenty-five years of *tropicalismo* and of the golden age of both artists. Gil implies here that Brazil is undergoing a different kind of "dictatorship," in the form of police brutality that targets the citizenry, and in particular the underclass, and is still a sad daily occurrence.

In a similar critical appraisal of Brazil, Gil seems to fault the ignorance of the people as much as governmental oppression, perhaps suggesting the need for more awareness of civil rights, as rendered in "Rep":

> The people know what they want
> But the people don't know what they want
> The people know what they want
> But the people don't know what they want. (356)

This knowing/not knowing is the dilemma of the living/dead that Gil finds so compelling and urgent. Looking inward does not deter Gil from looking outward in "La lune de Gorée" (The Moon of Gorée), in which Gil pays homage to the slave island in Senegal, recognizing the importance of liberty in the face of diasporic pain and the colonial yoke. On a forward-looking note, Gil explores the (un)happy marriage between technology and spirituality in the new millennium, as foregrounded in "Pop Wu Wei" "Quanta," and "Pela Internet." In spite of these mixed voices and feelings, Gil still takes pride in his Brazilianness, as synthesized in "The Green Giant, Part 1":

> Brazil is the biggest African country outside of Africa
> And the biggest Japanese country outside of Japan
> In Brazil there are farms the size of Belgium
> There are thirty million children in the streets of
> Brazil, more than the whole population of Canada
> Brazil is my home. (336)

Gil's patriotic sense of belonging to Brazil in spite of its contradictions reminds us of Ebenezer Obey, a Nigerian popular musician, who in the 1970s also came to terms with his Africanness after traveling the world performing:

I'm black and proud
I'm black and proud
I've traveled all over the lands and all over the seas
There is no place like Africa to me
Yea! Yea! Yea! Africa!
Africa is my home. (Ebenezer Obey, "Africa is My Home" [1973])

In this sense, Gil is an Afro-Brazilian ambassador.

The Tropicalist Visionary: Blending Music with Politics

Unlike Pelé, the world-renowned Brazilian soccer player, who "failed" to use his position and success to effect change for blacks in Brazil, Gil acts as the conscience of Afro-Brazilians. He takes this commitment not only to heart but into his music. In this sense, the "Gil phenomenon" goes beyond his artistic prowess to include his political savvy. Before his decisive entry into Brazilian politics in 1988, Gil always expressed his political sensibilities through his music, and was politically active beginning in the sixties. Now, as a member of the Brazilian elite who has succeeded against all odds, through "the barrel of a guitar," Gil, the current minister of culture in the Lula presidency, can be said to be among the very few Afro-Brazilians who have truly achieved social acceptance and political influence.

As Gil himself concedes, the masses do not have a voice without their leaders, and in the case of Afro-Brazilians, the leaders come from the same cultural organizations that depend on government subsidy in order to be visible. And this is the crux of the contradictions and pitfalls of black movements: having to be beholden to a government with which they do not agree is a double-bind. On the one hand, they must be critical, while on the other, they are forced to negotiate in silence. Gil's case is unique. As a self-made artist, his only allegiance to any group or government is by choice; his primary allegiance is to his audience. In this respect, he is fortunate to have been revered by all segments of Brazilian society, yet he remained an object of suspicion by elites and others who had reservations about his loyalty. This situation was tested in 1988 when Gil declared his candidacy for mayor of Bahia. In losing the race for mayor, he had to accept the lesser position of alderman, which also insinuates that he was not expected to aspire beyond certain level of political ambition and power.

Prior to 1988, he held the presidency of the Fundação Gregório de Matos (Bahia State Ministry of Culture), thus contributing to the positive image of blacks as among the first Afro-Brazilians to occupy political posts in the history of the country. In the early 1980s, Agnaldo Timóteu, a black singer from Rio de Janeiro, was elected to the national House of Representatives, and Benedita da Silva and Abdias do Nascimento were appointed to various political positions. Yet for Gil, blending music with politics was a feat, given the controversy that followed his announcement that he would contest the Bahian mayoral seat. Some claimed that Brazil was not ready for a black man to lead them, at least not at the mayoral level. It is equally probable that Gil's candidacy was rejected by his party due to his carefree way of life and attitude. Gil gave a series of interviews before and around the time of the election, some of which reveal him at his political best, sharing views from the challenges he faced and expressing his determination to make a difference by going all the way in this battle for the political realm in which blacks constantly were marginalized. The absence of blacks in Brazilian politics is not for a lack of viable candidates, even if they are few.

In an interview with *Jornal do Brasil* in 1988, Gil was asked why he wanted to be a mayor. His answer revealed his compassion for the downtrodden irrespective of race, color, class, sexual orientation, or political affiliation:

> Due to a willingness to do, a feeling that there is a need today to equip the Brazilian political project with the capacity for conciliation between the vision of rupture from institutions through revolution by the downtrodden lot who are all over—for I do not see this possibility in the near future—with the very strong resistance of the elites who try to maintain their interests without any concern for the emerging society. It is necessary to forge, as a matter of urgency in Brazil, an interaction between these two segments. The politically dispossessed all over need someone to fight for them, to at least give voice to their yearnings, conquer a political space in which we can begin to fulfill the minimal dreams, desires, and necessities of these people. (Risério and Gil, *O poético e o político*, 184).

It boils down to issues of power and empowerment. The powerless must understand what makes him or her subservient in order to ask for change. The question is: Are the powerful ready to share that same power along with the possibility of transferring its attendant privileges? This is the dilemma Gil faced in a country that preaches racial democracy while condemning a significant portion of its population to third-class citizenship. In fact, Gil went on to argue that no one is a full citizen in Brazil except the elites. Perhaps the way forward for Gil is not to be overwhelmed by this fact but as minister of culture to take on the challenges of the new millennium, especially renewal for the younger generation of Afro-Brazilians. Paradoxically, in 2008, Gil stepped down as Brazilian Minister of Culture.

To his credit, Gil used his five-year stint as Minister of Culture to expand on what he has called digital culture—a concern that may be said to be in the interest of the limited but growing middle class but not the majority. A full assessment of Gil's accomplishments is far from being easy to synthesize.

Although his official reason for resigning is the need for him to return to his artistic work from which he was feeling immense pressure, it is rumored in the news media that Gil was not able to get much done within the government in terms of his dreams, vision, and legacy as Minister of Culture. Having come full circle in his administrative aspirations, there was a special satisfaction in his resigning before being removed. Many speculate that another reason for Gil's resignation is that he was limited in his ability to translate dreams into concrete actions, hence was obliged to settle for enactment of policies that his successor would then implement. On the whole, Gil has applied the Tropicalist rebellion model to mobilize grassroots and non-governmental cultural forces to improve the image of Brazil abroad. Notwithstanding his detractors who claim that he was only a symbolic tool in the populist agenda of the Lula government, Gil has managed to survive at the top within a challenging racial and cultural democracy.

6

Afro-Brazilian Carnival

Partnership is the illusory ideal often aspired to by exponents of popular participation in development. With good intentions, they insist that participants in development must no longer live in "worlds apart"; rather, they must become neighbors and partners in the development enterprise. In an attempt to redefine development from a grassroots perspective, some scholars have elaborated alternative development paradigms and proposed a number of approaches.[1] The consensus is that beyond communication strategies, grassroots participation is the missing link in the development chain. In addition, the role of culture has been found to be essential as context and continuity for development. Indeed, a "cultural paradigm" that takes values and models of reality into account in any conceptualization of development has been advocated.[2] With this "model of reality" in mind, I propose that the participatory paradigm is a myth, especially when one considers the case study of Carnival (Port. *Carnaval*), with respect to communication and contradictions in Brazilian development.

This chapter borrows from Oakley and Marsden's "concept of participation"—outlined in their 1984 volume *Approaches to Participation in Rural Development*—and their conclusion that, in terms of redistribution of power or "empowerment," genuine popular participation hardly ever occurs. Oakley and Marsden identify three fundamental obstacles to empowerment—operational, cultural, and structural—that are not mutually exclusive. In this discussion, I will examine the limitations of the participatory paradigm in national development using Carnival as a case study, focusing primarily on the *blocos carnavalescos* (in the case of the Brazilian city of Salvador, Bahia) and the *escolas de samba* (samba schools of Rio de Janeiro) as community organizations each of which serves as a cultural entity in preparing the participants ("carnavalescos" and "sambistas," respectively) for Carnival. The chapter is divided into four parts. The first revisits the concept of participation or what I refer to as the "participatory paradigm"; the second examines participation in its cultural dimensions; the third poses the problem of Carnival and its contradictions; the fourth explores the myth of the participatory paradigm. The conclusion summarizes my proposal for redressing the imbalance in participation.

In this analysis, I draw principally from Roberto da Matta's 1979 work *Carnavais, malandros e heróis* (translated as *Carnivals, Rogues, and Heroes: An Interpretation of the Brazilian Dilemma*) and my own research in Brazil that included interviews with directors of community organizations, especially in the city of Salvador. My ultimate objective is to identify an approach that will possibly redress the imbalances and contradictions of the participatory paradigm that make partnership elusive and illusory.

The "Participatory Paradigm" Revisited

The inalienable goal of any development enterprise is the raising of the quality of life in the society, especially in rural areas. Salvador is a modern city with a long history and unique culture; indeed, it is the "Mecca" of Afro-Brazilian culture. The Brazilian Carnival as a national phenomenon is mostly urban; however, because of the huge gap between poor and rich, and the overall level of poverty in the inner city where the Ilê-Aiyê carnival organization, which is the focus of my study, is based, I would like to draw some parallels between rural and urban realities.

In order that development achieve the goal of improving the quality of life, scholars have identified some immediate and long-term objectives and constraints. Melkote has summarized six major areas of constraint: the lack of an effective system for delivering knowledge and skills to the rural population, the lack of an effective system for delivering financial and material inputs to small-scale farmers, inadequate market development, the lack of infrastructural development, the lack of employment opportunities, and the lack of significant involvement of the target population.[3] This last factor often leads people in certain situations to refuse to adopt innovations. Given the importance of popular involvement, there has been a call for an increase in participation as an alternative development paradigm in view of its strategic position as the so-called missing link in the development process.[4]

Oakley and Marsden identify five problems that inhibit the chances of improving the quality of life for the poor: a lack of access to resources for development; a lack of organizations to represent their interests; the dominant power of local moneylenders and traders; the dependent and marginalized nature of their social situation; and the air of despondency and despair that characterizes their lives.[5] Despite the obvious marginalization of the poor, the danger in radical reassessment and implementation, Oakley and Marsden observe, is the exclusion of external pressure groups both within and outside the community that might actually be responsible for its alienation and poverty. In other words, the concept of empowerment encourages the powerless to organize to protect their common interests in partnership with the powerful. Well reasoned as that may appear, such collaboration often leads to a top-down "empowerment" process, thereby causing a feeling of powerlessness on the part of the beneficiaries in relation to the benefactors.

In their attempt to theorize on the phenomenon, Oakley and Marsden have thoroughly engaged the concept of participation.[6] In addition to exploring different definitions, they also attempt to interpret them from a means-end perspective, contextualize their application, and identify potential constraints. They consider two main schools of thought: first, the advocacy of government intervention approach (mobilization and coercion), a top-down approach; and second, the argument for a nongovernmental solution, a bottom-up approach. Citing Pearse and Stiefel's view of participation as a "process of incorporation," they relate the process to some form of "political democracy" that ultimately brings about the societal change and growth that "development" implies. The key to ensuring an "authentic participation" is to have a bottom-up process that focuses on distribution, hence some form of partnership that is more grassroots oriented, and thus more participatory: "In this understanding of 'participation' the emphasis is upon education and the building up of the organizational basis with which certain groups within the rural sector might achieve their participation. Implicit also is some form of consciousness-raising and preparation for the task of participating" (*Approaches to Participation*, 17). The major criticism one might make of the theorization of "participation" concerns that it creates a dichotomy between the process and the beneficiaries. Oakley and Marsden contend that benefits of development have been inequitably distributed over the past two decades and "participation" is proposed as a means of reversing the pattern: "participation" is seen as the means for widening and redistributing opportunities to take part in societal decision making, to contribute to development, and to benefit from its fruits (18).

A scientific definition of participation is difficult to arrive at, but a review of the literature reveals a contrast of views that may help in the formulation of a working definition. Oakley and Marsden observe that definitions of participation move from the general to the more specific, from the dominant paradigm of development thinking to an alternative or participatory paradigm, yielding the following emphases: (*a*) voluntary popular participation; (*b*) encouragement of local initiatives; (*c*) involvement in decision making, implementation, and evaluation; (*d*) active involvement in a decision-making process; (*e*) rights and responsibilities in problem-solving; (*f*) an active process of initiative and authority; and (*g*) increased control over resources.

From an analytical perspective, the first three are still within the framework of the dominant paradigm while the last two reflect a shift toward the participatory paradigm: "Participation is considered to be an *active* process, meaning that the person or group in question takes *initiatives* and asserts his/her or its autonomy to do so."[7] Further, participation involves "the organized efforts to increase *control* over resources and regulative institutions in given social situations, on the part of groups and movements of those hitherto excluded from such control."[8] The importance of these two dynamic definitions, which best depict the participatory process and scope, is their focus on group dynamics and empowerment in terms of accessibility and control of resources.

Oakley and Marsden's categories for implementing the participatory paradigm are noteworthy: collaboration-input-sponsorship (mobilization), community development (delegation of responsibility), organization (need for meaningful local participation), and empowering (access to power and resources) (*Approaches to Participation,* 20). The understanding of participation from an empowerment perspective is particularly significant for my position that the participatory paradigm is a myth. Recent research sponsored by the United Institute of Research on Social Development (UNRISD) identifies three main elements of empowerment: power–scarce resources sharing, conscious efforts by groups to control their destinies and quality of life, and provision of opportunities at the bottom-up level.[9] If participation is to be both meaningful and an effective agent of change, involvement has to come from a position of power, not weakness, hence the critique of empowerment in the following cogent appraisal:

> The concept of "participation" as empowering *is* a radical departure from years of more traditional practice. Although its conceptualization is simple and its argument difficult to refute, it is correct to say that it both faces formidable barriers and that it is also difficult to imagine governments and locally established structures offering other than powerful opposition. Historical participation has rarely been willingly conceded to previously excluded groups and the encounter between opposing forces is the inevitable result. (*Approaches to Participation,* 27)

The issue here is not so much the end result of empowerment, but rather the means of achieving it, as well as the constraints that make such a goal nearly impossible to obtain without considerable concessions and negotiations that are often advantageous to the powerful.

I will discuss the limitations of the participatory paradigm more fully in my case analysis later in this chapter. At this point I will consider the question of participation as a means and as an end. By means, participation simply refers to a process of achieving the ultimate goal over a period of time, while end implies that participation is indeed the objective. Oakley and Marsden relate this distinction to the comparison of community development with formal organizations. While the former prepares the rural population for cooperation with government development plans, the latter provides the contractual structure for participation. The ideal situation is to have participation as both end and means, in order to achieve fruitful structural change and continued improvement. This ideal of participation is reflected in Rogers's definition of development, though more as a process and means than as an end in itself. Rogers credits the Latin American communication scholar Luis Ramiro Beltrán for this idea and suggests that his only addition would be to make it slightly revolutionary by including "empowerment" in the equation, thus increasing its radical potential. According to Rogers's definition, empowerment is "a widely participatory process of directed social change in society, intended to bring about both social and material advancement including greater equality, freedom and other valued qualities for the majority of the people through their gaining greater control over their environment."[10] A contrastive and far more radical view is that of participation as an end and inalienable right of the individual: "Participation is not a fringe benefit that authorities may grant as a concession but every human being's birthright that no authority may deny or prevent."[11]

The Cultural Dimensions of Participation

The impatience of development communication scholars with the dominant paradigm has led to a continued exploration of alternative viewpoints. Since the 1980s, the one-way communication theories of the last three decades are now giving way to such new paradigms as "multiplicity," "intercultural," "multicultural," and "pluralistic," all of which move in the direction of diversity and participation. In order to represent groups of people who were previously excluded from the development process, the new arguments center on inclusionary or participative perspectives in development communication.

Indeed, the central thesis of the alternative development paradigm draws principally from Rogers's *Communication of Innovation* (1971), Goulet's *The Cruel Choice* (1973), and Wang and Dissanayake's *Continuity and Change in Communication Systems* (1984), among others. Wang and Dissanayake define the new development model as "a process of social change which has as its goal the improvement in the quality of life of all or the majority of people without doing violence to the natural and cultural environment in which they exist, and which seeks to involve the majority of the people as closely as possible in this enterprise, making them masters of their own destiny."[12] From this perspective, the importance of culture in development communication cannot be overemphasized. Whereas Serveas advances the "multiplicity" challenge in the form of "two-way, interactive, participatory communication," in *Participatory Communication for Social Change* (1991), Fred Casmir's 1991 volume *Communication in Development* takes the participatory paradigm a step further by proposing a "cultural paradigm" whereby he establishes a triadic relationship between culture, communication, and development.

The cultural paradigm, in Casmir's view, refers to the "common, value-based interpretations, artifacts, organizational forms and practices of a group of human beings related to a specific environment" that has a shared system of "transmission and maintenance" and ultimately the ability to get its members involved in joint efforts or ventures considered to be crucial to their survival (7, 8). The role of culture becomes a driving force of popular and unforced participation. In this sense, culture becomes an energizing instrument of communication and development.

The distinction Casmir makes between the concepts of nation and state is relevant here, for if culture is considered "eternal," "long-longing and spiritual," it becomes comparable to a nation as compared to a state, which is characterized by its more temporary nature from the viewpoint of technology and innovation. Casmir goes on to clarify this fascinating distinction:

> Cultural efforts tend to include pride in accomplishing things in *traditional ways*. States, and the technologies they employ, take pride in doing things in *new* ways, in change, in development, in nonstatic endeavors. . . . Whereas *nations* deal with spiritual aspects and lasting values, *states* tend to deal with technological constructions which are limited in time. They pride themselves on not succumbing to traditional values, but rather, they point to the fact that in their "purest form," modern states are based on science and a "valueless reality." (10; emphasis added)

While it could be argued that Casmir is extremist in his call for a reassessment of earlier models of development and communication that focused on what he calls "Western injection-needle conceptualizations" (17) that are not always applicable to the non-Western world and culture, his views are worth examining for their holistic perspective. The meaninglessness of political independence without economic independence poignantly illustrates his argument and justifies his proposal for some form of interdependence in facing the "challenging task" of development that requires more than technological or political solutions" (21). Casmir seems to be suggesting that a culturally based participatory paradigm will be more rewarding than the dominant technologically based approach. Let us now examine what import Carnival as a popular and cultural phenomenon has for the participatory paradigm.

Carnival: Communication and Contradictions

Anyone with more than a casual exposure to the annual ritual of Brazilian Carnival will no doubt agree that this is one of the most spectacular events imaginable anywhere in the world in terms of national festivities. Seasoned observers, however, would also recognize the social, racial, and gender contradictions and conflicts that lie beyond the performative phenomenon. Brazil is often defined in terms of its three passions: Carnival, soccer, and *cachaça* (sugarcane gin). A closer analysis reveals that each of these social phenomena dramatizes the inherent contradictions of the Brazilian experience, be it from the viewpoint of sociology, anthropology, economics, culture, or communication. For the purpose of this chapter, I am exploring the role of communication and Carnival in Brazilian development drawing from what da Matta has rightly called "a rite of passage."[13]

The Afro-Brazilian samba schools, or *bloco carnavalesco*, are structured community organizations that function beyond preparing participants for Carnival. The carnival parade that lasts only three days may give the outsider-observer the illusion that its role is to promote fun/happiness and recuperation from the hardships of the previous year. The dynamics of popular participation may be analyzed from the viewpoint of these local organizations. The joint French-Brazilian film *Black Orpheus*, directed by Marcel Camus, is an interesting introduction for a carnival enthusiast.[14] It was produced at a time when Carnival was far less commercialized than it is today, yet the film still captured the popular flavor in its narrative depiction of the daily dramas that last all year, and not just on the three days of Carnival. While *Black Orpheus* has been criticized for its exoticism, idealism, and romantic view of life in the slums, it also provides a window into certain aspects of life that are not far removed from Carnival, such as the dreams and aspirations of both young and old to have a better life. Carlos Diegues's more recent version of the story, *Orfeu* (2000), also raises issues of participation. While this version is supposed to be the "authentically" Brazilian one, the issue of participation persists. Eurídice is now whitened, a significant commentary on racial democracy, and Orfeu, the classic lover, musician, and reveler, although still black, is now entangled in the world of drugs and gangs.

Samba is the primary musical form of Brazilian Carnival, and although its origins are in religious rituals that Africans brought to Brazil, it has become a popularly accepted music of "the greatest carnival of the world" through commercialization and tourism. Since the legitimization of samba and the commercialization of Carnival, the originality of composition and the camaraderie of the celebrants who get together to talk about life in general have given way to competition and individualism, thereby fostering exclusion of the poor who can not afford the luxury of paying for membership in samba schools or *blocos carnavalescos*.

The changing roles of the "escolas" have been attributed to a large-scale invasion by the middle class. Originally, participating in Carnival was simply a matter of social interaction, relaxation, and having fun.[15] As one of the elderly *sambistas* observed recalling the early years of Portela:[16] "Let me tell you what Carnival meant to me. It was our own thing. People made the greatest sacrifices; they even went hungry in order to parade on carnival day. They hocked their most precious possessions to buy their costumes and instruments. People wept when they couldn't parade. Once when my boss wouldn't give me the day off to parade, I quit my job! People really quit their jobs!" (*Escolas de samba em desfile*, 78).

From the development communication perspective, Casmir's notion that culture functions as a form of spirituality and model of reality is confirmed in the foregoing confession. For if Carnival becomes such a fanatical passion that it leads would-be-participants to quit their jobs to parade for only three days in Carnival, the question arises what happens after Carnival? The stressful daily routine is usually not worth the price versus losing a once-a-year opportunity to participate in Carnival. Hence, giving up one's job is. to the "traditional" person, something heroic and fulfilling, while by contrast, the "modern" person sees this as sheer insanity. It is this traditional thought process, especially when it comes to development, that communication strategies could be useful in transforming or enhancing. Although cultural and popular manifestations such as Carnival and soccer have been criticized in such films as Carlos Diegues's *Escola de samba, alegria de viver* and Joaquim Pedro de Andrade's *Garrincha, alegria do povo* as alienating and escapist, without such initial efforts at documenting popular culture, there would be no avenues for social commentary and criticism that eventually lead to change and transformation.

By contrast, modern Carnival, especially the parades in Rio de Janeiro, has lost traditional spontaneity and has become tourist oriented and overly structured, competitive, and regimented in order to comply with the rules of the parade. It is no longer a popular "street parade" where any interested party many join in; it is now a parade for show, for the hedonistic satisfaction of tourists who can afford expensive clubs, for personal (and corporate) promotion, for interschool competition, and for governmental grants and prizes awarded to samba schools. According to Jório and Araújo, this sharp contrast is appropriately highlighted in "the break with authenticity and spontaneity in the schools, [and] the imposition of artificial forms based on exaggerated luxury. The groups are humble and poor, in contrast to the sophisticated exhibitions of wealth by the middle class" (296).

From this comparative perspective, samba schools have evolved from being at the service of the soul (i.e., the music) to being at the service of economic gain and ultimately of the government, from being alienated from power to being included and "empowered" by the same instrument of alienation.[17] A Brazilian anthropologist has described the contradictory world of Carnival as the only period of the year when social inequalities are harmonized, when hierarchy becomes almost nonexistent and the marginalized poor become heroes and powerful, if even for just three days: "During Carnival, the marginal people of the hillsides, the outlying slums, and the samba school become 'teachers,' 'professors,' and 'doctors' of rhythm and the samba. They instruct the middle and the upper classes of the world of the samba, roguery, and tricky movement, a world forged by the effort to survive on a meager salary in a consumer society marked by exploitation."[18]

Blocos carnavalescos such as Ilê-Aiyê (House of the World), Olodum (Celebrant), and Filhos de Gandhi (Children of Gandhi) in Salvador, Bahia, reveal a similar contradictory pattern in terms of popular participation. Afro-Bahian Carnival has something peculiar and different that is also becoming a national phenomenon: the process of so-called re-Africanization of Carnival that also has its advantages and disadvantages from the viewpoint of development and communication. To illustrate my analysis, I will limit myself to the Ilê-Aiyê, the very first Afro-Bahian organization, founded in 1974. I had the opportunity to interview Ilê-Aiyê's director, Antônio C. dos Santos, popularly known as "Vovô," in the course of my research on Brazilian Carnival.[19]

The idea of founding an Afro-Bahian carnival group such as "Ilê-Aiyê" in the mid-1970s was espoused with enthusiasm by many Bahians, in particular those such as Apolônio and Vovô, who had always wanted an exclusively "African" organization to express their Africanness,. As Vovô puts it: "It was one of those nights in Curuzu that the idea came up. We were simply chatting, having some drinks. . . . It was at the time of the Black Power movement, you know; then we thought of forming an organization for blacks only and with African motives."[20] Due to a power struggle, the original founders of Ilê-Aiyê (Vovô and Apolônio) had a falling out resulting in Apolônio founding another group under the name of "Orunmila," which did not survive.

Ilê-Aiyê actually started as a political organization or pressure group, an offshoot of the Movimento Negro Unificado (MNU; Unified Black Movement), which is known for various political agitations and a nationwide consciousness-raising drive. Vovô opines that the "movement" was becoming ineffective and redundant as an agent of change and that it was time to replace it with a more significant cultural organization that could address the real problems of the poor instead of just holding constant meetings organized and distributing a lot of black-consciousness pamphlets all over the country without bringing any significant change or making any contributions to the overall quality of life of the marginalized poor.

Oepen rightly described this situation as a "dichotomy,"[21] while calling for "community communication" to bridge the gap between the old and the new paradigms of development communication.[22] Vovô seems to agree that Ilê-Aiyê was an organization formed as an effort to change the static intellectual and bureaucratic character of the MNU: "Our message was clearer and specific: it was the festival; it was the spectacle. The directorate of the Unified Black Movement meet and meet over and over without getting anything done. But we have changed a lot of things around here through

Carnival, without any discourse."[23] Vovô's disenchantment with the Unified Black Movement went beyond its function as an intellectual movement of change to its inability as an entity to take responsibility for effecting social change. The analogy Vovô is drawing here is intended to show the extent to which Ilê-Aiyê evolved as a social organization. My own reservation about such social change stems from my belief that the long-term achievements of Ilê-Aiyê as a community organization are questionable. Once a community organization achieves popular acceptance, it becomes more of a symbol than an actual agent of change, at least from the viewpoint of popular participation and beneficial community activities.

The "things" Vovô claims to have achieved through his community organization may be divided into two main phases: before becoming a carnival group to reckon with, and after. One of the major criticisms that could be leveled against Ilê-Aiyê as an organization is its irrevocable stance not to allow white membership, a policy that renders it a racially segregated community organization. Although there are more blacks in Salvador than whites, the trap of exclusionism is that it may turn the very people responsible for the marginalization of the poor—whom Ilê-Aiyê claims to defend—against them, thereby defeating its purpose. Oakley and Marsden have warned of the risk of focusing on a given group at the expense of another: "This focus poses the danger of actually excluding from analysis those groups in society who might be responsible for the process of impoverishment. We need to be able to see both sides of the coin" (*Approaches to Participation,* 11).

The year-long period between carnival celebrations represents a time for researching the theme of the next Carnival, organizing social activities, attending symposia, and releasing recordings with special social themes such as "Black Women and Empowerment," "Saving the Children and Their Future," "Black Beauty," "Drought and Hunger," "Blackness and Power," and so forth. The limitations I find in these social activities, however well intended, stem from their audience. Participants are often journalists, researchers, and active members of outside community organizations; therefore, they end up not meeting the immediate needs of the poor in terms of community participation and empowerment.

Moreover, publicity seems to be limited to pamphlets made available only at the headquarters of the organization on specific nights of *bênção* (blessing) or *ensaios* (rehearsals) and not through the mass media. Publicity seems to be restricted to the interpersonal, which may be acceptable and feasible for a smaller *bloco carnavalesco,* but for a medium-sized community organization such as the Ilê-Aiyê, such channels of communication are very limited indeed. This limitation is due in part to the undemocratic nature of the organization. Vovô is the director-president for life, his mother is the coordinator of operations, his wife is the chief costume designer, while other members of the family are involved with research on the costumes, design, and theme for the next Carnival.

Another limiting factor is that Ilê-Aiyê is unable to employ full-time employees when it is not carnival season, resulting in a typical family operation due to lack of funding other than what is generated by Carnival. The fact that Ilê-Aiyê must be self-sufficient in the carnival off-season makes it dependent on sale proceeds from T-shirts, organization paraphernalia, and postcarnival or other special recordings with renowned artists such as Gilberto Gil, Caetano Veloso, Maria Bethânia, and more recently, Daniela Mercury.

Intraorganizational communication is personal and is usually supportive of individual efforts toward achieving organizational goals. Although there is a frequent discontent about Vovô's ideals and leadership, such comments are only communicated discreetly, if at all. There is a risk of being perceived as disloyal if discontent is openly expressed. I observed an organizational culture that "enforced" a subtle code of silence and conformism. It is alleged, for example, that Vovô often gives the authorities lower figures in terms of the number of participants in the carnival parade, and by so doing is able to get more income from registering participants above the allowable limit. Ilê-Aiyê is expected to register only a thousand participants, but it is not unusual to register three thousand because of its popularity as the founding institution among Afro-Bahian groups. Moreover, since participants do not always participate every day of the parade, such fraud is more difficult to detect.

For his part, Vovô has become a symbol of achievement and entrepreneurial acumen that has brought pride to the wider community of Liberdade, Curuzu, and Salvador. Since coming of age in the mid-eighties, Ilê-Aiyê boasts two gigantic structures that it built from scratch. The buildings house employees, members of Vovô's immediate family, the organization's office, and a rehearsal hall. Despite this community pride, there is a wide socioeconomic gap between Ilê-Aiyê as an organization and its members and the rest of the community. While Vovô is able to travel abroad and attend international conferences and symposia, the rest of the organization rarely receives little by way of benefits. In the mid-nineties the group was able to travel to perform in the United States in such states as New York, California, and Louisiana. In addition, a few management-level members have also had the opportunity to travel to the United States for English as a Second Language training to enhance the emerging global nature of Bahian culture and marketing. The irony remains that the organization is held together by family members and mostly volunteer *sambistas* who derive their compensation from the popularity and applause they receive from the audience.

Shortly before Carnival, however, the entire atmosphere becomes more dynamic and involving. Publicity tends to increase and become more targeted, and the organization achieves greater financial stability members strive to catch up with their monthly contributions toward their *Fantasia* or Carnival costume. This is a time when interpersonal communication is at its best because of a heightened awareness, as the activities and themes of different community organizations take on aspects of a contest. Whoever has memorized the lyrics of the carnival music of a given *bloco* seems to gain the respect of community members, for in the final analysis, it is the popularity of a particular musical piece that often determines its success in the carnival parade competition.

In terms of thematic concerns, Ilê-Aiyê initiated a rotating focus on different African countries, from Egypt to Madagascar. This musical diffusion of African consciousness is fascinating. The orality of the medium makes it effective as it appeals to both literate and illiterate listeners. Aesthetically, Ilê-Aiyê also expresses its chosen theme through the costume design. For example, if the theme of a given year is "Egypt," the costume may bear the Nefertiti symbol, colorful Egyptian hieroglyphics, and related symbols. However, not everyone can afford the financial cost of the musical production or costumes. Other than listening to the music at rehearsals and on the radio, most community members, especially those earning the minimum wage, are unable to afford membership dues or costumes,. I remember the sheer surprise of many of my Brazilian friends when I paraded with Ilê-Aiyê in 1987 when the theme for that year was Nigeria.

While the ideal of "Africanization" of Carnival was part of the justification for forming Ilê-Aiyê, there is no indication that this process goes beyond the "propaganda" of Carnival. Indeed, Vovô is not considered a spokesperson for the Bahian black community; his jurisdiction is limited to Curuzu and to interstate and international organizations. His interorganizational communication seems very limited because each organization protects its ideas for the next Carnival. Organizational loyalty is also often a problem, since a treasured composer or *sambista* in one carnival group may be lured by a better offer from another group. The most common pattern is for such a member to become a solo artist or to start another *bloco,* which was the case for João Jorge Santos Rodrigues, who left his position as Ilê-Aiyê's director of education to join and strengthen Olodum in 1983.

From the educational perspective, Ilê-Aiyê often takes credit for getting children off the streets and turning them into drummers, composers, and singers. This claim may be valid in terms of protecting the youth from possible gang-related fights and violence, but it does not negate the fact that these children will then gradually be inducted into the Ilê-Aiyê organization as potential replacements for possible defectors. While Ilê-Aiyê has good intentions in terms of rescuing abandoned children from roaming the streets, these children should be helped to get back on their feet and be reintegrated into the school system, not merely into the samba school that only has an ephemeral function during Carnival. In 2001, through a thirty-minute educational video titled *Ilê Aiyê*,[24] the group provided an overview of its educational project, mission, challenges, and prospects for the future in terms of establishing an Afrocentric school already operating as "Escola Mãe Hilda," named after Vovô's mother.

Just like Brazil, Carnival is full of contradictions. Although Ilê-Aiyê was born out of cultural resistance and militancy, it seems that this community organization, initially dedicated to social change, has given way to a cultural industry that expands at the expense of its marginalized poor. As a community organization, Ilê-Aiyê is a cultural force in Salvador, but its role and methods in terms of improving the quality of life for the city's poor need to be redefined.

The Myth of the Participatory Paradigm

Considering the limitations and distortions inherent in the political application of the paradigm, all participation remains a myth. Although well-meaning exponents may see participation as a form of empowerment, it may serve as a manipulative tool for those who use the appearance of participation to fulfill a hidden agenda that, in essence, maintains the status quo—that is, the pretext of change through cosmetic adjustments instead of structural alterations that can actually redress poverty.

Meaningful participation at the grassroots level can only take place when structural constraints are removed and communication becomes an integral part of the process, rather than perpetuating top-down directives that alienate more than they integrate. As Mohiuddin Alamgir points out in his 1988 article "Poverty Alleviation through Participatory Development" obstacles that make participation difficult include an inhospitable political climate, inadequacy of local leadership, authoritarian structures that inhibit democratic decision making, alienation of the poor and powerless, unequal access to factors of production, inadequate government policies or financial support, lack of participation by women, and inadequate infrastructure for generating true participation (99). Yet, participation is not totally impossible since many Bahians and blacks from different parts of Brazil and the rest of the world participate in Ilê-Aiyê, Olodum, and other *blocos afro(s)*, as well as in such *afoxés* as the Filhos de Gandhi. Participation may not be politically contradictory, but it offers some avenues for empowerment if well channeled over the long term.

The contention that Carnival creates the ambience of popular participation where these contradictions and contrasts are somewhat harmonized and neutralized is debatable. My exploration of Ilê-Aiyê as a microcosmic carnival organization reveals what Oakley and Marsden have already identified as the obstacles of participation. Interestingly, the foregoing case study exposes the truism that the peculiarity of Carnival as a moment of illusion also implies that there is a price to pay for participation in those three days of illusion and dream. It follows, then, that it does not make much difference whether the context is Carnival for the contradictions remain constant, although they are more creatively disguised during Carnival.

As Ilê-Aiyê illustrates, when an external regulatory system is not in place to ensure conformity to certain standards, community organizations can grow into powerful enterprises and in the process may acquire the potential and disposition to alienate the very community they are supposed to serve. Such organizations create dehumanizing and frustrating environments resulting in wasted human talent.[25] Although Ilê-Aiyê may not be totally out of touch with the community, the concern here is that the only way community members can improve their lives is by deriving more fulfilling socioeconomic benefits and access to power and participation than can be gained by the mere symbolism and pride of belonging to the organization.

As Pearse and Stiefel rightly point out in *Inquiry into Participation,* despite concerted effort to enforce popular participation through United Nations development programs, "an examination of the performance is not encouraging.... Authentic popular participation seldom occurs," which is why it is worthwhile to examine the reasons for the disconnect between intentions and outcomes.[26] Oakley and Marsden suggest three fundamental obstacles to participation: operational, cultural, and structural. Among operational factors are 1) overcentralized planning; 2) inadequate delivery mechanisms; 3) lack of coordination; 4) inappropriateness of project technology; 5) irrelevant project content; and 6) lack of local structures (30). From an operational perspective, Ilê-Aiyê faces all of these obstacles, especially the first and the last two.

In the case of Ilê-Aiyê, cultural obstacles are not related to resisting change; rather, they are more the result of a cycle of disempowerment that can only be redressed by both understanding and overcoming marginalization and dependence. These obstacles are thus more structural than cultural and as Oakley and Marsden suggest, operational and cultural obstacles both are intertwined with the structural support, or opposition, they receive. When a structure becomes as symbolic as Ilê-Aiyê, community members may become docile and voiceless out of fear of being perceived as going "against the grain" in the community and may be met with stiff opposition, humiliation, and even oppression: "The structure dictates the terms of participation and reacts oppressively if those terms are redefined; its aim is to keep the rural people in their place, as labor power and possibly as consumers. Participation initiatives emanating from below, therefore, are faced with the dilemma of attempting to flourish within the context of the existing structure or seeking positively to influence the structure" (31).

While Ilê-Aiyê functions more as a family business than as a community organization, it is difficult for members to perceive their true situation for their thinking is "whatever is good for Ilê-Aiyê is good for us." This family loyalty is well intended, but when it makes the members blind to their exploited status, it makes it even harder for these immediate members to see how the extended membership is exploited in the name of Carnival. In *Pedagogy of the Oppressed*, Paulo Freire advocates that the goal of participation should be "raising the consciousness" of the oppressed. Through such a liberating type of communication, participation becomes a consciousness-raising process by which the powerless are enabled to "perceive their *real* needs, identify their *real* constraints and plan to overcome problems" as a form of liberation instead of depending on "elite-dominated rationality."[27]

The participatory paradigm, I insist, is a myth, and the demystification comes from the models of reality that have been explored in this chapter. In the case of Bahia, the supposed "Africanization" project through carnival manifestations did not go beyond the few years of its conception in the late 1970s in terms of originality and ideology. Since the 1980s, the trend has been toward large-scale capitalization of the cultural industry and "negritude," an explosion of Afro-Bahian carnival groups while using a rhetoric of simplification and mythification to capture the vulnerability of a poorly informed populace: "All of a sudden, it is luxury, energy, similarities of Egypt with Bahia, which take care of Salvador through the powerful voice of *Olodum* singers, the Lord of the Universe, in search of the lost ark and the knowledge that Egypt is part and parcel of African thought. However, we blacks of Bahia are no longer slaves; let us free ourselves from the psychological currents; yes, we are men and women of African civilization."[28]

A tourist or naive observer might react to this pamphlet, distributed by Olodum during the 1987 Carnival, with enthusiasm and appreciation for the Olodum organization, which competes with Ilê-Aiyê. However, such propaganda tragically is disseminated shortly before and during Carnival in order to get participants in tune with the theme for that year, with the result that it loses its impact as an instrument of change. Indeed, few carnival participants are in the mood for such intellectualization of Carnival as a possibly mentally liberating phenomenon: they are more interested in escaping daily routine through music and dance.

In this power struggle, Vovô became a theorist, talking about dichotomy between "culture producers" and "culture explorers." Indeed, he may be offering a self-criticism and self-demystification without realizing it. As Ilê-Aiyê's leader, he could be accused of the same alienating practices. He criticized, for example, the exploitation of singers by white recording artists who were making a fortune from the popular musical piece "Faraó" (Pharaoh), which was written by Olodum for Carnival in 1987. He also frowned on foreign journalists who came to Brazil to film documentaries on these organizations without paying Ilê-Aiyê' for the right to do so. Essentially, Vovô is accusing external exploiters but fails to see the internal ones that he represents at the expense of the poor:

> In Bahia there are those who produce and those who exploit black culture. The Olodum music "Faraó" is circulating widely, but the singers are not the ones making the money; the music has been taken over by others.... Afro-Bahian groups provide jobs for many people who work forty-eight hours to make things succeed. This whole issue that black entities are there for the money is sheer political gimmickry. It is okay for whites to make money, but we are supposed to do everything for principle's sake and the "ideals," in defense of culture. Then come foreigners wanting to film us without paying a nickel and then take the documentary to Europe to make a lot of money. I send them packing right away.[29]

So long as self-interested leadership, centralized planning, and misplaced objectives remain the norm in community organizations, and so long as socioeconomic gaps continue to widen, the idea of popular participation will continue to be illusory and elusive. There is no question about the achievements of Ilê-Aiyê and other community organizations such as Olodum and Filhos de Gandhi, but the central issue is the need to decentralize, to empower and involve people at all levels (operational, cultural, and structural).

The decentralization of communication and the use of multiple channels of communication will also go a long way toward complementing this desirable effort at community participation. While I have identified through Afro-Bahian Carnival the myth of the participatory paradigm, it is far from being a hopeless situation, and with the right remedial measures, the whole participatory paradigm can be redefined. Development scholars need not give up in their commitment to this ideal: "References to participation are all-pervasive in both academic literature and project documentation, and the term 'participation' is increasingly influencing development practice across the board. It is true, however, that to date the rhetoric far outweighs the substance of, as opposed to the commitment to, the practice. But this practice is expanding and can be examined to reveal its major approaches and content."[30]

Conclusion: The Quest for Participation

This chapter's case study has attempted to answer the following questions: To what extent are the *escola de samba* or *bloco carnavalesco* organizations involved in community development? What role do they play in the community beyond preparing members and participants for Carnival? What is the definition of a participant? What does it mean to participate? Does the role of the participant change before, during, and after Carnival? How do the *escolas* and *blocos* serve their members? How do they articulate their concerns to the government and other groups? What is the role of communication in Carnival at both inter- and intraorganizational levels? In answering these questions, it has become evident that participation is a desirable alternative paradigm to the dominant top-down paradigm. The genuine need for such an inclusive process is more valid than the radical pursuit of alternatives.

An interview with Vovô conducted in the summer of 1999 in his Curuzu residence confirmed that not much had changed since the emergence of the group in 1974 in terms of popular participation and empowerment:

> Popular participation exists, but is limited to those who can afford to pay for their costumes in order to parade with the group during Carnival. Popular participation is very restricted in this sense, but when you consider the beautiful colors that take over the streets, the enthusiasm of the people, and just the excitement of seeing themselves on the streets with such a pride in their African origins, it is a phenomenal spectacle for the people. Otherwise, Carnival has become very elitist and even racist. I have even been personally accused of being racist because I insist on keeping the group exclusively for blacks only to show that we can organize ourselves without some white opportunist coming to take advantage of our sweat. Perhaps we have not been recognized or ever won any carnival competition because we refuse to sell out our spiritual ideals and cultural beliefs. I think that what we are struggling with is how to obtain power without being co-opted by the system. That is our challenge. We want power. Carnival is only a means to an end.[31]

Ilê Aiyê is waging a cultural battle to retain its Afrocentric image and consciousness while at the same time struggling to compete for recognition from a system that sees its ideology as radical, revolutionary, and counter to the global market. But popular participation becomes a luxury, for the organization cannot afford to allow everyone who wants to parade to participate without some financial contribution. And this is where the paradox lies. Ilê Aiyê projects an image of cultural power, yet its lack of economic power forces the organization constantly to negotiate on the issue of popular participation. This weakness has severely affected its ability to include the people it claims to represent. Its challenge now is to expand the parameters of popular participation by enabling participants to generate economic power through improved educational opportunities and acquisition of skills that will make them more marketable.

To reverse the top-down process that has thwarted the realization of this paradigm, there will have to be continuous training and development. Another possibility is the use of external agents to complement this process as facilitators and agents of change through forming groups, gaining their trust, expressing solidarity with their concerns, and helping them develop at the grassroots level. In order to avoid a radical change that ends up isolating participants, a joint coalition of efforts may have the best chance of succeeding. The solution will not come from further isolation of those who should benefit from development; rather, it will be a result of forming a network of progressive popular organizations that foster participation and partnership. Without these structural changes, participation will indeed continue to be a myth.

7

Film and Fragmentation

> In Brazil, the apparent inclusionism of "racial democracy" masks fundamental exclusions from social power. Indeed, the phrase "racial democracy" itself encodes a blame-the-victim strategy. If Brazil is democratic, the phrase implies, then blacks have only themselves to blame if they do not succeed.
>
> —Robert Stam, *Tropical Multiculturalism*

The technologizing of the process of dehumanization through cinema provides a vivid window into the subtle reenactment of slavery in the Brazilian context. In this substitution of methods, chains are replaced with demeaning and caricatural costumes, padlocks with fragmentation and silencing of the voice, rape with the perverse desire of the mulatta (mixed-race woman), domestication with the "chickenization," "zombification," and "buffoonization" of black actors. As a result, while Brazil may be said to possess an Afro-Brazilian soul through African cultural presence, the political structure is dominantly and alienatingly white and this explains the fragmentation of that very soul as reflected in the Afro-Brazilian personality. In our examination of select films produced between 1950 and 2000 for the purpose of highlighting the gradual process of the caricaturizing of Afro-Brazilian actors as well as a very few cases of subtle resistance, heroism, and subversion, this chapter provides an exposé of the multiple representations of the Afro-Brazilian.

In film and other visual or print media, critical thinking is not necessarily common. The guardians and gatekeepers of culture in its dissemination and marketing are duly aware of this trap: fatal and yet attractive consumption of demeaning representations by the subject of that subtle dehumanization. The visual medium has always been construed as the most effective tool of mass communication, of the popularization and propagation of ideas. And therein lies its power and potential for the manipulative destruction or construction of the mind. The Afro-Brazilian in this sense has been a tool in the hands of foreign filmmakers who troop to Brazil in search of the documentation of newly found South American *exótica*. This explains why a mesmerizing film such as *Orfeu negro* (Black Orpheus), a 1958 Franco-Brazilian coproduction, still raises questions about stereotypical images though it was made seventy years after official abolition of slavery, especially the era of its production. It is as if anything other than distortion of reality is unmarketable and thus not worthy of representation. Even Brazilian filmmakers are so constrained by budgets and politics that they are compelled to self-censor their representations or be censored strategically. The result is the projection of customized and propagandist images that reduce the Afro-Brazilian to a less than equal object of cultural and commercial exploitation.

The counter-discursive framework that Afro-Brazilian cinema represents within the entire Brazilian film industry is politically stifled as it cannot truly exercise its function as the eye of the people it supposedly represents since the eye behind the camera is that of the other it contests and claims to displace. My position lies in the ongoing struggle between the beneficiary and the benefactor as well as in the problematic of representation that D. N. Rodowick captured as a "crisis of political modernism":

> For film theory in particular and theories of cultural representation in general, the decades of the sixties and seventies will deservedly be remembered as a singularly productive era. However, to the extent that particular correlations of "text" and "subject" are the most striking constants in the diverse theoretical formulations of this period, and to the extent that these discourses were defined as a form of "political" inquiry or activity, a curious relation was established between aesthetic practice and aesthetic theory. (*The Crisis of Political Modernism* 273)

If a "theory" is at work here, it is more in the cinematic "fragmentation" of both the text and the subject as they undergo a commercial transformation toward ultimate selective consumption by the elite for whom and by whom a given film is produced.

Historicizing "Afro-Brazilian" Cinema

The idea of mapping the history of "Black cinema" in Brazil is itself fraught with contradictions. The first is that of representation. Depending on the time frame of production, Afro-Brazilians were for the most part absent from the screen; then portrayed as "slaves," "domestics," and objectified or caricatural figures who barely represent local color; while finally graduating to "exotic" figures who, while attempting to be self-assertive, also face the distortion of that self through a compromise with official deracialized consciousness or racial democracy. The second contradiction is what Robert Stam has called "Hollywood-centrism," whereby similar to the case of the national cinema, Afro-Brazilians are still not in a position of power to project their own image except as rendered by foreign or national directors who have the financial means to market distorted reality as they please. The Hollywood reference captures the multinational and economic imperatives that determine the control of cultural production in Brazil today, whether in content or form.

Stam's *Tropical Multiculturalism* provides the most authoritative and comparative history of race in the Brazilian cinematic industry to date and in any language. Theorizing on "racialized representations" (22) of Brazilian cinema over a period of a hundred years, Stam debunks stereotypical images of Afro-Brazilians, questions their absence, and contrasts his assumptions and conclusions with the North American experience. Such a comparison, while enriching, ends up in an imposition or adaptation of concepts such as "multiculturalism" that are not actually applicable in Brazil. Here is Stam defining his methodology: "As a critical method, multiculturalism places diverse peoples and communities in relation, always bearing in mind the history of European domination over the last five centuries. In this sense, many Brazilian artistic movements—modernismo in the 1920s, Tropicalism in the 1960s—can be seen as multiculturalist *avant la lettre*" (17). The suggestion that Brazilian modernism and Tropicalism are "multiculturalist" is an absolutist generalization, for both movements were elitist and did not include the majority of Afro-Brazilians whose cultural manifestations are folklorically thematized and musically recuperated while still remaining marginalized and condemned to the favela lifestyle. *Tropical Multiculturalism's* claim of "shared history" of conquest and oppression between the United States and Brazil from the antiracist viewpoint of the author equally downplays the fundamental difference between these two countries, which Carl Degler examines in *Neither Black nor White*. The representation of the African American within the time frame engaged by Stam contrasts sharply with that of the Afro-Brazilian within the same period in terms of rapid political gains and visibility. While Afro-Brazilians continue to be portrayed as exotic, primitive, folkloric, and naive, they equally continue to be underrepresented in the overall Brazilian cinematic industry.

As was the case with Brazilian theater, the burden of "modernization" of Brazilian cinema fell into the hands of European immigrants such as Segreto who did not have any moral responsibility to correct the oppressive images of Afro-Brazilians, especially with regard to slavery and the implied "inferiority" of blacks in the racial "Eldorado." As a result, instead of portraying blacks as human, resistant, and courageous in the face of oppression, the film-makers turned to the exaltation of the Indian as a way of avoiding the complexity of slavery. In cases where Afro-Brazilians are portrayed—such as in *Sinhá moça* (1953), *João negrinho* (1954), *Orfeu negro* (1958), *Bahia de todos os santos* (1960), *O pagador de promessas* (1962), *Barravento* (1962),

Ganga Zumba (1963) *Antônio das mortes* (1969), *Macunaíma* (1969), *Amuleto de Ogum* (1975), *Tenda dos milagres* (1976), *Xica da Silva* (1976), *A força de Xangô* (1979), *Eles não usam Black Tie* (1981), *A prova de fogo* (1981), *Chico rei* (1982), *Quilombo* (1984), *Jubiabá* (1987), *Orfeu* (1999), and *Cidade de Deus* (2002)—the struggle continues to be with their representation, not as they would want to be portrayed but as the expediency of commercialization and reductionism dictates. Furthermore, the exigency of the exotica-conscious market that makes profit through willful distortion of reality seems alluring and increasingly insurmountable. In most of these films, the Afro-Brazilian is usually foregrounded, objectified, fragmented, manipulated into a symbolic heroism, and finally diminished to the function of local color. The presence of Afro-Brazilians is thus only useful to the extent of buttressing the diversity of Brazilian culture but not necessarily a significant political entity worth recognizing. In very few cases, such as *Jubiabá, Ganga Zumba, Quilombo,* and *Xica da Silva,* where rebellion and revolt clearly inform the plots, the subversion of the dominant hegemonic structure appears more cosmetic and symbolic than a concrete attainment of political power.

In his compelling study of Afro-Brazilian cinema, *O negro brasileiro e o cinema,* João Carlos Rodrigues goes beyond the traditional "stereotypical" images of blacks as "lazy," "savage," and "roguish" to a listing of twelve provocative and incisive "archetypes and caricatures" (15). In their diversity and interconnectedness, these denigrating images sum up the various characters and representations that define the Afro-Brazilian image in Brazilian cinema: old black sage or griot, black mammy, martyr, black skin/white heart, noble savage, rebellious black, nigger, "malandro" (rogue), slum-dweller, crazy black, good mulatta, and muse.

"Pretos velhos," or old black sages, represent the West African griot figure in the Afro-Brazilian context.[1] Unlike other negative figures and images, a "preto velho" is a noble storyteller who is able to recount tales, legends, and family genealogies through the oral tradition as passed down from generation to generation. As the guardian of collective memory, the "preto velho," who may be either male or female, narrates the conflicting relationships between masters and slaves, their tensions, expectations, and frustrations, while retaining a sense of dignity, wisdom, and humor in the delivery of these tales and accounts. While this archetypal figure is more common in Afro-Brazilian folklore and literature, its manifestation in cinema has been reduced to a conformist personality as opposed to a militant figure, as in the films *Sinhá moça* and *O saci.*

Of so many dehumanizing stereotypical images, that of the mammy figure is perhaps the most disturbing. As a result of overall oppressive status, Afro-Brazilian women have been defined and objectified by others, especially the dominant culture. The controlling image of the "mãe preta," or black mammy, in which a black slave woman is supposed to be giving her own milk to help raise white children instead of her own is doubly oppressive. While this figure has been romantically represented in Brazilian literature by José de Alencar, Jorge de Lima, and Machado de Assis, among many others, its popular manifestation in television and film is more provocative, as in many *telenovelas* (soap operas) celebrating the black mammy and in the film *João negrinho* (1958).

The martyr figure faces up to the caprices and atrocities of the masters by subjecting himself to their various forms of horrendous torture in the name of dignity and resistance to slavery and oppression. In *Xica da Silva*, Teodoro is one such figure; Zumbi also exudes a martyrlike personality in *Quilombo;* while the black labor activist Milton Gonçalves, in *Eles não usam Black Tie* (They Don't Wear Black Tie) is murdered not only for his activism but for his blackness. In the character referred to as "Negro de alma branca" (black skin/white heart) lies a sharp contrast to the martyr. This "good nigger" who seems to know his place and hurts no one, is the quintessential "traitor" of his race, as depicted by Ismael in Nelson Rodrigues's powerful play *Anjo negro* (1948) and in a number of films, such as *João negrinho* and *Também somos irmãos* (1949). Another contrast is found in the characters of the "noble savage" as opposed to the "rebellious black." While the former is depicted in the protagonist of *Xico rei* (1985), who pays with his own labor to buy the freedom of his people; the latter is the classic Zumbi in *Quilombo*, who kills himself in order to avoid arrest by whites.

In view of their susceptibility to manipulation and contextual appropriations, especially in Brazil's "racial paradise," these images may be totally negative in one situation, and absolutely "plausible" in another, but not without their subtle connotations of inferiority and negativity. The image of the "nigger," which connotes the "good for nothing" individual and "bloody rapist" as in *A Menina e o estuprador* (The Little Girl and the Rapist, 1983) or even the homosexual figure as in Adolfo Caminha's *O bom crioulo* (The Good Nigger, 1895), portrays the Afro-Brazilian in his most bestial and ridiculous state. Yet, the term "nigger" is used, among Afro-Brazilians, as a referential signifier for the resistant and "good black" who somehow resonates the figure of the "malandro" or "rogue" in terms of ambivalence, subversion, and ingenuity. Equally associated with Èṣù, the god of the crossroads, confusion, and freedom, this "roguish" figure, in films like *Macunaíma, Bahia de todos os santos,* and *Jubiabá* among others, suggests that the Afro-Brazilian, whether in the era of slavery or "modernity," is by nature "untrustworthy," "dubious," and "unreliable." These are the images that crush the mind while gradually dehumanizing the self into a manipulatable and vulnerable consciousness.

Unlike the images that are situated within the slavery era and its history, in modern times stereotypes have taken a more urban tonality in both the figures of the "favelado" (slum-dweller) and "crioulo doido" (crazy nigger) who are seen as marginal, infantile, and playful. In the case of the slum-dweller specifically, idealism, blind felicity, and revelry often combine with alienation to produce a figure best illustrated by most of the characters in *Orfeu negro* (Black Orpheus) and the music of Vinícius de Morães, in particular "Felicidade" (Happiness). This figure also manifests itself in abandoned children, the "street terrors" who will later graduate into rogues as they grow up on the streets learning survival skills as in *Moleque Tião* or *Rio 40*.

The mulatta constitutes the pivotal figure in whom Brazilian racial mythology is synthesized as the sum total of sensuality, promiscuity, and beauty. Both desirable and yet despicable given her "prostitute" figure, she is considered the ultimate necessary evil as she is often exploited in film, fiction, and reality. What Degler calls the "mulatto escape hatch" (*Neither Black nor White*, 219), on which the Brazilian racial utopia rests, serves as a theoretical and propagandist tool in both literature and popular culture, especially in such films as *Xica da Silva* (1976) and *Anjos da noite* (1987). A sharp contrast to the mulatta is the figure of the muse, who represents an idealist figure of the black prima donna. While such writers as Luís Gama, Cruz e Souza, and Abdias do Nascimento have attempted to represent this figure, it has yet to be popularized in Afro-Brazilian film. The Afro-Brazilian soul struggles not only for legitimacy on the screen but also for the recuperation of the fragmented self in day-to-day living. It is a struggle best captured in the conflict between whitening and self-preservation.

From Exoticism to Whitening

The idea of whitening may appear appealing to Afro-Brazilians who find themselves carrying the painful burden of blackness on a daily basis.[2] Yet, the whole story is yet to be told by critics who project this ideology as being acceptable to Afro-Brazilians without any form of struggle or resistance. As Twine points out, "the 'whitening ideology' was originally coined by the Brazilian elite to reconcile theories of scientific racism with the reality of the predominantly nonwhite population of the country" (*Racism* 87–88). Anything other than white must be "exoticized" to be acceptable and nonthreatening to that racist ideology of white supremacy. In the field of popular culture, especially the cinematic industry, that ideology is best illustrated by three popular films: *Orfeu negro, Macunaíma,* and *Xica da Silva*.

Comparatively, these films reenact societal prejudices and stereotypes—for example, the illusion of greatness and happiness during the three days of carnival in *Orfeu negro;* the stigma of color and laziness as in the portrayal of the eternal child Macunaíma whose only aspiration of bettering herself is to become white in *Macunaíma;* and the negotiation of power through mulatta sensuality and manipulation of the white master and conqueror, in *Xica da Silva*. In these three cases, death to self and negation of identity symbolize the ultimate imperative to regeneration and survival. Orfeu pays with his life in order to join Eurydice, his desired lover; Macunaíma dies at the end of his voyages around the nation in search of his identity; while Xica dies a spiritual death by realizing the insignificance of her superficial power as the lover of a powerful white man. The carnivalesque spirit runs through these transformations and deaths that serve as allegories of exoticism and whitening in the eye of the camera and that of the cineast.

Exoticism is mega-marketing, an appealing "Blaxploitation" tool that echoes a different plantation through the screen. The notion that Afro-Brazilians are "lazy" and "lascivious" is supposedly worth going to see at the movies—as Macunaíma is born, raised, and groomed as such, thus reinforcing the stereotype that was rampant throughout the slavery era. In the same vein, Orfeu could not be satisfied with one woman, Mira, to whom he is supposedly engaged. A powerful mythology, that of Orpheus and Eurydice, must be reinvented in order for Orfeu to be seen as "unfaithful" yet doomed to descend into hell with Eurydice in search of his true love. In her own right, Xica is the ultimate embodiment of "whitening" as she dramatically sells her body, through intelligence and manipulation of course, in order to seduce her white master—her only possible "savior" and "redeemer" from her misery and slavery. In spite of her given and won "freedom," she still discovers she is not allowed into the church like other whites. And herein lies the shock and fallacy of racial democracy. Her luxurious cosmetic gown and artificial freedom could not get her into the symbol of perfection and divinity which the church represents just as Zé-do-Burro was forbidden to pay his pledge in *O pagador de promessas* because he made it to a Candomblé goddess, Iansan, as opposed to a Catholic saint, Santa Barbara.[3] This artificial conflict is geared toward separating the "good" and the supreme race from the "evil" and inferior one, which nonetheless is stereotypically attractive due to its transnational market potential.

Cinematic Fragmentation and Questionable Contestation

Marilena Chaui's notion of duplicity and ambiguity in Brazilian popular culture as theorized in *Conformismo e resistência* holds true for the screen as well, especially when seen from the viewpoint of the challenges Afro-Brazilians face in the negotiation of their representation. The manipulation of blackness in all its ramifications into a source of entertainment and instrument of economic gain even when the ideology of resistance is apparently present makes representation very problematic. On the one hand, Afro-Brazilians want their culture to be represented yet they do not have any control over the manner by which those cultural values are used for counterideological motives and officially sponsored Brazilian racial mythology. On the other hand, to contest such a representation as racist is to evoke the wrath of the cultural power brokers, who may decide not to represent Afro-Brazilians at all. How do Afro-Brazilians negotiate their representation with cultural producers? Do they have the power of negotiation at all? An exploration of a number of "popular" films illustrates the mechanism of fragmentation, resistance, and recuperation of the Afro-Brazilian soul on screen.

Orfeu Negro: Carnival as Eroticism, Exoticism, and Rebirth

Directed by Marcel Camus and produced by a joint Franco-Brazilian venture in 1958, *Orfeu negro* (Black Orpheus), the cinematic adaptation of the play by Vinícius de Moraes, *Orfeu da conceição: Tragédia carioca*, has been praised as "a dazzling combination—a riotously colorful tapestry of carnival tumult and pulsating music"[4] and "well laced with exoticism."[5] And it is in this combination of the "dazzling" and the "exotic" that the film finds its folkloric and international appeal. The challenging process of defolklorization, which according to Michael Hanchard's argument, lies in critical historicism that confronts the prejudices of the Afro-Brazilian present and establishes experiential connections with global forces in the New World,[6] locates *Orfeu negro* as an Afro-Brazilian paradigmatic film of contestation and conformism. While the film was adapted from Vincius de Moraes's play, the focus here is more on the film version, which has taken on a more compelling yet reductionist life of its own.

The Orpheus myth, which has many variants, serves as an allegory of Afro-Brazilians' present descent into "hell" in search of their romantic past rooted in the love of Africa, represented by Eurydice. The film manipulates this metaphor of the past and that of the "backward glance," Orpheus's tragic flaw without which Eurydice will continue to be his, or at least will be found and recuperated. The story of love overlaps with that of Carnival and the Afro-Brazilian experience to produce perhaps a riveting documentary of legend, legacy, and history. The plot revolves around Orpheus, a trolley conductor, and Eurydice, his girlfriend who, mythically, has been his true lover since the beginning of time, and the conflict between her and Mira, who is engaged to Orpheus, hence jealous of the excessive attention Eurydice.

Orfeu negro opens and ends with the enchanting carnivalesque music composed by Vinícius de Moraes, "Felicidade" (Happiness), and sung by Antônio Carlos Jobim in which the irony and illusion of happiness that Carnival represents for most Brazilians are best captured in the contrastive refrain, "Sadness is unending; happiness for sure." The reality of working for a whole year, saving toward the dream of robing oneself with an ephemeral costume that disappears after Carnival, only to quickly return to the daily poverty that is the norm foregrounds the opposing socioeconomic forces operating in Brazil among the different social classes. The sharp contrastive image of poor Afro-Brazilians who live on the hilltop (*morro*) and that of those living in metropolitan Rio de Janeiro sets the tone for the value of Carnival as the moment of what da Matta calls "neutralization of hierarchies," a moment when "the barriers of social position are suspended" (*Carnivals* 207). Yet, from the beginning to the end of the film, the suspension of these hierarchies only points to an illusion as the poor are compelled to spend all their money on costumes for a momentary escape from poverty, as Serafina confesses to the bread-seller: "Thank you for the offer, but I spent everything on my carnival costume."

Structurally, the myth of Orpheus, the myth of Carnival, the myth of perfect love, and the myth of racial democracy all combine to complicate a story of love, carnival, and life. As Jared Banks notes in "Cinematic Adaptation," *Orfeu negro* symbolically engages the ritualistic dualities of ascent/descent, life/death, birth/rebirth, innocence/experience, degeneration/regeneration, and love/hate in a captivating rendering of the dramas of Rio de Janeiro's slum-dwellers (*favelados*)—a microcosm of the Brazilian dilemma. The principal characters—Orpheus, Eurydice, Mira, and Serafina—reinforce the racial democracy myth while the secondary ones—Chico, the costume makers, the revelers at rehearsals and real carnival parades—are depicted as "happy" and "content" in spite of their lowly status in the society. Chico, for example, is depicted as a fool who has no memory of his own, and who simply repeats what Serafina tells him although he belongs to the Naval Force and has come all the way from Montevideo to visit her lover. At work here is the process of Bakhtin's theory of carnivalization and transgression. As Stam points out:

> In carnival, all that is marginalized and excluded—the mad, the scandalous, the aleatory—takes over the center in a liberating explosion of otherness. The principle of material body—hunger, thirst, defecation, copulation—becomes a positively corrosive force, and festive laughter enjoys a symbolic victory over death, over all that is held sacred, over all that oppresses and restricts. (*Subversive Pleasures* 86)

In the final scene, when Orpheus is carrying the corpse of Eurydice in his arms, he sings to the lyrics of "Happiness" with which the film begins, as if betraying his own conscious subconscious, with the implication that it was all an illusion. In this dreamlike fantasy captured in the Carnival that has just ended and has handed him Eurydice's still body as opposed to the vibrant soul and energy to which he was first attracted, Orpheus is stuck in the middle: unable to move on and yet unable to forget the romantic past.

Taking each character or entity as a "liberating explosion of otherness" and a "symbolic victory over death" and, principally, over oppression in all its forms, one cannot say with all certainty that this "victory" goes beyond mere symbolism. Eurydice dies in the arms of the very lover who has done everything to save her, while Orpheus loses both his celestial love (Eurydice) and his terrestrial "passion" (Mira) through the "backward glance" and inevitable death. He must die in order to join Eurydice in heaven, or in hell. In both the Macumba ceremony and the final scene, Orpheus' lack of faith and his insistence on looking backward cost him the Eurydice of his life. Mira kills her beloved Orpheus through anger, jealousy, and the stone she throws at Orpheus, transferring all her hate into a decisive act of revenge. In that revenge, she also loses Orpheus to death. The grocery shop owner's love for kisses from his buyers who would rather kiss than pay for their purchases; Serafina's enchantment with visiting the buffoonized Chico; the boys' interest in knowing whether Orpheus could make the sun rise with his music; the revelers' dancing escapades and fantasies with the exuberant and alluring Mira; and the little girl at the end of the film who actually symbolizes the reinvention of Eurydice, all are located within the carnivalesque mode of temporary pleasures and permanent deaths. Every character operates within a mode of fragmentation, its temporary subversion, and a vicious return to a fragmentated state.

In spite of Marcel Camus' exotic rendering of tragedy, the appealing transformation of love into death, and the implied resurrection at the end of the film, Orpheus, the principal character, is far from being a hero. Of course, he commits a tragic flaw by killing his love unintentionally, yet his own "death" is more symbolic than real. Orpheus is torn throughout the film by the contradictory forces of love and life. In attempting to escape reality, he is further pushed into the abyss of myth, and in this sense, he remains a mythic hero even if he joins legendary Eurydice in death.

From the viewpoint of female representation, most of the women are portrayed as vain, superficial, and sensational. Mira, who is engaged to Orpheus, is a dominant figure; she is not only greedy but extremely jealous. She is obsessed with Orpheus's relationship with Eurydice and when she suspects Orpheus's infidelity, she quickly warns him: "If I see her with you, I will end her life." Mira's strong personality contrasts with that of Eurydice, who is passive and shy, but admirable. Serafina and other women in charge of carnival costume are manipulative and intriguing. It seems as if the cineast is suggesting that weak and obedient women are more attractive, while the likes of Mira are to be condemned. In fact, both Mira and Serafina seem to be dependent on their men for love and money. Mira bought her own engagement ring out of desperation, whereas Serafina was almost nostalgic of Chico's presence, and his return was quite a fulfilling event for Serafina. This representation of women as manipulative, sensuous, and naive is not restricted to Afro-Brazilian women—Brazilian women of other races are similarly portrayed in a denigrating and degrading manner in such films as *Macunaíma* and *Pixote*.

In a more recent version of the Orpheus mythology and its adaptations, the classical film version directed by Marcel Camus, *Orfeu negro* now gives way to Cacá Diegues's *Orfeu* (1999), which was previewed in New York. Unlike the tame and exotic rendition of the earlier version, Diegues's interpretation blends shocking realism with what Ivaldo Costa calls "banalization of violence" ("Orfeu...") in terms of the superimposition of the drug trafficking underworld on a rather festive and musical film. In the struggle to produce a realistic film, Diegues may be accused of excessive compensation and consciousness of the limitations of Camus' interpretation in the 1958 original. Yet, the fragmentation continues: Eurydice, played by Patrícia França, as opposed to Marpessa Dawn (black) in the Camus film, is now a mulatta while Orfeu, played by Toni Garrido, is black. The elimination of "black" in the title of the new version also raises a question. Does this mean that Brazil is becoming more and more racially democratic in the new millennium? I suggest that it simply means that Brazil will continue to grapple with socioeconomic, political, and racial inequalities that fragment not only the Afro-Brazilian population but the entire carnivalesque land of contrasts and ambiguities. The elimination of "black" from the title could also be interpreted as an attempt to claim the film as a "national" source of pride and shame and not an exclusively Afro-Brazilian experience.

O Pagador de Promessas: The Limits of Religious Syncretism

Produced by Anselmo Duarte within the context of the Cinema Novo movement of the early sixties, a period of opposition and contestation against dominant foreign models and commercial Brazilian cinema, *O pagador de promessas* (Payment as Pledged, 1962) was heralded as merging a nonconformist approach to the portrayal of contemporary Brazilian social problems with a rebellious regional consciousness. The religious syncretism that is already broached in the Macumba divination scene in *Orfeu negro* occupies center stage in the enactment of Zé-do-Burro's drama in *O pagador de promessas*. Afro-Brazilian religion manifests itself as Candomblé in many Brazilian *terreiros* (temples) where relics of African religious practices coexist with Catholic rites as a strategic means of cultural survival. In Anselmo Duarte's cinematic adaptation of Dias Gomes's play of the same name, the crafty blend of Bahian culture and Afro-Brazilian culture, with the story of innocence and transgression can be said to mirror faithfully the stage play. As Dias Gomes points out in his author's note, the play is completely fictional, a fable to be precise, and yet constructed on the basis of folkloric and sociological elements that translate an experience (10). But the play and film are definitely more than that.

O pagador de promessas is the story of a rural man who makes a promise at the Candomblé shrine to carry a big cross to the Church of Santa Barbara in Salvador in order to pay his vow if his donkey is cured. The donkey is cured and he feels a moral and religious obligation to pay his vow, but the Catholic priest, Father Olavo, will not let him enter the church since he concludes that having made his vow in the *terreiro*, the one who pledges must definitely have some satanic connection from which deliverance is sought. This central "conflict" between Iansan (the Afro-Brazilian goddess of storms) and Santa Barbara (a Catholic saint), between the priest and the rural man, between the Catholicism and Candomblé, will intensify toward the ultimate death of the protagonist, Zé-do-Burro, who pays his vow through resilience and the consciousness of the people who collectively carry his corpse on the cross into the church he was forbidden to enter while alive.

From the opening scene of the film, when Zé is portrayed making his vow in the *terreiro*, the practitioners of Candomblé are distanced, almost serving the function of local color, hence suggesting Zé's contradictory position: is he making a vow to a Catholic saint or to an Afro-Brazilian goddess? This ambivalence runs through the play and the film as Zé is never involved with the *terreiro* ceremonies but with simply paying his vow at a Santa Barbara church. The rationale for making a vow in the *terreiro* but ending up paying it in the Catholic church stems from the Afro-Brazilian religious blend with popular Catholicism. Since Santa Barbara and Iansan are equivalent entities, Zé did not seem to see any conflict of interest. Zé translates the tragic elements that the original play tried to convey, especially the irony of not succeeding in fulfilling his promise even though he labored so very hard. He only fulfills the pledge in death. Dias Gomes and Anselmo Duarte seem to explore this ambivalence to the fullest as Zé seems contradictory, naive, and rural, a figure unable to reconcile rural life and city life, innocence and experience, faithfulness and transgression and above all, flexibility and intransigence. In a sense, both Zé and Father Olavo are stubborn in their beliefs: Zé dies by refusing to compromise his pledge, and Father Olavo is ridiculed for demonizing the Candomblé to the fury of the *capoeiristas* and the people in general. In Zé's first encounter with the priest, they seem very opposite in their convictions. For Father Olavo, Zé's pledge is very exaggerated but for Zé, "a pledge is a pledge; it is like business."

Robert Stam's observation about the possibility of a Christian allegory is incisive, noteworthy, and well conceived. Zé-of-the-Donkey is associated with Christ: he rides into town on a donkey, he carries his cross, he is tested by temptation, and he is called a "new Christ" by the media. The monseigneur, meanwhile, is associated with Pontius Pilate; "Bonitão" with Judas; Marli with Mary Magdalene (*Tropical Multiculturalism* 217). This allegory is perhaps the most compelling in the film, a construction that will be the basis of the conflict between Zé and Father Olavo, as one recalls the opening of the film when passers-by pay their respects to Zé as he was doing his "via crucis" on the way to the Santa Barbara church. In addition, during the media "circus," the sick, elderly, and newborn babies were brought to Zé for blessing as if to confirm his Christ-like figure.

Although Zé is not necessarily an Afro-Brazilian character by virtue of color and African origins, he is an embodiment of Afro-Brazilian cultural values in terms of his allegiance to Candomblé and his regional location in the Northeast as a *caboclo* (of white-Indian descent). Brazilian racial complexity makes it problematic to define Afro-Brazilianness in absolute terms—fluidity and ambivalence serve their purpose in a multicultural society when convenient. The "African" elements in the film seem to serve as local color and authenticating props and are not necessarily essential elements such as in character development. Some of the traditional songs and practices such as capoeira, Candomblé, and samba attest to the affinity Brazil shares with Africa and the extent to which African experience has been transplanted across the Atlantic. Yet, Zé's fragmentation and ultimate sacrificial death is symptomatic of a larger societal malaise: religious intolerance, exploitation of his innocence by the media, Bonitão's seduction of Zé's wife, and his equally unbecoming betrayal of Zé to the police, all combine to make the protagonist a victim of his pledge and moral obligations. During his epiphanic moment of crisis, Zé laments that Santa Barbara, to whom he made his vow, has abandoned him at a crucial moment of need, but he resolves nonetheless not to abandon his pledge no matter the cost. In dying in order to pay his pledge, Zé responds to societal fragmentation of his soul and remains a mythic hero[7] to conscious members of the society represented by the *roda de capoeira* who share his beliefs and plight through their act of solidarity with him by carrying him on the cross into the church.

Macunaíma: Fragmentation as Identity

While Zé's fragmentation in *O pagador de promessas* relates more to his commitment to his pledge and its problematic interpretation by the Catholic Church than to his identity, Macunaíma's dilemma stems from his fragmented identity, hence the appellation of a "characterless hero" not only by virtue of his morality but by the trope of multiracial personality projected by Mário de Andrade. Directed by Joaquim Pedro de Andrade and based upon a book of adventures and transformations written by Mário de Andrade in 1928, *Macunaíma,* the film captures the essential contradictions of Brazilian identity through the prism of political allegory. Brazil is likened to the principal character, Macunaíma, who is born lazy, a baby already fifty years old, and who refuses to grow but basically is interested only in carnal pleasures throughout his "adventures." As David Haberly suggests, Mário de Andrade himself, struggled with his own multiplicity, a "somatic embodiment of the traditional racial trinity" (*Three Sad Races* 137), thus betraying his multivalent ancestral legacies and the search for such an identity in *Macunaíma*.

Through a crafty process of identity fragmentation (African-Indian-European), the film as well as the novel problematize and critique the Brazilian national character as represented in the protagonist. The complex internal structures that Haberly divides into ten codes elucidate a rather cryptic construction that in its picaresque and rhapsodic cosmogony redefines being Brazilian.[8] The chronological and cosmogonic codes refer to the multiplicity and simultaneity (atemporality) that engender the magical transformations in the novel and film. The petrologic code is the fixation of multiple identities within a native–foreigner dialectic. The celestial code is borrowed from Indian mythology and refers to the irreversibility of identity fixation, especially the ability of superior beings to become stars. The entomologic code relates primitivism with environment, especially the relationship between insects and primitive society. The epidemiological code refers to the susceptibility of the hero to the illnesses of civilization. The ornithological code encapsulates the nobility of Macunaíma as the birds symbolically serve as a canopy protecting him. The code of the machine refers to the mutually mechanical nature of men and industry. The racial code refers to the three races that Macunaíma embodies, white, black, and Indian. The sexual code refers to the lustful nature of Macunaíma. The linguistic code refers to Andrade's multiple borrowings from Africanisms, Europeanisms, and Indianisms, to construct what Haberly calls the "harlequinate lexicon" (156).

Joaquim Pedro de Andrade's attempt to capture the irreverent, the subversive, and the funny, in the cinematic adaptation of Macunaíma, reveals a problematic constant: the anthropophagical imperative that Oswald de Andrade elaborates in his modernist aesthetics of selective absorption of the good in all cultures.[9] Yet, Macunaíma, born black, was not "good" enough to be absorbed, eaten, or "cannibalized" until he was transformed into a white prince who then has occasional sexual escapades with an Indian. At birth, Macunaíma was greeted with repulsion: "How ugly!" On the contrary, when he turned into a white prince after smoking Sofará's cigarette, the treatment changed to "How beautiful you have become!" The multiplicity implied in Macunaíma makes it difficult to separate the *Afro*-Brazilian from the rest of the Brazilian identity. And therein lies the strategy of the novelistic and cinematic construction: ambiguity and multiplicity of identity. Macunaíma embodies the stereotypes associated with Indians, blacks, and whites: He is lazy, intelligent, stupid, and enterprising at the same time. On another level, Macunaíma is far from being a model Brazilian, particularly when represented as a black. In the limited representations or transformations of Macunaíma into the Afro-Brazilian, the protagonist becomes an allegory of the permanent childhood as his grotesque birth and six-year silence testify. In addition, Macunaíma is portrayed as an exotic figure who, through various race-mixing rituals and initiations, must be transformed into an acceptable creature in order to be accepted by a "whitened" society. By portraying him as a trickster who must use every opportunity to survive and subvert obstacles in his way, any guilt by association is minimized for in the final analysis, Macunaíma is not to be trusted. He is a "hero without any character" and thus his co-optation in order to be accepted by a "racist" society must be read as being in his own interest. He can only blame himself for the consequences of choosing not to be accepted by opting for the radical perspective, which is to see Brazil as racist and not totally welcoming of his original blackness.

Xica da Silva: Cosmetic Control, Problematic Power

While *Macunaíma* problematizes Brazilian identity, *Xica da Silva* interrogates power as an instrument of social and political authority and manipulation. The sensuous film version also betrays far-ranging stereotypes and misconceptions about black and mulattas. The illusion of greatness that the film creates in the representation of Xica must be critically examined within the larger historical context of slavery, subjugation, and dehumanization of Afro-Brazilians. There is no question that this is one of the most compelling Brazilian films of all times. Directed by Carlos Diegues, produced in 1976, and based in part on the play by Antônio Callado, *Xica da Silva*, like the film *Orfeu negro*, is not very faithful to the dramatic text. In fact, while the play focuses on the era of Xica's superficial empowerment and relative freedom, the film begins with a historical account of the making of Xica Silva, from her "chickenized" days as a slave to her intelligent manipulation through her sensuality and sexuality to gain her "freedom."

Antônio Callado's play, *O tesouro de Xica da Silva,* written in 1959, and the film both narrate the eighteenth-century experience of a slave woman, Xica, who became a legend and the most powerful woman through her relationship with the richest man in the region of Minas Gerais. João Fernandes de Oliveira, who had been delegated by the Portuguese Crown to oversee the mining of precious stones in Tijuca and Xica, succeeds in getting him to fall in love with her and thus becomes "the power behind the throne" (*Tropical Multiculturalism* 291). Henceforth, Xica achieves almost all her desires from her powerful lover: her freedom, her own slaves (*mucamas*), her personal ship and a lake to sail it on, and a certain compelling cultural presence in the city. A carnivalesque inversion seems to be at play as whites who used to control her are now under her "corporeal control"; they now sing and serve her, however reluctantly. In spite of the apparent power struggle, Xica da Silva does not attain full political power, as she discovers when she is not allowed to enter the church, a symbol of elitism, perfection, and whiteness.

While Xica protests this racist treatment, her actions are very naive, simply shouting at the priest and cursing rather than getting her wish fulfilled. She does not succeed in changing her lover's mind either. Instead, João Fernandes promises to build her a personal church, betraying the fact that their relationship has some limits when it comes to hegemonic symbols. And this is the crux of Xica's fragmentation as she goes through moments of discovery and revolt simultaneously.

Using her newfound freedom and cultural power, Xica often confronts João Fernandes about the treatment of slaves, asking for better treatment but having to negotiate with her body in all cases. The case of Teodoro is significant. An independent smuggler, he was shown at the beginning of the film equally "disempowering" João Fernandes by taking his white horse and leaving with his gang in reverse conquering posture. Although João Fernandes is sympathetic to Teodoro's plight, he is compelled to choose between Teodoro and the Crown during Teodoro's capture and torture—and of course, he chooses to side with the Crown. Compared to the greed and self-serving cultural "power" of Xica da Silva, Teodoro uses his ill-gotten wealth to personally buy slaves' freedom. His capture may also be traced to Xica, who was looking for Teodoro to call up an army but ends up leading Teodoro's captors to his abode. This image of Xica as a dubious personality is valid to the extent that she does not really bring about a revolution but effects only cosmetic changes that serve her own personal interests.

The framing of the film in a vicious circular construction (slave-"queen"-slave) suggests a dead-end situation from which a slave cannot escape. From the beginning, Xica is portrayed as a "sexually available slave" (293). She is seen in the midst of chickens she was feeding and is being called by a pampered D. Jorge as if she was a "chick" her self: "Xic, Xic, Xic, Xic. . . ." This scene is not only irritating in its debasement of her character; it also portrays Xica as a nymphomaniac slave who must be satisfied by all white men without any concern for her dignity or self-respect. Her body serves the carnal pleasures of various white men while she gradually becomes a respectable sex object in the bed of João Fernandes. Even to the Conde de Valardes, who has been sent to inspect João Fernandes's financial and erotic activities, Xica was at first irresistible as she prepared a feast and danced naked in front of the mesmerized Portuguese envoy. Yet, Xica's carnal hypnotism of the Count only lasted the night as the envoy resolved that João Fernandes still needed to return to Portugal, thus divesting Xica of her temporary, illusory, and cosmetic power. As Stam cogently puts it: "Cultural victories mask political defeats. And this situation will change only when the respect often accorded Afro-Brazilian *culture* is matched by a real change in the social situation of Afro-Brazilian *citizens,* a change that would necessarily involve a radical redistribution of that substance vital to the life of any community—political power" (296). As painful as that reality is, Xica fails to see beyond the passion and assurances of João Fernandes. And in that naiveté lies her tragic flaw. She believes too easily in the rhetorical promises; her white lover says, for example: "I will give you everything the diamonds of Tijuca can buy. I will cover you with diamonds. I will give you a whole palace just for you. Everything for you, Xica." Of course, this is too good to be true. "Everything" does not include Xica's equal integration into the hegemonic social order and hierarchy.

Xica's dilemma and fragmentation is equally a reflection of societal hypocrisy. From her first owner, Mr. Intende, who enjoys Xica's touch during on-demand massages, to D. Jorge's daily sexual escapades, to the contractor João Fernandes's passionate takeover of this "precious jewel" called Xica, the society reinforces the stereotype. Xica is damned if she is sexually exploited and damned if she is not. Even Xica herself plays into this stereotype as she proudly dramatizes in front of João Fernandes: "Xica knows how to do certain things that she alone knows how." D. Jorge's response to Xica's takeover from the first owner and himself was: "Now the sky is no longer the limit for her!" as if to suggest that she is in better hands, how lucky she is! Yet, for personal reasons stemming from her own thirst for "power" in any guise, even if it is a fantasy, Xica sells her body, sells her soul, and loses her mind and dignity. In the final analysis, she loses that same manipulated body for it becomes fragmented—a fragmentation captured in her rejection and disappointment in not being able to enter the symbolic world of purity and whiteness—the Catholic Church. She is the quintessential metaphor for Afro-Brazilian fragmentation.

Eles Não Usam Black Tie: From Revolt to Scapegoatism

Directed by Leon Hirszman and produced in 1981, *Eles não usam Black Tie* (They Don't Wear Black Tie) is one of those problematic films whose title easily misleads and whose content is subject to interrogation for its representation of the Afro-Brazilian on screen. Based on the play written by Gianfrancesco Guarnieri in 1955, the idealistic and romantic vision of how to effect a change in a dictatorship and oppressive working environment overlaps with the romance of two young individuals who are torn apart by their conflicting moral beliefs in the face of economic survival and ideological convictions. The urban context of São Paulo provides a unique milieu for the dramatization of a strike in which parents and lovers become antagonists in the name of ideological, generational, and class struggles. While on the surface the strike is the central problematic, beneath that conflict lie other enigmatic layers of plot structure such as the disintegration of the family, police repression, the impossible love between Tião and Maria, and finally but most compellingly for our purposes, the marginalization and death of Braúlio, the only significant Afro-Brazilian in the film. The title itself, *They Don't Wear Black Tie*, refers to the blue-collar workers who do not dress up like the factory owners who oppress them. It is a symbolic expression of protest and defiance in the face of unacceptable working conditions.

The supportive role of Braúlio in an obviously politically charged thesis play and film raises the question of the marginal role of Afro-Brazilians on the Brazilian screen and the related issue of police brutality that targets blacks for racist sport and psychological release from the tensions produced by the military dictatorship among the poor working class. On one day of the strike, while Otávio (the revolutionary who leads the strike, and father of Tião, who has just been turned away by his family and bride-to-be) is busy persuading his fellow workers not to enter the factory, Braúlio is seen counseling other fellow workers to be prudent, nonviolent, and aware of police reinforcement. It was as if he had a premonition; as an Afro-Brazilian, he knows, firsthand, not to be confrontational, but as he shares his concern with other workers, his voice of caution is the only one heard by the police. He becomes the easy target. A police officer whispers to the other, "Get the nigger!" and in no time, two shots are fired, and Braúlio falls and dies. During his funeral, Otávio considers Braúlio as a martyr who will be remembered in Brazilian history books. Yet, why must Afro-Brazilians be easy targets for elimination in the name of heroism and martyrdom? Unlike Tião, whom Otávio, his father, calls a "traitor not by cowardice but by conviction," Braúlio is a threat by virtue of his color.

Leon Hirszman's effective portrayal in *Eles não usam Black Tie* reveals a world of social dynamics among characters whose interaction indicates less of a racial divide and more of an ideological and class struggle—a case of a family members divided among themselves due to differences of political conviction. The role and place of the likes of Braúlio, an Afro-Brazilian, become secondary and insignificant. Reminiscent of the Cinema Novo neorealistic social exposé of dialectical tension between the workers and the factory owners, the film documents, however unfaithfully, the series of São Paulo strikes of the 1960s in protest of the military dictatorship. However, as Stam, Vieira, and Xavier[10] observe, "the São Paulo strikes were the product of a new generation typified by Luis Inácio da Silva ("Lula") and his Workers' Party rather than of the traditional left" (*Brazilian Cinema* 417). While the reality of the Brazilian worker has been neglected and is worth portraying, *Eles não usam Black Tie* reinforces the stereotypical image of the docile and passive Afro-Brazilian in contrast with the powerful women characters and leftist radicals such as Romana, Maria, and Otávio. Braúlio is a metaphor for the indictment of Brazilian police brutality and the specific fragmentation and scapegoatism of Afro-Brazilians.

Quilombo: The Vitality of Recuperated History

If in *Eles não usam Black Tie* Braúlio is sacrificed and scapegoated, *Quilombo* symbolizes the radical reinvention of resistant warriors embodied in the personalities of Ganga Zumba and Zumbi, his godson and leader of the *Palmares* (one of the self-governing black settlements or communities). Directed by Carlos Diegues and produced in 1984, *Quilombo* represents Afro-Brazilian resistance against colonial domination, slavery, and dehumanization. Gilberto Gil's music captures the spirit of the resistance through compelling and intermittent lyrics such as: "the happiness of the Afro-Brazilian is a warlike happiness" in "Zumbi (warlike happiness)." Gil goes on to end this cut with a homage to both Brazil and Zumbi highlighting the greatness of this warrior spirit to whom all Afro-Brazilians look for their hero:

> Brazil, my Brazilian Brazil
> My great shine, my root and nation
> Protector Zumbi, Patron Gatekeeper
> Send liberty to my heart. (*Gilberto Gil: Todas as letras* 276)

Historically situated between 1650 and 1695, *Quilombo* narrates the story of a rebellion led by Ganga Zumba in which the group escapes from the plantation to establish the Palmares. Self-sufficient and prosperous, Palmares ceases to be led by Ganga Zumba and is taken over by Zumbi due to internal conflicts and Ganga Zumba's compromise with the Portuguese. Zumbi is finally killed, but the resistance continues for another century, hence the importance of recuperating and valorizing this aspect of Afro-Brazilian history. In celebrating Afro-Brazilian culture and rebellion, *Quilombo* redefines the representation of Blacks in relation to slavery. The scene of the arrival of the Dutch to purchase slaves is quite violent and illuminating. One notes also that the Brazilian release of *Quilombo* totally eliminates this scene, while the American version retains it. It depicts the extent of Afro-Brazilians' resistance to slavery as opposed to the popular distortion that resistance was minimal or nonexistent. I believe the question usually asked by conservative critics, "Where is the resistance?" is best answered by this violent scene. Diegues shows the massacre of the Dutch with minimal casualties on the side of the Afro-Brazilians while at the same time depicting the gullibility of the slave buyers and sellers because they were taken by surprise.

Quilombo's attempt to recuperate Afro-Brazilian history and validate a long-denigrated and unacknowledged culture has many positive implications. First, by showing Afro-Brazilians as capable of organizing themselves into a governable and self-sufficient community, the film "corrects" their stereotypical and paternalistic image as a people who need to be governed in order to feel human—the slave needs his or her master to maintain that oppressive but convenient relationship. Second, the regeneration of African cultures and beliefs through such personalities as Acotirene who has spiritual powers and serves as a diviner and seer to the group; Dandara, who embodies the African spirit of Iansan; Zumbi, who is identified with Ògún (Yoruba god of metal, war, and justice); and Ganga Zumba, who is linked to Ṣàngó (Yoruba god of thunder) is empowering to the group. Finally, the colorful Afro-Brazilian costumes, musical interludes, and moments of linguistic resistance through the speaking and learning of an African language such as Yoruba all reinforce the cultural saga that the film represents. The violent destruction of the community by the colonizers notwithstanding, like Xica da Silva, the cultural victory may be a symbolic act toward a political act, historical reconstruction, and defragmentation. As the director of three compellingly "regenerative" yet problematic films—namely, *Ganga Zumba, Xica da Silva,* and *Quilombo*—Carlos Diegues may have set out to document Afro-Brazilian history, but in many instances in these films, he has actually reinforced stereotypes.

Jubiabá: The Limits of Afro-Brazilian Heroism

Afro-Brazilian heroes have this in common: they die for a cause that seems too overwhelmingly complex to comprehend, and too utopian to set the machinery of change in motion. Death thus becomes, in some cases, an escape from the frustration and faith in some symbolic and spiritual regeneration that will give the living and unborn hope to continue the struggle. Rosenfeld captures this problematic aspect adequately when he suggests that "we are not a happy people and that is why we need heroes." Baldo, the protagonist, manifests all the characteristics of a hero in *Jubiabá*. Even the title is somewhat questionable. Intended to pay homage to Candomblé worship and yet interrogate its contribution to modernity and progress, the film questions traditional values while praising them at the same time. Directed by Nelson Pereira dos Santos, and produced in 1987, *Jubiabá* follows the life of Baldo from his loss of his demented mother, to his temporary childhood crush on a white girl, to his ultimate expulsion from the house of Mr. Felipe, the commander.

Based on a novel of the same title by Jorge Amado and constructed in a similar mix of love story, resistance, and strike as in *Black Tie, Jubiabá* is richer in terms of Afro-Brazilian religious practices, music, and the strong Afro-Brazilian personality and hero captured in Antônio Balduíno (Baldo). The childhood love between Lindinalva and Baldo that is impossible due to racial differences and background turns ironic at the end of the film, as one sees Lindinalva, a formerly protected middle-class white girl living as a prostitute and begging for alms on the streets. Compared to Baldo, who despite his rites of passage as a wrongly accused runaway, becomes a successful boxer, circus performer, and activist who leads other workers to go on strike, Lindinalva dies a pauper, a prostitute, and homeless beggar. The contrast between her and Baldo is very significant and reveals naturalistic influences, or at least, dialectical orientation on the part of the filmic and narrative construct. Given the same circumstances, a white child can easily become delinquent the same way most Afro-Brazilian children are abandoned, homeless, and abused.

Baldo's revolt at the end of the film is against the celebration of African saints in the *Candomblé terreiro* but in favor of taking concrete and pragmatic steps toward transformation and change, indicating a complete rite of passage. Jubiabá, the *babalorixá* (Candomblé priest), kneels down in front of Baldo as if to pay his respects in a symbolic gesture of leadership transfer from the old to the new. This act is symbolic and strategic in that it accentuates the need for the young to assume leadership through mentorship from the elders. While Baldo's self-discovery may be seen as an exception to the rule, Jubiabá suggests that given the right combination of support, guidance, and opportunity, any Afro-Brazilian becomes endowed with innate "vital force" to overcome artificial and real barriers instituted by a racist society.

Tenda dos milagres: Rejecting and Promoting Racial Democracy

Representing the most racially controversial of his novels, Jorge Amado's *Tenda dos milagres* (Tent of Miracles), published in 1969, captures the debates surrounding the issue of being a mulatto in Brazilian society. In confronting the resistance on both sides of the argument, Amado seems to articulate a less popular position by proposing whitening and race mixture as the ultimate solution to the color problem. The film version, produced in 1977 and directed by Nelson Pereira dos Santos, offers a dual frame to uncover the life and times of Pedro Arcanjo, the mixed-race prototype, as well as the plight of the poet-filmmaker Fausto Pena, who is contracted by a North American anthropologist, Dr. Livingston, to research the life of Pedro Arcanjo. Nelson Pereira dos Santos, now honored with the first book written on him in English,[11] occupies a significant position in the Cinema Novo movement—concerned as it was with raising the consciousness of people through a delicate representation of racial complexity and poverty. As Santos indicated to Darlene Sadlier during an interview, "race is a theme that because of my upbringing is incorporated into my existence. . . . The other great issue, poverty, which is very linked to race, is a permanent theme in all my films; it is not possible to think about national identity without including the very serious problem of absolute poverty in some parts of Brazil" (Sadlier 159). As a seasoned film director who is considered the father and conscience of the Brazilian new wave of the early sixties that sought to establish an authentic portrayal of the marginalized poor, dos Santos offers in *Tenda dos milagres*, a sympathetic yet problematic interpretation of Brazil's racial dilemma.

Structured along two parallel storylines—one about the arrival of Dr. Livingston and the media frenzy that ensued; and the other, concerning the story of Pedro Arcanjo, the mulatto who lives what he preaches by engaging in sexual relations across racial lines. Nothing seems to be a coincidence here: sex, politics, sexism, racism, media manipulation, and intolerance—all are carefully worked into a tapestry of Afro-Brazilian culture in a setting that best represents the richness of that culture: Bahia. The viewer may not agree with the racial ideology propelling the original novel by Amado as well as dos Santos's interpretation, but what seems unquestionable is the paradoxical combination of irony, celebration, and sensuousness that exposes the myth of racial democracy. In addition to the implied dialogue on racial relations between a blend of historical figures represented by Pedro Arcanjo, and Professor Nilo Argilo's racist theories, Amado exposes the persecution of Candomblé devotees by the police.

The special attention given to the Nobel laureate American scholar by the media also speaks to the naïveté of some Brazilians in relation to foreign scholars. Not only is a press conference held in which Dr. Livingston unexpectedly declares Pedro Arcanjo, a lowly, totally obscure, dead, and long-forgotten Bahian mulatto functionary, as one of the greatest scientists of the twentieth century. Suddenly the investigation into the life of Arcanjo becomes a passion for Fausto Pena, a poet turned filmmaker, as he ransacks the archives in search of the enigmas of Arcanjo. In the same opening segment of the film, Ana Mercedes, a mixed-race woman, leaves the company of her boyfriend, Pena, and voluntarily submits herself into the arms of the newly arrived anthropologist in a self-fulfilling premonition of sexual union. Ironically, Fausto Pena takes both of the new lovers to a hotel room where Dr. Livingston is staying and leaves his girlfriend, Ana, with the anthropologist. As an indecent "payoff," Ana Mercedes convinces Dr. Livingston to contract Pena as his research assistant, and he agrees. Livingston helps Brazil rediscover the value of one of its scholars on racial relations, while confirming the validity of racial democracy as translated by Ana's sexual agility. Dos Santos criticizes the tendency of Brazil to recognize the contributions of blacks/mulattos only after they have been acclaimed abroad. In a sense, both Pedro Arcanjo and Ana Mercedes are victims of racial democracy—both representing "equality" but having nothing to show for it in life and death. Pedro Arcanjo was never recognized in his lifetime. He was a lowly functionary who died poor but was celebrated posthumously. Ana Mercedes, a "prostitute" at best—at least that is how she is portrayed—achieves social mobility and advancement through providing sexual favors. As for Dr. Livingston, Robert Stam appropriately reads him as a "two dimensional figure . . . suggestive of a pompous ass that he is than of the Nobel prize winner he is presumed to be" (*Tropical Multiculturalism* 304).

The story of Pedro Arcanjo is by far the more compelling in this film. Using a film-within a film technique, the viewer follows the life of Arcanjo as a clerk at the School of Medicine by day and a musician, dancer, and lover of women of all races by night, aiming to practicalize his theory of miscegenation. Proof of his commitment to Afro-Brazilian culture lies in his persistent research and publication of his findings with the help of a friend, Lídio Corró, who is a typesetter. Arcanjo's proposal for miscegenation against his ideological antagonist, Professor Argilo, faces stiff opposition from the white elite who were concerned about the new ideology derailing white supremacy and privilege. As an ardent defender of Afro-Brazilian culture in general, Arcanjo demonstrates strength and courage in the face of antagonisms against Afro-Brazilian religion and dignity, especially in the scene where the police arrive to disrupt a Candomblé rite and are confronted by the supernatural power of an African god. Arcanjo demonstrates that he is able to be a social scientist *pai-de-santo* (without any contradictions). The film confirms that Arcanjo "embodies cultural integrity and intellectual power" (301) through his consistent rejection of the racist theories that considered race mixture to be a form of degeneration. By complicating and exalting racial democracy at the same time, *Tenda dos milagres* proposes miscegenation as *the* ultimate solution to Brazil's racial problems. Stam sums up the irony and contradictions in the propositions of miscegenation as reflected in the figure of sexualized mulatta Ana Mercedes and the offspring of an interracial union, Tadeu, who continues in the tradition of persistent whitening as opposed to the reverse:

> In Brazilian ideology, miscegenation has been linked inextricably to "whitening," as the film itself suggests in the almost subliminal "progression" that takes us from Arcanjo, a mulatto, to his child by a white Scandinavian woman (Kirsi), to the marriage of another lighter-skinned son, Tadeu, to a rich white woman. The newlywed couples' move from Bahia to Tadeu's promised position in Rio reinforces this link between "whitening" and social success. The "epidermic meliorism" of the plot thus comes perilously close to the official ideology, by which blacks rise socially when they marry mulattoes, and mulattoes gain status when they infiltrate white families, precisely the formula that continually relegates blacks to the bottom of the hierarchy. (306)

In defending and celebrating Afro-Brazilian culture, *Tenda dos Milagres* ends up exalting racial democracy through a narrative plot which signals gradual elimination of blackness and reinforcement of white domination. A provocative, entertaining, and politically brilliant film, it succeeds in revisiting the myth of racial democracy, exposing its contradictions, and setting the tone for the need to move beyond this hypocrisy toward confronting the myth.

In Search of a Brazilian Spike Lee

The way forward for Afro-Brazilian cinema is the emergence of a Spike Lee who will transcend financial limitations, political censorship, and strategic fragmentation of actors through alternative outlets. With the exception of the dialogic contributions of Joel Zito Araújo, author of *A negação do Brasil* (The Negation of Brazil), to the discourse on racial democracy, the prospect of such a cinematic hero is still elusive in today's Brazil. João Rodrigues seems to believe that despite continued denial of racism, the emergence of such an Afro-Brazilian cinematic director is inevitable in the near future.[12] The eight films examined point more toward a gradual cultural conquest than a political achievement of social justice. The challenge to find a Spike Lee figure for Brazilian cinema may continue to be insurmountable if Brazil continues to blindly embrace the myth of racial democracy.

8

Ancestrality and the Dynamics of Afro-Modernity

To what extent is Roland Barthes relevant to a significant discussion of "Afro-modernity," especially as a theorist of language and culture? Barthes wrote, "To be modern is to know clearly what cannot be started over again."[1] This is the crux of the dilemma faced by theorists of modernism and postmodernism within the context of the African diaspora—an atemporal space of contestation. This chapter explores the problematic of ancestrality and the dynamics of Afro-modernity in the Brazilian context and by extension in the African diaspora. It ponders the legitimacy of "modernism" and "postmodernism" with particular emphasis on Afro-Brazilian cultural producers before and after the *Semana de Arte Moderna* of 1922. What is "modernity" for Afro-Brazilians? Why was the Afro-Brazilian excluded from participation in the significant literary and cultural movement of 1922? Why was the representation of the Afro-Brazilian limited to a cosmetic presence in Brazilian letters up to 1922 and after? How were the emerging writers of the time able to "correct" or challenge this situation? And how have contemporary writers defined themselves in terms of "modernity" and "postmodernity"? Roland Barthes's provocative assertion is indeed relevant, for it brings to the fore the dilemma of definition and application in the Brazilian context where these Western terminologies are not applicable. If "modernity" is defined as what cannot be started again, then it is the opposite of the African diaspora, by its own "definition" the regrouping of people of African descent in a new location other than where they originated. Africans have been able to "start again" in the New World—a location that carries the stigma of abuse and trauma that ordinarily should have prevented any form of "starting over." It is that resilience and strength that I associate with ancestrality, the spiritual linkage with ancestors and the consciousness of power entailed and implied by that awareness.

I first contemplated the notion of "Afro-modernity" while preparing for a conference in 2000 during which I was to present a paper on a terminology that suitably connects Portuguese African and Afro-Brazilian experiences. Since then, a seminal essay by Michael Hanchard, published a year later, helped me rethink my preliminary ideas. Hanchard's "Afro-Modernity:

Temporality, Politics, and the African Diaspora" provides a provocative assessment of the contradictions of Western modernity in relation to the African diaspora.[2] Hanchard's arguments can be summed up as follows: first, as an attempt to define how the people of the African diaspora can be considered modern subjects; second, as an interrogation of how modes of collective identity have reacted to or modified the discourses of modernity; third, as a definition of African diaspora scholarship in its dual model: the Herskovitsian and the mobilizational; fourth, as a critique of Paul Gilroy's proposal of Afro-modernism and the black Atlantic as a counterculture of modernity; and finally, as a dialectical proposal of Afro-modernity as "the negation of the idea of African and African-derived peoples as the antithesis of modernity" (274).

The thrust of Hanchard's thesis lies between a negation of the Herskovitsian model—that is, the limited focus on the survival of African cultures in the New World—and the emphasis on the mobilizational model, which implies what the critic calls "overt as well as veiled" (273) forms of resistance such as song, dance, revolts, rebellions, and civil rights movements. Hanchard further argues that there is a tendency to minimize the impact of African contributions to the West. Afro-modernity must thus be understood as the affirmation of how African peoples have departed from Western modernity despite their interlocking relationship with the same idea of renewal and their own need to be "countercultural" in the sense of negating modernity in order to affirm tradition without being contradictory. Indeed, Hanchard's main contention against Gilroy is the claim that Afro-modernism is "merely an appendage of Western modernity and European modernism" (274). For Hanchard, then, Afro-modernity is not an antithesis of Western modernity but an innovation of it, not a mimicry but a "normative *convergence* of two or more African and African-descended peoples and social movements in response to perceived commonalities of oppression" (275). This characteristic compels the oppressed to focus on the primacy of historical narrative in view of a common history of bondage and struggles for freedom. Hanchard provides many examples of what he calls "temporal politics and racial inequality" in Cuba, Brazil, the United States, and Ghana, while concluding that modernity can be seen from various vantage points: "as nightmare or utopia; as horrible past or present . . . , as a process of lived experience, with winners and losers, as well as strivings for redemption, recovery, retribution, and revolution, each experience tumbling into another and becoming . . . history" (298). The counterculture argument assumes that every attempt to define African diaspora people is a "reaction" to the West. This may be partly so in the context of slavery, colonialism, and other forms of human oppression, yet the act of subverting the mechanisms of oppression constitutes a natural process of survival through which positive elements of Western modernity combine with African elements in a process of adaptation and innovation. The new transcontinental "Africa," thus "invented," asserts itself as independent even within a territory that is not originally its own but that it claims as a legitimate result of its contribution throughout many centuries of oppression. Perhaps this explains Hanchard's position that Africans of the diaspora do not represent an antithesis or appendage of Western modernity.

Hanchard's thesis is relevant to the discussion of Afro-modernity in Brazil, for it sums up the notion of global African modernity as a process and not an end in itself. Afro-Brazilian culture is surely a pragmatic and shifting one, and the various cultural agencies possibly have been affected by African contributions whether acknowledged or not. From samba to Carnival, from capoeira to Candomblé, and from soccer to the *novelas* (soap operas), the memory of slavery and the revolutionary spirit of the *quilombo* continue to be imagined in many facets of Brazilian life. That modernist "process" goes back to the era of slavery when Africans were forcibly taken to Brazil. Consequently, Afro-modernity cannot be said to begin in 1922, the date that marks the beginning of Brazilian modernism. Instead, Afro-modernity began when the first slaves arrived in Brazil. As a result, the survival of African cultures and the mobilizational efforts toward freedom did not happen in a vacuum. While there are critics who suggest that the ancestral connection with the motherland is an "essentialist" argument, I insist that without such socially resistant cultural agencies as the Candomblé, samba, and capoeira, among others, the process of mobilization or of cultural survival would have been terminated. It is arguable, of course, that in the Brazilian context, "racial mixture" also accounted for the "survival," but in fact, the intended result was just the opposite. It was through the craftiness and resilience of the slaves that they were able to negotiate adapting African gods to Catholic saints, thereby forging what is called religious or cultural syncretism. Contrary to the fallacious racial democracy argument, the idea was to diminish or eliminate the blackness in African subjects by "maximizing" their whiteness through race-mixture. I do not intend to revisit the debates and schools of thought on racial democracy in this book; rather, I set out to draw connections between cultural production and strategies of resistance that I find in the concept of ancestrality.

Theorizing Ancestrality

The politics of Afro-modernity and its validation of African contributions to the West demand further reflection on the implication of ancestrality as a living social entity, an inextricable agency for modernizing processes. Ancestrality has a life of its own. As an ideology predicated on the vitality of cogent beliefs and shifting values due to a changing context, it must also be flexible to respond to conditions as they arise, hence its connection with modernity. How, for example, does ancestrality meet the fundamental needs of Africa and the African diaspora? Can the past be used to reinvent the present without opposing or contradicting it? I return here to Hanchard's *Orpheus and Power*, an interesting study of the black movements in Rio and São Paulo from 1945 through 1988. In arguing that the African past cannot be recuperated or remembered fully, Hanchard argues against the mythical gaze of Orpheus and proposes instead a necessity for dialogue and recognition of global forces in contemporary politics, and for a high degree of manipulation. While these propositions appear pragmatic and fit within the "Blaxploitation" of many of the cultural organizations in Brazil for election campaign purposes, I would like to differ with Hanchard by saying that any loss of African "memory" amounts to a spiritual death that cannot be saved by dialogue. Dialogue is only possible when each party is aware of identity and history of the other, hence confident about what each brings to the negotiation table, rather than when one party intends to erase that past in order to affirm the other's acceptability in the family of humanity.

The "reconstruction" of the past is not as negative as Hanchard suggests. It is far better than total loss of memory and far more relevant to a "conscious amnesia." A "continuous present" is equally meaningless without a profound understanding of the past. The present is not an ahistoric or decontextualized event but a continuation of a concrete and meaningful past. While the folklorization of the African cultural and historical past in Brazil is lamentable, the alternative of "forgetting" that past is unacceptable. Hanchard's suggestion that to avoid Orpheus's fate, Afro-Brazilians must be more self-critical as a way of ridding themselves of their "culturalism" or as a strategic ploy to reach integrity seems contradictory and defeatist. Organizations such as Brazilian social and cultural movements do not dialogue in a void if they do not feel a sense of equity during negotiations or even going into negotiations with those they perceive as their oppressors, that is, those who keep them from political power. As a matter of fact, governmental structures often work "against" themselves, when they see such an approach as a strategic manipulative edge or pretext to maintain themselves in power. Allowing Afro-Brazilian culture to exist "within conditioned limits" is a viable option for the tourist industry in economic terms. Therefore, not only are groups such as the Unified Black Movement "legitimized" within reason, they are often funded in the form of competition-and-reward as determined by white elites and institutions. "Racialized disjunctures" are a healthy terrain of struggle—further proof of the relevance of diversity and the imperative of tolerance. Conscious Afro-Brazilians see the past as prelude to the present and ancestrality as a proven source of inspiration and recuperation of that resistant past. Deciding whether that past is reconstructed in part or whole is not as crucial as accepting the European myth that Africans did not have any history, culture, or past.

In African diaspora scholarship, there is a general misconstruing of ancestrality as a notion limited to "ancestral spirits," especially as represented in ancestor worship.[3] In its broader sense, ancestrality echoes the sum total of reflections on the content and meaning of African cultures within the assimilated African diasporan reality, such as in Brazil. As Júlio Braga points out, from a theoretical viewpoint, "ancestrality can be constructed through a cultural and psychosocial specificity fundamentally based on an ancestral figure and which manifests itself through two distinct social areas, namely, recognized social formation of heritage and restructured religious communities" (*Ancestralidade afro-brasileira* 96). From this assumption, two levels of association can be identified: by African heritage and by religious affinity and practice. In this context, an African or an African diaspora subject who is alienated from his or her ancestral roots through denial or general lack of awareness cannot invoke ancestral power. Contrarily, an African or an African diaspora figure who adheres to the tenets of ancestral worship is welcome into the privileged domain of protection and empowerment. This is where ancestrality can become a "state of mind," because like any form of consciousness, it has to be attained through a belief system and awareness, not through imposition or coercion. Afro-Brazilian cultural production is inundated with ancestral manifestation in music, arts, festivals, and religious rites. Through the popularization of the sacred, African gods/goddesses or òrìṣàs are retained in all areas of Brazilian life. Beyond this retention, the òrìṣàs serve as both the source of inspiration and of strength. The ancestors need not "come out" as they would when remembered in the cult of Egungun, but they are already among the living since African culture supports the belief that the dead never depart in the first place, as captured in Birago Diop's "Souffles" (Breath):

Listen more to things
Than to words that are said.
The water's voice sings
And the flame cries
And the wind that brings
The woods to sighs
Is the breathing of the dead.
Those who are dead have never gone away.
They are in the shadows darkening around,
They are in the shadows fading into day,
The dead are not under the ground.
They are in the trees that quiver,
They are in the woods that weep,
They are in the waters of the rivers,
They are in the waters that sleep.
They are in the crowds, they are in the homestead.
The dead are never dead.[4]

Beyond the invocation of the "spirits of the ancestors," ancestrality challenges the trends in cultural study that want to do away with the past by expediently repackaging old truths into new and fashionable paradigms depending on who is professing and defining culture—a pattern Terry Eagleton, in *After Theory*, has appropriately termed "the politics of amnesia" (1–22).[5] As Eagleton notes, "the golden age of cultural theory is long past" (1), for nothing has been able to match the "founding mothers and fathers," such as Jacques Lacan, Claude Lévi-Strauss, Louis Althusser, Roland Barthes, Michel Foucault, Raymond Williams, Hélène Cixous, Fredric Jameson, Julia Kristeva, and Edward Said, among others. Even as we move beyond these ambitious and remarkable cultural thinkers (if we can actually move beyond them), we are finding that "the older generation had proved a hard act to follow" (2). It is within this politics of renewal that I situate Birago Diop's paradigmatic poem, "Souffles," as a point of entry into the interrogation of the African diaspora with particular emphasis on Brazil. Eagleton's ambivalent conclusion that "we can never be 'after theory,' in the sense that there can be no reflective human life without it" (221) aptly captures the dilemma of African and African Diaspora Studies. On the one hand, we need to ascertain the relevance of "traveling theories" to our own cultural, historical, and strategic realities and interests, while on the other hand, we must continue to make Herculean and often frustrating efforts to legitimize indigenous paradigms that are often dismissed as "unsophisticated," "uncomplicated," and "un-theoretical." If the offensive contention that Africans had no philosophy, no reasoning faculty, no thought process has now been laid to rest by able cultural critics such as Tempels, Kagame, Hountondji, Mudimbe, Senghor, and Soyinka, among others, we can at least begin to move in the direction of interrogating the African diaspora in what can now be called its golden age of consolidation where Africa at least continues to be signified, negotiated, and renegotiated within an expansive global framework of the dispersed children and cultures of Africa.

Eagleton's proposition that in order for cultural theory to dialogue with global history, it must have "answerable resources of its own, equal in depth and scope to the situation it confronts" (222) provides for some labor of analysis relevant to our own field of engagement. The situation that African and African Diaspora Studies confronts is comparable to Langston Hughes's poetic and paradigmatic question: "What happens to a dream deferred?" While some programs in Africana Studies or African American Studies are struggling to become departments, some are simply content with the approval of a major or a minor, while others rejoice at the notion of having a graduate curriculum.

I suggest that ancestrality as an embodiment of resilient, resourceful, imaginative, adaptive, and progressive force has sustained African peoples throughout their turbulent engagement with Western modernity beginning in the sixteenth century and continuing through the present. Whether it is in the context of the uniquely brutal experience of Atlantic slavery, or imperialism, colonialism, and institutional racism, Africans have consistently (whether consciously or unconsciously) grafted evolving conditions on their long-standing communal heritage. This is clearly expressed in complex strategies and ideologies of liberation, world-class cultural and artistic expressions, performance, music, religions, and political work that have brought us to where we are today. The few examples I provide later in the Brazilian context affirm these historical, cultural, and shifting processes. A viable African and African Diaspora Studies program must capture these forces from both local and global dimensions, while providing a pedagogy that will enhance analytical skills, evaluative skills, communication skills, writing skills, and critical thinking among our student populations.

Ancestrality is thus the theoretical and conceptual framework on which Africa and the African diaspora must consciously forge a sense of community from practical, economic, cultural, moral, and spiritual perspectives, despite the devastating impact of Atlantic slavery, imperialism, colonialism, fragmentation, authoritarianism, and other oppressive "isms." African and African Diaspora Studies departments or programs, if they are to be relevant to their local constituencies and the wider society, must articulate this deep sense of moral authority and legitimacy that can respond to substantive and pressing issues of race, class, and gender. In the rapidly shifting context of globalization, issues and courses on race, class, and gender remain central and nonnegotiable.

My differing with Eagleton over the issues that African and African Diaspora Studies confronts is not about new course offerings, for those of us operating in marginalized disciplines are very aware of both critical and curricular orthodoxy; hence, not to become creative much less esoteric at times in order to attract competitive students is basically to become resigned to our problematic fate. I suggest that the issue lies somewhere between the overall mission, vision, and resources of the establishment and the singular place of diversity in those strategic configurations. What is needed is to move beyond the "cosmetic" nature of these so-called area studies programs toward a move for their integration into the mainstream as viable academic departments and communities. It is when departments, programs, and their corresponding budgets are "equal in depth and scope" that we can begin to build alliances and partnerships on an equitable footing. Only then can some of these dreams be fulfilled and no longer deferred. Returning to Birago Diop's poem, "Souffles," ancestrality in Afro-Brazilian discourse emanates from the primacy of Yoruba cultural rootedness. For most Afro-Brazilians, Yoruba culture is the permanent reservoir from which they reach for meaning in the duality of knowledge and mysteries. They must not only continue to reach beyond words and inspiration to capture the "twists of souls" over many centuries of enslavement and oppression; they must also continue to reach for the Africa that refuses to be lost or forgotten, the Africa that has been a constant presence and companion throughout the transatlantic journey. That is why when Diop speaks in ancestral polyphony, it is prudent to listen beyond the words that are said. "Sarzan," a corrupted word for "sergeant," revisits the primitivism–civilization dialectic that problematizes the colonial mission in Africa and subjects the contradictions of modernity within the transgression of tradition to further rigorous scrutiny. The negritude movement and ideology of which Senghor and Césaire were founding fathers, and to which Diop significantly contributed, sought to assert the validity of African culture in response to the European image of African exoticism and barbarity. Emerging in the 1930s, this controversial ideology was instrumental to the cultural consciousness that developed later and to a certain degree the political emancipation of parts of the continent beginning in the 1950s. Yet, the earlier efforts since the turn of the twentieth century to give a global face to the African continent through the first Pan-African Congresses (1900, 1912, 1921, 1923) and much later in 1945 must also be seen as a search for the ancestors.

The protagonist of "Sarzan," formerly known as Thiémokho Kéita, and now simply called "Sarzan-the-Fool," was once a respectable "son of the soil" and a village chief in Dougouba, Senegal. He is returning to the village after many years of overseas exploits and travels that have taken him from Dougouba to Dakar, Sudan, Casablanca, Morocco, and Lebanon among other locations dictated by the French colonial administration. From a common "soldier" recruited in a rural village to a well-traveled and seasoned "sergeant" who has seen the world, he is now considered "civilized" and cosmopolitan, and returns in the company of the narrator, Birago Diop, to his home village. Although he intends to be employed as a district messenger or interpreter in the French colonial administration, he is instructed by the colonial administrator that he would do better to return to the village to civilize his own people "just a little bit" since the protagonist is now considered *assimilé*, or an "assimilated French Blackman," with all the alienating contradictions implied by that new identity. With this attitude of "superiority," he descends on his own community professing "civilization" and condemning his own African culture, including the celebrations, the drumming, the dances, and the initiation rites of passage. This is considered an act of disrespect and transgression of tradition, and the ancestors are not pleased. Consequently, in an act of exorcism and punishment, he becomes possessed to a point of delirium wherein he is now obliged to evoke the connections between the dead and the living in a process that brings the voice of the colonial administration in direct conflict with that of the ancestors. And that is what I mean about "ancestral sense"—a "cultural agency" through which the ancestors communicate with the living in practical, theoretical, and ideological sense. The morale of this tale goes beyond Sarzan's delirium and his therapeutic exorcism by the ancestors. Diop's tale, as figuratively enacted from the viewpoint of the psychological process of alienation and de-alienation that Sarzan goes through, is analogous to the reality of the African diaspora as a New World space characterized by its essential fragmentation and struggle for spiritual wholeness.

A case for an ancestral paradigm conjures up a series of debates on the validity of the backward gaze as signified in the Orpheus mythology—that of the permanent loss of Eurydice by Orpheus by disobeying the instructions from the gods that he not look back. If looking back into the African past and history is considered unproductive, deliberate amnesia of historical events may also be equally counterproductive. As my research moves from the interrogation of vital force and ancestral power to the politics of Afro-modernity, I remain convinced that in looking back we are actually looking forward, for as the saying goes, "Those who fail to learn from the lessons of history are bound to repeat it"—and that we cannot afford. Yet, Michael Hanchard in his conclusion to *Orpheus and Power* argues that "dialogue, however fragmented, was worth far more than memory" (167). But how can we dialogue when we are constantly persuaded to forget the past and move into the future of dreams deferred without interrogating the structural causes of this persistent deferment? I suggest that an ancestral paradigm is instrumental in the anthropophagic sense, that is, in the selective absorption of that which makes use of the historical past and of tradition in consonance with that which is modern as long as it is edifying and not degrading. A classic example is the new Brazilian version of *Black Orpheus* released in 2000, now simply titled *Orpheus* without the adjective "black"; in it, the Eurydice figure is now more whitened and more mulatta-looking than the black character of the 1958 version. Unlike the peaceful, festive, and harmonious ambience of carnival preparations and parades within a legendary love story, we now have a setting infested with violence, police brutality, and drug trafficking. While this may be a "realistic" portrayal of the new millennium as confirmed by another recent film, *City of God*, it seems to me that the black exoticism that was critiqued in the Franco-Brazilian version of *Black Orpheus* is now replaced with a mix of black utopia, dystopia, and an even more extravagant display of Carnival as the ultimate desirable Brazilian fantasy. These changes in the image of Brazil play into the official racial democracy mythology that goes against the reality of racism and social marginality.

African diasporan writers, cultural theorists, and cultural performers, such as Afro-Brazilians Abdias do Nascimento, Gilberto Gil, Antônio Olinto, Carolina Maria de Jesus, Benedita da Silva, Vinícius de Moraes, Jorge Amado, Miriam Alves, Esmeralda Ribeiro, and Aline França; African Americans W. E. B. DuBois, Martin Luther King Jr., Malcolm X, Harriet Tubman, Angela Davis, Toni Morrison, Alice Walker, Maya Angelou, Alex Haley, and Julie Dash;

Afro-Colombian Manuel Zapata Olivella; Afro-Panamanian Carlos Guillermo Wilson; Afro-Cuban Alejo Carpentier; Afro–Puerto Rican Lato Laviera; and Afro-Ecuadoran Adalberto Ortiz, have examined what I call "ancestral paradigm" in one form or the other. Although my research currently gravitates toward Afro-Brazilians specifically, the ancestral paradigm resonates across the entire Afro-diasporan world. For the purposes of a few close readings, I would like to engage some Afro-Brazilian echoes of ancestrality.

Abdias do Nascimento, a foremost Afro-Brazilian critic of racial democracy in Brazil, Pan-Africanist progressive activist, painter, dramatist, thinker, and a fascinating icon that I was privileged to meet in 1999, has spent a lifetime defending the dignity of Afro-Brazilians. He was the first Afro-Brazilian to champion black people's human and civil rights as a member of the National Legislature (1983–87), where he presented the first Brazilian proposal for affirmative action policies. A former senator in the federal senate and founder of the *Teatro Experimental do Negro* (Black Experimental Theater), in the 1940s he formulated a theory of *Quilombismo* inspired by the *Palmares* model of multicultural conviviality based on mutual respect and dignity among the different groups that make up Brazilian society. Afro-Brazilians are invited specifically to "develop their own 'liberation ideology,' based on their own historical experience, not in order to separate themselves from the rest of Brazil, but to prepare to lead the nation, as its majority population, in a democratic context" (*Africans in Brazil* 65).

While Nascimento's proposal may sound radical in some quarters, his efforts to bring about equality must be understood within the ancestral framework. Dr. Emmanuel, the *assimilado* protagonist in his thesis-play, *Sortilégio* (Sortilege), echoes the alienated *assimilé* referred to in Birago Diop's ancestral tale "Sarzan." Highly educated, sophisticated *but* black, divided between the love of black Ifigênia and white Margarida, Dr. Emmanuel chooses Margarida for the sake of upward social mobility. Problematizing the racial question, Nascimento frustrates Dr. Emmanuel by making him go through several rites of passage that will ultimately bring him into full consciousness of his own black identity, with particular emphasis on such issues as police brutality and the fact that Margarida does not want any mixed offspring—just the convenient warmth and intimacy of a black body. And this is where the racial democracy thesis falls apart. Margarida repeatedly kills the potential biracial offspring through self-inflicted abortions. By the time Dr. Emmanuel comes to his "ancestral senses," it is almost too late, for the ancestors are already angry with him and must be appeased. Appeasement means sacrifice. Dr. Emmanuel is sacrificed on the altar of Eüu (the trickster figure), but because the ancestors are such good supernatural spirits, they give him an opportunity to redeem himself by symbolically making him shed his three-piece suit for the "ancestral loincloth" symbolizing freedom from assimilation and alienation. His ritual sacrifice and inevitable redemption signal the possibility of regeneration for the likes of Dr. Emmanuel in our society and the potential for change and harmony in our chaotic, diversified, and fascinating world.

Following in the footsteps of Abdias do Nascimento and with a similar global vision of ethnicity in his music and politics, Gilberto Gil, the international musical maestro (who I prefer to call "Baba Alapala," a name echoed in the title of one of his albums), was until 2008 the Brazilian minister of culture in the Lula administration. His Pan-African consciousness reverberates in his forty-year musical career with more than five hundred musical pieces now collected under the title *Gilberto Gil: Todas as letras*. Often referred to as the "praise-singer of the gods" due to the primacy of spirituality and the recognition of the ancestors in most of his music, which may be described as a synthesis of the popular and the sacred, he occupies a leadership position in the preservation and renewal of re-Africanization waves in Brazil since the 1970s, especially in Bahia.

In "Baba Alapala," one of his paradigmatic songs on Pan-African consciousness, Gil transcends continental bounds and historical eras such as slavery. Here he has crafted a song that is simultaneously African, Brazilian, Bahian, and African diasporan, as it situates the music in divine history during the celebration of the *eguns*, the frightful ancestral spirits that are still worshipped in Brazil today, especially in Itaparica. Using the interrogative voice of a young man who wants to know his lineage since the god being worshipped, *Aganju*, is the youngest version of Ṣàngó, the god of thunder whose characteristics include cheerful, daring, fun-loving, restless, and hot tempered, the percussive and spirited rhythm of the melody signals the unruliness of Ṣàngó. It is as if the singer is an incarnation of Ṣàngó himself with his mystique of invincibility that led to the legendary story of the famous king of Oyo, who is euphemistically referenced as *Oba Koso* and fictionalized in a play written and performed by Duro Ladipo. By tracing the lineage of the young man to royalty and divinity since Ṣàngó later became an òrìṣà or god, Gil implies that Afro-Brazilians not only have a proud history and past but also have every reason to celebrate their mythical and divine dimensions based on that ancestral connection.

These two examples are united by a commonality of preoccupations defined by identity and sense of origin. In the African diaspora, the issue of identity remains a constant zone of contestation and negotiation. In Brazil, the mulatto/mulatta figure represented in official quarters as the synthesis of the cosmic race in the racial paradise ultimately symbolizes the quintessential problematic entity, "neither, nor, and both," thus creating a crisis of both consciousness and identity. In that confusion, often seen as an edge in terms of political fluidity and astuteness, the biracial character wants to have it both ways—to be accepted by both races as an ally. But in fact, both races are usually suspicious of and nervous about this problematic biracial figure.

Can he or she be trusted? To blacks, when male, he is a traitor; when female, she is a "superior" beauty but still not "blonde" enough. To whites, if female, she is an object of desire, a "prostitute" par excellence; but when male, he is the perfect go-between, the unprincipled multivocal negotiator who will not hesitate to betray his own people for a mere token—hence only good for contingency interests.

In the final analysis, ancestrality proposes a neutralization of social hierarchies—gender, race, class, and other conflicting and alienating interests—through respect for self, others, and nature through which the ancestors manifest themselves. It operates on the assumption and the possibility of harmony within a cosmic constellation that sees good and evil (*tibi-tire*) as complementary forces and not necessarily antithetical to one another.

Dynamics of Afro-Modernity

The understanding of Afro-modernity in its varied manifestations also demands a deeper appreciation of its dynamics in Afro-Brazilian life and culture. Afro-Brazilian cultural producers have always struggled with devising self-affirmative strategies in their works in the face of assimilationist forces. Wilson Martins, a foremost Brazilian critic, has this to say about the Brazilian Unified Black Movement as it relates to the quality of literary production: "The Black movement as well as the agrarian reform movement became more coherent in 1995, but still haven't produced first-quality literature. These groups along with human-rights movements have yet to transcend the polemical and circumstantial phase of artistic creation."

Martins's position echoes statements that have been made about Luso-African literature in its combative or revolutionary phase of the armed struggle when literature was seen more for being an "arma de combate" (combative arm of liberation) than for its capacity to the communicate aesthetic principles. We must, however, not be blind to the absolutist generalization and Eurocentrism in Wilson's statement. What does Martins mean by "first-quality" literature? And what does he mean by "transcend[ing] the polemical and circumstantial phase of artistic creation"? These questions are relevant to what I consider fundamental in the appreciation of Afro-Brazilian culture.

In applying the Afro-modernist model of ancestrality, what is "past" is inextricably linked with the present and the future. Thus, what is said to be "modern" is also culturally rooted in the "traditional" without necessarily being contradictory. In negotiating being modern and being ancestral or traditional at the same time, the intricate relationship and connections find their commonality in self-affirmation, self-definition toward a meaningful and cosmic wholeness, the valorization of memory, and resistance to all forms of subjugation. Afro-Brazilian cultural producers struggle with the "lusotropicalist" myth of racial paradise and miscegenation while drawing inspiration from the ancestral legacy, as illustrated by Abílio Ferreira's "A casa de Fayola" (Fayola's House). While the most natural affinity between Africa and Brazil echoes in the negritude consciousness, particularly in the New World, as well as the influence of Brazilian literature, on Lusophone African literature particularly in Cape Verde, contemporary literary works from both continents have continued to be mutually enriching. Examples are numerous with the most visible being the influence of Guimarães Rosa on Angolan Luandino Vieira and Mozambican Mia Couto; of Lusophone African and South African writers on modern Afro-Brazilian writers, especially the Quilombhoje, and even cultural groups such as Olodum and Ilê Aiyê whose members have either written or sang songs in homage to Nelson Mandela, Winnie Mandela, Samora Machel, Agostinho Neto, and Amilcar Cabral, among other African heroes, that resonate in Afro-Brazilian cultural production. We must also not forget the emblematic figure of Abdias do Nascimento, who has applied the Yoruba dramatic principle to his *Sortilégio* while advocating the continuity of Yoruba mythology in Afro-Brazilian theater and visual arts, as well as Gilberto Gil, the eminent musical maestro who continues to praise Yoruba gods in his music to the extent that he has earned the nickname of "Baba Alapala," that is, "master of Apala," referring to a Yoruba traditional rhythm. Of course, these are only examples, for to map all the African and Afro-Brazilian connections would require a different book.

The paradigmatic experience captured in "A casa de Fayola" as discussed in chapter 2 offers a relevant platform to understand the artificial dichotomy between ancestrality and modernity. In the global cultural sense, "modernity" as rejected by Fayola and as embraced by Alexandre need not be dichotomous. One need not "die" in order to affirm the other. The violent displacement and elimination of Fayola as an embodiment of resistant, ancestral model of the periphery begs the question: why does Fayola refuse to substitute Afro-Brazilian culture for global capitalism? Yet, Alexandre is equally naïve to assume that by merely killing Fayola, he has gotten rid of tradition and "backwardness" symbolized in Fayola's attachment to the Candomblé shrine that is situated within the "villa" or the metaphoric slum that she adamantly refused to leave. In the ancestral mode of thinking, Fayola's death is indeed a form of sacrifice, a form of regeneration and victory for cultural resistance as Fayola becomes a heroine who sacrificed her life for the continuity of African tradition in Brazil. In proposing a framework for exploring disjuncture and differences in the global cultural economy beyond the center–periphery models, Arjun Appadurai suggests that the key to untangling this complex formulation lies in the relationship between five dimensions of global cultural flows—what he calls *ethnoscapes, mediascapes, technoscapes, financescapes,* and *ideoscapes.* Through these "scapes," Appadurai proclaims, flows the "politics of the mutual effort of sameness and difference to cannibalize one another" (43). This global formulation provides a pertinent lesson for the assumed erasure of "difference" in the Brazilian context and a pretext of "sameness" as suggested by racial democracy. As a matter of fact, the cannibalization of Fayola, representing Afro-Brazilian culture, by Alexandre, representing a dominant Brazilian culture, illustrates how the process is not and cannot be mutual in Brazil. Afro-Brazilians are so marginalized and economically disempowered that they do not constitute an effective force of change in the political sense. The five "scapes" advanced by Appadurai can easily be collapsed into two in the Afro-Brazilian context: ethnoscape and ideoscape. The other "scapes" are structurally in the hands of the elite. Afro-Brazilian modernity is thus informed by cultural and ideological potentialities—areas that are unquestionably rich and viable yet economically and politically ill-equipped to bring about the kind of desirable revolution that would lead to the equality desperately needed in Brazil.

9

The Forerunners of Afro-Modernity

My various interview sessions with contemporary Afro-Brazilian writers revealed one issue that was controversial and contested among the interviewees: modernism and modernity. For reasons best explained by their resistance to any formulation emanating from the other—that is, the dominant Brazilian intellectual currents and traditions, and Western institutions in general, which marginalize whatever does not conveniently fit their neatly packaged "canonical" paradigms—these writers reject assertions, such as that by Wilson Martins, for example, that Afro-Brazilians are yet to produce "first-quality" literature.[1] As I pointed out in the preceding chapter, Afro-Brazilian writers were excluded from the most significant cultural and intellectual moment of Brazilian modernism, the *Semana de arte moderna* of 1922. Although writers like Cuti and Barbosa believe this movement has nothing to do with Afro-Brazilian modernity, I suggest that the fact that there were a number of mature writers, who were building on the legacies of Cruz e Souza and Lima Barreto of the turn of the century, such as Lino Guedes and later on Solano Trindade, was an indication of black literary expression deserving of acknowledgment. Instead, Afro-Brazilians were only thematized during that significant literary and cultural movement. As a result, many Afro-Brazilian writers remained marginalized well into the late 1970s. Through an examination of the works of Solano Trindade, Abdias do Nascimento, Eduardo de Oliveira, and Oswaldo de Camargo, this chapter gives due recognition to their contribution as forerunners of Afro-modernity.

In spite of their different backgrounds and exposure, a commonality of moral outrage and protest is found in the works of these writers, such as the concern for oppressed and poor blacks and the struggle to recuperate their African values as a source of inspiration. At the same time, it was necessary to show, however unconsciously, that they could write in the literary tradition that has been exclusively dominated by white and mulatto writers. Although they did not set out to write as Afro-modernists, the fact that the reality of urban life and the timing of political openness in Brazil put a burden on them to speak out against the injustices of racism, qualifies them as ushering in an era of cultural and literary nationalism for Afro-Brazilians. Of the four writers explored in this chapter, I interviewed three who are currently alive

(Nascimento, Camargo, and Oliveira) while Trindade passed away in 1974, ten years into the military dictatorship which lasted until 1985.

With the exception of Trindade, my criteria for selecting these writers were principally that they had contributed to the establishment of contemporary Afro-Brazilian modernity and were still alive to talk about their experiences through granted interviews. Whether during the era of Machado de Assis, Lima Barreto, Castro Alves, Cruz e Souza, and Luís Gama in the nineteenth century or of such writers as Jorge de Lima, Lino Guedes, and Abdias do Nascimento in the twentieth century, being black has been a burden to carry in Brazilian society. The strategies employed by writers to lighten that burden is the central concern of this critical endeavor.

Solano Trindade: An Afro-Brazilian Langston Hughes

Solano Trindade, whose surviving family in São Paulo took the trouble to acquaint me with the legacy of their father, was quite different in personality and poetic production from Lino Guedes, who is considered by many as the true pioneer of Afro-modernism. Although a contemporary of Guedes, Trindade transcends the burden of blackness seen by Guedes, who believed in assimilation and bourgeois education as the way out of poverty and oppression. Born in 1908 into a family of modest means, Trindade moved from Recife to Rio de Janeiro in 1939 after establishing the Centro de Cultura Afro-Brasileira and participating in the first Afro-Brazilian conferences in Recife and Salvador. After many failed efforts to start a theater production, he finally succeeded in 1950 when he set up the *Teatro Popular Brasileiro*. A poet, playwright, and folklorist, Trindade has not been given his due recognition in Brazilian letters as has been the case with most Afro-Brazilian writers before him and of his generation. He may be better known in cultural milieus of Europe than in his own country. Not only was he concerned with the Afro-Brazilian experience, he sought inspiration in such African writers of the diaspora as Aimé Césaire, Léon Damas, Langston Hughes, Léopold Senghor, and Nicolás Guillén. In essence, he was a negritudist writer who did not allow ideology to cloud his vision, but to enhance his values. Although he died poor and in ill health in 1974, his works remain a testament of his legacy as a gentle writer who sought the freedom and happiness of his people. Among these works are *Poemas negros* (Black Poems, 1936), *Poemas d'uma vida simples* (Poems of a Simple Life, 1944), *Seis tempos de poesia* (Six Eras of Poetry, 1958), and *Cantares ao meu povo* (Songs to My People, 1961).

Trindade's wailings in *Cantares ao meu povo* and *Tem gente com fome e outros poemas* (People Are Hungry and Other Poems) have their inspiration and origins in a deep consciousness of popular poetry and his belief that the poet must function not as an alienated sage singing to his people in esoteric tongues but as one that transforms his observations into a dialogue with racism and injustice. For Trindade, singing a simple poem about a simple people, in a simple language, and with a simple object of defending their dignity is all that matters. As he reminisced in his later years, "Poetry is my greatest legacy" (*Cantares* 96), Trindade captured the very essence of his life.

Belonging to the first generation of writers who lived in the aftermath of abolition (1888) amid its profound disillusionment, he was in the forefront of the movement to establish dignity and recognition for Afro-Brazilian writers, artists, and cultural producers in general. From his participation in the first Afro-Brazilian congresses in São Paulo and Recife, he became more inspired to dedicate his entire career to developing Afro-Brazilian culture. Instead of the dreams of the slaves and activists who fought for abolition being realized, freedom after abolition was only in principle, not in practice. Hence, twenty years after abolition when Solano Trindade was born, inequality was still a central fact of life for Afro-Brazilians. Growing up poor as the child of a shoemaker, limited to a basic education that may be compared to a high school level, Trindade tried to make the best of the limited opportunities available to him at the time but was bent on improving such a lifestyle for those who would come after him. He sarcastically presents the reader with an inside tour of his house in "poesia doméstica," where he confesses his material and scholarly deprivation:

A minha estante
É um caixão de cebola
E são poucos os livros
Que eu possuo. (*Cantares* 68)

[My book shelf / Is a box of onions. / And few are the books / That I can call mine.]

Yet, these limitations continue to drive the poet into further passionate engagement with the life and realities of his people: he is essentially a poet of the people.

Trindade's poetry may be divided into five broad topics in terms of recurrent thematic patterns and preoccupations: poetic art, negritudist sensibility and identity, hope despite racism and oppression, love and the women in his life, and old age, which concerned the poet in his later years. Although these poems speak for themselves, they also overlap in a few cases. A global view of his poetics reveals an accessible poetry robed in negritudist consciousness that is stoic enough to break the walls of racism toward love for every human being. In this sense, poetry is an instrument both of self-expression and of protest. The personal, autobiographical elements overlap with the collective to produce a genuine interest in the human condition and a belief in equality and justice for all regardless of the color of their skin.

Trindade professes his poetic art in a number of poems, in particular "Canto dos Palmares" (Chant of Palmares). That he calls his poetry a "song" and a "chant" makes obvious the concern of this poet with melody and ritual in spite of the simplicity of his poetic language. "Canto dos Palmares," by its very title, captures two images: song and freedom. Taken as a "song of freedom" by symbolic freedom fighters, "the *Palmares*" (runaway slaves), "Canto dos Palmares" is both a tribute and a poetic testament in which the twenty-five stanzas, Trindade's longest poetic composition, articulates a social vision and political awareness of blackness and the master-slave vision that requires awareness from the viewpoint of structural juxtaposition.

The poet begins by invoking classic poets whose poetry he contrasts to his own, which is more engaged:

Eu canto aos Palmares
sem inveja de Virgílio de Homero
e de Camões
porque o meu canto
é o grito de uma raça
em plena luta pela liberdade! (*Cantares* 23)

[I sing to the Palmares / without being envious of Homer, Virgil, / and Camões / for my chant / is a cry of a people / in plain struggle for freedom!]

In this provocative comparison between the classical and the popular, Trindade achieves two aesthetic and ideological effects. First, he ridicules Homer and Camões by suggesting that he is not envious of them for their commitment is totally different. Second, he defines his art as a "cry . . . for freedom," hence, himself as more of a popular wailer than a classical sonnetist.

The entire poem is declarative, enumerating the injustices of the slaveholders as well as the counteroffensives of the fugitive slaves who sacrificed for freedom and resisted the devastation of body and spirit in order to be free. Trindade captures the participation of nature in this resistance by referring to the voices of the palm trees, the ripples caused in the rivers they crossed, and the cries of the jungles they traversed in their search for freedom. Dramatizing this act of rebellion, Trindade shows the stoic position of the Palmares as he recounts the atrocities as well as the tragic flaw of the masters:

Fecham minha boca
Mas deixam abertos os meus olhos
Maltratam meu corpo
Minha consciência se purifica

Eu fujo das mãos
Do maldito senhor! (*Cantares* 23)

[They close my mouth / But they leave my eyes open / They mistreat my body / My conscience becomes purified / I escape from the hands / Of the accursed master!]

In a narrative yet poetic style, Trindade gives an account of the struggles of the Palmares as they fight the oppressor. Instead of enjoying the tranquil rest of the Palmares, the oppressors are sleepless and restless as they constantly conspire to invade and recapture the territories of the Palmares. Trindade celebrates the qualities of resistance, struggle, and protest possessed by the Palmares:

Ainda sou poeta
meu poema
levanta os meus irmãos . . .
Minhas amadas
se preparam para a luta (*Cantares* 25)

[I am still a poet / my poem / uplifts my brothers . . . / My beloved ones / prepare for the struggle.]

Confessing his poetry is as "simple as life itself" (26), Trindade uses this "simplicity" in a complex way by ridiculing the actions of the oppressor while praising the efforts of the oppressed to be free. This dialectical tension pervades the entire poem as "bloody civilization" and "false faith" contrast with images of the "shout of war" and "freedom." The long poem closes with the triumph of freedom over oppression, articulation over silence, and the redemption of Zumbi, the courageous leader of the Palmares.

Other poems which reflect Trindade's poetic art such as "Eu sou poeta negro" (I Am a Black Poet), "Estética" (Aesthetics), "Poeta" (Poet), "Amar é uma constante em mim" (Love Is a Constant in Me), and "Senhora Gramática" (Madam Grammar) reinforce the poet's penchant for love, resistance, and regeneration, as adequately explored in "Canto dos Palmares." Not only does the poet promise to fight against injustice, he also appreciates the fact that black oppression and struggle have lasted many centuries: "As minhas batalhas / Tem a duração de séculos" (94; My battles / Endure for centuries). For Trindade, in "Estética," poetry must not be limited in its expression since "aesthetic emotions" (60) need not be censored. The poet further sarcastically declares in "Senhora Gramática" that his "grammatical mistakes" must be pardoned since as a simple poet he will not be pressured to become an esoteric poet:

Senhora Gramática
perdoai os meus pecados gramaticais.
Se não perdoares,
senhora
eu errarei mais. (*Tem gente com fome* 22)

[Madam Grammar / Pardon my grammatical mistakes. / If you don't pardon me / Madam / I will make more mistakes.]

In summing up Trindade's poetic art, the place of love must not be overlooked for the poet declares in "Amar é uma constante em mim" that his present, past, and future have always been an affirmation of love. The centrality of love in Trindade's poem is more than a kiss, an affection, a desire, but a constancy that defines his being as the title appropriately suggests. In fact, love is a timeless and spaceless aesthetic principle for the poet:

O meu amor não está limitado ao tempo
E ao espaço
Tem um sentido estético
É eterno. (82)

[My love is not limited in time / and space / It has an aesthetic meaning / It is eternal.]

Another poetic constant in the poetry of Trindade is captured in his negritudist sensibility and identity that goes beyond the confines of Brazil to the black world in general. Of the many poems written about black identity, his most compelling is "Sou negro" (I Am Black), in which the poet pays homage to his ancestral African origin as well as the legacy of this transformation in Brazil as reflected in the music of samba and love of freedom:

Sou negro
meus avós foram queimados
pelo sol da África
minha'alma recebeu o batismo dos tambores
atabaques, gonguês e agogôs. (*Cantares* 32)

[I am black / my ancestors were burnt / by the African sun / my soul received the baptism of tam-tams / drums, gongs, and *agogos*.]

This musical legacy is further regionalized as in the Maracatu of the Northeast, which Trindade captures in "Tristes maracatus" (Sad Maracatus). Using this music as a unifying trope for all the African ethnic groups who were enslaved in Brazil (Keto, Jêje, Angola, Congo, Mozambique), Trindade captures their sadness and happiness in the divided selves that are part of their condition. The poet's love for *maracatu* music is further engaged in "Eu quero maracatucar" (I Want to Create Maracatu Music) as a pretext to transcend the sadness that accompanies slavery and old age:

> Eu não quero envelhecer
> Eu não quero escravidão
> Eu quero juventude e liberdade
> Eu quero Maracatucá. (*Cantares* 87)

> [I don't want to age / I don't want slavery / I want youthfulness and freedom / I want Maracatu.]

In addition to exploring the various folklore of different regions of Brazil where Afro-Brazilians live through music, Trindade pays homage to the cities that affected him the most from birth through his old age such as Recife, Rio de Janeiro, and Salvador. Praising his city of birth in "Canção à minha cidade natal" (Song to My Native City), Trindade enumerates memories of landscapes, images of his birth house, festivals, street vendors, workers on strike, and a statue of Şàngó (Yoruba god of thunder) in the middle of the city; all define what makes it the "world's best city" that parades the "world's best Carnival" (46). Apparently nostalgic and romantic about Recife, the poet's image of Rio is more of suffering and adaptation, even of indifference. Of all the significant tourist attractions in Rio, Trindade confesses that he has not visited any of them:

> Nunca me banhei no Copacabana
> nunca fui ao Corcovado
> nunca fui ao Pão de Açúcar
> por tudo quanto é sagrado. (*Cantares* 48)

> [I never swam in Copacabana beach / I never visited Corcovado (Statue of Christ the Redeemer) / I never went to the Sugarloaf Hill / even if they are such sacred places.]

By contrast, Bahia is not only alluring but enchanting. The poet longs to see Bahia again as he notes with emotion that Bahia lives in his soul:

> Bahia que vive em minha alma . . .
> criação maravilhosa
> de minha raça . . . (*Cantares* 49)

> [Bahia which lives in my soul . . . / marvelous creation / of my race.]

The poet's exploration of music and the city is a clever means of preserving individual, architectural, and folkloric identities through poetry. More engaging in Trindade's poetry is his exposition of the injustices against the oppressed, the downtrodden, and the average worker as well as the defiant hope that keeps them undaunted. "Tem gente com fome" (People Are Hungry) is an enactment of hunger as captured in the onomatopoeic train movement that equates deprivation with a certain anguish that is better communicated by the doubt created in the meaning of the train's dirt, noise, and velocity. There is an unspoken parallelism here between hungry people and the velocity of the train:

> Trem sujo da Leopoldina
> correndo correndo
> parece dizer
> tem gente com fome
> tem gente com fome
> tem gente com fome. (*Cantares* 35)

> [Dirty train from Leopoldina / running running / seems to be saying / people are hungry / people are hungry / people are hungry.]

The repetition of "people are hungry" accentuates the urgency of the situation: poverty corrupts the soul and deprives the hungry of their sanity and health. The train indeed is personified; it is a metaphor of the hungry people. And for the worker, labor is the only form of overcoming poverty. The irony lies in the fact that even for the worker, there are no guarantees; a better life is only a dream, the poet says in "O canto do trabalhador" (Worker's Song):

> Amanhã será melhor,
> é o canto do trabalhador,
> que sai cansado do campo,
> que sai cansado da fábrica,
> para o desconforto do lar. (*Tem gente com fome* 10)

> [Tomorrow will be better, / is the song of the worker, / who leaves tired from the field, / who leaves tired from the factory, / and returns to the discomfort of his home.]

Despite these injustices of life and living, Trindade sings of hope as in "Canto da esperança" (Song of Hope), in which the poet, close to his last days, affirms that "there is always a poem waiting for me . . . / I will never have time to die" (42) only to add in another poem whose title is self-explanatory, "Nem tudo está perdido" (Everything Is Not Lost) as if to remain stoic and optimistic.

Behind Trindade's optimism about life are the women to whom he has given and from whom he has also received affection and tenderness. He calls them "as amadas da minha ternura," as in the poem of the same title (The Lovers of My Tenderness) where he expresses the feeling that love conquers everything: misery, hunger, pain, wars, hypocrisy, mediocrity, and lies. For the poet, the consolation is here in these lines:

Vou abraçar
as minhas amadas
vou beijá-las ternamente
sentir seus olhos, seus seios. (*Cantares* 95)

[I will embrace / my lovers / I will kiss them tenderly / feel their eyes, their breasts.]

For Trindade, love, is not an emotional manifestation or satisfaction; it is a permanent state of mind that self-regenerates according to the needs of the poet:

Quando um amor no peito morre
outro amor no peito nasce
Coração de poeta é terra boa
para plantar o amor. (*Cantares* 55)

[When one love of the heart dies / another love of the heart is born / The poet's heart is a good land / to plant love.]

Love could even become revolutionary, as in the poem "Vida" (Life) where the poet takes a cursory look at his life reminiscing about his philosophy of life as captured in the essence of love:

Sou amante da revolução
Amo a paz
Amo a ternura . . .
Amo o oprimido
Odeio o opressor
Amo as mulheres. (*Cantares* 57)

[I am lover of revolution / I love peace / I love tenderness . . . / I love the oppressed / I hate the oppressor / I love women.]

These poems reveal a poet who combines his inner pain with passion that being a lover provides while at the same time remaining a revolutionary in the face of oppression and injustice.

In his last years, Trindade became obsessed with the problematic of aging, owing, especially to his illness that took him from one hospital bed to another in search of cure and tranquility. Three main poems capture this final phase of the poet's life: "Canção da minha velhice" (Song of My Old Age), "Meditações sobre o leito do hospital" (Meditations on the Hospital Bed), and "Velhice, tema poético" (Old Age, a Poetic Theme). Trindade sees his old age as a kind of rebirth so long as he is able to write about it, thus giving a new life to a slowly dying body, as in "Song of My Old Age":

> A minha velhice merece uma bonita canção
> A minha velhice
> é uma nova juventude
> cheia de um novo amor. (*Cantares* 81)

> [My old age deserves a beautiful song / my old age / is a new youthfulness / full of a new love.]

This positive and vibrant perspective on life echoes in Martinho da Vila's music when he says in "Canta, canta, minha gente" (Sing, Sing, My People) that "Death, for me, is no departure but death is life starting all over again." Yet, Trindade must face his drama of loneliness in the hospital as he struggles for his life, as captured in "Meditations" where the poet's tone turns melancholic:

> A amada distante está presente
> A rua é uma abstração
> O telefone não chama
> A amada não beija. (*Cantares* 80)

> [My distant lover is present / The street is an abstraction / The telephone does not ring / My lover kisses no more.]

Trindade's illness was so burdensome that he was living in a twilight zone: neither wishing to live nor quite ready to die. A time of both nostalgia about the past and sadness in the present, old age becomes a relevant poetic theme as time gradually passes the old warrior by, as he confesses in "Velhice, tema poético" so ambivalently:

> Não pararei de poetar
> sinto uma necessidade permanente de poesia
> Não pararei de lutar
> tenho obrigação de lutar até o fim da vida
> Não pararei de amar
> o amor é tudo em mim. (*Cantares* 90)

[I will not stop writing poetry / I feel a permanent need for poetry / I will not stop struggling / I have an obligation to struggle till the end of my life / I will not stop loving / Love means everything to me.]

The poet sums up his worldview in this enigmatic moment of the desire to live in the face of approaching death. Dangling between writing poetry, keeping the struggle alive, and not missing every opportunity to love, Trindade remains faithful to his poetic manifesto to the very end.

While the blues poetry of Langston Hughes echoes in Solano Trindade in the form of irony, humor, and such psychological complexities as the attempt to love the one that does him wrong, one must not forget the explicit humanism of both writers. In sharing the pain of the oppressor as well as the oppressed, in his disdain for humiliation and oppression, Trindade finds his own humanist niche.

Abdias do Nascimento: Chief Priest and Invocator of Yoruba Gods

Abdias do Nascimento, a champion of Afro-Brazilian theater beyond the imagination of Solano Trindade, and a crusader of true democracy that includes blacks, has achieved an emblematic stature in Brazilian politics and culture. An accomplished painter as well, Nascimento finds inspiration in African gods (òrìṣàs) as transplanted into the diaspora, where they serve as guiding lights for lost African children who hold on to this heritage with passionate spirituality. Born in São Paulo in 1914, he is known as the founder of the famous Experimental Black Theater (*Teatro Experimental do Negro*, or *TEN*), which served as a stage for the denunciation of racism and the mobilization of awareness among blacks in general. A global activist, writer, and scholar, Nascimento has lived and taught in Nigeria, the United States, Colombia, and Panama and continues to be an active and militant figure in Afro-Brazilian affairs. His works range from the culturally grounded to the politically charged, and his legacy has been recognized with honorary doctorates by two Brazilian universities, Rio de Janeiro and Bahia, and another from Ọbafẹmi Awolọwọ University in Ile-Ifẹ, Nigeria. He also served as secretary of culture in Rio de Janeiro and federal senator in Brasília from 1994 to 1997. His works include *Sortilégio, Dramas para negros e prólogo para brancos, O negro revoltado, O genocídio do negro brasileiro, Sitiado em Lagos, Orixas: Os deuses vivos da África*, and a series of edited journals such as *Thoth* and *Afrodiáspora*. Vibrant and full of life, Nascimento was living in Rio de Janeiro when I interviewed him in 2000 in the company of his wife, Elisa Larkin Nascimento, and his secretary, Éle Semog. This study focuses on his only poetry collection, *Axés do sangue e da esperança (orikis)* (Blessings of Blood and Hope).

The idea of considering Nascimento as a poet is quite fascinating and something of an anomaly, for as a literary figure he has always been associated more with theater and visual images, not lyrical poetry. Yet, Nascimento has always possessed the consciousness of the poet in his oratorical gifts and pronouncements. At the core of his's poetry lies the duality of life and death, a regenerative impulse embedded in the very title of the poetic collection under consideration: *Blessings of Blood and Hope*. The notion of *axé*, which is translated here as "blessing," has a more ritualistic and liturgical meaning in its Yoruba etymology: àṣẹ in Yoruba means "amen," "so be it," or a general sense of authoritative power to grant a supplication or make it come to pass. In invoking "blessings" of the gods, there is an ambivalence of meaning in the deployment of àṣẹs in the sense of both seeking blessing and also paying homage. It is this enriching ambivalence that makes the collection a compelling treatise on praise-poetry. In fact, part of the title, "orikis" betrays the notion of praise for Nascimento is deeply aware of the implication of praise in Yoruba cosmogony. *Oríkì* refers to Yoruba praise-poetry chanted to evoke the attributes of humans (living, dead, or unborn), animals, places, kings, and even gods.

In *Axés do sangue e da esperança*, myth and ideology collide with memories of people and places all over the world thus invoking a Pan-Africanist consciousness and humanism. The poems of this collection reveal the poetic side of an Afro-Brazilian political figure the way he has not been seen by many. From paying homage to African gods; discovering autobiographical mementos through memory; declaring the validity of love and regeneration; using the *oríkì* to capture the praise of family, friends, relatives and loved ones; immersing the reader in religious and ritualistic consciousness; and seeing poetry as an instrument of combat and freedom in all its possibilities, Abdias do Nascimento communicates with the living and the oppressed while bringing them into dialogue with their ancestors. As Lélia Gonzalez points out, Nascimento's tripartite artistic creation is supported by an inner strength that translates his feelings and ideas into poetic metaphors: "É dessa força vital doadora da existência e da transformação dos seres que ele retira a energia que perpassa os três registros em que sua criação artística se expressa"[2] (From this vital force, giver of existence, and transformer of beings, he recovers the energy that shapes the three areas through which he releases his artistic creation). Noted for his duality and indeterminacy as captured in the figure of the trickster in Yoruba mythology, Èṣù is revered by his worshippers and theorists alike.[3]

No one understands the importance of ritual better than the veteran priest and poet-worshipper of Èṣù himself. The entire book of poems may be called a celebration of the gods; the poet invokes, in different instances, the virtues of Èṣù, Òṣun, Yemoja, Ògún, Ṣàngó, and Òriṣànlá. Nascimento opens the collection with a homage to Èṣù, god of the crossroads and contradiction in

Yoruba mythology. In so doing, he basically gets permission before entering into the muse of poetry so that the energy so released will be positive, or if negative, intended to bring about balance, healing, and fulfillment. "Padê de Exu Libertador" (Èṣù the Liberator's Ritual Offering) is a powerful double-edged invocation where Èṣù is simultaneously praised and also asked a favor. Èṣù's qualities are enumerated, the injustices of his worshippers (Afro-Brazilians) are highlighted, and each stanza serves as an elaboration of gradually accumulating supplications to end these anomalies through the power of the word and action.

Divided into four movements, "Padê de Exu Libertador" is a call for action on the part of Èṣù. In order to have more dialogic effect, the poetic voice calls on Èṣù directly. One of the longest poems in the collection, it unmasks the poet in his moment of obsession and heightened spirituality as he submits totally to the will of this god while urging a better life for his people. Like an Afro-Brazilian Moses on top of Mount Sinai, Nascimento performs this ritual with dedication and passion while informing Èṣù of the wailings and tribulations of his people. The first movement recognizes the ferocious nature of this god as a praise meant to urge action:

Ó Exu
ao bruxoleio das velas
vejo-te comer a própria mãe . . .
nas veias humanas
no corrimento menstrual
à encruzilhada dos
teus três sangues
deposito este ebó
preparado para ti. (*Axés* 9)

[Oh Èṣù / during the unconscious moment of candle burning / I see you devour your own mother . . . / in the human veins / running like menstrual stream / at the crossroads of / your three bloods / I deposit this *ẹbọ*(offering) / prepared just for you.]

By describing Èṣù as a god that would not even spare his own mother, the poem portrays this god as so fearless and terrible that no one should dare provoke his wrath.

Having asked for "àṣẹ verbal" (verbal power) once stolen but now recuperated and regained, having recognized the voracious nature of Èṣù, having offered a ritual offering, and having asked for the offering to be accepted, the poet then goes on to ask for protection against all forces of evil, oppression, and inequalities through the laws of natural retribution and cosmic harmony controlled by Èṣù himself:

> Fecha meu corpo aos perigos
> transporta-me nas asas da
> tua mobilidade expansiva
> cresça-me à tua linhagem
> de ironia preventiva . . .
> amadureça-me à tua
> desabusada linguagem. (*Axés* 11)
>
> [Protect my body against dangers / transport me in the feathers / of your expansive mobility / let me grow in the lineage of / your preventive irony . . . / let me mature in your / ever blunt language.]

This second movement's closure with the recognition that Èṣù is the god of communication and message confirms the need to invoke his compassion and blessing before setting out on this poetic journey.

The third movement is a specific request for Èṣù to carry the supplication of Afro-Brazilians to the Supreme God by exposing such injustices and anguish as slavery and discrimination:

> Faça chegar ao Pai a
> notícia da nossa devoção . . .
> exiba ao Pai
> nossos corações
> feridos de angústia
> nossas costas
> chicoteadas
> ontem
> no pelourinho da escravidão
> hoje
> no pelourinho da discriminação. (*Axés* 13)
>
> [Let the news of our devotion / arrive at the feet of our Father . . . / expose to our Father / our hearts / full of anguish / our backs / flagellated / yesterday / at the Pelourinho of slavery / today / at the Pelourinho of discrimination.]

This exposition is accusatory since its object is to highlight oppression and to pay homage to Afro-Brazilian heroes who endured these injustices through personal sacrifices. In the last movement, Nascimento enumerates and shifts the *oríkì* from Èṣù to Afro-Brazilian heroes. In so doing, he recognizes some of the qualities of Èṣù in these heroes of freedom and struggle:

> Exu
> tu que és o senhor dos
> caminhos da libertação do teu povo

> sabes daqueles que empunharam
> teus ferros em brasa
> contra a injustiça e a opressão
> Zumbi Luiza Mahin Luiz Gama
> Cosme Isidore João Cândido
> sabes que em cada coração de negro
> há um quilombo pulsando. (*Axés* 13)

[Èṣù / you who are the lord of / the crossroads of your people's freedom / who know those who carried / your iron shield on their chest / against injustice and oppression / Zumbi Luiza Mahin Luís Gama / Cosme Isidoro João Cândido / who know that in the heart of every African Brazilian / there is a *quilombo* pulsating.]

This powerful opening sets the tone for the complexity and ambivalence of the collection as the reader struggles with praise and indictment, with worship and supplication, with combat as well as compassion.

In the remaining poems about homage to the òrìṣàs, Nascimento integrates the values of these gods with his yearnings for change in the so called Brazilian racial paradise. In "Escalando a Serra da Barriga" (Making a Stop at the Serra da Barriga), Nascimento documents his visit to a historic mount in Alagoas called "Serra da Barriga" (Mount of the Belly), one of the settlements of freed slaves in the late nineteenth century. A spiritual journey to undertake, Nascimento feels like a Yoruba diviner (*babalawo*) who consults the sixteen cowries to uncover the mysteries of what must have transpired on this sacred mountain of revolt, resistance, and death. He surmises ideologically and philosophically that this mount is like a temple, a heritage that must be preserved for future generations:

> Esta é minha herança prematura
> na integridade do seu amor
> na violência da luta passada
> no sacrifício certo do presente
> na certeza da vitória futura. (*Axés* 31)

[This is my premature heritage / in the integrity of its love / in the violence of past struggle / in the assured sacrifice of the present / in the certainty of its future victory.]

In "Prece a Oxum" (Invocation to Ọ̀ṣun) and "Axexê em Oxum" (Funeral Ritual to Ọ̀ṣun), Nascimento deploys the regenerative nature of Ọ̀ṣun to seek protection and guidance as he journeys from the origins into the future and back. Both poems were written in exile in Nigeria and in the United States, thus indicating the poet's ability to maintain spiritual connections between the continents through the central energy of àṣẹ that runs through his veins as well as his penchant for documenting his experiences in different parts of the world.

Of the different autobiographical moments in this collection, such as in "Autobiografia" (Autobiography), "Testemunhando búfalo" (Witnessing Buffalo), and "Brisas panamenenhas" (Panamanian Breeze), the most compelling is the visit to the historic island of Gorée in Senegal, the transitory depot of slaves before they were transported to the New World. In "Peregrinação à Gorea" (Pilgrimage to Gorée), dedicated symbolically to Kariamu and Molefi Asante, Nascimento blends his positive emotions with anger forced out of sheer memory of what it was like in the inner chambers of the Gorée fort. By calling it a pilgrimage, the poet suggests a spiritual endeavor with a dual purpose: purification and embrace as a way of coming to terms with history. The repetition of "descent" implies a downward journey into the abyss:

Desço aos abismos do ódio . . .
Pelo teu ventre aberto
Gorea
alcanço a rota dos navios negreiros
refaço a tragédia
o trajeto
a epopéia da minha raça. (*Axés* 74–75)

[I descend into the abysses of hate / Through your open belly / Gorée / I reach the route of the black ships / I revisit the tragedy / the journey / the epic poetry of my people.]

While autobiographical moments turn revolutionary in *Axés do sangue e da esperança*, erotic moments serve not only as memories but as a regenerative release perhaps from the pressure of daily stress as experienced by most Afro-Brazilians. Poems like "Lucinda," "Axexê em Oxum," and "O sangue e a esperança" have their moments not only of eroticism but of procreation. In its play on the double sense of the name of the loved protagonist emanating from *luz* (light), "Lucinda" becomes a metaphor for an invitation to illumination that people in love often share. There is a sense of urgency as the poetic voice invites Lucinda to come to fulfill an act of conjugation between sex, flower, and the moon:

Não partissem os enamorados
(viagem sem regresso)
em amor circumflexo

amplexo da rosa
lua
e sexo. (*Axés* 70)

[Lovers should not separate / (journey with no return) / in circumflex love / amplexus of rose / moon / and sex.]

Yet, the poetic voice is not an ordinary lover; he is also the pastor of those who struggle and of prostitutes. This concern for the humanity of all people of different classes and circumstances betrays a deeper consciousness that love goes beyond the erotic—it is universal. The last poem of the collection, "Axexê em Oxum," which is incidentally circular and erotic, suggests an endless journey such as the one that takes place during the act of lovemaking. Nascimento likens the staff of Òrìṣàńlá (*Paxorô*) to the penis that swings back and forth from heaven to earth like a pendulum as if to suggest life without end as well as regeneration of life in death. Lovemaking thus becomes a symbolic process of dying and living at the same time:

Sob teu opá do mistério
comando o mistério do
meu próprio funeral...
enquanto meu pênis-opá
toca o sagrado do
princípio-fim-princípio. (*Axés* 104)

[Under your mysterious staff / I command the mystery of / my own funeral... / while my penis-staff / touches the sacred in / the beginning-end-beginning.]

In these memories, often religious, mythological, and ideological, the family plays an important role as well as relatives and loved ones. Nascimento approaches his family with tenderness paying homage to them in the form of the *oríkì*. Like the opening poem, "Mãe" (Mother) is another long poem of invocation and supplication. This is a journey through familiar landscapes of Franca, the poet's birthplace as well as the guarding symbol of memories of his mother. The accompanying photograph of both parents, Dona Georgina and José Ferreira do Nascimento, is a compelling image of those who gave the poet life and to whom he honors. "Mother" here is more than just the biological mother; it is used as a trope for life itself since the mother is generally considered as the life-giving force. The poetic voice's need to "navigate" as repeated in the poem concedes an inner desire to revisit memories of childhood in Franca. The poet leads the reader through the "coffee plantations," "the primordial waters of Olokun," "the blood of the land," "the orange flower perfume," "slave martyrs," and finally pays respects at the mother's tomb, which he considers sacred for it feeds on her mother's milk and blood—essential liquid elements of motherhood and regeneration.

Aside from poetically paying homage to his mother in his poetry, Nascimento, in *Axés*, sings praise-songs to his wife, Elisa, and to their beloved daughter, Yemoja. It may well be puzzling to the reader that parents would consciously name their children after a Yoruba river goddess such as Yemoja, but this is actually common among devotees. The case of Nascimento, an Afro-Brazilian, is also explainable as he spent part of his years of exile in Nigeria. In "Evocação da rosa" (Evocation of the Rose), the poet refers to his daughter as "cat-rose" and "flower-rose," images of tenderness, care and affection which sum up his love for this lovable and multicolored child. In singing the praise of his daughter, the poet also tells a story within a story: that of an episode of sadness when she loses one of her kittens to a wild cat. The reader gets the sense that this episode may have been invented to illustrate the gentleness and sweetness of the daughter. Nascimento also salutes his wife in "Oriki da Elisa," in which the poet confesses his love through variations in health and in frailty, in bounty and in need, as if to suggest a symbol of perfection in Elisa. Here is Nascimento praising Elisa:

> Amor unijugado
> no trabalho a quatro mãos
> na luta compartilhada
> de esperança em comunhão
> ao ritmo das coisas belas
> ao gosto agreste do bom
> do belo que profetiza
> a ternura que és tu
> Elisa. (*Axés* 43)

[Joined together in love / in work with four hands / in the shared struggle / of hope and communion / in the rhythm of beautiful things / in the crude taste of goodness / and beauty that profess / the tenderness that you are / Elisa.]

Through these family portrayals, Nascimento reveals that, politics aside, he is only human. He loves and feels pain like all of us.

In *Axés do sangue e da esperança*, the ritual that opens the volume continues throughout the book as the poet makes continual references to African gods. But it is in "O agadá da transformação" (The Sword of Transformation) that we find an archetypal ritualistic poem similar to the depth of the opening poem, "Padê de Exu," which celebrates Èṣù. Transformation is indeed what this collection is all about: the transformation of oppression into rebellious energy where survival must be articulated through the power of the word. "The Sword of Transformation" is a testament to solidarity with fellow Afro-Brazilians; the symbolic poet–chief priest hands over the sword-staff as a gesture of the continuity of the struggle. Making allusions to Ọṣun, Orisanla, Ògún, and Ifa in the first movement of the poem, Nascimento educates his people about their rich past, their painful present, and the need to take advantage of ancestral virtues wherein true power lies:

> Somos a semente noturna do ritmo
> a consciência amarga da dor
> florescida nos toques anunciadores
> da perenidade das coisas vivas
> à batida dos tambores. (*Axés* 86)

[We are the nocturnal seed of rhythm / the bitter conscience of pain / flowering in clarion calls / of perennial and lively things / communicated through drumbeats.]

While "The Sword of Transformation" is the most structurally melodious and rhythmical poem of the entire collection, its politics are equally more engaging. The symbol of the "sword" must not be taken simplistically. It echoes an urgency that needs to be addressed as if calling for social intervention. The call for transformation is a call to action as the poetic voice urges his people to stop complaining and to take up the challenge to change their destiny that is in their own hands:

> Não é tempo de reclamar
> nem tempo de chorar
> tempo é de afirmar nosso direito ao poder
> tempo é de batalhar . . .
> sem temer a incompreensão
> do inimigo ou do irmão. (*Axés* 88)

[This is no time for complaints / nor is it time for crying / it's time to affirm our rights to power / it's time to struggle . . . / without worrying about misunderstandings / by enemies of brothers.]

This combative spirit in the quest for total freedom is what unites the collection as poetry of protest, and songs of hope. Other poems of combat and freedom in the collection indicate the consciousness of a revolutionary who cannot be disguised in the homage paid to the gods, to relatives, and to the poet's loved ones. Indeed, *Axés do sangue e da esperança* combines a considerable dose of revolutionary optimism with memories inspired by people, places, and the gods. As the poet contemplates the wizard of Palmares who calls for the continued independence of the people of Puerto Rico ("El brujo de Palmares"), as he questions whether Brazil deserves to be called his "country" in spite of its injustices ("Imagem noturna de Copacabana"), as he expresses his solidarity with the oppressed of Latin America in general ("Rumo a Bluefields"), Nascimento's Pan-Africanist consciousness is on display. This consciousness is best expressed in "Mucama-mor das estrelas" (Greatest Woman of the Stars), a multivalent poem of love, praise, solidarity, and protest:

> Meu ferro de três pontas
> aponta em ti
> mucama-mor das estrelas
> os punhais da libertação
> Zumbi
> Ginga
> Toussaint
> Malcolm X
> Amilcar. (*Axés* 80)

[My three-pronged weapon / points toward you / greatest woman of the stars / the daggers of freedom / Zumbi / Ginga / Toussaint / Malcolm X / Amilcar.]

Taken as a Pan-Africanist statement, *Axés do sangue e da esperança* represents a message of love and transformation toward an eqüitable Brazilian society devoid of racism and discrimination.

Eduardo de Oliveira: "Words of Fire," Acts of Freedom

Like Abdias do Nascimento, Eduardo de Oliveira's interests are varied. He is a sonnetist, an attorney, a militant, and one of the most compassionate visionaries and dedicated individuals that I have ever met. As president of the *Congresso Nacional Afro-Brasileiro* (Afro-Brazilian National Congress), and working with considerable financial limitations, Oliveira has embarked on a cultural recuperative project by publishing, through grants from the Ministry of Justice and Human Rights, a series of "who's who in Brazilian Negritude" (*Quem é quem na negritude brasileira*, 1998) containing five hundred entries in the first volume alone. This is a much needed addition to documentation of the cultural producers and political activists for the Afro-Brazilian cause. An octagenarian, Oliveira was born in 1926 and continues to be active with issues of racial relations and discrimination in Brazil. As a teacher, poet, and administrator, he is well respected by such established writers and critics as Antônio Cândido and Fábio Lucas. His literary output includes *Além do pó* (1958), *Ancoradouro* (1960), *Banzo* (1962), *Gestas líricas da negritude* (1966), *Cancioneiro das horas* (1967), *Evangelho da solidão* (1968), *Túnica de ébano* (1980), *A cólera dos generosos* (1988), and *Carrossel de sonetos* (1994).

His most recent collection of poems, *Carossel de sonetos*, brings the reader in contact with a very mature poet whose commitment to his blackness transcends the limits of Brazil to encompass Africa, the United States, and other parts of the world where his people are found. In addition, the recurrent themes range from concerns about the burden of being Afro-Brazilian to more universally humanistic concerns about the human condition. Oliveira often directs his sonnets to those he is writing about, such as "brothers," "Mother Africa, "the poor of the third world," among others, equally dedicating every poem to important figures in the world of struggle and human family, such as Rosa Parks, Mário de Andrade, Langston Hughes, Adão Ventura, Clementina de Jesus, Clara Nunes, and Oprah Winfrey. Oliveira's breadth of knowledge of such international actors who have contributed to humanity in one way or another informs what a critic has appropriately called the "poetic and symbolic transcendentalism" of his poetry,[4] for it is hard to classify this poet conveniently, say, into the simple category of a negritude writer. Essentially, Oliveira reaches out beyond his color to embrace the world from philosophical, religious, and humanistic perspectives.

Outlining what may be considered his poetic testament in the beginning of the collection, Oliveira evokes the names of classical poets such as Saint-Beuve, Shakespeare, Petraca, Camões, Du Bellay, and Ronsard and promises to renew their art. But Oliveira's homage to these poets does not limit his own originality, for in "Soneto dos Sonetos" (Sonnet of Sonnets), the poetic voice suggests his inspiration comes from the burden of his black race:

> Quantos sonhos de amor jazem imersos
> em ti que és dor, temor, glória e desgraça?
> Foste a expressão sentimental da raça
> de um povo que viveu fazendo versos. (*Carossel* 25)

[How many dreams of love ferment / in you who are pain, fright, glory, and disgrace? / You were the sentimental expression of the race / of a people who live making poems.]

Oliveira recognizes his poetry as the "sentimental expression of the race" and in so doing defines his own poetic art. Sentimental, lucid, and critical, Oliveira blends classical tradition with modernist concerns as he navigates between elegant form and compelling content in a struggle for convergence wherein there is often more contradiction and ambiguity than clarity of commitment.

Following in the footsteps of Castro Alves and Cruz e Souza, Eduardo de Oliveira sees in poetry an outlet to sing the frustrations of daily living in their allegorical and musical possibilities. His black consciousness is as clear as his spirituality is betrayed by his mystical worldview. As Rodrigues points out in his appreciation of Oliveira's oeuvre, the poet "never ceases to be a social poet of his century" ("O transcendentalismo poético" 125). Here is a poem from *Túnica de ébano*, "Negra é a minha pele" (Black Is My Skin), to prove that sensibility of his times:

> Nada fui! Nada sou! Nada serei,
> Só porque negra é a cor de minha pele!
> Mesmo que tudo eu dê, pouco terei,
> Nesta Sodoma em que a ambição a impele!
> Diante desses racistas é que eu hei
> de amar o bem, antes que a dor revele
> que, por ser negro, ainda sustentarei
> seu império que, há tempos, me repele! (126)

[Nothing I was! Nothing I am! Nothing will I be, / Just because black is my skin! / Though I give everything, I gain little in return, / In this Sodom where ambition robs me of all. / Before these racists I must / love goodness before pain reveals / that for being black, I still must nourish / their empire which, for ages, repulses me.]

This poem provides a window into the commitment of Oliveira as a poet of conscience who can actually indict the racists that make his life meaningless and burdensome. On the whole, Oliveira's means, that is, the sonnet, becomes less crucial but yet calls for respect for this poet of sonnets who unlike Cruz e Souza is not trying to prove he could write like any white, simply wants to communicate his pain in the best form accessible to him.

At the center of Oliveira's poetry lies his blackness, which he defends with wry humor and combative poignancy. In his "negritude" poems, he mobilizes his people, he indicts the injustices of racism, and pays homage to black Africa, the inspirational muse of his poetic declaration. By its very title, "Acorda, irmão" (Wake Up, Brother) is a wake-up call to action as if to suggest a dormant posture that needs revitalization:

> Acorda, irmão, que é tempo de combate!
> Há, nesta luta, um brilho flamejante
> glorificando a fronte de um gigante
> que a tudo vence porque não se abate. (29)

[Wake up, brother, for it is time to fight! / There is, in this struggle, a flaming brightness / glorifying the forehead of a giant / who conquers everything for not giving in.]

This call transcends Brazil and extends to Africa and Afro-America as the poet sees a binding destiny among all "brothers" throughout the world. In "África," Oliveira praises the resistance and persistence of Africa without which her people would all be dead in the hands of oppressors he calls assassins. These "assassins" are reflected in Eurocentrism and the proverbial Latin American plagues that devour and marginalize Africans all over the world, confining them to mental ghettos as if leading them gradually into exile as rejects of the society in which they live.[5]

In spite of the castigation of the black body, metaphorically and physically, through slavery and exploitation over the centuries, Oliveira sings of hope, love, and happiness and pays homage to the black female body, which provides solace and warmth to the male in times of anguish:

Trago-te, neste instante, um mundo de esperança,
um mundo de alegria para a tua paz,
ó tu, que és minha pomba solitária e mansa,
ó tu, que és sempre grata ao bem que alguém te faz. (37)

[I bring to you, at this moment, a world of hope, / a world of happiness for your peace, / Oh you, my solitary and peaceful dove, / Oh you, who always appreciate the good done to you by others.]

Yet, this body must face its anguish; it must recognize that beneath that semblance of happiness lies escapist self-deception that is necessary to deal with what the poet in "Negro e faminto" (Black and Hungry) calls "estigma que traz desde menino" (50; the stigma you carry since childhood"). Here, the poet refers to the stigma of being black as being almost synonymous to shame.

In "Desterro" (Exile), dedicated to Langston Hughes, Oliveira launches a series of emotional accusations and indictments against the stereotypes projected about the Afro-Brazilian. The poet acknowledges that just looking at his own face reveals a lot: he is not living in a paradise; he cannot lay claim to any possession, including language; and finally, he basically lives like an exile in his own land:

Vivo e padeço como um desterrado,
como um negro que nunca pode amar
porque, no mundo, nunca fora amado. (38)

230 *The Forerunners of Afro-Modernity*

[I live and suffer like an exile, / like a black who can never love / because I was never loved by the world.]

Oliveira attributes this treatment to racism for stigmatizing an individual on the basis of his/her color is to "limit the splendor of his/her destiny" ("Ódio cruento" [Bloody Hate]), and the hater as well as the hated suffer the same hurt and emptiness represented in a common cross they bear. Racism, as the poet points out in "Dunas do racismo" (Dunes of Racism), is a suffocating pain that has no cure, especially for the hurt and sadness that accompany its infliction.

To relive and relieve the pain of slavery and racism, the poet goes on a spiritual journey through "Pelourinho," the cultural center of Salvador in Bahia, exorcising himself of that old shame where Africans were, through forced labor, made to make roads in stone and to build churches that they were not allowed to worship in. In anguish, the poet accuses his oppressor in "Memória" (Memory) boldly calling him a racist:

Racista! Onde é que está tua vitória?
Teu triunfo, afinal, onde é que está
que não se vê, por onde quer que vá
teu cego egoísmo, na empreitada inglória? (47)

[Racist! Where is your glory? / Your triumph, where it is after all / that it cannot be seen / the direction of / your egoism in contracted without glory.]

This outburst of confrontation is mediated by the poet's search for consolation in Mother Africa, symbol of pain, sacrifice, and perseverance as captured in "Mãe negra" (45).

Beyond these racial concerns, Oliveira ponders many moral, philosophical, and romantic questions that may not necessarily be divorceable from blackness but that represent an attempt to see beyond it and engage the human condition as a whole. These reflections often take the form of spiritual journeys and allusions as in "Cristo-ano-2000" (Year 2000 Christ):

Cristo, ao voltar aqui, depois de dois mil anos,
ficou estarrecido, ao ver a humanidade,
perdida na ambição, na mesma crueldade
que O fez chicotear a cara dos tiranos. (122)

[Christ, upon returning here in the year 2000, / became terrified to see humanity, / lost in ambition, in the same cruelty / that made Him beat up the face of tyrants.]

In the face of these millennial injustices, the poet turns to supplication, asking God to be so kind to humanity as to compassionately fulfill their needs, their hunger, their anguish, and their imperfections for only the metaphoric "Jerusalém do amor" (Lovable Jerusalem), symbol of the Holy Land and the "Santas escrituras" (Holy Words; 127) can make humanity laugh again. Oliveira's poetry seems to find inspiration in existential questions. Often, when the poet does not find a down-to-earth explanation, he resorts to existential and mystical analysis. In the sonnet "Hino à dor" (Hymn to Pain), the poet sees in pain the indestructible element that makes life worth living in the first place:

A dor, no mundo, é a única verdade
que preserva o valor da própria vida.
Do contrário, o que a manteria unida
em sua indestrutível integridade? (123)

[Pain, unique truth in the world / which preserves the value of life itself. / Contrarily, what keeps it united / in its indestructible integrity?]

Although this may sound like a contradiction for a poet who condemns oppression, racism, and injustices, it reveals the totality of this Afro-Brazilian, Afro-modernist, universal poet.

The poet-philosopher is betrayed in many other poems, such as "Feiras de vaidade" (Markets of Vanity), "Balada dos vencidos" (Ballad of Losers), "Alma perdida" (Lost Soul), and "Alma apaixonada' (Enamored Soul). These poems are marked by a profound awareness of human vanity, frailty, and mortality, essences that the poet sees as the only truth "recognized by the UNO" (100).[6] The consciousness of death as dues that humanity must pay regardless of color explains the paradox of racism as well as the moral imperative of goodness articulated in "Feiras da vaidade":

O homem, diante da morte, é uma semente
que só quando morrer terá nascido
para poder viver eternamente. (100)

[Man, before death, is a seed / who, only dying will be reborn / in order to live eternally.]

The metaphor of the world as a marketplace echoes the Yoruba proverb "Ile Aiye l'oja, orun n'ile" (The world is a marketplace; the other world is home), suggesting the temporariness of our sojourn on Earth and the need to be good-natured as opposed to the temptation of doing evil.

Before enjoying heavenly pleasures, the poet is not oblivious to earthly pleasures as reflected in a number of romantic poems in the same collection. Oliveira sees the "affectionate-romantic" poet as a slave to pleasure and a figure who finds therapy in lovemaking as in "Terapia do amor" (Therapy of Love):

> O sexo sempre foi a terapia,
> no sucesso da vida em companhia
> de quem mais se deseja e que nos ama. (155)

[Sex was always the therapy / for life's success in the company / of one we love most and who loves us in return.]

The therapy of love and the passion of lovemaking are also found in the act of kissing, as prelude to the sexual act itself. Like a slave, the poetic voice offers a supplication in "Beijas-me, mais" (Kiss Me More) for fear of losing the priceless and almost divine moment:

> Beijas-me mais, embora eu não mereça
> esta tua nudez que me seduz,
> que é minha exaltação e é minha cruz . . .
> pois, teme-se que o amor desapareça. (144)

[Kiss me more, although I don't deserve it / this your nudity that seduces me / my exaltation and my cross . . . / since I fear the love may disappear.]

Lovemaking, in this sense, compensates for the frustrations of daily life. The significant participant in this passionate process is also not an ordinary woman, she is a "perfect woman," a "temple of virtues" who makes her man feel "strong and protected." As the title of the poem dedicated to his wife, Deise de Oliveira, "Esposa e santa" (147), suggests, she is "Wife and Saint." While this homage to a loved woman is tied to passionate feelings, it nonetheless reveals a virtuous side of Oliveira that may be hidden from his black consciousness poems.

Aside from the beauty, musicality, and sonority of his sonnets, Oliveira has a message of complex realism toward life. For the poet, old age, death, lovemaking, pain, beauty, and fantasy all form integral parts of the inevitable constellation of the world. There is a gradual coming to terms with what life is all about, partly due to his old age, partly to his religiosity, and partly to his Pan-Africanist consciousness. Here is the poet characterizing death to his readers:

> A morte, amigo, já não me impressiona
> como me impressionava, anos atrás.

pois, hoje eu sei o bem que ela nos faz
quando a doce ilusão nos abandona. (97)

[Death, my friend, no longer bothers me / as it used to years back. / for today, I do know the good it does / when the sweet illusion abandons us.]

The "sweet illusion" here is life that leaves us unprepared to face the mystery of death. Like someone who has defied and "overcome" death, Oliveira sings of life while realizing his own mortality. Yet, by contrast, life is a "profound prison" (107) that gradually kills and corrupts our human essence. Oliveira's poetry is varied, profound, thoughtful, and mystical.

Oswaldo de Camargo: A Writer in Search of Perfection

While Oliveira strives to be the perfect poet, Oswaldo de Camargo proves to be one of the significant critical consciences of contemporary Afro-Brazilian letters. Born on October 24, 1936, in Bragança Paulista, São Paulo, Camargo became a respectable journalist, poet, novelist, social critic, and musician. Some have called him the Edward Said of Afro-Brazilian literature and criticism for his fight to establish the Afro-Brazilian canon through such critical anthologies as *A razão da chama* (1986) and *O negro escrito* (1987) as well as for his penchant for creative perfection. In addition to these anthologies, he has published individual works including novels, *Um homem tenta ser um anjo* (A Man Tries to Be an Angel); poetry, *Quinze poemas negros* (Fifteen Black Poems) and *O estranho* (The Absurd, 1984); and novellas, *O carro do êxito* (The Car of Success, 1972) and *A descoberta do frio* (The Discovery of Coldness, 1979).

That Camargo represents a reinvented Olavo Bilac in twentieth-century Afro-Brazilian letters is a well-deserved characterization of this prolific writer and pianist who for many young Afro-Brazilian writers is one of the leading figures of Brazilian black modernity. My interview session with Camargo in the summer of 1999 in his middle-class house in São Paulo revealed a writer of precision who strives for perfection in every word, idea, and articulation. I was particularly impressed by his personal library that boasts more than ten thousand volumes of Afro-Brazilian literature ranging from Cruz e Souza to Cuti as well as rare titles like Romeu Crusoé's *A maldição de Canaan* (The Curse of Canaan) and specially commissioned volumes such as *A mão afro-brasileira* (Afro-Brazilian Hand) and *Negro brasileiro negro* (Black Brazilian Black). I cannot help but associate the stature of Camargo with that of Olavo Bilac who demanded such rigor and labor to produce the perfect verse in his poem "Profissão de fé" (Profession of Faith), which may be considered Bilac's artistic testament:

> Quero que a estrofe cristalina,
> Dobrada ao jeito
> Do ourives, saia da oficina
> Sem um defeito.[7]

[I want the crystal stanza, / craftily fabricated / in the smithian style, to roll out of the smithshop / without any defect.]

As a literary "gatekeeper," Camargo occupies a very respected position as the guardian of the Afro-Brazilian literary tradition dating from the nineteenth to the twentieth century. Although his association with the younger generation is as a symbolic father figure, his interaction within the group is very limited and unproductive. Yet, the likes of Camargo are rare: seasoned, critical, and opinionated—virtues that come with his background as a journalist. This analysis will focus primarily on his collection of poems, *O estranho*.

O estranho (The Absurd) reveals various facets of the poetic voice as Camargo goes through spiritual consciousness, racial affirmation, and philosophical-existential reflections that all converge in the duality of religious refuge and social indictment. In his poetic testament, which, interestingly, does not open the collection, "Antífona," the poet calls on Senhora da Aparecida (Holy Virgin Mary) to watch over a collective repugnance stemming from an overall tiredness that overwhelms him and his people. If the testament is ambiguous and unspecific, the title poem, "O estranho," is more direct when it challenges the interlocutor to see beyond merely calling his wailings "complaints" and to share in his burden that only the poetic voice carries and appreciates:

> Senhores, vós não sabeis
> quem sou
> não, não sabeis quem eu sou!
> . . . .
> Eu vos convidei, senhores!
> Provai, provai do meu pão! (*O estranho* 20)

[Gentlemen, you don't know / who I am / . . . / I invite you, gentlemen! / Taste, taste my daily bread!]

This invitation has multiple functions: the poet wants to be seen as black, human, and yet open to others in their difference so long as he is recognized and respected as an equal partner of the Cosmos.

Like an accused stranger wanting to reveal himself to the rest of the world while discovering himself at the same time, the poetic voice wanders around in enigmatic moments of self-revelation, reflection, and self-knowledge.

Using dark humor in the same poem, Camargo ridicules his "white" interlocutor whose "clarity" or whiteness makes him or her assume that it is possible to see from the perspective of the "black mind." For Camargo, behind the black smile lies a disguised and profound thought. Here is an intellectual poet who knows how to capture the intensity of feelings without being outrageous. In this call for dialogue and reconciliation, Camargo seems to depart from the historic dichotomous relationship between blacks and whites, that is, former slaves and their former masters, to a more coexistential and universal posture that often makes his intentions somewhat ambivalent.

In "Antigamente" (Long Ago) as in many other poems, Camargo enumerates the various figurative "valleys" that blacks find themselves struggling to come out of to no avail: tides, tempest, half-loaves, hate, long nights, and deep darkness. In all these realities, to sing a song will be soothing yet can not be done without much pain and anguish; even to sing is a challenge for the soul, a hesitation for the tongue:

Como quem quer cantar, mas não canta,
como quem quer falar, mas se cala,
eu venho fazendo escala
no porto de muita mágoa. (*O estranho* 69)

[Like the willing singer who does not sing, / like the willing speaker who keeps quiet, / I am making a quick stop / in the port of much anguish.]

No matter how the poet tries to dissimulate his feelings, he is at heart a man in anguish, truly tolerant and steadfast, but unable to negate his pain. It is this need to face his reality that the poet sees as a process in "Presença," where he is identified again as a "stranger" as if others know him better than himself. Taking responsibility for his own melancholy, his silence and ambivalence in the face of hurt and enslavement, the poet comes to terms with his hesitation and insecurity and affirms the need to take action toward consciousness and revolutionary engagement:

Eis-me aqui!
E convoco a vossa herança para um grande incêndio,
pois que ouso mirar-me, e já início! (*O estranho* 22)

[Here I am! / And I invite your family to a great burning, / since I dare look at myself, that's a start!]

These occasional outbursts will lead the poet to a more radical assessment of his reality as a black poet.

Camargo's efforts at ambivalence regarding his blackness and desire for universality are constantly at odds with his reality in a racist society in which he is consistently reminded of his racial burden. In "Lembro-me, sim, estive lá!" (I remember, Yes, I was there!), such a burden is unveiled when the poetic voice resorts to memory to capture one of his most purifying poetic moments:

> Lembro-me, estive lá . . .
> o contorno do grito desmaiado
> antanho na memória . . .
> Dor no território negro!
> Dor no território negro! (*O estranho* 33)

[I remember, I was there . . . / the contour of a fainted cry / long bygone in memory . . . / Pain in black country! / Pain in black country!]

Likewise in "Primeira lamentação de Cam" (First Lamentation of Cain], the poet alludes to the biblical Cain story of inequality and jealousy among brothers:

> Oh!
> Vós que passais!
> Vede se há caminho igual
> ao meu! Vede onde ando:
> entre o espanto e a cinza,
> entre o tropeço e o laço
> do alvo caçador. (*O estranho* 39)

[Oh! / You passers-by! / See if there is a pathway comparable to mine! See through my pathway: / between terror and ashes, / between stumbling and the trap / of the white hunter.]

Here, there is neither ambivalence nor ambiguity: the indictment is geared toward the feeling of entrapment by a lurking white hunter looking for a prey. And whether during the slavery era in the fields of plantations or on the streets of discrimination that surround urban Afro-Brazilians, Camargo ends up lamenting repetitively in "Cantilena dos negros da Fazenda Soledade" (Small Corner of Blacks of Soledade Farm): "Uma agonia sem jeito" (40; a helpless agony). It is somewhat ironic that the same poet who preaches reconciliation and dialogue is now pointing out the helplessness of blacks as if to reveal that ambivalence is only a mask and that Camargo is indeed a revolutionary poet in spite of himself.

"Em Maio" (In May) and "Oferenda" (Offering) are two poems that converge as the poet deals with being Afro-Brazilian and longing to feel the presence of Africa in a foreign and racist land. In "Em Maio," Camargo takes a controversial position by challenging an important date not only for Afro-Brazilians but for the rest of Brazil. The official date of the abolition of slavery is May, but many Afro-Brazilians have rejected the date opting for November in recognition of their leader, Zumbi, who was murdered in the same month. Hence, Camargo's poem raises issues of ideology and politics. Ideologically, opting for November is a bold move in terms of self-affirmation and resistance on the part of Afro-Brazilians. Politically, such an act reflects a larger sociocritical commentary on the date and event. For Camargo, the implied "liberty" attached to May offers nothing to the people: the weak, the old, and the decadent; instead, it provides memories of slavery, powerlessness, and humiliation. In this poem, celebration becomes an opportunity for reevaluation of such abstract celebrations while questioning their contradictory realities:

> Mas a Liberdade que desce à praça
> nos meados de maio,
> pedindo rumores,
> é uma senhora esquálida, seca, desvalida
> e nada sabe de nossa vida. (*O estranho* 51)

> [But the Liberty that marches toward the square / in the middle of May, / asking for attention, / is a squalid, dry, invalid woman / who knows nothing about our lives.]

For Camargo, the celebration of "liberty" is as contentious as the memory of Africa to the poet. In "Oferenda," the poet struggles with the split feeling of being Brazilian and being African at heart. The poet's loneliness in Brazil and longing for Africa are conflicting emotions that befall him in the middle of the night. Indicting both his immediate environment that makes him long for Africa and Africa that has "abandoned" him, the poetic voice wonders what such a lost soul can do:

> Que farei do meu reino: um terreno
> no peito,
> onde pensei pôr minh'África,
> a dos meus avôs, a do meu povo de lá que me deixam
> tão sozinho? (*O estranho* 52)

> [What do I do about my kingdom: a territory at heart, where I thought about my Africa, / Africa of my grandparents, Africa of my people who left me / so lonely?]

Camargo's passion for Africa is both an expression of affirmation of his identity and a protest against slavery and dispersal which have conditioned

Afro-Brazilians to an alienating way of life. In a global perspective, Camargo's poetry is seemingly contradictory, wanting to be nonracial while being bound by the burden of his color. In his search for perfection, Camargo exposes his imperfection, his humanity.

Divergence and Convergence

The four writers examined in this chapter not only exude modernist tendencies in language and sociospiritual commitment, but also use those concerns to advance the cause of black pride in their varied styles and political engagements. In this examination of the pioneers of Brazilian Afro-modernity, a convergence merges in the quest for the liberation of the Afro-Brazilian race. Solano Trindade's poetic simplicity captures the yearnings of the poor, the downtrodden, and the elderly while making a global cry for freedom. Abdias do Nascimento uses Afro-Brazilian religion to empower his people toward cultural and political consciousness. Eduardo de Oliveira is the poet of negritude for Afro-Brazilians. Although his style is Parnassian and sonnetist, he is nonetheless concerned with his people's freedom. Camargo's search for perfection may be likened to the burden of blackness itself: the need to prove his humanity. These four pioneers provide the path for the second generation of modernists that emerged and matured in the late seventies and eighties, including Luis Silva (Cuti), Miriam Alves, Márcio Barbosa, Adão Ventura, and Aline França.

10

(Un)Transgressed Tradition

> At times, I am my own suspicious police officer
> I ask myself for identity papers
> And after showing them
> I arrest myself
> And give myself a serious beating.
>
> —Cuti, "Quebranto"

The tenacity of Afro-Brazilian writers in general is unquestionable as they negotiate the stifling effects of the racial democracy mythology on their cultural production as well as on their threatened humanity. It must also be noted that the criticism of the new generation of Afro-Brazilian writers has been scanty at best, but also quite limited if not dismal when it comes to particular authors.[1] Hence, beyond the freedom to write, there is a constraining block on critical production due to a lack of sustained critical practice and development as well as limited publishing outlets for Afro-Brazilian issues.

Shortly after the Brazilian military dictatorship ended, cultural entities experienced relief from official censorship as well as self-censorship. It was during this wave of artistic "freedom" that the four writers under consideration in this chapter launched their writing careers only to mature and become "visible" two decades later. Cuti (Luiz Silva), Arnaldo Xavier, Ronald Tutuca, and Carlos de Assumpção may not all be contemporaries by age, but their works, linked by an ideological commonality, strike a common chord of disenchantment, rebellion, and transgression with the object of affirming their existence, dignity, and humanity. As much as these writers try to escape their ancestrality through conscious experimentation with multiple forms, they actually refine and reaffirm that same tradition. By ancestrality, I mean that vital source of kinship and heritage that links the Afro-Brazilian to his/her past as in such cultural and religious relics as Candomblé and certain styles or forms of music as well as dance—all of which may be subsumed under intellectual cum cultural production. On the reciprocal level, multiplicity is the experimentation with form as verifiable in visual poetry, multivocal poetic expressions, and performative manifestations.

Unlike some of their predecessors addressed in the previous chapter, who were obliged to deal with racism head on, and "by any means necessary" (in the words of Malcolm X), this new generation has often hidden behind language and symbolism in order to go beyond the tentacles of discrimination and push their imaginations to the extent where the "establishment" criteria of a quality production may well be subverted or outsmarted by their very own rules.

This chapter explores the connection between aesthetic experimentation in the works of Cuti, Arnaldo Xavier, and Ronald Tutuca as a means of liberation on the one hand, and the relevance of ancestrality or tradition through the multiple formalistic ventures on the other. In essence, I propose to examine the process of cultural production through a consistent struggle with form, identity, and ancestral consciousness. Often going beyond the racial problematic but entrenched in the discourse of origin, religion, and social problems, these writers seem to depart from the ideological constraints of their predecessors.

In my examination of Afro-modernist tendencies in these writers, I subscribe to the "mobilizational model" suggested by Michael Hanchard that involves focusing on "resistance, overt or veiled (song, dance, slave revolts, postemancipation rebellions, or civil rights movements)" ("Afro-Modernity" 273). As Hanchard further suggests, "only under conditions of modernity could people defined as African utilize the very mechanisms of their subjugation for their liberation" (273). The reverse appropriation of the tools of oppression is found in the use of language and varying stylistic strategies that dynamize these writers' poetic messages. As Manuel García-Castellón observes, the criticism of Afro-Brazilian works preabolition and even postabolition has been characterized by what he calls "caricatura racista" (racist caricature), that is, the commentaries that reinforce negative stereotypes such as "el negro, criatura sin cerebro ni valores morales, es el malandrín y pícaro que vive en las favelas" ("Luis Silva," 33; the Afro-Brazilian, a brainless and values-deficient creature, . . . a crook and parasite who lives in the slums). The subversion of the negative stereotypes and the reinvention of the true personality of the Afro-Brazilian lies at the crux of the discussion in this chapter.

Cuti: The Beautification of the Beastly Black Burden

Perhaps the most prolific of the younger generation of Afro-Brazilian writers, Cuti has experimented with at least four artistic media: poetry, short story, drama, and recently, music. Described as an "example of the role of the intellectual and writer in the struggle for social, economic, and psychological freedom,"[2] Cuti exudes a political consciousness of his blackness and the responsibility to organize others which led to the founding of *Cadernos negros* in 1978, and two years later, the literary movement known as Quilombhoje. While Michael Hanchard may be right that the historical narrative is crucial and "intrinsic to Afro-Modern consciousness and politics" ("Afro-Modernity" 277), such an expectation is actually a luxury for Afro-Brazilians whose immediate challenges with racism and inequalities do not allow them the time and peace of mind to think about or create a historical narrative. Most of the writings by modern writers, Cuti included, are restricted to day-to-day experiences such as police brutality, hunger, ghetto life, unfortunate or abortive love relationships, the treatment of women, and the importance of preserving the Afro-Brazilian family. Given this situation, Cuti's engagement with the deep-seated anguish and anger within a society that sees him as different is, at best, to "beautify" this burden through artistic and ideological response.

In the works under consideration—*Batuque de tocaia, Flash crioulo, Negros em conto, Dois nós na noite,* and *A pelada peluda no largo da bola*—Cuti seems to have evolved over the years from anger and rebellion, to a search for artistic finesse. A prolific reader and writer, Cuti has several published works to his credit along with various creative and critical works in journals and anthologies. In addition, he defended his master's degree in literary theory in 1999 with a thesis on Cruz e Souza, and completed his doctorate in the same area at the Universidade Estadual de Campinas (São Paulo) with a PhD thesis on Luís Gama in 2003. Born in 1951 in the city of Ourinhos, São Paulo, Cuti is best described as a native Paulistan whose African roots are not endangered in the least even though he is living in Brazil's most industrial city. Now in his fifties, he is less agitated than he used to be in the eighties when he first launched his writing career. He has traveled extensively within and outside Brazil to do readings of his works and participate in conferences. Cuti officially left the Quilombhoje group in 1995, but he helped organize the silver jubilee of the publication of *Cadernos negros* in 1998, with events and activities commemorating the series' production and resistance, after his departure.

Cuti's creative corpus has equally evolved from a need to respond to racism, as in the first wave of his poems and short stories in the *Cadernos negros* series, to a mixture of the search for the precise expression for the precise message or ideological penchant and of the resolution of the primary place and mode of struggle for his anguished and choleric spirit. Anthologized in many of the first attempts to document contemporary black writing, such as *O negro escrito* by Oswaldo de Camargo, *Axé: Antologia contemporânea da poesia negra brasileira* by Paulo Colina, *Schwarze poesie/Poesia negra* by Moema Parente Augel, and most recently, the special issue of *Callaloo* on African Brazilians, Cuti is gradually becoming a literary institution in his own right. Not only did he spearhead the creation, development, and maintenance of the Quilombhoje group for almost twenty years, he provided the necessary leadership and initiatives that led to getting individual authors published within the group. In an interview with Cuti in 2000 in São Paulo, the author lamented his exit from the group, which he attributed to the members' lack of dedication, consistency, and time-consciousness. Feeling he had contributed long enough to hold the fort together, he intended to turn his focus to individual work instead of, as he said, "wasting" his time with those who do not want to grow up and take responsibility for themselves. Although he continues to collaborate with the series (*Cadernos negros*), his departure has been called the beginning of the end of the group, both by current members and by those who have also left the group, although to everyone's surprise (and to the dismay of some), the group continues to function and produce in spite of limited collaborative and administrative help compared to what it used to enjoy.

A cursory look at Cuti's production over the twenty-five-year period 1978–2002 in *Cadernos negros* sets up, even as early as 1978, the aesthetic tone for what is to come from Cuti in later years. In the preface to the very first number of the series, the group establishes a "blueprint" for their association, their movement, and above all, their purpose and mission:

> *Cadernos negros* marca passos decisivos para nossa valorização e resulta de nossa vigilância contra as idéias que nos confundem, nos enfraquecem e nos sufocam... *Cadernos negros* é a viva imagem da África em nosso continente. É a Diáspora Negra dizendo que sobreviveu e sobriviverá, superando as cicatrizes que assinalaram sua dramática trajetória, trazendo em suas mãos o livro. (2–3)

> [*Cadernos negros* marks a decisive step toward our self-appreciation and springs from our vigilance against ideas which confuse, weaken, and suffocate us... *Cadernos negros* is the vivid image of Africa on our continent. It is the black diaspora saying that it survived, it will survive, overcoming the scars that marked its dramatic journey, reaching out with a book in hand.]

Like the collective ideological consciousness that evokes such an affirmative statement, the poems in that same collection speak to the wave of freedom and new resolve to chart new directions and destinies that came with the independence of the Lusophone African countries such as Angola, Mozambique, Guinea-Bissau, Cape Verde, and São Tomé and Príncipe as well as the internal dynamics of relief from Brazilian military dictatorship in Brazil. In a fifty-two-page anthology and comprising thirty-five poems written by eight poets—Cunha, Angela, Oliveira, Hugo, Célia, Minka, Camargo, and Cuti—this inaugural issue, with a cover depicting the slums of São Paulo, marks a definite new beginning for Afro-Brazilian literature. Fundamental to this shift or turn is the necessity to be "free" in all the various manifestations of the word: ideologically, intellectually, spiritually, physically, socially, and even economically. In order to be a free intellectual, the Afro-Brazilian cultural producer must no longer wait for or depend on the traditional presses in order to communicate his/her message. Hence the importance of *Cadernos negros* as an independent forum for publishing new voices.

As one of the "new voices" of the time, the poet Cuti combines ideological motifs with dialectical realism. His five poems in the first issue of *Cadernos negros*—"Meu verso" (My Poetry), "Impressão" (Impression), "Sapo engolido" (Swallowed Toad), "Vento" (Wind), and "Preconceito racial" (Racial Discrimination)—have a tone of urgency and resolve. They sum up the reality of the moment as the poet defines his poetry, comments on the independence of new African nations, laments the exploitation of the Afro-Brazilian self in a cosmopolitan setting, and above all, contests racial discrimination. Yet, "Meu verso" remains the most compelling poem since Cuti synthetically defines his 'arte poética' and political mission disguised in poetic form:

Meu verso fala do negro
Meu verso fala do grito
que os brancos não escutaram
porque fecharam os ouvidos
Meu verso fala do ódio encolhido
Do nosso olhar esprimido. (47)

[My poem speaks of blacks / My poem speaks of shout of protest / to which whites did not listen / Because they blocked their ears / My poem speaks of contained hate / In our constricted eyes.]

While this poem may be considered prosaic and "simple," it nonetheless captures the essence of Cuti in his formative years. Cuti's poetry speaks of the black experience, its pain and protest, its anguish as it dialogues with an other who is not listening, and the resulting frustration and anger that tends to linger on even after the presumably therapeutic writing process.

Published in 1998, the two commemorative editions of *Cadernos negros* (*Os melhores poemas/contos*) equally provide a window into a sample of the best in Cuti's imagination. In the poetry edition, the five anthologized poems capture Cuti's evolution from the strictly ideological to the amorous, that is, a poet who is appreciating the beauty of life even in a world of hate, brutality, and violence, thus coming to terms with the imperative of sanity in the midst of lunacy. In a sarcastic self-portrait, "Quebranto" dramatizes those evil eyes which follow Afro-Brazilians around: those of the police, the caretaker, and even of the snobbish "lover" all combine to frustrate the poetic voice as he succumbs to the reality of alcoholism to wish away his exhaustion and feeling of "solidão primitiva" (48; primitive solitude). Other than "Para ouvir e entender 'estrela,'" which ridicules the absence of black dolls for black children, the other poems focus on some form of erotica and pleasure. "Mar Glu-Glu" alludes to the eyes of the male that are captivated by the female buttocks to the point where the male gaze not only desires this metonymic female body but ends up in the "murmúrio no mar glu-glu / a forma do espaço repleto e nu" (50; murmuring of the sticky sea / the form of the full and naked space). Likewise, "Sedução," as the title suggests, evokes the effect of a kiss as an invitation to a more passionate encounter and journey into the eclipse of amorous plenitude. Finally, the graphic description of intercourse in "É tempo de mulher" (It Is the Woman's Turn) is a pretext to actually paint a picture of the participatory and empowering role of the woman in the sexual act as she seems to be in charge from the beginning to the end.

In the short story edition of *Cadernos negros: Os melhores* (1998), Cuti's "O batizado" (The Baptized) returns to his critique of alcoholism as an unviable "escape" for Afro-Brazilians since it causes complications and more destruction without resolving the problem. The story is intricately crafted as it juxtaposes female (Joana and Dona Isaltina) and male (Belmiro, Paulinho, and Tico) characters subjecting them to a discussion of many issues: from the question of identity and the use of African names to a larger issue of those destroyed by alcohol whom he euphemistically terms "o batizado." A metaphor for "immersed in water" and "soaked in beer," it captures what happens to the drunk as this figure loses all his senses and disrupts the peace and events organized by well-meaning people. The issue of the Unified Black Movement is also discussed since there is a sense that it does not offer practical solutions to serious problems. Of course, this is a short-sighted critique, and a committed Afro-Brazilian can see the actual impact of the movement from the viewpoint of basic awareness and agitation for fundamental human rights.

His second volume of poetry, following *Poemas de carapinha* (Crisply Black Poems, 1978), which, as Zilá Bernd suggests, deals with the phase of black poetry that rejects "alien" ideologies—namely, Marxism and Catholicism[3]— Cuti's *Batuque de tocaia* (Drumbeat of Ambush) offers a wide range of themes that focus mostly on protest of social injustices and an unresolved black–white dialectic. With the faith of the poets of the "geração de 80" (generation of the 1980s) turning from utopian ideals to the adoption of poetry as an instrument of combat against discrimination, the creative imagination is doubly burdened. On the one hand, the written word must now be potent enough to communicate anguish, and on the other hand, it must be subtle enough not to alienate the reader who is actually being invited to sympathize with the writer.

As one of the voices of the new generation, Cuti assumes a leadership position using his fearless and blunt words to confront the system that alienates him. As the poet declares in "Ela" (It) referring to his poetry:

A minha poesia
um susto que pula no pescoço
e procura
agarra esse medo
esse medo que nos espreita na lapela do riso. (17)

[My poetry / a fright that seizes one in the neck / and searches / captures this fear / this fear that pries into the lapel of laughter.]

Problematizing further the notion of fear, Cuti in "Medo medular" (Modular Fear) opines that fear is not only a burden for those who can predict the actions of blacks but even for blacks themselves:

Todo mundo tem medo
da vingança do preto
até o preto. (35)

[Everyone is afraid / of the revenge of blacks / even blacks.]

Yet the consciousness of this vague fear runs through the entire collection of *Batuque de tocaia*.

In "Com o vermelho da vergonha de ver, disse" (With a Shameful Gaze, She Said) and "Apenas" (Only), Cuti continues his engagement with fear as if this is something subconscious for the poet. The poetic voice is afraid of so many things: the unborn baby, macumba (traditional medicine or "witchcraft"), old age; and finally, in a subtle twist of tone, he declares abhorrence for racial democracy in Brazil:

negro, tenho medo
negra, tenho medo d'eu morrer branco
e renascer negro. (63)

[Black man, I am afraid / Black woman, I am afraid of dying white / And being reborn black.]

While the ideological intention here is ambivalent as far as the implication of dying white and being reborn black, one can also appreciate the dark humor as if the poetic voice is indicting all those who aspire to be white and their desire to remain white given the privileges of whiteness and the process of "whitening" that places more value on the lighter-skinned person in Brazilian society. At the same time, the poet may also be suggesting that the fear of being "reborn black" speaks to self-consciousness and the price of persecution and humiliation that comes with such a stoic posture of awareness. Beyond the preoccupation with color and the implicit deep-seated fear in both blacks and whites, Cuti's themes are defined by subconscious polarities: black–white, I–Them, indictment–withdrawal, fear–boldness, despair–hope, all operating within the framework of exposing the burden of blackness in Brazil. In *Batuque de tocaia*, Cuti not only beautifies the black burden, he transfigures it without minimizing its potential for self-destruction.

Following *Batuque de tocaia* five years later, *Flash crioulo: Sobre o sangue e o sonho* (1987) continues the poetic tradition of Cuti but with a refined twist. Collecting thirty-nine poems altogether, without titles, without punctuation, but suggestive titles highlighted within the poems, Cuti experiments with form once again. searching for the perfect visual effect on the page to translate his inner feelings be it of pain or of pleasure. At least two of his frequently anthologized poems ("Mar glu-glu" and "Quebranto") are found here, indicating a palpable maturity. The title itself is suggestive: "flash" is a brusque and sudden ray of light that illuminates exposure in the photographic parlance, an epiphanic moment of some sort. And perhaps that is why there are no titles since the reader is led into illumination through spontaneous outpourings controlled with craft and "cerebration." The opening poem succinctly defines and articulates the poet's art:

> as dores dum povo sou
> e as danças
> que dançam
> desvirginando o espaço no gozo dos movimentos . . . (9)

> [the pain of a people I am / and the dances / that they dance / deflowering the space in the pleasure of the movements . . .]

The rest of the poems seem to mobilize Afro-Brazilians and raise their consciousness: asking them to assume their responsibility and fight for their rights through the black speech as in "Falar sem receio a palavra negro" (Speak without Shame the Black Word), critiquing the living conditions that often give the air of squalor and degeneration as in "Prédio" (Building), condemning the fallacy of racial democracy as in "Veio" (Came), and defining his notion of fraternal revolution as in "Sobre as cicatrizes" (About the Wounds):

> irmão, minha irmandade
> nada tem de rosário
> meu deus
> é revolucionário. (55)

[brother, my brotherhood / has nothing to do with rosary / my god / it is revolutionary]

The reader may be tempted to see this as referring to Catholicism, but on a contrastive level the poetic voice is indeed juxtaposing the illusion of harmony with the reality of conflict that requires resolution through poetic combat as opposed to fantasy. This statement is the most declarative ever made by Cuti in terms of his overall poetic corpus and ideological vision.

Bringing together twenty-seven short stories and fragments of reflections, such as "Morro" (Slum) and "In-cura" (Without Cure), most of which had been previously unpublished, *Negros em contos* dramatizes Afro-Brazilian images in dealing with sadness and joy, economic poverty and human plenitude, alienation and de-alienation, discrimination and affirmation, discord and solidarity. In these polarities lies the cry for freedom and social integration without being apologetic. By their quality of composition and thematic relevance, these stories evince a sense of maturity from most of those published earlier in the *Cadernos negros* series. Perhaps, there is a sense of "arrival" and aesthetic accomplishment even as the cover indicates, where the author seems to be sitting in a relaxed posture, holding his glasses in hand, and posing for a portrait.

One of the most striking stories is "Negrinho" (Deep Black Man). Constructed around a group of friends who meet every now and then to have a drink and talk about life, amid some background music, and opportunity to turn the bar meeting into a party. The story gradually turns into a critique of police brutality as the Police come in every now and then looking for "Tremendão" (Biggie), a name that suggests intimidation and threat to the police. On one occasion, when the police came, one of the members of the group asked them to put their weapons away and quit harassing them; of course, he was arrested for "desacato à autoridade" (disregard for authority). As the group composed of Eliodoro, Odair, Isidro, and Senhor Jair continued their feast and conversation, it was announced that a new baby had just been born: Negrinho. Ironically, Negrinho is actually an adult, and soon to be a grandfather, as if the author is suggesting a cyclical process of birth and rebirth: "Todos brindamos o nascimento e uma renovada certeza florida entre nossos lábios" (70; We all celebrated our births with a renewed certainty flowering between our lips). Considered as a paradigmatic text, this story examines some of the fundamental issues facing the Afro-Brazilian people as they struggle with societal conflicts as well as their own internal conflicts ("quizila") while preserving their identity and containing their oppression.

The Afro-Brazilian experience is a primary concern for Cuti, and he engages this unique and challenging state of being in multiple aesthetic forms. Adding to his experimentation with poetry and the short story, Cuti is also a playwright. He has coauthored *Terramara* (1988) with Miriam Alves and Arnaldo Xavier, and published *Suspensão* (1983) a few years earlier, but *Dois nós na noite* remains his most accomplished play. Comprising a total of five plays (*Dois nós na noite, Transegun, Madrugada me proteja!, Canção da saga,* and *Nódoas*) mostly in one or two acts, the dramatic text marks a renewal of black theater since Abdias do Nascimento's *TEN* (*Teatro Experimental do Negro*/Experimental Black Theater) of the 1950s. The most accomplished of the five plays, *Dois nós na noite* (Two of Us at Night) exposes the drama of an Afro-Brazilian woman in crisis as she deals with the issue of estrangement and ill-treatment from her husband. It is curious that Cuti's choice is a female character, whose monologue contrasts with that of Emmanuel in Nascimento's *Sortilégio,* for example. Indeed, this contrast makes for a comparative study of both texts given their parallel dramatic tension and tragic vision. Could this be in response to the criticism of *TEN* that it consisted mostly of male playwrights portraying or looking at women subjects or having female characters only in secondary roles?

In his seminal article, perhaps "Individualidade e Colectividade em *Dois nós na noite* de Cuti," which is among very few (if any) other articles on this text, John Rex Amuzu Gadzekpo suggests that Cuti's text has possibly suffered some theoretical influences such as those of *TEN* and Augusto Boal's *Teatro do Oprimido*. He cannot be more accurate in his somewhat tentative declaration. For Gadzekpo:

> *Dois nós na noite* cabe à perfeição nesse esquema, mas vai além: em vez de ser apenas um instrumento da negritude, ele representa, a meu ver, o saudável ingresso na categoria de literatura universal feita por um negro brasileiro, desmistificando, não negando, a questão racial. Não se trata dum simples mundo de negros unidos contra demônios brancos opressores, mas sim uma complexidade do drama humano no qual o racial é apenas um elemento. (726)

[*Dois nós na noite* belongs perfectly to this scheme and goes even beyond: instead of being an instrument of negritude expression, it represents, from my perspective, the healthy integration within universal literature as produced by an Afro-Brazilian, demystifying, not denying, the racial problem. It is not simply a world of Afro-Brazilians against white demons-oppressors, but yes, a complexity of human drama in which the racial is just one element.]

Universality may well be implicit in Cuti's humanism in his character development of Judith, but the point must also be made that the primary target audience is consciously and explicitly Afro-Brazilian. By staging the crisis of the gendered and racial consciousness of Judith, Cuti is indeed exposing the internal conflicts of Afro-Brazilian women in general who have to move beyond condoning the excuses their lovers/husbands give for humiliating, exploiting, and abandoning them. The central conflict here is that of solitude, an anguishing and emotional state of mind when one is supposedly "loved" and yet lonely. The paradox is effective as the audience/reader sympathizes with Judith while also being drawn into the critique of her overall demeanor.

Structurally, the dialogic monologue creates an aesthetic challenge and novelty that is comparable only to the theater of the absurd. What can be more absurd than a woman dialoguing with herself instead of her "oppressor"?[4] Can the woman also be her own oppressor through her implied silence, self-alienation, and solitude? Or can she in fact be "blamed" for condoning the atrocities of her oppressor? The complexity here also extends to the fact that the reader/public does not see/hear Judith talk about her "husband" or even "female partner" (should that be the case)—in essence, the implied villain or antagonist. This ambiguity has many implications. First, the reader/public cannot ascertain if the "husband/partner" is white or black, male or female, nor can we be sure even with the symbolic ending where a black bird is motionless (dead) in a white cage. Second, by universalizing or relativizing color, is Cuti suggesting that the dilemma of the Afro-Brazilian is comparable to that of the white Brazilian woman? Third, the characteristics of the husband—he is drunk, unfaithful, and a womanizer—are not at all peculiar to Afro-Brazilians. In fact, Cuti is arguing that they constitute potential idiosyncrasies of every man.

From this universal tendency of Cuti emanates his empathy for the experience of young Afro-Brazilians, hence his incursion into the juvenile genre as well. In *A pelada peluda no largo da bola*, memory collides with introspection and reflections in furnishing the reader a slice of the author's own infancy. While one cannot be sure that the author is speaking strictly of his childhood, there is some textual evidence to suggest this is the case. The dedication to the copy I have reads: "Um retorno astral praquele garoto no canto de mim" (2; an astral return to that youngster in one corner of me).[5] The ability of an adult to capture the age of innocence has been one of the chief problematics of the autobiography. In this juvenile literary piece, the narrator is quite credible and the tone is mellow and less agitated or conflictual in terms of racial issues. There are occasional insinuations about other races such as the reference to Zé Carlos as "Japonês" (Japanese) as well as the argument whether Zé is white or yellow and thus capable of serving as a fair referee, that do revisit the racial question. In general, the experiences of the narrator are positive among other kids, and the language is quite appropriate for the elementary or even early secondary level. Cuti succeeds in creating effective dialogue and is very passionate about the subject matter, that is, soccer, which he uses as the focal point as well as pretext to narrate his childhood memories. From beginning to end, the structure is cyclical as we accompany the joys and adventures of these young boys and girls whose innocence is alluring. One of the most dramatic moments in the narration is the encounter of Maria da Conceição, a widow who is now afraid of men in general, with the drunk who asks her for cookies:

—Tem comida? Só quero comida. Não sou ladrão, não. Passou a mão num pacote de bolacha sobre a mesa da sala e saiu dando risada. No pequeno quintal dos fundos, abriu a braguilha e urinou no muro. (32)

["You have some food? All I want is food. No, I am not a thief." He dished his hand into a box of cookies sitting on the table in the room and went out laughing his head off. In the inner small backyard, he opened the slit of his trousers and urinated on the wall.]

Such humorous occasions give the story its flavor and candor as the narrator shares what he finds to be funny, hoping that the reader finds it equally hilarious. As in much of Cuti's works, especially in "O Batizado" and a number of poems, alcoholism is considered a vice and comes under ferocious attack, yet here the critique is done with a subtle humor befitting juvenile literature. It is this blend of artistry and personal reminiscences that make *A pelada* a unique accomplishment for the author.

As a production from their golden years, *Quilombo de Palavras* is a remarkable achievement by Cuti and Carlos de Assumpção. In the age of technological innovation, the transformation of the written word into the spoken is indeed a creative measure to recuperate the oral tradition. Since the members of the Quilombhoje group became used to reading their poetry during the launching of the *Cadernos negros* series, it should come as no surprise that these two comrades came together to recuperate and record ancestral voices that may not otherwise be captured on the page. The creative mix of poems widely considered to be the chefs d'oeuvre of these two poets—"Quebranto" and "Favela" (Cuti); "Presença," "Protesto," and "Auto-retrato" (Carlos de Assumpção)—and the opportunity to hear them aloud give new meaning to oral performance. Poetry is best when it is spoken and performed. Even before the age of rap and hip-hop aesthetics, which have gained currency in São Paulo, Rio de Janeiro, and Bahia, some Afro-Brazilian poets have always aspired to performative art in order to reach a wide audience since the printed text continues to be a product limited to the upper and middle classes, and even the educated. Hearing the evocative voice of Assumpção in "Presença," for example, is like listening to a live oral poetry performance:

É zum
É zum
É zum
É zumbi
Zumbi de Ogum
Guerreiro de Ogum. (*Quilombo* CD 6)

[It's zum / It's zum / It's zum / It's Zumbi / Ògún's Zumbi / Ògún's warrior].

When considered in its totality, Cuti's extensive aesthetic experimentation and productive synergy may well betray an internal struggle on the part of the writer to transcend his immediate and presumed limitations as an individual, collective role model, and family man and become an Afro-Brazilian artist with a mission. The beauty in Cuti's artistry lies somewhere between his ability to blend anguish with creative ingenuity to produce soothing music under cacophonic intensity and duress and a deep-seated search to transform himself into an icon to be remembered in Afro-Brazilian letters. Cuti's Afro-modernity, then, is nothing less than a desire to contribute to the improvement of the lot of Afro-Brazilians who remain disempowered, voiceless, and marginalized through systematic alienation that can only be subverted via ideological representation, not art for art's sake.

Arnaldo Xavier: At the Crossroads of Construction and Constriction

By all standards, Arnaldo Xavier is not your average Brazilian Afro-modernist writer. When Xavier affirms that "the black man is an island and a labyrinth lost within himself,"[6] he indeed provides the reader with a theoretical basis to appreciate his entire productive corpus as that of an artist trying to free himself from a social quagmire. I consider him an intellectual ahead of his time, whose intellectual potential has been subject to a stifling setting. Should he gain the same respect and recognition most writers in the West are accorded, he will be considered a postmodernist writer by his esoteric style and mesmerizing vision. Well read and versed in world literature just like Oswaldo Camargo of the first generation,[7] Xavier strikes me as a multiple experimentalist who is self-assured and simply needs urgent exposure. During my interviews with him, he confessed to a nagging frustration with the Brazilian publishing industry and expressed interest in exploring possibilities outside of Brazil.[8] As he showed me a range of innovative visual poems, colorful and intellectually challenging images recollected in "another world" of which only a few have been published in journals and books, I was saddened by the fate of this writer who is unfortunately wasting away and whose works are locked up somewhere between Avenida Paulista and the Universidade de São Paulo, where he lives.[9]

When compared to Cuti, there is a significant gap. Cuti, too experiments aesthetically, but he is not a visual artist. Indeed, Cuti uses words to capture and convey his ideological message; for Xavier, however, the word must be re-created and reappropriated through visual images and even the corruption of the word. Xavier struggles with a theory of form that he calls "Orikrítika," that is a combination of the Yoruba word, "Ori" (destiny), and a neologism of "criticism" derived from its Portuguese origin but rendered with a *k*—thus "krítica" instead of "crítica." While the unpublished essay does not necessarily define the concept, its claim is implied: that the criteria for the criticism of Afro-Brazilian culture must be set by Afro-Brazilians themselves.[10] The extent to which this is plausible and possible is questionable since most such critical ideas end up in the writer-critic's drawer without an avenue for publication. In this study, I propose to uncover the representative works of Xavier from his contributions to *Cadernos negros* (nos. 10, 12, 13), through his coauthored (*Manuel de sobrevivência, Terramara*) and individual works (*A roza da recvsa, Lud-Lud*), as well as samples from his unpublished collections of visual poetry in order to convey a totality of his artistry.

Contramão (Wrong Way, 1978), in which Arnaldo Xavier collaborated with other six poets, sheds more light on the mystery of this poet at least in his formative years. Xavier's prefatory note to his section of poetry, comprising nine poems, reveals his artistry as a "poema-proceso" (poem-process), a kind of "aesthetic-political alternative" (20) as well as the making of poetry as an act of "love and courage." While these poems are more socially and family oriented, there are, however, some indications of complexity as in "São Palido" (Pale São Paulo) and "Em busca de ouro" (Searching for Gold). In "São Palido," Xavier provokes the reader by invoking the Tietê River, the central river in São Paulo, in its possibility to produce blood confused with milk. The irony of course lies in the assumption that Paulistans need milk more than they need blood, but the reverse is the case. Blood here represents the toil, the violence, the indifference, and the brutality of the city. As for "Em busca de ouro," Xavier uses the image of the serpent eating another serpent as a metaphor for the capitalist system, which implies survival of the fittest.

Though Xavier's works are technically excluded from the two commemorative editions of the *Cadernos negros* in 1998, further points of entry to the appreciation of the complexity of his poetry come from his anthologized poem "Poema Juju" (*Cadernos negros* 13) and from a few short stories, "Os últimos dias de ressurreições de Cirillo La Ursa" (*Cadernos negros* 10) and "Um dia ela foi flor nos jardins" (*Cadernos negros* 12). These three examples share Xavier's idiosyncratic style of playing with visual effects, which are more glaring in "Poema Juju" (Juju Poem) than in the short stories. In this narrative poem, which starts with an "I-I" dialoguing with "You" and later shifts to descriptions, then reflections, without any punctuation whatsoever except for intentional blanks indicating beginning and end or continuity, emphasis is placed on such words written as "cOOração" (hEArt) and OONírico (ONeiric), without any intention to clarify the plot and meaning of the story. In the final analysis, the reader feels completely dumbfounded and bewitched, exactly as the title suggests ("Juju"), which could mean either traditional concoction or a style of music. The reader is partly bewildered and challenged, perhaps as the author intends. Allusions to Greek mythology, the Bible, the Koran, as well as to Eastern philosophy reveal a conscious effort to be linguistically difficult, obscure, abstruse, academic, esoteric, and intellectual. One longs to ask the author: What is the point of this poetic exercise? Only Arnaldo Xavier holds the key to that answer.

In not so sharp a contrast to "Poema Juju," "Os últimos dias de ressurreições de Cirillo La Ursa" translates this innovative soul of the writer as if he is attempting to write a classic or even a saga. Using roman numerals, especially the number thirty (xxx) as a crucial point of reference, the entire "short story" (or "sketches") pays homage to an unnamed deity or deities qualifying them with such accolades as "OONipresença" (14; Omnipresence), "GRANDÁRVORE" (14; Great Tree) and "Rio das ostras!" (16; River of Oysters) among others. On occasion, the narrative turns into a self-portrait as the narrator speaks of himself and his past:

> NAQUELA ÉPOCA Eu tinha vintemetros de altura. Daí o meu nome—Oriente! Tornei-me o guia para caça o auscultador dos ventos para pesca o mirante para coleta de frutos e de lenha. De minha mãe-Daluz poucoouquasenada melembro. Sua lembrança se resume até hoje. (16)

> [AT THAT TIME I was twenty meters in height. Hence my name. I became a hunting guide the stethoscope of the winds for fishing the harvest observer of fruits and cotton. Of my mother, Daluz, I hardly remember anything. Her memory remains a summary to this day.]

As in "Poema Juju," Xavier highlights certain words in this short story, such as the epithets and analogies associated with the Cirillo La Ursa, a mythological figure whose silence is seen as that of the "esCORpião" (SCORpion) and "SerpENTe" (SerpENT), and this characteristic is confirmed at the end of the story when the voice from below the earth says: "EU QUE DEVORO EU!" (30; I AM HE WHO DEVOURS MYSELF). The trope of resurrection and self-destruction/renewal explored in this story-reflection lends itself to Afro-Oriental philosophy and the belief in the image of the serpent biting its own tail for the sake of self-preservation and replenishment. If there is any moral in this story, one must not lose sight of the possibility that the mythological figure, indeed, represents the Afro-Brazilian who, from a Xavieresque perspective, is his/her own worst enemy, perhaps in a desperate attempt to survive.

In an even more absurd story, written in one very long paragraph over eight printed pages (59–66), "Um dia ela foi flor nos jardins" (*Cadernos negros* 12; One Day She Was a Flower in the Gardens), the narrator, Sr. Maltazar y Soldo, is a servant to Clair, a dying middle-aged lady in her middle-class home. Instead of the normal sense of compassion between a servant and a dying boss, their relationship is more intellectual if not philosophical. The more the reader learns about this dying lady, the more intense her state becomes, and the narrator turns epiphanic as if contemplating the oddness of life and death, birth and rebirth, conception of life and its destruction. In one of these contemplative moments, the narrator compares the lady to a fly that has only twenty-four hours to live as if reflecting on the fragility of life:

> A idéia da morte pesava como um território onde predominava o silêncio, e que para alcançá-lo tornava-se necessário se submeter a um trajeto desconhecido, a transformar a vida em algo destituído de ilusões, um camelo de batalha fatalmente perdida. (60)

> [The notion of death was weighing like a territory where silence was overwhelming, and to attain it, it was necessary to submit oneself to an unfamiliar outfit, transforming life into something destitute of illusions, a senseless battle already fatally lost.]

These morose reflections seem to prepare the reader for the climactic ending where the sick lady and her servant (the narrator) find themselves playing real Russian roulette as a way to take chance with life or to invite death to come sooner. What is puzzling for the reader is the fact that the narrator participates willingly yet reluctantly, and ends up killing the lady when it is his turn to shoot. And to make matters worse, at the tribunal, instead of defending himself, his only defense is: "Caguei na boca de Clair!" (66; I defecated in the mouth of Clair!). The absurdity of both the crime and the defense reminds one of Albert Camus' *L'Etranger* (*The Stranger*). But instead of Meursault's defense that he did not intend to kill, the narrator emphasizes the killing with a dramatic ironic twist without attempting to absolve himself, and therein lies the absurdity of the story, which does not correspond with the title unless perhaps, if the author intends to be humorous by linking "flower in the gardens" to the brutal act of "rape" and revenge on the level of Clair representing a sick nation, Brazil, and the narrator representing the Afro-Brazilian defending himself by any means necessary. From this perspective, the multiplicity of Xavier's imagination is partly illuminated.

The use of literature as self-defense is also evident in *Manuel de sobrevivência* (Survival Manual), a humorous but "volatile" comic book that attempts to expose the various situations in which Afro-Brazilians find themselves mistreated and marginalized in Brazilian society. Coauthored with Maurício Pestana, who illustrated the dialogue and commentary, Xavier seems to have reflected on how to reach the Afro-Brazilian audience more effectively since this medium contrasts sharply with that of poetry and short story where the writing is typically more complex and philosophical. The crux of this "manual" lies in demystifying the notion that Brazil is a deracialized and nondiscriminatory society. Of course, this claim is a myth. One very classic example is a situation where the white boss is looking for "excuses" to dismiss certain workers. Of the ten standing in front of him, seven are white and short in height while three are black and tall. Here is the boss making his case:

> —Terei que despedir alguns de vocês! Pra não dizerem que está havendo proteção, só despedirei os três mais altos da turma! (41)

> [I'll have to fire some of you folks! Just so that they don't say I'm being discriminatory, I'll fire the tallest three of the bunch.]

It is quite obvious from the illustration that these "tallest three" are blacks and that if they were the "shortest," that would have been the excuse to eliminate them. With this illustration, Xavier succeeds in painting a dismal picture of Brazilian racial relations and the potential for corruption, abuse, and illegality. Ironically, most Afro-Brazilians experience these injustices and hardly complain or seek recourse to any legal redress in part out of frustration and in part because they do not believe any remedies are likely.

Another of Xavier's cooperative ventures, *Terramara*, coauthored with Cuti and Miriam Alves, is a play that lends itself to the same strategy adopted by *Manual de sobrevivência:* exposure and awareness. Dedicated to the memory of Solano Trindade and to Abdias do Nascimento as well as to Grande Otelo (the trio who contributed in no small measure to the development of Afro-Brazilian theater), *Terramara* is ample proof not only that Afro-Brazilians can work together in solidarity of purpose but also that they can produce quality work. The story foregrounds an imaginary *afoxé omi Oxum,* a Candomblé house where Dona Joana washes the head of her daughter Marilda in a symbolic and religious ritual of cleansing the impurities and negativities in her life—a form of rebirth as Marilda even foretold: "Não . . . Tato, eu nasci de novo" (15; No . . . Tato, I was reborn). The song sung by Dona Joana is important because it confirms the ancestral connections between Africa and Brazil as well as the continuity of healing and spiritual tradition:

> É para curar
> É para curar
> Folha de guiné, auê
> É para curar
> É para curar. (16)

> [It is curative / It is curative / Leaves from Guinea, *auê* / It is curative.]

Also significant is the date of publication: the year 1988 marks one hundred years since the abolition of slavery in Brazil. While this may be coincidental, it is however worth noting that *Terramara* was published and launched amidst the euphoria and celebration of the abolition centennial. The resistance of Afro-Brazilians is remarkable in this play as the three acts contest the validity of the Catholic church with respect to the resolution of problems facing them. Using a dialogic approach, Xavier et al. contrast the values and virtues of Candomblé with those of the Catholic Church through sarcastic and ironic effects, such as in the declaration of Teófilo, a white evangelical figure preaching the need to indoctrinate "barbarians":

> O patrimônio é da igreja.... Tira! Tira! Tira o feitiço daqui!... Precisamos catequisar os negros. Doutrinar esses bárbaros. Temos que catequisar os negros. Os cultos ocultos. (45)

> [The patrimony belongs to the church.... Remove! Remove! Remove fetishism from here!... We need to catechize Afro-Brazilians. Indoctrinate these barbarians. We need to catechize Afro-Brazilians. Occult cults.]

While character development is deficient in this three-act play, the overall thematic structure of the struggle—between tradition and modernity, and between Catholicism/capitalism and Candomblé/"fetishism"—remains very well explored and sharply contrasted.

In line with the stylistic, linguistic, and graphic game he plays in most of his works, Arnaldo Xavier in *A roza da recvza* (The Rose of Withdrawal, 1986), attempts to create a "manifesto" on a new Afro-Brazilian literary language as if tapping on the validity of African oral tradition as an interfacial strategy deployable by writers between the written and the spoken word. Its very title, artistically engraved in the eagle-invoked, suggests a daring effort of the artist to rescue Afro-Brazilian writing from the fangs of colonial language: Portuguese. By re-working orthography and creating new symbols and signs, he proposes stylistic strategies of self-expression and cultural paradigms for the recuperation of Afro-Brazilian identity. The "withdrawal" is not necessarily negative; it is, in fact, an announcement of the emergence of a new language, hence the metaphor of springing forth to life as a romantic "rose." The notion of "withdrawal" may also be extended to mean "rejection" as in a new literary language that is formulated in order to displace the previous one. Every writing should be a statement of discovery. The neologistic style with its notable visual emphasis, as already discussed, makes Xavier's poetry and short stories difficult to grasp. In the case of *A roza da recvsa*, despite its lack of titles for the poems, it is impossible to call it a long poem in many voices; moreover, with its poems that obscure in order to reveal many interrelated thematic concerns, its interpretation makes for intellectual gymnastics. Luiza Lobo's laconic observation that "Arnaldo Xavier, em *A roza da recvsa* (1986), retrabalha as montagens de Mallarmé e dos concretistas com vocábulos iorubas" (163; Arnaldo Xavier, in *A roza da recvsa* [1986], reworks the collages of Mallarmé and the concretists with Yoruba words) is not only reductionist but limited. Arnaldo Xavier's work goes beyond refining the works of the nineteenth-century French poet Mallarmé and the Brazilian concretists alone. In its overall aesthetics, his work is a conscious effort to move the Afro-Brazilian from the stereotypical plane of objectification to a more dignified level of subjectivity through postmodernist experimentation and assertiveness. Xavier raises a number of critical questions in this innovative text: What should the language of Afro-Brazilian literature be—the same Portuguese used by the Portuguese colonizer or a new language imbued with Afro-descendant consciousness such as Yoruba language and philosophy? To prove Afro-Brazilians as human and capable of reasoning, must they be limited to their African roots alone? Why not tap similarities echoing in Oriental and Greek philosophies in order to justify that all (wo)men are born equal? These and many other questions form the interrogative basis for the understanding of Xavier's anger and the effort to domesticate it through creative rebellion.

In a recent interview with Arnaldo Xavier, the writer responded to my question about why his works are so "esoteric" and difficult: "I was born in an environment deeply rooted in oral tradition. When I came to the South of the county (Brazil) I tried to fuse the oral or the verbal with the visual and I have suffered so much due to this innovation. In the process, I realized that I was actually defining a language for Afro-Brazilian literature. All I try to do is to be a writer with autonomy and freedom, nothing more."[11] This statement illuminates some of the questions and enigmas that have not been answered or clarified by many critics to date. The opening "poem"/stanza of *A roza da recvsa* philosophizes about strategic survival and subversion:

```
se )num momento( A Faca
DESEJAR
ser beijada
—!a beije
)MAS
COM TANTA CRITICIDADE
QUE INCOMODE O PROPRIETÁRIO DA FACA (11)
```

[If)at a moment(A Knife / WANTS / to be kissed /—! Kiss it / (BUT / WITH SO MUCH CRITICALITY / THAT MAKES THE OWNER OF THE KNIFE UNCOMFORTABLE.]

Perhaps this is the key to Xavier's imagination: the need to subvert the established norm (status quo) with the very instrument of oppression and representation—language. The symbols of the knife and the kiss become two antagonistic forces that with skill and vigilance may meet. It is about domesticating the cobra without getting any of its poison.

But in other poems/stanzas, instead of playing the language game, the poet resorts to the imperative of hope while remaining conscious of his visual aesthetics, as in these lines:

> por mais Insólita que Seja a Primavera
> atravessarei
> do Roseiral à Rosa
> da Roseira à Semente
> antes que por Omissão
> ou Arbítro
>)o Sol(
> retifique o Seu Curso
> diante o Meu Medo e Minha Ilusão (18)

[No matter how unusual the Spring Is / I will pass / from rosebed to Rose / from Rosebud to Seed / before through Omission / or through Free Will / the Sun / corrects his Route / before My Fear and My Illusion]

In another poem/stanza, the poet talks about his "eternity" and perhaps immortality in view of his self-regenerative sense that makes him liken himself to powerful illuminative symbols of nature such as the sun and light:

>)enloqueci(Sou uma Luz Inapagável
> ... na manhã mocha
> semiamarela
> como uma simples laranja madura
>)e Eu não Sou apenas uma palavra
> de trinta e três anos
> Eu. Sou trinta e três anos(
> —Acordei-me bem antes
> do AntiSol. (31)

[)I became insane(I am The Unquenchable Light / ... in my semiyellow firearm / like a simple ripe orange /)and I am not just a / thirty-three-year word / I am thirty-three years(/ I woke up way before / the AntiSun.]

And finally, when the poet can no longer hide his pain in obscure images and words, he bursts into a confession and philosophy of pain, defining its scope, manifestations, and limits:

> AQUI
> debaixo dessas Cinco Estrelas
>)Agonia(

)Grito(
)Fome(
)Medo(
)Tristeza(
. . . .
—Não há mais como camuflar a Dor. (49)

[HERE / Under these Five Stars /)Agony(/)Shout of Pain(/)Hunger(/)Fear(/)Sadness(/ (. . .) /—Hardly is there a way to hide Pain.]

This confession, seemingly contradicting the claim made earlier about the difficulty in Xavier's poetry, uncovers the inner void of the poet and his search to fill that emptiness through artistic escapades. Of course, he can be in pain and still be artistic about the expression of that pain, and that is what makes Arnaldo Xavier's poetry totally innovative and thought provoking. Although the title of *A roza da recusa* suggests "withdrawal," I prefer to see it more as a form of resistance: that is, withdrawal from the norm and invention of an alternative tradition.

Along the same line of *A roza da recusa*, *LudLud* (1997), whose opening refers to "fabricanções" (factory/fabricated-songs), presents an ambivalence created through neologism that corrupts "fábrica" (factory) and "fabricações" (fabrications) with the word "canções" (songs), in Portuguese. Here is an example of the "crossroads" between construction and constriction in *LudLud:*

subsenhor . . . como se escada caminho fosse encruzilhada   Vazado
depend**urad'olh**ar foice contemplando a última batalha   Totém destrói
Tabu Terrestre demole Celeste   Flor trucida Fruta . . . Exuzíaco expurga
Dionisíaco . . . Diax**ética d**ilui Dialética . . . Axé devora Fé   E**nigma d**ecifra
Dogma . . . Abutre dilacera Ab**utre**   NegrRo engole Grego. (18)

[Underlord . . . / as if stairways were a crossroad / Teared-up dependent gaze were the last struggle / Totem destroys Taboo / Terrestrial demolishes the Celestial / Flower decapitates Fruit . . . / Exuziac expunges Dionysiac . . . / Diaxethics dilutes Dialectics . . . / Àṣẹ devours Faith / Enigma deciphers Dogma . . . / Vulture dilacerates Vulture / Black swallows Greek].

In a sense, the dilemma with Xavier's creation is his audience. To appreciate Xavier's art, the reader must be well read to identify and relate to the symbolisms of totem and aboo as in the Brazilian modernist and "Anthropophagic" project. Likewise, the idea of contrasting such powerful images of *àṣẹ* (vital energy) with faith, enigma with dogma, black with Greek requires some intellectual background that in all fairness, few Afro-Brazilians possess.

The reader must realize that Xavier's audience is not the average Afro-Brazilian but the more "cultured," "bourgeois," and "intellectual" among them. Even the title is not so simple to grasp. *LudLud* perhaps echoes the beats of the eagle's wings as it glides into the storm, as suggested by the visual images within which the entire volume is framed.[12]

Negotiating between tradition and rupture, between norm and deviation, between pain and its "domestication," Xavier concerns himself with a wide range of issues that tend to mythologize pain and the burden of blackness through poetic escapism. Whether the poet is talking about "abutres" (vultures); Ṣàngó, the god of thunder; "Juju" or ẹbọ and their implications for sacrifice and transformation; fire, light, ashes, and the imperative of renewal; the mythology of "Abiku," the liminal being oscillating between life and death, heaven and earth; the image of a bird setting itself free; the role of Èṣù, the god of the crossroads; and the recurring image of the serpent biting its own tail, *LudLud* continues the regenerative and resistant tradition of *A roza da recusa*, in which pain and sadness cannot be hidden in spite of the various strategies to minimize them. In comparison to Cuti, Xavier is more cerebral than ideological; he is also less direct than Cuti, who refuses to take the shortcut in articulating his anger. Indeed, for Xavier, to regenerate is to transcend the black burden through a state he calls "transnegrescência":

> Subsenhor Trazido por um pássaro muito antigo Aqui debaixo deste Baobah transn**egresc**ência asa levito e deponho minhas flores Cuia cheia de estrelas corpo líquido rio rubronegro Leão se águia No último dia de ressurreição. (96)

> [Underlord / Brought by a very ancient bird / Here under this Baobab tree / Transblackessence raised wing / and I lay my flowers / Gourd full of stars / liquid body black Rubicon river / Lion becomes eagle / On the last day of resurrection.]

While Xavier recognizes the mystical nature of ancient birds as well the relevance of the baobab tree, which serves as a meditative/spiritual refuge as the concept of "transblackessence" takes root in the mind of the poet as a form of self-preservation and renewal, the poet nonetheless comes to terms with his blackness even as he struggles to transcend it.

In his unique visual poetry, Arnaldo Xavier resorts to Òrìṣà or Candomblé (African religion) tradition in Brazil, symbolic African images, and the renovation of concretist aesthetics within an Africanist frame. In "1888,"[13] Xavier captures the date of abolition in Brazil as in the image of a crucifix as if to suggest that the date is only a myth and that Afro-Brazilians are still subjugated and are yet to be free. Problematizing the same date, Xavier invokes the image of chains[14] in the form of 1888 buttressing the view that the

Afro-Brazilian is still enchained despite one hundred years of abolition as celebrated in 1998.[15] As Ronald Augusto observes in "Transnegressão," the visuality of Arnaldo Xavier's 1888 collage demands of the reader "maior simpatia ocular" (54; the greatest ocular sympathy), whereby the reader must choose between "simbólo e ícone" (symbol and icon) since words seem to become more and more reduced and almost eliminated. Another remarkable image is that of Èṣù, the god of the crossroads.[16] In this image, reproduced in red and black with one side representing a three-pronged fork and one side of the X in red, while the other represents a two-pronged fork and the other part of the X in black. Capturing not only the essence of Èṣù, the image reenacts the sign and the signification since the first fork forms E while the other forms a U and the (red and black) X in-between integrates the divisive and dual essence of Èṣù. Integrating the verbal and the visual in a concretist mode is the illustration of one of the poetic movements in *A roza da recvsa* where the poetic voices states: "O PRETO é uma ilha e um labirinto em si mesmo"[17] (The Afro-Brazilian is an island and a labyrinth lost within himself), the only difference being that in the visual representation, "preto" becomes "negro," perhaps in preference for the affirmation of blackness in the subverted as opposed to the pejorative meaning of "negro."

In the appreciation of Xavier's total productive and creative corpus, the author's own conscious erudition and construction combines with the indifference about audience and critical reception to give the reader a truly dynamic devotee of Èṣù, a critic-creator oscillating between the hot temper of Ṣàngó and the creative tranquility of Òṣun, whose eyes radiate with the voracity of the sun and the relaxing aura cum illumination of the moon. It is in this tango of construction and constriction that I situate Arnaldo Xavier.

Ronald Tutuca: Ambivalence of Stylistic Sanity and Lunacy

In his "Transnegressão," a critical essay paying homage to a number of Afro-Brazilian writers, such as Cuti, Oliveira Silveira, and Arnaldo Xavier, Ronald Tutuca (Augusto[18]) provides some incisive insights into a compelling concept he calls "TransBlaxpression."[19] An anecdote of a German student he had come into contact with while in Salvador-Bahia, through a referral from Arnaldo Xavier and Éle Semog, provides Tutuca a point of entry into the discussion of this notion. Reacting to his "poema caligráfico-visual" (calligraphic-visual poem), the student asks: "Onde está o Negro neste poema?" (48; Where is the Afro-Brazilian in this poem?). Tutuca's understanding of the student's question leads to a series of other implied questions, such as "Where are black symbols and images in Afro-Brazilian writing (*quilombo,* freedom, corporal punishment, slavery, etc.)?" "Where is the pain and black magic?" In essence, "Where is the exotic?" In response to the German's question, and in defense of those writers who attempt to move beyond the black burden, Tutuca affirms:

> Uma pequena parcela de escritores negros vem fazendo, há algum tempo, os necessários escurecimentos. Através de suas obras, conseguimos vislumbrar o sentido mais radical ou plural da idéia de *transnegressão*. (. . .) Este autores e seus poemas vão aos poucos tomando cada vez mais complexa qualquer definição, pretensamente consistente e acabada, a respeito das linhas de força do total desta escritura. (48)

> [For a while now, a minuscule group of Afro-Brazilian writers have been employing certain necessary maskings. Through their works, we have been able to discern the most radical or plural meaning of the ideal of *TransBlaxpression*. . . . These authors and their poems are making it more and more difficult to define, with a final and consistent pretension, the major and total dynamics motivating this writing.]

Tutuca's declaration provides a useful critical position about his own philosophy and validation of visual poetry as an alternative tradition for a select few of Afro-Brazilian writers in the sense that it is a craft of an "elitist" group that can afford the artistic price of "alienating" their audience and vice versa. His own works, which were not discussed in the essay in question, equally attest to a consciousness of formalist radicalism and rebellion, as in *Homem ao rubro* (1983), *Puya* (1987), and *Vá de valha* (1992). In addition, a contemporary of Tutuca, Edimilson Pereira, sums up Tutuca's artistic work as "fragmentário com linguagem sarcástica, dura, e popular-cotidiana; poética de rupturas sintáticas agressivas"[20] (fragmentary with a sarcastic language, harsh, and contemporary-popular. Poetics of aggressive syntactical ruptures). When Tutuca's three volumes of poetry are seen as a shifting and cohesive whole, the voice of the chaotic Afro-Brazilian mind, the alienated member of a deracialized yet racist society comes alive in spite of the effort to syncopate the language, condense the words, and fragmentize the message.

In three movements—"Primeiras peças," "Quadras de destrinça," and "Voz feirante"—*Homem ao rubro* (Blood-Red Man) provides a somewhat lucid yet obscured alternative way of envisioning the Afro-Brazilian subject. Challenging the reader, the "prefatory" poem evokes the labor of the apprentice-pendulum as he swings between one work and the other, realizing the challenges of the moment and the inevitable "veio futebolístico" (footballistic vein) as if to suggest that the work of art is always a "game in process," a relatively tentative and unfinished product that is often called "poem-process." The illustration of this poem is curious: against the image of the Brazilian flag, a patriotic national symbol, the poem, situated in its tail in the form of an academic degree or pointer, oscillates from one end to the other as if to confirm the theory provided to the reader in this opening poem. The first movement, appropriately titled "Primeras peças" (First Plays), captures defamiliarized personal reminiscences and situations. One such moment lies in the sexual act as the (male) poetic voice makes a connection between pleasure and death where beauty is not so important since the feeling of sweetness and soothingness that comes from penetration and ejaculation is far more vital. As the poet affirms:

Ameaço
a favor da morte
contando ser esta a
maioridade do nosso desejo. (35)

[I threaten / in favor of death / hoping that this / is the ultimate of our desire.]

Another moment lies in a situation with the poetic voice's boss as the employee runs after a beautiful lady in the city:

Não prestei o menor esclarecimento
ao otário do meu chefe
fui na cidade faladeira me provalecer
com a bonitinha da botica. (36)

[I did not in the least open up / to my foolish boss / I went to the bubbling city to have a good time / with the beautiful lady of the pharmacy.]

The second movement, "Quadras de destrinça" (Disentangling Quatrains), becomes even less direct as the quatrains have nothing to do with each other as the title suggests. The movement consists of notes on the lover of soul music and the lover of memory and ancestral struggle and a commentary on the living conditions of the dwellers of *Pelourinho* whose music emanates from the *senzalas* (slave quarters). In spite of dissociating himself from these subjects and images, the poetic voice is indeed sympathetic as he identifies with these *Pelourinho* habitants who now remind him of history as in the allusion to *senzalas*. While the second movement does not reveal much, the third, "Voz feirante," is more informative, perhaps because the poet becomes a "market voice," as appropriately titled. Unlike the first two movements, which had accompanying illustrations, this section is stripped of any illustration. Even in this voice of the "marketplace," the reader/audience is not without a challenge as the poetic voice confesses in the very last poem of the movement:

> A poesia que eu fiz coroca e não
> deu porque rodava com aventurança
> e economicidade
> a precisão de escrever
> banditismo de negro olhando
> diferente as resoluções ocidentais. (38)
>
> [The poetry I have written fails / and did not succeed because it was going on in circles / about economics / and the precision of writing / the banditry of the gazing black / different from Western resolutions.]

Although more of an explanation for poetic deviation than an apology, the ending of *Homem ao rubro* weakens the overall effect of this volume. As the title suggests, "Blood-Red Man" may be an ambivalent invention to capture a restless or an angry soul taking out his frustration on his poetry through artistic violence. It is also a statement of defiance to poetic norm.

Published four years after *Homem ao rubro*, *Puya* (1987) reinforces the stylistic complexity of the former volume as it takes the reader over a quadripartite economy of words and images that culminate in a puzzling section termed "emere," a Yoruba word for the liminal being traveling between heaven and earth and belonging to the realm of nocturnal spirits. The first three sections are no less challenging: "Homem ao rubro apócrifo" (Blood-Red Apocryphal Man), "Noma," "Atradução como crítica" (Translation as Criticism), and "[ ]" (i.e., Empty Square). Overall, these poems are cryptic without any attempt to simplify or to communicate. As Van Hingo, the critic, observes, reading Ronald Augusto's poems may give one a sense of shame at the inability to decipher the meaning: "Será o reconhecimento de uma limitação do leitor. Uma limitação de vocabulário, de leituras, enfim, de informação" (10; This could be the realization of the reader's limitation. A limitation of vocabulary, of readership, in sum, of information). Perhaps even more compelling is Van Hingo's conclusion that Ronald Augusto's poems are devoid of soul: "São desalmados, sem coração" (9; They lack soul; they are heartless). If the title is close to any word in Portuguese, it is *Puxa!*—that is, "Surprise!"—as if the poet is mocking the reader to the extent of challenging: "Read if you dare!" Indeed, the attempt to analyze these poems has been frustrating, futile, and almost anger-invoking. The reader encounters lines like: "pés de papelão pretinto / envelhecendo a água" (16; sheets of precolored paper / aging the water). Although I interviewed the poet, I am still not convinced that this type of writing devoid of social function contributes in any way to the advancement of the Afro-Brazilian. If the goal is only to prove the "complexity" of the Afro-Brazilian mind, the question remains to what extent this realization transforms the oppressed subject from his/her alienation and deprivation.

By the time the reader gets to *Vá de valha* (Go Get Some Help,[21] 1992), his most recent volume of poetry, it is becoming obvious that the poet is reacting to the negative critical reception by now "simplifying" just a little bit and "communicating" more within the poem. The text is divided into three main parts: "vá de valha," "ciclo Salvador," and "poemas experimentais" (experimental poems).[22] These parts are not necessarily sequential—another "lunacy" of the author. The first is supposed to capture the poet's dialogue with Guimarães Rosa, Mário de Andrade, Machado de Assis, Raúl Pompéia, and Gregório de Matos in an attempt to praise or ridicule them as the case may be. Here is Ronald Tutuca commenting on Matos:

gregório de matos oco olho do cu do
inferno sermão cego naso
torcido asco . . .
um preto é um branco sem caráter
sem espírito sem um pensamento sequer
que se morda (que se meta) a si mesmo. (40)

[Gregório de Matos empty eye of / deep hell sermon born blind / twisted disgust . . . / a black is a white without character / without spirit without any thought / who bites (kills) himself.]

Conceivably, Tutuca is angry with Gregório de Matos for his portrayal of the Afro-Brazilian, especially as a pastor-preacher in Bahia, where a significant number of Afro-Brazilians live, yet Matos's representation is "colonial" at best, and bestial-inhuman overall. But is this pure sarcasm on the part of Tutuca? Is being angry with Matos enough without saying why? In the final analysis, the reader must not only know the background of Matos and his religio-political art; the reader is invited to unravel he mysteries of the poem, which are multiple and multilayered. This realization confirms my position that although Ronald Tutuca attempts to "escape" his negritude or to transcend it, he, like others in this group, still answer to and defend their blackness. I cannot agree more with the poet as he declares: "O tom dos poemas não é, apenas, de ressentimento; pelo contrário, estes criadores são apresentados como 'meus autores-inimigos preferidos,' em registro irônico" (The tone of the poems is not only resentful; on the contrary, these creators are presented as "my favorite authors-enemies" in ironic register).

The second part captures the poet's three-year sojourn in Salvador-Bahia, a period he calls a contradiction of expectations since the black capital still operates with a preabolitionist mentality in terms of its racial relations. Other than images/words invoked in the poems such as "musseque" (African ghetto), "favela" (Brazilian slum), "cubata" (plantation slave house), and "carapinha" (crisped-curled hair), these poems are neither evocative of

Salvador, Bahia, nor reflective of the experiences of discrimination or racism since the poetic voice does not communicate that. Similar to the third part that the poet calls "experimental," the poems with words are not so far away from the visual poems: their commonality lies in ideological silence/articulation and stylistic lunacy. Ronald Tutuca's poetic corpus marks a rupture in the poetic tradition of Solano Trindade, Abdias do Nascimento, Eduardo de Oliveira, Oswaldo de Camargo, and Carlos de Assumpção. However, although Tutuca's art seems to have multiple expressive dimensions, it has not totally succeeded in transgressing his blackness, despite his aggressive stylistic manipulations with which he hopes the reader can see beyond the color of his skin and focus on the beauty of his art.

Conclusion

The three poets examined, Cuti, Arnaldo Xavier, and Ronald Tutuca, communicate their anguish through a consistent struggle with form. While black consciousness and anger are the Cuti trademark, Arnaldo Xavier taps Yoruba ancestral ethos and mythology to uncover the parallels of Afro-Brazilian culture with Greek and Oriental philosophies. The most complicated and obscure of the three, Ronald Tutuca, takes poetic experimentation to an extreme, becoming silent in the process of economizing words, and challenging the reader to a point of frustration and even disgust. Regardless of their media, the three poets clearly demonstrate the complexity of Afro-Brazilian cultural production through the postmodern aesthetic that informs their productive and ideological agendas. Ultimately, these writers are seeking recognition and respect for both their artistry and their philosophy.

11

Ancestrality, Memory, and Citizenship

> The question of Africans' participation in Brazil is first and foremost a question of *citizenship*. The abolition of slavery did little or nothing to return the citizenship that the regime of chattel slavery stole from us along with our very humanity. On the contrary, the living conditions imposed on African Brazilians after the "Golden Law" of abolition stripped us of our citizenship for the second time. And since the Eurocentric elites could not tolerate the idea of a nation composed in its majority of blacks, they arranged for the arrival of immigrants recruited in Europe.
> —Abdias do Nascimento and Elisa Larkin Nascimento[1]

The notions of nation and citizenship are by nature complex since what constitutes each of these communities is defined equally by sociopolitical, cultural, and historical values that cannot be separated from the legacies of struggles to assert ownership, freedom, and eligibility to share in the distribution of national resources and benefits. The zero-sum political scenario is particularly informative to understand societies and peoples that have been historically oppressed and marginalized, such as inhabitants of the former colonies and their shifting conditions from the enslaved to the "emancipated" or from the colonized to the "postcolonial." As the above quote by Abdias do Nascimento and Elisa Nascimento affirms, the challenge for Brazil as a miscegenational society is less to ensure some form of participation by blacks in the society than to make "citizenship" an equitable right available to all those who participated in making Brazil a great nation through their travails, toils, and suffering over many years of enslavement. The slave cannot claim to belong to a nation, much less hold any claim to its citizenship. The slave is considered an object, an "owned" property that has no will or soul of "its" own.

Yet, after the abolition of slavery in 1888, the harsh realities in which Afro-Brazilians live even today suggest that abolition was only a cosmetic measure and that subtle forms of slavery and bondage—mental, financial, social, even spiritual—still exist in Brazil. Afro-Brazilians are then compelled to resort to their ancestrality and collective memory to recapture that lasting cultural legacy that was stripped but not totally lost through the Middle Passage. In such a process of revitalization and recuperation of self, it is inescapable that Africa remains an intertextual point of reference for the African diaspora. Like other African descendants in the diaspora, Afro-Brazilians are caught in the classic DuBoisian "double consciousness" and double bind: being Africans and being Brazilians all at the same time. Symbolically, the Orpheus gaze translates this duality of place and space as Afro-Brazilians must look back to Africa in order to look forward to their future within the contradictions of Brazilian modernity. This chapter situates within this paradigmatic shift and flexibility the relevant works of Esmeralda Ribeiro, Miriam Alves, Abílio Ferreira, and Geni Guimarães to ascertain how these modernist cultural producers negotiate their penchant for tradition within modernity on the one hand, as well as the combination of ancestral consciousness with collective memory on the other. Although spatially disconnected from Africa, Afro-Brazilians reconnect through many ritualistic media, especially the spiritual and the cultural, while masking these within expressive traditions that nonetheless have their political implications and resonances.

The hybridity-inspired paradigm of modernity and double-consciousness proposed by Paul Gilroy in *The Black Atlantic* comes with certain apprehensions, especially regarding the author's critique of "African purity," "authenticity," and his recognition of the "diverse processes of black cultural production" (190). In calling into question "the very desire to be centered" that may be taken for granted by a middle-class bourgeois intellectual comfortably insulated in the ivory tower against the hardships of daily struggles faced by Afro-Brazilians and other dispersed Africans of the diaspora, such as unemployment, discrimination, police brutality, violation of human rights, and violence in different degrees, Gilroy overstates the validity of his argument that the antiquity of African civilization in relation to Western civilization is a simplistic inversion of Eurocentricity, and by implication a claim of "superiority" by Afrocentrists. Alas, Gilroy misses the point. To challenge white superiority by emphasizing the legitimacy of one's culture and origin need not be a proposal for a reversal of position but is definitely a corrective to the sweeping misinformation disseminated about African cultures. Does anyone seriously suggest that proponents of Afrocentricity seek to make whites "inferior" or "subordinate" simply by claiming to be "superior" to whites? That argument reeks of a flawed and impossible possibility in the modern world of capital and financial control located in the hands of a white majority. The focus of this book does not allow for a thorough defense of Afrocentricity but recognizes the importance of Africans all over the world being or becoming conscious of their origins as a measure to deal with the alienation and hostility of the "New World" environment. While most Afro-Brazilians do not want to claim African nationality per se, they at least identify with their past in such rituals as Candomblé and the *afoxé* liturgical music of Filhos de Gandhi, and capoeira, among other artistic/religious/popular entities. Since Afro-Brazilians are far from being the majority in Brazil (except as defined by the notion of race common to North American racial history—the one-drop-of-blood rule to define "blackness"), it is inconceivable that they could become the majority through a theoretical or even ideological inversion. It is this freedom to connect, reconnect, and disconnect that Gilroy ridicules under the guise of problematization and intellectual challenge that begs the issue.

From the classical Orpheus gaze in Greek mythology to its various Brazilian interpretations, the resistance embedded in the action of Orpheus cannot be understated. The historicizing of the present at the expense of the past as suggested by Michael Hanchard will be meaningless without an understanding of the past.[2] For Orpheus, the backward gaze constitutes a point of departure for strategic dialogue and negotiation. The loss of Eurydice in that process recognizes the challenges of reconnecting with the past (Africa) but is not an excuse to dismiss the re-Africanization efforts of the black movements and groups in the seventies. Despite Eurydice's warning to Orpheus that looking back would mean losing her, it is arguable that Eurydice wanted it as such; the only way the legendary lovers could both be together is by Orpheus leaving the land of the living to join her in the spiritual realm of the dead. To keep looking forward without historical hindsight is to remain without cultural memory. The memories of Africa in several expressive manifestations that Afro-Brazil offers, particularly in Bahia, equally testify to this significant and transformative consciousness. If Brazilian Afro-modernity is taken to be atemporal, the different expressions of resistance during enslavement, such as the creation of *quilombos* and the cultivation of African traditional religions in their reconfigured structures in Candomblé, are as "modern" as more recent manifestations such as capoeira, samba, and Afro-Brazilian carnival. In *Race and Color in Brazilian Literature,* David Brookshaw captures the posture of Afro-Brazilians in their resistance against white Brazilian domination and the mythology of miscegenation in the chapter he appropriately titles "Retreat into the 'Quilombo.'"[3] The trope of the "quilombo" is not necessarily a rejection of Africa but rather a "type of African continuum, in which African traditions were preserved, but within the specific environment of the New World" (290). While "quilombo" continues as a constant creative muse, Africa is equally symbolically signified in the cultural production of Afro-Brazilians through African relics and icons in Brazilian reality.

Allegories of Identity, Ancestry, and Voice

Manipulating the ambivalence of the title "Ogun,"[4] Esmeralda Ribeiro crafts a story that Paul Gordon calls the "critical double."[5] Due to its tonal character, Yoruba language offers a multiplicity of meanings where one sign may have multiple signifiers. The title of Ribeiro's story captures this multiplicity. While in the context of the story the word means inheritance, it can also mean "god of iron," "war"/"struggle," "twenty," or even curative medicine depending on the intonation. In the specific context deployed by Ribeiro, the "critical double" lies in the multiple figurations of a black telephone as an element of inheritance, racial sign, and instrument of articulation or communication. The critical doublings are enhanced by the possibilities of interpretation the sign offers in the Brazilian miscegenational context. What is ambivalent is the actual authorial intention. The question is: Is the blackness of the telephone a representation of black voice or is it a problematization of blackness in the sense that on many occasions, through distorted perceptions, dreams, or hallucinations, the narrator sees the black telephone appearing "neither white nor black"?[6] This case study provides ample evidence of a racial dilemma, especially in the acceptance of the black telephone by a samba club (*casa de samba*), as the theme and allegory of its parade. On the one hand, the ambivalence of the blackness of the telephone raises a question of hybrid and shifting identity that defines the complexity of race in Brazil. On the other hand, the acceptance of the telephone as an allegory during carnival, by a black cultural institution that a samba club represents, speaks to the negotiation that most of these cultural organizations are compelled to make. The "whiteness" or "blackness" of the telephone notwithstanding, the samba club has given it legitimacy by adopting it as the voice of resistance, even if symbolically. The narrator, Mariana Cesário, actually expresses her disappointment when the phone finally arrives and she finds it to be black instead of the white she had expected. The allegories of race, ancestry, and voice are intertwined metaphorically within the title and the narrative. As Gordon points out, "One of the most outstanding anomalies of titles is that they are that part of a written text that is specifically meant to be quoted, spoken, or referred to" (*The Critical Double* 94).

Aside from the black telephone representing inheritance, it is also signified as an instrument of Afro-modernity in terms of its utility: communication. Though the oral tradition is still inherent in the use of a phone, the medium of that communication is no longer the same—there is indeed a new "medium"—the technological element that bridges the distance unlike in oral tradition where the communication is personal and unmediated from the speaker to the listener. Though Afro-Brazilians cannot lay claim to the telephone as their expression of modernity since such inventions are not patented by the first inventor, the idea of problematizing its color serves as a point of entry into the discussion of the relevance of race in modernity. The fact that the narrator temporally locates her own birth on November 20, 1964, is equally significant. November 20 is the anniversary of the death

Ancestrality, Memory, and Citizenship 271

of Zumbi dos Palmares, the official hero and leader of Afro-Brazilians who resisted Portuguese domination and slavery in the seventeenth century and founded the *quilombo* settlement of Palmares.

In "Ogun," the family setting provides crucial clues about the primacy of color, race, and identity in Brazilian life. As the narrator describes her house in contrast to the black telephone, the reader is as bewildered as the telephone company installers who have come to deliver the black telephone after twenty years of installment plan payments:

> Numa bela manhã de sábado quando completava vinte primaveris anos, eis que chegam os servidores da rapartição telefônica em sua residência, para instalarem o aparelho. Eles ficaram primeiro admirados pela fachada e depois pelo interior da casa. A frente era pintada toda de branco e no interior nenhum objeto da sala tinha combinação de qualquer outra cor. O branco predominava. (*Callaloo* 18.4 [1995]: 913)

> [On a beautiful Saturday morning when she was twenty years old, the telephone company installers arrived at her home to put in the phone. First they were surprised by the outside and then by the inside of the house. The exterior was painted entirely in white and inside there wasn't a single object of any other color.]⁷

While the choice of "white" as a favorite color may have nothing to do with racial complexities, it is inconceivable that a black family would consciously select all-white household effects unless they belong to the Candomblé faith.⁸ Even then, the worshippers of Òrìṣànlá usually limit their choice of white to their outfit on a special day. As the narrator clarifies, there were "constant fights about race" (741) in the household, a situation that led to the separation of Mariana Cesário's parents. A household with a white mother of Italian descent and a black father of African descent need not be problematic in a true racial democracy, but the reality in Brazil is different. In fact, both parents advise their daughter against marrying a black man under the pretext of the aversion of blacks to studying: "My parents always warned me. Don't marry a black because they only know about soccer and . . . nothing about studying" (741). Such an imposing caveat confirms the conviction and faith of some Afro-Brazilians in the principle of social mobility through racial stratification and mixture. It is the classical case of "marrying well" to improve one's social status and ensure a better life and future for one's offspring.

As a microcosmic Afro-Brazilian family, the Desários' interactions, concerns, and consciousness are permeated by the issue of racial identity. Even on the individual level, Mariana Cesário, on several delusionary and hallucinatory moments, resorts to discovering her own identity: "I have to find myself. I have to know who I am" (745). One instance is when she is making sure that she had covered all the bases in terms of a promotion possibility to General Coordinator—a position that was being competed for by other women, white and black. To make herself acceptable, she decides to "straighten her hair" in a beauty salon suggestively named Why Don't You Straighten Your Hair? Although she has constantly been praised by board members for her efficiency and consciousness (never missed work, never sick, never late, worked overtime for the same pay), she does not get the promotion. She then resorts to self-analysis about her identity as if wondering what else she could have done differently to be worthy and deserving of the promotion. In this particular contemplative instance, she resorts to ancestral strength by invoking her ancestors in a dream: "She dreamed that she wore her hair naturally and dressed in the clothes of her black ancestors" (745). Through this psychotherapeutic measure, she rehumanizes herself and thus leaves behind the feeling of discrimination and injustice.

Using inheritance or heritage as a trope of collective undertaking takes the black telephone to another doubling or metaphoric level. Could the black telephone represent the voice of Afro-Brazilian people? Indeed, in one of her dreams, the black telephone becomes a man to the extent that they hold each other's hands, make passionate love, and constantly caress each other. At a crucial moment when their eyes meet, they express pride in their own bodies and identity: "We are beautiful, beautiful" (744). Such a loving declaration among Afro-Brazilians is a constant struggle as the primordial struggle has been focused on daily survival against social inequalities and it has taken the efforts of Afro-Brazilian cultural entities such as Ilê-Aiyê, *Gélédé,* and Quilombhoje, among others, to resuscitate racial pride within the black community. Such identitarian awareness led to a recent research project cosponsored by Quilombhoje and *Amma—Psique e negritude* that has now been published as a book: *Gostando mais de nós mesmos* (Loving Ourselves More).[9] The black telephone represents such a collective possession that the entire family deliberates what to do with the phone since Mariana Cesário is so disappointed and dissatisfied with its black color. Even when it is decided to sell or get rid of it, Mariana finds out from the company that the contract has a clause put in by Mariana's father that the telephone is not to be sold but must be given away. If the consensus is that the phone remain in Mariana's room or be given away since it cannot be sold, the fact that the phone ceases to work also raises another issue of voicelessness and silencing. There is no evidence that the phone ever worked. The only time in the story where the phone could function was met with disappointment. As a representative of Afro-Brazilian voice, the silencing of the black telephone is symbolic of the silencing of all Afro-Brazilians, hence reflective of political implications that are embedded within the narrative.

Mariana's decision to donate the black telephone to a samba club, "Recreational Society—Popular Culture," makes a powerful statement about the creativity of Afro-Brazilians within a hostile environment. On a further subversive level, the donation itself translates into a subconscious utilitarian ideology: instead of simply throwing the phone away in anger and frustration, taking it to where it can at least serve the useful purpose of entities whose cultural values intersect with that of the "blackness" of the phone reveals Mariana's the intelligence. The samba club unsuccessfully paints the telephone white, turning it "neither white nor black" (746) in the process. That the samba club needed to paint the phone in the first place also makes the point that their "voice" must be acceptable to a wider community even though they are keeping Afro-Brazilian musical culture intact while also providing entertainment. As the theme of the samba club ("In Lands with White Laws We Have to Have Brown Solutions,") confirms, Afro-Brazilians must devise strategies of survival. Mariana finally comes to terms with the "critical double" that the black telephone represents, even as suggested by her father's voice, which she hears during the carnival parade telling her "their doubts will always be our certainties" (746), as if to testify to the permanent Brazilian racial dilemma—neither white nor black but both. Mariana's voice in the narrative is subsumed under a more dominant racist ideology from which she cannot escape or, rather, chooses not to escape. There is something of a dubious irony lurking behind this ambivalence. Is Mariana conscious of her racial "confusion" being an offspring of both Italian and African parentage or is her need to surround herself with "white" possessions a genuine desire for whiteness? Does Mariana have a choice in selecting a "comfortable" race of affiliation and does she really have to make a choice? Is she a victim of a society that does not allow her to promote her "Africanness" but permits her to negotiate a relatively more acceptable "mulatta" identity that she embodies? Mariana's rejection of the black phone, coupled with her frustration in procuring a white phone instead is a state of crisis in identity consciousness. The donation serves as the exorcism, a therapeutic process of liberation through her desire to observe the transformation and recasting of a rejected object by integrating it into the sacred and popular space that the *casa de samba* represents. Like the phone she rejects, she too is also rejected by the white establishment of work and influence that she struggles to be part of.

Throughout the dreamlike tale, a central problem revolves around race, identity, and racism. Using the work setting as well as the phone company setting, Ribeiro exposes and attacks the social inequalities that result from racial discrimination. Ribeiro's narrative strategy plays on ambivalence and ambiguity of color, symbol, and meaning. While coping with the startling experience of the black telephone both at the family level and at the individual, the ramifications of racism are equally played out when she contacts the phone company about the installation.[10] She is not well attended to until she informs the establishment of her status as a manager. In the company she works for, which ironically is called "Here There is No Racism," she is denied a well-deserved promotion, which was given to someone else who was less qualified. Interestingly, the story does not focus on the race of her competitors other than to say they are women. Although it is unclear if Mariana is actually living a reality or if she is dreaming since the cathartic point in the story creates an illusion that the telephone is still located in Mariana's room, as if the entire story were an undesirable enactment of a nightmare. The magic-realist approach is effective in that it provides possibilities of critical interpretation while challenging the reader to face the unresolved racial problematic throughout the story. Unlike *Malungos e milongas* (Brothers and Sisters) where Ribeiro directly appeals to heightened collective consciousness and solidarity between male and female Afro-Brazilian militants, "Ogun" is more of a metaphoric tale.[11] The fantasy-like approach in "Ogun" relies on memory and recollections to make the indictment of social inequalities subtle and effective—an ample evidence of Ribeiro's consciousness of the duality of resistance and negotiation within a larger marginalizing sociopolitical structure and its alienating effects on Afro-Brazilians.

The Intertext of Gender, Nation, and Cultural Identity

Of the entire generation of cultural producers who belong directly or indirectly to the Quilombhoje movement,[12] Geni Guimarães is one of the most mature and by far, the most accomplished.[13] With many literary and social awards to her credit, ranging from the coveted Jabuti Prize in 1988, to the Adolfo Aisen Prize in 1989, and the Black Personality Award in 1990, among others, she deftly oscillates between poetry and short stories without neglecting the novella, not to mention her recent return to children's literature. An examination of Guimarães's corpus of cultural production reveals a playful writer who on the one hand combats racism and sexism, and on the other situates the Afro-Brazilian experience within the totality of Brazilian reality in a nonthreatening manner. She skillfully engages issues of gender, cultural identity, and citizenship—which includes the children, who are the future of Brazil. Despite her productive record, the critical reception of her works is scanty, a situation that is not limited to Guimarães alone.

The criticism of Afro-Brazilian literature generally faces a dilemma Cuti qualifies as "intellectual orphanage," or what we may call critical orphanage.[14] The lack of a systematic body of critical works geared toward the recognition of valuable works and their authors makes the critical inquiry of an "outsider" (such as myself) particularly daunting.[15] Even among the "insiders" such as the authors themselves, criticism is an elitist endeavor that many writers cannot afford. The result is a plethora of panoramic reviews in local magazines, especially during a new book launching. The challenge for the individual and group producer such as Quilombhoje is how to validate their work among academic critics. It is arguable that individual Afro-Brazilian writers such as Miriam Alves, Geni Guimarães, Esmeralda Ribeiro, and Cuti are better known and recognized for their works outside of Brazil than in their own country. Compared to Ribeiro, Guimarães is more subtle in her language and ideological consciousness, less direct and provocative.

Born September 8, 1947, Guimarães belongs to the generation I have designated as "forerunners of Afro-modernity"[16] in the sense that they came to maturity at a time of political openness in Brazil—a period that led to the formation of many cultural and political entities such as the Movimento Negro Unificado (Unified Black Movement), Ilê-Aiyê, Olodum, and Quilombhoje, among many others. She qualifies as the "total" Afro-Brazilian writer in that she does not confine herself to labels of race and gender although her writings do manifest passionate sensibilities concerning the plights of Afro-Brazilian women, men, and children. In a response to a question about her function as writer in Brazilian society, she asserted:

> Acredito que o escritor, compromissado com seu povo e sua época, deve cumprir o dever de conscientizar, denunciar e reescrever a história de forma a provocar transformações sociais que impulsionem o indivíduo em busca de uma sociedade melhor e mais humana.[17]

> [I believe that a writer, committed to her people and her time, must fulfill the duty of raising consciousness, contesting and rewriting history in such a manner that provokes social changes that spur the individual into searching for a better and more humane society.]

This global perspective is essential as the Brazilian woman writer must not function in an esoteric feminist vacuum alienating herself from the community, but in the reality of home, work, society, culture, and racism. Celeste Dolores Mann captures the multiple function and responsibilities of the black woman writer in general when she posits that in addition to dealing with white male domination, Brazilian women writers must engage in a "constant process of debunking myths, deconstructing cultural paradigms, attacking stereotypes and defining their own voice. . . . Moreover, much of the writing is a search for racial, cultural, or female identity. Because of the dominant society's concept of racial identity, its myth of racial democracy, sexism, and paternalism, this quest is extremely complex for Afro-Brazilian women."[18] It is within this "complexity" that the literary corpus and significance of Geni Guimarães must be understood.

Woman as the "Continual Motion" of the World

In assessing the creative world of Geni Guimarães, Conceição Evaristo's poem "Eu-mulher" (I-Woman) provides several "epigraphic" insights that capture the ancestral linkage as well as the feminine strength of this multivalent writer—attributes that define, pervade, and illuminate the imagination in *Terceiro filho* (Third Child), *A cor da ternura* (Color of Tenderness), *Balé das emoções* (Ballet of Emotions), and *Leite do peito* (Milk from the Heart). Evaristo's poem is not only paradigmatic, it is fundamental:

> Uma gote de leite
> me escorre entre os seios.
> Uma mancha de sangue
> me enfeita entre as pernas
> (...)
> Eu—Mulher em rios vermelhos
> inaugura a vida.
> (...) Antevejo
> Antecipo
> Antes-vivo. (...)
> Eu—Mulher
> abrigo da semente
> moto-contínuo
> do mundo.[19]

[The following trans. is NOT by author]

[A drop of milk / runs down between my breasts. / A stain of blood / adorns me between my legs. / ... I foresee / I anticipate / I live beforehand. ... / I-Woman / shelter of the seed / continual motion / of the world.

The representation of the woman as life-giver, as the repository of strength, and as the "vital engine" that propels the world connects with the power of the ancestors to provide solace in times of weakness, vision in times of blurriness, and assurance in times of uncertainty, to the extent that the woman may be seen as protector of the "seed" of life just like the ancestors. Women and the ancestors are connected not only physically but spiritually, hence the analogy captured in the qualities of "foresight," "anticipation," and "life-before and life-after." A new child born has a lineage that transcends the immediate parents but continues his or her linkage with the grandparents and the ancestors. In African cosmological belief, these ancestors are not "dead" and gone but are still comingling with the living—manifesting themselves through animate and inanimate objects.

Guimarães's poetic corpus, from *Terceiro filho* through *Balé das emoções* as well as her anthologized poems,[20] shares the qualities of Conceição Evaristo's epigraphic poem. In the "continual motion" metaphor are embedded issues of love, life, death, anguish of racism, sexism, as well as efforts to make the world a saner and better place. The entire collection seems to be guided by a synesthetic sensibility between bondage and freedom, between a gendered tension and a penchant for compassionate humanity as illustrated in the poem "Livre" (Free), which may be regarded as her "arte poética." The poet comes to terms with the limits of the poetic word to capture the "heart of the poet," the "infinite sadness" of the world, the happiness of the universe," and concludes rebelliously that "all the goodness of the soul cannot be boxed into one sonnet." Guimarães's philosophy of poetry is evocative of what Harold Bloom calls "the anxiety of influence,"[21] or rather the internal tension suffered by the poet in the process of freeing himself/herself from other external "inevitable" influences in the poetic process. In "Livre," Guimarães asserts her rights and the imperative to be free:

> Por isso é que agora me liberto
> E liberto a profusão de alegrias que há em mim
> E liberto a liberdade de minha liberdade,
> E solto o mundo reprimido.
> (. . .)
> Na liberdade de meu verso eu vibro,
> Eu amo, eu canto!
> Eu me completo e completo o meu poema.
> Eu sou gente, eu sou mulher, criança.
> Livre!!! (*Terceiro filho* 56)

[That is why I set myself free / I set free the torrent of happiness within me / And I set free the freedom of my freedom / And I release the repressed world. / . . . / In the liberty of my poetry, I vibrate, / I love, I sing! / I complete myself and complete my poem. / I am people, I am a woman, I am a child. / Free!!!]

There is nothing else to add to this explicit poetic vision: Guimarães revels in her freedom within the inescapable bondage and conditionings of the world. In the Brazilian racial context where the potential for veiled discrimination is rampant, the freedom to self-express directly or indirectly is a powerful consolation that cannot be taken for granted.

Of the entire poetic collection in *Terceiro filho*, only a few poems address issues of blackness directly or indirectly. Instead, Guimarães focuses more on the frustrations of love, the freedom to express herself, the acceptance of death as an inevitable "nothingness" in life, and varied philosophical reflections that depict her wisdom and compassion for humanity. The freedom of expression that Guimarães holds so dear in "Livre" (Free) is contradicted in another poem, aptly titled "Contradição" (Contradiction"), where the poetic voice admits that faced with the immensity of the space in the universe, freedom becomes frightening, especially as she ponders the sensation that a poet is more often living "in prison" than living in freedom in the sense that the poet is constantly running away from herself as if she is afraid of discovering herself:

> Andei sob medidas,
> Com medo de me encontrar.
> (. . .)
> Mas tanto tempo estive presa,
> Que meteu-me medo a liberdade,
> E fiquei completamente accorrentada,
> Com todo este espaço que existe no universo. (86)

[I walked in calculated precision, / With the fear of finding myself. / . . . / But for a long time I was stuck, / That freedom gave me the fright, / And I was completely overwhelmed, / With all this space in the world.]

An explanation for this contradiction may be found in "Banalidades" (Banalities), the closing poem, in which the poet imagines what her legacy would be, expecting the reader to conclude: "Para cada louco, uma mania" (119; For every insane mind, a mania). On the contrary, Guimarães is not an insane poet; rather, she may be translating the traumatizing potential of the harsh realities of the world.

Beyond the contradictory freedom in "Contradição," only in "Palco da vida do crioulo" (Life Stages of the Biracial) does Guimarães critique the positive but romantic image of the biracial person, or *crioulo*, as the mixed-race figure or "native-born slave" who is supposed to be representative of the universal race that Brazilian race-mixture policy has supposedly created. Instead, Guimarães inverts and subverts that distorted image by portraying the anonymous bi-racial person as orphaned, poor, uneducated, miserable, homeless, and alcoholic. Here is an ideological poem—subtle yet effective as it ridicules the Brazilian myth of racial democracy. In the last stage of the bi-racial one's life, he dies of misery and hunger in the company of his friend and killer—*cachaça:*

> Um crioulo embriagado.
> E onde estava ele, lá se via ela:
> Na rua, no quarto, no bar, na calçada,
> Na fome, na sede, na dor, na miséria,

Morte-mulher em gota disfarçada,
Má companhia, namorada sincera. (13–14)

[A drunk native. / And where he was, there she was: / In the streets, in the room, in the bar, on the stairway, / In hunger, in thirst, in pain, in misery, / Mother-Death in veiled drops, / Bad company, honest girlfriend.]

"Palco da vida do crioulo" is ironically a simultaneous critique of Brazilian traditional rum (*cachaça*) in view of its potential to destroy its victim. For the alcoholic, the drink is a "friend" because it provides temporary relief from the anguish of daily living.

Guimarães's concern for the downtrodden and the marginalized is also echoed in "Você é responsável" (You Are Responsible) where the poetic voice shares with others her elation ("sentir-me árvore" [feeling like a tree]) at being pregnant, and upon the birth of the child, provides a piece of moral advice to all children about their role in shaping their own destinies:

Não vi no meu filho um marginalizado,
Um jovem ladrão, vadio, assassino.
Não me vi dando ao mundo um filho viciado! (10)

[I could not see my child as a marginal, / a young rogue, a loafer, an assassin. / I could not see myself giving birth to a corrupted child!]

Similarly, Guimarães critiques laziness and ignorance as represented in "Tereza molecada" (Frivolous Tereza), about a woman who spends her entire life having babies, one after the other, without any education, exposure, discretion, or wisdom. The poetic voice not only ridicules the rogue-marginal-assassin child; she equally condemns the fate of the irresponsible mother, who cannot control her own body and mind, with a sarcastic series of questions:

Oi Tereza, como vai a vida?
Já sarou a barriga do Matéus?
E ela, responde boca escancarada:
"Tá tudo bom, com as graças de Deus" (89)

[Hello, Tereza, how is life? / Has your stomach recovered from having Mateus? / And she replies, mouth wide opened: / "All is well, by the grace of God."]

The "Frivolous Tereza" figure goes against the notion of the woman as a "continual motion" of the world in the sense that instead of engineering the world wisely, Tereza, indeed, has become a danger to that process since the children she is giving birth to will not have adequate nurturing or provision but will end up as "at risk" children who may become the very assassins and rogues that Guimarães protests in "Você é responsável." A final message to the youth is found in "Droga... que droga, bicho?" (Damn... Damn, Dude?) where the poet advises young ones to be involved in their own future and not live a futile life:

> Voce simplesmente não está. Vocé néo é homem!
> ....
> Faça uso da sua mocidade.
> Não seja apenas uma desculpa na terra.
> Você pode nascer amanhã,
> E ser um presente para a sociedade. (36)

> [You are simply not present. You are not a man! / ... / Cultivate your youth / Do not be a sorry statistic on earth. / You can be born tomorrow, / And be a present to the society.]

Although these concerns relating to the youth and the single mother indicate a social consciousness on the part of Guimarães, her overall political consciousness is questionable.

Terceiro filho resonates in other socio-emotional and philosophical spheres in which Guimarães's "politics" seem blurred insofar as an agency of change and mobilization for equality and the attainment of political power is concerned. As most of her "reflective" poems aptly indicate ("Reflexão"; 15, 76, 88), the poet seems to be content with the status quo or practically frustrated by social conditions she cannot change. For a poet who belongs in the older generation I have termed "forerunners of Afro-modernity," it is revealing that the vicissitudes of life have brought a writer to a point of total withdrawal, where the only solution she proposes is to "make the best of life" (as in "Reflexão"):

> Se...
> Deus existe com sua misericórdia e com sua justiça, Não me preocupo com o que há de vir,
> Porque...
> Neste mundo em que vivi,
> Do modo em que as coisas são.
> Eu vivo do modo que me é possível. (76)

> [If... / There is a merciful and just God, / I do not worry about tomorrow, / Because.... / In this world that I live, / The way things are. / I live by the rule of possibility.]

While it is understandable to submit to the will of God in the face of overwhelming social injustices, it is also arguable that to be socially passive is escapist, for religion can only provide solace to a certain degree but the harsh realities that make life unlivable are experienced on a daily basis. Guimarães's indifference, however strategic within a very hostile environment, speaks to her "conservatism" as captured in "Indiferença" (Indifference). Her expression of a total disenchantment with life and her willingness to accept whatever life has to offer suggest a lethargic spirit conditioned by the shock of racism and limitations that she does not address directly in this collection, which she has interestingly titled "Third Child." "Indiferença" captures Guimarães's lethargy very vividly:

> Se eu tiver que ser feliz, que seja!
> Se tiver que sofrer, que sofra!
> Onde quer que eu esteja,
> Apenas faço questão desta indiferença. (114)

[If I have to be happy, so be it! / If I have to suffer, so be it! / Wherever I am, / I only insist on this indifference.]

A cursory look at the remaining poems reveals a tormented life challenged by a permanent search for love and the realization of nonfulfillment, such as in "Mãos vazias" (Empty Hands), where Guimarães is filled with pessimism in the face of emptiness since she is tired of constantly giving and not receiving in return. The question the poet seems to be asking is: How can I console others when I am tired and empty with nothing else to offer? The image of the "empty hands" symbolizes both the giver and the receiver. This total self-resignation is captured in the last stanza:

> Canso-me é certo, mas não paro nunca,
> Encarreguei-me de viver assim.
> Então, eu tenho que dar sempre o que não tenho,
> Resigno-me e vou: Exausta, pobre, indiferente.
> De braços abertos e mãos vazias. (78)

[I am tired of course, but I never stop, / I chose to live like this. / Hence, I have to give what I don't have, / In self-resignation, I continue: Exhausted, poor, indifferent. / With open arms and empty hands.]

Similar somber poems, such as "Constatação" (Realization), "Pensei" (I thought), "Meu grande pequeno mundo" (My Great Little World), "Morte" (Death), "Crise" (Crisis), "Final de buscas" (End of Searches), and "Consequência"—all depict the poetic voice contemplating and dealing with pain and suffering, death and its acceptance, as well as disillusionment, as if the poet were preparing the reader for the inevitable in this world: a peaceful death. Yet, the poet's worldview can be characterized as the pleasure of making others happy despite persistent obstacles, as in "Meu mundo" (My World).

What is saddening in this poetic trajectory lies in the poet's self-analysis in "Canstatação"—a feeling that the aggressive experiences of life and nature have schooled her to the extent of her becoming a thorn, a stone, a disgrace—negative attributes that reflect a stoic and indifferent posture in the face of life's adversities. As the poetic voice asserts: "Concluí a auto-avaliação:

> Longe dos rios me tornei o lodo,
> Fugindo das rosas me tornei o espinho.
> Sou pedra sem montanha.
> Sou bagagem dos caminhos em que andei. (16)

[I concluded the self-analysis: Far from the rivers I became the mud, / Running from flowers I became a thorn. / I am the stone without a mountain. / I am the street baggage on the paths I walked.]

It takes a strong woman to be an engine of "continual motion" in spite of the obstacles the world seems to put in the way of the poet. The motions and emotions in *Terceiro filho* call attention to the ancestral strength that Afro-Brazilian women may not even be aware of but that they nevertheless evoke through resilience and hope embodied in their works.

Many of these feelings of frustration and betrayal result from unreciprocated love that pervades *Terceiro filho*. At least half of the entire collection evokes emotions of love: desire, passion, regret or nostalgia for a lost lover. Guimarães, in this sense, is like a lover who never grows old. Indeed, she offers a theory of being a woman in "Para ser mulher" (To Be a Woman). According to her, a woman needs to play many roles at the same time: she is wife, lover, and mother while seeing beauty as a desirable complement, not an essence or requirement. In addition to having "girlish" looks, she must be womanly in her decisions, "dizer sim e sem dizer não, saber negar" (108; saying yes, and without saying no, knowing how to refuse). She must also be able to articulate a "maybe" with her head and have a "theorem" in her body—but in any instance must she be ignorant of her desires. While these words of wisdom qualify Guimarães as both a womanist and a feminist, one wonders why her own philosophy has not worked for her in love. A series of poems relates the pain and suffering of the poetic voice: "Dúvida" (Doubt), "Falando de amor" (Speaking of Love), "Orgulho" (Pride), "Dor sublime" (Sublime Pain), "O que amo em você" (What I Love about You), "O que digo e o que dizem" (What I Say and What They Say), "Meus dias felizes" (My Happy Days), "Meu fadário" (My Destiny), "Alegria de ser" (Joy of

Being), and "Comunhão" (Communion). As painful as most of these "love" poems are, they nevertheless provide a point of solidarity with all women as they share in the hardships and pleasures of loving in a patriarchal setting such as Brazilian society.

Terceiro filho may be considered a book of love presented to women in particular and to humanity as a whole. "Dúvida" expresses the sense of loss of a loved one and the love/hate memories that ensue. "Falando de Amor" is a definition of love by a passionate lover. "Orgulho" captures the ego of a lover that gets in the way of true expression of love but instead manifests itself as pretense and pretexts. "Dor Sublime" expresses the suffering of love during a conflict or unexpected disappointment. "O que eu amo em você" declares love in spite of the other's negation and indifference. "O que digo e o que dizem" evokes a poet in love and the suffering generated by love—the poet hides her feelings but her soul declares a deeper love. "Meus Dias Felizes" captures the sad nostalgia of a woman as she discovers an old love letter bringing back memories and the poetic voice's contemplation of where those "happy days" suddenly went. "Alegria de Ser" contends that being in love gives the poet a fascinating sensation of beauty, affection, and satisfaction. "Comunhão" describes the sexual act as a process of irrationality and insanity and yet, a desirable moment of exchange between two people in love or in lust:

> E fica sempre,
> Tapando-me a boca,
> Cegando-me a visão,
> Para que eu possa fingir o meu riso,
> E no meio dos meus gestos,
> Nos instantes de protestos,
> Não mostrar que a desrazão de te querer,
> Deixou-me louca. (104)

[And stay forever, / Tapping me in the mouth, / Blinding my vision, / In order to fake my smile, / And in the midst of my gestures, / During instants of protest, / Not to show the irrationality of wanting you, / Made me crazy.]

Despite the agony of love that runs through most of the poems in *Terceiro filho*, the poetic voice seems to be on a constant search for the ideal love, particularly in the poem Guimarães titled "Meu fadário" (My Destiny). Partly pessimistic, partly optimistic, "Meu fadário" is a poem of hope for love. Four structural movements can be identified. In the first, the poetic voice—poor, spiritually dead, and unloved—longs to know what her destiny is projected to be. In the second movement, a startling and hopeful destiny is revealed: an ardent passion and a sublime lover. In the third movement, the passionate love is lost, a sense of loss ensues, and the poet feels like dying. In the final movement, hope comes alive as a prediction is made: "Um dia virá quem tanto quero" (105; One day, the one I want so much will come). It is on this positive note that "Meu Fadário" projects a brighter future for the tired and disillusioned lover. The "continuous motion" in *Terceiro filho* is an explosive adventure domesticated through the power and subtlety of poetic language. Although not declared as autobiographical, it contains insights into the life and times of the poet—if the poetic voice is taken (hypothetically) as the poet herself. It is no surprise, then, when in "Consequência," Guimarães alludes to Cecília Meireles's poetry when she states:

Sou poeta.
Nao sou alegre nem triste.
Caí na indiferença,
Quando vi e ouvi a condição de existir nesta vida. (44)

[I am a poet. / I am neither happy nor sad. / I slid into indifference, / When I saw and heard the living condition of this world.]

This conclusion is similar to that reached by Cecília Meireles when in "Motivo" (Motive) she self-defines:

Eu canto porque o instante existe
e a minha vida está completa.
Nao sou alegre nem sou triste.
Sou poeta.

[I sing because the moment exists, / and my life is complete. / I am neither happy nor sad. / I am a poet.]

The blatant identification with Meireles partly explains the abstraction in Guimarães's poetry. Meireles lost her parents very early in life, while Guimarães lost many lovers and loved ones. Both dealt with their disillusionment through sensuous enchantment with nature and total liberty of the spirit couched in poetic outpourings and reminiscences.

Unlike *Terceiro filho*, which was dedicated to the poet's father, *Da flor o afeto, da pedra o protesto* (From Flower an Affection, from Stone a Protest), a second volume of Guimarães's poetry is dedicated to her mother and sister Cema—an interesting combination of affection for and homage to a parent and a sibling. The title offers some clues as "flower" represents affection while "stone" represents protest as if to suggest a poetic evolution or even paradigmatic shift from ideological conservatism[22] to consciousness and confrontation. While *Terceiro filho* "explodes" with inequalities in love and a sense of disenchantment with the world, *Da flor o afeto* takes a more pragmatic position in indicting racial oppression and discrimination. For poetry that has thus far been conservative, it is refreshing to have at least three poems (representing one-seventh of the entire collection) that strike a nerve in terms of Brazil's myth of racial democracy. "Integridade" (Integrity), "Negrinha" (Young Black Woman), and "Explicação" (Explanation) may be either appreciated separately or analyzed as a triad. They contribute to the intertext of gender, nation, and cultural identity that defines some of the concerns of Afro-Brazilian women writers. The first makes a declaratory statement in which the poet defines herself as a proud Afro-Brazilian woman. The second calls to awareness and action young black women and by extension, herself. The third poem explains her newfound consciousness to all who may be confused by this sudden change in poetic strategy and language. Both the title and the cover already prepare the reader: the young boy with an aggressive posture as if attacking an adversary symbolizes protest even if the title had not said it. Since Guimarães has insisted on poetic liberty, this analysis does not concern itself with what led to this change—for other poems in the volume also address issues of love, gerontology, and loneliness but they are overall less abstract and more pragmatic. As a "continuous motion" that moves the world, the reader is rolling along with the motions and emotions of Guimarães's poetic progression.

"Integridade," as the title suggests, is the totality of an individuality when assumed and defended. It is a cogent statement on identity—individual, collective, and cultural. "Integridade" enumerates what it takes to be considered an "Afro-Brazilian woman" without shame. The pride of being a "black Brazilian woman" runs through the poem, and most compellingly in the last stanza, where the poetic voice strikes a very "purist" note as she emphatically affirms:

Negra
Puro Afro sangue negro,
Saindo dos jorros,
Por todos os poros. (8)

[Black woman / Pure Afro black blood, / Gushing out, / Passing through all the pores.]

This call to assume one's identity, one's heritage, one's history, and one's past is a Pan-African sentiment since the poem refers to black blood in general. The qualities of blackness are enumerated in the crispy hair, shining back, rhythmic walk, black hands, black breasts, black soul, black sensibility, black truths and lies, black cries and smiles, and finally, black blood. The poem's title can be replaced with "identity" for ultimately that is what black integrity is all about. The first line of each stanza repeats "ser negra" (being a black woman) for rhythmic emphasis and musicality while finally breaking to the word "Negra" (black woman) as if referring to all black women.

In "Negrinha," the poetic voice dialogues with a young black woman she sees in a hanging portrait. In the portrait, this young woman is sitting in the lap of a Santa Claus, almost in a kneeling posture and looking in only one direction. The poet observes the youngster as sad despite her smile, with short curly hair and closed mouth. Her entire constricted and confined demeanor angers the poet to such a point of hurt and revolt that she critiques the little girl's silence and voicelessness:

Em pé negrinha!
Levanta os braços,
Estica as pernas!
Escancara a boca!
Diz que tem fome,
Grita que tem sede! (9)

[Get up, young black woman! / Raise your arms, / Move your legs! / Liven up your mouth! / Say that you are hungry, / Cry that you are thirsty!]

The context is ironic in the sense that though Santa Claus is usually a loving and caring figure who provides for the needy, in this case the girl is expected to ask for help and gifts. Likewise, what the girl needs is more than a gift: In fact, she is hungry, depressed, and voiceless as if she has suffered to the point of silence and lethargy. The awareness that the poetic voice is providing the girl is only an incentive, a call to action and to protest. It is only at the end of her poetic action that she realizes that she was speaking to a portrait and not the girl herself:

Perdão:
Quase me esqueço que a negrinha,
Só é um quadro pendurado na parede. (9)

[Sorry: / I almost forget that the young black woman, / Is only a portrait hanging on the wall.]

The poem is one more example of the shifting ideological consciousness of Geni Guimarães that locates her within the intertext of gender, nation, and cultural identity.

After these well-articulated poems about blackness, beauty, and sensibility, Guimarães feels the need to explain her ideological position—an uncomfortable plight that reinforces the tensions of racial relations in

Brazil. Without mentioning the word "racism" in "Explicação" (Explanation), Guimarães craftily indicts the myth of racial democracy, pointing out its hypocrisy and its debilitating effects on Afro-Brazilians. At the very beginning of the poem, the poetic voice declares: "Não sou racista" (13; I am not racist). The affirmation seems to be an answer to a charge or rumor circulating in the media or by critics in general concerning her ideology, but the response is curious and raises a question. On the one hand, every artist has the right to express himself or herself and to choose his or her subject matter freely. Yet, censorship was a normal occurrence in dictatorial Brazil, which only started changing in the mid-1970s. On the other hand, the burden to have to explain oneself on such an issue is a double bind. The usual recourse for critics of those who raise their voices against racism or any form of discrimination is to label those who speak out as "racist" or "segregationist" so as to put them on the defensive. If defending one's culture and identity is "racist," perhaps it is best to remain thus rather than to sell one's soul to the hegemonic other. By the same token, perhaps such a criticism leveled against Guimarães is plausible since she was somewhat complacent about race in her earlier work, *Terceiro filho*. To answer artistically, as she does in her second work, is a commendable creative response. After admitting that she may be considered "doida" (crazy), she confesses that she is only human, that she cries like everyone else, and that this poem is not even meant to avenge repression and social inequality. Rather, she simply wants to

> Banir dos nossos peitos,
> Este sentir hereditário e triste,
> Que muito me magoa
> E que tanto te envergonha. (13)

[Banish from our hearts, / This hereditary and sad feeling, / Which hurts me / And which shames you so much.]

It is instructive to note that instead of mentioning the word "racism" or "superiority complex," she hides her feelings behind euphemisms: "hereditary," "sad," "shameful," "hurtful." I consider Guimarães's choice not as "poetic" license per se but as a conscious and convenient effort not to offend anyone, especially since she already feels compelled to "explain" her ideological position. The use of the affective pronoun "te" also betrays this familiarity as if talking to a friend. Of course, the means is effective in the Brazilian context and the mission is completed, but the attitude of the poetic voice is (un)consciously condescending. Guimarães's *Da flor o afeto* announces a poet whose "motto" indeed is to be "free" to express herself as she pleases without constraints.

With *Balé das emoções* (Ballet of Emotions), Guimarães returns, once again, to a "sanitized" poetry where words are suggestive and racial or social-political issues must be read between the lines if at all. The volume opens with an epigraph by Paulo Bonfim that suggests, ironically, that we write in such a manner that posterity would be able to decipher effortlessly "a cor do nosso sangue" (10; the color of our blood). Perhaps this is an unconscious betrayal of guilt or a caveat for the reader who may raise questions after reading; for in actual fact, there is no art to determining the color of the blood—it is red. "Blood" in this context seems to mean origin, race, species, or temperament. As the title suggests, the collection is a "ballet of emotions" in terms of a theatrical dance performance characterized by movements and fluidity—indicating a lack of formal constraints and rules.

Published in 1994, fifteen years after her first book of poetry, *Terceiro filho*, *Balé das emoções* does not have the intensity of the first two collections in the sense that Guimarães's concerns have become quite banal and popular. An allusion to Adélia Prado's "Com licença poética" (With Poetic License) raises some expectations, especially with regard to the creative process as a "parto sem dor" (36; painless delivery), but upon a closer analysis, poetry is manipulated as a "warning finger"—a coded expression that has the potential to liberate or to indict. A few other poems are noteworthy, such as "Condição" (Condition), in which the poetic voice invites a lover to recognize her appeal as an "aroma of Africa" (66); "Lembranças" (Memories), in which the poet remembers and pays homage to older and contemporary intellectual artists like Camões, Drummond, Meireles, Cuti, Oswaldo, Colina, Semog, and Graciliano (84); "Magia negra" (Black Magic), which describes the value of unity and invisibility in love: "Somos um e ninguém vê. / Nem nós" (98; We are one and no one notices. / Not even us); and "Visão de mmim" (Vision of Myself), where she reflects on her life and achievements, yet feels so incomplete even as death approaches figuratively. One of the most compelling poems in *Balé das emoções* is "Queda do pássaro" (Fall of the Bird), a narrative of the tragic life of a bird that struggles with the currents of life, then without much struggle, falls into a dumpster. In empathy, the poetic voice identifies with the bird claiming personal knowledge of the bird's fate:

Comungo-me com ele
pois sei de sua sorte:
Morre da dor singular de ser sozinho. (80)

[I commune with it / for I know about its fate: / It dies of a singular pain of loneliness.]

In her mid-fifties, Guimarães seems concerned about her final years but she is not so frail as her contemplative poems suggest. Perhaps her evocation of death and acceptance of its inevitability is a direct inspiration from the ancestors with whom she is very much in communion.

While Guimarães may be cryptic and subtle in her poetry, she is fairly more revealing in her prose fiction, as confirmed by her autobiographical reminiscences in both *Leite do peito* and *A cor da ternura*, narratives about rites of passage of a black girl from infancy through adolescence in Brazil's so-called racial paradise. Since *A cor da ternura* (Color of Tenderness), a novella published in 1988, is a reworked version of *Leite do peito* (Milk from the Heart), a collection of short stories published two years earlier, I focus this analysis on *Leite do peito* as an "expanded" version of *A cor da ternura*. Both titles reflect the maternal and sensitive instincts of the young Guimarães as she recounts memories of growing up black and female in a racist society. As the *Jornal nacional do Movimento Negro Unificado* reports: "Espanta-me como a autora consegue colocar, purificar e cristalizar em formas literárias tão belas, momentos tão amargos da sua / nossa experiência com o racismo brasileiro"[23] (I am terrified how the author is able to translate, purify, and crystallize through such beautiful literary forms such bitter moments of her/our experience with Brazilian racism). Guimarães shares a "nutritional" prowess with the reader—like true maternal milk, a source of life and love that a mother passes to her children as if giving herself to the world through her book as the best gift of memories that may help other young ones cope with day-to-day racism.

In eleven short stories, from "Primeiras lembranças" (First Memories) through "Força flutuante" (Fluctuating Energy), Guimarães portrays the ugly faces of discrimination and the virtuous value in breaking racial barriers through loving oneself and each other. Guimarães recognizes that her memories have come not from "nothingness" but from her parents, siblings, and children to whom she pays homage for their contribution to her "tenderness and transparent soul" (11–12). In an interview with Guimarães, the writer stated: "Although many walls have been torn down all over the world, but for Afro-Brazilians especially other walls still need to be broken since they are cleverly disguised. We can only achieve this through unity of the race, and it is not enough to keep saying 'yes, sir' to everything and everyone, but we need to take our struggle to the political arena."[24] In real life, Guimarães is more down-to-earth; as a writer, she carries her artistry to the formal level—recounting memories with such great creative imagination that she seems simultaneously detached and attached to the events she narrates. The artistic distance does not limit her vision of infancy, femininity, blackness, or her curious questioning of the world of adults. In addition, Guimarães exposes other perplexing images, such as her thoughts on Christmas as a commercialized event, the irony of the omniscience of God, the violence perpetrated against black Brazilians through the myth of racial democracy, evocation of respect for the elderly and their wisdom, and a subtle critique of the educational system and educators. Such a broad scope of concerns is definitely not that of a child, and *Leito do peito* is a voice of a young Guimarães mediated by the adult.

"Primeiras lembranças" (First Memories) is a tapestry of domestic and urban events crystallized into one short story. Young Guimarães finds herself in a caring and loving family where her close attachment to her mother is fundamental, as echoed in their mother–child conversations, their playfulness in action and in words, her own realization of her challenged sister, Cema, whom she calls "exceptional, my stupid poem" (19), and her curiosities about childbirth and where babies come from—especially when her mother becomes pregnant. In this story, the qualities of tenderness are laid out as captured in the title *Leito do peito* itself, and even the novella later based on it, *A cor da ternura*. Tenderness is evident in the mother's witty patience in explaining and answering all questions raised by the young Guimarães; it is captured in the milk the young child reaches for in her mother's bosom, it is found in mother's answer to a child's moment of doubt about love:

—Mãe, a senhora gosta de mim?
—Ué, claro que gosto, filha.
—Que tamanho?—perguntava eu.
Ela, então, soltava minha cabeça, estendia os braços e respondia, sorrindo:
—Assim. (15)

["Mother, do you love me?" / "Don't be naughty! Of course, I do, my daughter." / "About what size?" I asked. / She will then stretch my hair and her arms, and answer with a smile: / "This big."]

Despite young Guimarães's innocence, she is also able to empathize with Cema by cleaning her with her own clothes when Cema, because of her mental disability, would eat dirt. In the later poem dedicated to Cema in *Da flor o afeto*, "Cema, Ceminha," Guimarães shares the wisdom of this "exceptional" sister: "Mentira do mundo que a Cema é bobinha. / A Cema é poeta" (2; A lie of the world that Cema is stupid. / Cema is a poet). Even when Guimarães is in doubt, she asks her sister about the existence of God, for example. Cema replies by pointing to objects around the house to suggest that God is everywhere and in everything.

While "Primeiras lembranças" sets up the family setting, a microcosmic Afro-Brazilian social reality, "Bairro da Cruz" (Da Cruz Neighborhood) expands that setting to the level of an entire neighborhood. Since Guimarães's mother is a school teacher, the family contemplates moving from the rural area to the city. Because the decision to move involves everyone in the family, a meeting is scheduled to discuss it. This is an indication of an enlightened family though one with humble means. A typical Sunday is described as a day of leisure for men—particularly playing soccer in the field.

Women, on the other hand, have their labor predetermined and divided: some clean the house, some prepare lunch, while others do the laundry and shine the shoes. Guimarães was charged with taking care of her siblings: her mentally challenged sister, Cema, and the younger Zézinho.

The discussion of the move is illuminative—it reveals the concerns of everyone as well as the collective support she gets to move to a new neighborhood and house. As usual, it is the mother of the house who raises concerns:

—O Bairro da Cruz e estranho, sei la. Tem um povo ma-encarado, esquisito. O vizinho da comadre, mesmo, ja teve preso. Parece que se apossou de coisa alheia. Tenho medo que as criancas peguem maus costumes. Deus me livre!—disse minha mae, se benzendo. (94)

["The Da Cruz neighborhood is strange, who knows. You have a strange kind of people there. Even a neighbor of our godmother got arrested. Seemed like he had possession of a controlled substance. I am afraid the children will pick up bad habits. Lord have mercy!" my mom stated, blessing herself.]

This episode exemplifies the rural-to-urban migration patterns even within a state. In addition, it mirrors the democratic setting of the Afro-Brazilian family against the stereotypically macho and autocratic lifestyle usually portrayed by biased writers.

Education, whether formal or informal, cannot be divorced from rites of passage. "Tempos escolares" (School Days) exposes the internalized violence and double standards caused by racial discrimination in Brazil. Discussions about Princesa Isabel, the historical figure who signed the abolition of slavery into law, make interesting instruction for the youngsters who listened attentively to Grandmother Rosária's tales—a white version of the slavery era where slaves are represented as "simple," "passive," and religious. By inserting this important episode in the history of Brazil, especially as it pertains to slavery, Guimarães succeeds in retelling the history to all who may want to forget its significance and ambivalence, especially in Brazil. The irony of the story lies in the fact that, despite this allusion to the abolition of slavery, the reality is that a form of slavery was still being practiced through racial discrimination. On at least two occasions, young Guimarães had a conversation with her mother about dress codes and hygiene. Her mother wanted her to be clean and well kept, but she wonders why Janete could be untidy and she could not. Her mother's response says it all: "—Mas a Janete é branca" (45; "But Janet is white")—suggesting that Janet could get away with what young Geni Guimarães could not. This "inferiority" complex becomes internalized as a code of conduct, as the young student unconsciously reminds herself every day:

Nariz limpo.
Eu era negra . . . a Janete, branca . . .
—*agora e na hora da nossa morte.* (49)

[Clean nose. / I was a black girl . . . Janet, white . . . /—*now and even till death.*]

Guimarães's painful realization of discrimination seems tragic and traumatic for the little black girl to the extent that reminding herself becomes the only way to cope with a social injustice she feels condemned to and that she cannot change—at least, that is the impression her mother gives her so that she would get accustomed to the normalized absurdity.

After the initial lessons on racial democracy in "Tempos escolares," other episodes crystallize the transition of Guimarães from a girl to a woman, especially "Metamórfose" (Metamorphosis) in *Leite do peito* and "Mulher" in *A cor da ternura*. These two interrelated stories provide the decisive moments in Guimarães maturing into a woman. In addition to being an intellectual guide for generations born and yet unborn, and as the "continual motion" of the world, a woman undergoes physical and hormonal changes to prepare her for reproduction, motherhood, and nurturing. "Metamórfose" continues where "Tempos escolares" leaves off in terms of additional details on the significance of Princesa Isabel. The young narrator quickly discovers a disparity between Grandmother Rosário's version and that told by her teacher:

Hoje, comemoramos a libertaçao dos escravos. Escravos eram negros que vinham da África. Aqui eram forçados a trabalhar e, pelos serviços prestados, nada recebiam. Eram amarrados nos troncos e espancados, às vezes, até a morte. (62)

[Today, we commemorate the freedom of slaves. Slaves were blacks who came from Africa. Here, they were forced to work and for their labor, they received nothing. They were tied to poles and beaten, at times till death.]

The conflicting versions did not stop her from internalizing racial inferiority as she questioned her own talent and courage to produce and read her own poetry. She went through mental agitation and insecurity thinking there were no black heroes or ancestors to draw inspiration and strength from. To the contrary, there are black heroes and heroines such as Zumbi dos Palmares and Luiza Mahin, but these were not taught in schools at the time. The narrator loses confidence in herself to the extent that she is unable to present her poetry on Princesa Isabel and tries to "wash off" her own blackness using a substance for cleaning dirty aluminum pots. In the final analysis, she only hurts herself to the point of bleeding but can not change her color. This episode parallels the conclusions of psychologists on the potential damage of discrimination on blacks in general.[25]

For a woman, the experience of life is incomplete without the ritual that confirms that femininity. Guimarães's day comes when she starts to menstruate and quickly seeks her mother's help as she faces a stream of blood which at the time was incomprehensible to her:

> Fiquei apavorada. Que seria aquilo, meu Deus? Por que saia tanto sangue de dentro de mim, sem mais nem menos? (. . .)
> —Mãe, olha . . . Acho que arrebentou tudo quanto e veia. Me ajuda! (. . .)
> —Você virou mulher, besta. Prá todo mundo e assim. Eu, a Arminda, a Iraci, a Maria, a Cecília, até a Cema passamos por isso. E assim mesmo que acontece. (*A cor da ternura* 79)

> [I became terrified. What could that be, my God? Why is so much blood gushing out from within me, no more no less? (. . .)
> "Mother, look . . . I think that all my veins have been ruptured. Help me! . . ."
> "You just became a woman, silly. For everyone it is the same. For me, Arminda, Iraci, Maria, Cecilia, and even Cema, we went through the same thing. That is how it happens."]

From this moment on, Guimarães is growing up to be a woman with the challenges and opportunities that accompany that transformation. Above all, she also realizes that discrimination does not end with graduation. Even as a teacher, she is observed more often than others and a few white students express concerns about having a black teacher: "Eu tenho medo de professora preta" (87; I am afraid of a black teacher). The fear, of course, comes from the negative and stereotypical instruction that this particular young white girl has received from the society—principally her white family. Guimarães's *Leite do peito* and *A cor da ternura* both capture the ingenuity of a writer struggling to achieve symphony and harmony in a racially discordant "paradise" such as Brazil.

A mature and award-winning writer, Guimarães has taken Afro-Brazilian (women's) writing to a visible and respectable level through a consistent outreach to the wider Brazilian society and her socioartistic efforts to bring all races and ages together. Along these lines, she has focused her attention on writing for children as a way of reaching them before society does. At least, three of her children's books have been published and adopted in schools in addition to *A cor da ternura*—which appeals to both adults and children. Others include *A dona das folhas* (1993), *O rádio de Gabriel* (1993), and *Aquilo que a mãe nao quer* (1998). These works are ample indication that Geni Guimarães is the classic embodiment of what Conceição Evaristo calls the "continual motion" of the world—especially in her determination to foster awareness in the hearts of those who still perpetuate racism, or claim that it does not exist. A remaining challenge to the appreciation of her literary corpus lies in translating her seven texts to date as well as her numerous collaborations with other writers in anthologies of which only a few are currently available in English.

Àṣẹ-Reconstructing Fragmented Bodies and Souls

Miriam Alves's discursive incursion into Afro-Brazilian life and culture is most salient in her attempt, through her many works, to bring into literary cohesion, the body and thought of the black female that she sees as fragmented. In resorting to the strategic power of the ancestors and her own magical hand as symbolized in the pen she uses, she proposes that the strength to counter these fragmentary forces comes from the ancestors. Alves, indeed, is one of the most articulate and effective voices of the ancestral paradigm in Afro-Brazilian discourse.[26] I use "àṣẹ-reconstructing" in this context as a pretext to express the process through which ancestral power is appropriated to reconfigure that which slavery and sexism have disintegrated—toward having a wholesome and reintegrated body and soul. Whether in critical discourse or creative imagination, Alves is dynamic and assertive in that she seems to be naturally in the vanguard of ideas and ancestral strength. Alves's "Pedaços de mulher" (Pieces of a Woman)[27] foregrounds the fragmented body and soul as they dialogue intertextually with those the poetic voice calls "prendedores" (captivators) as if contesting their hold on her and shaking off their fangs of bondage and captivity. The body and soul presented in this female figure point to a multivalent woman: she is the arduous lover, the tired and upset woman enjoying the absence of her lover, the same who breaks into "pieces" due to the pain of absence, who also sees herself as an "object" in the hands of her lover, and who feels "used," "discarded," and "forgotten" like the overused faded clothing—washed and rewashed to be reused again until it has become a useless rag. In the final analysis, the fragmented woman protests a setting that embodies a prelude to her defragmentation:

> Mulher—revolta
> Agito-me contra os prendedores
> que seguram-me firme neste varal . . .
> Eu mulher
> arranco a viseira da dor
> enganosa. (969)

> [Woman-revolt / I move against the clothes pins / that hold me on this clothesline . . . / I woman / I remove this helmet of / deceptive pain.]

The image of the clothesline captures the idea that many human "clothes" find themselves on the same line of use and abuse—the ones who protest are probably the ones and only ones that are set free. The poetic voice in "Pedaços de mulher" is just such a voice of protest. The question is: How and where does an "objectified" subject find her strength?

Miriam Alves's long poem, "Aro Boboi" provides an answer as she takes the reader on an esoteric and contemplative adventure epitomized through the four elements of nature—earth, water, air, and fire—as well as within a tripartite temporal space—morning, noon, and night.[28] In this ritualistic and performative poem, inspired by feminine òrìṣàs and anchored on ritual exaltation, oral tradition, cultural memory, and resistance, the poetic language translates the essential linkages between the human species and the elements of nature in a harmonious tango and dialogue with the artificial imposition of racial democracy. The key trope of reconstruction serves as the mediating energy that reorders the dismantled body and its soul. When the soul, which the Yoruba call èmí (soul), combines with the sanctity of ojú inú (inner mind, eye) is intact, it is possible for the body to resist a total fragmentation and bring about a gradual unity. Divided into three interrelated movements, the long poem reinvents time, space, and history. The first movement deals with the earth and the mythology of Odùduwà, or the creation of the world. Within this mythology, homage is paid to Yemọja (goddess of the sea), Ọṣun (goddess of the river), Ọya (goddess of storm and wind), and Ṣàngó ("Oba," or god of fire). The second movement, which is simultaneously a "rupture" from the descriptive qualities of each of the òrìṣàs in action, becomes performative in an esoteric dance captured through visual images in dotted lines breaking into a straight line that then drops into a slanting and progressive ritualistic possession as if tracing the duration and remembering the agonies of the Middle Passage. The third movement, titled "reconstruction," evokes once again the four elements of nature, insisting on the necessity of hope in order to put all the fragments together into wholeness and wisdom.

The poem starts with oríkì (praises), which serve as the antephonic introduction evoking the complexity of blackness under white imposition and the proposal to protect the millennial secrets of the ancestors. The choice of Yoruba oríkì is relevant for invoking the gods, who manifest themselves though the ritual possession of their devotees. In this case, the poet is the invocator, praising and paying homage to the ancestors. The "earth" goddess is saluted as the creator of the world:

Terra-fêmeo, natureza-deusa, senhora-criação . . .
Senhora-moldadora do mundo-terra.
Senhora Oduduwa a terra que pisamos . . .
Desrespeito à terra, desrespeito à procriação . . .

Terra-Senhora-Oduduwa-Terra-Senhora-Oduduwa-é-vida
Terra-Senhora-Oduduwa é morte-vida. Terra-Senhora-Oduduwa e continui-
dade, feminizando a criação. (8)

[Female Earth, Nature Goddess, Mother-Creator . . . / Mother-Molder of earth-world. / Mother Oduduwa the land we walk on . . . / Disrespect to the earth, disrespect to procreation . . . / Earth-Mother-Oduduwa Earth-Mother-Oduduwa is life / Earth-Mother-Oduduwa is death-life. Earth-Mother-Oduduwa is continuity, feminizing the creation.]

When a "shattered" body and soul come to terms with the powerful femininity of mother earth, the consciousness will bring about a healing energy that unifies body and soul. Without the earth there is no life; without "Mother-Creator," there is no creation; and hence all power of life and death is concentrated in this feminine god. The awareness produces courage, confidence, strength, hope, and power.

As the poem moves to the sea-goddess, Yemọja, the focus shifts to the mysteries and liquidity of this goddess as the poetic voice breaks into a dance of Yemọja in an oscillating cadence:

Senhora-Yemanjá-a-vida em vais e vens.
Senhora a guardar segredos. Vibralizar-mistérios
Senhora-mar-celulas-intensamente-vida.
Líquido
Aminiótico
da
Natureza
Terra
Senhoras alimentam vidas, bailando precioso. (9)

[Mother-Yemọja-life in to and fro. / Mother keeping secrets. Vibrating mysteries / Mother-Sea-Cells-intensely-Life. / Liquid / Amniotics / of / Nature / Earth / Mothers nurturing lives, dancing preciously.]

Likewise, Ọṣun, the river goddess, is praised as "Mother-Vitality," the "Crystal menstruation constant," "Millennial ancestral essence." Ọṣun shares certain common characteristics with Yemọja as both operate in an interconnected spiritual labyrinth, hence the analogy due to their complementarity:

Yemanjá e Oxum
águas-fêmeal-torrente.
Desrespeito às águas e desrespeito à vida
águas-nutrientes da geração feminiflora. (10)

[Yemọja and Oxun / female-torrential-waters. / Nutrient waters of the feminine-flora generation.]

Ọya (Yansã, goddess of the wind) represents the sphere of the winds and as such embodies

> a poderosa força do vento. Feminina poderosa. Inquietante movimento.
> desloca espaços-caminha livremente ao vento. . . .
> desrespeitar-a-força-do-vento é desrespeitar-se.
> Yansã-força-fêmeo-criação. (12)

[The powerful force of the wind. / Powerful female. Restless movement. / Dislocates spaces-roads freely to the winds. . . . / To disrespect the force of the wind is to disrespect oneself.]

By baring the secrets and qualities of Afro-Brazilian goddesses, one after the other, Miriam Alves symbolically provokes these òrìṣàs into protecting the living, that is, Afro-Brazilians. The caring, loving, nurturing, protective, and blissful nature of these goddesses gives their descendants hope and strength to continue their struggle. The long poem concludes that fragments must come together in unity, tomorrow must start today, and as Afro-Brazilians honor their ancestors, they become more knowledgeable and wiser about their past, present, and future. In immersing herself in and drawing nourishment from the poetics of gendered gods in the Yoruba pantheon, Alves is indeed calling attention to the validity of ancestrality in the decolonization of Afro-Brazilian modernity, which is defined by the tropes of racial discrimination, fragmentation, alienation, oppression, and disconsciousness, as captured in "Pedaços de mulher" (Pieces of a Woman).

Ancestral House within a Modern Kingdom

From Esmeralda Ribeiro to Miriam Alves, the multiple optics through which Afro-Brazilians engage modernity are further crystallized in the works of Abílio Ferreira, especially in his "A casa de Fayola" (Fayola's House) from *Fogo do olhar* (Volatile Gaze), which may be seen as a paradigmatic text for the analysis of the tensions between what I call the "ancestral house" represented by Fayola and the "modern kingdom" represented by Alexandre—the prototype of Brazilian racial democracy. A new direction in contemporary Afro-Brazilian writing and criticism is found in Ferreira. From his creative contributions to *Cadernos negros* and other anthologies such as *A razão da chama* and *O negro escrito*, through his critical interventions *in Criação crioula* and *Reflexões sobre a literatura afro-brasileira,* Ferreira has indicated a certain innovative imagination, a youthfulness and playfulness with ideas and concepts that have resulted in positions about national identity and the creative process. He is particularly apt at discovering urban images of blackness and the challenges faced by the Paulistan in particular. São Paulo, the cultural setting he knows best, serves as a muse as well as a burden—a passionate romance that always causes him pain be it in fugitive love or in the ongoing struggle for economic survival. In assessing Abílio Ferreira's place in contemporary Afro-Brazilian literature, Arnaldo Xavier affirms that Ferreira is oppositional in his artistry. Not only does he have a "deliberate inversion of axis,"[29] he invents new characters who challenge the black and female types created by Jorge Amado, resulting in what Xavier calls a "radical critical understanding" of Amado's exoticism.

In *Fogo do olhar,* Ferreira provides a panorama of his prose and poetry. While some of his creative works have been published in various anthologies, putting them together in one volume gives the reader a more profound sense of his worldview. Mostly addressing the pleasures and absurdities of loving and passion, the poems, chronicles, and short stories attest to the importance of loved ones in his life and give the text an autobiographical impulse. "As figuras da mamãe" (The Images of Mother) serves as a pretext to reflect on all mothers and their ability to transform "all the cruelty of life into amazing lessons of life" (23), but black mothers have a painful burden and experience: that of the destruction of and separation from their offspring and the agony of seeing their own children suffer. The narratives evoke moments of compassion, of passionate memories such as that of growing up, in "Estória no telespelho" (Story in the Mirror), the gaze of the woman captured in the enamored voice describing her lover, as in "O Fogo do olhar," the title story; and the definition of love, as in "Guria" and "Amar":

Amar não é bem a palavra
Talvez um borbulhar de histórias
Um renascer contínuo
E então direi—amar. (22)

[Loving is not really the word / Perhaps a burbling of stories / A continuous rebirth / And then I will say—loving.]

Amid all these evocative moments and experiences, "A casa de Fayola" stands out as a masterpiece. The collection would be incomplete without this particular story. A synthesis of all Afro-Brazilian issues coalesces in a love story immersed in the conflict between tradition and modernity—perhaps what Arnaldo Xavier calls the "quizila original" (original disagreement) ("O brilho de Abílio," *Antes do carnaval,* 22). As Xavier further points out:

Nestas encruzilhadas iluminadas mais de neon do que por velas, Abilio tem buscado centrar seus recortes do universo submerso da juventude pobre e negra da periferia. Há um encantamento com os seus mundos, sons, danças, gestos e fantasmas. (26)

[In these crossroads illuminated more by neon light than by candles, Abílio centers his images on the submerged world of poor black youths of the periphery. There is a certain enchantment about their world, music, dance, gestures, and fantasies.]

If *Fogo do olhar* dissects the conflicts within the "ancestral house" that Fayola's House represents, Ferreira's *Antes do carnaval* takes the reader even further into the complexities of this world where poor black youngsters become characters in the game of survival and affirmation of dignity. The subtitle to *Antes do carnaval*, "novella of maturity," suggests that the writer is also a participant in this story of growing up. "Contrastes" (Contrasts) compares the lives of two women (Catarina versus Clara) interwoven by family lineage in their generational gaps, opportunities, and circumstances. In addition to living in a disadvantaged apartment complex where squalor, poverty, and violence are the order of the day, uneducated but street smart" Catarina spends her time watching soap operas while encouraging her daughter, Clara, to get an education as a way out of poverty. Both are bound by their contrastive desires: the daughter wants her mother to be happy and appreciate her blessings and ample vision of the world, while her mother wants her daughter to be happy by attaining the education that she did not get. It is ironic that Catarina is only thirty years old but comports herself as if it is too late for her to return to school at that age. What is important for Catarina is that Clara have a better life than hers. Praising her lighter complexion and encouraging her to use beauty cream, she confirms the racial complexity in Brazil where to be of lighter complexion is an (illusory) assurance of better opportunities:

Você deu a sorte de puxar pelo lado do seu pai. Isso conta muito, sabia? Uma moça clarinha assim como você pode muito mais do que uma negra escura como a sua mãe. (39)

[You are lucky to have taken after your father's complexion. This is important, you know? A lighter-skinned girl like you can achieve more than a rather dark woman like your mother.]

Yet, the future Catarina envisages for her daughter is not necessarily what she will confront. Clara, even as her name suggests, is "clear" but will not be able easily to overcome the racial stigmas by virtue of light complexion alone—and as her mother clearly understands, she has to be educated as well. The disadvantaged context in which this underprivileged youth lives, which the author describes as a "city separated from the rest of the world" (35), does not help matters. The fear of stray bullets from violent encounters in the neighborhood, the odor coming from a week-old corpse disfigured with bullets and abandoned by the street corner, speaks to the degeneration of a community that can only be redressed through concerted progressive actions: education, economic development, an effective criminal justice system, and good policing.

As protective as mother Catarina is, Clara at sixteen faces a romantic situation where a young motorcyclist invites her to join him for a pleasure ride. Although she is receptive to the offer, she is cautious. She devises a way of completing her household chores before her mother returns home. Since the young chap is respectful and graceful, she accepts his invitation, only to be disappointed when he offers her a roll of Indian hemp during a visit to a park. She rejects the offer to smoke the illegal substance and brings the relationship to an end. "No meio do bosque" (In the Middle of the Forest) portrays Clara as a well-mannered young woman, who, despite her innocence and social limitations, succeeds in using her intelligence for cultural and political resistance. Her cautious nature is also observed in "Saturday Night Fever," which describes a confusing relationship between Clara and Cléber where one feels like a prisoner and the other, a free soul. In trying to make her mother happy and remembering her advice, she seems aware of the dangers of bad influence, especially at such a critical period of her life. Abílio Ferreira's positive portrayal of Clara suggests that in spite of social and peer pressures it is still possible for a young Brazilian woman to turn out well and be successful in life. Just like Clara in her relationship with her mother, Marcelo strives to please and provide for his frail adoptive mother, Dona Alexandrina. As a faithful child, Clara was a good companion to Dona Alexandrina until her death and later made sure that Marcelo succeeded in life through hard work, discipline, and will.

In spite of her protective nature toward her daughter, Clara, in "Um dia da caça, outro do caçador" (A Day for the Thief, the Other for the Hunter), Catarina is living a double life due to the fear of losing her only job with an abusive employer, Dr. Augusto. She is a nanny who also provides sexual favors to her employer when Dr. Augusto's wife is not at home. Clara finds out and decides to surprise the employer by coming to her mother's place of work at a critical time when Dr. Augusto typically comes around to exploit and abuse his employee. Dr. Augusto foolishly takes the bait and he pays—with pain inflicted by Clara on his privates. In this sense, Clara fulfills her promise to always protect her fragile and vulnerable mother:

> Como Clara previa, o Dr. Augusto logo sucumbiu e começou a passar mão na sua coxa. Não ofereceu resistência, apenas encolheu-se em pouco, e o Dr.

Augusto sentiu-se encorajado por essa reação, que lhe pareceu de desejo. E avançou para Clara. Mais e mais. Até que, de surpresa, ela agarrou os testículos e apertou muito forte, com uma força que não supunha ter. (83)

[As Clara expected, Dr. Augusto soon succumbed and started to caress her on her behind. She did not resist, only withdrew a little, and Dr. Augusto was encouraged by her reaction, that he read it like an expression of desire. And he approached Clara. Closer and closer. Suddenly, she grabbed him by his testicles and pressed so hard with an energy that he never thought she had.]

Clara's reaction to Dr. Augusto exuded her boldness to challenge sexual exploitation as well as an indication that she did not want to be a victim nor would she allow her mother to be one without resistance. Although the rest of the narrative follows the adventures and misadventures of Clara, there is no closure in her relationship with Cléber, which is unconsummated nor does it lead to marriage. In addition, the reader does not know more about the life of Catarina except that Clara takes her out with her occasionally. As the title suggests, *Antes do carnaval* (Before the Carnival) captures significant moments in the lives of youngsters before they become adults—a series of passage rites within the ancestral world of the favela and of challenges of modernity within the same city that is supposedly marginalized from the rest of the world, that is, the world where there is peace and harmony, as opposed to violence and poverty.

In their varied revisionist, stylistic, and ideological preoccupations, Ribeiro, Guimarães, Alves, and Ferreira all participate in the redirection of Afro-Brazilian letters and culture from their "stagnancy" toward renewed engagement with cultural tropes such as *casa de samba, quilombo, Candomblé*, and self-esteem—issues that have hitherto been treated on the exotic level by white writers or mulatto writers who found it more convenient to take a "hybrid" position on racial relations. The penchant for cultural heritage that Esmeralda Ribeiro's work "Ogun" embodies, the agony of racism that Guimarães's *A cor da ternura* addresses, the role of the òrişàs in the strengthening of the fragmented soul as captured in Miriam Alves's "Aro Boboi," and the self-esteem dramatized in the rite-of-passage narrative of Abílio Ferreira, *Antes do carnaval*, cogently display compelling strategies through which Afro-Brazilians negotiate "alternative citizenship"[30] in Brazil. Afro-Brazilian modernity is more of a negotiation of resistance than the rigid negation of the dominant structure. While working within the constraints of Brazil's official denial of racism and its social inequalities, Afro-Brazilians continue to tell their stories of strength, self-esteem, identity, and cultural values without any exhibition of shame of their origin or their current location.

12

Quilombo without Frontiers

Throughout Brazil, many Afro-Brazilian voices are clamoring for an audience and for inclusion within a racial divide and psychosocial fragmentation that continue to hinder political representation and empowerment of the vast majority. In spite of the challenges, it is satisfying to listen to these voices in many regions and come to the realization that regardless of the geographical disparateness, stylistic diversity, and differing thematic concerns, there is at least a sense of aesthetic unity among Afro-Brazilian cultural producers. Their respective location notwithstanding—be it Rio de Janeiro, Belo Horizonte, Porto Alegre, Salvador, Recife, or Maranhão—these cultural "Quilombolas" (dwellers of the runaway settlement during slavery) imagine a free world through their writings, attempting to move beyond the burden of blackness and prejudice, asserting a creative and spiritual energy even when the odds against cultural production are significant. Of about two dozen Afro-Brazilian writers I interviewed in my excursions into these "regional" cultural "Quilombos" (runaway settlements), I have selected only a few for in-depth analysis. Regardless of these writers' locations, to define them according to their region would be misleading, as most of their works do not display a particular regional consciousness but, rather, an aesthetic unity marked by the evocation of survival coupled with expressive protest against discrimination. Even when some of them, like Ricardo Aleixo of Minas Gerais and Ronald Tutuca of Rio Grande do Sul, experiment with visual images and postmodernist eccentricities, they remain bound by their African heritage and grounding—for example, Aleixo's evocation of *òrìṣàs* in *A roda do mundo*.

As Steven White notes, the objections of Ronald Tutuca against "pseudo proletarian literature of political engagement" and the need to go beyond the signs and stigmas of "blackness" in literature may be legitimate, yet such a "trans-blackness" movement has not effected any transformation or change in the perspectives of the elite establishment, which continues to be dominated by white values and strives to exclude black participation.[1] Tutuca may have gone beyond the problematic of blackness, but he, too, is a victim of a racial democracy that treats him less than equal to a white writer. As I pointed out in chapter 10, in the section titled "Ronald Tutuca: Ambivalence of Stylistic

Sanity and Lunacy," in spite of the fragmented language, syncopated structures, and obscured message, "the voice of the chaotic Afro-Brazilian mind . . . comes alive." In this sense, Tutuca goes beyond blackness only in what may be an artificial conviction that once you problematize the form, you end up with a "whitened" model acceptable to the establishment. The reality is that Tutuca is yet to be published by a mainstream publisher in Brazil. The figurative "*quilombo*" of the mind or of historical physical location is somewhat blurred given the denial of African contribution and racism, especially when society itself cannot see beyond skin color. The likes of Tutuca are experimenting with language and form for the sake of acceptability, transcendence, and vision, but the reality suggests that Afro-Brazilians belong to a *quilombo* without frontiers because their efforts, however varied, are geared toward freedom—be it mental, artistic-innovative, sociopolitical, or ideological.

Voices of Protest: The Bahian "Pelourinho" of Life

The new generation of Bahian writers sings of Africa not in the manner of Cruz e Souza, who contested the racist hypocrisy of intellectuals of his time, or Castro Alves, who sang about the plight of slaves in the Middle Passage, or Luís Gama whose poetry resonates passion for the abolition of slavery, for the reality these younger writers confront presently includes a sense of political and economic bondage that they strive to "escape" through fantastic and creative strategies. While these measures may offer symbolic empowerment, they also have the potential to liberate the mind to take bolder steps toward political mobilization—toward a reality that remains desirable but elusive. In the Lula presidency (2003–), there are serious discussions about the use of "quotas" in university admissions as a measure to redress inequalities and guarantee "equal access" for Afro-Brazilians. It must be noted, however, that even the potential beneficiaries of such measures are already "privileged" to a considerable degree. Hence "affirmative action—Brazilian style" will only redress inequalities at the middle-class level not at the grassroots level where such equality is fundamental and urgently needed. The fragmentation of the soul comes before that of the race, body, and class, and is the result of a persistently discriminatory status quo and a consequently pervasive disenchantment with social oppression. Of the many writers I interviewed for example, some cannot be represented in this study due to lack of publication outlets not because they have not been productive. Lindinalva Barbosa and Landê Onawale are two such cultural producers who have participated in various anthologies, such as *Cadernos negros* or *Poetas baianos da negritude,* but who are yet to publish their own individual works. While they may be hoping for a "celestial savior" who will sponsor their publications, the systematic social exclusion they face due to lack of access to the print media certainly constitutes a fragmentation of the soul in terms of deferred fulfillment. Like "Pelourinho," the place of flagellation where slaves were historically marketed and beaten, Bahian creative voices give account of their miseries while celebrating resistance and the triumph of the spirit at the same time.

Antônio Vieira, Jônatas Conceição da Silva, José Carlos Limeira, and Aline França are established Bahian writers who transcend generational gaps to address what Vieira calls "terrible nightmare and historical error" as manifest in the treatment of Afro-Brazilians over the years—and even to the present day. In the prefatory note to his collection of poetry, *Cantares d'África* (Songs of Africa), Vieira states his purpose: "I want to protest and show all my indignation for so many injustices and atrocities toward the black man" (15). He may well be speaking for the conscious spirits of Afro-Brazilians—dead and alive—as they deal with their estranged condition in a land that claims to be the "coryphaeus of racial tolerance" (15) but that systematically excludes them. Through varied strategies, each writer displays hate for injustice, love for transformation and transgression, and a feeling of strength in the face of daunting challenges. This "strength" manifests itself in forms of celebration, negation, protest, indictment, fantasy, playfulness, exorcism, and even ancestral connections between Africa and Brazil.

Cantares d'África is a collection of poems joyfully recollected and written in both English and Portuguese in many locations throughout the world: Africa, Brazil, and the Americas. Like his other two collections, *Areia, mar, poesia* (Sand, Sea, Poetry) and *Cantos, encantos, e desencantos d'alma* (Chants, Enchantments, and Disenchantments of the Soul), *Cantares* is partly reflective in tone and documentary in value, as well as partly autobiographical and celebratory. Unchronological in structure, it captures moments of fantasy and fulfillment, homage and nostalgia, misery and protest—thus inviting the reader to the hidden soul of the poet where his sadness blends with happiness in an oxymoronic symbiosis as reflected in "O poeta" (The Poet):

Poeta é um triste diabo
que transmite felicidade,
alegria, sorrisos, prosperidade.
No fundo, no fundo
é triste ente
e muito coerente
que transmite lamento
d'um coração solitário. (85)

[The poet is a sad devil / who transmits felicity. / Finally, finally / he exists to sing / the lament of the solitary heart.]

In sharing his soul with the reader concerning his melancholic background and "heritage" as the poet's English translation renders it in "Fruto, ventre, amém!" (Fruit, Belly, Amen), the poet laments poverty, critiques injustice, and challenges the younger generation to rise to the occasion by fighting for better living conditions:

> Nasci pobre
> e vou morrer miserável.
> Não quero que meus frutos
> sejam tão maltratados que nem eu,
> que sejam uns negrinhos instáveis
> como seu pai nesceu. (43)

[I was born wretched, / I will die miserable. / My black offspring, unstable / as their father, / will not suffer the same fate.]

Poverty begets sadness just like sadness can beget spiritual poverty if not positively channeled toward change, but Vieira's poetry is an overall attempt to transcend misery and attain happiness through liberation songs.

In a total of eighteen poems, mostly written in Ile Ife, Nigeria, and Dakar, Senegal, some in Madison, Wisconsin (USA), as well as Salvador, Bahia, the voice of the Pan-African poet is heard in his evocation of Africa, in his solidarity with the black struggle in Brazil and all over the world, in the homage he pays to Afro-Brazilian heroes, and in celebrations of such anniversaries as the abolition of slavery and the death of Castro Alves, expressions of solidarity with the downtrodden, homage to Yemọja, and passionate moments of love and the pain of lost love. The sensitive and sensuous poetic voice reveals a "sad devil" but also a "passionate patriot," a lover who cries when love disappears and the once warm bed turns cold as in "Paixão d'Othello" (Othello's Passion), and a conscious freedom fighter who sings about peace while calling for an end to oppression and death as in "Canto de paz" (Song of Peace). A lover of samba and jazz, which are one and the same for Vieira, a soul born to sing his joys and tribulations in a politicized cry for solidarity and mobilization for justice, such as in "Raízes: Samba e blues" (Roots: Samba and Blues) and "Canção do renascer" (Song of Rebirth).

One of the most compelling of these poems, "Em verdade vos digo" (In Truth I Say To You), written on Gorée Island (Senegal), betrays the politics of the poet as he reflects on the historic transit "slave-depot" on the coast of Africa from whence slaves, in chains, were transported to the New World. In this particular poem, evocative of biblical discourse, the poet's indignation is crystal clear, and his determination even more accented. He not only corrects the errors of history; he demands reparations:

> Que se quebram correntes
> elo após elo.
> Telas que vós pintastes em sangue
> da escravidão,
> nós negros brasileiros
> pintaremos em verde-amarelo.[. . .]
> O que vós chamastes hoje
> "democracia racial,"
> nós negro diremos:
> Injustiça social. (67)

[That they may break shackles / link by link. / Scenes that you paint / in blood of slavery, / we slaves of Brazil / paint in blue-yellow-green. . . . Today what you call / racial democracy / we blacks call / social injustice.]

Referring to the colors of Brazil's national flag, the poet contrasts the reddish color of slavery to the flag in the sense that although they are of different colors, it is as if the flag is blood-stained since Afro-Brazilians are not treated as full citizens due to racial discrimination. In his anguish and anger, he demands compensation for many years of agony: "You owe us everything" (69). Now deceased, the voice of Vieira (known as Da Silva in Ile-Ife, Nigeria) echoes not only in his poetry but in his acts of compassion toward fellow human beings. As a poet, he is a sensitive even direct evocator of pain and pleasure, calling sadness just what it is—the absence of happiness. In addition, Vieira joins hands with progressive comrades all over the world to call for an end to oppression and racial discrimination. As he aptly puts it in his prefatory note to *Cantares d'África,* "This is my humble homage to all the illustrious men from Brazil and elsewhere who fought and still fight vigorously for the progress and advancement of black people" (15).

While Antônio Vieira is a Pan-African with Afro-Brazilian roots in Bahia, Jônatas Conceição da Silva locates himself principally within Bahia with his two volumes of poetry, *Miragem de engenho* and *Outras miragens,* which capture the paradigmatic essence of the *engenho* (plantation) in its modern manifestation.[2] The poems in *Miragem de engenho* were written between 1978 and 1984, while those in *Outras miragens* were written between 1985 and 1988. Unlike *Miragem,* which is a shorter collection, *Outras miragens* is divided into three parts: "Notícias do engenho" (Plantation News), "O sopro da vela" (The Breath of the Candle), and "Domínio das pedras" (Mastery of Stones). In its poetic structure reminiscent of Carlos Drummond de Andrade and Manuel Bandeira, Da Silva's poetry is very economical in form and language. In both collections, the poet evokes, describes, reflects, and above all, interrogates. His politics lie in graceful articulation and cautious communication that leave the reader begging for more. Da Silva does not fill pages with words alone but with imagery and dialogue caught between the need for articulation and the desire to be silent—a forceful interaction of tensions between hesitation and determination. The three prefatory notes by Beatriz Nascimento, Oliveira Silveira, and Anamélia de Araújo Dantas attest to the maturity and refinement of Da Silva as well as his faithful place in the Unified Black Movement. As Silveira appraises:

> O Jônatas silencioso, operoso, cabeça consciente e madura, um dos militantes mais sérios do movimento negro do país. [. . .] Nas *Miragens* de Jônatas, o cuidadoso trato da palavra equilibrando consciência e emoção. Botando poesia na roda. Coisa prá gente saudar com palmas e tambor. (11–12)

[Silent Jônatas, operative, conscious and mature, one of the most serious militants of the nation's Black Movement. . . . In da Silva's *Miragens,* the careful treatment of the word balances conscience and emotion. Putting poetry within the circle. Something we should embrace with applause and tambourine.]

The tripartite construction of *Miragem de engenho* may be categorized thematically: autobiographical reminiscences in "Notícias de engenho"; spiritual reflections in "O sopro da vela"; and in "Domínio das pedras," in which both philosophical introspection and retrospection are engaged, where the poet examines the conflict between individual will and social forces. The *"engenho,"* or plantation, is a powerful trope for the living quarters of urban poor Bahians, Salvadorans in particular—a revitalized setting that used to be the location of slave labor in the production of sugar cane. Whether in Engenho Velho de Brotas or in Engenho Velho de Federação, the atmosphere of squalor and urgency, together with the contrast of abundant poverty in the midst of plenty translates the way of life of a people used and abused under slavery and now offering new forms of deprivation through economic stagnation. The notion of "miragem" (mirage) of the *engenho* captures both the colonial machinery of exploitation on the plantation as well as the pathetic conditions of modern life. It takes a native poet—a seasoned traveler who observes landscapes and looks ahead, knowledgeably, into the unknown—to perceive the various mirages that Bahia offers. In "O engenho" (The Plantation), the poet provides the social and economic history of slavery and the legacy of the name "engenho velho" (old plantation). In a contrasted poetic triad of plantation–new plantation–old plantation, Da Silva sums up the history of how the new locality came to be known as such. From the arrival of the Portuguese who constructed the plantation, through the slaves who constructed the new plantation under the colonials' supervision, to the ex-slaves who now live in the old plantation (i.e., the poorest sections of Salvador), Da Silva locates the setting of his poetic engagement: Salvador, Bahia.

The section "Notícias do engenho" (Plantation News) contains poems that capture memories of childhood—from family fraternal wishes, to school pranks, through lost love, and on to the creative contemplation of death. "Meus oito anos" (When I Was Eight Years Old) is a mirroring of the poet as seen through a photo portrait documenting the poet's eight-year-old frame:

> uma tarja no peito
> uma gravata borboleta
> uma camisa amarelada
> uma seriedade virtualíssima . . .
> O retrato na parede.
> Imagem do imemoriável,
> daquilo que foi
> Jônatas Conceição da Silva. (41)

> [A targe for the chest / a bow tie / a yellowish shirt / a virtual serious . . . / The portrait on the wall. / Unretractable image, / for what used to be / Jônatas Conceição da Silva.]

Within his childhood reminiscences, the poet critiques the poverty and misery that characterize *engenho* dwellers through a black sense of humor through which the contrasts between a river and a gutter take on a new meaning:

> Onde eu nasci não passa um rio,
> passa um rego.
> Refletindo toda miséria margeada. (40)

> [Where I was born flows no river / Flows a gutter. / Betraying all the hidden misery.]

But the social consciousness does not debar the poet from remembering moments of passion, as in his visit to an old love in "Visitação" (Visitation) where he peeps into the household of his former lover only to discover her with another man. Likewise, the poet pays homage to his father in spite of their difficult communication that often takes place in unusual moments, as in "Comunhão" (Communion):

> Velho, sei como é difícil
> dizer-te estas coisas.
> Nunca fomos afeiçoados
> a falar, a amar. (51)

> [Old man, I know how difficult it is / to tell you these things. / We were never enthusiastic / about speaking, about loving.]

On the subject of mortality, the poet finds consolation but demands a special way of being seen off this earth, as in "Verdejante" (Green Traveler)—not in a black coffin, nor in a white one, neither sinner nor angel, the poet prefers a green coffin, a symbol of an immortal tree planted by the living. All the poet wishes is to be watered on "nas manhãs de sol" (44; sunny mornings). The entire first section mixes memories and reflections as if there is no real separation between the perspective of the youth remembered and that of the adult remembering.

In the interluding section, "O sopro da vela" (The Breath of the Candle) which as its title suggests addresses the spiritual dimension of Bahia, of life, the poet evokes images of ironic supplication, as in "Estampas de Saubara" (Impressions of Saubara) where various normalized absurdities and immoralities are ridiculed and even desired in a strange mix of nostalgia and indignation. The entire section reflects on the passage of time and on the significance of December as the month of passion, of renewal, and of an end signaling a new beginning. It is a month of purification, full of festivities, sacrifices, and reunions. Parodying an epigraphic poem of Carlos Drummond de Andrade, "O último dia do ano não é o último dia do tempo" (The Last Day of the Year Is Not the Last Day of Time), the poet plays on the varied and ambivalent Portuguese usage of "all"—"all" men of the world (*homens todos*) from "all" over the world (*mundo todo*)—in order to suggest the universality of December, as in "Porque é dezembro" (Because It Is December). As the section title suggests, the "breath of the candle" symbolizes the ephemeral nature of life as evidenced in the month of December. Like the candle, the year comes to the end of its life and in order for life to continue, for there to be continued light, there is a need for another candle, another year. For the poet, life, like the burning candle, is a breeze and a breath at the same time—providing light against the potential of a total darkness. Da Silva's playful use of time and day/night duality makes this section a break from the past and a projection into the future. Like Drummond, Da Silva appreciates the brevity of life just like he believes in the many possibilities time offers in the continuation of life. The extinction of the burning candle is not necessarily the end of its life, but an opportunity to light another candle. The candle then serves as a spiritual metaphor for life and time.

The premonition of a philosophical end is thus set in motion within this section dealing with the brevity of life. The third section, "Domínio das pedras" (Mastery of Stones), takes its inspirational cue from Drummond's use of the metaphor of "pedra" (stone) in one of his modernist poems:

Tinha uma pedra
no meio do caminho
No meio do caminho
Tinha uma pedra. (Drummond, *Obra Completa*, 61–62)

[A stone there was / in the middle of the road / In the middle of the road / there was a stone.]

As for Drummond, for Da Silva the stone functions as a trope for "obstacles" in one's way during life's daily routines, adventures, and challenges. In order to "master" life, one must learn to use these obstacles as "opportunities" for growth, learn to remove the stones from one's path, and in some cases use them to construct a new path or a lasting monument. Da Silva's title ("Domínio das pedras") is not only philosophical; it is also spiritual. Perhaps he has in mind the biblical Peter, or "Pedro," whose name translates as "stone"; indeed, Jesus is quoted as saying "upon this rock, I will build my Church"—a reference to an unshakable "foundation." Although Da Silva may not necessarily be making biblical references, the poem lends itself to a sense of the need for perseverance and resistance in the midst of so much suffering. There is a sense of also carrying the burden of others or of having to overcome significant odds. Jesus Himself is referred to as the "Rock of Ages," that is, the One who is everlasting, as well as the "chief cornerstone." Within this multiplicity of meanings, the trope of "stone" is ambivalent at best—gearing simultaneously toward an obstacle as in "Lapidação" (Lapidation) as well as toward a necessary quality of the preacher when he delivers the "Word of God" with passion and swordlike penetration to effect transformation of mind and soul as in "Domínio das pedras" (Mastery of Stones). It is in this latter sense that the consciousness of the poet is revealed for "stones" here are synonymous with the "words" spoken with divine inspiration. As the title poem of the third section confirms, the preacher "masters" his art of words even before he mounts the pulpit. The art of preaching is described as words falling in silence, worked and reworked with elegance and precision in order to achieve the final objective—conversion and salvation of the soul. The clues of the church as context lie in the silence, the hesitation of lovers to hold hands, and ultimately, the conclusion of the poetic voice that:

No domingo
o domínio das pedras
era absoluto. (62)

[On Sundays / the mastery of stones / was absolute.]

With poetic skill, Da Silva plays on the ambivalence of the "stone." On the one hand, the preacher has absolute mastery of his words, and on the other hand, his congregants (the audience), for that moment, are also consoled as the poet identifies with their problems that are seen as "stones."

This ability to provide solace is premised on the masterly use of the spoken word that is inspired through the biblical Word. The poet, in this sense, is like the preacher.

Other allegories within the "mastery of stones" include the notion of inscription of stones as a point of remembrance as in "Itapira revista" (Itapira Revisited). Here the poet contemplates a beloved city with its music, noise, drums, and black percussionists. "Stone" then becomes a form of naming and identity, an evocative consolation for a nostalgic spirit commemorating his favorite city:

Daqui agora
resta-me o peso do teu nome
que ficará sempre guardado
em sílabas-pedras cravejadas. (63)

[From here now / All I have left is the weight of your name / which will be kept close to heart / in syllable-stones.]

Another is even closer to heart for a poet who is very serious about black militancy as embodied in "Zumbi e senhor dos caminhos" (Zumbi Is the Lord of the Roads). While Èṣù, the god of the crossroads, is usually associated with duality and ambivalence, the apellation as applied to Zumbi honors his role in resisting slavery and oppression and his bravery in setting up a "free" community welcoming Brazilian slaves who had not just run away but who chose freedom at the risk of their lives. The mythology of Zumbi has meaning beyond just for Afro-Brazilians. In this sense, the evocation of Zumbi translates into a well-deserved eulogy for a martyr who gave his life for the betterment of the condition of all black people—which Da Silva captures in these emotive words:

tua firmeza de propósito
de amor e liberdade
pela raça. (64)

[the firmness of your proposal / of love and freedom / for the race.]

Written over the three years leading to the centennial celebration of the abolition of slavery in 1988, *Outras miragens* follows in the style and sensitivity of *Miragem de engenho* where childhood memories combine with spirituality, religiosity, and political commitment, yet it differs in that it encompasses the poet's excursions to other parts of the country, especially São Paulo—thus providing a contrast to his confined location in Engenho Velho in Salvador.

In addition, a number of poems from *Miragem* dialogue with those in *Outras miragens*—"Verdejante-Odôia!" and "Minha máquina de bater" with "Minha máquina de bater Again," and "Meus Oito Anos" with "8 de dezembro"—reflecting a certain evolving maturity and an (un)conscious rewriting/revisiting of poems by an unsatisfied poet in search of artistic perfection. But the poet's penchants are on display: for the quotidian as in "Meu primeiro calçamento" (My First Shoes); for the trivial-historical, as in the homage paid to the old street car in "Naquele tempo tinha bonde" (At That Time There Was a Street Car); for the neologistic as in "Caosnaval," which combines the chaos of Carnival with the pleasures of the flesh in its poetry; and finally, for the cinematographic, as in the poet's impressions of the contradictions of São Paulo in its gigantesque presence in the mind and vision of a Northeasterner who is both awed and critical in "Poema da maioridade" (Poem of Bigness). In "Hai-Kai Prá L. B." (Hai-Kai for L. B.), Da Silva seems to be paying homage to "Lima Barreto," the nineteenth-century biracial writer who assumed his blackness as opposed to Machado de Assis, who denied his. I assume that the initials refer to Lima Barreto because the content of the poem claims to be "jealous of destiny" and refuses to indulge hatred. Knowing the troubled life of Lima Barreto and his struggle for acceptance in spite of his brilliance, the realization that he faced exclusion from the journalistic profession due to the color of his skin would be grounds enough for anger, but since destiny varies for all, jealousy may be a milder sentiment than hate. Instead of hate, Da Silva's poetry captures the love of the poet for his fellow human beings, identifies with the disadvantaged, the privileged, and the heroic alike, singing to them with feeling and protesting the plight of those who suffer, such as the honoring of a samba singer in "Canto de amor ao homem do samba batatinha" (Love Song to the Potato-Styled *Sambista*):

> Seu canto, nosso canto
> vem da profundeza do coração
> da dor. (28)

[His song, our song / comes from the innermost part of the heart / in pain.]

Aline França exudes a passionate aura in her fervent views regarding the female Afro-Brazilian voice. As a female and marginalized voice, França carries the burden of race, gender, and class. In addition, her achievements are commendable in the sense that she is able to manipulate the social condition of oppression by blending dreams with reality such as the aspiration of her characters to rise above the limitations of the social conditionings. As far back as the early eighties, when a new negritude was sweeping through Bahia with the renewed vigor of the re-Africanization and Black Power movements of the seventies, Aline França has been invested in the ancestral paradigm and its implications for the alienated souls in the Pelourinho of life in Bahia, and by extension Brazil. In her poem "Mensagem dos nossos ancestrais"[3] (Message of Our Ancestors), the poetic voice recounts a narrative of divine intervention in which in the midst of confusion and uncertainty generated by partygoers who were acting in an antagonistic manner towards the rest of the ensemble, the characters felt the energy and guidance of the ancestors through an agonizing and prophetic voice:

> Despertai negros de todo o mundo!
> Continuai
> lutando por melhores dias!
> Uni-vos Brasil e Africa!
> Continuaremos inspirando vossos corações,
> transmitindo a força que sustenta
> uma batalha gloriosa!
> Zumbi dos Palmares estará dentro de
> cada um de vós. (*Poetas baianos* 9)

> [Wake up blacks all over the world! / Continue / struggling for better days! / Unite Brazil and Africa! / We will continue to inspire your hearts, / transmitting the energy that sustains / a glorious battle! / Zumbi dos Palmares will be within / every one of you.]

As a poet, França lays out some of her fundamental preoccupations that will later be developed in narrative forms.

As Luiza Lobo points out in her discussion of the novelistic strain in Afro-Brazilian literary tradition, women have been "less represented in [the twentieth] century,"[4] and it is a matter for celebration that Aline França is cited in the company of Carolina Maria de Jesus, renowned author of *Quarto de despejo* (Child of the Dark), which documents the struggles of the poor and the oppressed in urban São Paulo. Added to this duo is Benedita da Silva, whose poignant and inspiring autobiography, *Benedita da Silva: An Afro-Brazilian Woman's Story of Politics and Love,* deserves to be adapted into film; in the words of Jesse Jackson, the book "disturbs the comfortable in order to promote social change."[5] It is remarkable that while the likes of de Jesus and França struggle with recognition and visibility at least in terms of international fame, Paulo Lins, author of *Cidade de Deus* (now available in cinematic adaptation), became an instant celebrity author not necessarily because of the subject matter that all three writers and their works share (representation of favela/*morro* life) but because of the rising wave and thirst for the violent and the exotic—which characterize the favela sociological imagination, especially as "documented" in the violent film *Cidade de Deus* (City of

God) by Ivan Lins. From *Negão Dony*, *A mulher de Aleduma*, and *Estandartes*, through a recent play, *As fontes antigas de Salvador e seus convidados*, the characters França portrays are marked by an ancestral consciousness; shocked by the tragedy and misery of their modern condition, they finally speak out loud against psychological and economic containment. In a 1996 interview with Femi Ojo-Ade, Aline França addresses the notion that her works often compel the spirit to oscillate "between dreams, fantasy and the secret power that lies in a world full of magic much unknown to us":

> Yes, indeed. In *A mulher de Aleduma*, I created an origin for Blacks. The first group of Blacks arrived on Earth. I ascertain the existence of *Ignum*. Ignum remains on a distant plain in a country occupied by Blacks, Black intellectuals, Blacks with advanced intellect.... They thought that the Earth needed to be occupied. They convened a meeting and decided to send a couple to occupy the Earth. This couple first landed in Africa and there appeared an old man (Aleduma) to choose a habitable place. When the old man arrived in Africa, he made a telepathic contact with both the people and *Ignum* in space and declared the place as the chosen land. The couple came to the Earth and procreated. We are descendants of that couple. Wild games were pacified and they respected Aleduma's presence. We are the fifth or sixth generation of that couple who procreated on Earth. (Ojo-Ade, Interview with Aline França, 285)

A mulher de Aleduma is a narrative typical of African mythology but also accentuated with a New World magical realist twist as well as a gendered perspective. The name Aleduma echoes the Yoruba word for the Creator, *Olodumare*, and signifies divine intervention in what would become a "primordial" event—the choice location reminiscent of the Yoruba creation myth of Oduduwa in Ile-Ife, Nigeria. There is a subtle parallel between this myth and França's creation of the myth of Afro-Brazilian origins. *A mulher de Aleduma* departs from the conventional creation myths, immersing the narrative in a complex configuration of ancestral imagination.

França's first novel, *Negão Dony* (Dony, the Black Boy), written in 1978, has all the qualities of a meta-narrative and autobiography. In both cases, França has created a totally imaginative work that may have autobiographical elements but operates principally by the conscious desire to establish linkages between Africa and Brazil, and by extension the rest of the African diaspora. Similar yet different to the first wave of autobiographical African novels of the 1960s and 1970s, such as Camara Laye's *L'Enfant noir* (The African Child), Ferdinand Oyono's *Une vie de boy* (Houseboy), Cheikh Hamidou Kane's *L'Aventure ambigüe* (Ambiguous Adventure), and Bernard Dadié's *Un negre à Paris* among many others. In these works, the African child is either estranged and disillusioned in Europe or traumatized and even ironically bemused under the colonial regime in Africa, as he feels torn between the

Africa he left behind in the search for educational advancement and the Europe that now forces him to be appreciative of and nostalgic for Africa, or the victim of a more traumatic experience—that of being alienated in one's own continent under an imposing and invading European "master." *Negão Dony* reverses the paradigm by making the protagonist representative of an entirely *new* generation of Africans born in the New World to African parents who voluntarily moved to Brazil to live. The reversal is innovative and makes a bold statement about the relativity of bondage and freedom. Instead of coming in chains, Dony has come as a free child, yet is orphaned in Bahia when his parents die. The orphan-slave analogy may be lost on those who do not see beyond constructs and conventions. On the one hand, an orphan is indeed someone who is unprotected, lost in the world without a caretaker and who either becomes a ward of the state or is adopted or taken in by a sympathetic citizen. The slave, on the other hand, is considered property for whom sympathy is an anomaly and who is expected to perform on demand without compensation and without feelings. The analogy may be far-fetched, but both share a commonality: a sense of lost kinship and lineage, a sense of stripped history, broken continuity, and a traumatic loss of identity.

That Negão Dony ultimately thrives in spite of his abandonment and orphanage makes a statement about the potential for triumph of the human spirit. Using dance as a weapon of advancement and professionalization, he succeeds in forming a performing arts group that facilitates his return journey to Africa to perform capoeira. Not only did Dony return to Africa in order to reconnect with the continent he never knew, he also returned to Brazil to perform a symbolic ancestral ritual—he blew the sand of Africa that he had brought with him into the sea as if to invoke the spirits of the ancestors both in Brazil and in Africa to join in the celebration of spiritual connections and emotions necessitated by alienation, memory, and the imperative of resistance. Underlying *Negão Dony* is the intertextual story of Aline França even as the author herself recognizes and confesses:

> I felt a pang as I was writing the story—the entire fiction I created became so real to me. This is because I really wanted the boy, I wanted to discover that lost identity which I do not know. I am so close to Africa but I know not where I came from. I don't know my country of origin. I created this story in order to reaffirm to myself that Africa is very near. It is thus something more of emotion. (Ojo-Ade, Interview with Aline França, 285)

The need to discover her past, discover her origin, and even rediscover her own identity were compelling reasons to write the novel—a therapeutic measure that may be taken for granted by those who have not tasted the trauma of separation on the massive scale of transatlantic slavery. To be "close to Africa" only in images preserved in Bahia, in memories told by others, or even through association with those who come from there voluntarily does not fill the emotional vacuum expressed by the author. In creating this fictional story, Aline França fulfills her desires and aspirations to heal her emotions and have a psychological balance by embarking on a fantastic journey of the imagination.

A mulher de Aleduma, unquestionably França's most accomplished work to date, transcends the semiautobiographical fantasy of *Negão Dony*, inscribing this mythological text with an epic dimension that has not been seen in Afro-Brazilian letters since the resistance of Zumbi, leader of the Quilombo de Palmares. As the title suggests, "Mother" here is the source of life, the origin of everything—creation, procreation, and regeneration. Not only does the text open new directions and vistas, it also challenges the traditional way of addressing racial issues in Brazil. Instead of the facile ideological pamphleteering geared toward the recuperation of Afro-Brazilian values and dignity, França appeals to all Brazilians to look beyond the racial surface and biases in order to see the intelligence of Afro-Brazilians as embodied in the character of the blacks in the fictitious land of Ignum: "Os negros de Ignum não possuíam células nervosas típicas mas uma bolsa localizada no cérebro, cheia de cargas elétricas, que regulavam todas as sensações do corpo, dando-lhes um potencial de inteligência muito elevado (12; The blacks of Ignum did not have typical nervous cells but a sack located in the brain, full of electrical charges that regulate all the bodily sensations, giving them a potential for higher intelligence). França is definitely not suggesting that Afro-Brazilians have extraterrestrial intelligence but that the ideological intent of the hyperbolic assumptions must be understood and well taken—that Afro-Brazilians or at least these "imaginary" genetic entities possess extrasensorial qualities that distinguish them from the rest of the human species. Likewise, Ignum dwellers have abnormal feet that are turned backward. All this to say that França uses magic, poetry, and high imagination to visualize a world surrealistically divine, prophetically futuristic, and yet conceivable in the ideological sense, as a counterdiscourse to slavery and racism.

Imagining a *new* Eden, where blacks live in harmony with nature and with themselves, without the oppression of either colonization or slavery, *A mulher de Aleduma* confronts slavery, exposes the sustaining value in Afro-Brazilian religious rites, such as Candomblé, and locates in the wise old Aleduma the prototype of the Afro-Brazilian prophet to whom inhabitants of Aleduma render desperate supplication when all hope is lost on planet Earth: "—Oh! Velho Aleduma, volte e salve-nos" (13; "Oh! Old Aleduma, return and save usAleduma serves as a messianic figure—one who must sojourn with his people for a short while, depart this world for a period of time, and then return to save his people. Although the notion of blacks living by themselves in some fantastic world where slavery and colonization are an anomaly may be seen as idealistic and "segregationist," the imperative of freedom and the necessity to live as a happy people through uninhibited celebrations, festivals, feasts, and singing in both sacred and popular spaces do accentuate an ideological commitment veiled in myth, fantasy, and imagination. This ideology is expressed in the same interview with Femi Ojo-Ade where França projects 2050 as the year when blacks will take global power: "Let's prepare the ground for the year 2050 when Blacks will seize power in the whole world. This is what I tried to reflect in my recent work. By the year 2050 we shall capture the world. Blacks shall control the majority in the United States, South Africa, Brazil, Europe, but that will not happen now.... The year 2050 is still some years away" (Ojo-Ade, Interview with Aline França, 292). Since França was referring to *A mulher de Aleduma* as the literary work in which she projects into the future, it stands to reason that it is a futuristic work to be celebrated, critiqued, and preserved for generations.

França's struggle for the betterment of Afro-Brazilians' quality of life in the present as well as in the future is consistent with her commitment to the environment as portrayed in *Os estandartes* (The Standards). Published in 1993, *Os estandartes* engages nature, raises ecological questions, and confronts those who engage in environmental destruction through corrosive critique, such as in the dialogue between Kaitamba and Cambira after the narrative voice condemns the increasing irresponsibility of human beings toward nature and the d effects of pollution on the atmosphere:

—O que está pensando?
—Existem esperanças para o mundo?
—Quando a natureza ficar em paz. Ela está agonizando, e passa todo o seu desequilíbrio para a humanidade, as plantas que curam estão sendo queimadas, destruídas. (54)

["What are you thinking about?"
"Any hope for the world?"
"When nature is at peace. She is agonizing and transfers her imbalance to humanity; the curative plants are being burnt, destroyed."]

As the title suggests, "the standards" of respect for nature have been lowered and compromised, and in order to have a lasting peace, there must be a restoration of respect and responsibility for mother earth. França, through *Os estandartes*, proposes that, instead of continuing to destroy nature by embarking on deforestation, a reforestation plan be implemented, a new planting sensibility and the preservation of vegetation symbolized in the "verde da floresta" (15; green forest). Using the philosophical voice of *Fortiafri*, representatives of ancient sages, an environmentalist consciousness is awakened in humans as a point of departure toward awareness and social change. The "planting" trope may also be applied to a cerebral process of planting knowledge in order for the inhabitants of the Earth to realize that destruction of the ecosystem is equally self-destruction through the transgression of the four basic elements of life: earth, water, air, and fire. Environmental consciousness is a concern not only in *Os estandartes*, but also in *As fontes antigas de Salvador e seus convidados*. It is remarkable that Aline França has taken it upon herself to combine the social, the environmental, and the racial with the artistic for many cultural producers do not seem to cross "frontiers" of social issues. Using water as a pretext to discuss history and environmental health with particular emphasis on the hygiene of water distributed throughout Salvador, Bahia, she condemns the lack of clean water in most homes. The characters, representing parts of Salvador as well as personifying its twelve "fontes" (water fountains)—Fonte Pereira, Fonte dos Padres, Fonte do Gravatá, Fonte da Muganga, Fonte Baixa dos Sapateiros, Fonte do Gabriel, Fonte Vila Velha, Fonte Água de Meninos, Fonte Nova, Fonte do Santo Antônio, Fonte do Gueto, and Fonte da Mãe d'Água—tell their histories and specific characteristics with musical background and dramatic intensity. Water, like blood, is the source of life, the nutritional element that may also destroy as in Jorge Amado's classic *Mar morto* (Sea of Death).

Structurally, the play takes the reader through many scenes: the twelve fountains present themselves and their histories; the *sábio* (wise man) encounters four fishermen in search of the beginning and end of the waters after traveling the Seven Seas; the blacks from *quilombos* dramatize the value of water with which they wash their clothes in chantlike rhythm; and in the last discourses, the twelve fountains of Salvador ask for respect, sensibility, and the preservation of the environment. As Fonte do Gabriel articulates: "Aqui deixo o meu protesto que deixem as águas respirarem em paz" (19; I hereby register my protest so that you can leave the waters in peace). The narrative structure adopted by França allows for the multiplicity of voices and a uniformity of purpose as all the characters come to terms with the value of environmental protection—especially water, the source of life and survival for all. Water has no enemy, nor does it tolerate an enemy. It flows with purificatory properties as well as vindictive-ritualistic-violent potentialities when unnatural elements stand in its way. Anyone familiar with Salvador, Bahia, will appreciate the cultural and political contribution of Aline França in her various efforts to connect Bahia with Africa, Brazil with the world, and Brazilians as well as Bahians with the absurdity of racist oppression.

The fascinating complexity of the Bahian imaginative landscape would be incomplete without a discussion of the artistry of José Carlos Limeira, one of Bahia's finest poets, who has been anthologized in *Axé*, *O negro escrito*, *Cadernos negros*, *Schwarze poesie/Poesia negra*, *Poesia negra brasileira*, and *Quilombo de Palavras* but whose single-authored works—namely, *Lembranças* (Memories) and *Zumbidos* (Zumbified)—are out of print. Limeira's coauthored works (with Éle Semog) such as *O arco-íris negro* (Black Rainbow) and *Atabaques* (African

Drums), as well as the anthologies, provide a gate of entry into his overall cultural production. Limeira belongs to a group of writers that David Brookshaw has identified as operating within a "structure of revolutionary solidarity" against an institutionalized macrostructure based on the myth of racial democracy and on systematic alienation.[6] As both titles of Limeira's single-authored works suggest, Africa is signified through memory and through the symbol of Zumbi, the leader of the Quilombo de Palmares, as Afro-Brazilians deal with the "here and now" of their condition. Such a frame of mind gives them the necessary "revolutionary energy" to deal with the trauma of slavery, the memories of Africa and of separation, and the continuing enslavement of the mind through subtle inculcation of an inferiority complex. Brookshaw contrasts Limeira's "bandeirante" (frontiersman) and Magdalena de Souza's "Zumbi" to illustrate how Afro-Brazilians rewrite official history (e.g., Domingos Jorge Velho is considered a "hero" in history books) and thus why the excluded unofficial history in books is now popular through oral tradition (Zumbi's heroism and resistance to slavery and colonial oppression).

Limeira's poem is particularly instructive for it challenges the official history through sarcasm, playing between the official image of Domingos Jorge Velho's "heroism" and Limeira's own reinterpretation of him as a "cheap murderer" who participated in the destruction of the Palmares in 1690:

Ontem, senti um tremendo nojo
quando te vi como herói no livro
de história do meu filho.
Mas foi no fim, muito bom
porque veio de novo a vontade
de reescrever tudo
e agora sem heróis como você
que seriam no máximo depois de revistos,
assassinos, e bem baratos.
Atenciosamente
UM NEGRO.

[Yesterday, I felt really sick / when I saw you portrayed as a hero in my / son's history book. / But it was, after all, good / because I got the urge once more / to rewrite everything / without heroes like you, / who would upon revision, / be termed murderers, and cheap ones at that. / Yours sincerely, / A NEGRO).[7]

Limeira's expressive cultural corpus is marked by the problematic of identity and the necessity to defend one's people and their history and culture—with a particular penchant for colors, symbols, seasons, blueslike-yet-accusatory confessions, and resistance against a pervasive socioeconomic and political suffocation and its potential for silencing and self-silencing. In a declaratory tone, and after pondering his characteristic black features in the reflection he sees in the mirror as well as the social constraints that debar him from being himself, Limeira affirms his blackness in "Identidade" (Identity) while rejecting the more acceptable official "brown" identity imposed by Brazilian society: "Morra de susto! / Sou, vou sempre ser: NEGRO!" (Bernd, *Poesia negra brasileira*, 133; Die from surprise! / I am, I will always be: BLACK!). In a similar poem, "Mais um negro" (One More Black), Limeira enumerates the qualities of being a black man as not accepting a "white soul," being "aware of our history," rejecting any imposed heroes, and being comfortable with black hair as it is. The four-stanza poem begins with a line repeated at the beginning of each stanza to create emphasis, rhythm, and affirmation: "Sou um negro" (I am a black man). In the last stanza, the poetic voice breaks into a carefree mode, calling himself "kind of crazy," "kind of strange," and looking for more Blacks like himself to challenge the conventional Brazilian racial democracy. A more formidable and humorous affirmation of identity lies in "Diariamente" (Dairy), where the poet confesses that it is enough in the course of his daily routine to be able to maintain his identity and keep his head up at all times and at any cost, even if it means a "suicidal" proposition:

Me basta mesmo
essa coragem quase suicida
de erguer a cabeça
e ser um negro
vinte e quatro horas por dia. (Da Silva and Barbosa, *Quilombo de Palavras*, 15)

[Simply enough for me / this semisuicidal courage / to raise up my head / and be a black man / twenty-four hours a day.]

In *O arco-iris negro*, a coauthored collection true to its "Black Rainbow" title, Limeira expands on his previous efforts while retaining at least the title poems, such as "Lembranças" and "Zumbi . . . dos"—which celebrate how poetry translates bad events into memorable mementos and the allegorical courage of resistance captured in the figure of Zumbi, respectively. Other poems with the symbolic dates of "Maio" (May) and "Treze" (Thirteenth) refer to the official date of abolition while insisting on the importance of inner happiness for Afro-Brazilians. Whether the poetic discourse is on hunger, memories of a loved one, celebration of a sunrise, an homage to the gods, or an appeal to identity consciousness, Limeira uses poetry as a vehicle of self-expression when he finds himself lost within himself, pondering why life could not be better. The simplicity of his diction coupled with his firm ideological consciousness and special regard for the day-to-day make his poetry quite similar to that of Solano Trindade. Indeed, he dedicates a poem to Trindade, "A Solano Trindade" (To Solano Trindade), in which he reports on what he had read of Trindade's poems about not allowing the children to be enslaved like their parents:

Hoje li de você
Que meu filho não será,
O escravo que hoje sou (66)

[Today I read from you / That my son will not be / The slave that I am today.]

The similar poetic collection, *Atabaques,* coauthored with Éle Semog, offers a fuller representation of the scope and vision of Limeira, as the poet evokes cultural entities, dates, and figures that enhance the struggle of Afro-Brazilians in their search for true freedom, such as *quilombos,* Ilê-Aiyê, Jonita Machel (from Mozambique), and the love and solidarity of the black woman. As Oliveira Silveira points out in his preface to this volume, oppression has only changed its outfit, not its social mission—hence the need to evoke seventeenth-century Palmares as a reminder of the historical struggle to be free and as an inspiration in the modern era: "Palmares, muito a ver com a luta de hoje, que é a mesma: luta por uma libertação ainda não conseguida, mas sempre buscada" (1; Palmares [is] very similar to the struggle today, which is the same: the struggle for an elusive freedom always sought after). In the title of the collection lies its proposition: that poetry is like a modern African drum that needs to continue to be beaten and heard—a call to solidarity that transcends ages and location in its action-based quest for reason, justice, and social transformation. In the poem "Ao ilê-aiyê (O bloco)" (To Ilê-Aiyê [The Group]), Limeira sees beyond Carnival but evokes the ideology and beauty of a group representing "nossa revolução de atabaques" (12; our revolution through African drums), as well as a group with leadership qualities that Ilê-Aiyê's president, Vovô, calls "Negritude Lucipotente" (12), that is, a potentially illuminating negritude that rediscovers African pride and reinvigorates Carnival as a continuum of *Ijexá* rhythm and dance. A revolted poet, tired of being a "domesticated animal" with a white boss even after ninety-one years of abolition of slavery, which he calls a "farse" (farce), as in "Consciência" (17; Conscience); sympathetic to the social plight of the anonymous and poor Jacintos living "racial hypocrisy," as in "Reflexão" (40); sensitive to older revolutionaries as in the homage to paid to "Quilombos" (19), written for Abdias do Nascimento and Lélia Gonzalez; and a Pan-Africanist in the homages he pays to Agostinho Neto (of Angola) and Jonita Machel (of Mozambique), as in "Os olhos dos nossos mortos" (45; The Eyes of Our Dead) and "Jonita Machel," respectively, Limeira drinks from the fountains of revolutionaries, eats in the kitchen of solidarity, and makes love on the bed of the black woman, in order to sustain the strength necessary for a persistent drumming for freedom.

Skin Color and (De)Colonized Consciousness

Like their comilitants in Salvador, Bahia, and with the exception of a very few who collaborate in anthologies, national meetings relating to the Unified Black Movement, or coauthorship, contemporary Afro-Brazilian *Afro-Mineiro* poets (that is, black poets from Minas Gerais) do not get the critical attention they deserve. Even the anthologies are not representative as they give only a limited taste of the larger world of the Afro-Brazilian imagination to which poets who are yet to publish their individual works also belong. Adão Ventura, Edimilson de Almeida Pereira, Marcos Dias, Ricardo Aleixo, Waldemar Euzébio Pereira, and Anelito de Oliveira are the most prominent ones. Adão Ventura is considered the "vanguardist" writer in Minas Gerais, and his leadership has been recognized by being appointed president of the Fundação Palmares in Brasília (1992–2002). The color of his skin continues to be a hindrance to Ventura's upward mobility as one of his works attests: *A cor da pele* (The Color of the Skin). Another work, *Texturaafro* (Afro-Texture), is equally a testament to his Black consciousness within a society that constantly denies black equality and representation. Aside from Ventura, Edimilson de Almeida Pereira occupies a significant place in Afro-Mineiro letters given his intellectual vocation coupled with a ritualistic-spiritual consciousness and a fluid disposition toward Brazilian culture. In Ricardo Aleixo, Marcos Dias, and Anelito de Oliveira, I find a trio preoccupied with modernity, postmodernity, visual experimentation, and metaphysics geared toward resolving the fragmentation of daily living and the contradictions of their corrosive existence. But in Waldemar Euzébio Pereira, poetry is both popular and musical—a dramatic labor of love that need not be complex or complicated in order to communicate simple truths of life—for in these truths lie wisdom and strength despite their sentimental and philosophical nature.

Afro-Mineiro cultural tradition continues to interest critics as three critical essays among others testify: Femi Ojo-Ade's "Black Brazil: African Notes on a New Negritude," Steven White's "Reinventing A Sacred Past in Contemporary Afro-Brazilian Poetry," and Maria José Somerlate Barbosa's "Strategies of Poetic Language in Afro-Mineiro Discourses." Ojo-Ade's essay focuses on the emergence of a new negritude in the cultural "synthesis" that Brazil represents, using as (con)textual support to refute the claim of racial democracy a number of cultural producers such as Abdias do Nascimento, Adão Ventura, Aline França, Hamilton Vieira, Arnaldo Lima, and Olodum. Aside from a detailed analysis of Ventura's works, Ojo-Ade insists that for Afro-Brazilians to begin to solve the problems of racism that are alive and will die hard, they must move beyond the complacency of a cultural politics that in the final analysis seem to be limited and lacking in leadership. For Ojo-Ade, "In spite of programs of such groups as Olodum, the Afrocentricity of Candomblé, the sporadic militant manifestations by poets and artists, and some linkages with Africa, there remains a lack of strong, dedicated, and focused leadership able to offer the people a sense of purpose and the strength to take charge of the state that they built . . . for the white man" (192). Like Ojo-Ade, White's essay focuses on a number of poets—Estevão Maya-Maya, Oliveira Silveira, Edimilson de Almeida Pereira, Ricardo Aleixo, and Lepê Correia—in order to establish a linkage between Afro-Brazilians' sacred past and their contemporary poetry. White's is a selective focus, for there are many more poets and writers whose works are influenced by Afro-Brazilian rituals and religions; its strength lies in the rebuttal of Roger Bastide's misguided and Eurocentric claim that "*white* writers discovered African culture in Brazil."[8] White's powerful conclusion that "the symbolic systems and divine 'sociology' of the diverse Afro-Brazilian religions offer these poets not only a rich source of aesthetic inspiration, but serve as a stimulus for a very Brazilian reinvention of a repressed and neglected, shared African heritage" testifies to the need to rewrite and even critically reexamine the intellectual history of Afro-Brazilians with an eye on their valued contributions as opposed to the "exotic" perspectives offered by a few privileged ethnocentric critics. To these cogent panoramic analyses, Maria Barbosa provides a study focused on the strategies of poetic language in Edimilson de Almeida Pereira's creative works, with particular emphasis on African origins and sacred survival in Minas Gerais. From these critical angles, Afro-Mineiro discourse may be said to be sacred, popular, racial, gendered, and experimental—all at once. The effort of each writer to anchor his or her perspective on a particular problematic and the commonality of "task" within a divergent "mask" is of interest to this critic.

Often identified as a member of the "Geração de 60," that is, the generation of Mineiro writers who founded the *Suplemento literário* in 1960, Adão Ventura Ferreira Reis represents (after Guimarães Rosa and Mirilo Rubião) the most anthologized, the most international, and the most celebrated (with covetous national awards) Afro-Brazilian writer of Minas Gerais. Author of about half a dozen volumes of poetry, including *Abrir-se um abutre ou mesmo depois de deduzir dele o azul* (Opening Up of a Vulture or Even after Deducing the Blue, 1970), *As musculaturas do arco do triunfo* (The Muscularity of the Triumph Arch, 1976), *Jequitinhonha* (1980), *A cor da pele* (The Color of the Skin, 1980), and *Texturaafro* (Afro-Texture, 1992), Ventura has evolved from "universal" poetry to a more race-conscious writing as testified by the latter two texts.

In addition to these "Afro-texts," Ventura, in *Jequitinhonha*, conducts a "cultural journey" in space and time to the Vale do Jequitinhonha in 1979, where his grandfather, Teodoro, presents him with the mysterious and sacred world of his childhood. The poetry of *Jequitinhonha* is defined by its concision, its penchant for the historical, the sacred, and the popular, as well as the necessity to mystify. Ventura invites the reader into the world of celebration of the departure of warriors for battle (in "Relâmpagos . . ."); the historical Tejuca, where João Fernandes de Oliveira (the Portuguese Contractor) loses his mind through the passionate manipulation of Chica da Silva (in "Tejuco"); the longing for Biribiri, as if to be there "como um raio de sol" (like a sun flash) (in "Biribiri"); a world of festivities such as the *Festa do rosário* (in "Dançantes do sêrro"); the colorful war dances of the "Caboclos" (Brazilian Indians) and the humbling Christmas celebrated without fanfare but with simple cheese, *cachaça* (sugarcane rum), and sweets (in "Noite de natal"/"Ainda natal") [Christmas Night/Christmas Still]. The poet's love for Jequitinhonha overflows in "Paisagens do Jequitinhonha" (Landscapes from Jequitinhonha), where in an interrogative tone, the poet wonders about the belly-dancing in the waters of Jequitinhonha, the liberating zigzagging flights of birds, and the artistry of the artists from Minas Novas. Finally, the poet ends the collection with "Circense" (Circus Fellow), a philosophical reflection on life as a circus where the jester is able to produce laughter with a sad face, and "Filosofia" (Philosophy), expressing the poet's penchant for a simplified life like the waves of the waters.

Like the jester figure in "Paisagens do Jequitinhonha," *A cor da pele* captures a poetic voice who is saddened and revolted by the color of his skin but who produces beautiful poetry expressing this predicament—while regenerating himself at the same time from the debilitating fangs of racist oppression. Signifying a phase in Ventura's evolution that can be termed "decolonized consciousness" in the sense that blackness is confronted with pride, without shame or hesitation, the poetic voice in *A cor da pele* sings, protests, indicts, ridicules, and embraces as if to take pride not only in his color and African ancestry but in the courage to confront all Afro-Brazilians who possess an "alma branca" (white soul) with the values of blackness. The title itself plays on analogies and paradoxes: "color" and "skin"—same yet different depending on the one bearing the burden or the pleasure of carrying around that stigma or pride. *A cor da pele* is a poetic collection about origins, a journey within in search for one's identity and its defense with absolute conviction. The volume is divided into four books or sections: Livro 1: Das biografias (Book 1: On Biographies), Livro 2: Da servidão e chumbo (Book 2: On Slavery and Common Sense), Livro 3: Raízes (Book 3: Roots) and Livro último (Final Book). In telegrammatic-cinematographic images, Ventura condenses history, evokes memories and flashbacks of the horrors of slavery, protests in subtle but effective language physical abuse in "senzala" (shanty town) in the service of the white enslaver, as well as the resistance captured in the image of Zumbi in "Quilombo" (Runaway Settlement). Through a multivocal long poem, *A cor da pele* defines the burden of black skin as a wrestling with the horrors of slavery, the shame of betrayal by unconscientious Afro-Brazilians, and lessons of history experienced by the suffering and tired hands of both grandmother Justina and grandfather Teodoro.

Ventura's ideological consciousness self-betrays in the contrastive irony between the figure of "Preto de Alma Branca" (Black with a White Soul) in book 2 and the evocation of the "color of the skin" in the last book of the volume. Through enumeration and repetition, the color of the skin, a trope for the Afro-Brazilian during slavery and to the present, is defined as "saqueada e vendida" (plundered and sold), "chicoteada e cuspida" (beaten and spilled out), "camuflada e despida" (camouflaged and stripped), "vomitada e engolida" (vomited and swallowed) as if the subject is an object without a soul, at the mercy of the "owner" who treats him or her with impunity and sadism. Such an anguishing portrayal of an oppressed slave contrasts sharply with a black with a white soul who has lost consciousness of blackness and only serves the whims and caprices of the oppressor for meager privileges. Here is the figure of treachery and betrayal—scolded and ridiculed by the poetic "bullets" of the poet:

o preto de alma branca
e seu saco de capacho.
o preto de alma branca
e seus culhões de cachorro.
o preto de alma branca
e sua cor de cameleão.
o preto de alma branca
e o seu sujar na entrada.
o preto de alma branca
e seu cagar na saída.
o preto de alma branca
e seu dangue de barata.
cada vez mais distante
do corpo da Grande Mãe-África. (40)

[Black with white soul / and his servile bag. / Black with white soul / and his doglike restlessness. / Black with white soul / and his chameleonic colors. / Black with white soul / and his soiling on entrance. / Black with white soul / and his defecation on leaving. / Black with white soul / and his cockroachlike blood. / Gradually more distant / from the body of Great Mother Africa.]

The evocation of Great Mother Africa equally establishes the Pan-African consciousness of Ventura as represented by a number of other poems, such as "Papai-Moçambique" (Mozambique-Father), which traces ancestry through cultural resistance; "Um" (One), which dreams of the old Africa from the trunk of the tree of a new Africa; and "Meu pai" (My Father), where references to an old father as well as Soweto and Johannesburg may indicate a homage to Nelson Mandela—the freedom fighter against South Africa's apartheid regime.

Through symbolic and contrastive poetic language, Adão Ventura gives new revolutionary meanings to the images of the "senzala" and the "quilombo." Evoking the image of the "scourgings" through routine and forced labor, the poetic voice subverts this image by imprisoning the shadow of the "senzala" within the "ghettos of his skin." "Senzala" becomes synonymous with black skin and all the negative images it evokes: slavery, oppression, rape, violence, abuse, and dehumanization. By contrast, "quilombo" is that safe haven where, like Zumbi, the poetic voice hibernates like a lurking, cautious, wise, and brave warrior looking out for its prey, with a declared readiness to shoot his defined enemy: the white oppressor. Not only is the revolted Afro-Brazilian determined to fight back, he must also resolve such pressing racial questions as why Jesus Christ is always portrayed as white while others—blacks, Indians, Asians, Chicanos, and mestizos are expected to accept this divine whiteness, as in "Por que Jesus Cristo é sempre branco?" (Why Is Jesus Christ Always White?). Another racial problematic for Ventura is resolved in "Meu sonho" (My Dream), in which he declares that his dream is not to marry a white woman for fear she will accuse him of "soiling" her white race or will call him "nigger" all his life. *A cor da pele* represents a subtle weapon of protest, mixed with cultural, historical, and racial references with the object of raising black consciousness and alerting the unwary about the double-edged nature of "skin color":

A cor da pele
é uma faca
que atinge
muito mais em cheio
o coração.

[The skin color / is a knife / that pierces / more incisively / the heart.]

Similar to *A cor da pele*—unpaginated, in four parts (origins, heroes, history, identity)—crafted together in a condensed and refined testament of protest accentuated with a sense of the complicity of the other as captured in the poem written by Manuel Bandeira and which Ventura cites as epigraph:

Somos duplamente prisioneiros:
de nós mesmos
e do tempo em que vivemos.

[We are conjoined prisoners / of ourselves / and of the time in which we live.]

The double bind in space and time that Bandeira refers to captures Ventura's exposé of the skin as a metaphor for the historical moment of slavery and its horrors.

In *Texturafro*, Ventura moves beyond the racial question as treated in *A cor a pele* to a recognition of heroes and that of history. The first part dramatizes his African origin through what is portrayed as a condemned life as in "Origem" (Origin), his black skin as a tool of exploitation during slavery, and a dance of supplication made to the queens, princes, and princesses of the "Cangado" (African Folk Dance). The second part, representing resistance, showcases a gallery of heroes: Chico-Rei, Escravo Isidoro, and Zumbi—all revolutionaries who challenged enslavement through direct confrontation or negotiation.

In the third part, which is more historicist and concerns the arousing of black consciousness toward action and emancipation, Afro-Brazilian history is summed up as

um traço
num abraço
de ferro e fogo

[a link / in an embrace / between iron and fire.]

Using this "smithing" metaphor of a forged union of labor and anguish, the poet goes on to establish a continuity of oppression, as in "Menino de rua" (Street Boy), whose street fights, verbal confrontations, and present-day police brutality are likened to the struggles of Zumbi in the seventeenth century. In a sudden tone of revulsion and protest in "AGORA" (NOW), the poetic voice calls his people to action in order to "cut the neck of the dog," that is, the oppressor:

É hora
de sair do gueto
eito,
senzala
e vir para sala
—Nosso lugar é junto ao Sol.

[It is time / to get out of the ghetto / plantation, / shanty town / and come to the room /—Our place is together with the sun.]

The final part is both a eulogy and an evocation of identity. Dedicated to his deceased father, José Ferreira dos Reis (1905–88), the poet, in "Poema da morte de um pai" (Poem of the Death of a Father), pays homage to him through the evocation of familiar landscapes of Serro, Santo António do Itambé, Baguari, Folha Larga, Itapanhoacanga, São Miguel, and Almas de Gunhães as if to recall old times on his journey to rejoin his father, Teodoro, and the poet's grandfather. So as not to leave his "mother" out of the picture, in "Identidade," the poet equally celebrates her through the enumeration of her duties: cleaning the floor, washing the clothes, cleaning the plates, and singing a nocturnal rhyme for her son. The suggestive title, *Texturaafro*, plays on the ambivalence of "text" and "texture" as if to see both text and the skin that produced it as inseparable in their color blindness. The declarative title as well as the poignant images within the volume attest to a poet who is no longer in search of his identity but is fighting to bring others—still lost within the confusion and conflict of racial democracy—to a state of awareness, illumination, and empowerment. Both *A cor da pele* and *Textuaafro* function as a "discourse of transgression" against the trope of slavery and exploitation as well as toward the imperative of freedom and black pride.[9]

In Afro-Brazilian discourse, Edimilson de Almeida Pereira, who is a generation apart from Adão Ventura, is one of the newer and most cogent cultural voices that belongs to the generation that came of age following the Brazilian military dictatorship. As an anthropologist, cultural critic, creative writer, and professor, Pereira expresses provocative perspectives on Afro-Brazilian cultural production and its future directions. A very prolific writer and critic with over a dozen works in print, he is by far the most productive and intellectually stimulating of his generation. Perhaps "transgression" captures Adão Ventura's poetics, but Edimilson de Almeida Pereira's poetry is not that simple to define. He oscillates between multivocality, multiculturality, existentiality, and transgression such that any one label does not suffice to capture his essence. Maria Barbosa notes that Pereira's poetic production "points to the impracticality of attempting to pin down a single moment when the ontological grounding occurs in historical time, in cultural heritage, or in language"[10]—confirming Pereira's fluid engagement in the evaluation and definition of Afro-Brazilian identity.

In 2001 I had the opportunity to interview a number of Afro-Mineiro poets, At that time, I was attempting to bring to a close my research, which had primarily taken me until then to São Paulo, Rio de Janeiro, and Salvador, Bahia, I decided, out of sheer curiosity, to discover those I have called, for lack of a better expression, "regional" poets. To my surprise, the reality confronting these Afro-Brazilians was not very different from their counterparts in other parts of Brazil: neglected, repressed, disempowered, struggling, yet undaunted. I felt a sense of solidarity with their plight as well as a sense of enrichment in moving beyond the São Paulo–Rio–Salvador axis. In an interview with Steven White, Edimilson de Almeida Pereira stated that "the influence of Minas in my poetry does not exist simply to make my work 'regional.' I attempt to write about my land and my culture, but I also hope my writing demonstrates a universal sense."[11] While I did not meet Pereira in person, we communicated and I acquired several of his works while in Belo Horizonte in addition to others he sent me while he was in Switzerland doing postdoctoral studies. One of his poems, "Nova Orleans"[12] reveals the Pan-African consciousness of a poet who though he has never been to the United States, is sensitive enough to capture the "transposition of hypocrisy" in comparing Brazil's racial relations to those of the United States:

A vida sabe o revés de uma tentativa
mas o incêndio da voz atenua a solidão
e o medo de um país incompreensivo. [. . .]
só um *blue*
é justo e completo como um abraço.[13]

[Life knows the negation of an effort / but the fire of the tongue overcomes loneliness / and the fear of an incomprehensable country. . . . / Only the *blues* / is fair and complete as an embrace.]

Given the multivalent perspectives of Pereira's cultural production,[14] I will focus on representative works of which I find *Corpo vivido* (Lived Body), *Ô lapassi e outros ritmos de ouvido* (Hey, Brother and Other Rhythms of the Ear), and *A roda do mundo* (Gyration of the World) the most compelling as they reveal the multiple "faces" of this enigmatic and provocative cultural producer. Maria Barbosa has already addressed the connection between Pereira's anthropological research and his poetic production—a symbiotic relationship that she calls "the rich cultural context from which he extracts his themes: Minas Gerais' colonial past; historical settings; cultural transformations; and cultural practices of African origin."[15] Without these "cultural contexts" where the sacred co-mingle with the anthropological, creative imagination is stifled. Not only do the contexts constitute "linguistic roads and rich cultural representations,"[16] they transform human experience into vivid cultural memory through creative documentation and imagination. Yet, characteristic of Pereira is the use of symbolic language to denounce injustice and oppression as opposed to the direct, documentary, declamatory posture found in the poetry of Cuti or Abdias do Nascimento. I find Pereira's argument, that since there are many blacks, there are bound to be many faces and thus the choice of ambivalence and multiplicity is a valid poetic strategy, to be a "convenient" explanation for his politically detached nature. Perhaps in this sense, the color of the skin may be said to be both "colonized" and "decolonized" in Pereira. While he should not have to defend himself, he nonetheless seems aware of the burden of blackness and the necessity and communal expectation for him to participate in what he calls "a literature of courage, strength, hope" (Steven White, "Edimilson de Almeida Pereira," 51). As Pereira openly admits:

> I'm sure there are people who want me to produce poems that are more engaged with the black cause.... My poetry is highly engaged with the defense of human rights, with the preservation of the dignity of individuals and social groups. It is certainly a poetry engaged with my history as a black man: what I want for us, and for all people, is respect, dignity and freedom. My work with popular culture taught me that people frequently use symbolic language to speak about their concrete and abstract problems. (51)

Pereira's penchant for the symbolic in the expression of his creative imagination deserves to be recognized to the extent that he not only recuperates the history and tradition of Minas Gerais, but by extension Afro-Brazilian culture; he attempts to renew that "tradition" by giving it the same qualities befitting a literary and cultural movement. In the same interview with White, Pereira cites numerous issues facing black poets in Brazil: a precarious educational system that translates into a lack of incentives for teachers, hence a lack of corresponding intellectual stimulation among students. This has resulted in a feduction of scholarly production, as well as serious publishing difficulties, distribution impediments, and the need for authors to become their own publishers, promoters, and distributors. Even more disappointing is the fact that an academic reviewer would hardly comment on Afro-Brazilian works, dismissing them as of insufficient "quality" to be of interest to the literati—a mixed-race elite Esmeralda Ribeiro has appropriately qualified as "the publishing Mafia." As a result, Afro-Brazilian cultural producers very often "must function as sociologists, anthropologists, historians—roles that come from the urgent need to present (from a black perspective) the history of blacks in Brazil. And these poets must also assume the role of being critics of each other's works, since the academic or university criticism still largely ignores this facet of Brazilian literature" (53).

In his own critical assessment of the Afro-Brazilian cultural tradition,[17] Pereira notes the pattern of invention and freedom in literature using the examples of Cuti, Oliveira Silveira, Adão Ventura, and Estevão Maya-Maya. On the one hand, Pereira identifies poets he calls "historicists" such as Cuti and Ventura. These are poets who consciously draw a connection between the literary text and social reality, and for whom the poetic text is "an instrument of social intervention" (140). On the other hand, the "inventors" such as Maya-Maya and Silveira depart from the cultural-documentary and socioritual value of their works, thus establishing "a certain way of creating poetry that is multiple in order to affirm and deny itself" (143). Pereira likens the "inventors" to Èṣù, the trickster figure in Candomblé: "sweet and acid, funny and dangerous, creator and devourer, someone who produces both understanding and misunderstanding.... The world of the orishas and of humanity needs Exu in order to understand opposites and generate attraction between them" (143).

If Pereira's "critical-theoretical" approach is anything to go by, he must be situated among the "inventors"—for his poetry not only invents, it disturbs the sensibilities through "metaphorical and magical conception of language ... refusing to anchor itself in any absolute and emblematic value."[18] I would also argue that Pereira belongs to the "historicists" as well. The notions of "historicist" and "inventor" need not be oppositional for each of the poets Pereira himself uses to illustrate these "categories" can easily be fit into both. To what extent is Cuti or Ventura more of a "historicist" than an "inventor"? And to what extent is Maya-Maya or Silveira more of an "inventor" than a "historicist"? While Cuti's poetry is necessarily and transformatively "vicious and cutting" (140), in other respects, it is sensuous, erotic, passionate, and even formalistic to a considerable degree, especially in his latter poetic evolution. Likewise, Ventura's apparent penchant for historical facts, figures, and heroes may be seen as creatively fostering the understanding of the present, not its "misunderstanding." As I have pointed out in examining Cuti, Ronald Tutuca, and Arnaldo Xavier, although these poets, especially Tutuca, attempt to transcend their blackness, they still end up defending that identity without consciously articulating the term.[19] It is in this sense that I agree partly with Pereira when he affirms that "we still haven't done enough in our poetry on the relation between tradition and modernity" (White, "Edimilson de Almeida Pereira," 54). I also must disagree with Pereira, however, on what needs to be done. I suggest that Afro-Brazilian literature and culture now have enough material to construct this critical relationship. My own notion of "Afro-modernity" in Brazilian literature and culture is a step in that direction. What I find currently lacking is the type of productive critical dialogue Pereira is pushing for on myriad Afro-Brazilian issues—a critical formulation in dire need of formulators if Afro-Brazilian literature is to move beyond speculative criticism.

True to his "magical conception of language," the poetic corpus of Pereira constantly undergoes a process of refinement as seen in *Corpo vivido*—which brings together eight previously published volumes in one collection, namely, *Hipocampo* (Sea Horse), *Corpo imprevisto* (Unforeseen Body), *Margem dos nomes* (Margin of Names), *Bailo* (I Dance), *Kianda* (Angolan Sea Goddess), *Árvore dos Arturos* (The Arturos' Genealogy Tree), *O livro de falas* (Book of Voices), and *Dormundo* (Pain of the World). A closer examination and comparison of some of the old volumes and the "collection" reveal significant changes, especially in *Árvores dos Arturos*. Originally published in 1988, it was then included in *Corpo vivido*, with the addition of "*and other poems*" to its title. In *Corpo vivido*, the "other poems" cover two separate sections; "Alguma dança com Nicolás Guillén" (Some Dances with Nicolás

Guillén) and "Contos Africanos: Reinvenção de imagens" (African Stories: Reinvention of Images) have been completely removed. Further, the syntax of the poems has also been changed, and their length considerably reduced as in the following example:

MATA DO CURIANGU	CURIANGU
silêncio veio no	Silêncio veio no
primeiro raio do espanto.	raio.
Os ossos nasceram rijos	Os ossos voltados
com os olhos voltados	Para o mundo.
Para o mundo.	
[CURIANGU JUNGLE	[CURIANGU
Silence came	Silence came
at the first exciting shine.	at sunshine.
Bones were born rigid	Bones gazing at
with the eyes watching	the world.]
the world.]	
(*Árvores dos Arturos* 75)	(*Corpo vivido* 97)

Only three years apart in terms of date of publication (1988 versus 1991), the reworked poem is remarkable in syntactic, lexical, and semantic terms. In the original version, the bones of the narrative voice are watching the world while in the "revised" version, the bones themselves, not those of the narrative voice are gazing at the world. I am unconvinced that the modifications have not changed the meaning. And if multiple meanings are intended, the reader must be provided with at least some clue as to what is meant. Multiplicity may be desirable in situations of ambiguity and ambivalence. The rest of the poem in the original version provides these clues. This portrait of a typical *Arturos* family in the Curiangu jungle depicts their harsh life as captured in their daily routine: "primitive" birth, toughness in forced growth, cold ambience and creative warmth in fire, sound, songs, and dance, full of memories even before old age. In the new version, Pereira's language is more concise and in comparison with the old version, social commitment is traded for linguistic finesse.

In *Corpo vivido,* the classic world of twisted fate, witchcraft, and spell captured in the figure of the sea horse (*Hipocampo*) encounters Angolan sea goddess mythology (*Kianda*). The ambivalent secrets of the lover in moments of indecision (*Corpo imprevisto*) together with philosophical reflections of the multiple meanings hidden in names of people and places and a penchant for the oracular and the divinatory potential of the word (*Margem dos nomes*) provide the necessary background for the celebration of life (*Bailo*) as well as a sense of shared burden at the "pain of the world" (*Dormundo*) as exemplified by two case studies on the Arturos (*Árvore dos Arturos*) and popular speeches heard and collected in the field (*O livro de falas*). As Carlos Nejar notes of this collection: "The totality of Edimilson's works introduces a thematic diversity ranging from metaphysical inquiry to dionysical ludism, from linguistic to symbolic divestment. The poet shares the pain of loss and the apprenticeship of poetry."[20] The poetic voice seems to have been forced to grow up very early, for in "Embruxados" (Bewitched), like a stoic soul, undeterred by the devouring and bewitching potential of life, he laments:

Com tantos abismos
nada perturba.
Inexoráveis as pontes. (26)

[With so many abysses / nothing startles. / The bridges, unmovable.]

Even when the subject is love, the poetic voice is reflective and philosophical, as in "Corpo imprevisto":

Tenho a instrução das aves,
mas o desejo
dos amantes. (81)

[I have the instruction of the birds, / but the desire / of lovers.]

This suggests that the choice is difficult to make between letting go and staying with the "body" of the "other" that also torments him. The world of magic—terrestrial and imaginary—is the world of the griot as he appeals to the sea goddess not to hurt his bones even if she takes him with her ("Kianda") to the world beyond. African mythology blends with the wisdom of the ancients as if Pereira is retelling Angolan folktales and folkways in poetic form. "Ouvido" (Hearing) provides an ample example of the man-animal world of confrontation where the "weakest" becomes the "strongest" and wisest:

O viajante recebe da cobra
um amuleto. [. . .]
Roubado em seu segredo
o viajante desaparece.
A cobra muda de veste,
o homem perde o corpo. (193)

[The traveler receives from the serpent / an amulet. . . . / Tricked by his own secret / the traveler disappears. / The serpent changes its skin, / the man loses his body.]

Here is a classical African tale in which the snake charmer is fooled by his own charm or forgets the magical words and becomes the victim of the snake, which usually kills the charmer. *Corpo vivido* is a powerful primer of the magical world that Pereira navigates in search of the meaning of life in its local and universal dimensions.

As the title indicates, *Árvore dos Arturos* (The Arturos' Genealogy Tree) translates a poet's anthropological-imaginative project in the midst of the Arturos—a search for origins, a search for identity and human bonding generated by the passion for discovery and commitment to knowledge. The Arturos community, family, and individuals belong to the same tree that was before them, still exists, and will always be there. Many poems refer to freedom, to the ancestors, to the communal spirit of the Arturos with which they deal with the challenges of life. Most of the poems are somber, melancholic, constantly evoking death, and passage of time, and yet echo the necessity for celebration, dance, and ritual in the midst of the chaos of life. When *Árvore dos Arturos* is compared closely with its anthropological-cultural reference work *Negras raízes Mineiras: Os Arturos* (coauthored with Núbia Pereira), there are a number of parallels as if the poetic work is a companion to the field work. The methodology section of *Negra raízes* outlines a ten-point premise that elucidates the creative work at the same time: the specificity of slavery in Minas Gerais; the dynamics of social process; global understanding of the phenomenon within a diachronic approach; refusal to consider black culture as subculture; the link between black religiosity and historical process; the link between Afro-Mineiros and the spatial dimension of their history; festival as location of reactualization of myth through the past, present, and future; multivalent nature of symbolic language; dance as one of the elements of religious sign through language and corporeal rhythm; and finally, the cultural resistance of the Arturos as a metonym for Afro-Brazilians in Minas Gerais.

The entire text of *Árvore dos Arturos* represents a historical and genealogical document. The structure reflects a consciousness of origins; of traditions, festivities, and rituals; and of the permanence of the ancestors. In a tripartite poem, "A árvore de Arthur Camilo" (The Genealogy Tree of Arthur Camilo), the poetic voice tells his own family history—how his father, Camilo, meets his mother, Felisbina, and the feeling of nostalgia about by-gone days; then, how he meets the love of his life, Carmelinda da Bela Vista, and his affection for her. Finally, he tells the young Arturos to continue the *Congado* tradition since he wonders for how much longer he will be alive:

Viverei até quando.
Meninos, segurem o Congado
e o tempo responde por todos" (78)

[How long shall I live. / Children, take care of the Congado / and time will answer to all.]

Following this family history "Mulheres Arturas" (Arturos Women) describes the fear and strength of women as they deal with the surprises of life, which they are well prepared to face. "Crianças Arturas" (Arturos Children) describes the rites of passage of the children as they go to school to learn about their historical past so as to have pride in their identity:

O pai que é capitão ensina:
"Auê, o povo do Congo é guerreiro!"
Meninos do Congo
Batuque e Moçambique! (81)

[Father who is chief teaches: / "Hurrah! Congo people are warriors!" / Congo children / Percussion and Mozambique!]

To this family structure, Pereira adds a definition by qualifying the Arturos as people who dance from within, as the poem "Os Arturos dançam por dentro" illustrates:

| Os santos se agradam do corpo! Há fogo no Congado! Os Arturos viram o mundo down em segredo do sagrado! Congo chama o Moçambique e os corpos se chamam. Auê! São os negros do rosário! Os santos dos negros Arturos! (82) | [Saints derive pleasure from The body! *Congado* is hot! The Arturos turn the world upside

In the secret of the sacred! Congo calls on Mozambique And bodies answer to the call. Hurrah! These are the blacks of the Rosary! The saints of black Arturos!] |

The Arturos do not simply dance and celebrate. Behind the celebrations is hidden cultural resistance as a measure of maintaining their culture and resisting oppression, as in "Festa de libertação" (Feast of Freedom)—a festivity marking May 13, 1888, the official date of the abolition of slavery in Brazil. This is a recent addition to popular Afro-Brazilian religious culture. Part of the enactment includes the era when there were still slaves and slavery in order to appreciate the full import of freedom captured in "music, festivity, and dance" (254). As Pereira and Gomes in *Negras raízes* conceive of this process of resistance as an existential act of survival as the practice of rituals of their ancestors "reaffirm their origin, force them to uphold the inherited tradition, while using the practices to critique social injustices, and finally, struggle to keep the knowledge of these rites alive" (510). In "Festa de Libertação," the five-part poem elaborates a complex ritualistic procession of liberation that leads to a Mass and a reunion. The first movement, "Cortejo de busca" (Procession Search), dramatizes the history of slavery through the enactments of its horrors and the resistance codified in songs, dances, and performance. Like a choreographed regalia reminiscent of a carnival procession with different "Alas" such as "Baianas" and "Bateria," the different groups, Congo, Moçambique, Kings, Queens, and "slaves" are dressed up for a search for origins. In protest, the drums call the names of the children whose destiny as "slaves" is death:

Os tambores gritam com esperanças
o nome dos filhos que a morte espera.
Os negros, os negros! (102)

[The drums cry out with hope / the names of children death is expecting. / Oh blacks, Oh blacks!]

The second movement, "Os escravos" (Slaves), describes the entire group as dispossessed: children with tired bodies even before they start their lives, the elderly with their ornaments weighing them down, the youngsters limited in their days, and the women with their dim eyes indicating aging sum up an empty life—used and abused, with their sweat rolling off their heads, and with their hands up in the air, in protest, asking for justice. The third movement, "A libertação" (Freedom), enacts the celebration of abolition based on the Golden Law signed by Princesa Isabel. A festive poem, full of excitement and reservation, but merriment all the same. In the fourth movement, "Missa Conga," perhaps the most important since it is a "Congo Mass," the poem queries the hypocrisy of praying to gods that cannot be worshipped openly since the devotees are still persecuted by the authorities and the language used in the rituals is foreign—an interrogation a critic has termed "part of the postmodern, meta-poetic discourse in which the self-reflexive and reflective elements of the text also examine the language" (Barbosa, "Strategies of Poetic Language," 71). The final movement, "Cortejo de encontro" (Reunion Procession), indicates a weary collective, smiling in the fulfillment of another year of celebration that is coming to an end.

In the world of the Arturos, the sacred cannot be separated from the popular, hence the primordial place of the ancestors in all festivities. The processions, rituals, dances, and feasts all are directly or indirectly an invocation and praise of the gods. Two poems in *Árvore dos Arturos,* "A igreja dos antepassados" (Ancestral Church) and "Os antepassados" (Ancestors), illustrate the centrality of the ancestors in the daily life of the Arturos. "A Igreja dos Antepassados" is a homage to a church that used to exist but is now in ruins.

No longer can there be a Mass or visits to the saints by devotees; all that is left of the church are memories of the walls and bells:

> Na capela em ruínas trabalha
> a herança dos negros antigos.
> Não há paredes nem domingos:
> há sinos, lembranças e Arturos. (99)

> [At the chapel in ruins / a heritage of ancient blacks. / No more walls nor Sundays: / but bells, memories, and Arturos.]

Like a cycle of life that begins with the ancestors and ends with them, the book, *Árvores dos Arturos,* ends with the Arturos portrayed as the embodiment of the spirit of their ancestors with whom they communicate and comingle in a permanent relationship. In the closing poem, "Os antepassados," the Arturos see a direct connection of their rituals and ceremonies as an attempt to evoke the history and spirits of the ancestors captured in the figure of Zumbi:

> E os Arturos de hoje—todos
> em torno do tempo—moverão
> no Cangado a vida dos negros.
> Zambi, ô Zambi!
> Olho do rosário!
> Os Arturos entram no meio
> e saem com o fogo do mundo! (126)

> [And the Arturos today—everyone
> with the passage of time—will evoke
> The life of blacks in *Congado* worship
> Zambi, oh Zambi!
> Eye of the rosary!
> The Arturos enter in the middle
> and exit with world's fire!]

The Arturos are strong people who address their condition with symbolic and performative ritual that is encoded in figurative language and sacred dance through which they pay homage to their ancestors. Pereira has performed a formidable feat by translating the Arturos experience into a legacy for future generations of historians and scholars alike, for in his words: "There is a saying in Os Arturos: 'A black person is an *aroeira.*'" An *aroeira* is a strong tree; blacks are as strong as the tree" (White, "Edimilson de Almeida Pereira," 52). In this sense, *Árvores dos Arturos* represents a poetic rendition of the ancestral strength of the Arturos.

In *A roda do mundo* (Gyration of the World), coauthored with Ricardo Aleixo, Pereira returns to his familiar Bantu world of *Congado,* Candomblé, and to the intertextual sacred-popular terrain of Our Lady of the Rosary, Saint Efigênia, Saint Benedict, Mama Kitaia, and Calunga—all operating within the conceptual Yoruba *oríkì* (praise) tradition in which Aleixo is even more engrossed. A declaration of identity resonates from the title, "Nós, os baianos" (We, Bahians), as if to see the world of *Candombe* in Minas Gerais as synonymous with that of Candomblé in Bahia, defining Afro-Brazilian identity as multiple yet basically united within a fragmented modernity. From the typical eye of the versed and committed *ethno-rapporteur*, Pereira creates a meeting ground for the ancients and the moderns, revealing the qualities and values that have remained unchanged over many generations. Each poem, or shall we say *oríkì* is an expression of the immortal beauty of the gods and the divinatory capacity of their speech. Pereira's poetic language possesses transpositional effects, as in "Família lugar" (Family Location) where a river is the "third margin" of two movements and abode of the living-dead, both cemetery and chapel. In the cemetery, the "dead" are resting, while in the chapel or shrine the saints-ancestors are being invoked and worshipped. The cemetery holds the bodies while the "capela" releases their spirits through music and dance—like the ancients in "Inquices" (The Inquisitors) who "die one way" and "live another way" using the human body, through spiritual possession as their bloodless abode. As the poem "Calunga lungara" (Mystery Revealed) confirms, Pereira uses poetic language to capture that which is not able to be captured; ideas that are considered "secrets" but that can only be rendered in poetic mystery, for "o que se diz não é Calunga" (what is spoken is not considered mystery). When considered in its totality, Pereira's cultural, critical, and creative corpus intersects skillfully within the nexus of tradition, modernity, and ancestrality, while respecting the sacredness and multiplicity of language. Unquestionably, Pereira's imagination occupies a primary place in Afro-Brazilian letters of both his own generation and that before it. He is bound to influence the critical intellectual voice of black Brazil for many years to come.

Marcos Dias is the Afro-Mineiro poet with whom I spent a considerable amount of time interviewing and who kept wanting me to return to have critical dialogues with him. His sheer enthusiasm as a poet is admirable—he lives for his creative "mission" and devotes much of his time to reflect on literature and culture. Of the same generation as Edimilson de Almeida Pereira, but possessing the consciousness of an Adão Ventura, and the profoundness of an Arnaldo Xavier, Dias has produced at least four poetic works. Of these, three have been published, namely, *Rebelamentos* (Rebellious Moments), *País indig(o blue)nação* (Indigo [Blue]Nation), and *Estudos sobre a cidade* (Studies on the City). Although *Perspectiva entre o movimento e o salto* (Perspective between the Movement and the Jump) has not yet been published, it is equally deserving of critical attention. As the poet explains in his bibliographic notes to *País indig(o blue)nação*, *Rebelamentos*, and *Estudos sobre a cidade,* the three poetic texts constitute a trilogy of "Negritude, Brazilianness, and Universality." In her own study, "Afrodicções" (Black Dictions), Jussara Santos remarks: "Dos três autores, cujos textos são analisados, creio que Adão Ventura e Marcos Dias, rincipalmente em *Rebelamentos*, sejam os que mais explicitam *um enuinciador que se quer negro* e que reivindica, em nome de um grupo, a reversão de valores, posições e estereótipos alocados nos segmentos de descendência negra africana (87; Of the three writers whose texts are analyzed here, I think that Adão Ventura and Marcos Dias, especially in *Rebelamentos,* are those who explicitly take the position of *enunciators who affirm their blackness* and who struggle on behalf of the group, the reversal of values, positions, and stereotypes assigned to African descendants [italics in original]). This is the group Edimilson de Almeida Pereira refers to as "historicists" or those "activist" writers who find it necessary to explicitly challenge the status quo by exposing the horrors of slavery and the imperative of freedom even in the present.

In *Rebelamentos,* Dias's first book of poetry published in 1990, he recuperates the intimate and refined pulsations gyrating from a tripartite consciousness of Africa, Afro-Brazil, and the African diaspora in general. The poems, in their fragments and aesthetic totality of a new negritude, indict and accuse while exposing images the poet calls "absconded Africas of my diaspora" as in the subtitle. By invoking activists—poets, religious leaders, even Afro-Brazilian icons and heroes—Dias reaches out to the entire world beyond the confines and conditions of the black experience in Brazil. Dias is a Pan-Africanist, a poet conscious of his roots, who bears the burden as a "silent" spokesperson whose articulation lies in the loud cry of his "rebellious," lucid, and experimental lamentation poems. In *Rebelamentos,* Dias fearlessly journeys first through the "*quilombo* of the mind" in order to recuperate the physical *quilombo,* which is often misunderstood as a passive symbol. The critical reception to Marcos Dias's first book has been phenomenal—from those like Fábio Lucas and Ricardo Aleixo who commend Dias's "poetic vision of life" to those like Márcio Almeida and João Maimona who identify his negritude and his attempt to reconcile "militantismo and aesthetics." A new Afro-Mineiro modernist voice can be said to have been born at a time of dire urgency for such a voice of reconciliation between poetic language and social commitment.

The *quilombo* painted by Dias is revolutionary and revolting, as in "Diário quilombola de lutas" (Diary of *Quilombo* Struggles):

O que pulsou em meu sangue
eram dores antigas—antigos ecos
de uma re-volta que se esculpiu
na plenitude deste meu gesto
de luta e de CORpo inteiro [...]
No território de minhas emoções
Palmares (de pé) resiste E contra
ataca" (26)

[What pulsated within my blood / were ancient pains—old echoes / of a revolt emanating / from the fullness of my action / of struggle and of my entire BODY... / In the territory of my emotions / Palmares (standing) resists And counter / attacks.]

This is a remarkable stance and evolution for a poetic voice, who in the first movement of the entire collection represents himself as the divided soul whose other part is on the other side of the ocean—that is, Africa, in "Interiores" (Intimacies]); or the "walled in" figure whose "anemic luck" in his daily routine in which he faces "insurmountable walls" forces him to submit himself to the caprices and consolation offered by alcohol: "jogar o siso na cachaça" (10; Give my reasoning to the rum). Struggling between lucidity and lethargy, Dias realizes the necessity to immerse himself in the warrior-like happiness of the ancestors in spite of the arduous journey and adverse conditions of life in the African diaspora, in "Dos lúcidos" (On the Lucid Ones). In "Entre o blues e o samba" (Between the Blues and Samba), Dias, a self-conscious "poet of the people," reflects on his options and choices: Is it worth spending time with the downtrodden? Is it worth raising questions without answers? Is it worth praising Africa, which is actually entangled in misery? These doubts, expressed as reflections, are resolved in the second movement ("Quizomba") where the poet declares his intention in "Bio/Grafia" (Bio/Graphy):

O Hoje das minhas Desgraças
tem sua gênesis no Tráfico [...]
Sou fato fruto espetáculo
de um tempo cujo opróbio
dos olhos ainda
não se apagou [...]
Porém o meu canto é fortE Pretenso
nos novos Quilombos que eu re/invento. (19)

[The Miseries of my Today / have their origins in the Slave Trade... / I am a tired fruit spectacle / of a time whose / shameful eyes / are yet to be blinded... / However my song is a strong Objective / in the new *quilombos* I re-create.]

In this reinvention of resistance, there is a dialogic companion, Adão Ventura, to whom Dias dedicates a poem ("Do axé" [On Blessing]) in the celebration of the ten years of the publication of *A cor da pele:* "As dores de todas as Áfricas / vos trago neste(s) poem(s)" (20; The pains of all Africas / I bring you in these poems). In this poem, Dias identifies himself as a fearless warrior who nonetheless enjoys the inspiration of his mentors such as Ventura. The remaining poems in *Rebelamentos*, especially in the third movement, are dedicated to Bishop Desmond Tutu of South Africa, another spiritual mentor whose courage and voice against apartheid gave Dias the necessary incentive to continue his intellectual-imaginative struggle against oppression and discrimination in Brazil.

País indig(o blue) nação follows in the footsteps of Rebelamentos but with a corrosive and incisive critical stance against Brazil's racial hypocrisy. It was written in 1995 in commemoration of the tercentennial of the death of Zumbi dos Palmares. In Rebelamentos, Zumbi has already been foregrounded, not only in the body of the collection ("Do axé"), a poem dedicated to Ventura, but in the epigraph by Éle Semog. The tercentennial of Zumbi's death provided ample opportunity to assess what has changed since Zumbi's heroic sacrifice in 1695. The pun of the title offers a clue: "indigo(blue)nation" evokes indignation and melancholy in the combination of "indigo" and "nation" with "blue" inserted between. If Brazil is repulsive and nauseating due to her social policies and official denial of racial discrimination, it is only in the text that the "truth" is revealed. Dias critiques invisibility, exclusionism, and the stereotypical treatment of Afro-Brazilians in Brazilian society. Humorously, the poetic voice confesses that he is rereading Brazilian official history in order to show its farce and hypocrisy, as in three related poems: "Cadernos da cilvilização brasileira" (Notes on Brazilian Civilization), "O país" (Country), and "Pátria" (Nation). In "Cadernos da cilvilização brasileira," the poetic voice attempts to reeducate white Brazil about the distortions in the Afro-Brazilian history they have been taught by evoking "countercurrents" of black heroes such as Ganga Zumba and Zumbi. Through literature and historical revision, the poetic voice is convinced that the ancestors recuperate from their invisibility over the years:

O crivo de minhas releituras atesta
que a história oficial mente
Até nas entrelinhas. (11)

[The riddle of my rereadings attests / that the official history lies / Even between the lines.]

As much as Brazil continues to maintain a lie as "truth" concerning her racial democracy, Dias contests that even if most people learn from what is said and written, the reality that the majority of her population is invisible cannot be ignored. For a true memory of the future, Dias campaigns for unofficial discourses that will counter and correct the official lies, as in "O país." In spite of his criticism of Brazil's hypocrisy concerning racial relations, Dias affirms his patriotic spirit in "Pátria"—although with the ambivalent feeling of an outsider in his very own country:

Aqui	[Here
finco raízes	I plant my roots
Mesmo desterrado	Although exiled
de seus espaços	from its most
mais nobres	noble spaces
Meus passos ainda	Still, my steps
caminhares de fogo	warmed by the fire
pelos contornos	in the contours
de seu corpo	of her body]
("Encruzilhada," 42)	(Crossroads)

Dedicated to Zumbi, the entire collection is an indictment of existing social inequalities in Brazil—a reminder that in 1995, three hundred years after the death of Zumbi, racial democracy continues to be a myth. The poetic voice's feeling of being at a crossroads must be understood as an expression of frustration with Brazil and her masked form of racism.

When compared to the discourses of Dias's first two volumes of poetry, *Estudos sobre a cidade* lacks the same thematic focus even if its concern remains social—the problems of unemployment and survival in a city gradually trading its humanity for capitalist gain. Dias confronts the agony of joblessness and the anguish of seeing street children being victimized by the very sector of the society that should protect them: adults and authorities. In this book of lamentation and tribulation, the poet is not at war with the city but with its insensitivity and selfishness. Two tropes seem to structure the collection: city life and economics. The book cover provides some clues: the eye of the poet gazing through images of civilization and urbanity—the computer, the buildings, the well-groomed worker in suit and tie—as opposed to the city's other side, with its favela, its *capoeirista* (Afro-Brazilian martial arts performer/dancer) and two poor half-naked kids looking back as if asking for something. Dias ridicules the city's "civilized" posturing while it disregards the health and dignity of the suffering masses, in "Quase ao jeito de Gregório de Matos" (Almost in Gregório de Matos's Style). In his opinion, the city is a modern model of the plantation and the slave quarters to which the modern worker is condemned:

Nesta c/idade o deus é o lucro	[In this city
O trabalho o mito do homem digno	Work the myth of the decent man
mas seu benefício (no vício	but his benefit (is the vice
da ImPrevidência) e o deficít fixo (46)	of the Unforeseen) and his constant debt.]

The economic life of the city is equally the concern of "Mercado de Trabalho" (Marketplace), in which the poetic voice enumerates a cycle of joblessness and its severe impacts on the unemployed individual—from underemployment and exhaustion through being made into a beast. The pun here is only discernible in the Portuguese for the poetic exercise is lost in translation; for example, the compound word "desemprego" (unemployment) could be broken down to several different words that capture the gradual degeneration of the unemployed figure (*desempregado*). As a result, one word degenerates into a fragmented body of words representing the unemployed person and his/her frustrations:

jan.	subemprego	[Jan.	underemployment
fev.	subemprego	Feb.	underemployment
mar.	subemprego	Mar.	underemployment
(...)		(...)	
dez.	prego	Dec.	exhaustion
jan.	prego	Jan.	exhaustion
fev.	desemprego	Feb.	unemployment
(...)		(...)	
do subempregado a sempre prego		from underemployment to constant exhaustion	
de sempre gado a desempregado (42–43)		from always being cattle to being unemployed]	

Unlike *Rebelamentos* and *País indig(o blue) nação*, which express black consciousness and issues of national identity, *Estudos sobre a cidade*, which completes the trilogy, is more universal in its concern with unemployment, poverty, hunger, and child abuse. The "trilogy" claim by Dias may be far-fetched for unemployment need not be a universal concern, although the effect of the city on the poor or the immigrant may be chilling and significant.

In *Perspectiva entre o movimento e o salto,* further experiments with poetic language and visual poetry and draws inspiration from the mentorship of Arnaldo Xavier and Ronald Tutuca, combining Dias's own poetic theory as defined in "Ars capoeirética II" (Capoeiristic-Ethical Art) as if to apply the self-defense strategies of capoeira dance within the artistic world he evokes.[21] In essence, for Marcos Dias, poetry becomes a modernist cultural weapon that uses the pretext of "movement" and rhythm to go on the offensive against the limits of articulation. As in capoeira, the *capoeirista* must always be vigilant for the tricks of the adversary. The hesitations and zigzags are part of the strategy of survival and of prowess in a game full of surprises and harmony. It takes the "ginga" (mastery of the swing) of the *capoeirista* to successfully compete:

Cabe a ginga do bailado
de alpargatas dos meninos
Seu vai-não-vai pontuado
de espreita a cada esquina. (60)

[It takes the swing of the dancer / the flexible childlike sandals / his go/no go vibration / his constant vigilance on every corner.]

From manifesto of blackness ("Manifesto ao negro experimental") to images of Ralph Ellison ("Rap Ralph"), Langston Hughes ("Langston Hughes revisitado"), Arnaldo Xavier ("Poema visual"), and Edimilson de Almeida Pereira and Milton Nascimento ("Letras e canções"), this collection serves as a homage to a number of cultural producers who have influenced the poet and whose admiration pushes the poet to higher heights. Dias does not want to be "boxed" into a theoretical corner but prefers to be "loose" in his movements and offensives to the extent of strategic fluidity that becomes a free-flowing art without barriers or limits. Dias accentuates this awareness of experimentalism and freedom in his title poem, "Perspectiva entre o movimento e o salto" (Perspective between the Movement and the Jump):

Vanguarda é risco: na cor da bamba do
desequilíbro e-r-r-a-r-i-s-c-a-r arisco?
À aridez branca do tudo está dito rever
berar a poética dos mitos Digo não digo
Des/equilibrar o jogo dos lugares fixos: A-risco arriscar um r-is-c-o no riscado (9)

[Vanguard is a risk: in the color of coolness / of the imbalance error-risk I take a risk / Against white aridity that all is said—to revisit / Bark the poetics of myths Say not say / Dis/rupt the game of fixed spaces: / With risk, take a risk on the draft copy.]

With this collection, Dias moves away from the strictly black consciousness (except through visual contrasts of white and black) to a more cerebral interplay between the poetical, the theoretical, and the philosophical—using this challenge to push himself, go beyond himself, and thereby discover himself as one of the compelling voices of Afro-Brazilian modernity.

When compared to Marcos Dias, Ricardo Aleixo de Brito, an Afro-Mineiro visual poet and plastic artist, is a more sophisticated thinker whose poetry forces the reader to contemplate and transgress the limits of meaning and form. Popularly known as Ricardo Aleixo, this poet finds complexity as normalcy. In the three works he has published to date, *Festim*, *A roda do mundo* (coauthored with Edimilson de Almeida Pereira), and *Trívio*, Aleixo displays a poetic evolution, maturity, and sophistication that remind one of the poetry of Ronald Tutuca in Porto Alegre and Arnaldo Xavier in São Paulo. Inspired by both French and Brazilian poets (Valéry, Haroldo de Campos, Oswald de Andrade, and Carlos Drummond de Andrade, among others), Aleixo defines his poetics ("Poética") as a process of instigation and mastication of "words, meat, and bones" as if to suggest that nothing escapes the artistic construction of images and the challenging deconstruction of meaning. With rigor and freedom, Aleixo creates difficulty and lucidity at the same time as he takes a cue from Valéry:

> Eu mordo o que posso"
> (palavra, carne ou osso)
> Me acho
> me acabo de vez
> me *disfarço*.

[I bite what I can / [(word, meat, or bone) / I discover myself / I terminate myself at once / I mask myself.]

The poetic act of "biting" and masticating the word is captured in the title poem, "Festim" (Little Feast):

> mut il   ar   otextoé só p   arte
> FORADEFOCO   EDER   OTA   ÇÃO
> do festi m.

[Mutilate the text is only / an out of focus and out of failure part / of a little feast.]

At first reading, Aleixo's poetry seeks to manipulate signs and meanings by reconstructing meaning at two levels: syntax and semantics. In so doing, the poetry is put out of focus in order to challenge the reader to see beyond the blurry focus and refocus the camera of meaning. Poetic "mutilation" sums up Aleixo's venture in *Festim*. All the poems are cryptic, postmodernist, and defamiliarizing as if deliberately withholding meaning, constantly subverting the norm, and reversing established poetic conventions and paradigms. The Cartesian adage, "I think therefore I am," is reworked as "EX / ISTO / LOGO AQUILO" (I exist / After that one) in "R (EX-ISTO)" (I Re-Exist). "Aquilo," which should refer to "I think" in the original maxim, is here neutralized and subverted. The reader is forced to recognize the poet at work within his world of complexities; dissimulating the known, and invoking the unknown. Through the enlargement, reduction, and collage of signs, Aleixo uses poetic language as a means to convey multiple meanings and the possibility of language to transcend its own meaning.

While Aleixo's first text addresses the problem of language, his second volume, coauthored with Pereira, *A roda do mundo* (Gyration of the World), shifts to the poetic celebration of Yoruba gods (*òrìṣàs*) through *oríkì* but with the same economy of words and structural concision. Aleixo describes each òrìṣà as a devotee would, paying attention to their specific qualities and character. Like in *Axés do sangue e da esperança* by Abdias do Nascimento, Aleixo begins his *oríkì* with a homage to Èṣù, the "master of easy speech" and "controller of paths" who negotiates between the gods and humanity as an intermediary and facilitator without whom contact is impossible. It is the same Èṣù in "Cine olho" (Camera-Eye) who, for Aleixo, is not a child but

a field,
an Exu hidden
sparkled
between
the
cars" (37)

This straight-line poem, composed as if the eye is looking through the lens, pushes the limits of poetic composition to a state of absurdity and pressured snapshots. After Èṣù, the warrior-like deameanor of Ògún comes to light:

Ele avança
e até a terra
treme. (. . .)
Ogun mata
o rei e o povo
e aí acampa.
(. . .)
Faz das cabeças
dos adultos
gongos
e usa as das crianças
como cabaças (38–39)

[He advances / and even the earth trembles. / (. . .) / Ògún kills / the king and his people / and there takes abode. / (. . .) / Uses heads / of adults / as gongs / and those of children / as drinking gourds.]

Ògún's bloodiness and ferocity only compare with the fearsome nature of Ṣàngó: he who releases stones of lightning, the Leopard, husband of Oya, and son of Yemoja. Unlike the terrestrial gods, the water spirits such as Òṣun and Yemoja are full of beauty, grace, and compassion. Òṣun cleanses the body of the sick and changes the fate of a bad destiny while Yemoja, the "grandmother of the universe," protects her children under and above the water. Of all these gods, one is supreme—Òrìṣànlá. The poetic voice makes a supplication to the supreme god in the Yoruba pantheon, to "quash the forces of my enemies," an ample evidence of Òrìṣàńlá's embodiment of justice and the faith his devotees have in him. In this intervocal, intertextual, and intercultural "translation" of the praise-songs of the gods, Aleixo's *oríkì* continue the millennial Yoruba tradition of the traditional griots who praised gods, kings, and even ordinary people who possessed compelling values or whose values needed to be changed through caustic criticism. Aleixo follows in the tradition of Birago Diop, Abdias do Nascimento, Pierre Fatumbi Verger, Gilberto Gil, Hermógenes Almeida, and Antônio Risério. Aleixo's *oríkì* is a poetic and appropriate collection of *ẹbọs* (offerings) to the gods.

Trívio (Trivium), the third collection of Aleixo's poetry to date, is in the words of the poet himself a "tri-path" poetry, a concept that explains the symbolism in the title. A prefatory note provided by the author explains that in the Middle Ages, the term referred to the inferior division of the liberal arts, which included grammar, rhetoric, and logic. Beyond this classical meaning, the author offers another: the "meeting of three paths," a concept that is called *Orita meta* in Yoruba cosmology—a location that is better termed as the marketplace to which three paths lead. If Aleixo's mission is to challenge grammar, redefine rhetoric, and reconfigure logic, the examples are ample in this collection where traditional language is first sacrificed in order to formulate a new way of conceiving of poetic language through visual images, assonances, and dissonances. In "Poética" (Poetics), Aleixo sums up his "ars poetica":

const
ruir
sobre
ruínas" (67)

[con / struct / over / ruins]

for only through the degeneration of an old language can a new one be born; only through the deformation of traditional form can a new form be born. Aleixo's poetry is again characterized by the experimental need to fragment not only syntactically but semantically—rearranging the rules of grammar and challenging the dialectics of meaning. Language then becomes fluid, a "process" not an end, as in "Língua" (Language):

(. . .) esplêndida língua
se formando
ainda
pode ser que se
decompondo. (31)

[(. . .) marvelous language / still / in formation / may be / decomposing.]

From songs and ballads of love; poem-reflections on body, hell, and homosexuality; homages to the gods and imaginative creators; a re-reading of the human species (human-angel); through a treatise on the logic of destiny, Aleixo enumerates a host of all-inclusive images. In such an extended poetic framing and landscape, the subject is decentralized and the poetic voice, preferring to be "nonexistent," elaborates on the poem as a formulation of a theory on language and myth as in the following poem in which identity is problematized. In the context of that poem, whites, machos, adults, Christians, and the rich are all participating in an absurd or even Brechtian game of being and nonbeing, of knowing and unknowing. Essentially, the reader is invited to explore the "three paths" of meaning through hearing, seeing, and reading strategies.

eles que são brancos e os que não são eles
que são machos e os que não são eles que
são adultos e os que não são eles que são
cristãos e os que não são eles que são
ricos e os que não são eles que são sãos e
os que não são todos os que são mas não (. . .)

[Those who are white and those who are not those / who are macho and those who are not who / are adults and those who are not those who are / Christians and those who are not those who are / rich and those who are not those who are sane and / those who are not fully who they are but . . .]

This is a solid example of Aleixo's artistry in its totality: language is musical, performative, lyrical, elliptical, cerebral, mythical, and philosophical as if in a state of endless flux, of becoming, and of negotiation captured in the tripartite essence embodied in the title. The untitled poem also alludes to the mythology of racial democracy and the hypocrisy of whiteness. Aleixo's three texts, when considered as a "trilogy," chart new directions in *concretismo* (a Brazilian poetry movement of the 1950s that focused on a new way of looking at poetry and life) and abstraction without succumbing to the pitfalls of identity consciousness but with an eye on the universal through Yoruba cosmology and the endless poetic possibilities, complexities, and subtleties it offers.

Beyond Ventura, Pereira, Dias, and Aleixo, who have produced a considerable number of works that evidence of maturity and accomplishment, there are other Afro-Mineiro cultural producers in Belo Horizonte who are no less important, such as Anelito de Oliveira, author of *Lama;* Waldemar Euzébio Pereira, author of *Prosoema* and *Do cinza ao negro;* and Leda Maria

Martins, author of *Os dias anônimos* and *Afrografia da memoria,* among others. Oliveira's *Lama* (Mud) evokes the haunting tragedy of the postabolition era in which the marginalized Brazilian, "roaming the world day and night like a desolate park," narrates his own encounter with alienation, disillusionment, misery, and dehumanization. The poetic voice is lost in his wanderings, often seeing "nothingness" in life and seemingly accepting his crude and lowly state:

sobre o chão na lama
do chão e na alma do
despe ferida e feridas. (10)

[On the floor in the mud / from the floor and in the soul of the mud / outfit of hurt and hurts is removed.]

The poetic voice is macabre and melancholic as if on the verge of death and conscious of the premonition of death through the symbolism of night even during the day. Death seems to be just around the corner, its urgency unmistakable in the following lines:

sinto flácido levando
nas mãos algo que
deve ser a morte com
sua sombra de aço . . . (22)

[I feel empty carrying / in my hands something that / must be death with / its steel shadow.]

Unlike the images of devastation that Oliveira shares of the *real* Brazil, Waldemar Pereira offers a counterpoint of sentimental poems with moments of passion, hope, and transcendence. While *Prosoema* may be considered a formative poetic collection, it contains concrete moments of maturity and understanding of the hardships of life that the poet seems to hide as "secrets of failures." In *Do cinza ao negro,* the poet evolves in his negritudist consciousness, but the crux of this second volume lies in the survival of the spirit in the midst of struggle; for life, after all, is an "act of will" (40). Beyond survival, Leda Martins's *Os dias anônimos* (Anonymous Days) shares poetic intimacies and passionate reminiscences of which "Humanitas" (Humanity) is exemplary. Aware of her African ancestry as in "Linhagem" (Lineage) even if she does not display any obvious black consciousness, Martins promotes, somewhat contradictorily, the drawing of linkages with the past without dwelling rigidly on racial identity. Her essence is simply to be free, as powerfully evoked in "Humanitas":

Liberdade
minha única ambição
impossibilidade fatal
de esquecer
no cárcere do outro
minha própria prisão. (19)

[Freedom / my only ambition / fatal ambition / to forget / within the prison of the other / my own very prison.]

In this collection, Martins revisits the controversy in Afro-Brazilian cultural production over the use by some of the word "Negro" or blackness as a sign of affirmation while others want to transcend the label. Her poetry, even when talking about African ancestry, does not mention Africa nor does she refer to white/black dichotomies. Instead, Martins sings of freedom within the veiled sign of universality and ambiguity—an attitude that is understandable and respectable given the complexities of social inequalities that disempower Afro-Brazilians as a people.

This critical survey of Afro-Brazilian cultural producers in Salvador and Belo Horizonte provides a point of departure for the analysis of cultural outpourings from other regions. Although regional consciousness is apparent in such writers as Aline França, Antônio Vieira da Silva, Edimilson de Almeida Pereira, Adão Ventura, and Jônatas Conceição da Silva, among others, their overall aesthetic convergence is undeniable despite their stylistic divergence.

This extended discussion of the notion of having a "Quilombo without frontiers" is premised on the fact that within such an analytical and metaphoric "settlement," as used in this chapter, there is unity in diversity. Pereira, Dias, and Aleixo, among other "experimentalists," may have a penchant for the poetic language without completely compromising their ultimate African consciousness and heritage even when they seem to be engaged in an intellectual struggle with form, yet others, like Oubi Kibuko, Jamu Minka, Abelardo Rodrigues, Carlos de Assumpção, among many others, are less ambiguous in their aesthetic and ideological missions. In *Canto à mulher amada* (Song for the Loved Woman), for example, Oubi Kibuko suggests that the black woman is the only essence left for him that has a healing power." Perhaps to reassure the reader of his sanity, the poet-lover affirms that his is a "fogo natural" (natural flame), as the title of the last poem indicates. Just as in the love poems in *Poemas*, the poet-persona sings an *oríkì* to the Afro-Brazilian woman in *Canto à negra mulher amada*, putting this special one on a pedestal:

Mulher negra, negra mulher   [Black woman, real black woman
no teu sorriso encontro alegria   In your smile I find happiness
no teu corpo compartilho amor   In your body I share love

tua fé me enche de esperança	Your faith fills me with hope
tua amizade me enche de calor	Your friendship fills me with warmth
teu carinho cura a minha dor. (33)	Your caress heals my pain.]

When considered as a totality, Kibuko's imaginative world translates faithfully the inner passions and anguish of the poet, differing only in a dialogic/conversational approach in the love poems and an impersonal, even angry approach in the revolutionary ones. Kibuko deserves recognition as a mature poet whose subject matter may be considered "superficial" but is truly "esoteric" and magical on a deeper level. He invokes the woman into modernity as a pretext for solidarity with the man, while the oppressive system that torments him equally obliges him to explore transformative strategies such as loving and forming solidarity with the Afro-Brazilian woman.

Jamu Minka, like Oubi Kibuko, belongs to the Quilombhoje generation, which founded *Cadernos negros* even before opting for the name of the group two years after the first issue of the series in 1978. A neonegritudist in orientation, Minka is closer to Cuti in temperament, and is equally nationalist as he is Pan-Africanist. Also like Kibuko, Minka has not received either the national or the international critical attention I believe he deserves. As noted by Marcio Damazio, who wrote the preface to Minka's *Teclas de ébano* (Harps of Ebony), a number of influences inspired young, idealistic, and romantic Afro-Brazilians of the 1970s, especially a sense of awareness about black struggles all over the world including the North American civil rights movement and the fight for liberation in Lusophone Africa—evoking such leaders as Martin Luther King Jr., Malcolm X, Angela Davis, Agostinho Neto, Frantz Fanon, and Amilcar Cabral. Instead of limiting himself to the imaginative world of his poetic explorations, Minka translates his commitment into a political involvement within the community where he participates in forums and conferences to help the cultivation of black consciousness among the underprivileged. Before the publication of *Teclas de ébano*, and the advent of *Cadernos negros*, Minka tried his creative hand in a number of journalistic and artistic endeavors through outlets such as *Árvore das Palavras*, *Versus-Afrolatinoamérica*, and *Jornegro*. In the special issue of *Cadernos negros: Os melhores poemas*, Minka's five poems demonstrate a cogent grasp of a wide variety of Afro-Brazilian issues: colonial exploitation, social and racial inequalities, interpersonal tensions, dashed hopes, and ancestral strength. In "Efeitos colaterais" (Collateral Effects), Minka takes a powerful jab at the mythology of racial democracy by calling it "deceiptful propaganda" that validates and reinforces the "dictatorship of whiteness" as well as the hegemonic resistance against all those who challenge the official position:

| Negros de alma negra se inscrevem | [Blacks with black soul self-inscribe |
| naquilo que escrevem | In what they write |

mas o Brasil nega	But Brazil denies
negro que não se nega. (76)	Blacks who do deny themselves.]

"Efeitos colaterais" testifies to Minka's consciousness and resolve to effect change in the country that he loves so much but which treats him like a stranger. The "collateral" trope adequately translates the dilemma of the conscious Afro-Brazilian and the price of persecution he/she pays by speaking up against oppression and hypocrisy.

As his only collection of poems, *Teclas de ébano* brings together poems written by Minka over ten years, 1975–85; while representative of a wide variety of concerns, it lacks a sustained thematization. Minka's imaginative world is multiple and committed, and includes: commentary on national politics defined by its crooked disposition ("O tanq credo!"); a critique of Brazil's world fame in soccer and the irony that there is no equality in Brazil and many blacks are far from being happy at home ("Gol contra [II]," "Batebola, bate vida"); a disenchantment with multinational companies, foreign debt, and environmental pollution ("Sangue-cola," "Dívida external"); provocative and sometimes sarcastic commentary on racial issues ("Alma e pele," "Identidade II," "Afro-América," "Malhação II"); and an express solidarity with the suffering people of South Africa under apartheid ("Apartheid"). Jamu Minka invokes the fact that on the one hand, Brazil is famous for soccer on the world stage and yet at "home" in Brazil, blacks are living as if they are in South Africa under apartheid regime, that is, under segregation. It is ironic that a country's fame beclouds its racial discrimination and social inequalities policies as veiled as they are under "racial democracy." Ultimately, Minka's most profound protest lies in "Identidade II" (Identity II) where, once again, he attacks race mixture with an autobiographical twist, affirming his blackness:

Mestiças sementes	[Mixed race seeds
planos entrelaçados de futuro	intertwined plans of the future
e eu o primeiro fruto	and I, the first fruit
(...)	(...)
Por fim, a praia da consciência	Finally, beach of consciousness
território seguro de nossa própria história	secure territory of our own history
trilhas, orientação amiga	Footpaths, friendly orientation
identidade resgatada	recuperated identity
negro	Black
negrice	Blackness
negris ... SOU! (10)	Darkness ... I AM!]

Here is a very mature, stylistically refined poet with an uncompromising attitude even despite the subtle irony in his indictment of racial oppression.

The sense of victory lies in knowing the self and affirming that self with pride and conviction without the shame that racial democracy seems to assert on the unknowing individual.

In the constellation of neonegritudist poets, Abelardo Rodrigues may be situated in the intertext between Africa and Afro-Brazil, not as the Èṣù figure who plays in the crossroads of both continents but as a synthetic voice that recuperates the memory of Africa in Brazil, as translated by his *Memória da Noite*. As Hélio Pinto Ferreira points out in the foreword to the collection, Rodrigues is often compared to Arlindo Barbeitos and Agostinho Neto, prominent Angolan poets, whose works seem to have influenced Rodrigues through "a texture of words in which the cry of the man of color is heard" (6). In contrast to this express comparative praise, Oswaldo de Camargo is more critical, questioning why Rodrigues chose to be influenced by African poets and not by the Afro-Brazilian literary tradition of Lino Guedes (1920s), Solano Trindade (1930s), and the host of poets of the 1950s such as Eduardo de Oliveira and Carlos de Assumpção. Camargo further notes a "dislocation of influences" in Abelardo Rodrigues. According to him, Rodrigues's poetry is marked by "Africanness as opposed to Afro-Brazilianness" (9). Although very critical, Camargo at least admits that Rodrigues represents the "African poetic whisper among us" (10). While Rodrigues may have been influenced by a search for form in African poetry, I disagree with Camargo's generalization about the totality of Rodrigues's creative imagination. Both *Memória da noite* and his poems included in *Cadernos negros: Os melhores poemas* embody a profound Afro-Brazilian sensibility on the issues as well as a critical eye toward them. In "Garganta" (Throat), the poetic voice appeals directly to his interlocutor to ensure that her/his throat is properly cleansed in order to receive a pure blackness. Indeed, the throat or "voice" must be subversive like the carnivalesque Ash Wednesday. Likewise, in "Zumbi," in the tradition of the hero to whom it is dedicated, the poetic voice calls for solidarity of speech, hands, and action in order to continue the legacy of the revolutionary-warrior because:

20 de novembro	[November 20
e uma canção	is a warrior
guerreira. (25)	song.]

Even if the style echoes "Africanness," that should not be a defect but a compliment to Pan-Africanism. The mention of the date alone should suffice for evidence of a conscious mind that innovates while paying homage to the ancestral African tradition.

Beyond renewing African tradition in Afro-Brazilian culture, Rodrigues captures a Pan-American sensibility as well in "Blues" when he contrasts slavery with samba, Afro-Brazilian history, and the blues, suggesting that nothing captures the profound significance of this injustice to humanity but history itself:

Esta escravidão, amigo	[This slavery, friend
não é como o samba	Is not like samba
ou nossa história	or our history
Estes lamentos, amigo	These laments, friend
não são como Blues	are not like Blues
Este sofrer irmão	This suffering, brother
(. . .)	(. . .)
é História. (31)	Is history.]

In his overall poetic cosmologic vision, Rodrigues is perplexed by the suffering and agonies of Afro-Brazilians from the era of slavery through the present and their perpetual existence in a condition best summed up by the trope of the "night." It takes the night to unleash unruly winds and tempests of evil spirits, wreaking so much havoc and pain on those quietly sleeping and unwary that they may wake-up literally dead. Rodrigues is the "wake up" call not to death but to life, as he calls attention to the memories of past "deaths" that need to be confronted so their atrocities are not repeated. Pan-Africanist and Pan-American, Rodrigues is a conscious poet, a cultural producer who recuperates memory as a way of staying alive in the shadow of death that the Afro-Brazilian condition symbolically represents.

Carlos de Assumpção, according to Oswaldo de Camargo, is one representative of the Afro-Brazilian tradition who needs to be celebrated. Critically, sociologically, and culturally, Assumpção is a rebellious poet, one who attacks the injustices against blackness in general and exposes black identity as beautiful in the negritude tradition of Léopold Senghor and Aimé Césaire. In the poems included in *Cadernos negros: Os melhores poemas,* Assumpção addresses the interrelated issues of *quilombo* and Zumbi. In "Batuque" (Percussion), the poet-persona adopts African oral tradition by combining assonance and alliteration in four main words: "quilombo," "tambor" (drum), "batuque," and "tenho" (I have). By repeating these words many times, the poem creates an auditory musical effect that is reminiscent of Mozambican José Craveirinha's "Quero ser tambor" (I Want to Be a Drum). The text is a song of protest and yet of praise and celebration, a clarion call to action and readiness, for whoever has a musical spirit will also be inspired to fight and protest when necessary:

Tenho um tambor	[I have a drum
Tenho um tambor	I have a drum
Tenho um tambor	I have a drum
Tenho um tambor	I have a drum

Dentro do peito	Within my heart
Tenho um tambor. (29)	I have a drum.]

The musicality is inescapable and this is where Assumpção is like few other Afro-Brazilian poets—exceptions being Solano Trindade and Oliveira Silveira who adopt a similar approach in their poetry. Perhaps this musicality also explains why Cuti collaborated with Assumpção to produce a music CD, entitled *Quilombo de Palavras,* its lyrics taken directly from one of Assumpção's poems in *Protesto,* "Meu Quilombo."

Protesto (Protest) embodies many liberation songs that provide strength to the poetic voice as he wanders through life, speaking up against social injustices, and articulating or maintaining a stoic posture against a seemingly invincible and invisible enemy. For Assumpção, the entire world must know that the Afro-Brazilian has a heart like anyone else, and indeed not just any heart but a "heart made of granite" (20). Attacking the mythology of racial democracy and the expectation that the "good" citizen, black or white, must have a white soul, Assumpção sarcastically asks: "Quem já viu a alma algum dia / Pra saber se ela tem cor?" (Who has seen the soul some day / To know that it has a color?). In addition to resistant echoes in many of the poems, the Afro-Brazilian woman is praised in "Mulher negra," in which her gracefulness, laughter, beauty, voice, and walk are each appreciated and celebrated as comprising a total song in the mouth of a passionate lover, it is in "Protesto," the title poem—a long composition which is part history, part declaration—that the poet-persona synthesizes his anguish and the pleasure of protest at the same time:

Mesmo que voltem as costas	[Even if they turn their backs
Às minhas palavras de fogo	On my words of fire
Não pararei de gritar	I will not stop shouting
(…)	(…)
A minha história é contada	My history is told
Com tintas de amargura	With ink of bitterness
(…)	(…)
Eu não quero mais viver	I no longer want to live
No porão da sociedade	In the basement of life
(…)	(…)
E nem a morte terá força	And not even death will have the power
Para me fazer calar. (49)	To silence me.]

The tone of the poem is so reassuring and convincing that through it the poet defies death as a witness of conscience and a victim of injustices who yet refuses to be a victim even in death. Assumpção's declarative voice embodies one of the allegories of Afro-modernity in the sense that the voice of the other is constantly being heard by the promoters of culture thus relegating the "marginal" voice to the zone of forgetfulness and irrelevance.

Regarding this extensive panorama of Afro-Brazilian modernist voices, it is on a sad note that I conclude that the Afro-Brazilian literary tradition continues to be conditioned by the exigencies of mainstream or canonical critical machinery that does not see any value in these cogent and viable cultural productions. The clarity of mind within the walls of prison that Joel Rufino dos Santos expresses, the revolutionary impulses of Éle Semog in his demand for social equality, the diverse manifestations of the *quilombo* in the songs to Palmares that Oliveira Silveira composes, the trope of betrayal aptly demonstrated as the duality of oppression in the Brazil exposed in Lepê Correia's imaginative world, the love for the Afro-Brazilian women painted in the works of Oubi Kibuko as well as other manifestations of protest and black pride by other cultural producers, are significant contributions to Afro-Brazilian modernity, and by extension to the human condition when perceived as an indictment of hate and a conviction of the necessity of love.

13

Ancestral Motherhood of Leci Brandão

> Mangueira made its debut as a samba school in the Carnival of 1930 and has since attracted many illustrious songwriters and singers, including Nelson Sargento, Elza Soares, Alcione, Leci Brandão, and Jamelão.
> —McGowan and Pessanha, *The Brazilian Sound*, 38

To qualify Leci Brandão as an "ancestral mother" is to suggest that she is both successful and powerful. Yet, unlike Daniela Mercury, the Bahian solo performer who has popularized the songs of many Afro-Bahian carnival groups, Leci Brandão's name is still not widely known—but she can no longer be neglected. Continuing the legacy of such eminent singers as Alcione and Beth Carvalho, whose samba lyrics continue to be sung by Brazilians, especially in *pagode* circles, Brandão's lyrical output and political sensibility deserve to be brought to light. Given the limited research done on her to date and the scant bibliographic resources, this essay situates her work within all of Brazilian popular music in order to assess her full import to Brazilian music and specifically her stature as a figurative ancestral mother. Born on September 12, 1944, the daughter of Pérola Negra, one of the leading artists who popularized Brazil *pagode* in Brazil and in the wider world, Leci Brandão da Silva has emerged as a voice of continuity in a musical tradition that is as old as slavery. Although she celebrated twenty-five years of singing samba in 2000[1] and has almost two dozen CDs or LPs to her credit, she is still not as popular as such figures as Martinho da Vila, Beth Carvalho, Aragão, or Alcione. Her performance in 2005 with other major *pagode* talents in *Raça brasileira/Casa do pagode (20 anos)* promised to launch her further into the global spotlight. Indeed, Leci Brandão has a newly released CD and a DVD, namely, *Raízes do Samba* (2007) and *Canções Afirmativas Ao Vivo* (2008), respectively.

For Helena Theodoro, Leci Brandão represents the energy of our mothers, the "great ancestral mothers" who, as sonorous and celestial birds, are able to illuminate our paths.[2] The power of our mothers is perhaps next to the divine, and while Leci Brandão cannot be considered divine except figuratively and musically, the characteristics of *aje,* or our mothers, provide some clues to her ancestrality and immediacy in power and potency of action:

Ìbà ìyàmi òsòròngà
Ati orí jẹ apá
Ati èdò jẹ ọkàn
Ati ìdí jẹ òrónro
Ìbà èyin ìyàmi:
Afínju ẹyẹ tii njẹ loju oloko
Afínju ẹyẹ tii nfiyẹ sapa, tii nfiko sẹhin
Afínju ẹyẹ tii nfegungun sapa tii nfi egungun sẹhin
Afínju ẹyẹ tii nfirin sapa tii nfirin sẹhin
Afínju ẹyẹ tii nfina sapa tii nfina sẹhin.

[Homage to "Iyami Osoronga" [the mother witch of the universe] / She is the spirit that feeds on the flesh of the hand of her victim / from the top down to the base. / She is the spirit that eats both the liver and the heart of her victim / She is the spirit that sucks the gall bladder of her victim through its anus.

Homage to our mother witch: / The beautiful witch bird that feeds in the presence of the owner / The beautiful witch bird with feathers and beak / The beautiful witch bird whose teeth are made of feathers and bones. / The beautiful witch bird whose teeth are made of iron feathers. / The beautiful witch bird with volatile feathers and teeth.][3]

While Theodoro may appear to have overrated Leci Brandão's ingenuity, a cursory analysis of her musical career over the last two decades does confirm her troubled love life combined with the politics of affirmation for her community and people. The enumeration of the qualities of our mothers, or *oríkì,* as in the preceding invocation, equally provides a paradigmatic essence from which to evaluate Brandão's popular music. In Yoruba culture, the spiritual core of diaspora cultures in Brazil, Cuba, the United States, and Trinidad and Tobago, among other countries, to be called an *àjé,* or "mother witch," is indeed to be feared and imbued with awe. As the spirit that practically devours her victims without mercy, she is usually praised in order to be appeased, the same way divinities are traditionally invoked—hence the repeated homage and account of her beauty despite the horrifically destructive actions she is capable of as a "witch bird." In essence, to associate anyone with ancestral motherhood in Yoruba thought is to elevate that person to the realm of the metaphysical, the mysterious, the enigmatic, the spiritual, and the political—for even kings must pay homage to these "mothers" in order to exercise rule over their people; they must acknowledge the presence of the mothers and seek their protection in order to be successful.

Mangueira: Beginnings and Beyond

Mangueira is the foremost *escola de samba* in Rio de Janeiro, which has featured such eminent singers and songwriters as Martinho da Vila, Leci Brandão, and Alcione, among others, during Carnival or special events. As McGowan and Pessanha note in *The Brazilian Sound*, the *escolas de samba* in Rio de Janeiro have evolved since 1928 to be a grand spectacle—with the carnival parades featuring dazzling floats, expensive costumes, thousands of revelers, and many orchestras. Following the founding of the short-lived *Deixar falar* in 1928, Mangueira, the most traditional and long-lived of the samba schools in Rio, was formed. Given the repression of Afro-Brazilian culture at the time, carnival celebrations downtown were discouraged by the police. It was thus within the context of repression that Mangueira emerged as a samba school and a cauldron for the preservation of Afro-Brazilian cultural values. Against this repressive background, it is even more remarkable that Leci Brandão was the first woman to be invited to join Mangueira's composers' section, in 1974.

Brandão's list of accomplishments starts from her teenage years. Her hits include "Antes Que eu volte a ser nada," "Olodum força divina," "Dengue," "Deixa pra lá," "Isso é fundo de quintal," and "Só Quero te namorar," among others, but she actually started composing sambas at age 19. She won many national awards, including a second place award in the Mangueira carnival parade contest for her samba-enredo in 1973. She recorded her first LP, *Antes que eu volte a ser nada*, and had her first national hit in 1980 with "Essa tal criatura." During the years of rejection by recording companies, Brandão intensified her international visibility by doing tours of the United States, Japan, France, Denmark, and Angola. Brandão also toured Brazil with Joyce and the Fundo de Quintal group. In 1988, following *Dignidade* (1987), which had one of her most popular songs, "Só quero te namorar," she recorded *Um beijo no seu coração*, her first gold record, which included "Olodum força divina." In 1990 Brandão received two Sharp Awards for *Cidadã brasileira*, fefaturing "Maravilha: Araketu, semente da memória." Additionally, her hits include "Café com pão," and "Papai vadiou."

In his own review of Brandão's performance, Jon Pareles hears the voice of a "pensive sensuality"—a characterization that captures the duality and ambivalence of the musician's fluidity. He goes on to say:

> Ms. Brandão's voice is low and husky; when she sings ballads, she has a pensive sensuality. But most of her set was up-tempo; her feet were almost always dancing in small, precise steps. When not performing her own songs, Ms. Brandão drew on the songs of the *blocos Afros*—huge community drumming and singing groups—of Bahia. Those songs have a martial swing and lyrics that address political and cultural concerns.[4]

While it is abundantly clear that Brandão's music comes from the heart, that her passion for love and politics is unmistakable, she is also quite philosophical in her acute perceptions of basic things of life that only someone who has experienced struggles can feel and communicate with such ease and understanding. The ability to sing about quotidian issues and yet find morality and amusement in them, despite the intense pain in some cases, is an indication of a sensitive artist. That sensitivity pervades a number of songs over the course of Brandão's career, such as "Negro Zumbi," "Rebeldia," "Sou Negão," "Casa Grande e Senzala," and "Batida no Coração." Underlying the pain in the lyrics are tributes to Afro-Brazilian heroes, affirmation, social criticism, rebelliousness, a search for peace, and a general sense of celebration—like a bird that instead of complaining about what it lacks, reaches for higher planes where peace and pleasure abound. Brandão's "Batida no coração" (Beat of the Heart) captures what can be considered her artistic impulse:

> Enquanto estiver batendo o coração
> Faço um canto popular. . . . pra agitar esta nação
> . . . . Podem perseguir minha cultura
> Dou um jeito com ternura, pela arte vou lutar[5]

> [As long as the heart beats / I sing a popular song to shake up this nation / . . . / You can persecute my culture / With tenderness and art, I choose to struggle.]

Although this song may be seen as simple and direct, its political implication against oppression is deep. By fighting social justice through her music, Leci Brandão is using her art as a political weapon of change.

On a personal level, Brandão critiques rebelliousness that hurts the other lover as opposed to a constructive sense of disagreement among lovers, as in "Rebeldia"; in this, she reveals her sensitivity and vulnerability when it comes to love. This same obsessive voice of love and passion becomes political when she evokes Zumbi, in "Negro Zumbi" (Black Zumbi), the leader of the Palmares settlement, praising his faith, courage, and glory in the midst of painful struggle:

> Contra a força inimiga
> A defesa da família
> Lá na Serra da Barriga
> Permanente uma vigícia . . .
> Negro Zumbi, negro Zumbi
> Negro Zumbi, negro Zumbi[6]

[Against the enemy force / The family defense / Over there in Serra da Barriga / The vigil was permanent . . . / Black Zumbi, black Zumbi / Black Zumbi, black Zumbi]

Brandão's humble beginnings in the favela and her struggles to ascend socially and move her family out of the slum did not sever or inhibit her connections with that same community, in which she remains well rooted. As appreciative as she is of her roots, she critiques the contradictions of the racism that pervades Brazilian society in the metaphor of "Casa grande e senzala" (Masters and the Slaves), in which she ridicules the double standard inherent in the attempt to live in two worlds in Brazil:

Nos salões elegantes
Dançavam sinhá, damas e senhores
E nas senzalas os escravos
Cantavam batucando seus tambores.[7]

[In elegant saloons / Madams, masters, and ladies danced / And in the shacks, the slaves / Sang, beating the drums.]

Brandão's sense of origins and identity is further highlighted in "Sou negão" (I Am Truly Black), where she pays homage to black achievements all over the world, including those of Bob Marley, Bezerra da Silva, Pelé, soul singer Bob King, Malcolm X, Djavan, Gilberto Gil, Sandra Sá, and Zumbi—defending black pride and condemning stereotypes of marginality and danger with which Afro-Brazilians and blacks in general have been associated. These lyrics provide a window into the ideological and artistic commitment of Leci Brandão.

The Mystery of Happiness within Social (Dis)organization: *Eu Sou Assim*

Given Brandão's tendency to reinsert old hits into her newer albums, *Eu sou assim* (The Way I Am), released in 2000, may well be considered as a synthesis or commemoration of her musical career. While lacking apparent systematic organization, an internal framing is notable as in the homage paid to a veteran *pagodista*, Martinho da Vila, in the opening song and to Afro-Brazilian carnival groups in Bahia in the closing. Brandão bridges generations while reaching out to younger people. The album comprises seventeen cuts, from which seven thematic concerns may be discerned: love and passion, family values, role models and socialization, native values of the Brazilian Indian, youth and the limits of freedom, Candomblé, and the Afro-Brazilian community and its leadership. Brandão's ideological mission seems to have come full circle in this paradigmatic recording. The circular frame between Martinho da Vila and the Afro-Bahian carnival groups equally approximates the message and mission of *pagode* and Afro-Bahian *Carnival*.[8]

During an extensive interview with Brandão, the artist comments on the sacrifices of being ideologically committed to the Afro-Brazilian cause, and on the suggestion that she has not been as successful as other musicians because she insists on being politically militant in her own way. To a question about what she thinks of the image of blacks on television, she responds rather comprehensively about the larger issues of invisibility and marginalization:

> Não entendo por que as outras pessoas não se sensibilizam. Uma vez, bateram no meu ombro, dizendo assim: "Sabe por que você não explode? Tem que largar essa negrada para lá, tem que fazer o seu trabalho e esquecer isso, senão você fica visada." Fui muito cobrada, muito marcada, estigmatizada por causa dessa minha luta. Saí na frente mandando ver, há muito tempo. Hoje, tem gente nova chegando. Tem um povo jovem bem consciente. Fico muito feliz de ver. Não só no plano artístico como fora também, nas ONGs em geral. Tem muita associação comunitária fazendo coisas legais. Às vezes, também leio entrevistas com cantoras negras, o pessoal de *rap* lá de São Paulo. Tem muita menina do *hip hop* falando coisas maravilhosas.[9]

> [I don't understand why others are not sensitive and conscious. Once, I was tapped on the shoulder and told: "You know why you are not as successful? You need to leave these black folks alone, just do your work and forget about this issue; otherwise you will be stigmatized." I have paid so such a price for my belief and struggles. I have been stigmatized and marginalized. I have been in the forefront for quite a while. Today, a new crop of people are coming along. There are very conscious young people. I am happy to see that this is the case. Not only on the artistic level, but also beyond and in the NGOs [nongovernmental organizations] in general. There are many community organizations doing great things. At times I read about black women singers in the newspapers; about rap folks in São Paulo. There are many young women saying marvelous things.]

This interview reveals a deeper side of Brandão that may be glossed over in her lyrics—perhaps in her attempt to reach a wider audience in a country she sees as guilty of miscegenation; hence all races must be included in the discussion of racism and exclusionism.

As clearly ideological as Brandão is in real life and in her subtle politics of protest against injustices, her most recurrent thematic concerns continue to be love and passion. About half of *Eu sou assim* deals, in one way or anther, with love. When considered within the *pagode* genre, the theme of love is what conquers all hardships and the poverty typical of slum life so familiar to the majority of Afro-Brazilians. The ability to love, to sing about love, is a therapeutic way to overcome painful memories and daily deprivations that Afro-Brazilians suffer silently. Singers of *pagode* see this samba genre as a way to adapt their music to their modest means as opposed to the more sophisticated and exuberant instrumentations of the bigger *escolas de samba* with whom they compete indirectly and inadvertently.[10] Perhaps this is why *pagode* is considered the more traditional and more localized form of samba. Perhaps it was no coincidence that the very first song on the album is a medley celebrating at least three hits by Martinho da Vila, a veteran *pagodista*—"Canta, canta minha gente," "Quem é do mar não enjoa," and "Casa de Bamba." This strategic homage may well be considered as an *oríkì* (praise-poetry). By referring to "minha gente" (my people) in her appeal to the neighborhood, the city, and the country, Brandão calls on the entire nation to heal sadness with happiness by singing and hoping for a better future:

Canta, canta, minha gente
Deixa tristeza pra lá
Canta forte, canta alto
Que a vida vai melhorar.
Mas a vida . . . vai melhorar[11]

[Sing, sing, my people / Let go of sadness / Sing passionately, sing loudly / And life will get better / I am sure . . . life will get better.]

Beyond this introductory celebration of life in the midst of sadness, the issues of love and passion resonate throughout *Eu sou assim*, such as in "Café com pão," "Eu só quero te namorar," "Fogueira de uma paixão," "Jeito de amar," "Meu oceano," "Barco a vela," "Lua diamante," "Você pode ceder," and "Valeu demais." In the first, the lover offers food to her lover while in the second, she asks for every opportunity to express her love. The third captures the singer's desire to live in a fantasy world of pure and romantic love, while the fourth she invokes more fantasies in a prescribed manifesto of love found only in the waves of the salty ocean. The remaining songs evoke memories of past happiness and effort to relive them through a journey in a candlelit boat of love in which the face of the lover is envisioned in the moon. Ultimately, the imaginative love escapade is seen as a marvelous journey that the singer-lover would rather not let go.

Despite the pain, the anguish, the homesickness, the frustrated dreams, a certain hope is present, a revitalizing element that keeps the lover even more determined to keep up the search for the lost or estranged love. If "Fogueira de uma paixão" (Fireplace of a Lover) describes the passionate preparations of a lover for a missed lover through an exteriorized affection and intimacy,

"Jeito de amar" (Way of Loving) advocates for happiness where there is love, while "Lua diamante" (Diamond-like Moon) relies on the face of the lover for her strength. It is in "Barco a vela" (Candlelight Boat) that one finds a committed lover who will go to any length and pay any price to be reunited with her lover.

While the personal love life of Leci Brandão is unknown or at least not public, she is not necessarily a melancholic person. Yet, issues of self-esteem and female empowerment resonate equally in her music, such as on *Autoestima* (Self-Esteem) and *Cidadã brasileira* (Brazilian Female Citizen), making us wonder if love for Brandão is not a general language of peace, acceptance, and solidarity with all humanity. As she speaks about the younger generation, about the oppressed, about women, and about the Afro-Brazilian community, Brandão seems to have reached the crossroads of her professional and personal search for validation under the rubric of love. Using "Barco a vela" as a case study, we may be able to reach certain preliminary conclusions about the presence or absence of love in Brandão.

Constructed as a ballad, a love song to a loved one, "Barco a vela" may well be an imaginary trip taken in order to exorcise the pain and burden of an absent lover. The idea of taking a trip on the sea is a self-conscious undertaking—one that requires sacrifices of time and emotions. While there is no guarantee that this trip will deliver the loved one, the process is at least therapeutic, that the lover will feel better about herself after this self-imposed journey. A metaphor for a love paradise that is seemingly elusive, the candlelit boat dramatizes the lover's inner wishes, using the romantic scenery to alleviate the pain:

> Pego um barco a vela entro pelo mar vejo gaivotas que voam que voam
> Que voam na minha cabeça
> Olho para o lado vejo o horizonte olho para o sol que queima que queima
> Que queima que queima meu rosto.[12]

> [I get on the candlelit boat; through the sea, I see seagulls flying and flying / Flying in my head / I look to the side, I see the horizon; I look at the sun, burning and burning / Burning and burning my face.]

The idea that seagulls are flying in the head of the singer-personage indicates a state of anxiety, confusion, and agitation. Everywhere she turns, whether sideways or into the future, there is a price to pay. The pain of the sun scorching her body, the psychological impasse and hurt from her loneliness without her lover—the trip may not resolve these but may merely alleviate the anguish. Taking the boat at night also speaks to a sense of mystery and self-imposed suffering as if the personage is taking deliberate risks in order to "find" her lover by any means necessary.

As the music progresses, the lyrics become even romantic as the singer/lover turns to nature to find the love that eludes her in real life. Through this synesthetic process, the singer uses the portrait of her lover to find an analogy between the beauty of nature, as in the sea and the nocturnal scenery, and that of the missed lover:

Maravilha beleza esse mar que linda é a natureza
Ô ô ô beleza esse mar que linda é a natureza
Pego o teu retrato fico comparando sinto a tua falta que falta me faz tanto
Como é bom sonhar com você como é bom estar com você
Isso me fascina.[13]

[What a marvelous beauty, this sea; what beautiful nature / Oh! Oh! Oh! What a beauty, this sea; what beautiful nature / I pick up your portrait, and as I compare, I feel your absence, I miss you so much / How nice to dream with you; how nice to be with you / I am fascinated by this.]

The duality of lover/lover of nature qualifies Brandão as a romantic poet—one who is able to find solace in nature in the absence of physical love. Through dreams and fantasies, through fantastical journeys and escapist lyrical invocations, Brandão steps into the realm of the supernatural where as an ancestral mother she can reach beyond the physical plane to the celestial or even subaltern spaces in order to recover her lover. Unlike Orpheus's descent into hell, his need to die in order to see his Eurydice once again, Brandão's choice is to live through fantasies and mysterious rituals that only the sea and the sky can bridge toward a new beginning of hope. Brandão succeeds in distracting her own anguish by the therapeutic presence of nature which she calls "marvelous beauty."

Love, as the element that overcomes all odds, can only be learned from the formative years of youth. Beyond love and passion, Brandão revisits family values as the point of departure to the development of her own personality. Two songs best illustrate these values: "Papai vadiou" (Daddy Perambulates) and "As coisas que mamãe me ensinou" (Things That Mommy Taught Me). Both cuts give the audience a window into the family life of the singer in her characterization of her father as a "perambulator-dancer," and her mother as her first teacher who taught her about manners, respect, courtesy, greetings, and an overall sense of decency and humanity.

At first listening, "Papai vadiou" chronicles a happy family setting where father and mother are having fun by dancing to *pagode*, each one appealing to the other in a rhythmic endless tango, since *pagode* always lasts till daybreak:

Mas papai vadiou mamãe gostou
Papai vadiou mamãe gostou

Papai vadiou mamãe gostou
Por isso eu aqui estou
Mais quero ver você sambar
Como sambou papai
Quero ver você dançar
Como dançou mamãe.[14]

[But daddy perambulated, mommy loved it / Daddy perambulated, mommy loved it / Daddy perambulated, mommy loved it / That is why I am here / I want to see you dance samba / Just as daddy danced samba / I want to see you dance / Just as mommy danced.]

At a second listening, the dance between mother and father must be seen as a figurative sexual act, for the singer then says, "That is why I am here"—as if to suggest that the result of the "dance" between both parents led to her birth. Such a cryptic and figurative exploration of birth as a result of a samba dance confirms Brandão as a philosophical singer.

Another critical song that explores family values is "As coisas que mamãe me ensinou." In this homage to motherhood, Brandão asks her audience to actually give a round of applause to mothers, saying that it is an emotional subject for her:

A mãe da gente
A mãe da gente . . . é um caso diferente
Muito mais que comovente, que não dá pra comprar
. . . .
Um bom dia, boa tarde
Com licença, por favor
Tudo isso é resultado das coisas
Que mamãe me ensinou. . . . (*Eu Sou Assim* Track #3)

[One's mother / One's mother . . . is a whole different matter / More than an emotional matter, is not easy to come by / .Good morning, good afternoon / Excuse me, please / All of this is the result of the things / That Mommy taught me. . . .]

Overall, the value of motherhood is placed on a pedestal, as the main source of family nurturing that gave her the fundamental values about life and survival.

Following the focus on family values, Brandão moves into another realm of socialization, that of the value of teachers in her life. Calling teachers "Anjos da guarda" (Guardian Angels) in a song of the same title, the singer praises teachers for their knowledge and power to transform a nation. The singer sees the classroom as an invaluable setting of producing leaders and productive citizens. For her, the quality of being a guardian angel ensures that the opportunity to better oneself is provided to all without respect for ethnicity, race, color, or belief system. The entire song is a call to respect teachers:

> Professores
> Protectores das crianças do meu país
> . . . . . .
> Na sala de aula
> Que se muda uma nação
> . . . . . .
> Batam palmas pra ele
> Que ele merece.[15]

[Teachers / Protectors of the children of my country / . . . / It's in the classroom / That a nation is transformed / . . . / Clap for them / For they deserve it.]

From birth to learning family values and social values through schooling, Brandão's formative years are laid out as a basis to talk about social issues in Brazil through popular music.

Interestingly, as ideologically committed as Brandão is to Afro-Brazilian culture, she takes time to sing about the native values of the Brazilian Indian through their special purple berry fruit, the *açai*, a fruit found in the Amazon rain forest that has now become a Brazillian "power drink." Considered the "tree of life" that gives passion or enhances it, this fruit is used to express a constant in the singer's music—love. Yet, the symbolism of "Sabor açai" (Açai Flavor) goes beyond an aphrodisiac, as the *açai* seems to represent satisfaction, deliciousness, and good taste—for it is a fruit that nourishes "the passion of our people." The singer describes it as a blessed goddess, a fruit whose plants beautify and adorn the neighborhood; and ultimately, she declares herself a "Marajuara flavor" as if suggesting her sweetness and deliciousness as a human being.[16]

But Brandão's sweetness is not limited to invoking the metaphor of delicacy; it also reaches out to the freedom accorded to the young ones. In "Menor abandonado" (Abandoned Youngster) and "Deixa deixa" (Leave Them Alone), Brandão evokes the plight of Brazilian children in general. While abandoned children are obliged to sleep under traffic bridges and survive at the mercy of passers-by who often ridicule them, this image of social squalor indicts the lack or insufficiency of social services in Brazil and also reflects a larger social dilemma faced by young people. In a twist of consciousness, the abandoned persona ponders what will become of him if he is to remain under the bridge; instead, he resolves to take his destiny in his own hands:

Quero estudar, me formar
Ter um lar pra viver
E apagar essa má impressão
Que em mim você vê.[17]

[I want to study and graduate / Have a place to live / And erase this negative impression / You have of me.]

When compared to "Deixa deixa," which advocates more freedom for the youth, "Menor abandonado" seems to be more demanding in terms of attributing responsibility. By desiring to study and make a good life for himself, the abandoned youngster has come to a state of consciousness in identifying his problem in order to solve it. By contrast, "Deixa deixa" is actually a plea to adults to give youngsters a break in order to keep them from being a danger to the society. Emphasizing that it is preferable for children to have the freedom they need so they don't become angry and hurt innocent people, Brandão may be tactfully presenting the extreme situation and the threat these youngsters constitute to the larger society. By indulging them, the singer hopes that they will grow, become wiser, and end up learning to make better choices in life:

Deixa ele beber, deixa ele fumar, deixa ele jogar
É melhor do que ele sacar uma arma pra nos matar
Deixa ele assumir, deixa ele transar, deixa ele amar
É melhor do que ele sacar uma arma pra nos matar
Deixa ele fazer tudo . . .

[Let them drink, let them smoke, let them play / Better than for them to use a weapon to kill us / Let them be responsible, let them have sex, let them love / Better than for them to use a weapon to kill us / Let them do everything . . .]

Brandão's logic of unlimited indulgence is certainly questionable, for in the final analysis, overindulgence may well lead to a crisis that may be irreversible and may even worsen the conditions of the youngsters, especially if they have to learn the hard way either in prison, through punishment, or worse. On a deeper level, the attitude of "letting them loose" is also paradoxical as if suggesting that life will teach them, that it is the best teacher. In essence, the singer is of the attitude that there is no point in trying to prevent them from making mistakes and lose one's own life in the process. It is best that these youngsters learn on their own even if that means suffering what could be avoided such as their own loss of freedom or life.

It is inconceivable that Brandão could sustain her energy of artistic production and coping strategies with other social pressures without some amount of spiritual strength. While this study has invoked her ancestral motherhood as a source of strength, a compliment indeed for an Afro-Brazilian who is already immersed in Candomblé and ecumenical religiosity without any contradictions, Brandão's spirituality must be seen as an agency through which she conducts her life makes and music. To a question about the role of religiosity in her life, she responded during an interview:

> Sempre acreditei em religião. . . . Foi muito importante para mim. Essa coisa de eu gravar em homenagem a um Orixá foi por causa do Seu Rei das Ervas, entidade com a qual ela trabalhava. Ela faleceu, mas minha relação com a casa continua a mesma. Descobri que sou filha de Ogun com Yansã, comecei a cuidar dos meus santos, das minhas obrigações. Não sou fanática, mas faço isso com a maior seriedade. Meu CD Dignidade foi dedicado a Yansã; Um beijo no seu coração, que me deu o primeiro disco de ouro, foi para Ogun, o dono da minha cabeça.[18]

> [I have always believed in religion. . . . It was very important to me. This idea of releasing an album in homage to an òrìṣà (god or goddess) was because of *Seu rei das ervas* (god of the leaves), the religious entity that she (Mother Alice) attended. She passed away but my connection with the entity remains the same. I found out that I am daughter of Ògún and Oya, and started observing my religious rites and duties. I am not fanatical, but I do this with all seriousness. My CD *Dignidade* (Dignity) was dedicated to Oya. Bless Ògún's heart, the owner of my head-destiny, for giving me my first golden album. It was dedicated to Ògún.]

Judging by this interview, the homage to Osanyin[19] and Agemọ[20] at the end of the album is remarkable, for Osanyin is the Yoruba god of healing and the entire album is therapeutic in its multidimensionality while the Agemọ invocation relates to a masquerade that women are forbidden to see. The combination speaks to the ancestral motherhood and strength with which Brandão has forged her musical essences. In the rendition of the Agemọ chant, the rhythm changes from that of *pagode* to that of *Ijesa*,[21] a rhythm typical of the Nago-Jeje nation of Candomblé. The lyrics are also non-Portuguese, sung in classical and corrupted Yoruba:

Agemo wina parada
Agemo wina parada
Ewe ewe ewe
Ta ba nisoro a daba
Ossain ye—Oro ye o

Ossain ye—Oro ye o
Ossain é de mokoso—Ossain ye.[22]

[Agemọ, transform yourself / Agemọ, transform yourself / Leaves, leaves, leaves—oracle of divination / When we are in difficulty, we consult / All hail Osanyin! Here is the issue! / All hail Osanyin! Here is the problem! / Only you can reveal to us. Osanyin please!][23]

In dedicating the album to Osanyin, Brandão has asked for revelation, healing, and success all at the same time—not just for herself but for all those who buy and listen to her album. It is in this blend of artistry, religiosity, and ancestral strength that Brandão sets herself apart as a Brazilian popular musical voice worthy of closer analysis and appreciation.

Brandão and Afro-Brazilian Carnival Groups: From Mangueira to Olodum to Ara Ketu

For Leci Brandão, who grew up around samba schools in Rio de Janeiro and started her professional career in Mangueira, it must have been a transition to be performing with Afro-Bahian carnaval groups such as Olodum and Araketu. There is no question that the singer is well rooted within the Afro-Brazilian community and has also had a stint as a candidate for political office although she did not win. Community leadership has become an added function for carnival groups in Salvador since they were initially set up to fight racism and to educate. Over the years these groups have become business organizations, having to create their own shows, prepare seminars, publish educational materials, honor social engagements, develop young men and women in the music business, and ultimately prepare for carnival parades. Within this context, Brandão's "Zé do Caroço" (John Stone) reflects the values of leadership of this hardworking and considerate resident of the Pau da Bandeira neighborhood in Rio de Janeiro. A bold and charismatic figure, Zé do Caroço announced publicly that he would cause commotion in the community in order to protest for better conditions. Wishing there were other Zé do Caroços in Mangueira who would have his courage, Brandão sings:

O Zé do Caroço trabalha
O Zé do Caroço batalha
. . . . .
Ele quer ver o bem da favela
Está nascendo um novo líder
No morro do Pau da Bandeira.

[Zé do Caroço works hard / Zé do Caroço struggles well / . . . / He wants the best for the slum / A new leader is emerging / In the Pau da Bandeira neighborhood.]

The leadership qualities of the iconic Zé do Caroço are found equally in the Afro-Bahian carnival groups such as Ilê-Aiyê, Badawê, Olodum, and Araketu. As a Rio artist, Brandão's participation in the Bahian musical scene is extraordinary in the sense that it unites the Afro-Brazilian community symbolically while also giving her more visibility as an artist whose fame has now become national.

From its very first line, the song creates a melody that is totally different from that of *pagode;* although instruments can still be heard in the background, the voiced rhythm is essentially that of Afro-Bahian Carnival. In "Olodum, Força Divina" (Olodum, Divine Energy), the singer pays tribute to Olodum as a revolutionary entity that promotes survival, dignity, and humanity, seeing the group as a kind of rainbow spreading over the people:

Olodum, Força Divina Da Fonte Da Vida
Que Com Seus Mistérios
Traz encantamentos Pro Nosso Cantar
. . . .
Olodum Representa a Cultura.[24]

[Olodum, divine energy of the source of life / Who with its mysteries / Brings enchantments to our songs /. . . . / Olodum represents culture.]

The next song on the CD dedicated to Ara Ketu, another significant Afro-Bahian carnival group in Bahia. In "Deus do fogo e da justiça" (God of Fire and Justice), obviously making reference to Ṣàngó, the singer pays homage to the mythological cradle of civilization in Ile-Ife as well as to the òrìṣàs, whose traditions Ara Ketu is promoting in its social, cultural, and political activities:

Gerado Vou Cantar No Meu Ifé
A Palavra Mais Justa De Um Rei
No Seu Culto de Candomblé
. . . . . .
Se Você Ainda Não Sabe
Agora Eu Vou Revelar
Falará No Ara Ketu.[25]

[Now mature, I am going to sing of my Ife / The ultimate just word of a king / In his Candomblé association / . . . / If you still don't know / I am now going to reveal the mysteries / I will speak about Ara Ketu.]

In essence, Ara Ketu is exalted as a leader in the cultural preservation of Candomblé rites during Afro-Bahian Carnival. While both of these cuts give more prominence to the Afro-Bahian Carnival through these two groups, they are not the only musical groups that promote African culture and defend the Afro-Brazilian community against discrimination and racism.

Another significant musical group to which Brandão pays homage is Fundo de Quintal.[26] The refrain says it all, posing a rhetorical question that is simultaneously answered in order to indicate the importance of the group:

> O que é isso meu amor?
> Venha me dizer ...
> Isso é Fundo de Quintal, é pagode pra valer![27]
>
> [What is this about my beloved? / Come and tell me ... / It is Fundo de Quintal in action!]

In lauding one of the best *pagode* bands in Brazil, the singer revives the origins of this musical form that was born not in competition with commercialized samba, which was becoming elusive to smaller groups in terms of recording and performing possibilities, but in the backyards of the city. The group embodies the possibility of dancing and singing for fun without any inhibitions or concerns for either censorship or promotion. On the whole, Brandão's album, *Eu sou assim*, is a multifaceted live show that synthesizes the career of this compelling and underrated heroine of Brazilian *pagode*.

The House of *Pagode*: A Collective Celebration

Marking twenty years of samba by such Brazilian greats as Beth Carvalho, Arlindo Cruz, Cassiana (daughter of Jovelina Perola Negra), Almir Guineto, Fundo de Quintal, Iceia (daughter of Zeca Pagodinho), and Leci Brandão, *Raça brasileira* proves to be a collective homecoming for many of these artists as the ambience of festivity and harmony is re-created in the overflowing hall.[28] In a musical parade of at least three generations—singers, soloists, percussionists, flutists, chorus, and audience—everyone seems to be having fun and making the most of this unique moment celebrating *pagode*. The DVD is consistently entertaining, and not just to the audience; one performance after another revisits such themes as love, passion, nostalgia, melancholy, happiness, and social criticism—demonstrating remarkable gifts of storytelling mixed with self-ridicule. The entire show has a carnival-like atmosphere, as if for *pagode*, every day is a celebration.

Of the nineteen sessions, Leci Brandão participates in the penultimate track—three songs in succession—with Cassiana.

In the tripartite performance, covering "Pomba Rolou," Feirinha da Pavuna," and "Bagaço da Laranja," Brandão shares the stage with an equally electrifying Cassiana. It is remarkable that when Brandão steps onto the stage, she does a ritual blessing by touching the floor of the stage and then her own forehead as if to ask the earth to bless the performance, proof of her connectedness with her ancestors. Brandão's songs seem to recap themes similar to those explored by previous performers, such as Beth Carvalho, who says:

Sou a raça brasileira
sou chão, sou pó, sou poeira
sou filha deste porão
vou mostrar que o morro também tem direito à felicidade.[29]

[I am Brazilian race / I am the floor, the powder, the dust / I am the daughter of this basement of life / I am going to prove that the slum also has the right to be happy.]

In addition, the Fundo de Quintal band sings of the child asking her reveling mother where she put his toys; the Partideiros no Cacique sing about a Maria who left her lover/naval officer because she could not handle the long separation and homesickness any longer; and Mauro Diniz, Ircéa, and Cassiana protest the absence of running water in the slum:

Toma banho na chuveira
Você sabe que no morro
Não há água de torneira.[30]

[Take your shower in the rain / You know that in the slum / We do not have pipe-borne water.]

Pagode in this sense can be considered "roots-samba," for the performers are singing of events that are close to the heart, issues that bother them but for which they have no practical solutions; instead of losing their minds over these problems, they put them to song as a form of therapy or a way of coping.

The three windows into Afro-Brazilian culture all relate to folklore and survival—namely, musical space, market space, and party space—an indication indeed that Afro-Brazilians see festivity as an important coping strategy for their own spiritual balance. In the first track of *Casa do Pagode* (House of Pagode), "Pomba rolou" (Fooled by the Parrot), a generally festive atmosphere is ruined by a dubious character who is literally "fooled by the parrot" in the sense that the party spoiler must have been deceived. If he had heard true music, he would not have been a spoiler. He crashed the party and spoiled it because he thought he heard noise. This implies that the spoiler is not a true lover of music:

Pagode estava bem animado
Todo mundo contando refrão
Estava tudo certo, tudo estava bom
Chegou um sujeito . . .
Daí então foi que tudo virou um balolo[31]

[*Pagode* was very electrifying / Everyone was singing along the chorus / All was well, all was great / A spoiler arrived . . . / Then everything turned upside down.]

While the first song is about confusion, the next track is equally about causing confusion in an already busy environment such as the open market. As in the previous track, all was going well until Magdalena steps into the market to disrupt the peace by knocking over the pepper as if she is trying to get the attention of the market folk. In both cases, invisibility and marginality force the party spoiler and Margarida to act in strange ways:

Na feirinha da pavuna
Houve uma grande confusão
Magdalena chegou
Dava um tapa no pimentão
Eu também faço parte deste tempero[32]

[In the Pavuna open market
Some confusion took place
When Magdalena arrived
She suddenly spilled the hot pepper
I am also part of the seasoning, she says.]

'In "Bagaço da laranja" [Orange Peels], the third song of the tripartite potpourri of marginality and invisibility, the "spoiler" in this context feels disillusioned once the good times are over. This frustrated figure's dilemma and regret is similar to that felt by most Afro-Brazilians as they grapple with exclusion in a society that claims they are included Feeling "left over" is a perfect metaphor for those disenfranchised from economic and political participation. In describing his melancholy, the persona of the story is dealing with a painful but ironic situation where everything good, from food to good music, was no longer available; all that remained was useless trash:

Acabou a comida
Acabou o pagode
Acabou a bebida
Sobrou pra mim
O bagaço da laranja[33]

[All the food was gone
The *pagode* music was over
The bottles were empty
All that was left for me
Were the orange peels.]

In this panoramic view of the challenges faced by Afro-Brazilians in their daily living, the *Casa do pagode* sings of pain and calls for intervention by exposing innermost feelings and the secret burdens that Afro-Brazilians carry. Yet, the joyfulness and sense of triumph is unmistakable, and therein perhaps lies the beauty of being able to sing to relieve the pain. The invocation of "ancestral motherhood" at the beginning of this study was hypothetical given its deep meaning beyond African origins to the realm of spirituality, gender, and the politics of empowerment. Yet, after coming full circle in the analysis of Brandão's musical career, with special focus on *Eu sou assim* and *Casa do pagode,* one can assert that Brandão has reached a milestone and owes that success to the strength of our mothers as well as to her own faith in her capacities. In connecting her music to Afro-Brazilian community issues, Brandão truly represents the best of ancestral motherhood and strength.

Conclusion

The Future of Afro-Brazilian Cultural Production

In 1997, Spike Lee gave an exclusive interview to *Raça* (Race), an Afro-Brazilian magazine, in Brooklyn, New York, at his 40 Acres & A Mule Filmworks studio. Lee provides his thoughts on his emergence as an American icon who influenced race relations in the film industry, as well as his views on Brazilian racial democracy, especially during his visit to Brazil with Michael Jackson:

> *Raça:* What was your impression about the situation of blacks in Brazil?
>
> Lee: Everyone tries to project the image that Brazilians are just one, same, and united people under one country but I don't think this is the truth. It is easy to see that blacks are in the lowest level in the society and white descendants are found on the top of the social pyramid. There is something faulty over there . . .
>
> *Raça:* What about the issue of racism in Brazil?
>
> Lee: I would say racism is prevalent but Brazilians act as though it does not exist. They are just deceiving themselves. (*Raça* 11 [July 1997]: 14)

This interview, while revealing views of Afro-Brazilians from an African American perspective, also proves the point that such North American–South American exchanges are fundamentally crucial in order to begin to move toward a transformative model for Brazil's dilemma. The African American experience may not make an ideal or perfect comparison to the Afro-Brazilian, but it does provide a case of generally successful struggle for racial equality.

The future of Afro-Brazilians in a country that continues to embrace and live the lie of racial democracy rests on correcting that "something" that has been faulty for several centuries. To talk about an uncertain future when the current achievements in the area of social change regarding the elusive place and dignity of Afro-Brazilians in Brazilian society are rather minimal, is to simplify the situation by insisting, as do many with the official perspective on racial democracy, that all it takes is the will to want to mix racially to solve the complex racial, social, economic, and political problems. Yet, in spite of their exclusion and marginalization from political power, Afro-Brazilians must be commended for maintaining that vital force that translates into artistic and political strategies of articulation and subversion in the face of oppression. Of utmost importance are the cultural strategies. I have elaborated some of these strategies from many perspectives of Afro-Brazilian cultural production, in order to establish transatlantic connections linking two worlds that are kin yet separated by accidents of history, performance, and celebration, as well as a critique of the fragmented images of the Afro-Brazilian as projected on the Brazilian screen and television. What is clearly missing in the racial debate in Brazil is captured in the cogency of the Spike Lee interview and its suggestion that "there is something faulty there" and that "they are just deceiving themselves," which by itself, translates as a lack of political presence and visibility for Afro-Brazilians as well as the denial of racism in Brazil When this analysis is contextualized to the current state of political affairs in Brazil, it is safe to say that despite the few strides made in terms newly introduced Affirmative Action and educational policies, significant structural changes are yet to be seen that will change the marginal world of Afro-Brazilians as we currently know it. For instance, of the few visibly "black" government officials in the Lula government in recent years, Benedita da Silva, now ex-Minister for Social Work, was indicted for exaggerated professional misconduct in 2004 and has since been ousted in shame, Gilberto Gil, now ex-Minister of Culture, resigned in 2008, and Matilde Ribeiro, now ex-Minister of Racial Equality, was equally accused of professional misconduct or abuse of public office which forced her to resign in 2008.

With the exception of Gilberto Gil who left the government voluntarily by claiming to want to return to his artistic passion (music), others were publicly humiliated and technically forced to resign. The issue here is not about condoning corruption, but as far as public opinion goes, it is more of the fact that the treatment of the respective cases and outcome would have been different had the ministers not been Afro-Brazilians, that is, had they been white Brazilians. It is indeed suggested that it is a "skin thing" and that what the Lula government wanted were the seats of these ministers. Their trumped up charges were only convenient excuses to ridicule and get rid of them. The downfall of these ministers may actually have something to do with the stigma of color in Brazil. What has not been made public is that some of these "racial, ethnic, or social welfare" ministries were starved of funds and could not accomplish much even though they were under pressure to justify their existence or be abolished or replaced. If these public humiliations are the lot of the few elected black public officials, one wonders what the motivation will then be for any future aspiring Afro-Brazilian politicians since they can basically learn from their predecessors that representing their people in government is one thing, the fear of public shame is another. This political synthesis partly explains why political participation has continued to be elusive since Afro-Brazilian cultural producers are still limited in their aspiration for political power. In the meantime, the reality is that the corridors of power for Afro-Brazilians are still confined to the cultural space.

The fact that a Spike Lee has yet to arise in Brazil testifies to the urgency of the situation and the enormity of the task ahead. In a country where one still needs to preach the beauty of one's color and to demand equal opportunities and access to education, public forums, and dignified work environments, where racially mixed individuals still see themselves as "superior" and "more beautiful" than their black brothers and sisters, a balance sheet of achievements resembles a reenactment of that "eternal childhood" captured in the figure of *Macunaíma*, as if the Afro-Brazilian needs help to grow up and develop. But for how long? The Yorubas have a saying: "Nígbàtí a bá fi ọdún mẹ̀wá pilè werè, nígbà wo ni a fẹ́ bu igi jẹ?"—that is, "When one spends an eternity learning the art of insanity, how much longer will it take to profess it?" I ask how long because Afro-Brazilians are still celebrating such achievements as being able to get an education, being able to write about themselves, being able to set up a magazine similar to the American *Ebony* such as *Raça*, and being able to be visible in popular culture other than by playing such demeaning roles as cooks, wet nurses, maids, and in some cases, slaves on screen. Understandable as the slow-but-steady journey may be, such self-fulfilling celebrations of derogatory roles assigned to Afro-Brazilians on the screen are still subtly present but gradually changing—not because the popular cultural machine wants to change—but because actors and actresses are demanding genuinely representative roles, and because it is in bad taste in the twenty-first century to celebrate slavery and racism.

The future requires a coordinated partnership between progressive entities not only in Brazil but in the diaspora. The visit of Spike Lee and Michael Jackson to Brazil imply connections between Afro-Brazilians and African Americans that need strengthening at the level of cultural, spiritual, intellectual, and commercial cooperation and exchanges. The positive images of success and accomplishment generated by these visits in the psyche of Afro-Brazilians will continue to challenge Afro-Brazilians to higher heights in their struggle for dignity and recognition.

The denial of racism in Brazil remains the fundamental barrier to constructive dialogue and progress. Afro-Brazilians must not continue to be seen as only successful in entertainment, dance, sports, and the culinary arts. To live by such achievements alone is to delay the long-term necessity to advance into the political arena. How can the cultural strategies that are currently pervasive in Brazilian life as manifested in Carnival, samba, capoeira, and Candomblé translate into a vital political force when these cultural manifestations are controlled by the power of publicity, marketing, and promotion?

If Brazil is still not ready for a black state governor or mayor, when is it going to be ready for a black president? I am referring here to the subversion of the candidacy of Gilberto Gil, an internationally renowned artist and accomplished Brazilian musician, whose mayoral candidacy in Bahia was rejected by his own party and who was advised to try instead for the post of alderman. The compromised and negotiated collaboration with a hostile, hypocritical, and oppressive system does nothing but minimize the sacrifices already made to challenge those inequalities over the years. The future of Afro-Brazilian cultural production must be seen as operating between the will of the government to accommodate what continues to be perceived as aggressive demands for racial equality and the strategic partnership forged by cultural entities and producers in order to mount a viable collective front against the vestiges of racism that continue to be veiled under the mythology of racial democracy in Brazil.

Notes

Introduction

1. Palmares is a settlement community of runaway slaves. Among many *quilombos*, Palmares, led by Zumbi dos Palmares, is the most popular. "Palmares" thus represents a physical as well as a spiritual location for all Afro-Brazilians in their struggle for freedom.

2. For a detailed discussion of the veil metaphor in the African American literary tradition, see Robert Stepto, *From behind the Veil* (Chicago: University of Illinois Press, 1979).

3. For a more detailed discussion of this growing debate and controversy, see Degler, *Neither Black nor White;* Nascimento, *Racial Democracy: Myth or Reality?;* Skidmore, *Black into White;* Medeiros, *O Elogio da Dominação;* Andrews, *Blacks and Whites in São Paulo: 1888–1988;* Hellwig, *African American Reflections on Brazil's Racial Paradise;* Hanchard, *Orpheus and Power;* and Twine, *Racism in a Racial Democracy.*

4. Except where otherwise noted, all translations in this book are mine.

5. See Solano Trindade, "Navio Negreiro," *Revista do Patrimônio Histórico e Artístico Nacional* 25.1 (1997): 122.

6. This collaboration with Paul Simon produced a fantastic compact disc released in 1990, *The Rhythms of the Saints.*

7. In spite of his series of ordeals in the media, especially the recent accusations of child molestation, Michael Jackson is still highly regarded in Brazil in the cultural circles as an icon for promotional and solidarity reasons. His artistic achievement helps him maintain international acceptance and awe, but he is indeed not a representative black icon.

8. Gregório de Matos, *Poemas Escolhidos* (São Paulo: Cultrix, 1976), 37. Matos lived between 1633 and 1696, mostly in Bahia, leaving behind a sizable collection of verses in which he described the different races within the colonial social structure.

9. Domingos Caldas Barbosa (1738–1800) was affiliated with the Arcadian school, which followed the Classical school. Along with Silva Alvarenga (1749–1814), these poets may be considered the transition into the nineteenth century when Afro-Brazilian literature flourished and gained international attention, especially due to the emergence of Machado de Assis and Lima Barreto.

10. See Elisa Larkin Nascimento, *Dois Negros Libertários: Luiz Gama and Abdias do Nascimento* (Rio de Janeiro: IPEAFRO, 1985), 68. Gama (1830–1882), who hailed from Bahia, died just six years before the abolition for which he fought so well. Nascimento was born in 1914 in São Paulo and currently lives in Rio de Janeiro.

11. A native of Rio de Janeiro, where he spent most of his life, Machado lived from 1839 to 1908.

12. Alves (1847–1871) is mostly cited for such poems as "The Slave Ship" and "Voices from Africa"; his statue in Praça Castro Alves, which faces the seaport in Salvador, Bahia, from where slaves entered Brazil, is a reminder and acknowledgment of his contribution to the abolitionist struggle.

13. During my personal interviews with more than a dozen writers in this group in the summers of 1998 and 1999, most of them insisted on not being associated with "postmodernity" since their existence has always drawn inspiration and strength from the past. The concept of ancestrality is the focus of my ongoing research on this rebellious and dynamic "generation of the seventies" and their resonance in popular culture, especially among emerging youth organizations.

14. This is not intended as an exhaustive list but an overview.

15. Márcio Barbosa, "*Cadernos negros* e Quilombhoje: Algumas Páginas de História," *Thoth* (1997): 218.

Chapter 1

1. "A Guerra do Paraguai" (1865–70), also called the war of the Tríplice Aliança (Triple Alliance—Brazil, Uruguay, and Argentina), against Francisco Solano López, is adeptly foregrounded to situate *Iaiá Garcia* in sociohistorical context.

2. See for example, Raymond Sayer, "The Negro in the Novels of Machado de Assis," in *The Negro in Brazilian Literature*, 201–8; Giorgio Marotti, "Machado de Assis and Slavery," in *Black Characters in the Brazilian Novel*, 113–31; and Maria Luisa Nunes, "An Artist's Identity," *CLA* 27.3 (1983): 187–96.

3. See Raymundo Faoro, *Machado de Assis: A pirâmide e o trapézio* (São Paulo: Nacional, 1974), 327.

4. Cited in Maria Figueiredo, *O romance de Lima Barreto* (Belo Horizonte: Editora Lê, 1995), 9.

Chapter 2

1. "*Cadernos negros* e Quilombhoje: Algumas Páginas de História," *Thoth* 2 (1997): 206–19.

2. Bernard Mouralis, *Les Contre-Littératures* (Paris: PUF, 1975), 11.

Chapter 3

1. See, for example, the discussion of Jamu Minka's "Efeitos colaterais" (Collateral Effects), in chapter 2.

2. Personal interview with Miriam Alves, São Paulo, June 12, 1998.

3. Zilá Bernd, "The Construction of Femininity and Black Consciousness in Brazilian Literature," *Journal of Afro-Latin American Studies and Literatures* 1.1 (1994): 28.

4. Movimento Negro Unificado (Unified Black Movement) is a national black movement that can be traced to the 1930s and the post–World War II period, made up mostly of union leaders, then university students, who emerged in the era following the postmilitary dictatorship to combat racism and racial discrimination in Brazil. The movement along with its contradictions, which Michael Hanchard addresses in *Orpheus and Power* (1994), is often compared to the civil rights movement in the United States.

Chapter 4

1. See, for example, *Flux e Reflux de la Traité de Negres entre le Golfe de Bénin et Bahia de Todos os Santos* (Paris: Mouton, 1968).

2. See *Contos Crioulos da Bahia* (Salvador: Corrupio, 1977).

3. Jorge Amado has over two dozen fictional works to his credit, and he is perhaps the most translated and popular South American writer. Although his fame is such that he has a foundation in Pelourinho (Salvador, Bahia), named in his honor even while he was still alive, he also has his critics who accuse him of exploiting African elements in the Brazilian lifestyle despite not assuming an Afro-Brazilian identity. Other critics accuse him of pornography and the exploitation of mulattas in his novels. His critics notwithstanding, Fundação Jorge Amado stands as a major tourist attraction among others in Pelourinho—confirming the overall contribution and recognition of Amado to Afro-Brazilian culture. Jorge Amado died in October 2001.

4. Simon Gikandi, "Chinua Achebe and the Poetics of Location," in *Essays on African Writing*, ed. Abdulrazak Gurnah, 1–12 (Oxford: Heinemann, 1993). As he rightly puts it: "We are still imprisoned in a critical tradition—whose most fervent advocate has been Georg Lukacs—in which the history and development of the novel is explicated in strictly temporal terms."

5. See *Times Literary Supplement,* April 2, 1971, 369. This is perhaps the only review available on this work in English to date. Aside from the "colonial criticism," the reviewer's penchant for Eurocentrism reduces Olinto's work to mere mechanics, thereby missing the entire point of the author's intentionality in terms of drawing the connections between Africa and Brazil.

6. Antônio Olinto, "The Negro Writer and the Negro Influence in Brazilian Literature," *African Forum* 2.4 (1967): 5–19. The justification for Brazil's right to membership in the Organization of African Unity stems from the reasoning that Brazil has the second-largest African population in the world with a third of her population having African ancestry.

7. In Yoruba culture, days of the week are associated with specific beliefs: *Ojó aíkú* (Sunday) means a day of immortality; *Ojó ajé* (Monday) means a day of business profit; *Ojó Ísẹ́gun* (Tuesday) means a day of victory; *Ojórú* (Wednesday) means a day of sacrifice; *Ojóbò* (Thursday) means a day of new creation; *Ojó etì* (Friday) means a day of difficulties; and *Ojó àbá méta* (Saturday) means a day of three meetings. The implication lies in the warning the different days give to the community depending on the venture one wants to carry out.

Chapter 5

1. The concept of anthropophagy derives from Oswald de Andrade's *Manifesto Antropofágico* (1928; Anthropophagic Manifesto), a major document of the Brazilian modernist movement that proposed the adaptation of useful Western values to Brazilian realities instead of an uncritical importation of models from Europe at the expense of indigenous values.
2. "Roda" (Circle) was composed by João Augusto but performed by Gilberto Gil.
3. Gil identifies this woman as a Spaniard he had met and fallen in love with in Madrid. For Gil, it is amazing how a simple encounter and act could inspire these lyrics. He considers the coincidence a resulting "manifestation of the poetic soul" (cited in Rennó, *Todas as letras*, 104).
4. "Alapala" translates as the "master of Apala" in Yoruba. *Apala* itself is a traditional music that developed in the 1930s in western Nigeria. Haruna Ishola, considered the chief maestro and exponent of Apala, would not use any guitars in his music, hence the quasi-traditional form of its percussions. A Yoruba music scholar, Christopher A. Waterman (see *JuJu* [1990: 85]), suggests that "Apala" has been influenced by Latin rhythms, but Gilberto Gil's appropriation of this rhythm to his distinctly "Afro-Latin" music in Brazil seems to contradict this assumption.

The *balafon* is a musical instrument common to the Francophone West African subregion, is called *marimba* in Portuguese-speaking Africa.

Chapter 6

1. See Luis Ramiro Beltrán, *National Communication Policies in Latin America: A Glance at the First Steps*. (n.p., 1976); Everett M. Rogers *Communication and Development* (Beverly Hills: Sage Publications, 1976); Georgette Wang and Wimal Dissanayake, "Culture, Development and Change: Some Explorative Observations," in *Continuity and Change in Communication Systems*, 3–20 (Norwood, NJ: Ablex, 1984); Juan E. Diaz-Bordenave, *O que é participação* (Saũo Paulo: Brasiliense,1989); and Srinivas R. Melkote, "Another Development: Strategies for Participation and Communication in the Eighties," in *Communication for Development in the Third World*, 228–71 (New Delhi: Sage Publications, 1991).
2. See Fred L. Casmir, "Culture, Communication, and Development," in *Communication in Development*, 5–26 (Norwood, NJ: Ablex, 1991)
3. Melkote, "Another Development," 231.
4. See Rogers, *Communication and Development;* Manfred Oepen, *Development Support Communication in Indonesia* (Jakarta: Friedrich Naumann-Stiftung and Indonesian Society for Peasants and Community Development, 1990 [1988]); J. Ascroft, and S. Masileka, "Participatory Decision-Making in Third World Development," in *Participatory Communication: Working for Change and Development*, ed. S. A. White, K. S. Nair, and J. Ascroft, 77–98 (New Delhi: Sage Publications, 1989); and Melkote, "Another Development."
5. Peter Oakley and David Marsden, *Approaches to Participation in Rural Development*, 11 (Geneva: International Labor Office, 1984).

6. Oakley and Marsden's incisive book explores the "context of participation," "concept of participation," "practice of participation," and "an emerging strategy." In this chapter, I am drawing from their conceptualization of participation.

7. Oakley and Marsden, *Approaches to Participation*, 19, quoted in M. A. Rahman, "Process-Oriented Rural Development Planning Integrated with Key Elements of Rationality (for the Developing World), " MES Major Paper (Toronto: Faculty of Environmental Studies, York University, 1996), 43; emphasis added.

8. Oakley and Marsden, *Approaches to Participation*, 19, quoted in Andrew Pearse and Matthias Stiefel, *Inquiry into Participation—A Research Approach*, 8 (Popular Participation Program, the United Nations Research Institute for Social Development, 1979); emphasis added.

9. *Dialogue About Participation* No. 4 (Geneva: UN Research Institute for Social Development; Popular Participation Programme, 1983.

10. Professor Everett M. Rogers was interviewed by Singhal and Domatob during a visit to Ohio University–Athens. See Singhal, Arvind and Jerry Domatob, "The Field of Development Communication: An Appraisal (A Conversation with Prof Everett M Rogers)," *Journal of Development Communication* 15.2 (2004): 51–55. For the original definition, see also "Communication and Development: The Passing of the Dominant Paradigm," in Rogers, *Communication and Development*, 133.

11. Diaz-Bordenave, *O que é participação*, 3; cited in Melkote, "Another Development," 237.

12. Georgette Wang and and Wimal Dissanayake, "Culture, Development and Change: Some Explorative Observations," in *Continuity and Change in Communication Systems,* ed. Goergette Wang and Wimal Dissanayake, 5 (Norwood, NJ: Ablex, 1984), cited in Melkote "Another Development," 193–94.

13. Roberto da Matta, *Ensaios de antropologia estrutural: O carnaval como um rito de passagem* (Petrópolis: Editora Vozes, 1977), 19.

14. In a cinematic adaptation of a play by the renowned Brazilian poet and playwright Vinícius de Moraes, titled *Orfeu da Conceição,* Moraes's samba "Felicidade," which opens the film, highlights the contradictions of Brazilian Carnival. The ironic title is intended to reflect the explicit sadness in the poem:

Tristeza nao tem fim/felicidade sim
(. . .)
A felicidade do pobre parece
A grande ilusão do carnaval
A gente trabalha o ano inteiro
Por um momento de sonho
Pra fazer fantasia
De rei, ou de pirata, ou jardineira
E tudo se acabar na quinta-feira.

[Sadness is endless/Happiness yes / (. . .) / A pauper's happiness it seems / The great illusion of carnival / One works the entire year / For a moment of fantasy / To make carnival costume / As king, rascal, or gardener / And everything ends on Wednesday.]

For the complete lyrics, see Vinícius de Moraes, *Os melhores poemas de Vinícius de Moraes*, selected by Renata Pallottini (São Paulo: Global Editora, 1984), 51.

15. Amaury Jório and Hiram Araújo, *Escolas de samba em desfile: vida, paixão e sorte* (Rio de Janeiro: Poligráf Editora, 1969), 295.

16. "Portela" is one of the oldest and biggest samba schools in Rio. For an in-depth examination of the commercialization of Carnival, see Alison Raphael, "Popular Culture to Microenterprise: The History of Brazilian Samba Schools," *Revista de Música Latinoamericana* 11.1 (1990): 25–40.

17. Emancipated slaves were still considered inferior by Brazilians of Portuguese descent during the postabolition period. Since samba came from Afro-Brazilian celebrations, it was considered a taboo the same way Candomblé worshippers were persecuted. Samba lovers were actually humiliated and arrested for practicing what was regarded as "witchcraft and sorcery," hence the powerless position of participants at that time.

18. Roberto da Matta, *Carnivals, Rogues, and Heroes: An Interpretation of the Brazilian Dilemma*, trans. John Drury (Notre Dame, IN: University of Notre Dame Press, 1991), 132.

19. I was in Brazil as an exchange student between 1982 and 1983 and as a scholar in 1986–87 during which time I researched the topic for an unpublished thesis, titled "Festança Brasileira: Carnaval em São Paulo, no Rio e na Bahia" (Brazilian Revelry: Carnival in São Paulo, Rio, and Bahia). My stay in Salvador gave me an ample opportunity to be involved in the Afro-Bahian carnival organizations, in particular Ilê-Aiyê, with which I participated and paraded in the Carnival of 1987. That year the group's theme was Nigeria. As an update to this study, I interviewed both Vovô, the director and president of Ilê-Aiyê, and João Jorge Santos Rodrigues of Olodum in the summer of 1999.

20. Interview with Antônio Carlos do Santos (Vovô), director of the Ilê-Aiyê carnival organization in Salvador, Bahia, January 2, 1983. Curuzu, where Ilê-Aiyê has its headquarters, is one of the most densely populated areas in Salvador, where most Afro-Bahians live.

21. Oepen, *Development Support Communication in Indonesia*. Oepen argues that any meaningful development communication strategy with the goal of democratic social change must incorporate interpersonal communication in small social groups, at least at the crucial stages.

22. Oepen, *Development Support Communication in Indonesia*, 55.

23. Interview with Vovô, January 2, 1983.

24. This video was made with additional support from Liceu de artes e ofícios da Bahia and Fundação Odebrecht, from which it can be purchased.

25. L. G. Bolman and T. E. Deal, *Modern Approaches to Understanding and Managing Organizations* (San Francisco: Jossy-Bass, 1990).

26. Andrew Pearse and Matthias Stiefel, *Inquiry into Participation—A Research Approach* (Popular Participation Program, the United Nations Research Institute for Social Development, 1979).

27. Melkote, "Another Development," 246.

28. Anamaria Morales, "Blocos negros em Salvador: Reelaboração cultural e símbolos de baianidade," *Caderno CRH* (1991): 81.

29. Morales, "Blocos negros em Salvado," 82.

30. Peter Oakley and David Marsden, *Projects with People: The Practice of Participation in Rural Development* (Geneva: International Labor Office, 1991), 24.

31. Interview with Vovô, Salvador, Bahia, August 12, 1999.

Chapter 7

1. The black sages are also common figures in Umbanda (an Afro-Brazilian religion more popular in the southeastern part of Brazil).

2. For more detailed discussions of "branqueamento" (whitening), see Abdias do Nascimento, *O genocídio do negro brasileiro* and *Racial Democracy: Myth or Reality?;* Thomas Skidmore, *Black into White;* and Carl Degler, *Neither Black nor White.*

3. In the case of Xica da Silva, she is denied entry into the church due to her black skin color and to confirm the racism of the period that she was only good in the master's bed—not good enough for the "holiness" and "whiteness" of the church. Comparatively, Zé-do-Burro was denied entrance into the church due to his "pagan" faith and not due to the color of his skin. Although Zé-do-Burro did not see any difference between Santa Barbara (Catholic saint) and Iansan (African goddess, equivalent of Santa Barbara), the Catholic priest marked a difference between "satanic" worship that he associated with Iansan and divine worship that he associated with Santa Barbara. In both cases, Xica and Zé are victims of societal intolerance.

4. See back cover of the Home Vision Cinema version of Marcel Camus' *Black Orpheus.*

5. See front cover of the Home Vision Cinema version of *Black Orpheus.*

6. See Hanchard, *Orpheus and Power,* 167.

7. Anatol Rosenfeld, in *O mito e o herói no moderno teatro brasileiro* (35), suggests that it is necessary to deform complex realities through mythicization. And this process transforms the hero into a mythic hero. This explains why Zé's tragedy is not that of an individual but representative of the societal tragedy as a whole due to a lack of communication between the two. As Rosenfeld puts it, "Zé and the people of Salvador seem to live in different planets" (60).

8. For a detailed elaboration of these codes, see Haberly, *Three Sad Races,* 147–60.

9. See "Manifesto Antropófago" (Anthropophagic Manifesto), in *Presença da Literatura Brasileira (Modernismo)* (São Paulo: Difel, 1979), 65–73.

10. See Ismail Xavier, "The Shape of Brazilian Cinema in the Postmodern Age," in *Brazilian Cinema,* ed. Randal Johnson and Robert Stam (New York: Columbia University Press, 1995), 387–470.

11. See Darlene J. Sadlier, *Nelson Pereira dos Santos* (Chicago: University of Illinois Press, 2003).

12. See Rodrigues, "Novas Visões do Negro Brasileiro e o Cinema," *Revista do Patrimônio Histórico e Artístico Nacional* 25 (1997): 99.

Chapter 8

1. Roland Barthes, "From Work to Text," *Textual Strategies* (Ithaca: Cornell University Press, 1979 [1971]).

2. See Michael Hanchard, "Afro-Modernity: Temporality, Politics, and the African Diaspora," in *Alternative Modernities*, ed. Dilip Parameshwar Gaonkar, 272–98 (Durham: Duke University Press, 2001).

3. The need to look back into the past is not a phenomenon unique to a given African culture. While the Yoruba of Nigeria worship òrişàs and the dead as a way of paying homage to the ancestors, the Akan of Ghana apply the notion of *Sankofa* to refer to the need to "return and retrieve" the past. Similarly, the ancient Greeks celebrated their gods, paid homage to them in a ritualistic and mythological manner, and consulted oracles who were seen as a form of guidance in moments of uncertainties.

4. Birago Diop, "Breath," in *Poems of Black Africa*, ed. Wole Soyinka, 44–46 (Suffolk: Heinemann, 1975). The poem is taken from an original tale by Diop, "Sarzan," and seems to be based on personal experience and not credited to Amadou Koumba. The tale critiques the colonial policy of assimilation and ultimately makes a case for respecting tradition. The original tale, written in French, may be found either in the original collection by Birago Diop, *Les Contes d'Amadou Koumba*, or in one of several anthologies, such as *Contes Choisis*, ed. Joyce A. Hutchinson, 96–109 (Cambridge University Press, 1967).

5. See Terry Eagleton, *After Theory* (London: Basic Books, 2003), in which the critic makes a case for a refreshing vista on theory and its current relevance, and not its total abandonment. What is problematic about Eagleton's proposal lies in the suggestion that we can offer more interesting cultural courses that transcend race, class, and gender.

Chapter 9

1. For Wilson Martins, as of 1995, Afro-Brazilians are still limited in their artistic accomplishment due to their inability to transcend the "polemical and circumstantial phase of artistic creation." For a detailed understanding of Martins's misleading position, see "Brazilian Literature in the 90s," *Latin American Literature and the Arts* 53 (1996): 5.

2. See Lelia Gonzalez, "Griot e Guerreiro," introduction to *Axés do sangue da esperança* (Rio de Janeiro: Achiamé, 1983), i.

3. See, for example, Henry Louis Gates's study of the relation between Èṣù-Elegbara and the signifying monkey in *The Signifying Monkey: A Theory of African-American Literary Criticism* (New York: Oxford University Press, 1988), 3–43.

4. Ironides Rodrigues, "O transcendalismo poético e simbólico na poesia negra de Eduardo de Oliveira," *Afrodiáspora* 3.6–7 (1985): 125–32.

5. See "América Afro-Negra" (Black Afro-America), a poem in the same collection, *Carrossel de sonetos*, 31.

6. "ONU" in the original text ("Reconhecida pela ONU") refers metaphorically to the United Nations Organization (UNO) as a world-community legislative body.

7. See Alceu Amoroso Lima, ed., *Olavo Bilac: Poesia*, Nossos Clássicos no. 2 (Rio de Janeiro: Agir Editora, 1968), 38.

Chapter 10

1. I am referring here to the generation of the 1980s and beyond. The panoramic analyses and commentaries about the Quilombhoje group or on individual writers, such as the commendable efforts of Zilá Bernd, *Introdução à Literatura Negra* (São Paulo: Brasiliense, 1988), and *Negritude e Literatura na América Latina* (Porto Alegre: Mercado Aberto, 1987); and Luiza Lobo, *Crítica Sem Juízo* (Rio de Janeiro: Livraria Francisco Alves Editora, 1993), are usually inadequate. Other efforts are generated by the writers themselves as they organize national conferences on their own works yielding such titles as *Reflexões sobre a literatura afro-brasileira* and *criação crioula, nu elefante branco*.

2. See the back cover of *Negros em Contos* (Belo Horizonte: Mazza Edições, 1996) written by Moema Parente Augel.

3. See Bernd, *Negritude e Literatura na América Latina*, 119. Bernd suggests that the poets of the earlier generation who have thus been influenced include Solano Trindade, Oswaldo de Camargo, and Eduardo de Oliveira.

4. By "oppressor" here I mean the duality of burden captured in her race and even black partner.

5. Written September 4, 1988, this is actually a dedication to Márcio Barbosa, a member-poet of the Quilombhoje group.

6. See cover of *A roza da recvsa* (São Paulo: Pindaíba, 1982): "O PRETO é uma)ilha(e um (labirinto) perdido em Si Mesmo."

7. See chapter 2, where Solano Trindade, Abdias do Nascimento, Eduardo de Oliveira, and Oswaldo de Camargo are discussed.

8. I conducted interviews with Arnaldo Xavier in the company of Abílio Ferreira in the summers of 1999 and 2001.

9. I am hoping that an American publisher interested in art history may take up this challenge since these visual poems are so compelling and marketable. Some of these visual poems will be analyzed in the latter part of this chapter.

10. See Arnaldo Xavier, "Literatura à Flor da Pele:)Orikrítica(" (unpublished essay, 1998).

11. Telephone interview with Arnaldo Xavier, August 4, 2002.

12. See pages **XX** and **XXX** of this volume. The title may also suggest double mockery as in "ludíbrio," from which "lud" may be derived or is derived.

13. See Moema Parente Augel, ed., *Schwarze Poesie/Poesia Negra* (St. Gallen/Koln: Day Edition, 1988), 157.

14. See Ronaldo Augusto, "Transnegressão," in *Presença Negra no Rio Grande do Sul*, ed. Fernando Seffner, 47 (Porto Alegre: UE/Porto Alegre, 1995).

15. It is remarkable that most of these images were produced in commemoration of one hundred years of abolition in 1988 and yet the author, who died in 2004, was never able to find a publisher for his visual work. . In an interview in August 2002 with the author, Xavier noted with optimism that the Fundação Palmares had indicated some interest but had not committed to publish the material.

16. See Arnaldo Xavier, "Exu," *Revista do Patrimônio Histórico e Artístico Nacional* 25 (1997): 148.

17. Ibid.

18. With the exception of *Vá de Valha* (1992), and "Transnegressão" (1995), where he adopts "Augusto" as his last name, Ronald Augusto's first two books of the three under consideration were originally published under Ronald Tutuca, hence this analysis will use both names interchangeably. "Tutuca" is a childhood nickname turned official and then reversed in later years. The poet's full name is Ronald Augusto da Costa.

19. This is the best translation I can come up with in terms of the idea of going beyond blackness and ideological pamphleteering to enter the world of artistic perfection and innovation.

20. Interview with Edimilson de Almeida Pereira in Minas Gerais, Brazil, April 2001.

21. The literal translation, "Go to the Asylum," does not capture the hidden meaning of someone needing mental health care.

22. Interview with author in Porto Alegre, July 2001. This is a one-page note that describes three parts making up the text.

Chapter 11

1. For the full text of the speech, delivered by Professor Abdias do Nascimento during his swearing-in ceremony as Secretary Extraordinary for the Defense and Promotion of Black Peoples on April 10, 1991; see *Africans in Brazil: A Pan-African Perspective*, 70–79.

2. See Hanchard, *Orpheus and Power*, 164–67.

3. See David Brookshaw, *Race and Color in Brazilian Literature* (Metuchen, NJ: Scarecrow Press, 1986), 277–309.

4. See Esmeralda Ribeiro, "Ogun," *Callaloo* 18.4 (1995): 913–19; 741–47 (trans. Phyllis Peres). Esmeralda Ribeiro is currently the president of the Quilombhoje group while Márcio Barbosa is the vice president. They are both coeditors of the *Cadernos negros* series.

5. See Paul Gordon, *The Critical Double: Figurative Meaning in Aesthetic Discourse* (Tuscaloosa: University of Alabama Press, 1995).

6. Ribeiro, "Ogun," 746.

7. See ibid., 741. "Ogun" has been translated by Phyllis Reisman for the special issue of *Callaloo* (18.4), and I am citing from both the original Portuguese and Reisman's English translation of this particular story.

8. For a detailed discussion of the connection of Candomblé to slavery and black identity in nineteenth-century Brazil, especially in Bahia, see Rachel E. Harding, *A Refuge in Thunder: Candomblé and Alternative Spaces of Blackness* (Bloomington: Indiana University Press, 2000).

9. See Ana Maria Silva et al., *Gostando mais de nós mesmos*, 2nd ed. (São Paulo: Editora Gente, 1999). This book focuses on issues of self-esteem using an interview-style research paradigm to solicit questions and answers about problems confronting Afro-Brazilians in general—from racism, to being gainfully employed, to political awareness about African history and the black family.

10. The notion of a twenty-year installment plan on a phone initiated by Mariana's father once she was born betrays a fundamental social malaise that emanates

primarily from poverty and low socioeconomic status. For the average European or American, owning a phone is a social necessity, not a privilege. Yet, in Brazil, at the time Esmeralda Ribeiro wrote "Ogun" (1995), owning a phone was a luxury that partly reflected social status. Mariana had to wait for twenty years after the initial installment payment by her father before she could take delivery of her "inheritance." Her disappointment and shock must be understood within this context of a long-deferred gratification and a betrayal when the color (white) she expected of the phone turned out to be black with the phone company's unacceptable explanation that they delivered the only phone they had left, which happened to be black.

11. For a fuller analysis of *Malungos e Milongas*, see Niyi Afolabi, "Beyond the Curtains: Unveiling Afro-Brazilian Women Writers," *Research in African Literatures* 32.4 (2001): 117–35. Ribeiro's call for solidarity between the sexes among Afro-Brazilians is equally accentuated in her critical imagination of "Afro-Brazilian participative writing" as contained in her critical piece "A Escritora Negra e o Seu Ato de Escrever Participando," in *Criação Crioula, Nu Elefante Branco* (São Paulo: Ministry of Culture, 1987), 59–65. She cogently posits: "Unity of efforts between Afro-Brazilian men and women is necessary to further strengthen the struggle in which both intervene in the process of political participation and build a new national consciousness" (65).

12. Quilombhoje is a literary and political organization located in São Paulo that emerged in 1978 through the publication of an annual literary journal, *Cadernos negros*. Although the group did not officially become known as Quilombhoje until 1980, most of the members shared the same ideology about the recuperation of African values and dignity for Afro-Brazilians in general.

13. Geni Guimarães's extensive literary corpus includes *Terceiro filho* (Third Child; poems, 1979), *Leite do peito* (Breastmilk; children's short stories, 1986), *A cor da ternura* (Color of Tenderness; novella, 1988), *Balé das emoções* (Ballet of Emotions, 1994), *A dona das folhas* (Goddess of Leaves; children's' literature, 1998), *O rádio de Gabriel* (Gabriel's Radio; children's literature, 1998), *Aquilo que a mãe não quer* (That Which Mother Doesn't Want; children's literature, 1998). Other poems and stories have been published in various anthologies.

14. See Cuti, "Fundo de Quintal nas Umbigadas," in *Criação crioula, nu elefante branco* (São Paulo: Ministry of Culture, 1987, 151–60). By "orfandade intelectual," Cuti is referring to the ignorance of most Afro-Brazilians about their own literary past as well as a certain shame and disdain by those who do know. He cites some examples of important writers of the past: Cruz e Souza, Lima Barreto, Machado de Assis, and Luís Gama—all of whom have been accused, myopically of course, of one form of "betrayal" or the other. According to Cuti, contemporary critics need to know Afro-Brazilian intellectual history in order to better comment on its literature and culture.

15. Other than works by Zilá Bernd, Luiza Lobo, and a few unpublished dissertations on Afro-Brazilian cultural production, Quilombhoje boasts two collective critical works, namely *Cadernos negros*, which, while lacking in depth, do serve as a useful introduction to the works of the group as a whole, *Cadernos negros*though not to those of individual writers.

16. See chapter 2 of the present book.

17. Interview with Geni Guimarães, Barra Bonita, São Paulo, Brazil, July 2001.

18. See Celeste Dolores Mann, "The Search for Identity in Afro-Brazilian Women's Writing: A Literary History," in *Moving Beyond Boundaries,* ed. Carole Boyce Davies, 2:173–74 (New York: New York University Press, 1995).

19. See Conceição Evaristo, "Eu—Mulher," in *Enfim Nós/Finally Us,* ed. Miriam Alves and Carolyn Richardson Durham, 71 (Colorado Springs, CO: Three Continents Press, 1995). The English translation cited is by Carolyn Durham.

20. See, for example, Paulo Colina, ed., *Axé: Antologia contemporânea da poesia negra brasileira* (1982); Oswaldo Camargo, ed., *A Razão da chama: Antologia de poetas negros brasileiros* (1986) and *O negro escrito* (1987); Moema Parente Augel, ed., *Schwarze Poesie—Poesia Negra* (1988); and Miriam Alves and Carolyn R. Durham, eds., *Enfim Nós/Finally Us* (1995).

21. In *The Anxiety of Influence,* Harold Bloom suggests that in the process of negating the influence of the previous generation, a given poet ends up affirming that generation even if the product of that negation seems to be new and different.

22. When compared to Esmeralda Ribeiro, Sônia Fátima Conceição, Miriam Alves, and Coceição Evaristo, Geni Guimarães seems less forceful in articulating racial issues, at least in *Terceiro filho.* Perhaps this explains why, to date, there is no study of a "racial" nature regarding Geni Guimarães. See, for example, Lesley Feracho, "Transgressive Acts: Race, Gender, and Class in the Poetry of Carolina Maria de Jesus and Miriam Alves," *Afro-Hispanic Review* 18.1 (1999): 38–45.

23. Editorial review quoted in *Jornal do Movimento do Negro Unificado,* no. 16 (June–August 1989; Salvador, Bahia, Brazil) during the launching of *Leite do peito.*

24. Interview with Guimarães, Barra Bonita, July 2001.

25. See, for example, Richard Majors and Janet Mancini Billson, *Cool Pose: The Dilemmas of Black Manhood in America* (New York: Touchstone, 1992).

26. See Afolabi, "Beyond the Curtains," 117–35.

27. See Miriam Alves, "Pedaços de mulher," *Callaloo* 18.4 (1995): 969, trans. Carolyn Richardson Durham with Reetika Vazirani and Chi Lam, 801.

28. See Miriam Alves, "Aro Boboi," a forty-page unpublished long poem. According to a note by Alves: "'Aro Boboi' is a homage to the Oxumaré god which is represented by a cobra and the movement of the air in the world. In choosing this title for this tripartite work, I have in mind a way of dealing with the doubts of the black population from Africa who were transformed into slaves and who, through the esoteric journey of this long poem, manifest the capacity to recuperate themselves through the existence of and their belief in the òrișàs. The key words in this book are: hope, faith, and necessity to recreate life."

29. Arnaldo Xavier, "O brilho de Abílio," in *Antes do carnaval* (São Paulo: Selinunte, 1990), 29. Ferreira's characters, by their very assertive nature, are "oppositional" to those created by Jorge Amado, who are flat, stereotypical, and exoticized.

30. See Harding, *Refuge in Thunder,* 157–61.

Chapter 12

1. Cited by Steven White in "Reinventing a Sacred Past in Contemporary Afro-Brazilian Poetry," *Callaloo* 20.1 (1997): 70.

2. Since *Outras miragens* (1989) also incorporates *Miragem de engenho* (1984), this analysis cites the later work.

3. See Hamilton de Jesus Vieira, ed., *Poetas baianos da negritude* (Salvador: CEAO-UFBA, 1982), 9.

4. See Luiza Lobo, *Crítica sem Juízo* (Rio de Janeiro: Livraria Francisco Alves Editora, 1993), 164.

5. Da Silva's story covers a wide range of issues facing Afro-Brazilians today—poverty, lack of representation, racism, political exploitation, and educational and economic deprivation—as well as her own contribution toward alleviating those frustrations; as a non-traditional politician, she used her mobilization skills to win the support of her community in becoming the first black female senator in Brazil. For fuller highlights, see Medea Benjamin and Maisa Mendonça, *Benedita da Silva: An Afro-Brazilian Woman's Story of Politics and Love* (Oakland, CA: Food First Books, 1997), vii.

6. David Brookshaw, *Race and Color in Brazilian Literature* (Metuchen, NJ: Scarecrow Press, 1985), 290.

7. Cited in ibid., 291. For original poem, "Para domingos Jorge Velho," see José Carlos Limeira and Éle Semog, *Atabaques* (Rio de Janeiro: Artes Gráficas e Editora Ltd., 1984).

8. See Steven White, "Reinventing a Sacred Past in Contemporary Afro-Brazilian Poetry: An Introduction," *Callaloo* 20.1 (1997): 69–82.

9. Jussara Santos, "Afrodicções," master's thesis (Pontífica Universidade Católica de Minas Gerais, 1998), 35.

10. See Maria Barbosa, "Strategies of Poetic Language in Afro-Mineiro Discourses," *Luso-Brazilian Review* 37.1 (2000): 78.

11. See Steven White, "Edimilson de Almeida Pereira: African Brazilian Poet," *Callaloo* 19.1 (1996): 51.

12. Edimilson de Almeida Pereira, *Ô lapassi e outros ritmos de ouvido* (Belo Horizonte: Editora UFMG, 1990), 67.

13. See ibid.

14. In addition to over two dozen critical articles and eight cultural volumes coauthored with Núbia Pereira, Pereira's poetic production now amounts to thirteen works, including *Dormundo* (1985), *Livro de falas* (1987), *Árvore dos Arturos e outros poemas* (1988), *Corpo imprevisto e margen dos nomes* (1989), *Ô lapassi e outros ritmos de ouvido* (1990), *Corpo vivido* (1991), *O homem da orelha furada* (1995), *Rebojo* (1995), *Águas de contendas* (1998), *A roda do mundo* (1996), and *Casa da palavra* (2001). Pereira has also written three works in the children's literature genre, while the critical bibliography on his own works is extensive. This is a quite remarkable ouput for so young a scholar and writer—and suggests greater things to come. Two cultural volumes (coauthored with Núbia Pereira) are particularly worth mentioning: *Negras raízes Mineiras: Os Arturos* (2000) and *Ardis da imagem: Exclusão étnica e violência da cultura brasileira* (2001)—classic works of great imagination that uncover Afro-Mineiro "slave confraternities," especially the *Cangada*, and refute the invisibility of Afro-Brazilians, respectively.

15. Maria Barbosa, "Strategies of Poetic Language in Afro-Mineiro Discourses," 63.

16. White, "Edimilson de Almeida Pereira," 50.

17. See Edimilson de Almeida Pereira, "Contemporary Brazilian Poetry: Invention and Freedom in the Afro-Brazilian Tradition," *Journal of Latin American Cultural Studies* 5.2 (1996): 139–54.
18. See Pereira, "Contemporary Brazilian Poetry," 143. Cited by Pereira from Leda Maria Martins, *A cena em sombras* (The Stage in Shadows) (São Paulo: Editora Perspectiva, 1995).
19. See chapter 10.
20. See back cover of *Corpo vivido* (Juiz de Fora: Mazza, 1991).
21. Dias, Marcos. 2001. "Ars capoeirética II" [Typescript].

Chapter 13

1. Brandão's discography is extensive, including *Canções Afirmativas Ao Vivo* (2008) [DVD], *Auto-estima* (1999), *Somos da mesma tribo* (1996), *Anjos da guarda* (1995), *Atitudes* (1993), *Comprometida* (1992), *Cidadão brasileira* (1990), *As coisas que mamãe ne ensinou* (1989), *Um beijo no seu coração* (1988), *Dignidade* (1987), *Leci Brandão* (1985), *Essa tal criatura* (1980), *Metades* (1978), *Coisas do meu pessoal* (1977), *Questão de gosto* (1976), and *Antes que eu volte a ser nada* (1975).
2. Helena Theodoro, "Mulher Negra, Arte e Poesia: Leci Brandão," in *Presença negra no Rio Grande do Sul,* ed. Fernando Seffner, 57 (Porto Alegre: Prefeitura Municipal de Porto Alegre, 1995).
3. The excerpt, in its original Yoruba and translation, has been taken from a fuller invocational *oríkì* of our mothers; see "Invocational Prayer of Iyami Osoronga," http://www.awostudycenter.com/forum/lofiversion/index.php/t188.html (accessed February 25, 2007).
4. Jon Pareles, "Songs of Love and Politics from Brazil and Beyond," *New York Times,* March 10, 1993.
5. Leci Brandão. "Batida no coração." *Raízes do Samba*. Rio de Janeiro: EMI, 2007. CD. #B000031R33.
6. Leci Brandão, "Negro Zumbi." *A Cara do Povo*. Wallingford, CT: Phantom Sound, 2003. CD. [Track #15].
7. "Casa Grande e Senzala" (Masters and the Slaves) *Questão de Gosto.*
8. 'The "circular" frame comes from the way the album is arranged: starting with homage paid to veteran musician, Martinho da Vila and ending with homage paid to Afro-Bahian cultural groups, such as Olodum and Araketu. I read this as "circular" in terms of solidarity Leci Brandão shows for these individuals and groups. The commonality is about Afro-Bahian cause and dignity.'
9. See Betinho Ibase, "Entrevista: Leci Brandão," http://www.ibase.org.br (accessed August 21, 2006). The following individuals conducted the interview on the thirtieth anniversary of Brandão's career in 2005: AnaCris Bittencourt, Flávia Mattar, Iracema Dantas, Jamile Chequer, Lúcia Xavier (coordinator of "ONG Criola" [Crioula NGO]) and Marcelo Carvalho.
10. *Pagode* is a variation of samba, a traditional style begun in the 1970s in a poor suburb of Rio that has since become very popular and gradually commercialized.
11. "Canta, canta, minha gente" (Sing, Sing, My People) *Eu Sou Assim* [Track #1].

12. "Barco a vela" (Candlelit Boat) *Eu Sou Assim* [Track #1].
13. "Barco a vela" (Candlelit Boat) *Eu Sou Assim* [Track #1].
14. "Papa vadiou" (Daddy Loiters) *Eu Sou Assim* [Track #3].
15. "Anjos da guarda" (Guardian Angels) *Eu Sou Assim* [Track #12].
16. "Marajuara" refers to the juice from the Marajá palm fruit from the Brazilian Amazon region.
17. "Menor abandonado" (Abandoned Youngster) *Eu Sou Assim* [Track #11].
18. See Ibase, "Entrevista: Leci Brandão."
19. Osanyin is the Yoruba oracular god of revelation and healing.
20. Originally from the Ijebu Yoruba tradition, Agemọ is one of the many Yoruba deities. As a masquerade, it is valued for the ability to convince its audience that it has no hands, feet, or body—thus suggesting its supernatural self-sufficiency.
21. *Ijesa* refers to a particular rhythm that is named after the Ijesha of southwestern Nigeria—being among the religious styles that different "nations" or ethnic groups (Ketu, Gege, Dahoman, and Kongo-Angolan) brought with them from Africa to Brazil.
22. "Saudação a Ossain" (Homage to Osanyin, Medicinal Plant Goddess) *Eu Sou Assim* [Track #17].
23. My attempt at a translation here is only as good as the corruption of the classical Yoruba that I am able to tease out from the chant. The singer may not necessarily know the meaning either, but she is at least aware that she is paying homage to an oracular god, especially since she believes in the religion.
24. Deus do fogo da justice (Ara Ketu)" (God of Fiery Justice-Ara Ketu) *Eu Sou Assim* [Track #15].
25. Deus do fogo da justice (Ara Ketu)" (God of Fiery Justice-Ara Ketu) *Eu Sou Assim* [Track #15].
26. Fundo do Quintal is considered the group that revolutionized samba by introducing harmonic and instrumental innovations to *pagode* in relation to samba.
27. "Isso é fundo de quintal" (This is 'Fundo de Quintal') *Eu Sou Assim* [Track #16].
28. See the Disco/Video/Filmography section of the bibliography, *Casa do pagode/Raça brasileira (20 anos)*. This was a live performance recorded on November 29, 2004, at the Circo Voador in Lapa, Rio de Janeiro, and released in 2005.
29. Raça brasileira" (Brazilian Race) *Casa do Pagode* [Track #3].
30. Raça brasileira" (Brazilian Race) *Casa do Pagode* [Track #3].
31. "Pomba rolou" (Fooled by the Parrot) *Casa do Pagode* [Track #18].
32. "Feirinha da pavuna" (Pavuna Market) *Casa do Pagode* [Track #18].
33. "Bagaço da laranja" (Orange Peels) *Casa do Pagode* [Track #18].

Bibliography

Abodunrin, Femi. *Blackness: Culture, Ideology, and Discourse.* Bayreuth: Bayreuth African Studies no. 44., 1996.
Achebe, Chinua. *Things Fall Apart.* New York: Anchor Books/Doubleday, 1959.
Afolabi, Niyi. "Beyond the Curtains: Unveiling Afro-Brazilian Women Writers." *Research in African Literatures* 32.4 (2001): 117–35.
Afolabi, Niyi, Márcio Barbosa and Esmeralda Ribeiro, eds. *The Afro-Brazilian Mind: Contemporary Afro-Brazilian Literary and Cultural Criticism.* Trenton: NJ, 2007.
———. *Cadernos Negros / Black Notebooks: Afro-Brazilian Literary Movement.* Trenton: NJ, 2007.
Alamgir, Mohiuddin. "Poverty Alleviation through Participatory Development." *Development* 2/3 (1988): 97–102.
Aleixo, Ricardo. *Trívio: Poemas.* Belo Horizonte: Scriptum Livros, 2001.
Alonso, Carlos J. *The Burden of Modernity: The Rhetoric of Cultural Discourse in Spanish America.* New York: Oxford, 1998.
Aluko, T. M. *One Man, One Wife.* London: Heinemann, 1967.
Alves, Antônio de Castro. *O navio negreiro.* Rio de Janeiro: Paz e Terra, 1971.
Alves, Miriam. *Momentos de busca.* São Paulo: Self-Edition, 1983.
———. *Estrelas no dedo.* São Paulo: Self-edition, 1985.
———."Aro Boboi." 2003.
Alves, Miriam, Cuti, and Arnaldo Xavier. *Terramara.* São Paulo: Self-edition, 1988.
Alves, Miriam, and Carolyn Richards Durham, eds. *Enfim Nós/Finally Us: Contemporary Black Women Writers.* Colorado Springs, CO: Three Continents, 1995.
Amado, Jorge. *Jubiabá.* Rio de Janeiro: Record, 1997.
Amos, Alcione M. "Afro-Brazilians in Togo: The Case of the Olympio Family, 1882–1945." *Cahiers d'Études Africaines* 41.162 (2001): 293–314.
Amosu, Tundonu A. "The Jaded Heritage: Nigeria's Brazilian Connection." *África: Revista do Centro de Estudos Africanos* 10 (1987):43–51.
Andrade, Carlos Drummond de. "No meio do caminho." *Obra Completa.* Rio de Janeiro: Companhia Aguilar, 1964.
Andrade, Inaldete Pinheiro de. *Pai adão era nagô.* Recife: Produção Alternativa, 1989.
———. *Cinco cantigas para você cantar.* Recife: Produção Alternativa, 1989.
Andrade, Mário de. *Aspectos da literatura brasileira.* Brasilia: Livraria Martins Editora/INL/MEC, 1972.
Andrews, George Reid. *Blacks and Whites in São Paulo, Brazil: 1888–1988.* Madison: University of Wisconsin Press, 1991.
Appadurai, Arjun. *Modernity at Large: Cultural Dimensions of Globalization.* Minneapolis: University of Minnesota Press, 1998.
Appiah, Kwame A. *In My Father's House: Africa in the Philosophy of Culture.* New York: Oxford University Press, 1992.

Araújo, Joel Zito. *A negação do Brasil: O Brasil na telenovela brasileira.* São Paulo: Editora SENAC, 2000.
Arnold, A. James. *Modernism and Negritude: The Poetry and Poetics of Aimé Césaire.* Cambridge: Harvard University Press, 1981.
Ascroft, J., and S. Masileka. "Participatory Decision-Making in Third World Development." In *Participatory Communication: Working for Change and Development*, ed. S. A. White, K. S. Nair, and J. Ascroft, 77–98. New Delhi: Sage Publications, 1989.
Assis, Machado de. *Iaiá Garcia.* São Paulo: Editora Ática, 1994.
Assis, Machado de. *Iaiá Garcia.* Translated by Albert I. Bagby Jr. Lexington: University Press of Kentucky, 1977.
Assumpção, Carlos de. *Protesto.* São Paulo: Sociedade Impressora, 1982.
Assumpção, Euzébio, and Mário Maestri, eds. *Nós, os afro-gaúchos.* Porto Alegre: Editora da Universidade, 1996.
Augel, Moema Parente, ed. *Schwarze Poesie/Poesia Negra.* St. Gallen/Koln: Day Edition, 1988.
———. "A imagem da África na poesia afro-brasileira contemporânea." *Afro-Ásia* 19–20 (1997):183–99.
Augusto, Ronald. *Vá de valha.* Porto Alegre: Coleção petit poa, 1983.
———. "Transnegressão." In *Presença begra no Rio Grande do Sul*, ed. Fernando Seffner, 47–55. Porto Alegre:UE/Porto Alegre, 1995.
Azevedo, Thales de. "A possibilidade de uma literatura 'afro-brasileira.'" In *Democracia racial*, 85–107. Petrópolis: Vozes, 1975.
Banks, Jared. "Cinematic Adaptation: Orfeu negro da Conceição." *Canadian Review of Comparative Literature* 23.3 (1996): 791–801.
Barbosa, Francisco de Assis. *Lima Barreto e a reforma da sociedade.* Recife: Pool, 1987.
Barbosa, Márcio. *Paixões crioulas.* São Paulo: Quilombhoje, 1987.
———. "*Cadernos negros* e Quilombhoje: Algumas páginas de história." *Thoth* 2 (1997): 206–19.
———. "Quando o malandro vacila." *Cadernos negros: Os melhores contos.* São Paulo: Quilombhoje/Ministério da Cultura, 1998.
———, ed. *Frente negra brasileira: Depoimentos.* São Paulo: Quilombhoje/Ministério da Cultura, 1998.
Barbosa, Márcio, and Esmeralda Ribeiro, eds. *Bailes: Soul, Samba-Rock, Hip Hop e Identidade em São Paulo.* São Paulo: Quilombhoje, 2007.
Barbosa, Maria José Somerlate. "Strategies of Poetic Language in Afro Mineiro Discourses." *Luso-Brazilian Review* 37.1 (2000): 63–82.
———. "Exu: Verbo devoluto." In *Brasil Afro-Brasileiro*, ed. Maria Nazareth Soares Fonseca, 153–71. Belo Horizonte: Autêntica, 2001.
Barbosa, Rogério Andrade. *Bichos da África*, 1–4. São Paulo: Melhoramentos, 1987.
———. *Sundjata: O príncipe Leão.* Rio de Janeiro: Agir, 1995.
———. *Viva o Boi-Bumbá.* Rio de Janeiro: Agir, 1999.
Barreto, Lima. *Clara dos Anjos.* São Paulo: Ática, 1998.
———. *Recordações do escrivão Isaías Caminha.* São Paulo: Ática, 1998.
Barros Mott, Maria Lúcia de. *Escritoras negras: Resgatando a nossa história.* Occasional Paper no. 13. Rio de Janeiro: Centro Interdisciplinar de Estudos Contemporâneos/Escola de Comunicação/UFRJ, 1989.

Barthes, Roland. "From Work to Text." *Textual Strategies*. Ithaca: Cornell University Press, 1979 [1971].
Bastide, Roger. *The African Religions of Brazil*. Translated by Helen Sebba. Baltimore: Johns Hopkins University Press, 1978.
Béhague, Gerard. "Brazilian Musical Values of the 1960s and 1970s: Popular Urban Music from Bossa Nova to Tropicália." *Journal of Popular Culture* 14.3 (1980): 437–52.
———. "Popular Music in Latin America." *Studies in Latin American Popular Culture* 5 (1986): 41–66.
Beltrán, Luis Ramiro. *National Communication Policies in Latin America: A Glance at the First Steps*. N.p., 1976.
———. "Mass Media and Cultural Domination." *Quarterly Review of Education* 10.1 (1980): 76–89.
Beltrão, Luiz. "Communicaçao popular e região no Brasil." In *Comunicação/Incomunicação no Brasil*, 37–47. São Paulo: Edições Loyola, 1976.
Benjamin, Medea, and Maisa Mendonça. *Benedita da Silva: An Afro-Brazilian Woman's Story of Politics and Love*. Monroe: Food First Books, 1977.
Bernd, Zilá. *Negritude e literatura na América Latina*. Porto Alegre: Mercado Aberto, 1987.
———. "Negritude e gauchidade: Oliveira Silveira (1941–)." In *Negritude e literatura na América Latina*, 125–29. Porto Alegre: Mercado Aberto, 1987.
———. *Introdução à literatura negra*. São Paulo: Brasiliense, 1988.
———, ed. *Poesia negra brasileira: Antologia*. Porto Alegre: Editora AGE, 1992.
———. "The Consciousness of Femininity and Black Consciousness in Brazilian Literature." *Journal of Afro-Latin American Studies and Literatures* 1.1 (1993–94): 25–31.
Bernd, Zilá, and Margaret M. Bakos. *O negro: Consciência e trabalho*. Porto Alegre: Editora da Universidade, 1991.
Bhabha, Homi. *The Location of Culture*. London: Routledge, 1994.
Bolman, L. G., and T. E. Deal. *Modern Approaches to Understanding and Managing Organizations*. San Francisco: Jossy-Bass, 1990.
Braga, Júlio. *Ancestralidade afro-brasileira: O culto de Babá Egum*. Salvador: EDUFBA/IANAMÁ, 1995.
Brito, Edalvado. "Uma ode aos valores culturais da raça negra." Introduction to *A mulher de Aleduma* by Aline França, 7–8. Salvador: IANAMÁ, 1985.
Brito, Maria da Conceição Evaristo de. "Literatura negra: Uma poética de nossa Afro-Brasilidade." Master's thesis, Pontífica Universidade Católica do Rio de Janeiro, Brazil, 1996.
Brito, Ricardo Aleixo de. *Festim*. Belo Horizonte: Editora Oriki, 1992.
Brito, Ricardo Aleixo de, and Edimilson de Almeida Pereira. *A roda do mundo*. Belo Horizonte: Mazza Edições, 1997.
Brookshaw, David. *Race and Color in Brazilian Literature*. Metuchen, NJ: Scarecrow Press, 1986.
Butler, Judith. "Desire." In *Critical Terms for Literary Study*, ed. Frank Lentricchia and Thomas McLaughlin, 369–86. Chicago: University of Chicago Press, 1995.
Butler, Kim D. *Freedoms Given, Freedom Won: Afro-Brazilians in Post-Abolition São Paulo and Salvador*. New Brunswick, NJ: Rutgers University Press, 1998.

Callado, Antônio. "O tesouro de Chica da Silva." In *A revolta da cachaça*, 107–96. Rio de Janeiro: Nova Fronteira Editora, 1983.
Callado, Carlos. *Tropicália: A história de uma revolução musical*. São Paulo: Editora 34, 1997.
Callaloo 18.4 (1995). Special issue on African-Brazilian literature.
Camargo, Oswaldo de. *Um homem tenta ser anjo*. São Paulo: Self-edition, 1959.
———. *O carro do êxito*. São Paulo: Martins, 1972.
———. *A descoberta do frio*. São Paulo: Populares, 1978.
———. *O estranho*. São Paulo: Roswitha Kempf Editores, 1982.
———, ed. *A razão da chama: Antologia de poetas negros brasileiros*. São Paulo: Edições GRD, 1986.
———. *O negro escrito*. São Paulo: Imprensa Oficial do Estado, 1987.
Canclini, García. *Hybrid Cultures: Strategies for Entering and Leaving Modernity*. Minneapolis: University of Minnesota Press, 1995.
Carvalho, José Jorge de. "Black Music of All Colors: The Construction of Black Ethnicity in Ritual and Popular Genres of Afro-Brazilian Music." Essay, University of Brasília Anthropology Series no. 145, Brasília, 1993.
Casmir, Fred L. "Culture, Communication, and Development." In *Communication in Development*, ed. Fred L. Casmir, 5–26. Norwood, NJ: Ablex, 1991.
Chaui, Marilena. *Conformismo e resistência: Aspectos da cultura popular no Brasil*. São Paulo: Brasiliense, 1986.
Chilcote, Ronald H. "Politics and Ideology in the Popular Poetry of Brazil." *Studies in Latin American Popular Culture* 2 (1983): 88–98.
Coco, Fusco. "Choosing between Legend and History: An Interview with Carlos Diegues." *Cineaste: America's Leading Magazine on the Art and Politics of the Cinema*. 15.1 (1986): 12–14.
Cohen, Keith, ed. *Writing in a Film Age*. Boulder: University Press of Colorado, 1991.
Colina, Paulo. *Axé: Antologia contemporânea da poesia negra brasileira*. São Paulo: Global Editora, 1982.
———. *Plano de vôo*. São Paulo: Roswitha Kempf Editores, 1984.
———. *A noite não pede licença*. São Paulo: Roswitha Kempf Editores, 1987.
———. *Todo o fogo da luta*. São Paulo: João Scortecci Editora, 1989.
Conceição, Jônatas, and Lindinalva Barbosa, eds. *Quilombo de Palavras: A literatura dos Afro-descedentes*. Salvador: Centro dos Estudos Afro-Orientais/UFBA, 2000.
Conceição, Sônia Fátima da. *Marcas, sonhos e raízes*. São Paulo: Quilombhoje/Edição da Autora, 1991.
Conniff, Michael L., and Thomas J. Davis. *Africans in the Americas*. New York: St. Martin's Press, 1994.
Correia, Lepê. *Caxinguelê*. Recife: Sambaxé Consultaria, 1993.
Costa, Haroldo. "O negro na MPB: Breve panorama." *Revista do Patrimônio Histórico e Artístico Nacional* 25 (1997): 159–77.
Costa, Ivaldo. "Orfeu e o contínuo renascer da cinedramaturgia nacional." *The Brasilians* 29.300 (January 2000): 14P.
Crook, Larry, and Randal Johnson, eds. *Black Brazil: Culture, Identity, and Social Mobilization*. Los Angeles: UCLA Latin American Center Publications, 1999.
Cummings, M., and O. Taylor. *Communications and Development in Africa and the African Diaspora*. Needham Heights, MA: Ginn Press, 1992.

Cuti (Luiz Silva). *Poemas da carapinha*. São Paulo: Self-edition, 1978.
———. *Batuque de tocaia*. São Paulo: Self-edition, 1982.
———. *Suspensão* (play). São Paulo: Self-edition, 1983.
———. *Flash crioulo sobre o sangue e o sonho* (poems). Belo Horizonte: Mazza Edições, 1987.
———. *Quizila* (short stories). São Paulo: Self-edition, 1987.
———. *A pelada peluda no largo da bola* (juvenile novella). São Paulo: Editora do Brasil, 1988.
———. *Dois nós na noite e outras peças de teatro negro brasileiro*. São Paulo: Eboh, 1991.
———. *Negros em contos*. Belo Horizonte: Mazza Edições, 1996.
———. "Poesia erótica nos *Cadernos negros*." In *Brasil Afro-Brasileiro*, ed. Maria Nazareth Soares Fonseca, 269–84. Belo Horizonte: Autêntica, 2000.
Damasceno, Benedita Gouvéia. *Poesia negra no modernismo brasileiro*. São Paulo: Ponte Editores, 1988.
Davies, Carole Boyce. *Black Women, Writing and Identity*. London and New York: Routledge, 1994.
Dávila, Jerry. *Diploma of Whiteness: Race and Social Policy in Brazil, 1917–1945*. Durham: Duke University Press, 2003.
Degler, Carl N. *Neither Black nor White: Slavery and Race Relations in Brazil and the United States*. New York: Macmillan, 1971.
Dialogue About Participation. No. 4. Geneva: UN Research Institute for Social Development: Popular Participation Programme, 1983.
Dias, Marcos. *Rebelamentos*. Belo Horizonte: Mazza Edições, 1990.
———. *País indig(o blue)nação*. Belo Horizonte: Mazza Edições, 1995.
———. *Estudos sobre a cidade*. Belo Horizonte: Mazza Edições, 1997.
———. "Perspectiva entre o movimento e o salto" Typescript, volume of poetry, 2001.
Diaz-Bordenave, Juan E. *Communication and Development*. Paris: Unesco, 1977.
———. *O que é participação*. Saũo Paulo: Brasiliense,1989.
Didi, Mestre. *Contos crioulos da Bahia*. Salvador: Corrupio, 1977.
Diégues, Manuel, Jr. "A África na vida e na cultura do Brasil." *Revista do Patrimônio Histórico e Artístico Nacional* 25 (1997): 11–27.
Diop, Cheikh Anta. *The Cultural Unity of Black Africa*. Chicago: Third World Press, 1978.
duCille, Anne. *The Coupling Convention: Sex, Text, and Tradition in Black Women's Fiction*. New York: Oxford University Press, 1993.
Dunn, Christopher. "Tropicalist Rebellion: A Conversation with Caetano Veloso." *Callaloo* 70 (1996): 116–38.
Durham, Carolyn R. "Sônia Fátima da Conceição's Literature for Social Change." *Afro-Hispanic Review* 11.1–3 (1992): 21–25.
———. "The Beat of a Different Drum: Resistance in Contemporary Poetry by Afro-Brazilian Women." *Afro-Hispanic Review* 14.2 (1995): 21–26.
———. "Space and Time: Afro-Brazilian History in the Poetry of Miriam Alves." *CLA Journal* 16.2 (1997): 185–96.
———. "Art for Life's Sake: Literature by Esmeralda Ribeiro, Sônia Fátima da Conceição, and Miriam Alves." *Palara* 1 (1997):36–42.
Dzidzienyo, Anani. *The Position of Blacks in Brazilian Society*. London: Minority Rights Group, 1971.

Eagleton, Terry. *After Theory*. London: Basic Books, 2003.
Esman, Milton J. "Popular Participation and Feedback Systems in Rural Development." In *Communication Strategies for Rural* Development, 70–78. Ithaca: Cornell University, 1974.
Esman, Milton J., and Norman T. Uphoff. *Local Organizations: Intermediaries in Rural Development*. Ithaca: Cornell University Press, 1984.
Evaristo, Conceição. *Ponciá Vicêncio*. Belo Horizonte: Mazza Edições, 2003.
Fantinati, Carlos Erivany. *O profeta e o escrivão: Estudo sobre Lima Barreto*. São Paulo: ILPHA/HUCITEC, 1978.
Faoro, Raymundo. *Machado de Assis: A pirâmide e o trapézio*. São Paulo: Nacional, 1974.
Favaretto, Celso. *Tropicália, alegoria, alegria*. São Paulo: Ateliê, 1996.
Feracho, Lesley. "Transgressive Acts: Race, Gender, and Class in the Poetry of Carolina Maria de Jesus and Miriam Alves." *Afro-Hispanic Review* 18.1 (1999): 38–45.
Ferreira, Abílio. *Fogo do olhar*. São Paulo: Quilombhoje/Mazza, 1989.
———. *Contralamúria—o livro*. São Paulo: Casa Pyndahba, 1994.
———. *Antes do carnaval*. São Paulo: Selinute/Convivência, 1995.
Ferreira, Antônio Mário "Toninho." *Na Própria pele: Os negros no Rio Grande do Sul*. Porto Alegre: Companhia Rio-grandense de Artes Gráfica, 2000.
Figueiredo, Maria do Carmo L. *O romance de Lima Barreto: Uma recepção*. Belo Horizonte: Editora Lê, 1995.
Filho, Adonias. "The Negro in Brazilian Literature." In *The African Contribution to Brazil*, trans. John Knox, 91–100. Special edition of the Brazilian Ministry of Foreign Relations on the occasion of the First Festival of Negro Arts in Dakar, Senegal. Rio de Janeiro: Edigraf, 1966.
Fischer, Luís Augusto. *Um passado pela frente: Poesia gaúcha ontem e hoje*. Porto Alegre: Editora da Universidade, 1992.
Fonseca, Maria Nazareth Soares, ed. *Brasil Afro-Brasileiro*. Belo Horizonte: Autêntica, 2000.
Fontaine, Pierre-Michel. *Race, Class, and Power in Brazil*. Berkeley: University of California Press, 1985.
França, Aline. *Negão Dony*. Salvador: Prefeitura de Salvador, 1979.
———. *A mulher de Aleduma*. Salvador: Clarindo Silva, 1981.
———. *Os estandartes*. Rio de Janeiro: Littera, 1993.
———. "As fontes de Salvador e seus convidados." Typescript play, premiered in Salvador in 1998.
Freire, Paulo. *Pedagogy of the Oppressed*. Trans. Myra Bergman Ramos. New York: Herder and Herder, 1971 [1970].
Gadzekpo, John Rex Amuzu. "Individualidade e Coletividade em *Dois Nós na Noite* de Cuti." *ACTAS do V Congresso da Associação Internacional de Lusitanistas*. Oxford: LIDEL, 1999. 718–30.
Galinsky, Philip. "Co-option, Cultural Resistance, and Afro-Brazilian Identity: A History of the *Pagode* Samba Movement in Rio de Janeiro." *Latin American Music Review* 17.2 (1996): 120–49.
Garcia-Castellón, Manuel. "Luis Silva (Cuti), Afro-Brasileno, paladín de dignidad étnica y poeta de liberación." *Journal of Afro-American Studies and Literatures* 1.1 (1993): 33–45.
Gates, Henry Louis, Jr. *The Signifying Monkey: A Theory of African-American Literary Criticism*. New York: Oxford University Press, 1988.

Gilroy, Paul. *The Black Atlantic: Modernity and Double Consciousness.* Cambridge: Harvard University Press, 1993.
Gomes, Dias. *O pagador de promessas.* 34th ed. Rio de Janeiro: Bertrand, 1997.
Gomes, Núbia Pereira de Magalhães, and Edimilson de Almeida Pereira. *Assim se benze em Minas Gerais: Um estudo sobre a cura através da palavra.* Belo Horizonte: Mazza Edições, 1982.
———. *Negras Raízes Mineiras: os Arturos.* Juiz de Fora: Ministério da Educação/Editora da Universidade de Juiz de For a, 1988.
Gonzalez, Leila. "Griô e Guerreiro." Abdias Nascimento. *Axés do sangue e da esperança* (oríkìs). Rio de Janeiro, RJ, Brasil: Achiamé, 1983.
Good, James, and Irving Velody. *The Politics of Postmodernity.* Cambridge: Cambridge University Press, 1998.
Gordon, Paul. *The Critical Double: Figurative Meaning in Aesthetic Discourse.* Tuscaloosa: University of Alabama Press, 1995.
Goulet, Denis. *The Cruel Choice: A New Concept in the Theory of Development.* New York: Anthenaeum, 1973.
Gow, David D., and Donald Jackson. *Local Organizations and Rural Development: A Comparative Reappraisal.* 2 vols. Washington DC: Development Alternatives Inc., 1978.
Gow, David D., and Jerry Van Sant. "Decentralization in Participation: Concepts in Need of Implementation Strategies." In *Implementing Rural Development Projects,* ed. Elliot R. Morss and David D. Gow, 107–47. Detroit: Westview Press, 1985.
Grunig, James E. "A General Systems Theory of Communication, Poverty, and Underdevelopment." In *Intercultural and International Communication,* ed. Fred L. Casmir, 72–104. Washington DC: University Press of America, 1978.
Guarnieri, Gianfrancesco. *Eles não usam Black Tie.* São Paulo: Editora Brasiliense, 1966.
Guerreiro, Goli. *A trama dos tambores: A música Afro-Pop de Salvador.* São Paulo: Editora 34, 2000.
Guimarães, Geni. *Terceiro filho.* São Paulo: Jalovi, 1979.
———. *Da flor o afeto, da pedra o protesto.* São Paulo: Self-edition, 1981.
———. *Balé das emoções.* Barra Bonita/São Paulo: Evergraf, 1985.
———. *Leite do Peito.* Belo Horizonte: Mazza Edições, 2001.
Haberly, David T. "Abolitionism in Brazil: Anti-Slavery and Anti-Slave." *Luso-Brazilian Review* 9.2 (1972): 30–46.
———. *Three Sad Races: Racial Identity and National Consciousness in Brazilian Literature.* Cambridge: Cambridge University Press, 1983.
Hall, Stuart, David Held, Don Hubert, and Kenneth Thompson. *Modernity: An Introduction to Modern Societies.* Cambridge, MA: Blackwell Publishers, 1996.
———. *A identidade cultural na pós-modernidade.* Translated by Tomaz Tadeu da Silva and Guarcira Lopes Louro. Rio de Janeiro: DP&A Editora, 2001.
Hanchard, Michael G. *Orpheus and Power: The Movimento Negro of Rio de Janeiro and São Paulo, Brazil, 1945–1988.* Princeton: Princeton University Press, 1998.
———. "Afro-Modernity: Temporality, Politics, and the African Diaspora." In *Alternative Modernities,* ed. Dilip Parameshwar Gaonkar, 272–98. Durham: Duke University Press, 2001.
Harding, Rachel E. *A Refuge in Thunder: Candomblé and Alternative Spaces of Blackness.* Bloomington: Indiana University Press, 2000.

Hellwig, David. *African-American Reflections on Brazil's Racial Paradise.* Philadelphia: Temple University Press, 1992.
Herron, Robert. "Lima Barreto's *Isaías Caminha* as a Psychological Novel." *Luso-Brazilian Review* 8.2 (1971): 26–38.
Hohlfeldt, Antônio. *Literatura e vida social.* Porto Alegre: Editora da Universidade, 1996.
Hollanda, Heloisa Burque de. "Two Poetics, Two Moments." *Portuguese Literary and Cultural Studies* 4 (2000): 245–54.
Homero, Rita. "Elisa Lucinda abre o verso." *Raça* 2.10 (1997): 46–49.
Hornik, Robert. "Communication as Complement in Development." In *World Communications: A Handbook,* ed. George Gerbner and Marsha Siefert, 330–45. New York: Longman, 1984.
Howe, Irvin, ed. *The Idea of the Modern in Literature and the Arts.* New York: Horizon Press, 1967.
Htun, Mala. "From 'Racial Democracy' to Affirmative Action: Changing State Policy on Race in Brazil." *Latin American Research Review* 39.1 (2004): 60–89.
Irele, Abiola. "The African Imagination." *Research in African Literatures* 21.2 (1989): 49–67.
Jehlen, Myra. "Gender." In *Critical Terms for Literary Study,* ed. Frank Lentricchia and Thomas McLaughlin, 263–73. Chicago: University of Chicago Press, 1995.
Jesus, Carolina Maria de. *Beyond All Pity.* Translated by David St Clair. London: Earthscan, 1990.
Johnson, Randal. *Cinema Novo X 5: Masters of Contemporary Brazilian Film.* Austin: University of Texas Press, 1984.
Johnson, Randal, and Robert Stam, eds. *Brazilian Cinema.* New York: Columbia University Press, 1995.
Jones, Jermaine. "The Repatriation of Brazilian *Libertos* in Nineteenth-Century Lagos." Master's thesis, University of Wisconsin, 1996.
Jório, Amaury, and Hiram Araújo. *Escolas de samba em desfile: vida, paixão e sorte.* Rio de Janeiro: Poligráf Editora, 1969.
Kamalu, Chukwunyere. *Foundations of African Thought.* London: Karnak House, 1990.
Kang, Joon-Mann. "The Politics of Communication in Rural Development: An Overview." *Media Asia* 15.2 (1988): 92–99.
Kennedy, James H. "Recent Afro-Brazilian Literature: A Tentative Bibliography." *Current Bibliography on African Affairs* 17.4 (1984–85): 327–45.
Kibuko, Oubi Inaê. *Como se fosse pecado.* São Paulo: Self-edition, 1980.
———. *Sobrevivência.* São Paulo: Self-edition, 1981.
———. *Mergulho.* São Paulo: Self-edition, 1981.
———. *Poemas para o meu amor.* São Paulo: Self-edition, 1984.
———. *Canto à negra mulher amada.* São Paulo: Self-edition, 1986.
Kibuko, Oubi Inaê, Cuti, Miriam Alves, and Arnaldo Xavier. *Semeando.* São Paulo: Self-edition, 1983.
Kleymeyer, Chuck. "What Is 'Grassroots Development'?" *Grassroots Development* 15.1 (1991): 38–39.
Laotan, A. B. "Brazilian Influences on Lagos." *Nigeria* 69 (1961):156–65.
———. *The Torch Bearers; or, Old Brazilian Colony in Lagos.* Lagos: Ife-Olu Printing Works, 1943.

Lemke, Sieglinde. *Primitivist Modernism: Black Culture and the Origin of Transatlantic Modernism.* New York: Oxford University Press, 1998.
Lima, Alceu Amoroso, ed., *Olavo Bilac: Poesia,* Nossos Clássicos no. 2. Rio de Janeiro: Agir Editora, 1968.
Limeira, José Carlos. *Lembranças.* Rio de Janeiro: Self-edition, 1971.
———. *Zumbidos.* Rio de Janeiro: Self-edition, 1979.
Limeira, José Carlos, and Éle Semog. *O arco-íris.* Rio de Janeiro: Self-edition, 1979.
———. *Atabaques.* Rio de Janeiro: Self-edition, 1984.
Lindsay, Lisa A. "'To Return to the Bosom of Their Fatherland': Brazilian Immigrants in Nineteenth-Century Lagos." *Slavery and Abolition.* 15.1 (1994): 22–50.
Lins, Osmans. *Lima Barreto e o espaço romanesco.* São Paulo: Editora Ática, 1976.
Lobo, Luiza. *Crítica sem Juízo.* Rio de Janeiro: Livraria Francisco Alves Editora, 1993.
Magaldi, Cristina. "Adopting Imports: New Images and Alliances in Brazilian Popular Music of the 1990s." *Popular Music* 18.3 (1999): 309–29.
Majors, Richard, and Janet Mancini Billson. *Cool Pose: The Dilemmas of Black Manhood in America.* New York: Touchstone, 1992.
Mamdani, Mahmood. *Citizen and Subject: Contemporary Africa and the Legacy of Late Colonialism.* Princeton: Princeton University Press, 1996.
Mann, Celeste Dolores. "The Search for Identity in Afro-Brazilian Women's Writing: A Literary History." In *Moving Beyond Boundaries: Black Women's Diaspora,* ed. Carole Boyce Davies, 2:173–78. New York: New York University Press, 1995.
Mann, Kristin. *Marrying Well: Marriage, Status, and Social Change among the Educated Elite in Colonial Lagos.* Cambridge: Cambridge University Press, 1985.
Maranhão, Salgado, ed. *Ebulição da escrivatura.* Rio de Janeiro: Civilização Brasileira, 1978.
———. *Punhos da serpente.* Rio de Janeiro: Achiamé, 1989.
———. *Mural de ventos.* Rio de Janeiro: José Olympio Editora, 1998.
Marotti, Giorgio. *Black Characters in the Brazilian Novel.* Translated by Maria O. Marotti and Harry Lawton. Los Angeles: Center for Afro-American Studies/University of California, 1987.
Martins, Leda Maria. *Afrografias da memória.* Belo Horizonte: Mazza Edições, 1997.
Martins, Maria. *A cena em sombras.* São Paulo: Editora Perspectiva, 1995.
Martins, Wilson. "Brazilian Literature in the 90s." *Latin American Literature and the Arts* 53 (1996).
Masilela, Ntongela, ed. *Black Modernity: 20th-Century Discourses between the United States and South Africa.* Trenton, NJ: Africa World Press, 1998.
Mata Machado Filho, Aires da. *O negro e o garimpo em Minas Gerais.* São Paulo: Editora da Universidade de São Paulo, 1985.
Matta, Roberto da. *Ensaios de antropologia estrutural: O carnaval como um rito de passagem.* Petrópolis: Editora Vozes, 1977.
———. "*Carnaval* as a Cultural Problem: Towards a Theory of Formal Events and their Magic." *Working Paper no. 79, The Helen Kellogg Institute for International Studies,* 1–35. Notre Dame, IN: University of Notre Dame, 1986.
———. "O sentido do carnaval," "Um carnaval legal," and "A democracia do carnaval." In *Explorações: Ensaios de sociologia interpretativa,* 74–87. Rio de Janeiro: Editora Roccó, 1986.
———. *Carnivals, Rogues, and Heroes: An Interpretation of the Brazilian Dilemma.* Translated by John Drury. Notre Dame, IN: University of Notre Dame Press, 1991.

McGowan, Chris, and Ricardo Pessanha. *The Brazilian Sound: Samba, Bossa Nova and the Popular Music of Brazil.* Philadelphia: Temple University Press, 1998.

Melim, Angela, Carlos Lima, and Renato Casimiro. *Os arcos e a lira.* Rio de Janeiro: Oficina de Poesia/Letras-UERJ, 1998.

Melkote, Srinivas R. "Another Development: Strategies for Participation and Communication in the Eighties." In *Communication for Development in the Third World*, 228–71. New Delhi: Sage Publications, 1991.

Minka, Jamu. *Teclas de ébano.* São Paulo: Quilombhoje, 1986.

Mitchel, Angelyn. *Within the Circle.* Durham: Duke University Press, 1994.

Moi, Toril. *Sexual/Textual Politics.* London: Routledge, 1995.

Moore, Zelbert L. "Solano Trindade Remembered, 1908–1974." *Luso-Brazilian Review* 16.2 (1979): 233–38.

Moraes, Malú, ed. *Perspectivas estéticas do cinema brasileiro.* Brasília: Editora Universidade de Brasília, 1986.

Moraes, Paulo Ricardo. "Mister Marraketh." *Cadernos negros* 4 (1981): 87–96.

———. "Sabor bem brasileiro." *Cadernos negros* 6 (1983): 46–50.

———. *Eunuco.* Porto Alegre: Editora Ponto Negro Brasileiro, 1991.

Moraes, Paulo Ricardo, and Paulo Naval. *O garçom e o cliente—No balcão do naval.* Porto Alegre: Editora Ponto Negro Brasileiro, 1999.

———. *João cândido.* Porto Alegre: Prefeitura de Municipal de Porto Alegre, 2000.

Moraes, Vinícius de. *Os melhores poemas de Vinícius de Moraes.* Selected by Renata Pallottini. São Paulo: Global Editora, 1984.

Morales, Anamaria. "Blocos negros em Salvador: Reelaboração cultural e símbolos de baianidade." *Caderno CRH* (1991): 72–92.

Moura, Clóvis. *Sociologia do negro brasileiro.* São Paulo: Editora Ática, 1988.

———. *Dialética radical do Brasil negro.* São Paulo: Editora Anita, 1994.

Mudimbe, V. Y. *The Idea of Africa.* Bloomington: Indiana University Press, 1994.

Meyers, Robert. "Brazilian Popular Music in Bahia 'The Politics of the Future': An Interview with Gilberto Gil." *Studies In Latin American Culture* 9 (1990): 297–309.

Nascimento, Abdias do. *O negro revoltado.* Rio de Janeiro: GRD, 1968.

———. *Racial Democracy in Brazil: Myth or Reality?* Translated by ELisa Larkin Nascimento. Ibadan, Nigeria: Sketch Publishers, 1977.

———. *O genocídio do negro brasileiro.* Rio de Janeiro: Paz e Terra, 1978.

———. *Sortilégio.* Rio de Janeiro: Paz e Terra, 1979.

———. *O quilombismo: Documentos de uma militância pan-africanista.* Petrópolis: Vozes, 1980.

———. *Axés do sangue e da esperança (orikis).* Rio de Janeiro: Achiamé, 1985.

———. *Brazil: Mixture or Massacre?* 2nd ed. Translated by Elisa Larkin Nascimento. Dover, MA: Majority Press, 1989.

———. *Africans in Brazil: A Pan-African Perspective.* Trenton, NJ: Africa World Press, 1992.

———. "Teatro Experimental do Negro." *Revista do Patrimônio Histórico e Artístico Nacional* 25 (1997): 71–81.

Nunes, Maria Luisa. "An Artist's Identity versus the Social Role of the Writer: The Case for Joaquim Maria Machado de Assis." *College Language Association Journal* 27.2 (1983): 187–96.

———. *The Craft of an Absolute Winner.* Westport, CT: Greenwood Press, 1983.
Oakley, Peter, and David Marsden. *Approaches to Participation in Rural Development.* Geneva: International Labor Office, 1984.
———. "The Concept of Participation." In Oakley and Marsden, *Approaches to Participation in Rural Development,* 1984.
———. *Projects with People: The Practice of Participation in Rural Development.* Geneva: International Labor Office, 1991.
Oepen, Manfred, ed. *Development Support Communication in Indonesia.* Jakarta: Friedrich Naumann-Stiftung and Indonesian Society for Peasants and Community Development, 1990 [1988].
Ojo-Ade, Femi. *On Black Culture.* Ile-Ife, Nigeria: Obafemi Awolowo University Press, 1989.
———. "Interview with Aline Fraça, Afro-Brazilian Woman Writer." In *Being Black, Being Human,* 283–304. Ile-Ife, Nigeria: Obafemi Awolowo University Press, 1996.
———. "Black Brazil: African Notes on a New Negritude." In *Black Brazil: Culture, Identity, and Social Mobilization,* ed. Larry Crook and Randal Johnson, 175–97. Los Angeles: UCLA Latin American Center Publications, 1999.
Olinto, Antônio. *Nagasaki.* São Paulo: José Olympio Editora, 1956.
———. *O dia da ira.* São Paulo: José Olympio Editora, 1959.
———. *Brasileiros na África.* Rio de Janeiro: Edições GRD, 1964.
———. "The Negro Writer and the Negro Influence in Brazilian Literature." *African Forum* 2.4 (1967): 5–19.
———. *A casa da água.* Rio de Janeiro: BLOCH, 1969.
———. *The Water House.* London: Rex Collins, 1970.
———. *Early Relations and Cultural Links between Brazil and Nigeria.* Lagos: Nigerian Institute of International Affairs, 1975.
———. *A casa da água.* Rio de Janeiro: DIFEL/INL, 1978.
———. *O rei de Keto.* Rio de Janeiro: Nórdica, 1980.
———. *Trono de vidro.* Rio de Janeiro: Nórdica, 1987.
———. *Tempo de palhaço.* Rio de Janeiro: Nórdica, 1989.
———. *Sangue na floresta.* Rio de Janeiro: Nórdica, 1992.
Oliveira, Eduardo. *Carrossel de sonetos.* São Paulo: Pannartz, 1985.
———. *Carrossel de sonetos.* São Paulo: Pannartz, 1994.
Oliveira, Emanuelle. *Writing Identity: The Politics of Contemporary Afro-Brazilian Literature.* West Lafayette, IN: Purdue University Press, 2008.
Oliveira, Omar S. "Mass Media, Culture, and Communication in Brazil: The Heritage of Dependency." In *Communication in Development,* ed. Fred L. Casmir, 200–233. Norwood, NJ: Ablex, 1991.
Ortiz, Renato. *Cultura brasileira e identidade nacional.* São Paulo: Brasiliense, 1985.
Patai, Daphne. *Brazilian Women Speak.* New Brunsick: Rutgers University Press, 1989.
Pearse, Andrew and Matthias Stiefel. *Inquiry into Participation—A Research Approach.* Popular Participation Program, the United Nations Research Institute for Social Development, 1979.
Pereira, Edimilson de Almeida. *Árvore dos Arturos.* Juiz de Fora, Brazil: D'Lira, 1988.
———. *Ô lapassi e outros ritmos de ouvido.* Belo Horizonte: Editora UFMG, 1990.
———. *Corpo vivido.* Juiz de Fora, Brazil: Mazza, 1991.

———. *O homem da orelha furada.* Juiz de Fora, Brazil: D'Lira, 1995.
———. *Rebojo.* Juiz de Fora, Brazil: D'Lira, 1995.
———. "Survey of African-Brazilian Literature." *Callaloo* 18.4 (1995): 875–80.
———. *A roda do mundo.* Belo Horizonte: Mazza Edições, 1996.
———. "Contemporary Brazilian Poetry: Invention and Freedom in the Afro-Brazilian Cultural Tradition." *Journal of Latin American Cultural Studies* 5.2 (1996): 139–54.
———. "Poems." *Journal of Latin American Cultural Studies.* 8.2 (1999): 165–70.
Pereira, Edimilson de Almeida, and Núbia Pereira de Magalhães Gomes. *Arturos: olhos do Rosário.* Belo Horizonte: Mazza Edições, 1990.
Pereira, Edimilson de Almeida, and Steven White. "Brazil: Interactions and Conflicts in a Multicultural Society." In *Global Multiculturalism: Comparative Perspectives on Ethnicity, Race and Nation,* ed. Grant H. Cornwell and Eve Walsh Stoddard, 123–41. Lanham, MD: Rowman and Littlefield, 2001.
Perrone, Charles A. "*Axé, Ijexá, Olodum:* The Rise of Afro-and African Currents in Brazilian Popular Music." *Afro-Hispanic Review* 11.1–3 (1992): 42–50.
Perrone, Charles A., and Christopher Dunn. *Brazilian Popular Music and Globalization.* New York: Routledge, 2002.
Prado, Antônio. *Lima Barreto: O crítico e a crise.* Rio de Janeiro: Editora Cátedra, 1976.
Proença Filho, Domício. "A trajetória do negro na literatura brasileira." *Revista do Patrimônio Histórico e Artístico Nacional* 25 (1997): 159–77.
Quilombhoje. *Reflexões: Sobre a literatura afro-brasileira.* São Paulo: Quilombhoje/Conselho de Participação e Desenvolvimento da Comunidade Negra, 1985.
———. *Criação crioula, nu elefante branco.* São Paulo: Ministry of Culture, 1987.
———. *Cadernos negros: Os melhores contos.* São Paulo: Quilombhoje/ Ministry of Culture, 1998.
———. *Cadernos negros: Os melhores poemas.* São Paulo: Quilombhoje/Ministério da Cultura, 1998.
———. *Frente negra brasileira: Depoimentos.* Compiled by Márcio Barbosa (interviews and texts). São Paulo: Fundo Nacional da Cultura, Ministério da Cultura, 1998.
Quinlan, Susan Canty. *The Female Voice in Contemporary Brazilian Narrative.* New York: Peter Lang, 1991.
Quintas, Fátima, ed. *Mulher negra: Preconceito, sexualidade e imaginário.* Recife: Fundação Joaquim Nabuco, 1995.
———. *Gilberto Freyre: A obra em tempos vários.* Recife: Fundação Joaquim Nabuco, 1999.
Rabassa, Gregory. *O negro na ficção brasileira.* Rio de Janeiro: Tempo Brasileiro, 1965.
Raça. "Interview with Spike Lee." *Raça* 11 (July 1997): 10–14.
Rahman, M. A. "Process-Oriented Rural Development Planning Integrated with Key Elements of Rationality (for the Developing World)." MES Major Paper. Toronto: Faculty of Environmental Studies, York University, 1996.
Raphael, Alison. "From Popular Culture to Microenterprise: The History of Brazilian Samba Schools." *Revista de Música Latinoamericana* 11.1 (1990): 25–40.
Rassner, Ronald M. "Palmares and the Freed Slave in Afro-Brazilian Literature." In *Voices from Under: Black Narrative in Latin America and the Caribbean,* ed. William Luis, 201–22. Wesport, CT: Greenwood Press, 1984.

Rego, Enylton de Sá, and Charles A. Perrone. *MPB: Contemporary Brazilian Popular Music*. Albuquerque, NM: Latin American Institute/University of New Mexico, 1985.
Rennó, Carlos, ed. *Gilberto Gil: Todas as letras*. São Paulo: Companhia das Letras, 1996.
Ribeiro, Esmeralda. *Malungos e milongas*. São Paulo: Quilombhoje/Edição da Autora, 1988.
———. "Ogun." *Callaloo* 18.4 (1995): 913–19; 741–47.
Risério, Antônio. *Carnaval Ijexá: Notas sobre afoxés e blocos do novo carnaval afrobaiano*. Salvador: Corrupio, 1981.
———, ed. *Gilberto Gil Expresso 2222*. Salvador: Corrupio, 1982.
Risério Antônio, and Gilberto Gil. *O poético e o político e outros escritos*. Rio de Janeiro: Paz e Terra, 1988.
Rodowick, D. N. *The Crisis of Political Modernism: Criticism and Ideology in Contemporary Film Theory*. Urbana: University of Illinois Press, 1988.
Rodrigues, Abelardo. *Memória da noite*. São José dos Campos, Brazil: Self-edition, 1978.
Rodrigues, Ironildes. "O transcendentalismo poético e simbólico na poesia negra de Eduardo de Oliveira." *Afrodiáspora* 3.6–7 (1985): 125–32.
Rodrigues, João Carlos. *O negro brasileiro e o cinema*. Rio de Janeiro: Globo, 1988.
———. "Novas Visões do negro brasileiro e o cinema." *Revista do Patrimônio Histórico e Artístico Nacional* 25 (1997): 91–99.
Rodrigues, João Jorge Santos. *Olodum: Estrada da paixão*. Salvador: Grupo Cultural Olodum/Fundação Casa de Jorge Amado, 1996.
Rogers, Everett M. *Communication of Innovation: A Cross-Cultural Approach*. New York: The Free Press, 1971.
———. *Communication and Development: Critical Perspectives*. Beverly Hills, CA: Sage Publications, 1976.
———. "Communication and Development: The Passing of the Dominant Paradigm." *Communication Research* 3.2 (1976): 213–240.
Rolim, Cândido. *Exemplos alados*. Fortaleza, Brazil: Gráfica Rabôni, 1997.
———. *Pedra habitada*. Porto Alegre: Age Editora, 2002.
Rosenfeld, Anatol. *O mito e o herói no moderno teatro brasileiro*. São Paulo: Perspectiva, 1982.
Rowell, Charles H., ed. *Ancestral House: The Black Short Story in the Americas and Europe*. Boulder, CO: Westview Press, 1995.
Ruttan, Vernon W. "Integrated Rural Development Programs: A Skeptical Perspective." *International Development Review* 2 (1975):129–51.
———. "Integrated Rural Development Programmes: A Historical Perspective." *World Development* 12.4 (1984): 393–401.
Sadlier, Darlene J. *Nelson Pereira dos Santos*. Urbana: University of Illinois Press, 2003.
Sansone, Lívio. *From Africa to Afro: Use and Abuse of Africa in Brazil*. Amsterdam/Dakar: SEPHIS/CODESRIA, 1999.
Sansone, Lívio, and Jocélio Teles dos Santos. *Ritmos em trânsito: Sócio-antropologia da música baiana*. São Paulo: Dynamis Editorial, 1998.
Santos, Joel Rufino dos. *História de trancaso*. São Paulo: Editora Ática, 1983.
———. *A botija de ouro*. São Paulo: Editora Ática, 1984.

———. *O saci e o curupira*. São Paulo: Editora Ática, 1984.
———. *Dudu calunga*. São Paulo: Editora Ática, 1986.
———. *Cururu virou pajé*. São Paulo: Editora Ática, 1986.
———. *Quatros dias de rebelião*. Rio de Janeiro: José Olympio Editora, 1989.
———. *Crônica de indomáveis Delírios*. Rio de Janeiro: Rocco, 1997.
———. *Quando eu voltei, tive uma surpresa*. Rio de Janeiro: Rocco, 2000.
Santos, John F. "A Psychologist Reflects on Brazil and Brazilians." In *New Perspectives of Brazil*, ed. Eric Baklanoff, 233–63. Nashville: Vanderbilt University Press, 1966.
Santos, Jussara. "Afrodicções: Identidade e alteridade na construção poética de três escritores negros brasileiros." Master's thesis, Pontifífica Universidade Católica de Minas Gerais, 1998.
———. *De flores artificiais*. Belo Horizonte: Sobá/O Meio, 2000.
Santos e Silva, Alessandra. "O exercício de cidadania na prosa de Inaldete Pinheiro de Andrade e Rogério Andrade Barbosa." Paper, Universidade de Pernambuco, Recife, 2000.
Sayers, Raymond S. *The Negro in Brazilian Literature*. New York: Hispanic Institute, 1956.
Schaeber, Petra. "Música negra nos tempos de globalização: Produção musical e management da identidade étnica—o caso do Olodum." In *Ritmos em trânsito: Sócio-antropologia da música baiana*, ed. Livio Sansone and Jocélio Teles dos Santos, 145–59. São Paulo: Dynamis Editorial, 1998.
Schnabel, Tom. *Rhythm Planet: The Great World Music Makers*. New York: Universe Publishing, 1998.
Schwartz, Ronald. *Latin American Films, 1932–1994: A Critical Filmography*. Jefferson, NC: McFarland, 1997.
Schwarz, Roberto. *Ao vencedor as batatas*. São Paulo: Duas Cidades, 1977.
———. *Misplaced Ideas*. London: Verso, 1992.
Seffner, Fernando, ed. *Presença negra no Rio Grande do Sul*. Porto Alegre: Prefeitura Municipal de Porto Alegre, 1995.
———. *Curetagem (poemas doloridos)*. Rio de Janeiro: Edição Independente, 1986.
———. *A cor da demanda: Poesia afro-brasileira*. Rio de Janeiro: Letra Capital, 1997.
———. "A selva da vida." In *Cadernos negros: Os melhores contos*, 51–64. São Paulo: Quilombhoje/Ministério da Cultura, 1998.
Serveas, J., ed. *Participatory Communication for Social Change*. Thousand Oaks, CA: Sage Publications, 1991.
———. *Development Communication in Action: Report of the Inter-Agency Meeting on Advocacy Strategies for Health and Development*. World Health Organization Conference, Geneva, November 9–13, 1992.
Sheriff, Robin E. *Dreaming Equality: Color, Race, and Racism in Urban Brazil*. New Jersey: Rutgers University Press, 2001.
Silva, Ana Maria Silva et al., *Gostando mais de nós mesmos*, 2nd ed. São Paulo: Editora Gente, 1999.
Silva, Jônatas Conceição da. *miragem de engenho*. Salvador: Instituto da radiofusão educativa da Bahia, 1984.
———. *Outras miragens*. São Paulo: Confraria do Livro, 1989.
Silveira, Maria Helena Vargas da. *O sol de fevereiro*. Porto Alegre: Evangraf, 1991.

———. *Tipuana*. Porto Alegre: Grup Editorial Rainha Ginga, 1997.
———. *O encontro*. Porto Alegre: Grupo Cultural Rainha Ginga, 2000.
Silveira, Oliveira. *Germinou*. Porto Alegre: Self-edition, 1962.
———. *Banzo saudade negra*. Porto Alegre: Self-edition, 1970.
———. *Décima do negro peão*. Porto Alegre: Self-edition, 1974.
———. *Praça da palavra*. Porto Alegre: Self-edition, 1976.
———. *Pêlo escuro*. Porto Alegre: Self-edition, 1977.
———. *Roteiro dos tantãs*. Porto Alegre: Self-edition, 1981.
———. *Poemas sobre Palmares*. Porto Alegre: Self-edition, 1987.
———. "Notícia sobre autores negros na literatura gaúcha." *Boletim Bibliográfico* 49.1–4 (1988): 159–62.
———. "Ser e não ser" and "Outra nega fulô." In *Cadernos negros: Os melhores poemas*, ed. Quilombhoje, 108–10. São Paulo: Ministério da Cultura, 1998.
———. "O desafio cultural." In *Na própria pele: Os negros no Rio Grande do Sul*, ed. Antônio Mário Ferreira, 103–12. Porto Alegre: Companhia Rio-grandense de Artes Gráficas, 2000.
Singhal, Arvind, and Jerry Domatob. "The Field of Development Communication: An Appraisal (A Conversation with Prof Everett M Rogers)." *Journal of Development Communication* 15.2 (2004): 51–55.
Skidmore, Thomas. *Black into White: Race and Nationality in Brazilian Thought*. Durham: Duke University Press, 1993.
Soyinka, Wole, ed. *Poems of Black Africa*. London: Heinemann, 1975.
———. *The Burden of Memory, the Muse of Forgiveness*. New York: Oxford University Press, 1999.
Sparks, David. "Gilberto Gil: Praise Singer of the Gods." *Afro-Hispanic Review* 11.1–3 (1992): 70–75.
Spivak, Gayatri C. *Outside in the Teaching Machine*. London: Routledge, 1993.
Stam, Robert. "Slow Fade to Afro: The Black Presence in Brazilian Cinema." *Film Quarterly* 36.2 (1982): 16–32.
———. *Subversive Pleasures: Bakhtin, Cultural Criticism, and Film*. Baltimore: Johns Hopkins University Press, 1989.
———. "Cross-Cultural Dialogisms: Race and Multiculturalism in Brazilian Cinema." In *Mediating Two Worlds: Cinematic Encounters in the Americas*, ed. John King, Ana M. López, and Manuel Alvarado, 175–203. London: British Film Institute, 1993.
———. *Tropical Multiculturalism: A Comparative History of Race in Brazilian Cinema and Culture*. Durham: Duke University Press, 1997.
———. "The Flash of Spirit: Cinematic Representations of Afro-Brazilian Religion." In *Black Brazil: Culture, Identity, and Social Mobilization*, ed. Larry Crook and Randal Johnson, 313–38. Los Angeles: UCLA Latin American Center Publications, 1999.
Stepto, Robert. *From Behind the Veil: A Study of Afro-American Narrative*. Urbana: University of Illinois Press, 1991.
Telles, Edward E. *Race in Another America: The Significance of Skin Color in Brazil*. New Jersey: Princeton University Press, 2004.
Theodoro, Helena. "Mulher negra, arte e poesia: Leci Brandão." In *Presença negra no Rio Grande do Sul*, ed. Fernando Seffner, 21–29. Porto Alegre: UE/Porto Alegre and Prefeitura Municipal de Porto Alegre, 1995.

Torres, Wagner. *Cantária*. Porto Alegre: Plurarts, 2000.
Trindade, Solano. *Poemas de uma vida simples*. Rio de Janeiro: Self-edition, 1944.
———. *Cantares ao meu povo*. São Paulo: Brasiliense, 1981.
———. *Tem gente com fome e outros poemas: Antologia poética*. Rio de Janeiro: Prefeitura da Cidade de Rio de Janeiro, 1988.
Turner, Jerry M. "Les Brésiliens: The Impact of Former Brazilian Slaves upon Dahomey." PhD diss., Boston University, 1975.
Turner, Lorenzo D. "Some Contacts of Brazilian Ex-Slaves with Nigeria, West Africa." *Journal of Negro History* 30.2 (1942): 55–67.
Tutuca, Ronald. *O paquiderme com asa de água*. Porto Alegre: Self-edition, 1981.
———. *Mortoalegrense*. Porto Alegre: Self-edition, 1982.
———. *Homem ao rubro*. Porto Alegre: Grupo Pró-Texto, 1983.
———. *Puya*. Porto Alegre: Biblos Livros, 1992.
Tutuca, Ronald, with Jaime da Silva and Paulo Ricardo de Moraes. *Negro três vezes negro*. Porto Alegre: Self-edition, 1984.
Twine, France Winddance. *Racism in a Racial Democracy: The Maintenance of White Supremacy in Brazil*. New Brunswick, NJ: Rutgers University Press, 1998.
Twine, France Winddance, and Jonathan W. Warren, eds. *Racing Research, Researching Race: Methodological Dilemmas in Critical Race Studies*. New York: New York University Press, 2000.
Ulhôa Carvalho, Maria de. "Tupi or Not Tupi MPB: Popular Music and Identity in Brazil." In *The Brazilian Puzzle: Culture on the Borderlands of the Western World*, ed. David J. Hess and Roberto A. da Matta, 159–79. New York: Columbia University Press, 1995.
Veiga, Manuel, ed. *Cabo verde: Insularidade e literatura*. Paris: Karthala, 1998.
Veloso, Caetano. *Verdade tropical*. São Paulo: Companhia das Letras, 1997.
Ventura, Adão. *Abrir-se um abutre ou mesmo depois de deduzir dele o azul*. Belo Horizonte: Oficina, 1970.
———. *As musculatras do arco do triunfo*. Belo Horizonte: Comunicação, 1976.
———. *A cor da pele*. Belo Horizonte: Self-edition, 1980.
———. *Texturaafro*. Belo Horizonte: Self-edition, 1992.
———. *Jequitinhonha*. Belo Horizonte: Mulheres Emergentes, 1997.
Ventura, Roberto. *Estilo tropical*. São Paulo: Companhia das Letras, 1991.
Verger, Pierre. "Nigeria, Brazil, and Cuba." A Special Independence issue of *Nigeria* magazine, October 1960.
———. *Flux et reflux de la traité des nègres entre le Golfe de Benin et Bahia de todos os santos du 17ème au 19ème siècle*. Paris: Mouton and Co., 1968.
Vieira, Antônio. *Cantares d'África*. Rio de Janeiro: Gráfica Riex Editora, 1980.
Vieira, Hamilton de Jesus. *Poetas baianos da negritude*. Salvador: Centro de Estudos Afro-Orientais, Universidade Federal da Bahia, 1982.
Vieira, Rosângela Maria. "Brazil." In *No Longer Invisible: Afro-Latin Americans Today*, ed. Minority Rights Group, 19–46. London: Minority Rights Publications, 1995.
Waldemar, Euzébio Pereira. *Do cinza ao negro*. Belo Horizonte: Mazza Edições, 1993.
Wang, Georgette, and Wimal Dissanayake. "Culture, Development and Change: Some Explorative Observations." In *Continuity and Change in Communication Systems*, ed. Goergette Wang and Wimal Dissanayake, 3–20. Norwood, NJ: Ablex, 1984.

Washington, Teresa N. *Our Mothers, Our Powers, Our Texts: Manifestations of Àjé in Africana Literature*. Bloomington: Indiana University Press, 2005.
West, Dennis. *Contemporary Brazilian Cinema*. Albuquerque: Latin American Institute/University of New Mexico, 1993.
White, Steven F. "Contemporary Brazilian Poetry: Invention and Freedom in the Afro-Brazilian Cultural Tradition." *Journal of Latin American Cultural Studies* 5.2 (1996): 139–54.
———, ed. "Edimilson de Almeida Pereira: African Brazilian Poet." *Callaloo* 19.1 (1996): 31–54.
———. "Reinventing a Sacred Past in Contemporary Afro-Brazilian Poetry: An Introduction." *Callaloo* 20.1 (1997): 69–82.
———. "Poems." *Journal of Latin American Cultural Studies* 8.2 (1999): 165–70.
———. "Brazil: Interactions and Conflicts in a Multicultural Society." In *Global Multiculturalism: Comparative Perspectives on Ethnicity, Race and Nation*, ed. Grant H. Cornwell and Eve Walsh Stoddard, 122–40. Lanham, MD: Rowman and Littlefield, 2001.
Williams, Raymond. *The Long Revolution*. Harmondsworth: Penguin Books, 1961.
Woods, John L. "Integrated Development Programmes Can Be Counter-Productive." Paper presented to ESCAP Expert Group Meeting on Organizational Aspects of Integrating Family Planning with Development Programmes, Bangkok, 1976.
Xavier, Arnaldo. "Various Poems." In *Contramão*, ed. Aristides Klafke, Arnaldo Xavier, and Celso Luiz. São Paulo: Edições Pindaiba, 1978/
———. Xavier, Arnaldo. *A roza da recvsa*. São Paulo: Pindaíba, 1986 [1981, 1982].
———. "Dha lamba à qvizila—a busca dhe hvma expressão literária negra." In *Criação crioula, nu elefante branco*, 89–100. São Paulo: Quilombhoje/Ministry of Culture, 1987.
———. "Literatura à flor da pele (Orikrítica)" Typescript essay. São Paulo, Brazil, 1987–88.
———. "O brilho de Abílio." Introduction to *Antes do carnaval* by Abílio Ferreira, 9–32. São Paulo: Selinunte, 1990.
———. *Ludlud*. São Paulo: Casa Pyndahyba, 1997
Xavier, Ismail. "The Shape of Brazilian Cinema in the Postmodern Age." In *Brazilian Cinema*, ed. Randal Johnson and Robert Stam, 387–470. New York: Columbia University Press, 1995
———. *Allegories of Underdevelopment: Aesthetics and Politics in Modern Brazilian Cinema*. Minneapolis: University of Minnesota, 1997.
Zilberman, Regina. *Roteiro de uma literatura singular*. Porto Alegre: Editora da Universidade, 1992.

Disco/Video/Filmography

Andrade, Joaquim Pedro de. *Macunaíma*. Brazil, 1969. 90 min., color. Portuguese/English subtitles. VHS.
Barros, Aramis. *Casa do pagode/Raça brasileira (20 anos)* (House of Pagode/Brazilian Race [20 years]). Rio de Janeiro: Som Livre, 2004. 0073-9. DVD.

Brandão, Leci. "Casa Grande e Senzala" (Masters and the Slaves) *Questão de Gosto* (Matter of Taste). Rio de Janeiro: Polydor, 1976.

———. "Canta, canta, minha gente" (Sing, Sing, My People) *Eu Sou Assim* (This is the Way I Am). São Paulo: Trama, 2000. CD #84.494.129. [Track #1]

———. "Papa vadiou" (Daddy Loiters) *Eu Sou Assim* (This is the Way I Am). São Paulo: Trama, 2000. CD #84.494.129. [Track #3]

———. "Barco a vela" (Candlelit Boat) *Eu Sou Assim* (This is the Way I Am). São Paulo: Trama, 2000. CD #84.494.129. [Track #8]

———. "Menor abandonado" (Abandoned Youngster) *Eu Sou Assim* (This is the Way I Am). São Paulo: Trama, 2000. CD #84.494.129. [Track #11]

———. "Deixa deixa" (Leave Them Alone) *Eu Sou Assim* (This is the Way I Am). São Paulo: Trama, 2000. CD #84.494.129. [Track #11]

———. "Anjos da guarda" (Guardian Angels) *Eu Sou Assim*. São Paulo: Trama, 2000. CD #84.494.129. [Track #12]

———. "Deus do fogo da justiça" (Ara Ketu) (God of Fiery Justice-Ara Ketu) *Eu Sou Assim*. (This is the Way I Am). Trama, 2000. CD #84.494.129. [Track #15]

———. "Saudação a Ossain" (Homage to Osanyin, Medicinal Plant Goddess) *Eu Sou Assim*. (This is the Way I Am). São Paulo: Trama, 2000. CD #84.494.129. [Track #17]

———. "Negro Zumbi" (Black Zumbi) *A Cara do Povo* (The Face of the People). Wallingford, CT: Phantom Sound, 2003. CD. [Track #15]

———. "Feirinha da pavuna" (Pavuna Market) *Casa do Pagode* (House of Pagoda).Rio de Janeiro: Som Livre, 2005. [Track #18]

———. "Batida no coração" (Beating of the Heart) *Raízes do Samba* (Roots-Samba). Rio de Janeiro: EMI, 2007. CD. #B000031R33. [Track #7]

Brandão, Leci and Cassiana. "Pomba rolou" (Fooled by the Parrot) *Casa do Pagode*. Rio de Janeiro: Som Livre, 2005. [Track #18]

Burle, José Carlos. *Também somos irmãos* (We are also Brothers). Brazil, 1949. 90 min., Black-and-White. Portuguese. VHS.

Camus, Marcel. *Orfeu negro* (Black Orpheus). Brazil/France, 1958. 106 min., color. Portuguese/English subtitles. DVD.

Censoni, Osvaldo. *João negrinho*. (Black John) Brazil, 1958. 89 min., color. Portuguese. VHS.

Cuti and Carlos de Assumpção. *Quilombo de Palavras: Poemas* (Runaway Settlement of Words: Poems). Manaus: Microservice, 1997. CGC 34.525.444/0001–62. CD.

Diegues. Carlos. *Xica da Silva* (Chica da Silva). Brazil, 1976. 117 min., color. Portuguese/English subtitles. VHS.

Diegues, Carlos. *Quilombo* (Runaway Settlement). Brazil, 1984. 127 min., color. Portuguese/English subtitles. DVD.

Diegues, Carlos. *Orfeu* (Orpheus). Original sound track of film. Rio de Janeiro: Sony Music Ltd (Brazil)/Natasha Records, 1999. CNPJ 43.203.520/0001–04. CD.

Diegues, Carlos. *Orfeu* (Orpheus). Brazil, 2000. 112 min., color. Portuguese/English subtitles. DVD.

Duarte, Anselmo. *O pagador de promessas* (Keeper of Promises). Brazil, 1962. 90 min., black-and-white. Portuguese. DVD.

Gil, Gilberto. *Le troubadour du Brésil* (Brazilian Trobador). Warner Music–France, 1997. 3984–21185–2. CD.

———. *Tropicália 2: Caetano e Gil* (Tropicália 2: Caetano and Gil). Polygram-Brasil, 1993. 518.178–2. CD.

———. *Quanta*. Warner Music–Brasil, 1997. 92770–2. CD.

———. *Gilberto Gil*. Polygram-Brasil (Millennium series), 1999. 538.204–2. CD.

———. *Leci Brandão e os convidados* (Leci Brandão and the Invitees), 2003. 898133064975. CD.

Hirszman, Leon. *Eles não usam Black Tie* (They Don't Wear Black Tie). Brazil, 1981. 120 min., color. Portuguese/English subtitles. VHS.

Lima Júnior, Walter. *Xico rei*. (King Chico). Brazil, 1985. 110 min., color. Portuguese. VHS.

Marre, Jeremy. *The Spirit of Samba: Black Music of Brazil*. Brazil/USA, 1998. 60 min., color. English. DVD.

Meirelles, Fernando and Kátia Lund. *Cidade de Deus* (City of God). Brazil, 2004. 130 min., color. Portuguese/English subtitles. DVD.

Santos, Juana Elbein dos. *Ancestralidade Africana no Brasil: Commemorative CD in Honor of Mestre Didi's 80th Birthday*. São Paulo: Axis, SECNEB, 1999. CD-ROM.

Santos, Nelson Pereira dos. *Tenda dos milagres* (Tent of Miracles). Brazil, 1977. 130 min., color. Portuguese/English subtitles. VHS.

Santos, Nelson Pereira dos. *Jubiabá*. Brazil, 1986. 108 min., color. Portuguese. VHS.

Veloso, Caetano. *Sem lenço, sem documento: O melhor de Caetano Veloso* (Without Handkerchief, Without Identity Papers: The Best of Caetano Veloso). Polygram-Brasil, 1989. 836.528–2. CD.

Index

Abeokuta, Nigeria, 114
Abiku, 260
Abionan, 120, 121, 122, 123, 124
abolition, 25, 27, 30, 31, 36, 38, 51, 52, 55, 58, 63, 102, 108, 111, 112, 116, 119, 261, 265, 267, 291, 303, 305, 311, 320, 321, 335, 336, 349, 381, 382, 386, 389, 399, 403, 405, 417
Açai, 367
Acotirene, 188
Ademolá, 122
Aduké (Abionan's mother), 122
Afanu, Germana, 111
Afoxés, 71, 129, 138, 143, 163, 255, 268, 409
African and African Diaspora Studies program, 199
Afro-Bahian carnival, 20, 129, 151–68, 357, 362, 371, 372, 386
Afro-Bahian epic, 90
Afro-Bahians, 386
Afro-Brazilian: carnival, 5, 8, 143, 151–68, 269, 361, 370, 372, 386; cause, 5, 8, 9, 26, 226, 362; cinema, 6, 169–92; community, 52, 62, 68, 69, 70, 74, 75, 77, 78, 90, 91, 95, 97, 98, 101, 102, 103, 106, 361, 364, 370, 371, 372, 375; culture, 2, 3, 5, 7, 10, 13, 17, 18, 21, 65, 73, 110, 152, 179, 184, 187, 190, 191, 195, 196, 204, 205, 206, 209, 252, 266, 330, 353, 359, 367, 373, 383; dignity, 37; discourse, 5, 7, 199, 294, 328; heroine, 90; identity, 2, 3, 14, 24, 65, 97, 256, 328, 338, 383, 402; image, 3, 172, 247; letters, 6, 110, 233, 251, 301, 316, 338; modernity, 18, 193–206, 207–38, 297, 301, 344, 356; music, 273, 400; personality, 6, 45, 59, 169, 188; religion, 90, 179, 191, 238, 323, 387, 411; roots, 10, 129, 306; soul, 169, 174, 176; struggles, 13; trilogy, 7, 110; voice, 4, 11, 12, 60, 85, 96, 272, 302, 312; women writers, 7, 19, 80, 91, 103, 107, 285, 391, 392
Afro-Brazilianness, 3, 181, 353
Afrocentricity, 70, 163, 167, 268, 322
Afrocentrists, 268
Afro-consciousness, 139, 141, 143
Afro-Mineiro, 20, 322, 323, 328, 334, 338, 339, 344, 348, 393, 398
Afro-modernity, 193–206, 207–38, 240, 241, 251, 269, 270, 275, 280, 331, 355, 388, 403
Agemo, 369
Agogos, 212
Àjé, 358, 413
Akan, the, 388
Alagoas, 221
Alaketu, 120
Alamgir, 163, 397
Alcione, 10, 20, 130, 357, 359, 397
Alencar, José de, 173
Alexandre, 10, 70–75, 205, 206, 297
Aliança (Alliance), 112, 382
allegories, 175, 269–74, 311, 355, 413
Almas de Gunhães, 328
Almeida, Hermógenes, 347
Almeida, Márcio, 339
Alvarenga, Silva, 381
Alves, Castro, 5, 12, 20, 52, 208, 228, 303, 305, 382
Alves, Miriam, 69, 76, 80, 90, 91, 95, 97, 99, 107, 201, 238, 247, 255, 268, 275, 294, 295, 297, 301, 382, 392, 401, 402, 404
Amado, Jorge, 3, 5–7, 13, 110, 188, 189, 201, 298, 318, 383, 392, 409
ambiguity, 3, 23, 25, 30, 31, 38, 48, 91, 175, 182, 227, 236, 249, 273, 332, 350

amnesia, 24, 92, 196, 198, 201
Amosu, Tudonou, 109, 397
ancestral house, 297, 299, 409
ancestral linkages, 7
ancestral motherhood, 20, 357–75
ancestral paradigm, 14, 17, 201, 202, 294, 313
ancestral sense, 190, 60, 102, 200, 202
Ancestralidade, 14, 197, 267–301, 399, 415
ancestrality, 193–206, 267–301, 338, 358, 382
Andrade, Carlos Drummond de, 306, 309, 344
Andrade, Joaquim Pedro de, 158, 181, 182
Andrade, Mário de, 5, 6, 12, 26, 181, 227, 265
Andrade, Oswald de, 182, 344, 384
anthropophagize, 128
anthropophagy, 384
antigo senhor (old master), 31–33
antithesis of modernity, 194
Ao vencedor as batatas!, 27, 410
Apolônio, 159
Appadurai, Arjun, 205, 206, 397
Aragão, Jorge, 357
Araketu, 359, 370, 371, 394
Ara Orun (ancestors), 123, 231
Araújo Dantas, Anamélia de, 307
Arcanjo, Pedro, 189–91
archetypes, 172, 417
Argilo, Nilo, 190
Asante, Molefi, 222
àṣẹ, 1, 2, 143, 217, 218, 226, 241, 318, 340, 341, 346, 388, 392, 400, 403. See also *axé*
assimilado, 406, 408, 417
assimilé, 202
Assis, Machado de, 6, 9, 10, 11, 23–26, 37, 38, 49, 50, 55, 173, 208, 265, 312, 381, 391, 402, 406
Assumpção, Carlos de, 14, 57, 65, 89, 239, 250, 266, 350, 353, 354, 414
Atlantic passage, 5, 18, 19, 20
Atlantic slavery, 199, 319
Augel, Moema Parente, 398

Augusto, João, 134, 384
authenticity, 3, 158, 268
Avenida Paulista, 251
axé, 1, 2, 143, 217, 218, 226, 241, 318, 340, 341, 346, 388, 392, 400, 403, 406, 408, 417
Azevedo, Cassi Jones de, 49, 50, 77
Azevedo, Thales de, 51

Baba Alapala, 127, 139, 203, 205
babalawo (diviner), 122, 221
babalorixá (Candomblé priest), 189
Bacharel, 44
Badagry, 112
Badawê, 371
Baguari, 328
Bahian identity, 133
Baianos (Bahians) 3, 134, 303, 313, 337, 393, 412
Bakhtin, Mikhail, 177, 411
Balduíno, Antônio (Baldo), 188
Bamgbose Street, 108, 112
Bandeira, Manuel, 306, 326
Banks, Jared, 177
Barbeitos, Arlindo, 353
Barbosa, Lindinalva, 188, 189, 303, 400
Barbosa, Márcio, 16, 54, 57, 68, 69, 77, 78, 90, 97, 99, 238, 382, 389, 390, 397
Barbosa, Maria José Somerlate, 323, 328, 329, 393
Barra Bonita, São Paulo, Brazil, 391, 392, 403
Barreto, Lima, 37–50, 52, 55, 207, 208, 312, 381, 382, 391, 398, 402, 404, 405, 408
Barthes, Roland, 193, 198, 387
Bastide, Roger, 15, 323
Béhague, Gerard, 128, 129, 399
Beltrán, Luis Ramiro, 155, 384, 399
bênção (blessing), 160
Benedict, Saint, 337
Beokis, 104
Bernd, Zilá, 399
Bethânia, Maria, 130, 132, 161
Bhabha, Homi, 399
Bilac, Olavo, 233, 388, 405

Biribiri, 324
Bittencourt, AnaCris, 394
black mammy, 80, 172, 173
Black Personality Award, 274
black-and-white, 54, 111, 414, 416
blackness, 3, 12, 18, 23, 25, 37, 50, 58, 61, 62, 68, 82, 102, 131, 160, 173, 174, 175, 183, 191, 195, 208, 210, 227, 228, 230, 236, 238, 260, 261, 265, 266, 269, 270, 273, 277, 285, 286, 289, 292, 295, 298, 302, 303, 312, 320, 324, 325, 329, 331, 339, 344, 350, 352, 353, 354, 390, 397, 403
black–white dialectic, 244
Blaxploitation, 175, 196
blocos afro(s), 359
blocos carnavalescos, 151, 157, 159
Boal, Augusto, 248
bohemian sensibility, 133
bondage, 18, 27, 37, 194, 267, 277, 294, 303, 315
bossa nova, 128, 130, 131, 399, 406
Braga, Júlio, 17, 197
Brandão, Leci, 20, 357–75, 394, 395, 411, 415
Braúlio, 186, 187
Braz Cubas, 36
Brazilian architecture, 108, 111
Brazilian development, 151, 157
Brazilian Embassy, 110, 112
Brazilian filmmakers, 170
Brazilian hip-hop, 10
Brazilian modernism, 129
Brazilian popular music, 128
Brazilian Quarter (*Popo Aguda*), 108, 111
Brazilian regionalism, 135
Brazilian theater, 171
Brazilians in Africa, 110
bread seller, 42, 177
Brito, Ricardo Aleixo de, 20, 302, 322, 323, 337, 339, 344, 399
Brown, Carlinhos, 10
Buarque, Chico, 128, 137, 138
"buffoonization," 8, 69, 110, 169, 178
bumba-meu-boi, 109, 111, 113

burden of blackness, 18, 20, 62, 174, 208, 238, 246, 260, 302, 329

caboclo (white and Indian), 181, 324
Cabral, Amilcar, 205, 351
Cachaça, 66, 157, 278, 279, 324, 340, 400
Cadernos negros, 78, 85, 91, 97, 98, 102, 241, 243–52, 354, 382, 390, 391, 397, 398, 401, 406, 408, 410, 411
Callado, Antônio, 227
Calunga, 337, 338, 410
Cambira, 317
Caminha, Adolfo, 173
Camargo, Oswaldo de, 69, 233–38, 251, 392
Camões, Luís de, 1, 210, 227, 288
Campos, Augusto de, 128
Campos, Haroldo de, 344
Campos Square (*Praça campos*), 108, 111
Camus, Albert, 254
Cândido, Antônio, 227
Cândido, João, 221, 406
Candomblé, 2, 53, 66, 70, 71, 113, 122, 175, 179, 180, 181, 188, 189, 190, 195, 205, 239, 255, 256, 260, 268, 269, 271, 301, 316, 322, 330, 337, 338, 361, 369, 371, 372, 378, 390, 403
Capinam, José Carlos, 128
Capoeira, 9, 22, 54, 65, 72, 135, 181, 195, 269, 315, 345, 378
capoeiristas, 180
Cardoso, Fernando Henrique, 16
Cardoso, Hamilton, 55
caricatures, 172
carioca, 24, 38, 48, 176
Carvalho, Marcelo, 394
Carmelinda da Bela Vista, 334
carnaval (Portuguese), 10, 151, 151, 157, 157, 159, 160, 166, 298, 299, 301, 370, 385, 386, 392, 402, 405, 409, 413
Carneiro, Edson, 12
carnival (adj.)/carnival (n.), 151–68
Carrena Street, 111
Cartola, 10

Carvalho, Beth, 20, 357, 372, 373
Casa grande e senzala (Masters and the Slaves), 3, 360, 361, 394, 414
Cassiana, 372, 373, 414
Catarina, 114, 115, 299, 300, 301
Catholicism, 113, 180, 244, 247, 256
Caymi, Dorival, 10, 130
celestial code, 182
Celinha, 61, 64, 82, 83
center–periphery models, 205
Centro de Cultura Afro-Brasileira, 208
Césaire, Aimé, 55, 208, 354, 398
Cesário, Mariana, 270, 271, 272
Chauí, Marilena, 80, 175, 400
chefs d'oeuvre, 250
Chequer, Jamile, 394
Chica da Silva, 324, 400, 414. *See also* Xica da Silva
"chickenization," 169
Christ-like figure, 181
Cinema Novo, 179, 186, 189, 404
cinematic fragmentation, 175–76
cinematic industry, 8, 171, 174
Cintra, Benedito, 54, 58, 59, 85
Circo Voador, 395
citizenship, 267–301
Cixous, Hélène, 198
Clarim da Alvorada, 12, 65
class discrimination, 28, 67, 74
Cléber, 300, 301
Colina, Paulo, 400
collective memory, 172
color-blind, 3, 328
communication, 151–68
community organizations, 151, 152, 157, 160, 162, 163, 164, 166, 362
Conceição, Romana da, 111, 112, 113, 186
Conceição, Sônia Fátima da, 401
concretismo, 128, 348
concretists, 257
Conde de Valardes, 184
conformism, 176
Congado tradition, 334, 335, 337
Congresso Nacional Afro-Brasileiro (Afro-Brazilian National Congress), 227
continentalism, 135

contradictions, 13, 17, 19, 50, 52, 53, 59, 63, 68, 77, 80, 102, 105, 129, 134, 141, 147, 148, 151, 152, 156, 157, 163, 164, 170, 181, 191, 194, 200, 268, 312, 322, 361, 369, 383, 385
contradictory forces, 178
cooptation, 101
Corcovado (Statue of Christ the Redeemer), 213
Correia, Djalma, 130
Correia, Lepê, 61, 323, 356, 400
Corró, Lídio, 171
cosmogonic code, 182
Costa, Gal, 128, 130
Costa, Ivaldo, 179
Costa, Júlia da, 111
Cotonou (Republic of Benin), 7
counter-discursive framework, 170
Couto, Mia, 205
Craveirinha, José, 354
Crespo, Antônio Gonçalves, 12
Crioulo, 14, 173, 241, 246, 278, 279, 383, 401
Cruz, Arlindo, 372
Cruz, Clément da, 111
Cruz e Souza, João da, 5, 9, 10, 12, 52, 55, 174, 207, 208, 228, 233, 241, 303, 391
cultural affirmation, 60
cultural collective, 6, 51–79
cultural dimensions, 155–56
cultural heritage, 52, 53, 111, 301, 328
culural memory, 7, 125, 269, 295, 329
cultural object, 138
cultural production, 1–21,
Curiangu jungle, 332
Curuzu, 159, 161, 162, 167, 386
Cuti (Luíz Silva), 240–51

Dadié, Bernard, 314
Dahomey, 114, 121, 412
Damas, Léon, 208
Damasceno, Benedita Gouveia, 12, 15, 40
DaMatta, Roberto, 152, 157, 177, 385, 386, 412
Damazio, Marcio, 351

Index 421

Dandara, 188
Dandet, 37, 38
Dantas, Iracema, 394
d'Ávila, Aires, 46
Dawn, Marpessa, 65, 179
Deglar, Carl, 15, 22, 171, 174, 381, 387, 401
dehumanization, 1, 8, 39, 169, 183, 187, 326, 349
development enterprise, 152
diabolical instinct, 144
dialectical writing, 102
dialogic approach, 2
Diop, Birago, 197
Dias, Gonçalves, 11, 131
Dias, Marcos, 394, 401
Dias, Procópio, 28, 29, 33, 34
Diègues, Cacá, 179
Diègues, Carlos, 15, 157, 158, 183, 187, 188, 400
Diniz, Mauro, 373
Diop, Birago, 17, 197, 198, 199, 200, 201, 202, 347, 388, 401
disalienation, 18
disconsciousness, 297
discriminatory attitudes, 3
diversity, 172
Djavan, 361
Dom Casmurros, 36
dominant culture, 63
Duarte, Anselmo, 414
Du Bellay, 227
DuBoisian, 119
duCille, Anne, 75, 401
duplicity, 175
Duprat, Rogério, 128

Eagleton, Terry, 198–199
ẹbọ (Offering), 219, 347, 401
Eduardo, Mr., 79, 99, 100, 101
Egungun, 197
eguns, 203
Eliodoro, 247
Emmanuel, Dr., 202
empowerment, 8, 17, 76, 107, 117, 149, 151–83, 197, 302, 303, 328, 364, 375
Enfim nós/Finally Us, 392

Engenho Velho de Brotas, 307
Engenho Velho de Federação, 307
engenhos (plantations), 60, 307–11, 393, 410
entomological code, 182
epidemiological code, 182
Epifania, 117
escolas de samba (samba schools), 10, 151, 158, 359, 363, 386, 404
Èṣù or Exu (god of the crossroads), 219, 220, 224, 259, 331, 346, 389
Esu-Elegbara, 388
ethno-rapporteur, 338
Eurídice *or* Eurydice, 157
Eurocentricity, 268
Evaristo, Conceição, 14, 57, 69, 74, 75, 76, 82, 83, 85, 86, 89, 103, 276, 277, 293, 392, 399, 402
ex-escravo (ex-slave), 27, 28, 32, 37, 51, 53, 82, 307, 412
exoticism, 174, 200, 273, 304
Expresso 2222, 137, 138, 409
exotica, 169, 172

façade, 24, 172
Face da Morte, 10
Fanonian, 117
Faoro, Raymundo, 31, 382, 402
Fátima, Sônia. 6, 14, 4, 57, 77, 85, 88, 102, 107, 392, 400, 401
Favela, 10, 73, 74, 75, 129, 139, 171, 173, 177, 240, 250, 265, 301, 313, 342, 361, 370
Fayola, 19, 69–76, 103, 205, 206, 297, 298, 299
Fayola's House, 205
FECONEZU (Festival Comunitário Negro Zumbi—Black Zumbi Community Festival), 55
Felisbina, 334
Feminine discourse, 103
Ferreira, Abílio, 205
Ferreira, Hélio Pinto, 353
FESTAC, 109
Figueiredo, 37, 382, 402
Filhos de Gandhi, 129, 137, 138, 143, 159, 163, 166, 269

film, 169–92
film theory, 170
Floc, 46
Folha Larga, 328
folklorization, 17
footballistic, 262
Fortiafri, 317
Foucault, Michel, 198
fractured tradition, 59
fragmentation, 169–92
fragmented bodies, 294–97
fragmented construction, 80
França, Aline, 402
França, Patrícia, 179
freed African slaves, 7
freedom: people's, 221; symbolic, 210; total, 225
Frente Negra Brasileira, 12, 52, 398, 408
Freyre, Gilberto, 3, 128, 408
Fundação Gregório de Matos (Secretariat of Culture in Bahia), 148
Fundação Jorge Amado, 383
Fundação Odebrecht, 386
Fundação Palmares, 322, 389
Fundo de Quintal, 359, 372, 373, 391, 395

Gabriel, Fonte, 318
Gadzekpo, John Rex Amuzu, 248, 402
Gama, Luís, 221, 381
Gansallo, Albino Taiwo, 111
Gaonkar, Dilip Parameshwar, 388, 403
Garcia, Iaiá (character), 12, 23, 24, 27, 28–30, 36, 37, 50, 382, 398
Garcia, Luís, 28–37
García-Castellón, Manuel, 240, 402
Garrido, Toni, 179
Géléde, 272
gender, 274–94
generation of returnees, 109
Gerônimo, 10
Gikandi, Simon, 116, 383
Gil consciousness, 128
Gil, Gilberto, 127–50
Gilberto, João
Gilian, 145
"Gilmania," 129

Gilroy, Paul, 194
Glass Throne, 110, 113, 120, 123
GOG, 10
Gomes, Edson, 10
Gonzales, Lélia, 218, 321, 388
Gorée, 147, 222, 305
Grande Otelo, 255
Gregoróvitch, 45, 46
Grupo Palmares, 55
Guarnieri, Gianfrancesco, 6, 185, 403
Guedes, Lino, 13, 52, 55, 207, 208, 353
Guillén, Nicolás, 208, 331, 332
Guimarães, Geni, 391, 392
Guineto, Almir, 372

Haiti, 146, 147
Hanchard, Michael, 9, 15, 17, 53, 54, 78, 79, 176, 193, 194, 195, 196, 201, 240, 241, 259, 381, 383, 387, 388, 390, 403
harmonious coexistence, 3
harmonious relations, 1
heroism, 90, 107, 169, 172, 186, 188, 319
Herskovits, Melville, 194
Herskovitsian model, 194
Hingo, Van, 264
Hirszman, Leon, 185, 186, 415
Hountondji, Paulin, 198
Htun, Mala, 16, 404
human degradation, 27
humanitas, philosophy of, 27, 349
humor, 44, 46, 84, 172, 217, 228, 235, 245, 250, 254, 308, 320, 341

Iaiá Garcia (novel)
Iassan (Afro-Brazilian Goddess of the storms) 175, 180, 181, 387. See also Santa Barbara
ideological consciousness, 242, 275, 286, 320, 325
ideological paradigm, 50
Iemanjá (Yemǫja), 133, 134
Ifa system of divination, 118, 121, 122, 131, 156, 225
Igbosere Street, 111
Ijebu Yoruba tradition, 395
Ijesa, 369, 395

Ijesha, 395
Ijexá, 321, 408, 409
Ilê Aiyê, 8, 10, 123, 129, 152, 159–67, 205, 231, 272, 275, 321, 371, 386
Ile-Ife, 217, 305, 306, 314, 371, 407
Indianism, 11, 182
inequalities, 2, 4, 15, 16, 22, 23, 32, 37, 38, 48, 60, 158, 179, 219, 241, 272, 273, 274, 285, 301, 303, 342, 350, 351, 352, 379
intergenerational, 63
interorganizational, 162
interracial solidarity, 89
Intende, Mr., 185
interstate, 162
Invenção de Orfeu, 13
Irele, Abiola, 119, 404
Isabel, Princesa, 291, 292, 336
Ishola, Haruna, 384
Isidoro, Cosme, 221
Itapanhoacanga, 328
Itaparica, 203
Ituaçu, 128

Jabuti Prize, 274
Jacino, Ramatis, 57, 77
Jacintos, 321
Jackson, Michael, 10, 376, 378, 381
Jaded Heritage, 109, 397
Jameson, Fredric, 198
Janete (Janet), 291–92
Jesus, Carolina Maria de, 15, 84, 201, 313, 392, 402, 404
Jesus, Clementina de, 227
Jobim, Antônio Carlos, 128, 176
Joana, Dona, 255
Jofre, 103–6
Jorge and Estela, 27–28
Jório and Araújo, 158, 386, 404
Jubiabá, 6, 8, 13, 172, 173, 188, 189, 397, 415
Juju, 129, 252, 253, 260, 384
Justina, 325

Kagame, 198
Kaitamba, 317
Kakawa Street, 108, 111

Kane, Cheikh Hamidou, 314
Kariamu, 222
Ketu, King of, 110, 113, 120, 122, 123
Kibuko, Oubi Inaê, 14, 57, 60, 69, 77, 99, 350, 351, 356, 404
Kongo-Angolan, 395
Koumba, Amadou, 388
Kristeva, Julia, 198
Kuti, Fela Anikulapo, 109, 127

Ladipo, Duro, 203
Lagos (Nigeria), 108, 404, 407
Lagosian, 108, 111
Lapa, 395
Last Supper, 137
Laye, Camara, 314
Leira, Carlos, 77
Leopoldina, 214
Leporace, 46
Lévi-Strauss, Claude, 198
Liceu de artes e ofícios da Bahia, 386
life-force, 142
life-giver, 276
Lima, Arnaldo, 322
Lima, Jorge de, 5, 13, 52, 173, 208
Limeira, José Carlos, 14, 20, 57, 69, 304, 318, 319, 320, 321, 393, 405
Lindinalva, 188, 189, 303, 400
Lins, Paulo, 15, 313
Livingston, Dr., 189, 190
Lobo, Fernando, 130
López, Francisco Solano, 382, 411
Lucas, Fábio, 227, 339
Lukacs, Georg, 116, 383
Loberant, 46
Lobo, Luiza, 256, 313, 389, 391, 393
Lomé (Togo), 7
Losque and Lara, 46
"ludíbrio," 389
Lukacsian, 116
Lula, 8, 16, 17, 148, 150, 186, 203, 296, 303, 316, 377
Lusophone African literature, 205
Lusotropicalism, 205
Lusotropicalismo, 128

Machel, Jonita (of Mozambique), 321

Machel, Samora, 205, 321
machismo, 84, 88
Macumba, 178
Macunaíma, 181–83
Mahin, Luiza, 20, 90, 221, 292
Maimona, João, 339
Malês (muslim slaves) Rebellion of 1835, 90
Mallarmé, 256–57
Malungos e milongas (Brothers and Sisters), 79, 81, 98, 99, 101, 102, 274, 391, 409
Mama Kitaia, 337
Mangueira, 357, 359, 370
maracatu music, 212, 213
"Marajuara flavor," 367, 395
Maranhão, 8, 302, 405
Margarida, 202, 374
marginality, 21, 69, 132, 142, 201, 361, 374
Maria, Elza, 112, 357
Marilda, 255
Marotti, Giorgio, 15, 382, 405
Martins, Lêda Maria, 349
master-slave relationship, 9, 30, 31, 210
Matos, Gregório de, 11, 148, 265, 342, 381
Mattar, Flávia, 394
Maurício, Father José, 10, 327
Maya-Maya, Estevão, 323, 330, 331
Medeiros, Maria Alice de Aguiar, 3, 381
memory, 267–301
Mercury, Daniela, 10, 20, 161, 357
Meireles, Cecília, 284, 288
Menezes, Tobias Barreto de, 12
Mercedes, Ana, 190
mestiçagem or *miscigenação* (race mixture), 23
Meursault, 254
miscegenation, 9, 191, 205, 267, 269, 270, 362
Meyers, Robert, 131
Migué, 112, 328
milieus (pl.), 208
military dictatorship, 18, 55, 127, 128, 132, 137, 138, 186, 208, 239, 242, 328, 383

Minas Gerais, 8, 19, 20, 57, 85, 110, 120, 183, 302, 322, 329, 330, 334, 337, 390, 393, 403, 405, 410
Mineira, 85, 334, 393, 403
Minka, Jamu, 14, 56, 57, 62, 64, 66, 67, 85, 99, 242, 50, 351, 352, 382 406
MNUCDR (Movimento Negro Unificado Contra a Discriminação Racial—Unified Black Movement Against Racial Discrimination), 55
modernism, 12, 15, 2, 116 129, 130, 131 170, 171, 193, 194, 195, 207, 208, 387, 398, 401 405, 409
modernismo, 15, 52, 129, 130, 171, 387, 401
Moraes, Vinícius de, 6, 128, 174, 176, 201, 385, 386, 406
Moreira, Gilberto Passos Gil, 136–87, 201, 203, 205, 347, 361, 377, 379, 384, 406, 409, 411, 415
morro (hilltop-slum), 247, 313, 370, 373
mother earth, 296, 317
motherhood, 107
Moulero, Padre Thomas, 111
Moura, Clóvis, 4, 6, 24, 406
Mouralis, Bernard, 58, 382
Movimento Negro Unificado (MNU), 62, 103, 159
mucamas (slaves), 183
Mudimbe, 198, 406
mulatto escape hatch, 174
mulatta, 22, 50 80 81, 169, 172, 174, 179, 183, 191, 201, 203, 273, 383
mulattoes, 3, 5, 9, 11, 68, 146, 191
multicultural society, 181
musical legitimacy, 130
Myth of Orpheus, 176–79
myth of racial democracy, 1, 12, 15, 23 82, 177, 190, 191, 192, 275, 278, 285, 287, 289, 319, 419
mythic hero, 178, 181, 387

Nago-Jeje, 369
Nascimento, Abdias do, 217–33
Nascimento, Beatriz, 307
Nascimento, Milton, 10, 344
Nazaré das Farinhas, 112

Ndee Naldinho, 10
negation of identity, 174
negotiating, 1-21
Negra, Jovelina Perola, 372
negritude, 8, 61, 129, 16, 200, 272, 303, 312, 321, 322, 338, 339, 354, 389, 393, 398, 399, 407, 412
negritudist, 208, 209, 212, 349, 351, 353
Nejar, Carlos, 333
neo-abstraction, 38, 216, 284, 348
neocolonialism, 116
neo-concretism, 128, 348
Neto, Agostinho, 205, 321, 351, 353
Neto, Torquato, 128, 131, 132
neutralization of hierarchies, 177
New Diaspora, 111
Nicholas, Joseph Sebastian, 111
Nigerian-Brazilian identity, 112
Nigerian-Brazilian relations, 412
Nigerian Institute of International Affairs (NIIA), 407
noble savage, 172
Northeasternness, 108, 109, 128, 132, 134, 181, 212, 312,
Núbia Pereira, 334, 393, 403, 408
Nunes, Clara, 227
Nunes, Maria Luisa, 25, 227, 382, 406

Oba Koso, 203
Obafemi Awolowo University, 217, 407
objectification, 71, 81
Odair, 247
Odunlami Street, 111
Oduduwa, 295, 296, 314
official mythology, 5
Ojelabi, Maria, 111, 112
Ojo-Ade, Femi, 31, 322
Okri, Ben, 120
Olinto, Antônio, 5, 108, 110, 111, 201, 383
Oliveira, Anélito de, 20, 322, 348
Oliveira, Eduardo de, 14, 18, 207, 226, 228, 238, 266, 353, 388, 389, 409
Oliveira, João Fernandes de, 183, 184, 185, 324
O Elogio da Dominação (In Praise of Domination), 3, 4, 381

Ogum (Port.), 66, 172, 250
Ògún, 121, 269, 271, 274, 301, 346, 369, 390, 391, 409
Ojó àbá méta (Saturday), 383
Ojó àíkú (Sunday), 383
Ojó ajé (Monday), 383
Ojo Awo, 383
Ojóbò (Thursday), 383
Ojó etì (Friday), 383
Ojó Îségun (Tuesday), 383
Ojo Jacuta, 121
Ojo Obatala, 121
Ojo Ogun, 121
Ojórú (Wednesday), 383
ojú inú (inner mind, eye, or soul), 95
Okesuna Street, 111
Olavo, Father, 180
Olinto, Antônio, 5, 108, 110, 111, 201, 383
Olodum, 10, 79, 159, 162, 163, 165, 166, 205, 275, 314, 322, 359, 370, 371, 386, 394, 408, 09, 410
Olodumare, 314
Olympio, Epiphanio, 108, 111, 397, 405, 407, 410
Onawale, Landê, 14, 57, 303
O navio negreiro (The Black Slaveship), 5, 397
optimism, 9, 36, 39, 57, 64, 65, 68, 72, 79, 91, 94, 97, 215, 225, 389
Orientalism, 137
Oríki, 118, 120, 121, 217, 218, 220, 223, 224, 295, 337, 338, 345, 346, 347, 350, 358, 363, 394, 399, 403, 406
ornithological code, 182
Orpheus and Power, 9, 15, 53, 78, 79, 196, 201, 381, 383, 387, 390, 403
Òrìṣàńlá, 225
Orita Meta, 347
Orixá, 15, 90, 100, 189, 217, 369
Ortiz, Renato, 65
Osanyin, 369, 370, 395, 414
osumare (also *Oxumaré*—rainbow), 122
Òṣun (also *Oxum*—goddess of the river), 221, 222, 223, 255, 296, 392
Otávio, 186

Our Lady of the Rosary, 367
Oxalá (the supreme god), 143
Oyono, Ferdinand, 314

Pagodinho, Zeca, 372
Pagoda, 20, 21, 357, 362, 363, 365, 69, 371, 372, 373, 374, 375
Pagodista, 361, 363
pai-de-santo, 191
Palmares, 20, 37, 55, 58, 187, 202, 210, 211, 226, 271, 292, 313, 316, 319, 321, 322, 339, 340, 341, 356, 360, 381, 389, 408, 411
Pan African heroes, 60
Pan Africanism, 201–2
Pan African consciousness, 82
Pan African vision, 64
paradox, 3
Pareles, Jon, 359, 394
participation, 107
participatory paradigm, 152–56
Patrocínio, José, 12
Paulista, Bragança, 233
Pena, Fausto, 189, 190
Paraguaian War, 28
Parnassianism, 18
Partideiros no Cacique, 373
passers-by (pl.), 68, 181, 236, 367
Pau da Bandeira, 370, 371
Paulistan, 241, 252, 298
Pelé, 106, 148
Pelourinho, 303
Pereira, Edimilson de Almeida, 262
Pereira, Waldemar Euzébio, 20, 57, 322, 348, 349, 412
Pérola Negra, 357, 372
pessi-optimism, 57
Pestana, Maurício, 254
Petraca, 227
petrologic, 182
Pixote, 15, 178
poet–chief priest, 225
political allegory, 181
political power, 171, 185, 196
political transformation, 128
politicizing, 97–102
politics of return, 108–13

Pompéia, Raúl, 265
Portela, 157, 386
post–Cold War era, 116
postcolonial theory, 7, 113, 118
postcoloniality, 114, 116, 117, 119
postmodernism, 116, 131, 193
postmodernity, 130
post-Tropicalism, 132
Potiguara, Eliana, 84
Praça Castro Alves, 382
Prado, Adélia, 288
praise-poetry, 118, 120, 121, 217, 218, 220, 223, 224, 295, 337, 338, 345, 346, 347, 350, 358, 363, 394, 399, 403, 406. *See also* Oríki
praise-singer, 203, 411
praise-singing, 46, 132, 139
preto velho, 172
pre-Tropicalism, 133
Pré-Tropicalismo, 133
Princesa Isabel, 291, 292, 336
problematization, 119, 269, 270
protest, 303–56
Puzo, Mario, 146

Quilombhoje, 51–79
Quilombismo, 18, 202, 406
Quilombo, 302–56
"Quilombolas," 302

race studies, 412
race-bound, 102
race-mixture, 3, 23, 189, 191, 195, 278, 352
racial absolutism, 26
racial consciousness, 50
racial democracy, 1–21, 22–50
racial discrimination, 59
racial domination, 3
racial Eldorado, 171
racial hypocrisy, 97, 321, 341
racial mythology, 175
racial paradise, 23
racial relations, 3
racial utopia, 174
racialized representations, 171
Racionais MCs, 10

racism, 3
racist society, 39, 49, 50, 55, 56, 68, 69, 183, 189, 236, 262, 289
racist stereotypes, 4
Raimundo (character), 35
Ramos, Guerreiro, 12
re-Africanization, 159, 203, 269, 312
rebellious impulse, 31, 136
rebelliousness, 81
Rebelo, Aldo, 54, 69
recuperated history, 187–88
redignifying, 91–97
reformulation, 94
religious syncretism, 179–81
Rennó, Carlos, 127, 132, 384, 409
Republic of Zorei, 114, 123, 124
resistance, 1, 2, 8, 9, 22, 35, 55, 57, 68, 70, 80, 83, 90, 92, 96, 97, 118, 144, 149, 163, 173–76, 187–89, 194–95, 204–5, 207, 210, 211, 221, 229, 237, 240, 256 259, 269, 270, 274, 295, 300, 301, 327, 334, 335, 336, 340, 351, 401, 402
reverse diaspora, 20
revisionist, 24, 60, 301
Ribeiro, Esmeralda, 6, 14, 19, 54, 57, 66, 77, 80, 81, 84, 97, 107, 201, 268, 269 275, 297, 301, 330, 390, 397, 398, 401
Rio Grande do Sul, 57, 302, 389, 394
Risério, Antônio, 347, 409
Risério and Gil, 149
roda de capoeira, 181
Rodrigues, Abelardo, 14, 60, 89, 9, 350, 353, 409
Rodrigues, Eustáquio José, 57, 77
Rodrigues, João Jorge Santos, 162, 386, 409
roguish or trickster figure, 69, 152, 172, 173, 398
Romeu Crusoé, 233
Ronsard, 227
Rosária, 291
Rosa, Guimarães, 205, 265, 323
Rosenfeld, Anatol, 188, 387, 409
Rubião, Mirilo, 323
Rubiãos, 36
Rufino, Alzira, 7, 82

Sá, Sandra, 361
sacrificial death, 181
Said, Edward, 198
Saint Benedict, 337
Saint-Beuve, 227
samba schools, 10, 151, 157, 158, 359, 370, 386, 408
samba-reggae, 140
Sambistas, 151, 157, 161
Sango (Yoruba god of thunder), 203
Sankofa, 388
Santa Barbara, 175, 180, 181, 387
Santo Antônio do Itambé, 328
Santos, Antônio Carlos dos, 129, 159–67, 321, 386, 387. *See also* Vovô
Santos, Deoscoredes Maxililiano dos (Mestre Didi), 14, 110, 415
Santos, Jussara, 338, 393
Santos, Nelson Pereira dos, 188, 189, 387, 409, 415
São Miguel, 328
Sarzan, 200, 201, 202, 388
Sayers, Raymond, 27
scapegoatism, 185–86
scapes, 205–6
Schwarz, Roberto, 22
Sebastianism, 124
segregation, 1, 83, 287, 316 352
Segreto, 171
self-dignity, 30, 44, 45, 59
self-liberation, 102
self-mystification, 80
Seljan, Zora, 111
Semana de arte moderna (Modern Art Week), 12, 52, 193, 207
Semog, Éle, 57, 61, 69, 77, 217, 261, 318, 321, 341, 356, 393, 405
Senghor, Léopold, 208, 354
Senhor Jair, 247
senzalas (slave quarters), 3, 263, 324, 326, 327, 360, 361, 394, 414
Serra da Barriga, 221, 360, 361
Serro, 324, 328
Sertanejo, 134
sertão (backlands), 134
Serveas, 15, 410

Seu Machado, 118
sexual object, 138
sexualized mulatta, 191
Sharp Awards, 359
Shohat, Ella, 116, 118
Silva, Bezerra da, 361
Silva, Chica da, 34, 400, 414
Silva, Jônatas Conceição da, 14, 20, 57, 304, 306, 307, 308, 350, 400, 410
Silva, Laje da, 42
Silva, Lázaro Borges da, 111
Silva, Luis Inácio da (Lula), 186
Silva, Sebastian, 115, 117, 124
Silva, Dona Sophia Marilewa da, 111
Simon, Paul, 10, 381
slum-dwellers (*favelados*), 177
social commitment, 128
social tensions, 50
societal corruption, 38
societal fragmentation, 181
socio-emotional, 280
Sofará, 182
Souza, Isabel, 111
Soyinka, Wole, 198, 388, 411
spiritual awakening, 77
spiritual consciousness, 139
Stepto, Robert, 2
stereotypical roles, 81
strategies of survival, 1
subjectivity, 11, 30, 257
subservience, 30, 37, 47
sugarcane, 9, 62, 64, 66, 157, 324
Suzana, 104
symbolic actions, 2
symbolic representation, 172
symbolism, 73, 164, 178, 240, 259, 347, 349, 367
syncopative, 140

Tadeu, Teresinha, 57
Teatro do Oprimido, 248
Tejuca, 324
Tempels, 198
TEN (*Teatro Experimental do Negro*/Experimental Black Theater), 11, 12, 202, 217, 248, 406
Teodoro, 173, 184, 323, 325, 328

Terramara, 247, 252, 255, 397
terreiro (shrine), 2, 71, 179, 180, 189
thematization, 11, 352
Theodoro, Helena, 357, 394
theorizing ancestrality, 193–206
Thiémokho Kéita, 200
third world (adj.), 116, 118, 227, 384, 398, 401, 406
Thomas, Dona Angêlica, 111
Tietê River, 252
Tijuca, 183
Timotéu, Agnaldo, 148
Tinubu Square, 111
Tokunbo Street, 111
Tolstoy, 38
trans black essence, 302
"TransBlaxpression," 261, 262
transnationalization, 141
Trindade, Solano, 208–17
Tríplice Aliança, 382
Tropicália, 127–32
Tropicalismo, 128
tropical multiculturalism, 171
Tropicalist legacy, 127–50
Tropicalist Manifesto, 131
Topicalist pioneer, 127
Tropicalist visionary, 148–50
Tropicalists, 129
Turgenev, 38
Turton, Dona Luiza Ebun, 111
Tutuca, Ronald, 261–66
Twine, Winddance, 1, 15, 164, 174, 270, 352, 381, 412

Ubá, Minas Gerais, 110
Umbanda, 387
(Un)Broken Linkages, 108–26
Unified Black Movement, 383
United Institute of Research on Social Development (UNRISD), 154
Universidade de São Paulo, 252, 405
University of Ife, 109

Vale do Jequitinhonha, 323
Valéria, 28, 36
Valery, 344, 345
Vazirani, Reetika, 392

Veloso, Caetano, 3, 7, 127, 128, 130, 132, 146, 147, 161, 401, 412, 415
Ventura, Adão, 14, 20, 227, 238, 322, 323, 326, 328, 330, 338, 339, 340, 350
Verger, Pierre Fatumbi, 15
Vieira, Antônio, 20, 304, 306, 350
Vieira, Hamilton, 322, 393, 412
Vieira, Lia, 57, 77, 85, 87, 88
Vieira, Luandino, 205
Vila, Martinho da, 10, 216, 357, 359, 361, 362, 363, 394
Villa-Lobos, 10
vital force, 1, 2, 125, 189, 201, 218, 377
Viveiros, Captain, 44
Vovô, 129, 159–67, 321, 386, 387

warrior-like happiness, 140
Water House, 110, 111, 113, 114, 115, 117, 118, 120, 121, 123, 124, 407
West Africa, 5
West African griot, 172
white dominance, 53
whitening, 3
Williams, Raymond, 4
womanhood, 86
Wright, Richard, 55, 208, 247, 248, 385

Xangô (*Oba,* or god of fire), 172
Xavier, Arnaldo, 251–61
Xavier, Lúcia, 394
Xavieresque, 253
Xaxá de Souza I, 111
Xica da Silva, 6, 8, 172, 173, 174, 183, 184, 188, 387, 414

Yansã (goddess of storm and wind), 297, 369
Yoruba diaspora (writer), 7, 108, 110
Yoruba gods (Orisa), 118, 122, 205, 217, 345
Yorubaland, 108, 126

Zé, Tom, 128, 130, 132
Zé Kéti, 10
Zé-do-Burro (Zé-of-the-Donkey), 175, 179, 180, 387
Zés do Caroço, 370, 371
Zézinho, 291
"zombification," 169
Zumba, Ganga, 37, 143, 72, 87, 188, 341
Zumbi dos Palmares, 20, 37, 58, 271, 92, 313, 341, 381

Rochester Studies in African History and the Diaspora

Power Relations in Nigeria: Ilorin Slaves and their Successors
Ann O'Hear

Dilemmas of Democracy in Nigeria
Edited by Paul Beckett and Crawford Young

Science and Power in Colonial Mauritius
William Kelleher Storey

Namibia's Post-Apartheid Regional Institutions: The Founding Year
Joshua B. Forrest

A Saro Community in the Niger Delta, 1912–1984: The Potts-Johnsons of Port Harcourt and Their Heirs
Mac Dixon-Fyle

Contested Power in Angola, 1840s to the Present
Linda Heywood

Nigerian Chiefs: Traditional Power in Modern Politics, 1890s–1990s
Olufemi Vaughan

West Indians in West Africa, 1808–1880: The African Diaspora in Reverse
Nemata Blyden

The United States and Decolonization in West Africa, 1950–1960
Ebere Nwaubani

Health, State, and Society in Kenya
George Oduor Ndege

Black Business and Economic Power
Edited by Alusine Jalloh and Toyin Falola

Voices of the Poor in Africa
Elizabeth Isichei

Colonial Rule and Crisis in Equatorial Africa: Southern Gabon ca. 1850–1940
Christopher J. Gray

The Politics of Frenchness in Colonial Algeria, 1930–1954
Jonathan K. Gosnell

Sources and Methods in African History: Spoken, Written, Unearthed
Edited by Toyin Falola and Christian Jennings

Sudan's Blood Memory: The Legacy of War, Ethnicity, and Slavery in Early South Sudan
Stephanie Beswick

Writing Ghana, Imagining Africa: Nation and African Modernity
Kwaku Larbi Korang

Labour, Land and Capital in Ghana: From Slavery to Free Labour in Asante, 1807–1956
Gareth Austin

Not So Plain as Black and White: Afro-German Culture and History, 1890–2000
Edited by Patricia Mazón and Reinhild Steingröver

Writing African History
Edited by John Edward Philips

African Urban Spaces in Historical Perspective
Edited by Steven J. Salm and Toyin Falola

Yorùbá Identity and Power Politics
Edited by Toyin Falola and Ann Genova

*Constructions of Belonging:
Igbo Communities and the Nigerian
State in the Twentieth Century*
Axel Harneit-Sievers

*Sufi City: Urban Design and
Archetypes in Touba*
Eric Ross

A Political History of The Gambia, 1816–1994
Arnold Hughes and David Perfect

*The Abolition of the Slave Trade in
Southeastern Nigeria, 1885–1950*
A. E. Afigbo

HIV/AIDS, Illness, and African Well-Being
Edited by Toyin Falola and
Matthew M. Heaton

Ira Aldridge: The African Roscius
Edited by Bernth Lindfors

*Natural Resources and Conflict in Africa:
The Tragedy of Endowment*
Abiodun Alao

*Crafting Identity in Zimbabwe and
Mozambique*
Elizabeth MacGonagle

*Locality, Mobility, and "Nation":
Periurban Colonialism in Togo's Eweland,
1900–1960*
Benjamin N. Lawrance

*Sufism and Jihad in Modern Senegal:
The Murid Order*
John Glover

*Indirect Rule in South Africa:
Tradition, Modernity, and the
Costuming of Political Power*
J. C. Myers

*The Urban Roots of Democracy and
Political Violence in Zimbabwe:
Harare and Highfield, 1940–1964*
Timothy Scarnecchia

*Radicalism and Cultural Dislocation in
Ethiopia, 1960–1974*
Messay Kebede

*The United States and West Africa:
Interactions and Relations*
Edited by Alusine Jalloh and
Toyin Falola

*Ben Enwonwu:
The Making of an African Modernist*
Sylvester Okwunodu Ogbechie

*Representing Bushmen:
South Africa and the Origin of Language*
Shane Moran

*Afro-Brazilians:
Cultural Production in a Racial Democracy*
Niyi Afolabi